P9-DBJ-590

Information Security Intelligence: Cryptographic Principles and Applications

Thomas Calabrese

THOMSON

DELMAR LEARNING

Australia • Canada • Mexico • Singapore • Spain • United Kingdom • United States

THOMSON
DELMAR LEARNING

Information Security Intelligence: Cryptographic Principles and Applications
Thomas Calabrese

Vice President, Technology and Trades SBU:
Alar Elken

Editorial Director:
Sandy Clark

Acquisitions Editor:
Dave Garza

Development:
Dawn Daugherty

Marketing Director:
Cynthia Eichelman

Channel Manager:
Fair Huntoon

Marketing Coordinator:
Casey Bruno

Production Director:
Mary Ellen Black

Production Manager:
Larry Main

Production Coordinator:
Dawn Jacobson

Senior Project Editor:
Christopher Chien

Art/Design Coordinator:
Francis Hogan

Senior Editorial Assistant:
Dawn Daugherty

COPYRIGHT © 2004 by Delmar Learning, a division of Thomson Learning, Inc. Thomson Learning™ is a trademark used herein under license.

Printed in the United States of America
1 2 3 4 5 XXX 05 04 03

For more information contact
Delmar Learning
Executive Woods
5 Maxwell Drive, PO Box 8007
Clifton Park, NY 12065-8007.
Or find us on the World Wide Web at
http://delmarlearning.com

All rights reserved. No part of this work covered by the copyright hereon may be reproduced or used in any form or by any means—graphic, electronic, or mechanical, including photocopying, recording, taping, Web distribution or information storage and retrieval systems—without the written permission of the publisher.

For permission to use material from this text or product, contact us by
Tel 1-800-730-2214
Fax 1-800-730-2215
www.thomsonrights.com

Library of Congress Cataloging-in-Publication Data
Calabrese, Tom.
  Information security intelligence : cryptographic principles and applications / Tom Calabrese.—1st ed.
    p. cm.
  ISBN 1-4018-3727-1
  1. Computer security. 2. Data protection. 3. Information technology—Security measures. 4. Cryptography. I. Title.
QA76.9.A25C3418 2003
005.8—dc22

2003023227

Notice To The Reader
Publisher and author do not warrant or guarantee any of the products described herein or perform any independent analysis in connection with any of the product information contained herein. Publisher and author do not assume and expressly disclaim any obligation to obtain and include information other than that provided to it by the manufacturer.

The reader is expressly warned to consider and adopt all safety precautions that might be indicated by the activities herein and to avoid all potential hazards. By following the instructions contained herein, the reader willingly assumes all risks in connection with such instructions.

Publisher and author make no representation or warranties of any kind, including but not limited to, the warranties of fitness for particular purpose or merchantability, nor are any such representations implied with respect to the material set forth herein, and the publisher takes no responsibility with respect to such material. Publisher and author shall not be liable for any special, consequential, or exemplary damages resulting, in whole or part, from the readers' use of, or reliance upon, this material.

Table of Contents

Preface ix
Acknowledgments xiii

Section One: Information and Security Planning I
    Overview 1
    Section Goals 2
    Key Elements to Success in Mastering This Section 2

    CHAPTER I: Introduction to Information Theory **3**
    Securing Information 6
    Data to Information 15
    Information Systems 23
    Information Movement 27
    Information Management 33
    Summary 35
    Study Questions 36

    CHAPTER 2:   Threat Agents and Risk **41**
    Common Myths and Misconceptions 42
    The Numbers Do Not Lie 47
    The Perpetrators 51
    What Is Risk? 55
    The Threats 60
    Risk Assessment and Vulnerability Analysis 74
    Risk Management 87
    Summary 89
    Study Questions 90

    CHAPTER 3:   Information and The Law **95**
    A Reasonable Expectation of Privacy 97
    Privacy from Law Enforcement and Privacy at Work 98
    What Constitutes a Crime? 103
    Crime Prevention, Detection, and Prosecution 105
    The Law 117
    Summary 137
    Study Questions 139

CHAPTER 4: A Model for Information Security Planning **143**
An Information Security Model 144
Security Planning and Policy Creation 157
Education and Management 167
Summary 168
Study Questions 170

Section Two: Cryptographic Principles and Methods **175**
Overview 175
Section Goals 176
Key Elements to Success in Mastering This Section 177

CHAPTER 5: Cryptographic Philosophy **179**
Cryptography Evolving 180
The History of Cryptography 182
The Study of Language 203
Protecting Information 205
Strength of Method 210
Summary 215
Study Questions 217

CHAPTER 6: Mathematical Principles of Cryptography **223**
Mathematical Properties of Information 224
Number Representation 226
Exponentiation and Logarithms 231
Mathematical Logic 232
Basic Number Theory 235
Computational Complexity 250
Cryptographic Principles 256
Summary 257
Study Questions 258

CHAPTER 7: Symmetrical Key Cryptography **265**
Symmetrical Cryptography Basics 267
Software Keys 272
Symmetrical Operations 276
TEA: a Tiny Encryption Algorithm 281
Other Symmetrical Algorithms 291
Summary 292
Study Questions 295

CHAPTER 8: Public Key Infrastructure **299**
Asymmetrical Key Cryptography 301

Digital Signatures 310
Attacks against Encryption 317
The Need for a Public Key Infrastructure 318
Summary 335
Study Questions 337

Section Three: Information System Security **341**
Overview 341
Section Goals 342
Key Elements to Success in Mastering This Section 343

CHAPTER 9:   Securing the Information System **345**
Physical Security 347
Application and File Protection 358
System Security 361
Network Security 364
Intrusion Detection 375
Summary 380
Study Questions 381

CHAPTER 10:   Viruses, Worms, and Malicious Software **387**
Harmful Code 388
NonMalicious Code 389
Malicious Software 395
Malware Defenses 403
Summary 405
Study Questions 405

CHAPTER 11:   Securing the Digital Marketplace **409**
Web Businesses and Security Requirements 411
Web Technology Basics 413
Using Cryptography to Build a Web Trust 417
Making the Right Choice 432
Where to from Here? 439
Summary 440
Study Questions 441

Glossary 447
Appendix A 473
Appendix B 521
Appendix C 529
Appendix D 535
Bibliography 539
Index 545

DEDICATION

As a young boy, my best friend was my dad. He was a perfect role model. He was a mechanical engineer, so he could seemingly make anything work. He loved baseball, he loved electric trains, and most important, he loved me and made me feel important. He always had "cool stuff" to play with from his job, and he always let me experiment. He worked on submarines for the U.S. Navy and made sure I always had a fresh supply of pictures and toys. Regrettably, he passed away while I was young so we never "talked technical" as adults. Alhough I was young, he had already piqued my interest in technology.

Luckily for me, I had a great family who comforted me and spent time with me after he passed. I wish that I had the space to list them all and mention all the wonderful things they did for me. My grandfather took over and filled in for most of the "dad stuff." I spent a considerable amount of time with my grandfather, watching as he did the outdoor chores. I always wanted to help but was told I was much too young to use the lawn mower and other power tools. Finally, after years of waiting, my grandpa asked me to mow the lawn. I was thrilled and quite eager to start mowing. My family lived in a modest home with a small lawn. It usually did not take long to mow the lawn (a half hour, tops). My grandfather was meticulous in everything he did. While cutting the lawn, he always made a beautiful design in the grass. When he was done cutting, we would joke that he had put the "Hollywood cut" on the lawn. On my first day at the controls, it was strictly sheets to the wind. Three hours later I was done, and the lawn was a terrible mess. There were missed spots and a design that only Picasso could appreciate. Grandpa was understandably upset. What he said to me that day has been with me ever since. He just stared at the lawn and without even glancing over at me he simply said, with a heavy Italian accent, "You no tinka, you only do!"

At the time I had no idea what he meant. Twenty-five years later, I realized he was telling me that I needed a plan to guide me. He wanted me to be organized and to have a method in my approach to projects. Today my wife says I have a plan for everything. This lesson took a while to learn but has been a great asset to me in both my personal and professional life. A good portion of what is needed in the security consulting field is setting strategic direction and planning security implementations.

I would like to dedicate this book to two people: my dad, who was a great friend, a professional role model, and a lifelong inspiration to me; and to my grandfather, whose simple words of wisdom transcended age, language, and educational boundaries. I love you both and you are missed.

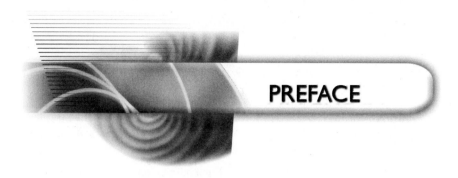

PREFACE

Every day, Internet traffic and the number of online users continue to grow. The Internet is the standard for electronic information transport. Ultra high-speed processors on the desktop, advances in systems and network technologies, and a generalized acceptance of the TCP/IP suite of protocols have all enabled cyberusers to fully participate in the digital marketplace. Information is data processed by its associated applications. Information is often an underappreciated corporate asset of great value. The electronic flow and circulation of digital information has reached levels never previously anticipated. After a decade of computing and networking standardization, information has emerged as an entity unto itself, free of the bounds of system-compatibility requirements. Information travels independently through the networking fabric of our electronic domain.

During this same period, cybercrime has become rampant because cybercriminals have grown more sophisticated in their methods. The same spirit of openness and standardization that fostered the growth of the Internet and widespread information sharing also created a new venue for criminals. Securing electronic information is a new field and can be a daunting task for information system managers. While we struggle to adequately prepare security professionals with the most up-to-date technologies and strategies, our adversaries continue to launch varied and innovative new attacks at an astounding pace. Viruses, electronic eavesdropping, electronic identity fraud, denial-of-service attacks, malware, and cracking are but a handful of the techniques used by hackers, crackers, script kiddies, and cyberterrorists.

In the wake of the September 11th tragedy is a heightened awareness of physical and infrastructure security. It is equally important, however, to keep vigil over our electronic frontier. Cyberterrorists represent a clear and present danger and can affect us in multiple ways. They can use our open Internet to conduct clandestine operations (cloaked by the very cryptographic techniques we use for protection). They can obtain sensitive information about every element of our personal lives, financial status, medical history, and correspondence. This information can be used to fraudulently obtain documents, assume false electronic identities, slander reputations, or track an individual's movements. Cybercriminals can falsify information, deny service, or launch widespread viral attacks in an attempt to destabilize infrastructure, disrupt financial or social services, or interrupt communication pathways. By using the vast open resources of the Internet, the cyberterrorist has access to ubiquitous communication systems and information resources. It is widely known that the perpetrators of the September 11th attacks used sophisticated cryptographic methods to code and disseminate information to their operatives.

Therefore, in the midst of our rapidly evolving, technologically-laden world, the need for securing our electronic information is essential. The development of the engineering talent required to support such an endeavor is critical. The industry standards for computer security are no longer rooted simply in system or networking technologies. Rather, they must focus on protecting the information entity wherever it resides. We must gain a full appreciation of exactly what information is (its properties), where it lives, how it moves, and what methods are available to protect it.

As the name implies, *Information Security Intelligence: Cryptographic Principles and Applications* is a book that focuses on information rather than exclusively on information system infrastructure. This text is designed for the undergraduate information science or computer science student as an introduction to the information security or computer forensics fields. Many colleges and universities now offer courses and programs focused on information security and computer forensics. The focus is on protecting information, authenticating information and users, and securing the information systems through which information must pass. Because this is an emerging area of technology, there is a definite shortage of material suitable for use as an introductory college text in this discipline. This project fills that void. A goal of this text is to be both easy to read yet provide significant depth. The textbook is divided into the following three sections:

    I Information and Security Planning

    II Cryptographic Principles and Methods

    III Information System Security

The first goal of the text is to provide students with a foundation in basic information theory. Students need to understand the properties of information and how to take advantage of them in developing a protection scheme. This preliminary material presupposes only minimal knowledge of the information technology area. Once this theme is developed, the difference between the information and the information system becomes clear. This will help the student understand how to separate and prioritize the various entities that we are trying to protect.

Developing an information security orientation versus an information system orientation is crucial. This text is oriented strongly toward the information security domain. This leads to a presentation of an information security model. The information security model provides a visual aid that details the layers of security required to adequately protect our information and guarantee its authenticity. This model is used in a persistent fashion throughout the text. It is a symbolic representation of the goals we are trying to achieve.

Once the reader is grounded in the need for information security, it is necessary to provide the reader with an understanding of exactly what constitutes a successful "hack." Chapter 2 provides a detailed review of the most common hacks, their signatures, as well as pointers to online resources with current updates on hacker tactics and examples of cybercrime. Chapter 2 also presents a methodology for identifying risk, conducting vulnerability assessments, and mitigating risk. Mastering this material presents a significant first step in developing a security requirements document. Understanding the risks to information, and what can be done to minimize those risks, is the foundation of any security plan. Risk analysis is a critical step in developing return-on-investment statements, which will become important as we implement our plan.

Another important aspect of information security is understanding the legislative initiatives undertaken to help ensure information security, privacy, and confidentiality. The laws governing electronic crime are complex and, at times, vague. Students should develop a feel for the legislation and its strengths and weaknesses. A broader understanding of this information can lead to informed discussion, debate, and constructive change. Through this material, the student will learn how electronic security legislation, while aimed at preventing crime, may infringe on our personal rights as citizens.

Next, the text provides an overview of computer forensics and creating information audit trails in the context of evidence. This is important because prosecuting information security crime is especially difficult. The FBI model for investigating electronic crime is presented and reviewed. In particular, two areas that require advanced expertise to enable successful prosecution are evidence handling and courtroom technical presentations.

Section One, "Information and Security Planning," concludes with a discussion of security plan development. Such plans should represent the cornerstone of any security initiative. It is important for organizations to embrace such strategies and develop cost-effective information security plans. Information security implementation can be expensive if it is not well thought out. Today's management paradigm has shifted from a liberal, outspend-the-competition stance to a far more conservative, spend-when-justified position. Executive management justifiably requires fiscal appropriations to be coincident with sound, return-on-investment metrics. This chapter presents a series of best practices designed to accomplish this goal. Information security does not have to be expensive to be effective.

Section Two, "Cryptographic Principles and Methods," represents a detailed look at the underlying technological enablers of information security. In this section, students will first be presented with a general discussion of cryptographic principles and the benefits of encryption. As information travels through the network, there is no guarantee it will always travel through a secure path. Encrypted information retains its integrity regardless of the security levels present on a given system (where the information may reside) or on a particular network segment (where information may travel). The concept of Confidentiality, Authenticity, Integrity, and Nonrepudiation (CAIN) will be explored. CAIN concisely expresses the goals of a solid information security plan and, as such, represents the yardstick by which our information security model must be measured.

In Chapter 5, students will be introduced to the concepts of substitution and transposition through a review of early encryption works. A detailed discussion follows in Chapters 7 and 8 regarding popular cryptographic algorithms, protocols, methods, and related security applications. Section Two includes a detailed analysis of symmetrical and asymmetrical cryptography, digital signatures, and the mathematics of cryptography. Students will be provided a detailed review of several of the most predominant protocols used in the industry.

We will closely examine the concept of "applying a key" to data by a comprehensive review of the Tiny Encryption Algorithm (TEA) code. This code enables students to gain a full appreciation of Feistel ciphers and the power of key strength. Section Two concludes by examining the effectiveness and appropriateness of all of these methods.

Section Three, "Information System Security," addresses the practical issues of large-scale planning and deployment of the information security plan as it pertains to the information system. This part of the text is organized around the remaining layers of the information security model presented in Section One of the text. Although this section is not meant as a comprehensive study of network, systems, or Web security (all worthy of a full text unto themselves), it is meant to help students garner an understanding of these areas because they are critical to the secure flow and warehousing of information. Information systems comprise all the infrastructure and methods that enable information creation, storage, and movement. A concise technology overview of network architecture security standards and strategies, Web-enabled information security protocols and protections, physical site defense, system-level security protections, and effective malware countermeasures is presented. We conclude with a comparison of popular methods for implementing large-scale security deployments.

This project is targeted to fill the void of available classroom text for a college-level information security course. It can be used as part of either a single-term or two-term course. The textbook covers an introduction to information security, basic security countermeasures, and advanced cryptographic systems. This text presupposes a prerequisite knowledge of fundamental college mathematics, computing technology, introduction to networking, introduction to programming, and operating systems concepts. The book uses a rigorous and consistent method of presentation of this material.

In particular, each section of the text specifies the learning goals for the section to provide students with the proper focus. Then, for each section, is a list of key enablers, which are the tasks that students should master to confirm their knowledge before going to the field. Each chapter has a list of key points, which call out the important messages presented. Finally, each chapter ends with a chapter summary, recommended reading, and a set of study questions for self-examination. Lab experiments in Appendix A can be run to gain valuable, hands-on experiences[1] and mixed and matched with custom lesson plans.

It is strongly suggested that the labs be run in conjunction with the course because they have been designed to reinforce the written concepts and will prove interesting for the student.

The text concludes with other useful appendixes, a glossary, and a list of recommended resources for further studies.

Additional information can be found at *www.informationsecurityintel.com.*

---

[1] It is recommended that labs be performed using noncritical and isolated systems because much of the software that is downloaded from the Internet may contain harmful code and viruses that can cause damage to information and infrastructure. It is important to experiment with these labs, but the control of the network-based software is not always reliable. Every effort has been made to focus on materials from only the most reputable sites. The author and publisher of this book, however, cannot be held responsible for the adverse effects of any lab detailed in this text.

ACKNOWLEDGMENTS

When I first started writing, I looked at the acknowledgements from many texts for ideas. Most started out with special regards and thanks to the author's family, usually thanking them for their patience. Now I know why. My family provided incredible support throughout this project. Thanks to my oldest son, Nick, for the great neck massages before he went to bed, and for his interest in my work. Thanks to my twins, Peter and Alyson, for letting daddy work. Special thanks to my wife, Sharon, for her tireless proofreading, typing, and general support. I love you all very much.

I would also like to thank the many people who contributed in so many different ways to the compilation of this book. Bill Dwyer, thank you for the ideas and the thought-provoking conversation. Michael Feeny, thanks for reviewing and working with me on the math section of the book. Thanks to Dr. Joyce Oster, Ph.D. and Professor Eric Oster for taking the time to carefully review and detail the mathematics section. I would also like to thank Professor Mike Gendron for his review, support, enthusiasm, and contributions. Thanks to my colleagues at Johnson and Wales University who made contributions and guided the student workers: Professor Steven Andrade, Professor Al Benoit, Dean Everett Zurlinden, Dr. Kenneth Schneyer, Professor Chris Briggs, Professor Dave Sanzaro, and the administrative staff of the School of Technology.

I would like to give special recognition to Joseph Porreca, Matthew Little, and Karen Labonte for so many hours of crunch-time support and a do-anything attitude. The unselfish sharing of your time is an incredible statement regarding your character and your friendship. I truly appreciate it.

I would also like to thank David Wheeler for his help and support with the Tiny Encryption Algorithm (TEA), and Chris Venesse for his wonderful Javascript implementation of TEA.

Thanks to the many student researchers, lab developers, and programmers from JWU who played a role, in particular: Brendon Moll, Sanjay Uttam, Jesse Derick, Brandon Bendall, Magnus Hansson, William Robsky, Saana Kerroumi, Luis Aranguren, Jason Cabral, Matt Sidla, Kevin Fanion, Albert Hilliard, John Caminiti, Louis Pittsley Jr., Scott Borowy, Melanie Burgess, William McEttrick, Janine Buonomo, Lori Dumas, Colin Finnan, Nicole Kanner, Briane Hume, Alina Fivilay, and Matthew Shaub. I would also like to thank my many industry contacts for their insight and suggestions, in particular: Henry Hodge, Robert Cooper, Bob Hutzley, and also to my many security consulting clients who have been generous in sharing their time and stories.

An old adage observes that, throughout your life, you are lucky if you have one or two really great friends. If that is so, than I am truly blessed. I would like to thank four of my very best friends: Barry Driks, Ed Dena, Jude Horoski, and John Horoski for their continuous support, prayers, and fellowship. In particular the Barry voicemail joke of the day helped me laugh during the year it took to write this book.

Last, but most definitely not least, the credit for the incredible CD that accompanies this text goes largely to Chris Gregson. Chris spent countless hours creating this piece, editing film, programming, managing the other contributors, and handling my countless change requests. Thanks so much for this unbelievable effort.

Thanks to Dawn Daugherty and the staff at Delmar for your support, and to Melissa Sabella for getting me started.

"CSYV HIXIVQMREXMSR AMPP FVMRK CSY QYGL WYGGIWW"
—An encrypted fortune from a fortune cookie I ate during the final
stages of book development. I hope it will guide the readers.

Delmar Learning and the author would like to thank the review panel for their suggestions and comments during the development process. Thanks go to:

William Dwyer
Whitehall, PA

Ryan McCaigue
DeVry University
Phoenix, AZ

Judson Miers
DeVry University
Kansas City, MO

Eric Salveggio
Virginia College
Birmingham, AL

Brent Williams
Purdue University
West Lafayette, IN

SECTION I

Information and Security Planning

OVERVIEW

The essence of any security plan is understanding the properties and behavior of the asset being protected. Information is the single most important element of any computing infrastructure. Given today's modern networks and high-speed processors, large amounts of information can be moved or accessed over thousands of miles in microseconds. Information is processed data and has semantic meaning when paired with the requisite application. Information content has value to its owner.

Information also has an identity. By this we mean that it can be validated, authenticated, and addressed. This identity, combined with the values content, remains valid as long as it does not change without authorization. This is called integrity. Information's integrity must be understood and preserved for data to maintain its value.

Confidentiality, Authenticity, Integrity, and Nonrepudiation (CAIN) is a term that captures the essence of, and describes the four main principles regarding, information security.

The study of the properties of information form the crux of Section One. More specifically, this section of the text details the following five points:

- The properties of information
- The viable threats to that information
- Information risk evaluation techniques
- The information security planning process
- An information security model required to address the CAIN parameters

Section One lays the groundwork for a detailed discussion of how to invoke and enforce information security. The desired outcome of Section One is to synthesize all the elements mentioned with the goal of developing a proper information security plan. With this ability mastered, students will then focus on Section Two of the text. Section Two concerns the information security technique of cryptography.

SECTION GOALS

Upon completion of this section, students should be able to

- Describe the information abstraction
- Understand how to qualitatively and quantitatively characterize information
- List various threats and threat agents to information
- Describe the information architecture model
- Understand basic hacking and cracking techniques
- List the various pieces of legislation that have been introduced and adopted to deal with electronic crime
- Perform a methodical information security risk analysis
- Write a standards-based security plan (e.g., ISO 17799 standard)
- Develop policy statements tying the information security plan to the technologies and security best practices required to successfully implement the plan

KEY ELEMENTS TO SUCCESS IN MASTERING THIS SECTION

To master the topics in this section, students should do the following:

- Pay particular attention to the properties of information. It is important to understand the value of information and why it is the essential focus of our plan
- Focus on the key relationships between information and systems, information and networks, and information and people. By correctly interpreting these relationships, readers can appropriately assess the role of each in the context of a security plan
- Identify and categorize threat agents. Readers should hone their ability to categorize threat agents. Readers should be able to differentiate those posing a clear and present danger to the confidentiality and integrity of information, from those causing disruption/denial of service, and from those presenting minimal danger and being more of a nuisance than a real threat
- Grasp the gist of the federal and local legislation enacted to fight cybercrime and cyberterrorism. It is not necessary to quote verse and chapter of the legal statutes; rather, it is important to grasp the intent and the spirit of the legislation. Students should be able to identify when the laws have been broken, explain how to collect evidence, and suggest appropriate legal recourse
- Create a risk assessment plan based on the ownership, threat, and value tree analysis technique. This is a critical outcome of Section One of this text
- Document a security plan according to ISO17799, based on a proper risk analysis. This is the ultimate goal of Section One

By setting these goals, you will be able to customize your learning plan. It is also highly recommended that you attempt the learning exercises and lab experiments throughout this text to solidify your knowledge with hands-on experiences.

Introduction to Information Theory

He who wants to defend everything, defends nothing.
—Frederick the Great

If your home was on fire, what is the first action you would take? Would you call the fire department, gather your belongings, grab your wallet, and look for your homeowners policy? No, you would most certainly leave the structure, get your family to safety, and then address your property concerns. In a disaster scenario, the preservation of human life is obviously most important. This is so because we value human life above all other possessions.

The first step in creating a personal security plan is to list the items that you need protected and rank them in order of their importance. Undoubtedly, you would put yourself and your family on the top of that list. Try and make a list of everything required to completely secure your home. A few of the items that might come to mind are door locks, window locks, an alarm system, a fire safety plan, fire extinguishers, upper-floor escape ladders, and emergency numbers programmed into your phone. These are the beginnings of a reasonable strategy. But how about more extreme precautions: a bodyguard, weapons, a personal army? For most of us, these measures are impractical and unnecessary.

KEY POINT

Prioritization, scope, and practicality are important concerns in developing a security plan, as shown in Figure 1-1.

Prioritization means that under most circumstances you want to afford an appropriate degree of protection for all items of importance. However, under catastrophic circumstances, lower-priority items can be sacrificed (i.e., the contents of your home or the home itself) to afford maximum protection to the highest-priority items (your personal well being).

Practicality refers to the feasibility of your plan. Nothing in life can be absolutely guaranteed. Thus, overcommitting to one aspect of your plan will surely cause unreasonable sacrifices to be made for another.

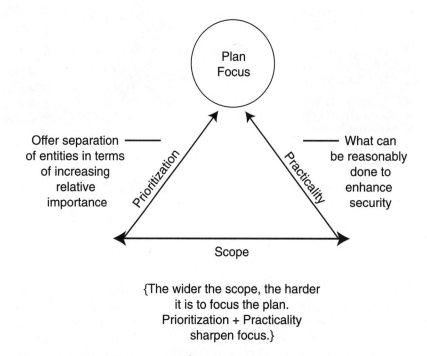

Offer separation of entities in terms of increasing relative importance — Prioritization

What can be reasonably done to enhance security — Practicality

Plan Focus

Scope

{The wider the scope, the harder
it is to focus the plan.
Prioritization + Practicality
sharpen focus.}

Figure 1-1   Prioritization and practicality sharpen focus.

Finally, **scope** is the breadth of your plan. As the scope of your plan increases, the potential for absolute security diminishes proportionately. Take, for example, the securing of a shopping mall or a university campus as compared to personal home security. We now have to consider the volume of occupants and escape routes, the number of security checkpoints, the availability of medical personnel, the protection of store egresses, the handling of large sums of cash and receipts, and more. If done correctly, your security checklist grows rapidly. Further, if you extend this thinking to the local, state, and federal levels, then the checklist is no longer a list. Instead, it is volumes of books of important actions to take and policies to follow. Is it more likely that a national security plan will be breached than a home security plan? Absolutely it is. We see proof of that every time a crime (of any magnitude) is committed.

Securing your person, physical surroundings, or your at-large environment is really not all that different in scope from securing your information infrastructure. As you will learn, both tasks have obvious sets of actionable items when presented on a small scale: They both have many specialty requirements, they require users' cooperation, and they each can be big mountains to climb when looked at from the strategic level "in the large." But most importantly, a security plan has to be devised so that if worst-case scenarios develop, the plan would fail gracefully with respect to the highest-priority security requirements. In other words, if the situation deteriorates (e.g., our house is burning out of control), our plan—while it cannot save the house—allows us to escape to safety.

Chapter 1 acquaints students with the persona of information—what its properties are, how it moves, where it exists, and why protecting it should be the highest-level requirement of our computing security plans. Studying information theory helps us learn about these challenges and provides a foundation for our information security plan.

As you move through this chapter, pay particular attention to the following thirteen properties of information and how we can take advantage of them in devising our security plan:

- Information is hierarchically evolved from data (or, information is processed data)
- Information has an identity
- Information has its roots in numbers and can be mathematically manipulated
- Information's semantic value is from associated applications and storage formats
- Information is presented through data abstractions to users
- Information has an owner(s) and history
- Information can be altered
- Information can be copied
- Information can move
- Information can be authenticated
- Information has integrity
- Information can be self-describing through the use of metatags.
- Information can have associated access controls
- Information can be disguised through the use of encoding schemes

 To successfully complete this chapter, students should pay particular attention to:

- The definition of information
- The properties of information, being sure to understand why each property makes information unique
- The mathematical properties of information, especially the binary representation of data
- The computer organization of information, in particular the relationship between bits, bytes, data, fields, records, files, and information. This property becomes critical later in the text
- The separation of information from the information system. Pay careful attention to the differences between the two and how information is more focused than the information system and, thus, easier to protect
- The use of abstractions throughout the history of computing and how we can take advantage of this strategy to encourage the implementation of information security
- The need for metadata so that information can be treated as an independent entity
- The definition and intent of the CAIN principles
- The components of the information system
- How information travels and is moved
- How information is stored and represented on a computer and other digital devices

It is also important that readers understand the relationships between information and data, information and systems, information and networks, and information and people. Once these relationships and properties are mastered, readers will have a firm grasp on the psychology of information and be better prepared to understand the threats it may encounter. This understanding prepares students to plan effectively for information security.

SECURING INFORMATION

Why do we consider information to be the primary focus of our security plan? As we have alluded to thus far, security planning cannot be considered an absolute guarantee. In life, bad things happen to good people all the time. Even under the tightest of security, crime occurs. Presidents have been assassinated even though the U.S. Secret Service assigns considerable, dedicated resources to their protection. As we have discussed, we need to prioritize our thinking and our planning. What is most important? Can it be protected? Is this plan overly restrictive of movement, access, and freedom?

KEY POINT

To maximize security, it is necessary to isolate and restrict the object of the protection. It is imperative, however, to weigh the cost of this isolation and restriction against the benefit gained from that particular measure of protection.

In our computing security plan, as with our example of a house on fire, it is unlikely we will face a complete catastrophe. It is possible , however, and we must be prepared for this scenario. In our electronic protection scheme, we must set priorities, understand the scope of potential losses (**risk**), and plan accordingly.

The notion of securing computing infrastructures, networks, premises, and identities can seem daunting from the outset. Given even the most modest of computing infrastructures, it is obvious that the number of security measures required to provide a "safe" environment can be large. In most Fortune 500 commercial applications, that number can be overwhelming. Completely securing the Internet would be impossible, just as it is impossible to protect every citizen of the United States or the world from being victimized by crime. As shown in Table 1-1, numerous destructive virus attacks were launched in 2002 and 2003. These attacks have infected countless thousands of computers and are hard to stop—or even predict—because they are launched indiscriminately against the computer populace at large.

Most of us feel safe in our own homes, are not afraid to participate openly in local social events, use the public facilities provided by the state and private enterprises, travel comfortably within the borders of the United States, and feel empowered to explore the world. Similarly, most computer users work on their personal computers without much concern. They utilize the computing environments of their employers, educational institutions, or private enterprise. And most persons enjoy exploring the boundaries of our electronic world through the Internet.

Most computer crime is of the nuisance type. By this, we mean that a website can be defaced, or access to a service denied, or unauthorized access achieved with no intent of damaging information. In most of these cases, the crimes are committed by curious, immature people who have too much free time. Generally, the intent is to see if they *can* commit cybercrime, not to destroy information. This behavior can be terribly inconvenient, even expensive (e.g., lost productivity), but it generally will not cause a company to go bankrupt. On the other hand, the complete loss of financial data at a bank, the complete loss of student information at a university, or the disruption of health care service caused by the alteration or loss of patient data could have long-term implications for the survival of an institution.

As seen in Table 1-2, fraud and identity theft have become the largest sector of new computer crime. In the case of fraud, the perpetrator is typically utilizing the medium to gain access to personal information about the user. This information can then be used to scam money from legitimate organizations, credit card companies, and the like.

Table 1-1 Example of Viruses and Worms

Virus/Worm	Month Discovered	Features
I Love You	May 2000	Delivered in an e-mail with "I Love You" in the subject line. Opening the attachment starts its execution. Sends itself to everyone in the host's address book. Writes over music and picture files. Created by a Filipino student.
SirCam	July 2001	Delivered in an e-mail with a subject based on a document in a previously infected machine. Requests advice from the recipient in an attachment that looks like a document or other file. Sends itself to everyone in the host's address book and hides in the Recycle Bin so it is not found by all antivirus software.
Code Red	August 2001	Attacks a flaw in Internet Informatin System (IIS) Web server software. Defaces Web pages and degrades system performance, and can cause overload on other servers.
Nimda	October 2001	Spreads via e-mail, websites, or shared hard disks on networks. Hits computers running Windows operating systems and repropagates periodically, reinfecting machines. Slowed the Internet down as it affected Web servers.
Goner	December 2001	Delivered in an e-mail that invites the recipient to look at a screen saver attachment. Attacks antivirus software on the host computer as well as firewalls on servers.

Table 1-2 Types of Internet Fraud

Type of IT Fraud	Primary Group Affected	Fraudulent Activities
Credit card fraud	Business	Web sites skim credit card numbers and use them to charge purchases or cash advances that are disallowed by the credit card company.
Investor fraud	Consumer and business	Criminals use chat rooms to pump up the price of an almost worthless stock, which they then dump at a high price.
Illegal IDs	Business	Underage individuals use IT to create IDs, which they use to purchase tobacco and alcohol.
Online auction fraud	Consumer and business	The seller does not provide the goods after receiving payment or the buyer does not make payment after receiving the goods
Identity theft	Consumers	Information about an individual is stolen and used to set up a new identity for the criminal or other person
Travel fraud	Consumers	Websites promise great ticket prices or trips and then do not provide them to the buyer
Telephone fraud	Consumers	Users are lured into unknowingly downloading software that calls an international number, resulting in huge telephone charges

Identity theft techniques can be used for far more malicious activities, including obtaining false documents for criminals and terrorists. Table 1-3 lists the broad categories of information technology crime that can cause the greatest financial damage.

Table 1-3 Types of Computer Crime

Type of IT Crime	Purpose
Theft	Steal hardware, data, or information from individuals or organizations, either directly or through networks.
Fraud	Use computers and the Internet to steal money or other valuable items by deceiving victims.
Copyright infringement	Use software, music, or trademarks, which in many cases are obtained illegally over the Internet.
Attacks	Damage hardware, data, or information.

To confirm our commitment to the vital role of information, we will examine how it is used. As seen in Figure 1-2, data represents our historical representation of events. Information is created from this data to achieve a view of our present condition. This same information forms the basis for our decisions about the future. This cycle continues with respect to time and ultimately determines if our business survives or fails. Thus, if we lose our information, we have no basis upon which to form future decisions. Given the extent to which our businesses are tied to the electronic representation of information, protecting it is essential.

In our electronic world, many security implementations are focused on the systems and network components (information systems). Some plans treat information systems, as opposed to the information as the object of the security model. This approach is often breached because it fails to focus the security plan on what is most important to the organization—the information it possesses. Over the last five years, the prevailing security focus has shifted toward information. Emerging companies such as VeriSign provide information-focused security solutions. Given the events of recent history, this information awareness was evident in the stability of our financial markets after the September 11th attacks. The World Trade Center attacks took a high toll on human life and dealt a blow to our national infrastructure. One might have thought that such a strike at the infrastructure of the world's financial capital would have devastated the world's ability to transact business and would have introduced chaos into the securities community. However, it did not. Why do you suppose that was? It comes down to two reasons. First, there was an increased awareness of the vulnerability of our information after the World Trade Center bombing in 1993. Many companies made a complete reassessment of their information security requirements and opted to decentralize their data stores, move the primary processing facilities to remote and hardened sites, and create "hot backup sites," which could be brought online in an emergency.

The second reason lies in our current computing styles. With the maturity of personal computing, many people maintain their regular work information locally. This work style allows people's information to remain with them wherever they go. Copies of this information are maintained on a widely distributed infrastructure of various kinds of servers. As opposed to the electronic world we knew just ten to fifteen years ago, the current emphasis has shifted from centralized data warehousing to diverse, decentralized information-based personal computing, utilizing extensive client-server relationships.

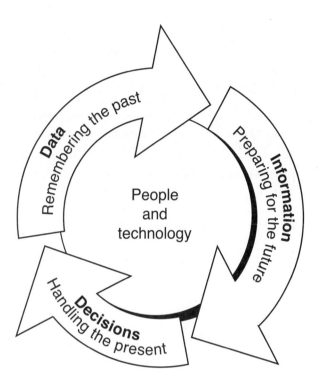

Figure 1-2   The IS cycle.

As a result of these two paradigm shifts, significant infrastructure was destroyed, phone systems were affected, and some data services were lost. Yet the information archive, which was distributed and protected, remained intact. Many of the affected organizations had remote and redundant data centers. Much organizational information was local to the users. Because the information survived and remained available, it was possible to redistribute it so that business could resume (in a slightly limited capacity) while the affected infrastructure was quickly rebuilt elsewhere and reactivated.

KEY POINT

Information, not systems and networks (information system), needs to be at the core of our security plan.

Even though the information survived, critical systems were lost. This distinction was the enabler that allowed us to restart our businesses and our economy. The lesson is that the security emphasis in this new era of computing has to be focused on the information, which is at the core of our information security architecture.

KEY POINT

According to *Information Security* magazine, sixty-four percent of companies will be investing in intrusion-detection software this year and a projected sixty percent increase in U.S. federal spending on IT security is expected in 2003. A projected growth rate of 117 percent is expected in worldwide Virtual Private Networks (VPNs—encryption tunnels through the Internet) by 2006 (Infonetics Research). All of these predictions are significant because they point to an unheralded focus in overall electronic security, on information security protection, and on the need for privacy.

http://www.misti.com/08/tris0802sp.html

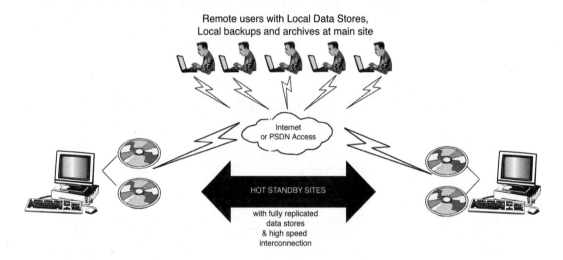

Figure 1-3   Large corporation infomation disaster recovery strategy.

PLANNING INFORMATION SECURITY

Successful security planning of any kind first requires a detailed understanding of the entity being protected. In our case, that entity is **information.** Information should be treated as a living being within our computer systems and networks. Information moves, changes, and grows (figuratively speaking). Information has meaning, purpose, and value, and it can be irrecoverably damaged by accidents or acts of malice. Information is not data. Information is actually processed data and has power and worth.

After examining ways to protect information and understand the properties of information, which enhance our protection strategies, we must formulate a security plan (see Figure 1-3). This plan is necessary to coordinate the implementation of all the parts of our security model across the enterprise. This plan must be adhered to and strictly enforced to ensure success. The plan must be adaptable to various technologies already in place. The plan must be adopted by our management and user communities.

A security plan has three essential parts:

- Protection of the information itself at the core
- Hardening of our resources (systems and networks)
- Authentication of those accessing the information

As seen in Figure 1-4, these three parts break down further and form the basis for the information security architecture model seen in Figure 1-5.

For all the reasons previously discussed, information is at the core of the model. We then introduce layer upon layer of areas of security defenses, which would need to be compromised before the data could be affected. We coat the core information with a protective covering—cryptography—that is tightly bonded with the information and follows it wherever it goes. Next, we require authentication using digital certificates for information access control. These inner three layers address protection of the information at the core.

Hardening of resources is addressed through the next three layers: OS hardening, system and network configurations, and information system architecture. These three areas need to be addressed to minimize the possibility of the information being destroyed, stolen, or altered while "at home." The internal network and systems need to be considered a safe haven for information. Further, we wish to provide safeguards

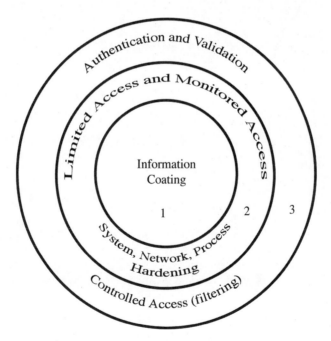

Users are forced to penetrate
layers of security
This optimizes security and maximizes
the opportunity to
control access

Figure 1-4   Three core parts of information security.

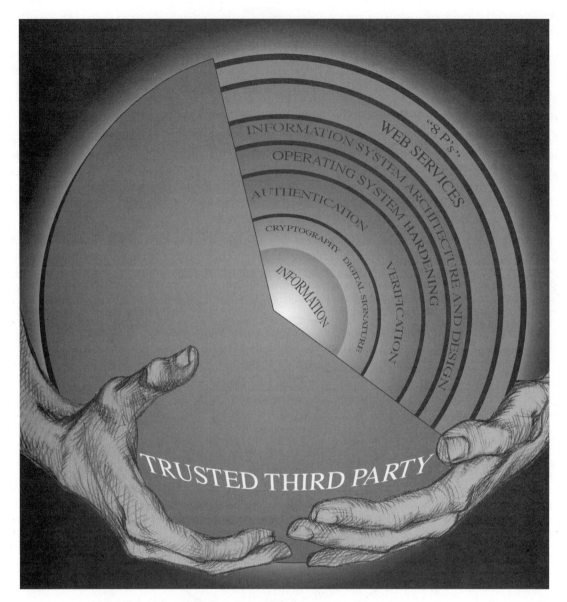

Figure 1-5 Information Security model.

that enable the information to travel between remote locations of the organization safely over the public network.

Finally, through our World Wide Web layer and our eight Ps layer, the control of public access to the information and user-level security controls are addressed. In these two layers, we allow for the requisite viewing and manipulation of the information within established and acceptable guidelines. It is also in these two layers that we address the public aspects of our information's exposure, physical defenses, access policies, availability, and management. The outermost layer defines access controls, user behavior, and policy development.

If we look at Figure 1-6, we see that an organization must address the degree of security required to meet the requirements of the organization. They range from ultrarestrictive to extremely permissive. The degree of security the organization wants will directly influence the degree to which any layer in the model is implemented. We will return to this important consideration in Chapter 2.

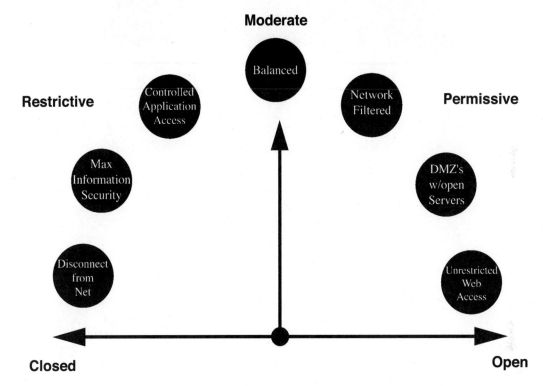

Figure 1-6   Degrees of security.

Just as the OSI model is to network planning, the information security architecture (a security reference model) is to developing information security plans and implementations. This model focuses more on information than on infrastructure. As you will see in the chapters and sections that follow, the approach is aimed at protecting the information's **confidentiality, authenticity, integrity, and nonrepudiation (CAIN)**. CAIN, as shown in Figure 1-7, is an industry standard principle that is the base upon which the model stands. We will explore the CAIN principle in detail later in this section.

For our plan and model to be successful, we need to embrace the concept of a **trusted third party**. A trusted third party is a neutral participant—whose integrity is beyond reproach—in an information transaction. This third party enables validation of the transaction, authentication of the information/participants, and confidence in a predictable, controlled outcome. For example, this concept has

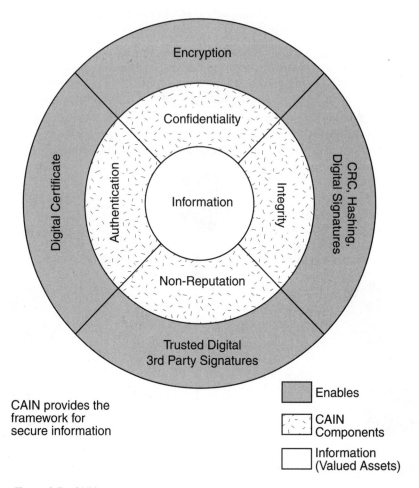

Figure 1-7   CAIN.

long been the premise of a successful monetary system, which requires that the exchange of a note be backed by a promise to the bearer (and receiver) of the note as to its worth. The government, in this case, is the trusted third party. When we write a check, the bank is the trusted third party that promises payment. When we use a credit card, the credit card company is the trusted third party. For information to be of value, a similar set of promises must be made and kept to establish trust.

All these elements need to be brought together in the form of a well thought-out security plan. This plan will form the basis for a successful information security implementation. It will also be used as a guide to developing a cohesive set of information security management policies. Notice that information is the central theme of our security plan. After learning the material in Section One of this text, students should be able to derive this plan and these policies from the organizational requirements, with the information security architecture model as a guide. We will review the layers of our model throughout the text. This model forms the industry foundations of information security. The balance of Chapter 1 will focus on the nature of information.

DATA TO INFORMATION

As was mentioned previously, you need to know a lot about what you are protecting and how it is likely to behave to provide the best possible security. In the case of securing the family before purchasing an alarm system, for example, it is helpful to know the makeup and behavior of the family. Are there small children? Where do they play? Is there a pool or other potentially dangerous area? Where does each person sleep? Who is the last person to arrive home? Who is the most responsible person in an emergency? Is the family away from home a lot? By knowing these answers, you can begin to build a profile of family behaviors. This profile can be useful in helping detect vulnerabilities and, subsequently, build a security plan that best fits the lifestyle of the family. Notice that the emphasis is on the family and their actions, not on their possessions. Obviously, possessions will be secured and addressed as part of the plan, but our plan is primarily concerned with the safety of the family.

Information sits at the core of our model. We begin our exploration of the properties of information by understanding where information comes from. Information is made up of one or more data elements. So, the first question that must be answered is this: "What exactly *is* data?"

As seen in Figure 1-8, data should be thought of as a logical collection of bits (ones and zeros) that represent a byte (8 bits) or bytes (multiples of 8 bits), as defined by the data type. A byte is the smallest addressable unit in most operating systems. This does not mean that we cannot have bit-wise operations. Rather, we refer to bits with respect to their position within bytes.

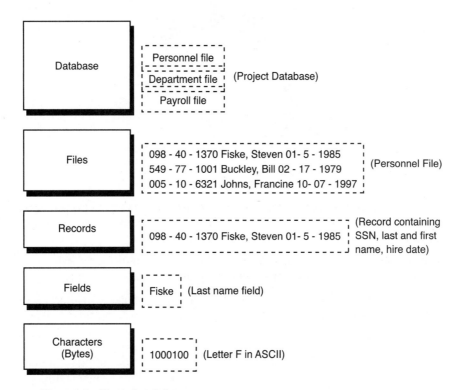

Figure 1-8   Hierarchy of data.

Bytes of data can be accessed in two ways: Individually, as is the case if the byte represents an ASCII character; or in groups, as in the representation of simple or complex numbers. For example, 2 bytes (16 bits) represent an integer value in most systems, while 4 bytes (32 bits) might represent a long integer. Numbers can use specific bits within the bytes assigned to represent the sign of the number, positive or negative. The location of the bytes can be thought of as an address in the computer memory. An address points to a particular memory location that can contain a value or a part of a value (determined by the type—character or numeric).

Figure 1-8 shows how data is made up of varying numbers of addressable byte-wise-typed units. Programs and databases require the user to predefine the type of data for use prior to execution. This requirement allows the operating system to understand the application's data requirements so that sufficient supplies of data units can be allocated.

This explanation is the strictest definition of data. Currently, most people define data more loosely and are actually misusing it. Data and information are not the same. This assumption is incorrect and is an important distinction to make. Data are the building blocks of information, as shown in Figure 1-9. Data are combined and manipulated by the applications to give meaning and value.

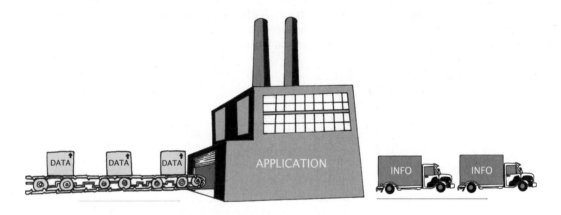

Figure 1-9 Data to information.

File-based applications allow for the combination of data elements to form fields. For example, an address is a field that is formed by the combination of data that represent the individual characters of the street and number of a house.

These fields can also be combined to form records. These records combine related fields to describe some entity. This combining of related fields is the core concept in most database applications.

The compilation of related records is found in files. These files are then placed in folders, which are accessible to the user for continued use. These files and folders can be shared, moved, or manipulated.

ABSTRACTIONS

To understand the properties of information, we need to first understand the concept of **abstraction**. Abstraction means to hide the details. Abstractions are used in computers, engineering, product development, and many other technology-based disciplines. For example, when you use Windows XP[1] (shown in Figure 1-10), you are using an abstraction. By clicking on the "My Computer" icon and the Folders option, you are able to move files through the standard click-and-drag method. However, in reality, the file is actually moved through the execution of many CPU and memory interactions. These details are hidden from the user and, thus, we have an abstraction. This concept forms the basis of every user interface ever developed.

The goal of an abstraction is to create a higher-level, simpler interface. Upon implementation, the user invokes this abstraction whenever it is necessary to handle the details of the lower-level, and more complex, system. This allows the user to focus on the high-level task and not become overwhelmed by the details of the tool they are trying to use. This concept has served as the catalyst for the unparalleled growth in the computer industry.

All of computing has been affected by the power of abstractions. It is the single biggest reason computing is as popular as it is today. People use what they understand and therein lies the power of abstractions.

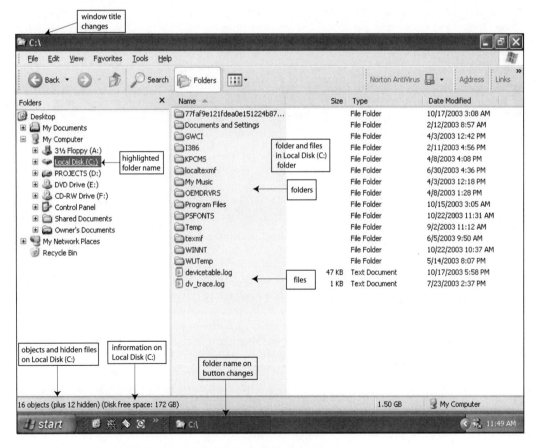

Figure 1-10   Viewing the data hierarchy.

[1.] Windows XP is a registered trademark of Microsoft Corporation.

A computer consists of a central processing unit (CPU), the arithmetic logic unit (ALU), the bus that connects all of the hardware components to a common communication pathway, the computer memory, network interfaces, off-line storage devices, peripherals, and more. These internal devices—when activated via computer instructions executed in the CPU—combine to perform the functions required to execute the applications. Even for those who have studied the details of computer architecture, it is difficult to formulate a concise explanation of how even the most routine tasks (e.g., printing to a printer) are actually carried out. So, imagine if the average user had to communicate the details of those operations every time they wanted to print something. The thought of having to coordinate those activities each and every time you need them would dishearten even the most ardent among us. As a result, the concept of an operating system was introduced more than forty years ago. Its primary purpose was to hide the details of the underlying computer architecture from the user, making operation of the computer easy and efficient. This is our first example of an abstraction in the computer science field.

Since then, this particular abstraction has continued to improve. No longer must we utilize the cryptic commands of the conventional operating system. Today we use point-and-click, icon-driven technology. Our movements of the mouse initiate programs containing thousands of lines of code with the click of a button. Today, the casual user needs limited (or even no) understanding of the underlying computer architecture. This is a key point of which we must be mindful. Users rely on abstractions.

KEY POINT

Information is stored and maintained in many remote computers operated by those who have little actual computer knowledge.

Programming languages also have evolved over the years. They, too, have benefited from the abstraction paradigm. Programming in machine code or assembly code is no longer necessary to gain control over system elements.[2] Currently, we program in third- and fourth-generation languages (commonly referred to as 3GL and 4GL). These languages provide the necessary abstractions for programmers to program the applications. The programming language abstraction hides the details and intricacies of implementing routine system, memory, and network interfaces.

DATA ABSTRACTION

Information, like programming languages and operating systems, also relies heavily on abstraction techniques. As previously discussed, computers understand the differences between ones and zeros. A one is created through the presence of an electrical charge (in memory or on a wire) and the zero is created by the absence of that charge. These ones and zeros (bits) form the basis of all data. Computers address memory in terms of **bytes.** Bytes are formed by grouping eight of these **bits** (ones and zeros) together. As far as the CPU and memory are concerned, this is the extent of data. Computers place no semantic value on data. That is to say, the computer does not know what the data represent, only that it exists. However, we know that this data, these bytes, actually have semantic value. For example, a collection of bytes, when taken as a group, might represent information concerning your bank account. Once we (not the machine) know what it represents, we can apply an application to it, creating an environment in which it makes semantic sense and has value. We do this through a combination of data abstraction and programming abstraction (i.e., creating applications).

---

2. In some instances of real-time programming and programming microdevices, it is still more efficient to program in assembly-level code.

Remember that data abstraction is relatively simple: Bits are grouped to make bytes. Bytes, or collections of bytes, can be typed. Typing allows us to understand that the bytes represent different kinds of numbers (integers, floating points, long integers) or characters. Collections of these common types of bytes are used to form **fields**. For example, your first name is a collection of bytes of the type character, which could be used to form a first name field. Fields are then combined to form **records.** Records are logically connected groups of fields. For example, your first name, last name, address, and phone number form a directory record. Collections of logically connected records describe **entities.** An entity is a real-world object. For example, a collection of these directory records could be grouped to form a phone book. This represents our data abstraction. Entities at the computer level are a collection of ones and zeros, with limited meaning. Entities at the application level take that same collection of ones and zeros and can be used to model real world objects.

Let us take a step back. We have uncovered yet another important trait of information. *The semantic meaning of the data is implied, and is revealed only through additional application processing.*

KEY POINT

Information is processed data. The combination of data and applications gives information its value.

Without an implied meaning, the data itself appears to have limited or no meaning. The semantic value of data is introduced through its requisite application. Therefore, information has an inherent security quality: You need the correct interpretation (application awareness) of the data, plus the data itself, to make information. The absence of either of these qualities reduces the worth or usefulness of the information.

Moving forward with this concept, we see that information is far greater than simply a collection of bits or bytes or even data. Information has semantic value based on the applications, which establish intent for use within the computer. It is important to note that computer hardware executes what can be considered a simplistic set of instructions, which provides basic logic for the manipulation and movement of data. Therefore, those who build a security plan around the computer environment are protecting something that is not only a commodity (easily replaced), but also of little real importance if taken apart from the information. Conversely, the information (the processed data and the application) can be utilized on any properly matched machine and, thus, it has a value that far exceeds that of the hardware it runs on or the networks that it moves on (see Figure 1-11).

KEY POINT

We will define information to mean the combination of processed data and its associated application.

We have discussed value with how it relates to information. The semantic interpretations of processed data by the applications yield information, which is of value. But we have yet to define value itself. What makes information valuable to the consumer? Ask this question: "Why is money valuable?" Most would agree that money is valuable because we believe the promise made by the government that lets us trade the currency for goods. Simply put, the more money you have, the more goods you can purchase.

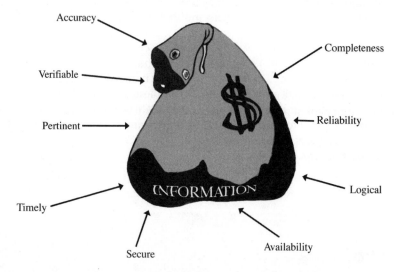

Figure 1-11 Making information valuable.

According to a variation of an old saying, information is power. The more information you have the more control you have over uncertain outcomes. Like money, however, a promise must be kept: The information must be of use to have value. For information to be of use, it must be all of the following: accurate, complete, reliable, logical, verifiable, available, timely, pertinent, and secure. Notice that security is like a blanket that covers all of the other qualities. Just like money in the bank, users need to believe that the information has not been altered, manipulated, stolen, or destroyed. The information needs to be valid for making the decisions required by the organization. Information, like money, must be held to a certain standard to have value.

METADATA

A term that has recently become popular is **metadata**. Literally translated, metadata means "data about the data." As we continue to develop the information abstraction, it is fashionable to incorporate metatags into the information. Metatags describe qualities about the data and its intended use. These characteristics can be viewed by the applications, by operating systems, and by network devices separately from the information so that direct actions can be taken by those components with respect to the information.

These tags range from primitive cyclical redundancy checks, used as part of the error control process, to sophisticated authentication and configuration parameters. Tags are useful in speeding up processing by predetermining the amount of storage the incoming information will require. Metadata is popular in **Hypertext Transport Protocol**. In this particular instance, the metatags are incorporated in the protocol headers along with the data to reference:

- Status codes regarding the condition of a file transfer
- Information expiration data
- Client or server authentication information
- An explanation of the information
- Information size and resource requirements

HTTP and S-HTTP for secure Web access are important parts of information access and are discussed in detail in Chapter 11.

Other examples of metadata are digital signatures, encryption keys, and protocol header information. E-mail, for example, layers a significant amount of metadata onto a message to guarantee proper delivery of the message and application (mail use) affiliation.

Metadata is a powerful component of information and, therefore, must be protected. We will repeatedly address the metadata component of information, particularly regarding information ciphering and S-HTTP.

CAIN

It is important to understand the dynamics of secure information. What is the litmus test for information security readiness? As was previously mentioned, information security and our subsequent security plan must be closely tied to the CAIN paradigm. CAIN is a principle that assists us in the evaluation of our security posture (see Risk Management in Chapter 2). For now, we will look at the intent of the CAIN components.

Confidentiality reflects the necessity to keep information private. We must understand the privacy requirements of the information's owner and reflect them in information security controls. Information confidentiality controls can be implemented through the use of encryption, file access controls, file system privacy features, system access controls, and public key cryptography. These controls are discussed at length in this text.

Authenticity is the ability to determine if the information you receive or use is the original information as it was intended to be presented. Information becomes suspect when, for example, spoofed e-mail—the process of replacing the true identity of the sender with a fake one—occurs. This deception misleads the user and can result in a serious crisis.

Integrity is the property of the information being complete and uncorrupted. Integrity is closely related to authenticity. Authenticity fraud is the deliberate intent to deceive. Integrity problems are focused more on the usability of the information, based on consistency in the original bit pattern with respect to time. Viruses, worms, and other malware can create integrity issues with data. In addition, integrity problems can arise from other nonsecurity-related problems, such as a noisy transmission system, a bad data storage device, or exposure of information to noncompatible versions of our applications.

Nonrepudiation concerns the undisputed ownership of information, or the undisputed initiator of an information transaction. Therefore, the information's originator should be able to prove ownership without question, and not deny ownership for the sake of convenience. The Digital Signature Bill discussed in Chapter 3 allows us to utilize our digital correspondence and actions as we would our own signature. Thus, information gains power.

Understanding and embracing these principles helps us understand why we take certain particular actions while developing our security posture.

INFORMATION AND NUMBERS

As we just discussed, information is created or takes its semantic value from processed data. Data is ultimately just collections of ones and zeros—binary numbers. Information is hierarchically evolved from data and thus inherits all of its most basic attributes.

KEY POINT

Information in the most primitive sense can also be thought of as a collection of numbers.

Because all electronic information can be thought of as numbers, it can be manipulated using all forms of mathematics. Mathematics, or the study of numbers, is based on proven theories, axioms, and lemmas. Proofs are any mathematical principle that is **idempodent** across the set of real numbers. This means that given a basic mathematical principle (e.g., addition, subtraction, multiplication, division, Boolean operations) the corresponding operation, when applied to any numbers, will yield the same answers for the same numbers every time. Stated another way: Given the addition operation as an example, we can prove that addition, when applied to any two numbers, yields the following:

- An answer for a given pair that will always yield the same result (e.g., 2 + 2 = 4 every time)
- A principle that can be extended to include all real numbers, x and y, such that we can perform the operation x + y on any real number. This provides a confidence that this addition operation will work the same way on all real numbers and need not be put to the test for the complete set of numbers (which would obviously be impossible)
- A principle that is extensible to include additional axioms such as the commutative law x + y = y + x

The manipulation of data remains consistent with the laws of mathematics. These laws allow us to guarantee that the process applied to the data can be reversed, thus allowing us to regenerate the original message from the ciphertext. This is an important property of information because it is the very basis of **cryptography**. Cryptography, as we will see later in the text, capitalizes on these very mathematical laws to create disguises for information. Cryptography can be used to protect information's confidentiality, integrity, authenticity, and nonrepudiation. These disguises become a companion to the information, traveling with the information wherever it goes.

KEY POINT

Cryptography fundamentally exploits both mathematical logic and properties to disguise, protect, and authenticate information. It is a crucial CAIN enabler.

Some of the mathematics we will discuss in Section Two of the text revolve around special numbers. These special numbers include pi (π), the golden ratio, prime numbers, and the like. We will see that these numbers have interesting properties that can help us **encrypt** (the process of cloaking or encoding our information) and **decrypt** (the process of decoding) our information.

These special numbers are used in conjunction with specialized numerical methods which, when taken together, form powerful cryptographic algorithms. These methods include modular arithmetic, Fermat's theorem, Euclid's theorem, Chinese remainder theorem, and orthogonal mathematics. All of these methods are discussed in detail in Section Two of the book.

INFORMATION SYSTEMS

We previously defined information as both the set of related processed data and the associated applications. These two work together to give information its value. They form the information entity. To be accessed by information users, the information entity does require an information system. The information system can be thought of as an information access and control platform. If you recall, we have already alluded to the idea that computers, in the absence of information, are of limited use. In fact, computers offer only the fundamental instruction set required to run applications that turn data into information. The information system can also be thought of as combinations of these computers and networks so they are able to **input** the information, **access** the information, **process** the information, **output** information, and provide **feedback** regarding the process that is running. This process is shown in Figure 1-12.

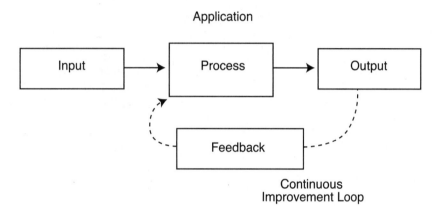

Figure 1-12   Continuous process improvement.

Each component of the information system has to be examined and controlled so that the information can be protected from unapproved access.

This system may comprise one or more subsystems: computers, storage arrays, memory components, networks and network components, and a variety of support applications (e.g., Microsoft applications, browsers, OSs). The system is defended in the middle tiers of our security model because each of these components, while important to the access, development, and use of information, is not mission critical and can be replaced.

The final topic of this chapter deals with understanding the relationships between information and the various components of the information system. This information system, while not as high a security priority as the information itself, is also an important component of our security plan.

KEY POINT

The information and the information system are two separate entities with different sets of security requirements.

STORAGE DEVICES

The most basic component of the information system is the storage devices that contain the data to be processed. Many types of storage options exist in three broad classes: short-term memory, permanent or longer-term storage, and network-accessible (shared) storage.

The four primary types of memory are Random Access Memory (RAM), Read-Only Memory (ROM), Programmable RAM (PRAM), and cache.

RAM is considered a volatile memory, meaning that it is temporary. This memory is used to track instructions (executable code) and data during application execution. RAM is considered a series of switches that are manipulated by placing electrical charges on them. Once the power to the unit and the RAM is removed, the data and instructions that were previously executing are lost.

ROM is nonvolatile, or memory that does not change. In this memory configuration, the memory does not lose its contents when the power to the system is removed.

Cache is a special high-speed access memory available to the CPU. This memory is faster to access than RAM and offers many performance advantages to the computing power of a machine.

From a security perspective, it is important to realize that remnants of all processed data and applications will remain in RAM or cache until the memory is recycled. These remnants of information have formed the basis of many successful attacks that have resulted in unwanted disclosure of information. For this reason, we must include the management of these OS controlled storage areas as part of our information security plans.

It is also important to note that the ROM or PROM is where our base applications (i.e., operating systems, vendor-supplied programs, network protocols, and memory management routines) are stored. This information controls the operation of the environment and the access to information stored in this machine.

Permanent storage can be achieved through many external devices attached to the computer, as shown in Figure 1-13. These devices include magnetic tape, magnetic disks, Redundant Array of Independent Disks (RAIDs), Storage Area Networks (SANs), optical disks, Digital Video Disks (DVDs), memory cards and memory sticks, and flash memory, among others. These devices archive our information for longer-term access and for backup and recovery purposes. It is important that we control access to these devices in a secure manner to prevent our information from being compromised. Long-term memory is vulnerable to attack. When you delete a file from long-term memory, only the pointer to the file is deleted. The contents remain on the disk until it is properly cleared. Disk- recovery tools can retrieve previously deleted files.

ACCESS METHODS

The device types mentioned previously have various access methods for retrieving data. In general, computer operating systems control data processing and information generation. Data are input from one of the various sources previously mentioned and brought into the RAM or main computer memory for the CPU to access. Once the data and the application are present, the processor can apply the prescribed logic (program), which then creates the semantic value and produces information.

These access methods are important because each one implies how much of the storage device's contents is accessed by a particular application. In the case of **Sequential Access Method (SAM)**, data are retrieved in the order in which they reside on the storage medium. This means that for the application to use any

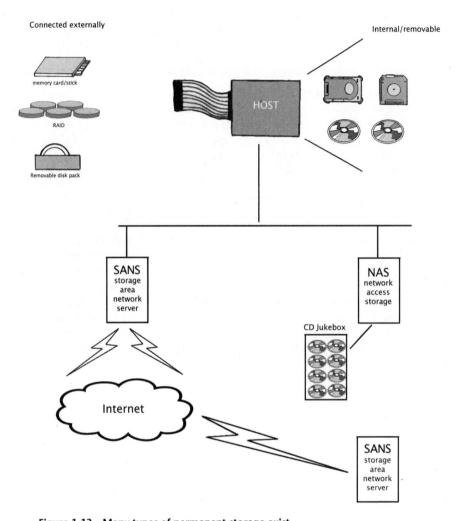

Figure 1-13   Many types of permanent storage exist.

part of the data, it must sift through all of the contents between the first data elements and the one sought. This process is slow and less secure. By processing in this fashion, the data are placed into volatile memory for this cursory examination. The result is exposing the information to the types of remnant searches that were discussed earlier.

Direct access methods provide a more efficient search and retrieval algorithm, which is far more secure than SAM. The memory contents are directly accessed based on indexes pointing to particular data elements based on **keys** to that data.

Additionally, information is stored in various formats that are OS dependent. These are important considerations to examine when determining with whom you want to share information and whether or not your systems are compatible. These storage formats are the focus of companies such as EMC Corporation.

EMC produces a line of products that allows for conversion of these formats so that information on non-homogeneous systems can be shared. These formats include NFS for UNIX systems, NTFS for XP and NT systems, FATS 16 and FATS 32 for Windows 98/2000, and CIFS for network attached storage.

DATA STRUCTURES, DATABASES, DATA WAREHOUSES, AND DATA MINING

Programmers and computer scientists create most of the applications we use in our information systems. These programmers and software engineers utilize standard programming practices, which enable the modeling of real-world entities through software. Most recently, the object-oriented model has evolved. In this model, software objects are created for the purpose of modeling. These objects have attributes and methods. For example, if we were to model a bank account, we might create attributes such as the account number, the name on the account, and the balance of the account. Methods or actions might include deposits, withdrawals, and inquiries. At run time, processes that access the information required to populate these objects are created. The objects are then enabled and work independently. Currently, objects include methods for information security (e.g., encryption).

Databases are similar in nature but have a much broader scope. Information is archived and accessed through a database. The most popular type of database is known as the **relational database**. This type of database stores information in **tables**. These tables are of a familiar row and column format as shown in Figure 1-14. The rows in the tables represent entities. An entity is the real-world object we are trying to model. The columns are attributes, which describe the entity. One or more of these attributes can be considered to be a **key**. Keys are required by the database so individual entities or groups of entities can be identified. A key that uniquely identifies an entity is considered a **primary key**. Primary keys are important because they ensure proper database development and, consequently, eliminate the potential for duplicate entities (redundancy).

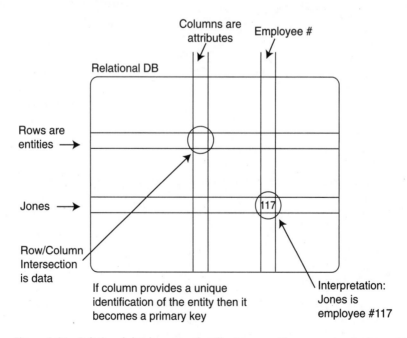

Figure 1-14   Relational databases are familiar to users. They are extensively used in industry.

Databases are widely used and are the source of much of the data we use to form information upon which we base our decisions. Databases are important parts of the information system. Attacks on databases often affect the integrity and confidentiality of data, two key CAIN components. Database security is a high-priority item in our security model.

HIPAA

As an example of the highly restrictive requirements of databases, we will briefly examine medical records databases. Recently, the Health Insurance Portability and Accountability Act (HIPAA) legislation was passed at the federal level. This set of laws requires health care providers to protect all forms of patient information and confidentiality. As of the writing of this text, most states are preparing to enforce this legislation, and most health care providers are seeking ways to comply. The legislation prohibits charts on patient doors, hallway or elevator conversation regarding patient care, and unauthorized access to patient records. These records are for the most part maintained electronically and provide the basis for care and treatment. These records usually are accessed by physicians, medical staff, administration, insurance providers, and others involved in the diagnostic and rehabilitation process. According to HIPAA, a person viewing a patient record must be permitted to view only that portion of the contents relevant to his function. For example, a hospital financial administrator really has no need to know the prognosis of a patient's illness. Thus, the hospital information services departments at most every hospital in the United States are currently trying to cope with this new legislation and devise methods for its enforcement. The majority of these databases are vast and have long histories. Therefore, they will be difficult to retrofit. One possible solution involves the implementation of row/column access restrictions. Many companies are currently researching solutions to this interesting security problem.

INFORMATION MOVEMENT

Another key component of our information system is the networks upon which information is transported. The information is first passed to the network stack where it is passed from the application to lower network-centric layers. At these layers the information is **encapsulated** in a series of **protocols** as it is prepared for transport. We will reference the **OSI model**, shown in Figure 1-15, often throughout this text because it is an excellent framework for our discussion. This model depicts seven distinct layers that control various functions of the communications architecture.

The layer closest to the user is the application layer. At this layer, information is presented to the transport architecture by the controlling application. This application places a request for the information to be sent to a peer application on a remote host. An example of this is when you send a message via Microsoft Outlook to a friend's e-mail account. Pressing the send key enables the network.

The next layer is the presentation layer. Here, information is converted (if necessary) to a predetermined requisite format (i.e., ASCII to EBCDIC). This layer is reserved for information-type conversion and may be adapted by specific architecture (i.e., TCP/IP) as required to support the given application.

The presentation layer interfaces with the session layer. The session layer is responsible for session management and network security functions. This layer is used to keep track of logical connections (between

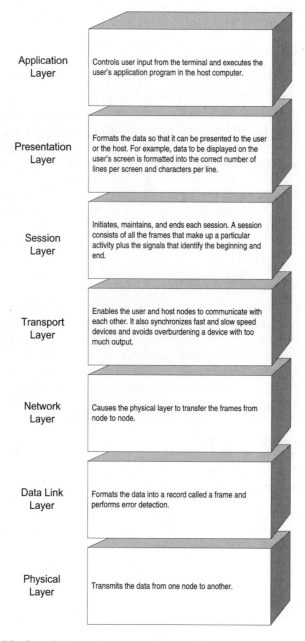

Figure 1-15   Open Systems Interconnection model.

applications and the network interface), manage them, and provide for a secure set of connections. This is obviously going to be a critical layer for our studies.

The transport layer is the lowest level of the model to have a complete end-to-end view of the connection. At the transport layer, network connections (between hosts) are formed and maintained. This is a significant layer, especially in the TCP architecture because it is the layer most often compromised by hackers. It is at this layer that network identity theft, port scanning (for illegal access), and network denial-of-service attacks most frequently occur.

The network layer is the layer that routes individual data packets. This is also the layer that tracks the in-place network configuration. The network layer is often the place that hackers go to "map" our networks for predetermining the location from which information emanates.

The data link layer provides point-to-point, error-free transmission between any two nodes in the network. The physical level describes the connectivity of the media (e.g., wires, radio wave, fiber optics) over which information travels at the bit-wise level.

To illustrate the importance of this model, let us use an analogy of the U.S. Postal Service. When we are writing a letter and preparing it for a long-distance friend, we play the part of the application layer. This is where our information is created. If our friend speaks Spanish and we speak English, we might have our letter translated by a friend who is bilingual. This represents the function of the presentation layer. Also, the presentation layer is at work when we fold the letter and seal the envelope.

Placing the letter inside an envelope is what encapsulation really looks like. This envelope must have a set of source and destination addresses and the requisite postage. This is the equivalent of the session layer. We now want to send the letter or form a connection, as shown in Figure 1-16, so we drop it in the mailbox and raise the red flag. This is the job of the transport layer. The letter is now inside the postal system where it is "routed" from office to office until it arrives at the destination post office. At that point it is routed locally to the recipient's mailbox. These steps are the equivalent of the lower three layers of the OSI model: the network, data link, and physical layers.

Once the letter is at the destination post office, the process is reversed and the letter makes its way back up the protocol stack until our friend receives it. The whole process is elegant and simple. In fact, it works exceptionally well for all forms of communication. This is the enduring quality of the model. It can evolve with the changes in the underlying technologies because the primary mission of our networks— information transfer—remains the same. Information transfer is a key component of our information system and needs to be carefully reviewed and protected.

INFORMATION "IN THE CLEAR"

In the infancy of networks, the idea of information theft or information altering was not an important concern. This lack of concern was because most networks were constructed out of private lines. As a result, we have become used to a network in which information is transmitted "in the clear." This means that to most network users, even today, we do not take the necessary precautions of encrypting (disguising) our information to help keep it private and controlled.

Transmitting in the clear allows anyone with a network sniffer (a device created to view the information flowing over the wire for trouble-shooting purposes) to read our most guarded secrets. This is the primary reason this book is so focused on cryptography as the main enabling technology. Networks bring to the surface the need for information privacy more than any other area of our information system. We can control our laptops to a large extent, password protect our files, and keep others out of our e-mail

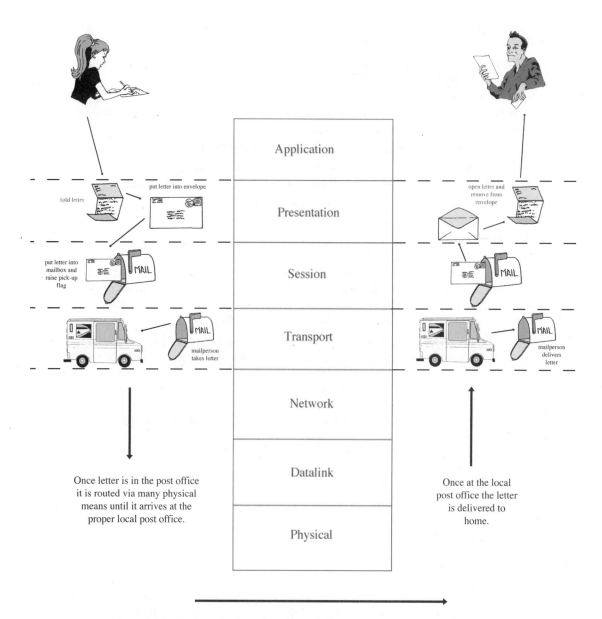

Figure 1-16 Communications transport analogy.

accounts, but we cannot control the millions of miles of network infrastructure that is shared throughout the world.

When we send e-mail from Boston to Sydney, through how many network devices will the message pass? How many routers will examine the routing information? How many systems will temporarily cache our information? How many persons will have access to those temporary stores of information? Do you trust everyone that works in every IT department connected to the Internet? Do you trust every worker at the phone company? If not, then you are leaving a lot to chance by transmitting in the clear.

As we progress with our studies, we will begin to build a methodology that will help us avoid unnecessary and unwanted information exposure. Encryption, digital signatures, and digital certificates are a great first step in this process.

This is also a good opportunity to point out the various traffic types we will encounter in the network. Data transfer is usually slow and bulky. It comprises many large data packets that move through the network infrastructure while awaiting reassembly later at the destination host.

We will also encounter voice and real-time video traffic. This is a relatively new blending of real-time information, called **isochronous** traffic, with the traditional data payloads. This recent phenomenon is caused by the ultra-high speeds of today's modern networks.

Finally, we also see true **multimedia** (non-real-time voice, data, and video) packaged together to create unique user experiences. These file sizes are generally massive and are downloaded from servers to local viewers at run time.

All of these are part of what we refer to as information. All of these parts require the same degree of security, and all can be compromised if things are left to chance. Most important, all have different characteristics, which makes devising a standard network security policy difficult.

ELECTRONIC MAIL AND HYPERTEXT

Two kinds of applications have dominated the literature: e-mail and hypertext. Together, these two applications generate the majority of Internet traffic. Accordingly, they deserve special consideration.

E-mail has become the primary mode of communication in most businesses (aside from the telephone). Most corporations use integrated mail, messaging, and calendaring platforms to assist the busy executive in time and communication management. E-mail traffic dominates the Internet. Unfortunately, it is one of the easiest systems to compromise. **E-mail spoofing** (sending a message using a different person's name as the sender) can cause confusion and harm to an organization. Most people do not know how to detect a spoofed e-mail and can be caught up in the ruse.

Other kinds of issues can occur with e-mail identity theft, stolen e-mail (trespass), and content manipulation. Today, e-mail is so popular that many organizations and people use it to exchange files instead of the traditional copy procedures. Although this is convenient, it can be fraught with issues if the data is transmitted in the clear.

E-mail also creates privacy issues. Federal law permits e-mail monitoring if it is sent or received from inside the organization or if it is created on company computers. However, some civil rights experts argue that these electronic communications are privileged. This creates not only a legal but also a moral paradox for the security-conscious employer. As with any important advance in communication (e.g., the telephone), once the novelty of the idea wears off, people take the tool for granted. Why should reading someone's e-mail transmission be any different from eavesdropping on a phone call? In essence, the concept of privilege will continue to evolve as e-mail and instant messaging continue to gain momentum. In large part, these laws require being tested in our legal system. This process will undoubtedly take a long time.

Hypertext Markup Language (HTML) was designed to make information homogeneous in its presentation so that it could be utilized by any platform without regard to its storage and use characteristics.

HTML is a script language, meaning that all of the commands for processing the text are built in to the information. Most people forget how recently browsers were developed to view HTML files. This phenomenon has truly blossomed only in the last fifteen years. For many of the younger readers, this technology for accessing Web files has always been in place. HTML works over the network through its relationship with HTTP. HTTP creates connections between client browsers and Internet servers that store the HTML code. These connections are purposefully simple in nature. The client requests a resource (a particular file or image) and the server responds by transmitting either that resource or a series of codes (a review in detail will follow in Chapter 10), which are used by the browser to ascertain and communicate the source of a problem. This interaction is shown in Figure 1-17.

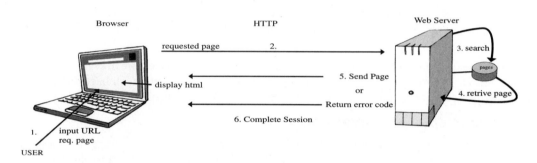

Figure 1-17   HTML and HTTP are the basis for a ubiquitous document management system.

In most systems running TCP/IP, the most popular Internet communications protocol, all server access for the Web is handled on PORT 80. A port is a predefined spot where an application grants access to a particular application. For example, PORT 23 is the TELNET port, which allows access to the system login routines. PORT 80 is considered a "well-known port." Leaving ports unprotected can cause irreparable harm to information by those who seek unlawful access. Because the premise of Web technology is based on the concept of openness, and because this technology is obviously popular, another paradox is created: Do we permit wide-scale access knowing that threats are looming near, or do we restrict access, thereby negating the effectiveness of the site? This particular paradox continues to be the focus of Internet security product development and security planning. We will come back to this topic in detail because it is a critical component of the information system.

In 2001, Microsoft embraced **Extensible Markup Language (XML)** and called it the XML revolution. HTML does an adequate job of describing how a Web page will look and function, but HTML has no idea what the words on the page mean. The page could be an advertisement for a new skateboard or the plans for making a bomb. HTML does not know the difference because it is just a language to set up and use this information. XML, however, is an application-aware language. XML makes Web content intelligent. Pages and content that are XML aware can identify themselves to search engines. For example, with HTML the search is a category or keyword search. (In some cases, semantic searches are conducted by intelligent search engines.) These searches are slow and not overly comprehensive. With XML, requests will be made to say "all pages about topic X, identify yourself." Pages that are content aware will then introduce themselves into the search. XML is a strong user of metadata. The net result of using XML is spending more time on the creation and management of information and far less time worrying about the presentation of it. All this means that Web pages will be dynamically created and tailored to the users' needs, and the servers will be truly store-and-serve devices, rather than the control-and-present devices they are currently. When combined with the power of sharing that the .Net environment encourages, you will increase the flow of information on the Internet to levels never before anticipated. What does all this mean to us? Information security on the Web will be more important than ever.

INFORMATION MANAGEMENT

Information and information systems require management so they are preserved in a known state. As was previously discussed, information's value increases as its reliability increases. Reliability and stability over long periods of time need to be managed.

We have established that information and information systems are not the same. Information systems comprise the computer systems, the networks, and the processes (executing applications) and must be managed. Managing these components requires considerable resources, planning, and perseverance. Information systems management must be methodically carried out and constantly monitored. Most organizations have mastered the art of keeping their information systems available. Managing information systems is a topic that can span many volumes and is, for the most part, beyond the scope of this text.

Information itself also requires management. Two main areas of information management are of interest to us. The first is disaster planning. The second is controlling access to our information.

Currently, many interesting kinds of applications produce information, including traditional kinds, such as databases and "number-crunching" applications. Decision-support systems help direct us through the plethora of information an organization can amass via directed searching and prioritization. Data-mining applications create sophisticated views of information based on complex relationships that exist within databases and data warehouses. Finally, artificial intelligence applications and expert systems use information to make decisions based on expert heuristics (rules of thumb). All of these applications create or enhance information for us. Once the information is created, we must preserve it and protect it.

On September 11th, a large portion of our information base was threatened. As a result of good planning and conscious efforts to minimize the exposure of that information, the long-term effects of the devastation were averted, and the information was recovered.

DISASTER RECOVERY AND BACKUP

Most of us realize the need to back up our information. We create several versions of the data and the applications and store them in separate and secure places. The more copies we have and the more frequently we perform the backup the more we are immune to the devastating effects of loss. Most of us have had the experience of working on a report or an article, when, for no apparent reason, the application or the system failed and hours of work were lost. If it has not happened to you, chances are someday it will. Many applications have proven unreliable and can malfunction during normal operation.

The important point is that whether the destruction of information was deliberate or by accident (e.g., fire, flood, power outage, hardware failure, software failure) the preservation of information and the subsequent resumption of business is your responsibility. More important, it is one of the few areas of information security that you really can control.

This information backup is not always a simple task. Suppose, for example, a business with fifty thousand distributed global users wanted to keep track of information and back it up. This task can be quite difficult because it involves many complex processes, procedures, and automation. One method for handling this request is to have the data backup handled by an independent third party. Many companies specialize in maintaining off-site storage and backup of corporations' information.

Today with the advent of **Storage Area Networks (SANS)**, it is much easier for remote users to archive their information in central repositories. Information backups can be automated and regularly scheduled.

Disaster recovery represents the backbone of any security plan. A valid security plan starts with the assumption that the information currently "in play" will become corrupt and that a backup copy will be required to restore it.

KEY POINT

A basic assumption of any security plan should be that information will be corrupted (intentionally or accidentally), and that restoration of that information will become necessary.

Disaster recovery planning, while separate from security planning, is just as important. One must establish the following thresholds for disaster recovery:

- How much down time or recovery time can a business sustain before any financial impact becomes unrecoverable? Many businesses cannot fully function without access to their electronic information. Many companies do not have—or it would not be feasible for them to have—a manual process to temporarily recover (albeit at a slower rate).
- How frequently should the data be completely archived? Can the company perform partial backups, based only on backing up the files that change?
- Where should the archive be kept? Should it be in one place or in multiple places? Remember that natural disasters (e.g., earthquakes) can affect areas thousands of miles wide.
- Should disaster recovery be handled internally or by an outside firm? Both have pros and cons. If internally handled, you will need at least two locations that are networked together but are many miles apart. You will want high-speed connections between the sites, and that could mean significant extra cost. You will need someone to manage the process. If externally handled, you will incur added (but predictable) expenses. You must place trust in the third party to do the job and to keep your information private. Remember that each additional person or group with access to your information is one more potential source of a security breach.

Proper disaster recovery planning cannot be stressed enough regarding the stability of your business and the preservation of your information.

INFORMATION ACCESS CONTROL

As we will see, another critical topic that repeatedly comes up is the type and degree of access to information that we permit. Access is a part of both the information security plan and the information system security plan. In Section Two of this text, we will examine the encryption process. This process will allow us to tightly control the access to information on an intimate basis. Each piece of information can be encrypted and only those individuals or programs on a need-to-know basis will be granted access. This access is controlled with passwords and keys. Additionally, these same encryption techniques can be employed to provide validation and authentication of the information's sender and user. This topic is one of the most important concepts in the text and is fully covered in Section Two.

Information systems also provide access control to information, including system access password protections, network screen and packet filtering protections, file access control lists at the operating system level, Virtual Private Networks (VPNs), Virtual Local Area Networks (VLANs), Secure Hypertext Transfer Protocol (S-HTTP), Secure Socket Layer (SSL), Point-to-Point Tunneling Protocol (PPTP), Secure Electronic Transfer (SET), and many other systemic protections can be offered. These factors are covered in Section Three of the text.

Finally, volumes of text have been published on the physical security of corporations, employees, and physical assets. This branch of security is quite mature. These components need to be secured to the same degree as our information. But how do physical security processes impact information security? Suppose, for example, we spent a fortune protecting our information and spent no money or time protecting our office space. If that were true, and you had information of value, you would almost certainly get hacked. Why? The answer is simple. **Hacking and cracking** (as we will see in the next chapter) is as much a social art form as it is a technical craft. **Social engineering**, as its name implies, is an important part of hacking. It refers to the perpetrator's ability to be able to gain useful information and insight into the corporation or the person to be hacked via interpersonal communication, physical theft, or even sifting through your garbage.

Therefore, it is critical that physical access to your records, offices, computers, networks, and in-place assets be limited and monitored. Many strategies exist for restricting access to these assets, ranging from barriers and fences to sophisticated biometric access controls. Many of these considerations are outlined in Section Three of this text.

SUMMARY

Information is a valuable asset that must be protected to ensure businesses' viability. The value of information is determined by its semantic meaning. Information is the combination of processed data and the applications that add semantic value. Information is an abstraction, which is more valuable than the underlying data from which it was developed. Data tell us about the past; information tells us about where we are and about the trends of which we are a part. This information influences the decisions that we make about the future. Metadata is data about data. It is often attached to information to increase the efficiency, access, and control of information use. It adds value and power to information.

Information is strongly related to numbers. Numbers and the properties of numbers are important characteristics in helping us protect information. Cryptography fundamentally exploits mathematical logic and properties to disguise, protect, and authenticate information and is an important CAIN enabler.

Proper planning for the preservation of information in the event of a disaster must be paramount. Prioritization, scope, and practicality are important concerns in developing such a security plan. Information contains fourteen properties, which affect how we can best protect information. These properties allow us to predict the information's behavior and thus plan for the viable disaster scenarios. Information can move, change, be stolen, be corrupted or altered, and it has identity.

Security plans become more complex as the scope of the plan increases. The broader our concerns, the less effective our security plan will be. These characteristics lead us to the conclusion that the best security posture is to "security coat" the information so that it is constantly protected regardless of location. It is equally important to weigh the costs associated with isolation and restriction versus security. The more security we impose, the less open we can be with our information.

The events of September 11th have, in general, raised the national awareness of security. Recently the Department of Homeland Security placed an emphasis on information security. This act should make it obvious that information, not systems and networks (the information system), needs to be at the core of our security plan.

Our seven-layer information security model forms the basis for comprehensive security planning. This model encompasses

1 Information

2 Cryptography and digital signatures

3 Authentication and verification

4 OS hardening

5 Information system architecture and design

6 Web services layer

7 The 8 Ps of protection

This model adequately addresses the CAIN requirements detailing the core components of information security. The model also emphasizes the need for a trusted third party to ensure that actions between interested parties have integrity.

Information systems should be distinct from the information itself. The information system can be thought of as combinations of computers and networks that are able to access (input) information, process information, output information, and provide feedback regarding the process that is running. Information systems protection is to information protection as homeland security is to personal protection. Information systems are the places that hackers and crackers go to find access to and copies of our data. It is important to understand how these systems work to prevent intrusion and malice.

Disaster recovery and backup, although they are primitive, proactive prevention considerations, should form the basis of any security plan. Disaster recovery planning should be done in conjunction with security planning.

STUDY QUESTIONS

The following questions will serve as a guide in confirming your understanding of this chapter. The answers to the odd-numbered problems are in the back of the text.

1 List the fourteen properties of information.

2 Draw the information security model.

3 Define information abstraction.

4 Why does mathematics play such a critical role in information security?

5 Information is at the core of our model because: (choose one)
   a. Networks and systems are impossible to protect adequately.
   b. Information is the asset with the greatest organizational value.

    c. Information is the easiest asset to protect.

    d. Information is the most difficult asset to protect.

6 Which of the following are properties of information? (choose one)

    a. It has evolved from data and is processed data.

    b. It has identity.

    c. It can be mathematically manipulated.

    d. All of the above.

7 What is the most important aspect of a security plan? (choose one)

    a. The details of the location

    b. To isolate and understand the object of protection

    c. To understand the surrounding infrastructure

    d. To understand the present capabilities

8 What is the core of any security plan? (choose one)

    a. Systems

    b. Networks

    c. Information

    d. Atmosphere and location

9 **True___ False___**   The projected growth rate in worldwide VPNs (encryption tunnels through the Internet) is 117 percent by 2006.

10 Which out of the following four choices is **not** part of a suggested information security plan? (choose one)

    a. Protection of the information itself at the core

    b. Hardening of our resources (systems and networks)

    c. Authentication of those accessing the information

    d. Distributing predetermined strong passwords

11 **True___ False___**   The paradigm that would validate and measure the effectiveness of a security plan would contain a framework that includes confidentiality, authenticity, integrity, and nonrepudiation of information security plans.

12 A trusted third party is a neutral participant; which of the following are examples? (choose one)

    a. Bank

    b. The government

    c. A stranger

    d. Answers A and B

13 True____ False____   The combination of data and applications gives information its value.

14 Metatags are used in protocol headers to reference which of the following? (choose one)
  a. Status codes regarding the condition of a file transfer
  b. Information expiration data
  c. Client server authentication information
  d. An explanation of information
  e. All of the above

15 What is the basis of cryptography? (choose one)
  a. The laws of mathematics
  b. Manipulation of data
  c. Creating disguises for information
  d. None of the above

16 How is data using Sequential Access Method (SAM) retrieved? (choose one)
  a. It allows you to retrieve data from anywhere on the drive.
  b. It retrieves data in the order in which it resides on the storage medium.
  c. It retrieves data using the point and click method.
  d. None of the above.

17 True____ False____   Direct access methods separate the contents of the memory into indexes and use keys to point to specific parts in the data.

18 What is the most popular type of database? (choose one)
  a. Object oriented database
  b. Hierarchical
  c. Relational
  d. Network

19 True____ False____   An abstraction is a technique used to hide complexity.

20 Most users have the most knowledge of what takes place on which layer of the OSI model? (choose one)
  a. Presentation
  b. Network
  c. Transport
  d. Application

21 What is the U.S. Postal Service compared to in Chapter 1? (choose one)
- **a.** The system architecture model
- **b.** The OSI model
- **c.** The information security model
- **d.** None of the above

22 Sending a message using a different person's name as the sender is called what? (choose one)
- **a.** Electronic interception
- **b.** E-mail spoofing
- **c.** E-mail hacking
- **d.** E-mail impersonalization

23 What does HTTP stand for? (choose one)
- **a.** Hypertext Transfer Protocol
- **b.** Hypertext Transport Protocol
- **c.** Hypertext TELNET Protocol
- **d.** Hypertext Technology Protocol

24 What port is the well-known port for TELNET? (choose one)
- **a.** PORT 80
- **b.** PORT 23
- **c.** PORT 111
- **d.** PORT 13

25 **True___ False___**   A basic assumption of any security plan is that the corruption of information is not something to worry about.

26 The ability of a user to gain information, statistics, or valuable information about a company through interpersonal communication. is called what? (choose one)
- **a.** Hacking
- **b.** Cracking
- **c.** Social engineering
- **d.** Information vulnerability

CASE STUDY

It is important for students to explore the concepts in this text through the use of both a hands-on experience (labs in Appendix A) and via a practicum. Throughout this text will be exercises that allow students to role-play the part of the security consultant. The majority of these exercises requires the completion of some research and the development of a short paper or essay.

These exercises focus on the HIPAA (Health Insurance Portability and Accountability Act) legislation presented in Chapter 3. A tremendous amount of opportunity exists for security plan development in this area. Thus, exposure to this topic is relevant.

For our case you will play the role of a senior network consultant from Security Inc. Your assignment is to help Cureme Hospital evaluate its information security posture and determine its HIPAA readiness. Given that stance it will be your job to create, justify, and recommend a security plan. If you procure management's approval (by the end of the text), you will be required to develop an implementation plan.

So let's get started!

It is your first day and you begin your assignment by interviewing the CIO of the hospital, I.M. Hurtin. Mr. Hurtin has expressed a serious concern about his organization's readiness for HIPAA. Primarily, he is concerned that the information from the many disparate systems in the hospital are not currently confidential or secure. In fact, he is not even sure what information the hospital has. He asks you to help him better understand HIPAA and to develop a list of information that he might want to think about protecting.

Research and comment:

- Review the HIPAA guidelines and frequently asked questions on *http://www.hipaa.org*. What strikes you as important considerations? What is the legislation aimed at protecting? How do these nontechnical guidelines appear to affect hospital information systems and the associated technologies?
- Describe what you believe HIPAA means from a technological point of view.
- Go to the Web sites of some local hospitals and search for the typical departments hospitals normally have. Can you identify ten departments that hospitals have in common?
- What information do you suspect is kept about patients? Research and catalog the types of tests that various diagnostic services run within the hospital.
- HIPAA stipulates that patient information is to be kept private. Only those persons on a need-to-know basis should be allowed to view this information. Based on your research, who needs to know?
- Does the hospital information systems staff need to know?
- Summarize your thoughts by creating a one-page abstract regarding how difficult you believe this assignment will be. Describe what you believe is an appropriate action plan. Write it down and see how your thoughts on this plan change as you progress in your studies. You will be amazed at how well you will be able to complete this assignment as we go through the text.

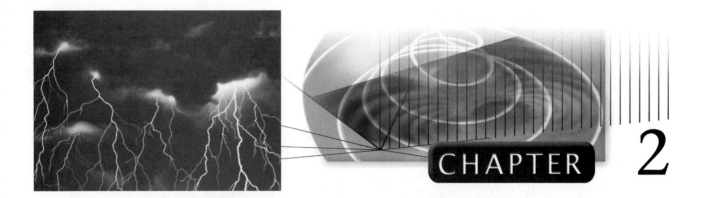

Threat Agents and Risk

One of the most time-consuming things is to have an enemy.
—E.B. White

With respect to our personal security, we are willing to tolerate a certain amount of **risk** to enjoy life. We understand these risks, we plan reasonable measures to mitigate them, and we exercise caution when warranted to avoid risk. But, most important, we carry on with the normal actions of our lives. This reasoning is also true as it applies to information security. We must analyze the criticality of the information, understand how it will *live* inside our information system, anticipate the enemy's strategy, create and execute a reasonable security plan, and carry on with our normal business activities.

In Chapter 1, we defined information and how it behaves. We examined its properties, how it evolves, and how it interacts with the core components of the information system. This gave us an understanding of the nature of our most valued asset. Given that background, Chapter 2 expands our investigation to develop an understanding of information security risks and what can be done to reduce or eliminate them. This chapter helps students develop an understanding of specific threats, how they are developed and delivered, and the type of damage they can cause to information and the information system. Chapter 2 focuses on three important topics:

- Common threats to information
- Perpetrators and intent
- Risk and risk management

These topics are supported by numerous statistics from the FBI, government-sponsored studies, and the U.S. Department of Justice. It is important to understand how real these threats are, and how easily these crimes are committed. Therefore, a security professional needs a strong set of sources for garnering such statistics.

One of the key skills required to develop a security plan is the ability to perform a **risk analysis**. This type of analysis includes the qualitative and quantitative measurement of risk. Furthermore, this analysis enables us to perform required risk management tasks. These essential skills are stressed in this chapter.

Information security planning and risk avoidance comes with a substantial financial cost. In today's volatile market, companies are skeptical of making such investments without significant cost justification. Most upper management is aware of the need for information security, but often they have no idea what this security should cost or the cost of inaction. Therefore, it is impossible for them to make appropriate decisions. Corporate executives often reason that "the company has never been victimized before" or "there would be no reason for us to be attacked." As we will learn, these statements represent faulty logic and can lead to disaster.

 To successfully complete this chapter, students should pay particular attention to the following:

- The definitions of risk, risk event, risk entities, and threat agent
- The identification of the types of perpetrators and their intent
- Understanding the types of attacks, which attacks are most common, and how they are constructed and carried out
- The identification of the risk management techniques of identification, minimization, mitigation, and transference
- The creation of risk analysis reports that provide rationale and justification in support of information security planning
- Establishing a habit of reviewing the literature (e.g., the many sources presented in this section) to remain current on the ever-changing nature and methods of attacks, and to remain up to date with the latest defense strategies
- Develop a strong set of reliable resources for gathering statistical data required for most justifications

Far too many security professionals focus purely on the technical challenges of implementing cybersecurity. They often lose focus on the most important issue in the establishment of any information plan: gaining acceptance and participation in the implementation of the plan. The goal of this chapter is to establish the requisite background in the realities of cybercrime and to dispel the common myths of corporate America in accepting and preparing for these realities. Security professionals should establish a work ethic, which includes utilizing the resources mentioned in this chapter to continually refine their skills and enhance their awareness in this area.

COMMON MYTHS AND MISCONCEPTIONS

One of the problems security consultants have when developing information security plans is overcoming the commonly held beliefs and misconceptions regarding security risks and threats. We will start our examination of risk and threats by evaluating each of these myths.

The most popular reason given for not investing in information security measures is this: "We have never been hacked before, why would it start now?" This rationale often produces disastrous results. Three broad categories of hacks that often occur to people or corporations for no apparent reason follow:

- Random attacks not directed at anyone in particular
- Attacks committed by a malicious insider
- Springboard attacks

The first type of random attack is usually committed by a **script kiddie**, or someone unleashing a **virus**. Script kiddies are usually youthful offenders that utilize previously scripted hacks written by accomplished and skilled hackers to generally create a nuisance. Sometimes script kiddies simply want to know if they *can* hack into a site. Although these attacks are often innocuous, they can create problems in the operations of a site and interfere with information flow. Break-ins can lead to inadvertent damage to the information system, shaken confidence in the integrity of information, or actual damage to the information itself. Anyone can be victimized by a script kiddie.

Similarly, viruses are generally implemented without regard to the spread rate or focus (the more people affected the better.) Viruses can be found and replicated without having any specific programming knowledge. A virus or a **worm** can cause tremendous damage to systems, data, and the effectiveness of our communications medium.

A second source of unexpected—and dangerous—attacks arise from disgruntled employees. This type of attack is common in the current weak economy, where businesses have cut back on employees and their benefits. Disgruntled employees usually are careful to plan an attack or steal information (e.g., taking a customer list to a new sales job) long before anyone suspects them. A disgruntled employee is dangerous for several reasons:

- They are already inside the perimeter security
- They know which information to target in their attacks and where to cause the most damage
- They can leave **backdoors** into the site, which they can use for future attacks
- Most important, they are usually angry when committing these crimes. They are not just curious; they are purposefully malicious

Finally, an attack often committed using unprotected (and unsuspecting) sites is called a **springboard attack**. In a springboard attack, the hacker gains access to your site for the purpose of using it to launch attacks as part of a widespread offensive against the actual target site. In this scenario, your site is penetrated by the hacker, who then loads programs with **triggers** used to release a coordinated set of attacks from your site and many similarly "set-up" sites. Being used as part of a springboard attack is usually accomplished without your ever knowing you were involved.

Thus, this myth of "We have never been attacked before, why should it start now?" can be dispelled by simply stating that every site can be compromised for the purpose of being used as part of one of these types of attacks. Further, you have limited ways of knowing if you ever have been attacked, especially if you have no **intrusion detection system (IDS)** in place. As we will see in the next chapter, being used by a cybercriminal in a springboard attack also makes you partly responsible for the damages. That alone should motivate you to action.

KEY POINT

Because of the variety of attackers (e.g., malicious insiders, script-oriented attacks, and highly skilled technicians) and places from which an attack can come, it is always possible that you could be attacked. Therefore, it is vital to protect the information with far more than just a perimeter defense so we can maintain confidence in its integrity even after an attack.

Another misguided claim revolves around who is actually charged with security. When an executive says, "Information security is handled by the IS department, they've got it covered," it probably means too much faith is placed in the department. Information is the property of the organization, not an individual or group. We cannot just assume that the IS department is capable of handling the security for our information on its own. We will look at a hypothetical example to help us understand why this is not possible. Assume that a pharmaceutical company is busy working on the development of a new drug therapy for arthritis. Because arthritis is a debilitating disease that affects a large segment of the population, the drug is worth a considerable amount of money to the company that develops the best treatments. Most pharmaceutical companies have competing development efforts. Each of these development efforts has a discovery phase, a development phase, a clinical trial phase, and a go-to-market phase of product development.

Let us now think of the information that is being developed secretly: statistical data on the affected population; chemical formulas for the various compounds tested; clinical trial data collected from the subjects tested; vast amounts of drug interaction information that must be submitted to the FDA; numerous papers, proposals and counterproposals to guide the development process and more. The information and raw data assembled generate boxcars of paper—and therefore a copious electronic—trail. Once the product goes into production, a tremendous amount of new information needs to be reviewed and protected.

For any IS department, this is a staggering amount of information to understand and catalog. From the research group's perspective, a secret is best kept by not even acknowledging that there is a secret. The development effort should be hidden from nonessential personnel. By telling the IS department about a developed secret, many people who do not need to know, will know, and that could be dangerous. The local research staff needs to be involved because to protect information, you need to understand it. Therefore, it might be best to handle information security on a project or departmental basis.

KEY POINT

The role of the IT department is to develop policies, procedures, guidelines, and best practices that serve the entire organization's security needs. IT is required to educate the user community, put in place requisite technologies, and then assist in implementing best security practices. The IT department does not have all the information necessary to develop a security plan in a vacuum. All of the departments in the organization contribute to the security plan. IT is like the orchestra leader conducting the musicians.

Another widely held myth is this: "Why should we be a target for attack? We don't do anything that encourages this behavior." This thinking creates a false feeling of security. In fact, most intrusions are done for the fun or the challenge of it. Few hacks are designed with a specific target in mind. Take for example most common viruses. These viruses are meant to cause widespread disruption of service. In addition, viruses are meant to be generally distributed and are rarely focused on a particular business entity. Also, as was previously mentioned, springboard attacks can be done to anyone, especially the least-secure sites.

When an organization asks "Why me?" look no further than brand. Think about how your **brand**, or market reputation, will be affected by an electronic prank. Brand, as most marketing experts will tell you, is the most important element of a company's success. This theory is supported when you watch television.

What does a thirty-second spot during the Super Bowl cost? Would you believe that during the 2003 Super Bowl, a thirty-second spot cost $2.2 million? Why would any company spend that kind of money? Because name recognition and name association are two important elements of branding. Your Web site also represents the brand. A random hack or a hack that purposely wants to deface your Web site may have a significant impact on your brand. How often do you check to see if your Web has been attacked? How often do legitimate users contact your site? How would your organization handle a harmful message posted on your home page? For many corporations, a site hack can cause a devaluation of the brand, thereby costing the firm money.

To go back to the original statement, "why would I represent an attractive site to hack?" it should be obvious that any site may be an attractive target based on brand, company function, or based simply on a random attack. However, the price paid because of brand defamation, let alone the potential loss or destruction of information, could be considerable.

Possibly the most dangerous of all the misconceptions is "We already invested in products, so I think we have it covered." This products-solve-problems philosophy produces confusion after a significant hack has occurred. Similar comments after a hack are: "We use anti-virus software," "We can detect intrusions with our intrusion-detection software," or the classic, "But we already have a firewall installed," are all difficult for the security adviser to address. These comments are examples of a process without a plan. Far too many people believe that these "security products" are guarantees against attacks. Unfortunately, no such remedy exists. For example, think of the company that utilizes a firewall for security. This firewall was placed by well-intentioned engineers who were trying to isolate, screen, and hide details from would-be attackers. As we will see in Section Three of this text, firewalling is an effective technique in security enhancement. But it must be part of a comprehensive security plan and not a stand-alone solution. Why? Suppose that you implement a firewall at the electronic front door of your company, between you and the Internet. Your goal, as previously stated, is to protect your site from possible intrusion. Now, suppose that you have a mobile workforce. Each of your sales executives carries a laptop. Every night, your sales team takes their laptops home. If just one of your salespeople connects to the Internet from home with an unprotected connection (no personal firewall) and is hacked, the results to your corporation could be devastating. If one of the salespeople's laptops is infected with a **Trojan**, a malicious software package that triggers at another time, then the Trojan could be triggered the next time that a LAN connection is established. This LAN connection would likely happen when your salesperson is back inside the firm. When the salesperson establishes the local LAN connection, the **malware** triggers and starts destroying and attacking from within. The firewall will not protect you. The firewall itself was compromised, not by the hacker, but rather by the unsuspecting salesperson.

The biggest obstacle in any corporation is money. The availability of funding drives the implementation and completeness of your security plan. Possibly the most difficult myth to overcome involves money already spent. Statements such as "We have already exceeded our security budget" or "We have outspent our competition on security," means that persuading the corporation to allocate more funds is going to be challenging. Information security protection is expensive, persistent, and ever increasing. For every person trying to protect information, one hundred are trying to compromise it. The number of possible hacks changes constantly, and their nature is increasingly complex. Thus, it is the responsibility of every security manager and team to understand the threats and to be able to provide statistics and vulnerability assessments to the upper management to help quantify their impact. Later in this chapter, many important sources of statistical information are discussed. Also, in this chapter we will spend a considerable amount of time discussing vulnerability assessments.

Another myth that frustrates information security professionals concerns the data's proximity to the organization. Many organizations have started outsourcing their computing infrastructure. Moving Web services to an **Internet Service Provider (ISP)** is common. The problem is that ISPs get hacked regularly. The concept of colocation has many business benefits, but a blanket assurance of information security is not one of them. First, ISPs and Application Service Providers (ASPs) are prime targets for hackers. Hackers can achieve much by penetrating the defenses of a single entity, which in turn opens many other doors. It is a challenge, but hackers find this challenge rewarding. Second, you may find yourself totally out of the security loop. You have little input to the security protocol. Finally, as we have stated earlier, the information is not on a particular Web server or backup site. Rather, the information is part of the organization. So, even if the data are not stored on-site, it starts within the confines of our corporation and is manipulated from there, where it is then exposed to suspect activity. The benefit of colocation—from a security perspective—is that it is backed up off-site in case of a disaster. The greatest benefit from a business perspective is that it is in close proximity to clients and partners. Those are good reasons to buy into such an activity. But do not buy into colocation as a substitute for a solid corporate-wide security plan because that will leave your assets at risk.

In the United States, the debate over big government versus small government has raged for years. Many people feel that the government needs to play a stronger role in the security of the Internet and the protection of our information. Some people believe that the government keeps the Internet safe and there is no need to worry. However, this belief promotes a false sense of security. Cybercrime, as we will see in the next chapter, is very much in its infancy. The FBI, the Department of Justice, and many other government agencies are only just beginning to make headway in the capture and prosecution of cybercriminals. Cyberterrorism is a major concern, with destructive capabilities far beyond our imaginations. In November 2002, President Bush signed a $900 million cybersecurity bill, which promotes awareness training, research, and product development to prevent cyberterrorism. This bill represents the first tangible evidence of our government's growing concern. Its significance lies in its influencing top minds to conduct much-needed research into the question of preparedness. Today, many books on the subject refer to cyberterrorism by a different name: information warfare. The primary concerns currently are the modalities of such a conflict, what it will look like when it comes, and where it will come from.

No one is really sure where it will come from or who will initiate the action. Given the high degree of interconnection of our information system, an attack of significant proportion could come from anywhere, and more disturbingly everywhere. The Defense Information Systems Agency (DISA) constantly tests the penetrability of government security systems. As we will see later in the chapter, even the government falls victim to successful hacks. The government plays an important role in the detection and the prosecution of all crime. In the case of cybercrime and information warfare, government involvement is essential for there to be any chance of curtailing such an attack. However, crime prevention is a different matter. By looking at various sites, including the FBI site, it is obvious that prevention education and early detection are stressed. In later sections of the text, a considerable amount of this material is listed for your review. It is important to point out that in an open and highly interconnected society, too much monitoring by the government would potentially deprive us of our privacy and many of our freedoms. The rights of the people are always in conflict with the effectiveness of our law enforcement processes. We strive to constantly balance and test the limits of these processes with respect to our expected freedoms. It is, then, inappropriate to assume that the government is prepared or able to prevent all attacks against our personal or business interests. In fact, it is up to us to understand the legislation, the elements of the government's security recommendations, and the processes in place for early detection and prosecution before incorporating them into our own plans.

Another myth that is difficult for the security consultant to overcome is when a company places too much emphasis on one area of their security plan at the expense of others. "We have a fantastic disaster recovery strategy, and we frequently back up our information. What else is there to do?" This hypothetical executive is only half right. It is important to maintain backups and have a comprehensive disaster recovery strategy. However, it is only part of the plan. Disaster recovery does not salvage all damage. For example, compromising the brand or reputation of the company, identity theft, and e-mail spoofing are just a few of the problems that cannot be addressed strictly through disaster recovery. These types of intrusions cause unwanted chaos, confusion, and the loss of millions of dollars. A plan must be balanced and multidimensional. As we will see in Chapter 4, by evaluating all of the risk elements affecting your business and by prioritizing your security commensurate with the security model followed in this text, a balanced plan will be achieved. Physical security, security of systems and networks, information security, and identity security all need to be addressed in our plan.

Many more examples of myths are presented to security consultants in this industry. It is important to listen to our users and eloquently confront these erroneous claims. We must rigorously examine each one and advise clients through the use of facts and well-documented information. This approach will raise the levels of awareness and allow for an appropriate amount of planning and prevention to be implemented. It will also drive corporate acceptance.

THE NUMBERS DO NOT LIE

Carl Sagan once said, "Extraordinary claims demand extraordinary evidence." This is especially true with respect to the current state of information security. Incredible information security breaches happen every day, yet few organizations are truly committed to information security planning. Many senior managers are aware of the threat, but they insist that the extent of the breaches is overstated. In an effort to assist readers in understanding the gravity of information security threats, consider the statistics available on the subject. Many sources of statistics are available regarding cybercrime, information theft, viruses and malware, prosecutions, financial liability and loss, and government activities. It is important for students to be armed with the most recent and most reliable statistics upon which to build justifications and propose plans and budgets. It is equally important for students to have command of their sources. Statistics and figures change constantly. Most of the statistics presented in this text will change after publication. Therefore, a significant part of this chapter is devoted to assisting students in building both a research orientation and a significant collection of sources to draw on for reliable statistics.

Almost without exception, all of the sources point out that the data presented are based only on reported crime. Most cybercrime goes unreported. As a result of this underreporting, precise metrics for most of the aforementioned statistics categories are largely understated. According to an FBI press release, "New Report Shows What Internet Scams Cost Americans" dated April 2002, Richard L. Johnston, Director of NW3C[1], states with regard to the number of complaints concerning Internet fraud and scams, "We anticipate the number of complaints to rise from 1,000 a week to 1,000 a day. We know more Internet crime is out there, it's just a matter of victims knowing where to go to report it and actually reporting it." Statements such as this are recorded throughout the literature. They point to a serious deficiency in our ability to accurately

---

[1] Funded by a grant from the Department of Justice, Office of Justice Programs, Bureau of Justice Assistance, the NW3C is a nonprofit organization that provides a national support network for state and local law enforcement agencies involved in the prevention, investigation, and prosecution of economic and high-tech crime. See *http://www.nw3c.org* for more information.

depict the current condition of information security. This tendency of significantly understated data diminishes the effectiveness of our predictions regarding trends and outcomes.

As is the case with all emerging areas of study, a large portion of early research investment is made in the area of data collection. Numerous government-funded research groups exist to accomplish just such a purpose. The FBI, the National Infrastructure Protection Agency, CERT[2] from Carnegie Mellon University, GOCSI, DISA, Computer Security Institute, The Office of the Attorney General for the United States, local and state law enforcement, and others conduct much of this data collection. Other reliable sources include the SANS Institute, McAfee, Riptech, and other worldwide government surveys.

The data collection process depends heavily on the contributions of the practicing field security professional. Appendix C of this text includes an electronic crime-reporting form as developed by the National Infrastructure Protection Agency. After you review this form, you will know why many of the risk evaluation techniques and security planning priorities presented in this book are carefully aligned with this type of reporting document.(For a list of useful resources, which can help keep students current on the state of information security, please refer to the bibliography at the end of the text.)

In many texts focused on information security, authors spread out many of the statistics that substantiate the need for information security planning and implementations. In this work, however, many of these commonly referenced measurements are concentrated in this chapter.

A good way to measure the need for a new technology is to look at the market analysis of the sector in terms of product development. According to *http://www.idc.com*, the market for Web intrusion services and products is expected to increase to nearly $700 million by the year 2006. This is a significant number for securing Web sites and services. Remember, this is only one aspect of information security. Couple this with the $911 million that President Bush allocated for the development of Internet threat analysis tools and studies and you can see that the Internet portion of the information security product and services spectrum will develop at a brisk pace.

The first area that software vendors need to be dedicated to is the testing and patching of available product. It is estimated that by exploiting vulnerabilities in Microsoft's IIS Web server product, more than 250,000 Web sites may have been compromised by the Code Red worm in the course of a nine-hour period (source: *http://www.cert.org/advisories/ca-2001-19.html* and *ca-2001-23*). This points to the need to develop a system for applying all vendor software patches as expeditiously as possible. A large amount of manufacturer cost, especially for software manufacturers, must be applied to the constant and comprehensive testing and updating of the product set. When selecting a vendor for critical infrastructure software, ask how they plan to address the challenge of due diligence required to reduce your risk of exposure. You should make inquiries with the vendor regarding the amount of development budget they intend to allocate to this task.

Another important metric to utilize in developing your risk analysis is the average cost per incident of a security breach. According to a UK Department of Trade and Industry study, the average cost of a "serious" security incident was approximately $50,000. When you consider the amount of incidents per year that the average business experiences, the cost could be devastating to a corporation. In the same survey 78 percent of companies had experienced at least one malicious security incident, with forty-four percent of them occurring in the last year. (Source: UK Department of Trade and Industry—Pricewaterhouse-Coopers *http://www.survey.gov.uk/view2002surveyresults.htm*)

[2.] CERT is not an acronym. Rather, it is a trademark of Carnegie Mellon University.

Another survey of 538 respondents conducted by The Computer Security Institute, with the participation of the San Francisco FBI's Computer Intrusion Squad, obtained the following data, which largely validates the UK survey:

- 85 percent (primarily large corporations and government agencies) detected computer security breaches in the last twelve months).
- 64 percent acknowledged financial loss as a result of the attack.
- The total financial loss reported totaled $377,828,700.
- 40 percent detected a penetration from the outside (up from 25 percent in 2000).
- 95 percent detected computer viruses.[3]

Based on these two sets of figures, it is likely that any organization can experience some form of a financial impact as the result of an information security breach. Few of the firms surveyed in the UK study were prepared for these financial liabilities. Fifty-six percent of those attacked were not covered (or were unsure of coverage) by cyberinsurance. (Source: UK Department of Trade and Industry – PricewaterhouseCoopers *http://www.survey.gov.uk/view2002surveyresults.htm*)

Most companies were also unprepared for the possibility of an information security problem. Only 27 percent of those surveyed claimed to have a documented security policy (Source: UK Department of Trade and Industry—PricewaterhouseCoopers survey.*gov.uk/view2002surveyresults.htm*). This number is consistent with other such metrics regarding the most fundamental precaution a company can take: a well-developed security plan.

To make matters worse, far too many companies do not allocate enough of their IT budgets to information security. In the same UK report, it is suggested that the benchmark for information security spending should be between 3 percent and 5 percent of the total IT budget for non-high-risk business and as much as 10 percent of the total IT budget for high risk sectors (e.g., financial). (Source: UK Department of Trade and Industry—PricewaterhouseCoopers *http://www.survey.gov.uk/view2002surveyresults.htm*) In most of the corroborating reports, few if any of the respondents come anywhere close to these numbers.

These kinds of budgetary estimates are considerable (5 percent of an IT budget) and surely weigh heavily on corporate executives. Take for example the cost requirements for information security in the health care industry. With the adoption of HIPAA legislation, most health care providers are being forced, under federal and state guidelines, to take information security more seriously. Experts estimate that implementing IT and management solutions to ensure the minimum compliance with HIPAA regulations could cost hospitals in the United States $22.5 billion over the next five years. (Source: *http://www.aha.org/ar/comment*) Given the minimal profitability of most health care organizations, numbers of this magnitude can be staggering. Most health care organizations are still evolving plans for HIPAA-related information security and have barely begun to understand the technological ramifications of this legislation.

Next we need to address the frequency and probability of cybercrime. According to a recent CERT report, computer security vulnerabilities more than doubled, with 1,090 separate security holes reported in 2000, and 2,437 reported in 2001. The number of reported incidents rose from 21,756 in 2000 to 52,658 reported in 2002. (Source: *http://www.cert.org/stats*) What do statistics like these tell us? Given that nearly every report suggests an increase in cybercrime and information security breaches, we cannot consider

---

[3.] *http://www.gocsi.com*

ourselves to be beyond the reach of, or more sophisticated than, those committing the crimes. Remember, these crimes are happening to someone—maybe even you or your organization.

The FBI estimates that the worldwide Internet population exceeds 349 million users (commerceNet Research Council 2000). In more recent surveys the number is believed to exceed 500 million users. These numbers provide ample targets for the cybercriminal, script kiddie, hacker, or cracker to attack. Many of us are worried about conducting financial transactions on the Web, and with good reason. According to an FBI report published in April 2002, Internet fraud is on the rise. During 2001, 56,000 victims reported cumulative losses of more than $117 million. This is an average of approximately $2,400 per incident. These crimes are difficult to prosecute. Even those that have been prosecuted have defrauded hundreds if not thousands of unsuspecting people. That money is rarely recovered. These types of crimes often go unreported at the federal level or are misreported in terms of where the statistics are logged. Thus, it is likely that this number is growing at an even more alarming rate than the data suggest.

Is anybody's information safe on the Internet? The answer, I am sorry to say, is: not really. It is surprising that the government of the United States, which takes great pride in matters of security, is not immune from the perils of these follies. In a candid Department Of Defense survey released several years ago, we can see that not even the government is safe. In a study conducted by the U.S. Department of Defense Information Systems Agency titled "Attacks Against DOD Computers (1992–995)," the following staggering results were released:

- 38,000 attacks were attempted on DOD computers
- 13,300 attacks were successfully blocked (35 percent)
- 24,700 attacks succeeded (65 percent)
- 23,712 of the successful attacks were undetected (96 percent of successful attacks)
- 988 of the successful attacks were detected (4 percent of successful attacks)
- Only 267 of the detected attacks were reported
- 721 of the detected attacks were not reported

The last of these numbers is most disturbing, considering the emphasis placed on the code of conduct required with respect to all matters of national security. These numbers illustrate that not only is the government prone to being attacked (a favorite challenge to hackers), but also the attacks are difficult to recognize. Trained people are responsible for constantly monitoring these systems and networks. Often the attacks are so subtle that the forensic process is slow and difficult to focus.

Computer forensics is an entirely different field of study (and beyond the scope of this text). As is suggested by the following data preparedness of the individual and the firm, and the incorporation of National Information Protection Agency, guidelines (see Appendix B) for reporting a crime can dramatically improve your chances of apprehending a cybercriminal. From a U.S. Department of Justice FBI report entitled "Recovering and Examining Computer Forensic Evidence," the following facts were revealed:

- In 1995, a survey conducted by the U.S. Secret Service indicated that only 48 percent of the agencies had computer forensic laboratories and that 68 percent of computer evidence seized was forwarded to one of those laboratories
- In the same survey, the U.S. Secret Service reported that 70 percent of law enforcement agencies were conducting computer forensic investigations without a written procedures manual, pointing to the continued need for standardization
- Refining and focusing an investigation is a considerably difficult task. It is time consuming (given a 30-GB hard drive) to scan every file on a computer system. It also creates an

unthinkable paper trail: To print a 12-GB set of text data would create a stack of paper twenty-four stories high. Therefore, for matters of practicality, it is the breadth of information presented to the forensic examiner that must be limited

■ Courts are requiring that more information rather than equipment be seized. This complicates the writing and execution of search warrants. Notice the focus on information as stated in the report

Other statistics analyze the threats themselves. In a 1998 FBI/CSI Computer Crime and Security survey ("Computer Security Issues and Trends," Vol. III, No. 2, Spring 1997 and Vol. IV, No 1, Winter 1998) the top ten types of attacks or misuse identified were as follows:

■ 73 percent reported being attacked by a computer virus
■ 68 percent had problems with insider abuse of the Net
■ 57 percent reported the theft of a laptop
■ 39 percent reported unauthorized insider access
■ 21 percent reported an unauthorized system penetration
■ 16 percent reported theft of proprietary information
■ 14 percent reported telecommunications fraud
■ 13 percent reported financial fraud
■ 13 percent reported sabotage
■ 9 percent reported passive wiretap

Of those surveyed, eighty-nine percent felt strongly that the likely source of an attack could be traced to a disgruntled employee; seventy-two percent felt independent hackers were a high risk to their business; and forty-eight percent felt threatened by U.S. domestic corporations. Of those surveyed, forty-seven percent felt that the Internet was perceived as the most probable point of attack (1997), up from thirty-seven percent in the 1996 survey.

As stated in the FBI August 2001 Law Enforcement Bulletin,

> *'Businesses and individuals rely on law enforcement crime statistics when making important decisions about their safety. Many citizens contact a local police station prior to purchasing of a home in a particular neighborhood to inquire about the number of burglaries and violent crimes in the area. Just as these data provide important information for communities in the real world, the same is true in cyberspace. For individuals and organizations to intelligently assess their risk level, agencies must provide accurate data about criminal threats. Access to reliable and timely computer crime statistics allows individuals to determine their own probability of victimization and the threat level they face. It also helps them estimate probable recovery costs. Law enforcement organizations traditionally have taken a leading role in providing crime data and crime prevention education to the public, which now should be updated to include duties in cyberspace."*

THE PERPETRATORS

So far, we have referenced cybercriminals by a variety of names. Throughout the literature, security professionals and the cybercriminals themselves have better defined these various classifications. Each has its own modus operandi, which can be key to better understanding the threats we face.

The term hacker has been used unilaterally to indicate anyone who gains unauthorized access into computer systems and data. Today, the refined definition of the terms has many subcategories of computer and phone system adversaries. Much of the classification arises from either the intent of the individual to do harm, or the type of system upon which the attacker works. Originally the term hacker was touted as a badge of honor for the people who possessed significant computer programming skills. Hacking evolved and became more or less a game of skill to take over a system. For the purposes of this book, we will use the term **hacker** to refer to the class of people who have no malicious intent and are more interested in the technological challenges of system information manipulation than causing harm. However, as we shall see in the next chapter, the new and updated laws make no such differentiation. Regardless of the motive, trespassing is trespassing .

On November 2-3, 1988, a landmark event occurred that forever changed the meaning of the term "hacker." Robert Morris Jr., a Cornell University student who was also the son of a Bell Labs Internet designer, unleashed the Morris worm from an MIT computer into the Web. The worm sought out vulnerable systems and infected them, creating thousands of shell programs that utilized all of the computer's resources. Once the worm was in place, it spread rapidly to new systems. Before long the worm had infected thousands of computers from coast to coast and brought down much of the research community's computing facilities. Because Morris did not anticipate this outcome, he ultimately distributed a solution. However, he was prosecuted and convicted under federal statutes and sentenced to three years probation and heavy fines. His appeal fell short and, as a result, gave credence to the new federal statute. The media hype and coverage of this event created the misconception that all hackers have malicious intent and aspire to be criminals.

To help clarify this, we will use the term "crackers' to identify people use their hacker skills with malicious intent. Crackers are accustomed to causing damage to vital information, creating disruptions of service, executing denial-of-service attacks, stealing information, and causing damage. Crackers more recently have been known to work for hire, as part of corporate espionage or cyberterrorist plots.

Hacker Sentenced in New York City for Hacking into Two NASA Jet Propulsion Lab Computers Located in Pasadena, California

RAYMOND TORRICELLI, a/k/a "rolex," the head of a hacker group known as "#conflict," was sentenced to four months in prison and four months of home confinement for, among other things, breaking into two computers owned and maintained by the National Aeronautics and Space Administration's Jet Propulsion Laboratory ("JPL"), located in Pasadena, California, and using one of those computers to host an Internet chat-room devoted to hacking. Chief United States District Judge MICHAEL B. MUKASEY also ordered TORRICELLI to pay a $4,400 in restitution to NASA.

At his plea to five separate charges on December 1, 2000, TORRICELLI admitted that, in 1998, he was a computer hacker, and a member of a hacking organization known as "#conflict." TORRICELLI admitted that he used his personal computer to run programs designed to search the Internet, and seek out computers which were vulnerable to intrusion. Once such computers were located, TORRICELLI's computer obtained unauthorized access to the computers by uploading a program known as "rootkit."

According to the Information and Complaint, one of the computers TORRICELLI accessed was used by NASA to perform satellite design and mission analysis concerning future space missions, another was used by JPL's Communications Ground Systems Section as an e-mail and internal web server. According to the Complaint, and his plea allocution, after gaining this unauthorized access to computers and loading "rootkit," TORRICELLI under his alias "rolex," used many of the computers to host chat-room discussions.

According to the Complaint, TORRICELLI admitted that, in these discussions, he invited other chat participants to visit a website which enabled them to view pornographic images and that he earned 18 cents for each visit a person made to that website. According to the Complaint, TORRICELLI earned approximately $300-400 from per week from this activity.

TORRICELLI also pled guilty to intercepting usernames and passwords traversing the computer networks of a computer owned by San Jose State University. In addition, TORRICELLI pled guilty to possession of stolen passwords and usernames which he used to gain free Internet access, or to gain unauthorized access to still more computers. According to the Complaint, TORRICELLI admitted that when he obtained passwords which were encrypted, he would use a password cracking program known as "John-the-Ripper" to decrypt the passwords.

In addition, TORRICELLI pled guilty to possessing stolen credit card numbers, he admitted obtaining from other individuals and stored them on his computer. TORRICELLI admitted that he used one such credit card number to purchase long distance telephone service.

According to the Complaint, much of the evidence obtained against TORRICELLI was obtained through a search of his personal computer. According to the Complaint, in addition to thousands of stolen passwords and numerous credit card numbers, investigators found transcripts of chat-room discussions in which TORRICELLI and members of "#conflict" discussed, among other things, (1) breaking into other computers (a practice known as "hacking"); (2) obtaining credit card numbers belonging to other persons and using those numbers to make unauthorized purchases (a practice known as "carding"); and (3) using their computers to electronically alter the results of the annual MTV Movie Awards."

The above is an excerpt of a document contained at:
http://www.cybercrime.gov/torricellisent.htm.

Another term that has its roots deep in technology subculture is "phreaker." A phreaker is a person who has detailed knowledge of how the phone system works and exploits that knowledge to gain unauthorized access. Phreakers began by utilizing discrete tone generators (red boxes), which would allow them to mimic the tone-base protocols of the phone system. By tricking the phone circuitry, phreakers were able to gain free phone access. One of the two best-known phreakers is John Draper, aka "Cap'n Crunch," (whose nickname refers to his use of a whistle from a box of the like-named cereal to generate the tones of 2600 Hz, which are used to grant operator privileges). The other is Kevin Pouslen, who used his skills to take over the phone line to a radio station to win a call-in contest. The term "phreaker" is now used to describe people who steal phone card information and service.

Long-Distance Phone Service Fraud

"Corey Lindsly and Calvin Cantrell we re sentenced today in federal court by the Honorable Chief District Judge Jerry Buchmeyer for hacking into computer systems belonging to Sprint Corporation, Southwestern Bell and GTE, illegally obtaining long distance calling card numbers and selling these stolen calling card numbers.

Corey Lindsly, age 32, of Portland, Oregon, was sentenced to forty-one months imprisonment and ordered to pay $10,000 to the victim corporations. Calvin Cantrell, age 30, of Grand Prairie, Texas, was sentenced to two years imprisonment and ordered to pay $10,000 to the victim corporations. Both defendants pleaded guilty in late spring to criminal fraud and related activity in connection with Access Devices and Computers, in violation of Title 18, United States Code, Sections 1029(a)(3) and 1030(a)(4).

Lindsly and Cantrell are the major ringleaders in a computer hacker organization known as the 'Phone Masters," whose ultimate goal was to own the telecommunications infrastructure from coast to coast. In addition to the numerous telecommunications systems that were penetrated, the group also penetrated computer systems owned by credit reporting agencies, utility providers, and systems owned by state and federal governmental agencies, to include the National Crime Information Center (NCIC) computer. These hackers organized their assaults on the computers through teleconferencing and utilized the encryption program PGP to hide the data that they traded with each other."

The above is an excerpt of a document contained at *http://ww.cybercrime.gov/phonmast.htm*

Script kiddies are a relatively new class of cybercriminals, more appropriately referred to as cybernuisances. It is not illegal to create malicious software. In fact, people do it regularly to test products and conduct vulnerability assessments. Script kiddies are generally teenagers with access to computers and the Net. They obtain these programs to occupy their time and have fun. Generally, they are being mischievous and have no malicious intent. The two main problems with script kiddies are 1) they do not understand the serious nature of the scripts and software they are running, and 2) they have a significant amount of free time to use them.

One of the most common methods for obtaining critical information to gain access to systems is social engineering. **Social engineers** are people practiced at the art of deception. They are masters at manipulating the social structure in an organization to gain computer passwords, critical phone numbers, and configuration files, as well as infiltrating an organization's trust.

Unfortunately, what started out as a hacking game has become an extremely dangerous practice. **Cyberterrorists** are the most recent addition to the growing lists of computer criminals. Many significant works are available regarding the growing threat of cyberterrorists, including the book *Information Warfare and Security* by Dorothy E. Denning. Cyberterrorism is the act of manipulating systems in the worldwide computer community to cause mass confusion, disrupt critical infrastructure, destabilize financial mechanisms, obtain false documents, conduct covert operations, or, in extreme cases, actually cause harm or death. The U.S. government is uncertain as to the extent to which our infrastructure is vulnerable to cyberterrorism. It is widely known that the perpetrators of September 11th used the Internet extensively to conduct covert operations and for concealed communications.

Trusted insiders are perhaps the most prolific and destructive of the cybercriminals. Statistics point out that disgruntled employees account for more than 50 percent of all known attacks and information disruption or damage. Further, these people lay the groundwork for their forays usually long before anyone suspects a problem. For example, a person can deploy a backdoor to be used later for unauthorized access, remove or manipulate critical files, steal customer lists or financial information, embezzle funds, or deploy malware of various kinds.

As can be seen when conducting a risk assessment, we should anticipate attacks from some or all of these groups and take proactive actions to minimize or remove these risks. Many companies and organizations do not even conduct the proper background investigations of perspective employees. It is surprising how many personnel departments fail to verify resumes, let alone conduct criminal background checks, on their employees.

By structuring and classifying our information and our personnel, many security breaches can be avoided.

WHAT IS RISK?

What does it mean to keep something safe? Many would argue that being safe is the equivalent of minimizing or removing risk. Exploring safety as it relates to information is important. As with the house fire example from Chapter 1 where evaluating the risks to people was paramount, it is also important to understand the risks our information faces. We must have a methodical approach to evaluating risk and capturing that analysis. By understanding the threats to our information, we can make informed decisions regarding the disposition of security measures. Remember that good security is rarely inexpensive or convenient. It is impossible and impractical to account for and protect against all forms of risk. Thus, we need a valid risk assessment to focus our planning and implementation efforts. A comprehensive risk evaluation increases participation in the security plan and confidence in the expenditures likely to be incurred.

> **KEY POINT**
>
> Risk is the possibility of loss or harm to something valued, based on the uncertainty of particular events or outcomes. Risk is measured by understanding the probability of a particular risk event, the frequency with which the event is likely to occur, and the dollar value of the item to be protected.

It is important to note that risk can be **voluntary** or **involuntary**. A voluntary risk is one that we know about and decide to take anyway. An example of this is driving in a car, even though we know that certain additional risks to our safety are likely to exist. We know that we can mitigate these risks and that the benefit of travel outweighs risk. We also know enough not to get in the car if the person driving has been drinking because statistics show that the risk will then too high. Therefore, we make an informed decision and either take or not take the risk.

Involuntary risks are caused by factors we cannot control, or possibilities that are affected by more variables than we can account for. Examples of involuntary risks are Earth being destroyed by an asteroid, or the world financial markets crashing. These risks, although certainly possible, are both remote and completely outside of our control.

Therefore, when assessing risk, we want to focus on the voluntary or controllable risks and be sure to take generalized precautions (usually insurance) against the involuntary risks that our information is likely to face.

Risk, by definition, is established in the context of both

- Risk events that we call **threats**
- And things valued that we call **risk entities**

The first step in understanding risk is to have a comprehensive understanding of your risk entities. Risk entities include physical surroundings (e.g., buildings, infrastructure) and personal items (self, communications pathways, operational assets, brand, financial assets, and information).

As we demonstrated in Chapter 1, information security is normally concerned with the security of the information and the information system. The value of the information system is rapidly declining. Products such as computer platforms, PDAs, laptops, networking hardware and infrastructure, and data storage devices have become commoditized. Often it is cheaper to replace these parts rather than to fix them if damaged or worn. In most cases they are replaced for underperformance long before they wear out. More important, the value of the information system is usually stable and predictable. Understanding this value is important because we can then predict our replacement costs.

Information, however, can be elusive and hard to quantify. The value of information is based on the cost of obtaining and producing the information, as well as its semantic value to the organization based on how it is used. The cost of obtaining and producing information can be derived from the man-hours and processing cycles required to obtain and input the raw data, and from the processing and application costs required to convert the data into useful information. Retaining these metrics can be helpful in determining the replacement time and costs to an organization in the event of a catastrophic failure. Additionally, many organizations (once converted to fully automated processes) rarely retain the original manpower and expertise available to reproduce the initial conversion effort in a timely fashion. Although this is easily overcome (via a consultative arrangement to obtain the skills and numbers of resources required) in the event of an isolated outage, what happens if the outage is widespread? You may not be able to garner the appropriately skilled resources because they may have already been engaged by other clients facing a similar problem. This is where careful planning and appropriate disaster recovery precautions play such a vital role.

As previously discussed, brand value is a combination of the use of information and the stability of the information system. The value of the brand must be determined and factored into any information value equation. Brand value can be easily obtained through the marketing department and is closely related to the market share (global and regional) indexes, which guide product development and distribution.

Information use is also measured through the sales metrics of an organization. We can look at variations in sales and marketing numbers based on the quality of information utilized by the sales and marketing staff. A powerful metric that can help us understand the value of information is found through an analysis of when an organization is deprived of requisite information for varied periods of time. Normally, this type of metric is associated with a time that marks **tcritical information failure**. This is when an organization suffers a loss (partial, ongoing, or total) in revenue based on its inability to retrieve, produce, or modify information critical to serving customer needs.

This analysis not only helps us understand the value of information use, but also helps us identify and prioritize the most critical information elements. Often in conducting this sort of an analysis, a security professional will hear statements such as, "As long as this particular information is available, we can survive," or "This process can no longer be accomplished without automation." These red flags should help us focus our attention on areas of greatest risk to the well being of the organization.

One outcome of analysis of this type is the cataloging and classifying of the information. It is helpful to classify information as the report is developed so that its relative importance can be understood as the information base evolves. For many years, asset management projects have helped corporations and organizations classify their risk elements. Many organizations are now beginning to utilize classification methods for the comprehensive inventory of information as well. Perhaps no organization has structured its documentation and information archives better than the U.S. military.

This classification strategy is well documented. Access to classified information is tightly controlled both from the perspective of personnel, as well as with respect to technology.

Five Tiers of Classification Used by the U.S. Military[4]

- Unclassified data is meant for public consumption
- Sensitive But Unclassified (SBU) data is meant for official use only. The improper release of the information could affect the privacy of personnel or in some way affect the disposition of the Department of Defense
- Confidential data could cause a breach in national security. This type of information includes activities regarding the movement of troops, munitions test results, resources consumptions statistics, and more
- Secret data is information that, if released, would cause serious damage to national security
- Top Secret data is information that, if released, would cause extreme damage to national security. This information requires recipients of the information to exercise complete confidentiality for life

Most organizations rarely need this detailed of a classification scheme. A minimum three-tier policy should be adopted:

- Public domain: This information has been determined suitable and appropriate for public consumption
- Internal use only: This is information used to run the business or to discuss improvements in products and services, which may prove embarrassing or disruptive to the company if revealed
- Confidential: Information of a personal or strategic nature to the business or employee

Another key area of risk evaluation lies in identifying the sources of the risk or **threat agents**. The potential perpetrators of the threats are varied, and their intent ranges from mischievous to malicious and calculated. These perpetrators can employ many types of attacks or threat agents. Information is likely to be targeted by one or more of these threat agents. We will examine the various types of the broad classes of these threat agents later in this chapter. However, for now it is important to realize that (as the statistics provided earlier support), the most dangerous source of the threat agents is the trusted insider. As we develop our security plans, we should not make the mistake of having an exclusively outward (Internet) focus.

[4.] U.S. ARMY School of Information Technology

KEY POINT

The source of risk involves identifying the type of perpetrator, whether the attack will come from inside or outside the organization's information system, and the type of attack.

Assessing the **attack probability** is partly determined by understanding the threat profile, the intent of the perpetrator (motive), and by understanding the nature of your business and your exposure to the attackers. Attack probability metrics can be best derived from historical data (logs). In the absence of, or in conjunction with, such empirical proprietary information, we can make projections based on broad-based data sources and our own instincts.

It is important for all security professionals to establish a consistent base of information to reinforce their security position. This information is often helpful in determining **attack frequency**. Trends can be captured by attack type (e.g., rate of spread of a virus, see *http://www.mcafee.com* for a global virus chart), by industry sector, by prosecutions and investigations, by dollar value, or combinations of the above. This analysis can then be used to isolate a particular trend and understand the frequency with which it is likely to occur.

In risk evaluations, we will see a tendency to equate risk assessments with the degree of organizational openness. This is a misconception. Determining our risk posture has more to do with the value of our information than with where it resides. We will notice that the degree of risk is directly related to the value of our risk entity, and has only a casual relationship to openness. As Figure 2-1 shows, the assessed level of risk decreases commensurate with the value of the information. This relationship is said to be proportional: As value increases, so then does risk.

Upon careful examination, we can see that the need for openness modestly affects our risk assessment. Conversely, the degree of openness significantly affects our security posture and plan. In an open environment with high-value information, we take somewhat different security measures than with high-value information in a nonconnected environment. The reasons for this set of deductions follow:

- A network should be viewed as nothing more than a transient storage environment. It is a place where information travels and lives. As we saw in Chapter 1, a bit is an electrical charge or a signal. Whether it is in the memory of our computer, on a floppy disk being toted to work, or traveling near the speed of light down a communications pathway, its value of the bit to our organization has not changed. If we were to ride in an airplane, we would still value our lives the same as if we were sitting in our living rooms. The only difference is that we take different precautions (e.g. wearing a seat belt versus locking the front door to the house)
- Most information breaches and most cybercrime is still regularly committed by trusted insiders. The disgruntled employee will use proprietary methods for intrusions and will do the most damage while still a trusted member of the community. These attacks might have little or nothing to do with the use of the Internet or the degree of openness
- Cryptographic methods, digital signatures, and secure Internet protocols are tremendous equalizers to the vast numbers of people with access to our public domain who would wish to do us harm. As will become clear in Section Two of this text, cryptography can be a powerful tool when utilized correctly. Today, the use of public cryptography methods can bring this capability to the most casual of users. Internet privacy is a huge concern. Low-cost solutions exist to comprehensively address this concern

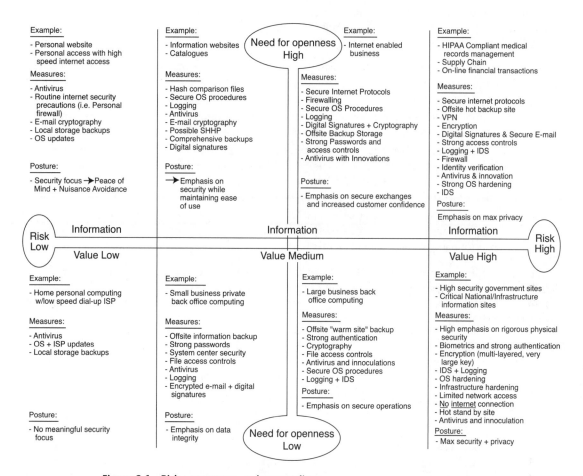

Figure 2-1   Risk—openness—value paradigm.

What we have shown here is that risk assessments are important. Risk assessments can help us decide between action and inaction. Once we understand our risks, the next logical question has to be "What can be done about them?"

KEY POINT

Risk measurements have to be based on the following: a quantification of the value of the risk entity; the probability the given event (which may cause the loss) will even occur, combined with the probability this event will have a negative (harmful) outcome; and the frequency prediction for how often such an event or series of events will occur.

Obviously, the better we understand our **risk factors**, the greater the probability that we can control or influence the outcomes of events to be favorable. Once we have identified the likely sources of the risk or the threats, it is important that we manage them. Risk management can be broken up into four parts:

1 **Identification**—As we have shown, the identification of risk factors can be a powerful exercise to help us understand security cost projections and also influence our risk entity prioritization.

2 **Removal**—After a risk has been identified, it should be evaluated to determine if it can be removed. Risks that can be removed should be removed. An example is a worker with a criminal history who is not permitted to work in trusted areas.

3 **Minimization**—For those risks that cannot be completely removed, we should focus on risk minimization. This is where security professionals spend the majority of their time. Examples of this include the implementation of firewalls or intrusion-detection devices or simple locks on a door to areas containing secure materials or assets.

4 **Transfer**—For those risks that cannot be cost-effectively reduced or removed, we should consider a transfer of the risk to a party with broader concerns. This transfer could be insurance, outsourcing, or off-site management.

Later in this chapter and throughout the text, extensive detail on the risk management process as it relates to information, security planning, and implementing defenses will be provided. However, we must first understand the threats we are likely to encounter and the perpetrator's motivations in committing cybercrime.

THE THREATS

True hackers don't give up. They explore every possible way into
a network, not just the well-known ones.
—the hacker Jericho

The aforementioned hackers, crackers, phreakers, cyberterrorists, script kiddies, social engineers, and industrial spies are all masters of manipulating our information system, our personnel, and our information itself. Their reasons for committing cybercrimes range from being a nuisance to committing industrial espionage. However, what they all have in common is a consistent set of tactics for practicing their craft. As expressed in the above quotation, hackers are constantly seeking new ways to penetrate our defenses. To effectively counter these threats, students of information security must also be well acquainted with these evolving exploits. You cannot defend against what you do not understand. By building our attack knowledge base, we can better prepare for the variants of these attacks, which are sure to come in the future. Obviously, no list of attacks and **vulnerabilities** will ever be complete. The intention here is to present the fundamental attacks and vulnerabilities upon which many others are based. A continuously updated list of attacks, the so-called SANS Top 10, can be found at *http://www.sans.org/topten.htm*.

Information can be attacked in a variety of ways. Availability of information can be affected making the access to information difficult or impossible. The very existence of information can be compromised if a cybercriminal deletes or removes files from the system or network. Confidentiality can be breached if information is intercepted and accessed by people other than the intended recipient. Information integrity can be compromised via destructive viruses. The authenticity of information can be compromised by attacks that cause the fabrication or alteration of the information ownership credentials. The evidence of online transaction can be compromised if an organization fails to involve a trusted third party for identity verification. Any of these can affect an organization at any time and without warning. What is more difficult to cope with is that these general categories of attacks can come in so many different forms. Categorizing these forms is important if the security professional is going to be successful in overcoming the attacks.

In general, attacks are organized into two broad categories: **passive attacks** and **active attacks**. Passive attacks involve the hacker eavesdropping or spying on the exchange or processing of information and access routines. Passive attacks also can involve the simple creation of an unrealized threat of a breach, thus reducing the confidence in an organization or their information.

Active attacks require the attacker to take overt action to disrupt, manipulate, corrupt, or access the information system in an effort to compromise the information itself. Active attacks receive the most notoriety in the press and are most often the focus of security products.

TCP/IP and Security

A closely related discipline to information security is networking. It is expected of security professionals to have a comprehensive understanding of network architectures and network protocols. Based on today's highly interconnected communications infrastructure, attacks originating on the Internet are increasing in frequency.

Students need to understand the **TCP/IP** model because this is by far the most predominantly used Internet access architecture. For many of these attack descriptions to have meaning, the reader should have a sound understanding of IP protocol and packet structure, TCP protocol and header structures, ports, sockets, well-known ports, and related application protocols (e.g. FTP, Telnet, ICMP, SMTP, SNMP). TCP/IP is complex and is a whole course unto itself. It is strongly recommended that the reader unfamiliar with these topics acquire the requisite information to be better able to function as an information security professional. A brief review of TCP/IP is presented in Appendix B.

These broad categories can be further broken down as seen in Figure 2-2.

While it is beyond the scope of this text to dissect every attack type, it is important for students to understand how to categorize these attacks, the basics of how they are implemented, and how they are deployed (and subsequently recognized).

CAUTIONARY NOTE

It is illegal to carry out an attack on any site, computer, source of information, person, network, or computer entity, for any reason. Not even as a joke! Perpetrators of hacks, attacks, and pranks are subject to prosecution under the law and can be fined or imprisoned. This information is provided exclusively for the instructional use of students. Please take this warning seriously. It is recommended that course instructors utilize "safe labs" (see the Building a Safe Lab appendix at the back of the text) for conducting experiments with various attacks. It is also important to note that many of the web sites available for gathering prepackaged attacks are booby-trapped and can infect the target systems and networks requesting the download. Using a "safe lab" can isolate problems and minimize exposure to attacks.

```
┌─────────────────────────┐   ┌─────────────────────────┐
│    Active Attacks       │   │    Passive Attacks      │
│                         │   │                         │
│  • DOS & DDOS           │   │  • Eaves dropping       │
│  • Instrusion attacks   │   │  • Shoulder surfing     │
│  • Hijacking            │   │  • Mapping              │
│  • Malicious code       │   │  • Release of message   │
│     - Viruses           │   │     content             │
│     - Worms             │   │  • Unrealized threats   │
│     - Trojans           │   │                         │
│     - Poison Cookies    │   │                         │
│  • Attacks against      │   │                         │
│    Encryption           │   │                         │
│  • Web based attacks     │   │                         │
└─────────────────────────┘   └─────────────────────────┘
```

Techniques used by hackers to:
  - Block services
  - Gain Information
  - Damage the Information
    System
  - Damage Information

Techniques used by hackers to:
  - Gain Information
  - Gain access to mechanism
  - Create fear
  - Cause confusion

Figure 2-2   To understand hacker operations, we must first understand hacker methods and tactics.

The following are descriptions of some of the most common active attacks. The reader should pay particular attention to the type names and the class of attack to which they belong. Each class of attack affects information differently. Understanding the various classes' characteristics is key to understanding why it is impossible to assume that you can successfully defend the information system against them all. Rather, it is suggested as the central theme of this work that protection of the information itself (as opposed to the information system) would better serve an organization.

Six classes of active attacks are likely to be used to against targets:

1 Denial-of-service and distributed-denial-of-service attacks

2 Intrusion attacks and information theft

3 Hijacking

4 Malicious code

5 Attacks against encryption

6 Web-based attacks

KEY POINT

These attacks are active and passive. Active attacks can be classified into six categories.

DENIAL-OF-SERVICE ATTACKS

The class of attacks known as **denial-of-service (DOS) attacks**, and **distributed-denial-of-service (DDOS) attacks** are among the most important to study and protect against. DOS attacks are devised to prevent access to information by authorized users. A DOS attack can occur when an attacker sends a large number of connection requests, information requests, or synchronization messages that overwhelm the host, thereby rendering it inoperable. A DOS attack can also be carried out at the system level by blocking account access. A DDOS attack involves the coordinated effort of DOS attacks from many locations simultaneously against the same host or site. The DDOS attack often involves the use of springboard attacks (malware planted on unsuspecting hosts set to trigger at such a time as to participate in or prolong a DDOS-style attack). These unsuspecting springboard hosts are known as **zombies**.

A DOS attack usually takes advantage of a weakness in the system or networking software, which causes the operating system or network driver to take an action or repeated action resulting in the denial of service to a legitimate user. These attacks often involve very simple but effective methods. Examples of DOS attacks might include

- Locking users out of their accounts by attempting to log in to their systems using the proper user ID with incorrect passwords. Most systems limit the number of attempts to log in so that any attempt to crack a password and gain unauthorized access is stopped. This DOS attack uses that knowledge to prevent an authorized user from accessing the system. One purpose of this style attack on a large scale could be to overwhelm the help desk busily trying to issue new passwords to irate users
- Overrunning a DNS server with lookup requests, causing it to use valuable resources (memory). This can cause slow response or a complete system-wide outage (in the event of a system crash)
- Repeatedly requesting the download of a large image from a Web server can be easily accomplished using the commands:

  <html>

  <meta http-equiv = "refresh" content = "100">

  <img scr= http://site.com/picture.jpg>

  </html>

  This can cause a server to significantly slow down or crash.
- Sending network control messages (requiring network responses) that tie up a communication interface. An example of this is the repeated pinging of a remote site. To do this, you could use the command

  >:looper

  >ping remotesite.com

  >goto looper

In recent years, many distributed versions of these attacks were successfully launched against large corporations, including several ISPs and prominent Internet-based clearinghouses. As you can see, there are several types of DOS and DDOS strategies with which the security professional should become familiar.

Flooding is a strategy used to overload the target system or network device with an unreasonable amount of legitimate messages that require action. The key to understanding this type of attack is to notice that all of the actions taken by the hacker are legitimate in terms of the syntax and construct of the activity. These types of attacks exploit weaknesses in the strategy upon which the service is based.

Three specific examples of DOS attacks are the SYN Flood, teardrop, and Smurf attacks.

A **SYN Flood** takes advantage of the simple and open nature of the TCP connection establishment protocol. As is often the case, older networking protocols (such as TCP/IP) were not designed with security in mind. In fact, most of these older protocols were designed to be run over a closed or private network where both the users and the infrastructure could be trusted. A key design principle of many such network protocols was to keep the required protocol actions simple. It is in this simplicity that the modern-day hacker gains advantage. As is shown in Figure 2-3, the network connection between two hosts is built on a three-way protocol exchange. First, a TCP packet is sent from the client to the host requesting the connection with the SYN flag set. The server then responds with both the SYN and ACK flags set. Finally, the client responds with the ACK flag set signaling the session is established. If the client does not respond or does not set the ACK flag in the response, the server will time out and close the session.

A SYN Flood attack exploits this handshaking process by submitting a large number of connect requests in excess of what the system can handle. Obviously, every system has an upper limit to the amount of resources it can commit to any activity. By occupying those resources, the attacker essentially shuts out any legitimate requests for connection.

Many firewall companies employ strategies to lessen the effects of a SYN Flood attack. Because the firewall sits between the attacker and the target host, it can intervene and satisfy (or act as a proxy on behalf of) the server and weed out malicious attacks. Many varied strategies to accomplish this exist, but they are beyond the scope of this text.

A **teardrop attack** essentially exploits the IP sequencing strategy. When IP packets are too long for the router to handle, they can be broken down into smaller packets, each of which is assigned a number. These packets are then sent individually and chained together via this numbering sequence. These individual parts are called fragments. When the receiver of the fragments gathers all of the parts, he then tries to reassemble them according to the packet sequence numbering. A hacker can construct a teardrop attack by sending such a series of fragments and simply putting a confusing offset into the second or later packets. Then, when the receiver tries to reassemble the original packet, it may have trouble dealing with the incorrect numbering sequence and subsequently crash or fail in some way. This of course causes a denial of service to all other users.

A **Smurf attack** is an attack that exploits the TCP/IP (see Appendix B) echo request or **ping** command behavioral design flaws. The ping command is designed to allow a user to test both the reachability and response times of remote nodes. This is done by typing

   >*ping www.nodename.ext*

via the command line interface. However, in the case of a Smurf attack, the hacker directs the ping command to the network broadcast address (meaning every node on the subnet will attempt to respond at the same time). Additionally, the attacker fakes the source address of the packet to be that of the victim and all of the responses will simultaneously converge on the target system. This will lock up the target network interface and slow the network performance on that segment.

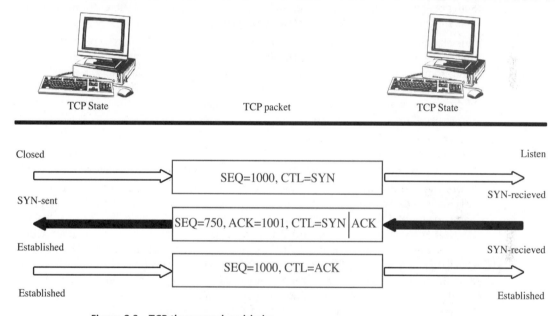

Figure 2-3   TCP three-way handshake.

Lockouts are attacks that result in legitimate users being unable to access the system and thus become isolated from their information. This is often accomplished using simple methods, such as exceeding the failed login attempts' parameter of the operating system.

E-mail floods or **mail bombing** are attacks that render a user's e-mail system unmanageable by filling it with huge amounts of unsolicited e-mail messages. Mail bombing can be a serious problem if it disrupts the normal flow of business activities inside a company.

Obviously, the attacker wants to remain anonymous. Anonymity can be accomplished by taking advantage of naïve code in the **simple mail transport protocol (SMTP)**. The e-mail spoofing lab presented at the end of this text provides a good example of how easy it is to spoof (falsify) an e-mail address.

Buffer overflows are one of the oldest hacker tricks known. Buffer overflows can cause devastating damage and disruption. A buffer is a piece of memory in the computer that is set aside to handle data in transit. This can be between two networked hosts, between clients and servers, or between internal computer processes. This memory is reserved, and the space dedicated to the buffer is predetermined at run time. Overflowing the buffer occurs when faulty application or system programming allows a peer program or user to input more data to the buffer than it was designed to handle. This can potentially cause two serious problems. First, the overflow can cause the application or the operating system to crash, resulting in a denial of service to all users. A second, and potentially more devastating, problem is that the overflow data may contain executable code (planted by the hacker), which is inadvertently executed. Hackers use this tactic to gain control of your system. The attacker may issue commands to change a system or network configuration. Worse yet, the attack may destroy or alter data. Buffer overflows almost always target software design flaws, especially in older applications or operating systems designed when security concerns were minimal .

One example of such a design flaw was the failure of protocol designers to properly confirm the length of an arriving IP packet. The IP packet header (see Appendix B) contains a length field. Some early versions of the protocol accepted the count when allocating buffer space and never actually counted the bytes in the packet. The programmers' failure to confirm the length of the packet allowed the hacker to add malicious code to the end of the packet, thereby causing an overflow.

Another example of a buffer overflow was caused by a bug in version 4.0 of Microsoft's Internet Explorer. If the user typed a *res://* URL with more than 256 characters, the program crashed. Moreover, hackers could add malware after the 256th character, which would then be executed.

Malformed commands are legitimate network commands (ICMP packets)that are purposefully malformed, resulting in programmatic confusion caused by incorrect error handling logic. These malformed commands will often cause the program or the system to crash. The **ping of death** is one such attack. In this attack the hacker creates an oversized ping request, which forces the network to fragment the packet into many smaller packets. Because of poor error checking and trusting program logic, the reassembled fragments (the total of which is greater than the maximum allowable packet size) are placed into the input buffer, causing a buffer overflow and subsequent system crash. In the early years of IP networking, this attack had an exceptionally high rate of success. Since then, vendors have updated their programs, removed the programmatic defects, and performed more adequate error checking.

INTRUSION ATTACKS

The next class of threat is broadly categorized as an **intrusion attack**. The intrusion attack is a deliberate attempt by the attacker to penetrate the defenses of the information security system and to gain unrestricted access to the information itself. Unlike a DOS attack, where the aim is to keep others from accessing information, the intrusion attack is seeking to steal or alter the information itself. Typically, these attacks are aimed at achieving one of three possible outcomes:

1 Steal information
2 **Sabotage** information
3 Fraudulently use an identity

Information theft is a serious problem, often occurring after the dismissal of a formerly trusted employee. Items such as customer lists, account plans, and product engineering specifications are but a few of the frequently targeted items. Industrial espionage is often conducted electronically and results in materials being accessed, often without the owner ever being aware of the trespass.

The sabotage of information results in a loss of confidence in the information's reliability and in a loss of confidence in the business itself. Sabotage can occur via unwarranted modifications to information, deletion of information, or the unintended release of information. In many cases, sabotage of information is a worse problem than information theft.

As we will examine in close detail in Chapter 3, **identity theft** is the most frequently committed electronic crime. This type of crime occurs when the attacker obtains personal information from the victim and uses it to falsely represent himself as that person. The most common form of electronic identity theft is the theft of credit information. Other identity theft crimes involve accessing personal accounts, falsifying loan papers, improperly releasing information under the assumed name, and releasing false information under the assumed name. These are difficult crimes to prosecute and equally difficult to defend against.

The following three categories of crime are focused on the improper use of information or the unwarranted access and manipulation of information. Each of these can be used alone or in tandem to perpetrate an intrusion attack.

Name spoofing is one of the oldest hacker tricks known. In the computer field, naming people, software, hardware, and network services is common and expected. In past generations of computer development, the use of such names was considered a valid method of identification, and it was often done without any verification. In this type of attack, the perpetrator utilizes the name of the attacked party (including people, machines, and software) to falsely represent themselves as that party. This can lead to the dissemination of erroneous information, the distribution of corrupted software, and the infiltration of systems, networks, or applications.

A simple example of name spoofing is detailed in the labs section at the end of the text. In the lab at the end of the text, the user utilizes Microsoft Outlook Express software to change the FROM: field of an e-mail message to represent any person they like. While it is true that the real identity of the sender is still available in the header of the mail message (although many people do not know how to determine what is in the header), the shock value of seeing a message entitled "the unfortunate terminatio n of your services" can be devastating.

Password cracking is a real set of attacks, supported by many freeware tools. Password cracking is a blatant attack on access to either the information or the information system. Protecting information and the information system with passwords is a common first line of defense in computer security. However, for many it is the only defense that is employed. As we shall explore in detail in Section Two of this text, the ability to crack a password is mathematically deterministic. This means the complexity of the password, the speed of the processor, and the method of the attack can yield a predictable time to password failure. It is not a matter of *if* the password can be cracked, simply a matter of *how long* the cracking process will take. Later in the text, we will perform a lab experiment demonstrating how various password lengths and constructs will take more or less time to penetrate.

Tools such as "John-the-Ripper," "Advanced NT Security Explorer," "Passfinder" for the Mac, "Crack" for UNIX, and many more are readily acce ssible. Password cracking is done via several methods. Brute force attacks simply try every combination of characters for every length of password. These are generally slow but effective. Dictionary attacks utilize a list of common words and phrases in an attempt to expedite the process. These are often quite effective because most people utilize common words or phrases to enhance their ability to remember the password. Rule-based cracking software utilizes common heuristics (rules of thumb) to better enable the cracking process. Such rules include trying a dictionary attack with words spelled backward, or using upper- and lowercase letters (effective in UNIX), or inserting a $ at the beginning or end of the possible password. No matter which of these methods are deployed, the exclusive use of passwords to provide security is obviously a mistake.

Identity theft is not an attack on information or the information system. Rather, it is an attack on the entity or owner of the information. As we shall see in Chapter 3, identity theft has become the designer crime of the hacker in the recent years. The reason for this is obvious: Successful identity theft can be profitable. The use of personal information to steal someone's credit card or bank account to purchase items or services has an immediate benefit to the cybercriminal. Given the relative ease of access to security hacking tools—which enable access to information—and to social engineering techniques, a technologically unsophisticated hacker can participate in this emerging crime area.

Identity theft can utilize name spoofing as previously discussed, or it can take a more subtle form such as Web spoofing (setting up a Web-like site to procure information). Further, identity theft can affect the software distribution process when an attacker distributes an unauthorized code (complete with malicious code) update on behalf of a vendor.

Identity theft is a crime that illustrates the need for authentication and verification of identity—two topics discussed in great detail in Chapter 3.

Social engineering is a hacker technique more about savvy than technical ability. This should be considered a bridge between the technology world and the common criminal world. Social engineering is the art of manipulating a person or organization to break policy and to disclose secrets or permit access, under the guise of a legitimate request.

For example, rather than crack a password, just ask for it. A common technique for this type of attack is for the hacker to contact the subject of the attack and represent himself as a member of the organization's system support team. Then the hacker simply tells the victim that there has been a problem with security, and that the employee's password is needed to correct some flaws in the account. The hacker then tells the victim to choose a new password and to wait twenty minutes before changing the password. The hacker concludes by telling the victim that the password will be reset. Often this type of interaction will go unchallenged.

Dumpster diving is a form of social engineering where the hacker searches the garbage or desk of the victim, searching for access codes, names of files, or the information itself. A nontechnical example of this is to search someone's personal garbage to find an unwanted credit card application that has been discarded. These are frequently sent to homes in an unsolicited manner. The perpetrator then completes and mails the application. By monitoring the victim's mail, the criminal can then steal the credit card and begin using it without the victim ever knowing (until the bills show up).

Port scanning is a relatively simple attack where the hacker uses the Telnet service to randomly try and connect to ports on a target system. By issuing the command

>*telnet www.somehost.com {port number}*

the attacker can probe the remote system for unprotected ports, which can yield access to the information system. This attack, in conjunction with a password cracking attack, can be effective in gaining entry to a system or network.

SESSION HIJACKING

Hijacking or the **man-in-the-middle** attack is yet another category of attacks difficult to defend against. In this type of attack, the hacker begins by "listening in" on the electronic conversation between two communicating hosts. This category of attack has both an active and passive version. The active version of the man-in-the-middle attack is utilized to assume control of a communication's path for one of several purposes:

- Redirecting information from the intended party to the hacker
- Changing the information as it is being sent and received to suit the hacker's purpose
- Preventing the transmission of information
- Disseminating incorrect information
- Misusing information

The easiest of these attacks is the **replay attack**. The replay attack involves capturing information, via the use of a network sniffer. The hacker captures a password and username (still encrypted) transaction over the Internet. The attacker then replays the information to gain access or to trigger some event. Notice the transaction need not be decoded.

Sequence number prediction, ARP cache poisoning (ARP spoofing), DNS spoofing, and **packet redirection** are more sophisticated methods of session hijacking. They involve using tools to manipulate the communication's protocols to take control of a session. In these attacks, the underlying purpose is to assume the electronic identity of a trusted host.

In the case of ARP cache poisoning, the attacker assumes the IP host identity of a trusted host while substituting the attackers MAC address for that of the attacker.   In the case of the DNS spoofing attack, the attacker directly manipulates the DNS server entry, which redirects connection requests to the attacker, who poses as the trusted host.

Sequence number prediction is somewhat more difficult. In sequence number prediction attacks, the hacker waits until a session between two trusting hosts is under way. Once the client gains access to the server (this is what the attacker cannot accomplish on his own), the attacker attempts to assume control of the session in place of the trusted client. This attacker must accomplish three tasks:

1 Have the IP identity of the targets

2 Keep the real client from responding to the series of transactions

3 Properly insert the sequence of bogus packets into the precise sequence of the TCP/IP data stream

The first two of these parameters are easily accomplished. Using a sniffer, the hacker can obtain the IP addresses of both the client and the server. The attacker can occupy the real client via a DOS attack on the client, thus satisfying the second requirement.

The third requirement requires more sophisticated technical prowess and the use of tools designed for the insertion purpose. These tools do exist. "Spoofit" and "rbone" are examples of such tools and can be utilized for this purpose.

The point of this discussion is that any of these attacks can compromise many of the security measures deployed because the attacks take advantage of unverified trust relationships. These type of attacks are difficult, although not impossible, to defend against. More important, they demonstrate the need for tighter information security precautions rather than just information system precautions.

MALICIOUS CODE

Malicious code or malware constitutes a prolific series of threats to information and the information system. These attacks include viruses, worms, Trojan horses, logic bombs, and backdoors to spread malicious code. When the malware is activated, it steals or destroys information.

Of these, viruses and worms are the most common and often do the most damage. A virus is software that attaches itself to another program on the user system. When the host activates the known application, the virus software is invoked and the destructive process begins.

A worm is a computer program that replicates itself, spreading from host to host over a network. This software is not always malicious. It can occur as the result of a logic error in a well-intentioned program. Worms are known to take up significant resources on both networks and systems and can therefore cause effects similar to denial-of-service attacks.

These types of attacks can spread at an alarming rate and overwhelm not just a single host but whole networks and industries. The Nimda virus in September 2001 spread across the Internet in just twenty-five minutes. The more recent SQL Hell virus spread with incomprehensible speed and disabled key interfaces from host systems to ATM machines on a worldwide basis.

Hoaxes are a new problem causing considerable issues in the e-mail virus and worm attack domain. Essentially, many well-intentioned people hear of a potential problem and immediately post messages to various distribution lists warning of the problem. This can lead to many hours of unnecessary work attempting to research and solve a nonexistent problem. A variant on this is a hoax attack, where the person spreading the false information includes a real virus in the warning message.

A **logic bomb** is a piece of code that causes the operating system to lock up and subsequently fail. This can be done purposefully via a buffer overflow, database dead lock, or excessive consumption of resources.

Code vulnerabilities are done through both the intentional development of **backdoors** (application entry points purposely left unclosed so that the developer can gain unobstructed access at their convenience) and the identification of coding flaws that can be exploited. The latter of these represent the most common reason that security breaches occur at all. Code vulnerabilities, whether intentional or simply design oversights, leave the user completely defenseless until the vendor takes corrective action. This is a dangerous situation for the user because once the hacker becomes aware of the potential of the attack, the victims must take the risk of operating with the known security hole or deny themselves the service until it is clear what countermeasure is available.

Trojans are pieces of seemingly harmless software planted on the victim's system. Later, based on some predetermined trigger, the software is activated and performs surreptitious actions, which can be malicious and breach security. Malicious software is studied in detail in Chapter 10. For now, students should understand the profile of each type of attack. Later we will review the programmatic details.

ATTACKS AGAINST ENCRYPTION

A class of attack that greatly concerns the audience of this text is **attacks against encryption**. These attacks strike at the essence of our security model. It is important that students understand these tactics so they can be anticipated and avoided.

Section Two of this text focuses on the use of varied cryptographic methods, which can safeguard our information. Essentially, cryptography is a process of encoding and decoding messages so that the ciphertext can be transmitted publicly but understood only by the intended recipient, who is in possession of the decode key and algorithm (method of decryption). This secret coding process is highly secure.

The encryption/decryption process is one part of the cryptographic process and specifically deals with the encoding of plain text and the decoding of ciphertext. For now, let us think of encryption as simply disguising our electronic secrets (plain text) as a coded message (ciphertext). Encryption techniques can be vulnerable to cracking given poor key choices and the requisite amount of time and tactics necessary to penetrate a given encryption method. Cryptanalysis is the process of breaking codes. Breaking codes is a difficult task and is often time consuming. We use this fact to enhance our cryptographic policy. In general, we shall see that cryptographic methods should meet two important criteria to be successful:

- The time required to break the cipher needs to be greater than the useful lifetime of the information
- The cost of breaking the code needs to be greater than the worth of the information.

If we can meet those two criteria, then breaking the code would serve no useful purpose. These criteria should be used to drive the selection of cryptographic method. We will spend considerable time on this process in Section Two of the text.

Several generalized methods are used to attack encryption:

- **Plain text attacks** occur when the attacker has access to a piece of ciphertext and a corresponding piece of plain text. Given this information, the cryptanalyst attempts to discover the key and the encryption algorithm, from which the message was originally coded. These attacks are not always intuitive and require enormous skill and patience. A variant of this attack includes the **chosen plain text attack**, in which the attacker has the ability to force the source to generate a cryptographic message containing a specific known term or phrase. This makes attacking the cipher easier
- **Mathematical attacks** require the cryptanalyst to know the algorithm being used. Given this information, the attacker can mathematically produce lists of valid keys and use a brute-force approach to determining which one is in use. These computations are highly complex
- **Weak keys** are keys whose numerical properties cause the encryption algorithm to falter or diminish. Given certain algorithms (TEA, for example) and a weak key, it is possible that multiple keys can be used to decrypt the same message. Further, it is possible to find a key (with the DES encryption algorithm) which, when repeatedly applied to the algorithm, can undo itself on alternating cycles. In either case, if a user randomly picks one of these weak key types, the security offered during this cryptographic session will be compromised. A good cryptanalyst already knows the effects of weak keys and will be prepared to try those types of keys in deciphering the text before attempting the arduous process of a mathematical attack. The percentage of such keys is relatively small and can be guarded against

WEB-BASED ATTACKS

Web attacks constitute the final classification of attacks that warrant examination. The explosive growth of the World Wide Web has opened tremendous sources of information and communication to Internet users. However, the mechanisms that we use to enable this technology can be compromised or used against us to cripple our systems, disseminate misleading information, perpetrate hoaxes, and gain access to information. The following are several types of web-based attacks:

- **HTTPD overflow and bypass attacks** are attacks that target the HTTPD protocol that manages the ports and buffers used by Web servers. Just as in the previously discussed buffer overflows, buffers exist in the HTTPD domain. These buffers are prone to attack, especially in the UNIX environment. By intentionally overflowing these buffers, the attacker can cause the overflow data to be executed, thus providing access to the system infrastructure. HTTPD bypass attacks are attacks that allow the attacker to alter the content of a Web page in an undetectable fashion
- **Poison cookies** and **cross scripting** are attacks that utilize the Web cookie as the vehicle for the attack. In each of these attack scenarios, the attacker plants a script that can change the appearance of the Web site or cause login information to be divulged
- **Timing attacks** are attacks that exploit the availability of cached information on the Web browser. This type of attack can enable an attacker to collect information regarding Internet usage, password and account information, or to create and deposit poison cookies on a victim's system
- **Code vulnerabilities** exist in many of the newest Web site development tools and programming languages. These include Visual C++, Visual Basic, CGI, Cold Fusion, XML, Perl, ASP, and others. These code vulnerabilities include not checking input and the unauthorized granting of privileges. Another more recent development is the idea of shared libraries. In an attempt to promote code reuse, we may open ourselves up to a high-risk security area. If a library becomes contaminated and the code reused in widespread applications, it is possible to proliferate the spread of a significant amount of malware
- **URL** or **image floods** are attacks meant to cause a denial of service. These occur any time PORT 80 becomes inundated with repeated rapid reload requests. An example of this was discussed earlier in this section

KEY POINT

Most of the attacks just discussed are caused by programmatic logic flaws, lapses in error or parameter checking, trustful protocol or product design, and the openness of networks. To prevent such problems, due diligence must be given to performing all required software updates. This is the vendor's only mechanism for closing holes in the code and protecting the user community.

PASSIVE ATTACKS

Passive attacks are attacks that usually target the people using the information system. Passive attacks also target the open communications pathways. These attacks often are used as a prelude to an active attack. The following passive attacks are common and can be the source of serious problems. In some cases, passive attacks cause problems that are difficult to solve because you may not even know that these attacks are happening to you or your organization.

Eavesdropping can be accomplished in a variety of ways: socially and electronically. When eavesdropping electronically, a number of devices known as **sniffers** can be used to monitor network activity. These devices can record the content of network messages, which can be reviewed to reveal information, usernames and passwords, network addresses of critical resources, and more.

A social equivalent to this is **shoulder surfing**, where the attacker literally watches the keystrokes of a user to determine usernames, passwords, telephone card numbers, MAC security codes, and other private information. Sometimes the attacker can use a small device such as KeyKatcher Keystroke Recording Device, between the keyboard and the computer to record as many as sixty-four thousand keystrokes. This type of device is passive (it listens) in nature and the attacker can recover the information later.

Mapping is another passive technique. It refers to the monitoring of network connections for the sole purpose of determining the network map of the victims' private network. A network map is an important part of the information system because it details the location of key resources and those resources deployed to protect it. By obtaining a clear picture of the user's network, the hacker can more specifically target appropriate systems, for example the mail server or a particular department's file server.

Release of message content is the distribution of information that is meant to be kept private. For example, if an executive correspondence is prematurely revealed announcing a particular stance during a contract negotiation, the subsequent meeting could be compromised. This distribution can be done effectively in an electronic medium because it is possible to reach a large number of recipients with a single keystroke.

Unrealized threats can reduce the confidence in information and damage the integrity of an organization without even executing an attack of any kind. An example of this is to circulate an unsubstantiated rumor regarding a fake vulnerability of an online service or software product. The power of the media is a tremendous force to reckon with, especially if a potential outcome of such an attack (were it to actually happen) would pose a substantial crisis. Another potentially bad outcome of such an unrealized threat is the unnecessary expenditure of funding to show a response proportional to the threat.

Social engineering also can be passive. Asking questions, observing behavior, and listening to conversations you were not meant to hear are all examples of social engineering. Gaining access to a secure facility by walking into the facility behind an authorized person (tailgating) is a whole lot easier than defeating a network firewall.

In summary, this section is presented not as a comprehensive list of all possible security threats, but as a means to illustrate the relative ease with which our information systems can be compromised. Further, this material should also demonstrate the vast number of truly diverse attack methods that can be deployed. This supports the underlying premise of this text: The perimeter defenses and the information system security architectures can be easily compromised. Thus, it is vital to provide security measures that are attached to and remain with the information. This will yield maximum protection of the valued asset—information.

RISK ASSESSMENT AND VULNERABILITY ANALYSIS

Risk assessment and vulnerability analysis, with regard to information security, is an evolving art. Risk assessment and vulnerability analysis is, at best, an imprecise science in the computer security domain. The **actuarial** formulas and risk assessment methodologies are well defined, but the information security risk event phenomenon is poorly understood, and data collection methods and sources are only now evolving. Whenever we deal with any type of security issue, there is a tendency to be secretive about the severity of the problem. Thus, while much data are collected, most of the collection is proprietary and secret. Little information is shared regarding security breaches. Consequences of this secrecy are that little data are available in the public domain and inconsistencies may be found in the collection methods. This yields a nonuniform distribution of data and leads to biased or faulty predictions.

In many industries, actuarial science is quite mature. Actuarial accountants and mathematicians work to develop risk analysis by guiding decision makers through the risk management process. The insurance industry is the best example of actuarial analysis determining both product availability and cost. For example, when a person buys life insurance, underwriters can determine (based on current health, age, sex, and lifestyle choices) the probable life expectancy of a person. The risk in this case is that a client will die before a reasonable amount of premium is collected to offset the death benefit. Because of the highly evolved data repository regarding illness, accidents, and causes of death, a person can be evaluated and assigned an index with a high degree of accuracy. This index points to a probable outcome based on the vast data resource available on the subject.

What is accuracy in statistical terms? All actuarial mathematics are concerned with **forecasting** outcomes of events where certain (isolated) situational inputs are unknown, based on either highly evolved historical data or by means of experimentation. These situational inputs can be expressed as variables within certain "anticipated" ranges. **Uncertainty** is the lack of information about an object of interest. Uncertainty is called probabilistic if one knows the finite set of outcomes likely to occur. **Variance** reflects the dispersion of input values around the mean (average) value of the solution set for these random variables. **Standard deviation** calculations are another method of quantifying dispersion (square root from variance). Good forecasting methods require the minimization of variance, or standard deviation, of input. In simpler terms, the modeling equations and the definition of the variables are constructed (chosen) to properly reflect the probabilistic real-world event, and the data must "fit" the model. This means the data must be of significant size and granularity to "smooth" the anomalies, and the data must be focused (isolated) with respect to the random variable in question. When standard deviation and variance indicate a clustering of the data around the **mean**, our forecasts will be highly useful—meaning that predictable outcomes are achieved by accomplishing three tasks:

1 The variables must be focused (well designed)
2 The data collection methods must be sound
3 The data sources should be vast and unbiased

As we can see, our understanding of the life sciences, mortality rates, accidents, census, and lifestyle variables are well defined and measured in specific data sets. This allows the insurance industry actuarial mathematician to construct models and equations, which truly reflect the real-word events. Given the vast, unbiased, and accurate data collection methods of coroners, hospitals, centers for disease control, police departments, and the like, we have a manageable data set to utilize. This combination makes this branch of actuarial science sound. Thus, the underwriters of life insurance can make high-quality decisions.

The same will someday be true with respect to information security risks. However, at this time the amount of data available is relatively immature and inconsistent. Consequently, a reliable risk event catalog and indexing system does not yet exist. Many government-sponsored studies are capturing much-needed data, which can be brought into the information security actuarial process.

This in no way minimizes the need for risk assessment and vulnerability analysis or for learning the necessary skills for implementing them. These are important processes and tools that can be a tremendous asset to the security professional. Students need to learn to apply the methods described in this section to the body of data currently available and accept the results in relative, rather than absolute, terms. As the data are refined and normalized, these skills will prove even more useful.

A good starting place is to review two important documents published by the National Institute of Standards and Technology:

- *SP 800-26 Security Self-Assessment Guide for Information Technology Systems*, November 2001
- *SP 800-27 Engineering Principles for Information Technology Security*, June 2001

Both of these documents can be obtained from *http://www.csrc.nist.gov/publications/nistpubs*. These two documents provide a framework and ideas for performing the analysis. Remember, no two corporations or organizations are exactly alike. Security is a custom science and vulnerability analysis needs to be done with that in mind.

KEY POINT

When creating a vulnerability analysis process, it is strongly recommended that comprehensive documentation techniques be employed. Additionally, the process should be repeatable (in that the company will continue to utilize the process), affordable (such that the organization will be able to conduct the process regularly), and appropriate (well suited for the organization.)

It is best to formally establish the criteria for the risk analysis. Start by setting parameters for the study. These might include determining

- Asset valuations and threats to those assets
- Effective security protocols with respect to those assets
- Specific security policies and proper-use criteria
- Baselines for security posture
- Effectiveness of a newly introduced security tool or product
- Organizational comparisons to the industry norm (a rapidly growing area)

These parameters can be used to drive data collection, to focus models, and to interpret outcomes. These parameters should be constructed to have long-term value to the organization. Studies need to be focused on a theme. Thus, a general statement of security purpose needs to accompany these parameters.

As part of stipulating this formal philosophy, the security professional should suggest a logical risk analysis process, which will guide the company successfully to its goal. Since risk analysis is a self-improving process, it is necessary for the process to be repeatable and adaptable. During the planning process, models can be constructed and applied to continually assess and improve the information security posture. As a result, strong documentation practices should be established.

The process shown in Figure 2-4 can be used to fit any of the criteria mentioned previously. In essence it is a seven-step process:

1 Set goals or establish a philosophy.
2 Capture the current state of security via the asset audit.
3 Determine availability and reliability of data sources.
4 Conduct **quantitative analysis**.
5 Conduct **qualitative analysis.**
6 Construct security posture metrics.
7 Refine and repeat the process until satisfied.

We must conduct an asset audit early in the process. This audit should consider both hard (tangible) physical assets, as well as soft assets (e.g. brand, intellectual property, information). This can be a daunting task because many of the corporate assets may not be obvious. Collecting physical assets and cataloging them can be done in both an automated and a manual fashion. Most network and system management products have the capability to capture the computer and network assets in your environment. Using most database tools, organizations can create summary reports regarding the content and size of the data set.

For example, a key factor in creating valuations of databases is the same as the amount of time it took to build the repository. The effects of not having access to software must be calculated. It is also important to capture the cost of connectivity methods used for accessing key resources. Remote applications are not of much use without a way to access them.

OTV TREES

Some assets, such as brand and intellectual property, are hard to capture and quantify. To capture the more important soft assets, use a proven technique called an **Ownership Threat Value (OTV)** tree analysis, shown in Figure 2-5. In this model, the security specialist begins by establishing the owner of overall organizational security. Together, they can define a requisite security posture statement commensurate with the corporate mission

Level Two of the tree assigns a more detailed ownership/asset relationship on a more compartmentalized basis. Take a look at each department in an organization and work with the department resources to understand their assets (hard and soft). This information can be obtained via a properly constructed interview process. It is important to probe the interviewee to uncover hidden sources of information. Examining the applications used and tracing the output of that application can be helpful. As we discussed earlier, many sources of information are taken for granted and often overlooked.

Level Three of the model aligns likely risks with each of the assets defined. Further, this level of the model provides a reference to the effectiveness of countermeasures generally applicable to protect this type of asset against the associated risks. Finally, Level Three defines the asset access requirements. Access requirements define who should have access to what and when they should have access to it. These three elements will allow the security professional to assess the risk and develop a prioritization of security requirements.

Level Four of the model is used to quantify (in absolute or in relative terms) the value or replacement cost of the asset in question. As mentioned earlier in this section, it is important to consider the asset creation process and the availability of resource requirements when creating cost estimates.

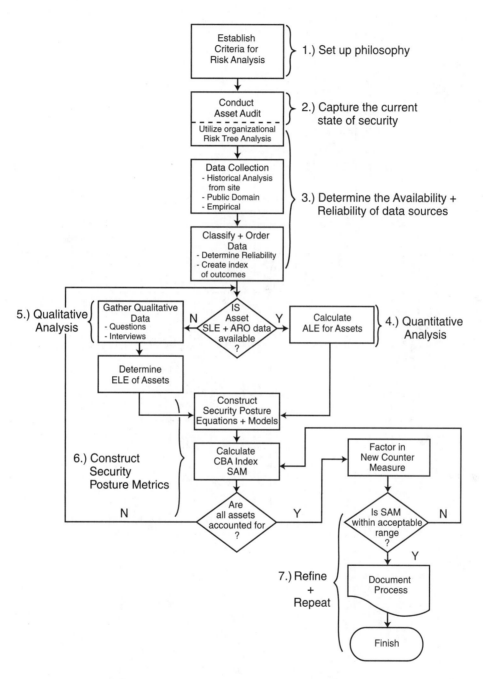

Figure 2-4   Risk analysis process diagram.

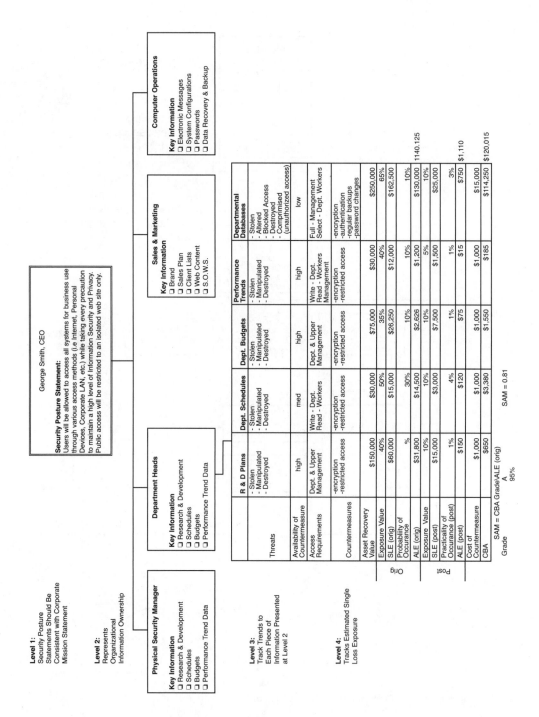

Figure 2-5   Ownership threat value tree example.

Conducting Productive Interviews

A large percentage of data collection involves conducting and recording interviews. This is a skill that requires practice and planning. It is best to begin the interview process by preparing a list of people who you feel are important to have participate in the process. Associated with each name should be the function and the reason for wanting the interview. This list should be presented to upper management for approval and input. The second step in successful interviewing is to prepare a preinterview questionnaire. This questionnaire should be sent in advance of the interview to each subject along with a letter (from a senior company official, preferably) detailing the reason for the interview. This type of preplanning will help the subjects prepare their thoughts and organize materials that may be helpful to you. Finally, prior to starting the interview process you should have several items likely to be referenced during the interview. These include:

- A network map
- System, router, and firewall configurations
- Any previously established security plan
- Any available asset inventory

You should proceed with interviewing either one-on-one, or in a group setting. Both can work well. It is generally good form to interview senior personnel in a one-on-one setting. Group dynamics theory dictates that having a senior person mixed in the interview process can reduce or influence participation of other group members.

The tempo of the interview is important. It is best to limit interviews to one hour (or multiple sessions of one hour.) This is usually an agreeable amount of time during which the atmosphere remains low stress. Also, have someone else (a secretary or administrator) set up the interviews. This will help you stay on schedule and will give the subjects a fairly static point of contact to speak with if necessary.

You should follow the guide that you previously sent out. Remember that most people like to be interviewed by someone who is prepared. Try not to let the interview drift. Keep the subject on topic. Sidebar conversations can reveal a lot about the attitude of the organization or department. However, these conversations need to be controlled.

It is important to take the following steps to ensure accuracy in the interview process:

1. Take copious notes during the interview and transcribe them immediately after the interview (while the ideas are fresh in your mind).
2. Create an affinity matrix. This tool lists interview members or departments across the top and issues along the side. Each time a subject feels strongly about a topic, note it in the affinity matrix (at the appropriate row/column box). These are generally scaled from 1 to 10, where 1 indicates a strong dislike and 10 indicates a strong preference. This type of tool allows you to isolate potential

3. Create a summary sheet for each of the interviews. This sheet should include an abstract of what the interview focused on, a rating as to the overall confidence you had in the interview (how reliable the information is), special concerns that came up (which may be outside the scope of your project), and a bulleted list of important thoughts. This sheet should be attached to the raw interview summary.

4. Send all subjects a copy of their interview so they can make revisions. It is easy to misunderstand someone during a brief meeting, especially when so many important topics are discussed.

The OTV model is often an effective first step in defining the security plan for your organization. An interesting initial test of security preparedness is to ask a perspective client to produce such a document. If the client cannot, it is almost a certainty that many assets have been overlooked and are unprotected. This document also provides the additional benefit of assigning ownership to each data element.

Assessing Information Value

Consider the following list when assessing the value of information:

- Cost of creating the information
- Cost to replace or reconstruct information
- Maintenance cost of the information
- Direct market value of information
- Value of copyrighted material, trade secrets (information can achieve this official status via legal petition), or intellectual property that can be directly measured in terms of direct sales or market segment comparisons
- Value of your information to the competition
- Loss of productivity based on unavailability of information
- Loss incurred by critical information failure

ESTABLISHING A RISK BASELINE

The next step in our security assessment is the establishment of data sources. The amount and quality of data available to complete the assessment is vital to the process of vulnerability assessment. In general, the data sources will come from the public record, or privately logged historical data, or via experimentation.

Be careful when taking data from the public record. The information should come from a reliable source (a list of such sources is at the end of this text). Also make sure to investigate the acquisition techniques employed by the researchers. Understand any bias in the subject group. Trend data are important, especially if data can be obtained based on a particular industry segment. Again, make sure the sampling is from a wide array of sources and does not reflect the views of only a minimal number of respondents.

Logged data, which your organization may record, are useful in understanding your security posture. If you are not currently using this information, take this opportunity to begin a collection process. Many host-based or router-based tools run on the firewall, which can record all types of security data.

Experimentation and vulnerability test scripts/products are widely used in determining the security readiness of an organization. These types of tools and methods are usually implemented after the first wave of security planning and implementation is complete. Vulnerability test software is readily available and is quite good at detecting holes in systems and networks of various types. Additionally, password-cracking software can help you and your users in assessing access. You should take this opportunity to review several of these tools to incorporate them into your vulnerability analysis. The following is a list of tools that are widely used:

- **Security Administration Tool for Analyzing Networks (SATAN)** was one of the first security assessment tools ever released. It is fairly old but can still be used. It is a TCP/IP port scanner that checks remote hosts for security vulnerabilities. It was designed to be used on UNIX systems. SATAN is available at *http://packetstorm.icx.fr/filedesc/sara-4.1.1.html* or *http://www.trouble.org/~zen/satan/satan.html*
- **Courtney** is a logging tool meant to detect SATAN scans. This tool should be installed to prevent unauthorized SATAN scans. The tool is available at *http://ciac.llnl.gov/ciac/ToolUnixNetMon.html*
- **Websense** is a screening/logging tool designed to work closely with the Cisco PIX firewall. Websense is available at *http://www.netpart.com*
- **ANTex** is a program that dumps password hashes from the NT registry. The program then attempts to crack the password (users can choose the cracking method). This tool can be used to detect soft passwords and to determine the average time to crack passwords
- **L0phtcrack/LC3** is a Windows password cracker
- **Security Administrator's Integrated Network Tool (SAINT)** is the next generation of SATAN. It is a much stronger and more up-to-date tool. It uses a Web browser interface and allows you to conduct attacks on your system. The tool then creates reports, which detail vulnerabilities. This tool is available at *http://www.saintcorporation.com*
- **LANguard Network Scanner** is a tool that allows you to evaluate holes in the Windows systems (e.g., password weakness, open shares, open network ports, configuration vulnerabilities) and is available at *http://www.gfisoftware.com*

RISK ANALYSIS

The next phase involves the analysis of data collected. Risk analysis is closely related to the study of probability and statistics, given that decisions are made under conditions of uncertainty. Probability and statistics are heavily influenced by the methods of data collection and experimentation. Therefore, it is logical that the study of risk be divided into two parts: a precise quantitative part featuring mathematical analysis of risk; and a more accommodating, qualitative part utilizing relative positioning of risk events based on perceived severity. In this section, we will study both.

Qualitative measures of risk can take many forms. We have already discussed the use of OTV trees as a method of capturing assets and identifying their associated risks and loss estimates. Another common qualitative technique is the Delphi technique, which presupposes that a group of people engaged in an estimation effort will perform better than an individual. In using this technique, the surveyor presents the group with an asset to appraise. The group members discuss and debate the merits of all the arguments and assign a value to the asset. The group measurements are statistically tested so an appropriate level of standard deviation from the norm is achieved. If this level is not achieved, the process repeats and the group works out differences and goes deeper into the analysis. Sessions such as these can yield many interesting findings and reasonable assessments.

Obviously a basic questionnaire can be utilized to collect and assess information. However, the problem with this approach is that if the questionnaire is not effectively administered, information can be skewed because of respondents' errors. If you use questionnaires, it is best to circulate several, which tends to smooth out data irregularities.

Regardless of the data collection method employed, the researcher needs to scale, rank, or index the data so they can be used in further studies. Qualitative information can be further refined through a modeling and benchmarking process, or through comparisons to industry segment data on like topics.

Quantitative analysis is based on measurements and mathematical models of our risk situation. The following explains the basic theory required in an actuarial analysis. The explanation is meant as a primer for students. There are entire books and courses of study dedicated to just this topic. Quantitative analysis has two inputs: the probability of an event occurring; and a one-time loss estimate, if it occurs. This yields the following value for **Annual Loss Expectancy (ALE)**:

$$ALE = ProbabilityOf\ Occurance \bullet SingleLossExposure$$

The single loss exposure can be further broken down into two parts: the asset value and the exposure factor. The asset value is obtained as detailed earlier in this section and reflects the amount of loss for a single event. The exposure factor expresses the probability that an attack will ever happen (just one time). Thus, the single loss exposure can be expressed as

$$SLE = AssetRecoveryValue \bullet ExposureFactor$$

The resulting ALEs (one for each asset) can be ranked and indexed to be used in conjunction with available qualitative estimates and models. We can also examine groupings of ALEs, which can be used to simulate the loss exposure to a more widespread attack.

Based on our earlier discussions of tree analysis and qualitative data acquisition, we can use this data to form estimates of asset valuations and loss exposure. We denote these as **Estimated Annual Loss Expectancies (EALEs)**.

Because we usually do not have the kinds of precise, industry-wide actuarial data required to perfect our forecasts, we can employ modeling techniques to improve our analysis and blend the qualitative and quantitative results. Modeling tools abound in conducting such analysis and are continually improving. Most are based on the Monte Carlo method of stochastic investigation. The term was coined by Stanislaw Ulam during the Manhattan project because of his interests in gambling and games of chance.

How Monte Carlo Works: A Simple Experiment

Bufton's needle problem 1768 (a variant of dart throwing) demonstrates that through empirical study of random stochastic events, we can derive good approximations of real-world phenomena. This experiment is a valuable example of a simple Monte Carlo analysis using a simple hit-or-miss technique for data presentation. We will use the modern-day equivalent of dart throwing to conduct our simulation. Given the dartboard depicted in Figure 2-6, we will attempt to derive an approximation of π.

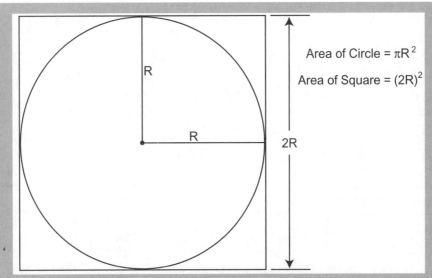

Figure 2-6   Dartboard.

We will start by throwing darts randomly at the dartboard, then comparing the number of darts landing in the target area versus the number of total darts thrown. It is best to use someone who is a poor dart player because this will yield a random and uniform distribution of darts. Thus we obtain a ratio

$$\frac{\#\,of\_darts\_hitting\_inside\_circle}{Total\_number\_of\_darts\_thrown}$$

yielding the ratio of hits to darts thrown. It is obvious that the number of darts in the target area will be somewhat lower than the total darts thrown because there is more total area in the square than in the circle. We can express the ratio of the two areas as the area of the circle over the area of the square.

$$\frac{\pi R^2}{(2R)^2} = \frac{AreaOfCircle(radius R)}{AreaOfSquare(side = 2R)} = \frac{\pi R^2}{4R^2} = \frac{\pi}{4}$$

These two ratios (circle/square and target hits/total darts) can be thought of as related, and proportional, as expressed through the equation shown as

$$\frac{\#\_of\_darts\_in\_circle}{\#\_of\_total\_darts} = \frac{\pi}{4}.$$

Through simple algebra, this relationship can be reduced to

$$\pi = 4(\frac{\#\_of\_darts\_in\_circle}{\#\_of\_total\_darts}),$$

giving us an equation for calculating p using the evidence collected in out dart-throwing experiment.

The more random dart events executed, the better the approximation. As we can see the number of darts in the target area will be less than the total number of darts thrown (those anywhere in the square), which will guarantee a fraction less than 1. This experiment, when simulated on a computer, actually yields an accurate approximation of π, given that we simulate the throwing of hundreds of thousands (if not millions) of darts. This method of setting up equations, isolating the element to be estimated, and conducting a large experiment is the essence of stochastic modeling.

Using such methods, we can create our models and test our security theories. The first step is to create a set of equations, which reflect our risk model. A primitive definition of risk can be expressed as

$$Risk = \{(O_1,Pt_1),(O_2,Pt_2),...,(O_n,Pt_n)\},$$

that is, risk is the set of ordered pairs of possible risk outcomes (O_n) with respect to the probability of occurrence (Pt_n). From this, we can express each outcome in terms of its required input. Those variables that are known (quantifiable) can be tested within a certain range. Those variables that are random can be tested using our modeling software to obtain a broad set of outcomes. Once the data set is broken down and analyzed, forecasts about outcome can likely be made. Part of the reason for doing this is that, usually, it is unclear as to what extent potential inputs will affect the outcomes.

We can also utilize Monte Carlo simulations to test what-if scenarios done by "shaping" the input data. The advantage here is that this is our experiment and we can change the rules to capture trends that we believe may occur, or those suggested in the public domain.

Notice that there are many ways to shape data sets, as illustrated in Figure 2-7. A normal distribution is shown in Figure 2-7a. This is an ideal data set with the majority of data points clustered around the mean and a balanced fall-off to the extremes. A focused distribution is pictured in Figure 2-7b. In this case, the clustering is more specific and illustrates a strong tendency to a particular value rather than a range. In Figure 2-7c we are using a uniform distribution. This curve provides us an opportunity to observe the outcomes of risk under a completely random set of inputs. In Figure 2-7d, we are biasing the data around a particular data value. This is useful in understanding how our model will perform when the data are strongly influenced or biased in a certain direction. This also allows us to test a model established toward a particular bias.

COST-BENEFIT ANALYSIS

Upper management will want to evaluate the effectiveness of your plan with a **Cost-Benefit Analysis (CBA)**. The CBA compares the annual loss expectancy prior to implementation of security countermeasures, with the ALE plus the annual cost of the countermeasure (ACC). This can be expressed as:

$$CBA = ALE(original) - (ALE(post) + ACC),$$

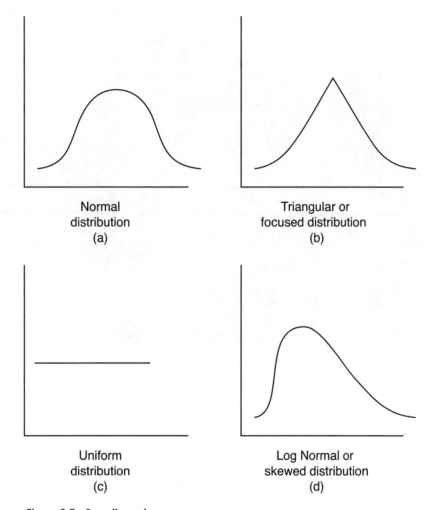

Figure 2-7   Sampling rules.

or simplified as

$$CBA = ALE(original) - ALE(post) - ACC.$$

This formula tells us how cost effective our security measure is compared to how much it reduces our risk.

Ultimately, the decision maker is trying to assess acceptable risk and the security posture. I advocate each organization crafting a **Security Acceptability Metric (SAM)**, which is an index of security posture. This index should be formed by utilizing the CBA and "security grade," which measures the current state of readiness as compared to the original ALE.

Importance of Random Number Generation

Several important topics in this text require the use of a random number generator to achieve success. The Monte Carlo simulation technique is one of those. Another is certain encryption algorithms, discussed in section two. Creating random numbers is not as easy as it seems. A weak random number generator can allow for predictability and can ruin studies and forecasts, or worse, cause encryption codes to be weak and broken.

The only way to create a truly random number is to base the creation of the number on a naturally occurring event (e.g., the time of the next lightning strike.) Given that information, we would have a truly random **seed** upon which to generate random numbers. Computers are deterministic; therefore, they are not prone to producing truly random events and, consequently, random numbers. Computers are, however, adept at computing complex mathematical equations. Thus, if we can provide a random seed we will be able to disguise the pattern in our random numbers well enough that they are imperceptible. These are called **pseudorandom numbers**. The algorithms to produce such numbers are constantly studied and improved.

Quite often, studies of random number generator outputs in large applications (millions of data points) can reveal a trend. The great computer scientist Donald Knuth stated, "Random number generators should not be chosen randomly." As you will discover, security professionals and those that study cryptography are concerned with the quality of random number generators. It is important that you research the literature for anomalies in particular implementations prior to basing security or forecasting choices on one.

- **A** (95 percent) indicates a high degree of readiness. This rating implies constant vigilance over systems, networks, information, passwords, and keys. To achieve this rating, an organization should have a permanent and dedicated security staff, monitoring structure, and affiliations with trusted third parties who have a vested interest in your organization's security posture
- **B** (85 percent) indicates a ready standard aligned with your industry segment and meeting your security posture. At this level, the organization conducts regular security audits. The organization must maintain a valid and comprehensive information security plan and well- defined security policies
- **C** (75 percent) is an outwardly focused security posture mainly concerned with network and system security. At this level, the organization fails to take explicit steps for guaranteeing the security of information. Organizations at this level may have portions of a security plan, but generally they are not comprehensive
- **D** (65 percent) achieves minimal security (e.g. virus control, address filtering, strong passwords), and invests little in security planning or implementation
- **F** (0 – 60 percent) indicates that the organization is unprotected or minimally protected. Organizations achieving this rating are in serious trouble

Thus we can express the SAM in the formula: $SAM = \dfrac{CBA \bullet Grade}{Ale(original)}$.

This index can then be used to understand how much value your organization is achieving from its current methods. Each organization will develop its own index categories. The top tier of the index should match the security posture requirement within budget, as stated early on in the tree analysis.

For example, a typical index may have a look and feel similar to the one shown in Figure 2-8

Remember that these assessments provide us with guidance for achieving our ultimate goal: an appropriate level of security for our business. As we manage the security process, decrease our risk exposure, transfer risk, and take serious planning and implementation steps, these metrics will improve. Risk is a constant, which must be continuously managed and reviewed:

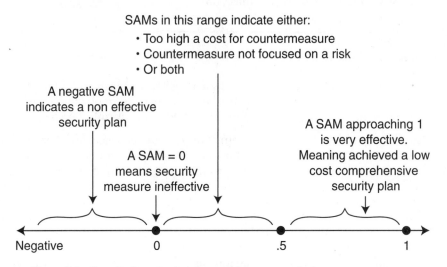

Figure 2-8   Security Security Assessment Measurement Index.

RISK MANAGEMENT

Once the security team has completed a risk assessment, the organization's exposure is generally well understood, the assets of the organization are complete and documented, and the threats have been recognized. Another benefit of this activity is quantifying financial loss. All of this analysis should provide management with the proper motivation to take action and the basis upon which to form good judgments.

The next logical step in our strategizing is to determine what we should do about these risks and threats. It is an obvious and foregone conclusion that it is impossible to offer 100 percent immunity from ever being successfully attacked. The data suggests that the sheer number of attackers and the coincident number of new attacks developed presents a clear and ever-present danger. Even the unrealized threat of impropriety can compromise the integrity of information and make it suspect. That threat is why a constant vigilance over information security is required.

A suggestion that may help an organization in determining the appropriate course of action is to test if the security plan better positions an organization to meet the CAIN challenge. CAIN can be used as an information security litmus test. If you recall in Chapter 1, we reviewed the CAIN principles of confidentiality, authenticity, integrity and nonrepudiation. As part of any vulnerability assessment, a sound methodology includes a statement of purpose. Regarding information, this security posture should most definitely focus on the CAIN principles.

As you progress through the text, many specific information security techniques will be presented, which you can use to minimize risk. These techniques, in conjunction with strong policies and plans, can derail many attacks.

However, minimization of threats and risks is only one course of action from which information security decision makers can choose. In general, risk management includes four basic strategies, which can be combined to tailor an appropriate course of action commensurate with the organizational security requirements:

1 Constant vigilance and **risk identification**
2 **Risk minimization** and avoidance
3 **Risk mitigation**
4 **Risk transference**

Each of these strategies should be examined to understand what is and what is not applicable to your situation. These strategies are meant to complement one another. By employing some measure of all four, we are likely to achieve a more acceptable risk threshold in the organization.

Constant vigilance is a key part of successful information security management. The risk assessment process described earlier in the chapter was used to establish a baseline for our security risk. However, once complete, we can take advantage of it so we can track progress toward our goal. A reassessment should become part of the regular risk management routine. The first assessment is always the hardest. Subsequent iterations take less time and are more easily focused. By continually performing this analysis, an organization can develop a deeper understanding of risks and security posture. This analysis has two residual effects. First, the individuals in the organization become increasingly sensitized to the elements of the risk profile that they can affect. Second, the organization has a better sense of its return on investment. This strategy should include automation as a key component to more accurately track

- The effectiveness of security measures
- The realized threat the organization faces (the number of actual attacks)

The second key strategy is risk minimization and avoidance. By this we mean to apply the information security model to identified potential risks so that successful countermeasures can be deployed.

Third, risk mitigation plays a key role. Risk mitigation defines what we do after a break-in has already occurred. How do we reduce the impact of the attack on our information condition? As we will discuss later in the text, having a sound information backup and recovery plan is one of the most important steps an organization can take to lessen the effects of information loss.

Fourth, we should consider risk transfer as a viable option when our own methods seem unlikely to stop the perpetrator, or when the recovery value of our assets would be prohibitively high. Companies such as Counterpane and Lloyd's of London offer this type of insurance. When the cost of reproducing the information is high, transference of the risk via insurance becomes a viable option. Another option in this same category is the outsourcing of information management. Although this does not guarantee that no one will tamper with the information, it does offer companies with lesser experience and resources the protections offered larger organizations. Essentially, this is a form of resource sharing.

These four strategies not withstanding, we also must realize that accepting what we cannot control is part of life and part of technology. Consequently, a central theme of this book is to form a layered approach to information security with an increasing emphasis on comprehensive implementation of those items closest to the center of the model. If we have taken the proper precautions to safeguard the information itself to the greatest possible extent, and we have implemented reasonable and balanced security measures to protect the information system, then we should feel satisfied with the security effort.

The more we actively manage risk, the greater the trust will be in our information. As previously mentioned, to achieve a security grade of A, and a SAM close to 1, our goals must be realistic and our investments in proportion to (and not in excess of) the reasonable threat.

SUMMARY

Chapter 2 focused on the reasons for embracing information security as both a discipline of study and an area of focus for organizations. Risk is defined as the possibility of loss or harm to something valued, based on the uncertainty of particular events or outcomes. Given that definition, Chapter 2 examined methods for quantifying, classifying, understanding, and addressing risk.

The chapter addressed the common misconceptions regarding the need for information security. Through a rigorous discussion of these myths and the subsequent assertion of factual statistics, the reader can successfully campaign for the inclusion of an information security plan. Achieving organizational buy-in is a significant component of securing information.

Another byproduct of gathering this compelling statistical data is for students to develop a network of resources upon which they can effectively garner information and remain current in this changeable area. The use of these resources is required in developing annualized rate of occurrence metrics.

A seven-step risk evaluation method was presented to guide the security professional through an examination of risk potential. This process is supported by the OTV tree tool, which can be used to guide and document the threat factors, most-affected organizational components, organizational ownership, and cost benefit analysis of a potential countermeasure. The chapter details calculations for annual loss expectancy, single loss expectancy, security acceptability metric, and cost benefit analysis.

In addition to the theoretical discussion of risk, materials were presented outlining the various types of attackers and their motivation. Additionally, the six most common types of hacker attacks were discussed in some detail. These include DOS and DDOS attacks, intrusion attacks, hijacking, malicious code, attacks against encryption, and Web-based attacks.

The chapter concludes with a discussion of the four-step process for managing risk: identification, minimization, mitigation, and risk transfer. This discussion leads us to the need for the development of both an information security plan and an information recovery plan.

This chapter should help raise students' awareness of the severity of the problem of information security is our open Internet community. Students should realize that hackers are not magicians or wizards. Rather, hackers are significant students of software algorithms and development, computational methods, networks, and Web technologies, who are constantly testing and probing the system for vulnerabilities. Depending on the hackers' motivation, they can exploit these vulnerabilities. There is nothing mystical about hacking. To compete with a hacker, you have to be as dedicated to technology as they are to cybercrime.

Students should be able to use this material as a launching pad for more extensive study and examination. Chapter 3 highlights how the legislation has regulated information and information security. In Chapter 4, we will review the creation of information security plans and policies.

One point that is worth raising is that it is counterproductive to generate unnecessary fear and worry. Although cybercrime is a significant threat, it can be dealt with through the use of reasonable measures and precautions. As we go through the planning process, we must be mindful that information security, like personnel security, can be taken too far. Excessive security measures can create wanton expenses, limit access to vital information, and curtail its usefulness.

STUDY QUESTIONS

1 Which of the following methods of breaching system security needs no computer to access to the desired information? (choose one)

   a. Man-in-the-middle attack

   b. Denial-of-service attack

   c. Social engineering attack

   d. Springboard attack

2 _____ attacks happen to people or corporations for no apparent reason. (choose one)

   a. Targeted

   b. Random

   c. Quantum phase

   d. Degenerative

3 What type of attacker is statistically most likely to cause problems to an organization? (choose one)

   a. Disgruntled employee

   b. Script kiddie

   c. Person using your computer for a springboard attack

   d. Phreaker

4 **True___ False___** Risk assessments need to be conducted only one time in the life of a security plan.

5 Which of the following is a valuable asset that is often overlooked in an information security plan? (choose one)

   a. Product development information

   b. Stock information

   c. Customer satisfaction information

   d. Brand

6 Which of the following is an example of a comprehensive security strategy? (choose one)

   a. We have security software and hardware, an information security officer, a security budget, employee training, and a disaster recovery system in place.

   b. We use anti-virus software and a firewall.

   c. We can detect intrusions with our intrusion-detection software, and we have a firewall. These are supplemented by our use of cryptography.

   d. We already invested in products so we have it covered.

7 _____ occurs when an organization suffers a loss in revenue based on its inability to retrieve, produce, or modify information critical to serving customer needs. (choose one)

   a. Data system failure

   b. Information intrusion

   c. Critical information failure

   d. Network connection loss

8 Which of the following is **not** one of the four parts of risk management? (choose one)

   a. Transfer

   b. Reconnaissance

   c. Minimization

   d. Identification

9 _____ can involve the simple creation of an unrealized threat of a breach. (choose one)

   a. Worms

   b. Trojans

   c. Passive attacks

   d. Active attacks

10 **True___ False___**   TCP/IP is the most predominantly used Internet access architecture.

11 An unsuspecting springboard host is known as a _____. (choose one)

   a. Zombie

   b. Slave

   c. Remote trigger

   d. Servant

12 What type of device monitors network activity? (choose one)

   a. Data logger

   b. Byte watcher

   c. Snooper

   d. Sniffer

13 _____ occurs when a faulty application or system programming allows a program or user to input more data to the buffer than it was designed to handle. (choose one)

a. Buffer bombing

b. Buffer overflow

c. Social engineering

d. Inflated buffering

14 The ping of death is an example of _____? (choose one)

a. A malformed command

b. A password-cracking attempt

c. A virus

d. An intrusion attack

15 In _____, the perpetrator utilizes the name of the attacked party to falsely represent themselves as that party. (choose one)

a. Port scanning

b. Buffer overflow

c. Name scanning

d. Name spoofing

16 Web spoofing, name spoofing, and the use of someone else's personal information are all examples of _____. (choose one)

a. Identity theft

b. Social engineering

c. Hidden-man attacks

d. Hijacking

17 The easiest type of man-in-the-middle attack to accomplish is_____. (choose one)

a. Sequence number prediction

b. Dumpster diving

c. The decrypting of packets

d. The replay attack

18 Which is **not** a form of session hijacking? (choose one)

a. Springboard attack

b. Sequence number prediction

c. DNS spoofing

d. Packet redirection

19 Which of the following is **not** malware? (choose one)

   a. Logic bomb

   b. Virus

   c. Hoax

   d. Worm

20 What is a logic bomb? (choose one)

   a. It is a piece of code that causes the operating system to lock up and subsequently fail.

   b. It is a type of session hijacking.

   c. It causes passwords and other information to be transmitted to an attacker.

   d. It causes control of a machine to be transferred to an attacker.

21 What is the one type of system weakness that the user does not have the ability to repair? (choose one)

   a. Trojans

   b. Attacks against encryption

   c. OS code vulnerabilities

   d. Packet redirection

22 If you want to gain access to or disable a system quickly, which type of attack would you **not** choose? (choose one)

   a. Man-in-the–middle attack

   b. Plain text attack

   c. Denial-of-service attack

   d. Buffer overflow attack

23 _____ keys are those with numerical properties that cause the encryption algorithm to falter or diminish. (choose one)

   a. Weak

   b. Algebraic

   c. Quantum

   d. Fragile

24 A time, system event, or user action that sets a piece of malware into action is called a_____. (choose one)

   a. Wake-up call

   b. Trap door

   c. Bear trap

   d. Trigger

25 To evaluate the effectiveness of your security plan, what will upper management want and expect? (choose one)

a. A business plan

b. A cost benefit analysis

c. A comprehensive security audit

d. An employee personality analysis

CASE STUDY

Back at Cureme Hospital, you are now tasked with constructing the OTV tree as the next deliverable to the hospital. Consider the following themes, people, and departments to begin the organizational section of the tree.

- I.M. Hurtin, CIO, whose mission statement is "To create a secure information environment that respects all facets of patient privacy in compliance with HIPAA requirements"
- Phil D. Memory, head of Cureme Hospital Information Systems, maintains all servers, network and communications environment, telephone network, basic office applications, and all clinical applications
- Eileen D. Pendonyou is in charge of patient scheduling and information. Requires that all in-patient and outpatient services be arranged through the scheduling system
- Dr. Looksee is the head of physician services and patient care
- Nurse Ratchet is the head of nursing
- Mr. Tobius Everything is the head of business administration, finance, and legal services
- Dr. Love is the chief of cardiology
- Dr. Ting Lee is the chief of neurology
- Dr. Kidd is the chief of pediatrics
- Dr. Mash is the chief of emergency services
- Dr. Xaviar Raye is the chief of radiology
- Ms. Pills runs the pharmacy
- Ms. Goodlunch is the head of dietary services
- Mr. Clean is the head of housekeeping and maintenance
- Mr. Debus is the head of transportation

Research and comment

For this assignment, go to some local hospitals' websites and research the information requirements of similar departments. Try to isolate the ownership of information by department. Assess the worth of the information and assign some arbitrary values to the information in your tree in line with your research. What are the threats to the information in your tree? Using Excel, construct a tree similar to the one in Figure 2-5. Complete the analysis and calculations for ALE and SLE. Consider some possible countermeasures to the threats listed. Research the costs of those countermeasures. Now calculate the CBA per item of information.

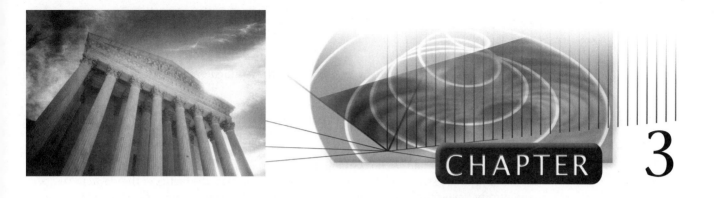

CHAPTER 3

Information and The Law

No law or ordinance is mightier than understanding.
—Plato (427 B.C.–347 B.C.)

Prosecuting attorneys are continually faced with the challenge of presenting criminal cases to a jury and explaining the motivation and intent of parties accused of criminal offenses. Juries are required to pass judgment on the defendant based on both the facts in evidence and the intent of those charged with the offense. It is sometimes difficult to determine if a suspect intended to act maliciously or if they were unaware that a crime was being committed. In our society, ignorance of the law cannot be used as an excuse for breaking the law. However, we are human and can make mistakes and err in judgment. For this reason, the courts and the legislation support various degrees of criminal charges, giving the prosecuting attorney a wide latitude in dealing with crime. *Mens rea* is a Latin term meaning "the guilty mind" and defines the test criteria that prosecuting attorneys use when deciding what charges, if any, to file against a suspect party. For example, if the party knowingly committed a crime and realized that what they did was wrong, then the intent was criminal and the charges are justifiable. If the person was truly unaware that a crime was being committed, or if the damage was the result of an accident, then there is no criminal intent and usually no criminal charges are pressed.

In the case of computer crimes, these decisions are perhaps more difficult to make than in most common criminal offenses. The nature of computer crimes and the intent of the accused cover a wide spectrum of possibilities. These crimes range from juvenile offenders testing out a new program that inadvertently causes damage to a computing infrastructure, to common criminals taking advantage of new technology to commit the new millennium version of an age-old crime (i.e., fraud), to sophisticated crackers stealing corporate or government secrets and selling them to cyberterrorists for a fee.

Alternatively, how do juries and prosecutors distinguish between criminal actions and the actions of a computer professional resulting in accidental damage? What constitutes professional malpractice?

In addition to determining criminal intent, prosecutors find presenting technology crime cases difficult even under the most clear-cut circumstances. This is true for several reasons:

- The area of litigation is extremely technical and, thus, difficult for most nonpractitioners to understand.
- The laws themselves are relatively new and to a large extent untested. These prosecutions are pioneering efforts that must sustain the rigors of numerous appeals. Daily, we hear of whole new categories of computer crime that are difficult to categorize under existing laws.
- The technology is dynamic and the tactics of the perpetrators are constantly changing. By the time a successful prosecution is completed in one case, the tactics of the cracker community have changed, making it difficult to draw precedent from previous cases.
- The quality of computer forensic evidence varies widely and the presentation of expert testimony is often less than effective.
- In many cases, computer records that document criminal activity are considered hearsay and are often excluded from evidence, which significantly hinders prosecutions. An exception to this is Federal Rules of Evidence 803(6): Records of regularly conducted activity, which implies that if the computer records were authentic, continuous, and accumulated during the normal operation, then they can be used. This is often a difficult standard to meet.
- Civil actions disputing ownership of information or assessing damages often face difficult issues of authenticity and verification.

Information security's primary goals are protecting information and preventing crime. However, the information security professional will often be faced with difficult security design, implementation, and reporting decisions regarding privacy, ownership, criminal activity, usage of technology, and policy/planning development where knowledge of the laws applying to the field become relevant. Further, some information security professionals may become law enforcement officials or become litigators in this field and will find this information valuable.

While this text is by no means a substitute for proper legal training, it should serve those interested in the technological aspects of information security with a sufficient background to fulfill the professional requirements of an information security analyst or consultant.

This chapter serves to overview four main areas focused on the legal aspects of information security:

- Evaluating privacy requirements
- The distinction between criminal and noncriminal activities
- The prevention, detection, and prosecution of cybercrime
- Familiarization with the primary pieces of legislation that define the bounds of information security

 To successfully complete this chapter, students should pay particular attention to the following:

- Learning the basic tenets of The Computer Fraud and Abuse Act of 1986 and the amended version, The National Information Infrastructure Protection Act of 1996 Title 18 USC 1029 and 1030. These acts form the cornerstone of information security legislation.
- Understanding the gist of the USA PATRIOT (Providing Appropriate Tools Required to Intercept and Obstruct Terrorism) Act of 2001 (H.R. 3162), the Economic Espionage Act of 1996, HIPAA legislation, The Computer Security Act of 1987, The Digital Signature Bill, and the Electronic Communications Privacy Act of 1986.
- The need for policy to clearly define user and organization expectations of privacy.
- The FBI model for handling evidence and for contributing to prosecutions.
- The professional ethics and code of conduct expected of information security professionals.
- The National Infrastructure Protection Center procedures for victims of computer crime.

In addition to the review provided of these key legal areas, this chapter offers interesting case reviews to support and reinforce the information provided. I would like to thank the National Infrastructure Protection Center, United States Attorney General's Office, and the Federal Bureau of Investigation for providing such a tremendous wealth of information on this subject in the public domain. I encourage readers of this text to visit their respective Web sites (listed in the bibliography section of this text) for more detailed reading on these topics.

A REASONABLE EXPECTATION OF PRIVACY

In the words of the eighteenth-century British politician William Pitt, "The poorest man may in his cottage bid defiance to all the force of the Crown." Paraphrased for the twenty-first century, our opinions, conversations, political views, habits, correspondence, and private information are ours alone to use and express, especially in the privacy of our home. No government official should have the right to invade our privacy or tell us how we shall conduct personal business in a private setting.

As we go through our daily lives, we maintain both a public and a private life. Generally, people take considerable care to safeguard their privacy. By this we mean that they do not openly reveal private thoughts and bad habits, and they keep correspondence, financial records, medical records, school records, and valuable items safe.

Notions of privacy are as old as the written word. In the Bible's Book of Proverbs 25:17, King Solomon states, "Make your foot rare at the house of your fellowman, that he may not have his sufficiency of you and certainly hate you." In more modern times, the U.S. Constitution and a plethora of additional legislation, which has been amassed over two and a half centuries, represent countless hours of efforts to safeguard our reasonable expectation of privacy.

Webster's New Collegiate Dictionary defines **privacy** as "freedom from unauthorized intrusion" and "a state of being apart from company or observation." As it relates to our property and personal existence, this seems reasonably straightforward. We expect that our homes will not be searched without cause. We expect that our phones will not be tapped. We expect that our trusted relationships (e.g., doctor to patient, clergy to layperson, lawyer to client) will be treated with respect.

These definitions, however, are blurry and difficult to apply particularly with respect to information in general, and to information accessed over the Internet in particular. If you recall, information is processed data, something that possesses semantic value and hence has an assessable real value. Thus, it is proper to perceive information as something quantifiable rather than as an idea. Tangible items are generally kept private by locking them away and storing them out of sight. Ideas, thoughts, and conversations, on the other hand, are usually kept private via discretion on the part of the correspondents. We trust that our secrets will not be revealed. The unique aspect of maintaining our electronic information privacy is that it must be treated both like tangible items and ideas. Information privacy is maintained by locking it away and sharing a trust with concerned parties. Subjecting electronic information to eavesdropping, unwanted disclosure, unauthorized manipulation or tampering, or theft, violates our privacy. Information privacy and the security of our electronic identity will be carefully examined throughout this text. It is imperative that we clearly understand how to:

- Protect our electronic privacy from those wishing to do us harm
- Understand legislation concerned with safeguarding our privacy
- Respect the privacy of others as we interact with them electronically

The following privacy issues will be the focus of our studies:

- Protections from unwarranted government intrusion of computers, information storage devices, files, and networks
- Expectation of information privacy at the workplace
- Public versus private information on the Internet
- Electronic privacy of customer, medical, and financial information
- Privacy of electronic communications over the Internet
- Freedom from observation on the Internet
- Protection of our electronic identity

PRIVACY FROM LAW ENFORCEMENT AND PRIVACY AT WORK

Protections from unwarranted government intrusion are perhaps the most important area of privacy protections. Even in the face of terrorism and sophisticated electronic crime, we should limit the government's ability to examine private correspondence and to eavesdrop on its citizens. Many instances throughout history remind us of just how oppressive our government can be when citizens yield these basic rights. As we shall see below, it has taken considerable time for the laws to catch up with the technology of the day. The **Digital Telephony Act of 1994**, for example, states that monitoring electronic transmissions is the same as wiretapping and that people engaged in this behavior on the Internet must issue a warning to users alerting them to that fact. Under current U.S. law, 42 USC Section 2000AA prevents the government from illegally searching and seizing computer records, work product materials, and the like unless law enforcement has a warrant issued by the court, or unless there is probable cause, or if law enforcement believes that the action will prevent an imminent death. These laws are necessary to maintain our right to privacy. Our government currently has and uses tools such as the FBI Carnivore system to monitor e-mails, instant messages, and digital phone calls. These tools are necessary to catch cybercriminals in cybertime, but their use must be regulated to prevent these tools from being used inappropriately.

What expectation of information privacy should we expect at the workplace? To a large extent, the answer to that question depends on the information security policies and usage policies that have been established. Not properly stating usage and privacy policies can lead to trouble for the organization. In organizations where no policies are publicly established, the users have a reasonable expectation of privacy because our legal system demands privacy as a right unless we explicitly surrender it.

For example, if you are issued an e-mail account at work, you have a right to expect personal correspondence to remain private. If you are assigned a file share on a server that is marked as yours alone (not part of a public file or work group), then you should be permitted to store personal information there even if it has nothing to do with the operation of the business. Likewise, the use of company or school computers for nonorganizational business would be authorized without policies to the contrary. Most organizations today require new employees, students, or members to sign affidavits affirming that they have read and agree with the policies of the organization, including those that allow the organization to invade (to a certain extent) the privacy of the individual.

The misconception most businesses have regarding privacy lies in the belief that because it is the organization's computer hardware and software, then the organization has a right to invade privacy. Further, the assumption is made that the user should not be able to use the system for any personal use. It turns out that if you issue computer hardware, software, applications, and accounts to a user, then the organization must explicitly determine the usage constraints and properly communicate them to the users. The same is true for Web sites. In many organizations today, newly hired personnel are required to sign documents specifically detailing computer and e-mail usage policies. This includes statements regarding limitations on the use of the Web (e.g., The Web shall not be used to view pornographic materials).

Cybercriminals are not the only ones using modern technology to their advantage. Currently, it is a common practice for employers to spy on their employees. Many employers have established electronic monitoring practices—some of which border on either unethical or illegal—to influence best use of company resources and employee activity. According to a *Sales and Marketing Management* magazine survey (from *USA Today* 2002, Darryl Haralson and Sam Ward), "twenty-seven percent of companies have terminated employees as a result of employee monitoring." Companies monitor employees' e-mail accounts to monitor how employees spend their time. Companies even watch to see if employees are attempting to seek employment opportunities elsewhere. The Annual American Management Survey for 2001 found "nearly three quarters (73.5%) of major U.S. firms...record and review their employees' communications and activities on the job including their phone calls, e-mails, Internet connections, and computer files." They monitor Internet use and are cracking down on the improper use of the network by the employees. They eavesdrop on conversations with clients to "ensure quality." While this seems like justifiable rationale, it treads close to the limits of legality. We often hear of people videotaping their babysitters' interactions with their kids, but the question remains: Is that kind of spying legal? In the case of electronic surveillance by businesses, the answer is yes. If the business has the proper policies in place to alert employees as to their expected conduct, the possibility exists that employees are being watched.

PRIVACY AS A CUSTOMER OR CLIENT

The electronic privacy of customer, medical, and financial information is closely monitored and regulated by the government. Several issues are of concern in this area. The first deals with the ease with which information can be gathered by simply forming a connection with a potential client. Just like the phone system's Caller ID, the communications protocols used on the Internet allow a called party to obtain information regarding who you are and where you are physically located. This information can be used by the business in many different ways, including its resale. The **Privacy of Customer Information Section** of the common carrier regulations explains that client information can be used only for the provisioning of service and not for marketing concerns.

A second concern revolves around the use of the computers in the processing, storage, and communication of medical and financial records. You'll remember from Chapter 2 that HIPAA is legislation that details the privacy requirements with which medical records and patient information must be handled. These regulations have significant implications for the electronic handling of this information, as well as the administration of policy and paper documentation. **Graham-Leach-Bliley Act of 1999 (GLB)** or **The Financial Services Modernization Act** articulates the privacy requirements of banks, insurance companies, and securities firms with regard to the disclosure of personal information. Again, this law translates to all electronic representations and communication of this personal information.

PRIVACY AND THE WEB

The next area to address is the extent to which we should expect or deserve privacy while **surfing** the Internet. Privacy and the Internet are two terms that do not go well together. As I tell most of my clients, when using the Internet, it is best to proceed as though you expect to be watched, hacked, and tracked. As we pointed out in the previous chapter, a growing number of hacks originate via an Internet-based entry point. The typical hacker will spend considerable time observing the target's behavior to understand what the target does on the Internet, with whom the target corresponds, and where the target spends most of his or her time.

Much of what you do on the Web is automatically monitored. It is very difficult, if not impossible, to know that you are being watched. Your own system, and most of the firewalls you pass through, collects all of the URLs you have requested. But surprisingly, it is the information that you voluntarily give up to Web sites that can prove to be the most damaging. Because you never know who is watching (monitoring) your Web transactions, you must be sure to never disclose vital personal information over a non-encrypted link. Chapter 11 of this text provides an enhanced discussion of these topics.

Keystroke monitors allow attackers to capture usernames and passwords via electronic eavesdropping. This information can provide a hacker with valuable user details, which can be the enablers of break-ins and other sophisticated hacks.

Along these same lines are **network mapping attacks**, where hackers monitor the flow of traffic into and out of a site for the sole purpose of capturing IP addresses and identifying key hosts and TCP ports of services they wish to compromise.

It is safe to assume that the Internet is an open forum, and you should treat your information the same way you treat your wallet on a crowded subway. Appropriate precautions should be taken on the Internet, and you will have very little recourse if your privacy is compromised.

Protection of our **electronic identity** is an area of growing concern. Electronic identity is the information that uniquely identifies an **entity**. An entity can be a person, computer, piece of information, file, software package, network component, or other principal that can be uniquely labeled. As we have seen, our electronic identity can be easily compromised if the proper precautions are not taken. The primary precaution that one needs to take is to reveal as little information as possible while surfing the Net. However, by just being on the Net, your movements, preferences, and personal information are more available than you might realize.

Los Angeles Man Sentenced to Prison for Role in International Computer Hacking and Internet Fraud Scheme

A Los Angeles man who admitted to defrauding computer distributor Ingram Micro, Inc. and numerous online retailers, including Hewlett-Packard.Com and OfficeDepot.Com, was sentenced to 33 months in federal prison.

Thomas Pae, 20, was sentenced on charges of wire fraud, conspiracy, and credit card fraud for his involvement in an international computer hacking and Internet fraud scheme targeting Ingram Micro. Pae pleaded guilty to the charges and admitted that in 2001 he participated in a scheme involving computer hackers in Romania who had gained unauthorized access to Ingram Micro's online ordering system and placed hundreds of thousands of dollars of fraudulent orders for computer equipment.

Pae also admitted that he purchased credit card numbers from hackers on the Internet and used the cards to purchase computer chips, hard drives, personal digital assistants, and other items from Handspring.Com, Amazon.Com, and Egghead.Com. Pae admitted that he and his co-conspirators attempted to purchase over $500,000 in computer equipment and other items from Ingram Micro and other online retailers.

Pae was sentenced by U.S. District Judge Lourdes G. Baird, who also ordered Pae to pay $324,061 in restitution to the victims of his crimes. In addition, once released from prison, Judge Baird imposed significant restrictions on his use of computers while he is under supervised release for a period of three years.

The above is an excerpt of a document contained at *http://www.cybercrime.gov/paeSent.htm*

An example of this monitoring is the improper use of cookies. Cookies help give the HTTP protocol a sense of **state**. State is a way of maintaining context and flow to an Internet Web session. Because HTTP is stateless (each command to obtain a page is separate and without relation to the next), by its very design it is difficult for Web designers to evaluate the context of a given exchange with a client. To help the designers, the cookie protocol was created. Cookies are a way of adding session context to the flow of a series of Web site exchanges. However, when Web advertisers create pop-ups that you browse, you may have your privacy invaded. The first time you click on a pop-up, you are randomly assigned an ID in a cookie that the firm transmits to your system. On every subsequent connection to any of its other marketing partners sites, that identifier will be collected (in accord with the protocol) and the marketing company begins to build a profile of your Internet preferences. Subsequently, all new pop-ups and marketing opportunities will begin to be customized to your particular tastes. Although this does not sound too serious, it is. You are being manipulated and tracked, and your privacy is being invaded.

Even through inadvertent programming acts, such as CGI scripting errors, confidential information can be accidentally revealed. Scripting errors have become a major problem in the Web design space, with respect to security. Cross-site scripting, for example, betrays the trust relationship between two parties. You can post information to a bulletin board application, for example, that contains malicious software in the javascript. When someone downloads that software, they are immediately hacked.

People can commit fraud by illegally accessing our electronic identities and misusing the information. As you will remember from Chapter 2, e-mail spoofing allows hackers to electronically pass themselves off as their intended victims. Invasions of privacy and the compromise of electronic identity can be quite costly and warrant increased caution.

A key concept we will review is authentication. **Authentication** is the act of binding an entity to a representation of identity. This is a powerful concept that, when used correctly, can curtail and often prevent identity theft.

As stated earlier, identity theft is the single fastest-growing crime in the world. Later in this chapter we will review important tips from the FBI regarding how to safeguard your personal information and prevent identity theft.

PRIVACY POLICIES AND STRONG ETHICS

As we roll out our information security plan, the organizational management should construct **usage policies**. Policies are expectations set by the organization to encourage certain behavior and to prohibit other behavior. When properly enforced, these policies can be used to assess penalties (e.g., termination of employment or garnishing of wages) commensurate with the offense. For a policy to be enforceable and to withstand all legal challenges, an organization must take great care to properly distribute the policy, train the user community on the policy, carefully choose unambiguous language in crafting the policy, explicitly state the penalties for breaking the policy, unilaterally enforce the policy with consistency, and in most cases document that employees acknowledge—in writing—receipt and understanding of the policy. These policies then become a part of the security plan and implementation. They play an important role in driving the behavior of the user community. Regarding information privacy, these policies play an even larger role. Policies become a part of the privacy contract between the users and the organization providing service. Even on your favorite Web site, you will notice restrictions and copyright information posted on most home pages.

Given the heightened state of sensitivity regarding crime, terrorism, and economically sound business development, it is understandable that organizations will use technology to improve their workers' productivity and performance, as well as check for illegal activities. It is also reasonable for organizations to take these same actions to eliminate waste and to ensure the proper use of company resources.

However, to keep from crossing that fine line between prudent and unethical behavior, organizations should investigate and subscribe to a code of ethics. This code can help guide the organization in developing both policy and tactics with respect to privacy issues, ownership issues, and usage permissions. The following steps should serve as a starting point in developing or adopting an ethics code:

1. All policy must be openly communicated and equally applied throughout the organization.
2. Restrictions on privacy should be specifically stated in policy.
3. The organization should encourage users to abide by all software licensing agreements and avoid infringement indiscretions.
4. The organization must never breach the privacy commitments that it makes and should respect users' privacy as is publicly stated in the policy of record.
5. The organization should regularly log all network and system activity, not just select instances of work flow.
6. Users should be issued separate public/private key pairs (see Section Two for more detail) for encryption and digital signing. The organization should keep a duplicate of the private encryption

key of each employee so that the organization can decrypt any file or correspondence in accordance with policy. The organization should not maintain a copy of the digital signature key because this would allow for forged signatures and would undermine the confidence of the **public key infrastructure**.

7 Organizations and contributors should have a clear understanding of ownership of intellectual property.

Although it may be reassuring to know that laws exist that are applicable to the area of electronic privacy, these laws are of little comfort when a trust is broken or our privacy is somehow invaded, especially if the courts are liberal in their interpretation of the statute. The laws, which we have mentioned, are effective in limiting government access to our private electronic information. They are also effective in regulating certain industry use of our personal electronic information. Unfortunately, the law itself does not constitute a significant deterrent to those in the private sector or to potential attackers that wish to do us harm.

On the other end of the legal spectrum, privacy laws seem to protect would-be criminals and terrorists who use the World Wide Web as a vehicle for their criminal activity. The modern terrorist hides behind the right of privacy while undermining our very system. This was never more evident than on 9/11. The legislature must balance our laws between the needs of law enforcement and the rights of individuals. They must also enable law enforcement officials to carry out effective investigations of cybercriminals. The privacy statutes currently require that you demonstrate that you had a "reasonable" expectation of privacy. The law allows for significant latitude, the extent of which is determined by the court's interpretation of reasonable.

Later in the text, we will review how the application of cryptographic techniques can establish both confidence in our trust relationships and control over the confidentiality of our information. Information security plans should be concerned with privacy. We should not use legislation as a shield. We can employ methods to keep information as private as we want while leaving little or nothing to chance.

WHAT CONSTITUTES A CRIME?

One of the key problems the legislature is currently addressing is in determining when hacking is a crime, and when it is not. As we mentioned earlier, the primary test of *mens rea* is one way a prosecutor will determine (based on intent) if a crime has been committed. But can we demonstrate clear intent, or even who is responsible, when the perpetrator's acts are cleverly disguised against the electronic backdrop? By examining the laws throughout this chapter, it is easy enough to prove intent in an electronic financial fraud case. But what about discovering the intent in a case concerning criminal trespass, denial-of-service attacks, social engineering attacks, information theft, identity theft (other than credit card), or the use of malicious software?

For example, is it a crime to write malicious software? This interesting question has generated much discussion. There are many reasons that someone might produce a computer virus. The obvious reason is to use it for malicious purposes. An alternate reason could be that the development of the virus or the worm occurred as a legitimate byproduct of a proper development effort. A third possibility is that the code was written to test new anti-virus software. Interestingly, the answer to whether the development process was criminal or not is "no" in all of those situations. It is the malicious use of software that constitutes a crime, the conscious act of trying to do harm or create loss, not the process of creating software in a lab.

But what about the software engineer that develops a killer virus and makes it available on the Net for script kiddies to use for destructive deeds? Is this act not comparable to a person providing a weapon to someone to use while committing a crime? While providing someone the means to commit a crime is usually a punishable offense, the formation of a linkage to a culpable accomplice is far more difficult to make in the cyber-arena. This is disturbing when we realize that the true engineering genius behind many of these scripted attacks often goes unpunished because the attacker did not release the attack. Rather, the attacker created the software and made it available to less-skilled hackers for them to use maliciously. Although most would agree that this is ethically wrong, it is difficult to bring charges, much less win the case.

Another troubling area is that of identifying crimes committed by people with permission to utilize computer facilities or who have legitimate access to information. This is difficult to sort out, especially when we remember that a large portion of cybercrime is committed by current or formerly trusted insiders.

The difficult task of sorting out this dilemma again goes back to the concept of intent. Apart from those meaning to do harm, we must consider the possibility that a loss may have occurred as the result of **errors and omissions** on the part of computer programmers, analysts, project managers, database managers, and communications experts. The computer professional and information technologist have extremely difficult technical jobs. Often these jobs require that they make decisions where the outcomes of their actions are uncertain. These experts are often the last line of defense in solving technology problems or producing a viable product. They can make honest mistakes. Most professional consultants carry errors and omissions insurance to protect them in the event a mistake is made. This is the equivalent of malpractice insurance for a physician.

The abusive form of a mistake is caused by **negligence**. Negligence refers to the willful disregard of potential bad outcomes in carrying out or failing to carry out a task. Negligence is sometimes punishable as a crime if it results in loss or harm to a person. More often than not, negligence is remedied through a civil action where some form of compensation is sought.

Another possible insider problem stems from the unauthorized use of information. Again, this can be difficult to prove. The unauthorized use of information refers to a wide spectrum of possible activities ranging from reading classified memos, to stealing corporate client lists, to copyright infringement.

Copyright infringement and intellectual property laws play a large role in forging a security policy. U.S. copyright laws extend the rights of protected intellectual information to their electronic representations. Thus, this area of information crime seems better defined than privacy or trespass. However, piracy continues to run rampant through our society. Illegally downloading music files, stealing software, and illegally copying movies are causing significant monetary losses across several major industries. These acts of piracy are illegal and create a difficult series of problems for information security professionals. Tools abound for creating second-generation copies of digital information (including music, movies, literature, and programs and software products).

The copyright and trademark laws also include creation of products and services, naming of products and services, and ownership of URLs. During the browser wars of the early 1990s, it was common practice for everyday people to register major corporate URLs and resell them back to the corporations at overinflated prices. Companies now often file for Web ID name protection at the same time they trademark or copyright a product.

Misuse of information is a problem frequently created by trusted insiders. This type of crime can be serious if the intent is to manipulate the financial worth or reputation of a business. Misuse of information can include releasing secret information, illegally selling information to rival companies, or misrepresenting information.

While it is true that some spectacular cases have been prosecuted in criminal court, the majority of information crime is dealt with either under tort law (where an individual seeks compensation for damages) or via out-of-court settlements. Organizational liability can be high and the need for counsel is important. It is wise to have your security policies and plans reviewed by an attorney specializing in this area. You should also retain the services of the law firm to ensure that all products, names, and intellectual property are properly registered with the appropriate government agencies.

CRIME PREVENTION, DETECTION, AND PROSECUTION

Crime prevention, detection, and prosecution are closely related topics. Whole areas of study are dedicated to each. The legal system is still adjusting to the age of cybercrime and a fascinating field appealing to most technologists is computer forensics. This area of techno–crime fighting is one of the most critical areas in building cases with a reasonably good chance of success. Computer forensics can also be used to understand the nuances of information security breaches and thus aid in the prevention of cybercrime. Computer forensic scientists are very much in demand and can have tremendous earning potential. This section of the text focuses on the role law enforcement plays with respect to cybercrime. It also addresses how organizations can assist in this process. The FBI has developed a multi-step model used to provide education on the correct handling of computer crime. The model will be examined in this text, as shown in Figure 3-1, and it is based in large part on the FBI model. It has been embellished to include areas of interest beyond those originally presented in the FBI model. The model has been extended to include the role of the legislature, deterrence, and the advancement of a valid crime statistics summary.

PREVENTION

As is shown in Figure 3-1, the first step in the crime-fighting process is crime prevention. Pursuing criminals and subsequently prosecuting them is a rather expensive process. Combine these costs with the mounting costs of the loss incurred by the victims and insurance carriers, and it is easy to understand why there is such an emphasis placed on prevention. The prevention process involves creating effective legislation, educating the public regarding the applicable laws and proven prevention techniques, emphasizing planning and policy creation, and providing threat analysis/data to security managers.

The legislature's role is extremely important because the current laws give the law enforcement process authority. During the last fifteen years, the legislation has crafted most of the cybercrime laws outlined later in the chapter. For the most part, these are solid laws that have evolved and adapted to the rapid change in technology. Work still needs to be done, especially in the area of rules of evidence. The majority of this chapter is dedicated to reviewing these laws and examining actual cases in which these various laws have been tested. Also, several selections from the FBI and NIPC Web sites are provided to offer expert interpretation of these laws.

The importance of education is easily overlooked when planning for information security. The government has begun pushing education as both a means of prevention and as a way of gaining widespread acceptance of the laws. As practitioners, we also have an obligation to educate those inside our organizations, as well as those outside the company that we choose to interact with electronically. By raising the awareness level of the user community, you should notice a greater level of compliance with policy and procedure. You may also notice that suspicious acts will be reported more frequently.

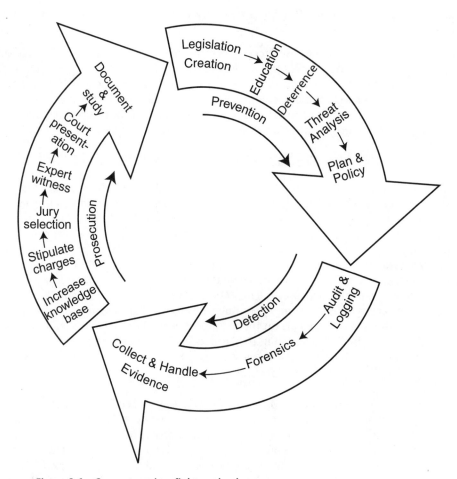

Figure 3-1 Computer crime fighter wheel.

Deterrence is the next step in the prevention process. If a person contemplates committing a crime, it is a goal of law enforcement and the legislation to make that person consider the possible penalties for committing this crime. The theory is that if the penalty outweighs the gain, then the person is less likely to commit the crime. By enforcing these laws, we set examples that should have the specific effect of deterring others.

However, two problems exist with this theory:

- The statement, "crime does not pay" is a misnomer. Not only does it pay, but it also pays well (especially white-collar crime).
- Many computer crimes go unpunished to avoid unwanted publicity and an undermining of confidence in the organization attacked.

We have already examined the need for an organization to conduct a threat analysis. A threat analysis will help focus the security plan. By understanding not only the threat agents likely to be encountered, but also the profile of the attacker and the valuation of a successful attack, we can develop security plans and implement countermeasures that make sense. Additionally, the threat analysis can be useful if an organization is successfully attacked. A threat analysis can provide a detailed road map (via OTV trees) of the likely impact of the attack on the organization that will be affected, and the level of attention required to address the problem.

Security planning is a key step in the prevention of cybercrime. As we shall see in Chapter 4, the implementation of a well-positioned security plan can help plug holes, educate the user base, secure information, and make the organization quicker to respond to an attack.

Building a Crisis-Management Team

Team building is a key area in any security plan. A security response team needs to be in place to best respond to trouble. The sooner a hacker can be stopped, the better. Once a system perimeter is penetrated, it is only a matter of time until the information becomes vulnerable. It is important to note that the security plan is built from the inside out, meaning that we address the core of the model, cryptography, authentication, and verification first. Then we implement the operating system hardening, secure information system design and architecture implementation, and provide secure Web services. Finally, we address the outer layer of the model, which includes physical security, educating and communicating the plan to the user community, and establishing the operational processes and procedures.

Once the strategy is implemented, the steps should unfold from the outside in. The perimeter defenses must be defeated and the information system successfully penetrated before the information is at any risk. By the time the hacker accesses the information and runs into the formidable wall of encryption, the security team should have sufficient time to respond to the threat and limit any damage.

One of the key components of the information security plan is to determine the organization's **fail-safe** stance. This stance is intended to be the default security posture of an organization under attack. One fail-safe stance is required for each information system entity in the organization. There are two possible fail-safe stances: opened and closed. In the open posture, the organization permits all activity regarding the information entity, even in the face of a security failure. An example of this is a university network. It is not reasonable to take Internet access off-line and deprive students of that access just because there is an attack via that connection in progress. In this example, it might be more prudent to track the intruder, limit the intruder's access, and initiate an investigative process.

By contrast, a closed stance is warranted in the case of a research and development facility, or a sensitive government site under attack. In either of these cases, it might be wise for the organization to disconnect a connection and close access to the information system being infiltrated.

Once we have our plan and our fail-safe stances, we need to understand the crisis management-process for our organization. Determining who is on the crisis management team and how the team will respond to an attack represent important decisions. The functions of the players on these teams are rarely the same for any two organizations. This decision will depend on a variety of factors including the nature of the business, the total amount of users and information, the need to protect clients, and the available resources to support team leadership.

In general, the team needs to have an executive sponsor. This should be a senior organizational member with decision-making authority. This person becomes useful in deciding what trade-offs need to be made under worst-case scenarios. The team also should include a technical advisor. This person is the technical lead, someone that possesses an in-depth knowledge of the technology areas as well as information security hacker tactics. The technical adviser is the most valuable member of the team and often assumes command of tactical operations during a crisis.

Additionally, the team will require an auditor. The auditor is useful to the team because typically the auditor has intimate knowledge of the assets being protected and understands the details of in-place logging activities. The auditor can help during the investigation phase by assisting in capturing evidence and determining valuation of the assets affected.

Finally, in large organizations, people from security, marketing, and human resources should be included to interact with outside law enforcement agencies, effected staff, and even the press, if required.

Intrusion Detection

The final step of the security implementation process is putting technology in place to complement the security team. This technology makes the initial determination that a break-in has occurred or that an attack is under way. Putting detection measures in place to alert you when you have been attacked helps increase efficiency in the initial phases of an alert by narrowing the possibilities of what is happening.

Two types of **intrusion detection systems (IDSs)** are available: proactive and reactive. A proactive system continually monitors the information system and takes action based on a detected weakness in IS before an attack is in progress. A reactive system uses various recognition techniques to identify an attack in progress and then sound the alarm. In either case, these systems are the enablers of our alert capability. Without these systems in place, a team might not realize there is a problem (and often do not) until long after the attack is over.

Intrusion detection systems are discussed in greater detail in Chapter 9. They constitute a significant piece of the technology required to safeguard the information system.

Operational Policies and Plans

Finally, the development of operational policies rounds out the prevention portfolio. Policies differ from plans because policies are focused on a particular topic and detail the operational and procedural steps required of users, systems, and administrators to ensure the safety of the information. As we shall see in Chapter 4, the security professional will attempt to create policies for the operation of information system components, behavior of users, information archiving and restoration, administrative tasks, use of cryptography, care of electronic identity, crisis-management team roles and responsibilities, and the use of all applications and services.

Prevention works, especially when there is a focus on education, individual roles, and organizational direction to complement the enablers (the laws, techniques, plans, and procedures). The National Infrastructure Protection Center offers these tips (*http://www.oww.nipc.gov*) to help organizations minimize their potential vulnerabilities and enhance their effective responses:

- Join your local InfraGard chapter (contact local FBI field office for details).
- Establish a liaison with law enforcement.
- Educate the users.
- Maintain backups of all original operating systems software.
- Maintain backups of all important data.
- Maintain and enforce corporate information systems security policies.
- Install adequate security software to recognize an attack.
- Enable packet filtering and access control lists on routers.

- Ensure that audit trails are turned on.
- Place a banner on your system to notify unauthorized users that they may be subject to monitoring.
- Routinely test your system for vulnerabilities.
- Change logins and passwords frequently.
- Require that passwords contain special alphanumeric character combinations and/or one-time tokens.
- Cancel logins and passwords when employees leave your organization.
- Install vendor patches for known vulnerabilities.
- Maintain the most current updates to anti-virus software.
- Restrict and monitor network access to Internet hosts.
- Utilize remote access authorization tools.
- Consider establishing an emergency response team or a contact with an existing incident response organization.
- Develop an organizational computer incident response plan/policy.

INVESTIGATION

By way of definition from the U.S. Department of Justice Web site article, "Recovering and Examining Computer Forensic Evidence," by Noblett, Pollitt, and Presley, **computer forensic science** can be defined as a science "created to address the specific and articulated needs of law enforcement to make the most of this new form of electronic evidence. Computer forensic science is the science of acquiring, preserving, retrieving, and presenting data that has been processed electronically and stored on computer media."

The article describes two interesting aspects of the computer forensic scientist's job that point to the need for this person to have a significant background in information security: "Courts are requiring that more information, rather than equipment, be seized. This requires cooperative efforts between law enforcement officers and the computer forensic scientist to ensure that the technical resources necessary for the execution of the search warrant are sufficient to address both the scope and complexity of the search." The article continues, "Computers may logically contain both information identified in the warrant as well as information that may be constitutionally protected. The computer forensic scientist is probably the most qualified person to advise both the investigator and prosecutor as to how to identify technical solutions to these intricate situations."

Investigating cybercrime is a different process than investigating a traditional crime. As was previously mentioned, cybercrime investigations require an advanced knowledge of computer science and information technology. An electronics crime investigation requires knowledge of databases, computing hardware, networking and communication systems, and various types of electronic media. The type of evidence that the cyberinvestigator must collect, catalog, and discover is of a different nature than the physical evidence (e.g., a fingerprint) collected in a routine criminal investigation.

Another significant problem is the sheer volume of information that criminologists sift through. Consider that today the average hard drive is a minimum of 20 GB. If you were able to print out that much information, you would produce a pile of paper fifty stories high. Therefore, it is not only important for computer forensic scientists to be able to obtain the data, but they must also be able to use algorithmic methods for isolating those portions of the data that are pertinent to the case. This extrication is done through the use of advanced searching and sorting algorithms, keyword searches, and **computational**

linguistic algorithms (those algorithms that use heuristic methods to express language relationships programmatically).

Some forms of the investigative process are similar: interviewing witnesses and experts, evaluating financial records, preparing and executing a search warrant, and actually processing the criminals. Law enforcement from the state and local level all the way to federal and international levels have increased their awareness of the investigation of cybercrime. It is important to note that cybercrime investigators are in short supply and that the federal government has many programs under way to train agents in this field. This is clearly an emerging growth area in technology.

There are whole texts and courses dedicated to the study of the investigative process. With respect to information security (as one area of cyberinvestigations), there are several aspects of the investigative process that we will highlight:

- Audit trails and **logging**
- Collecting and analyzing evidence
- Securing the crime scene

Audit Trails and Logging

The use of audit trails and logging tools are important parts of a criminal investigation, which, by necessity, are required to begin long before a crime ever takes place. Information systems typically monitor the following: account activity, login attempts, file modification/creation/deletion activities, network activities, and performance fluctuations. By carefully examining a well-kept set of logs, the computer forensic scientist can construct both the timeline of attacker activities, as well as the identity of the intruder.

An important part of every information security plan should include statements regarding the type and frequency of regularly scheduled logging and monitoring activities. Without those statements, the very logs that show a pattern of activity of the perpetrator may be excluded as **hearsay**. Hearsay is a legal term that implies that any statement made outside of court and without the benefit of either cross-examination (of the witness who made the statement, not the person who heard it) or corroborating evidence that clearly connects the statements to the context in which they were made is considered suspect. The courts have addressed the hearsay issue of computer records many times during the last fifteen years. Depending on the case in question, we see varying degrees of latitude offered the prosecutors regarding this matter. According to Federal Rules of Evidence 801(a), "A 'statement' is (1) an oral or written assertion or (2) nonverbal conduct of a person, if it is intended by the person as an assertion," By strict definition, the evidence cannot contain hearsay if the "statement" were not made by a person. The courts only partially agree. The key is that the statement made as a matter of computer process must be (1) a record of regularly conducted activity and (2) untouched by human hands. Any computer record that contains the written correspondence or thoughts of a person (a Word document containing a letter, for example) can be considered hearsay because it was proverbially penned by a human. As a result, the document without supporting testimony is considered hearsay. However, an IDS that automatically logs a report regarding the state of the information system at any moment in time *can* be used as evidence because it is untouched by human hands. The one caveat that exists in this latter case is that the record or log must be part of the well-established business practice of the organization. Any computer-generated log that is created by law enforcement for the sole purpose of being used as evidence is considered hearsay. According to the Seventh Circuit Court of Appeals in the case of the *United States v. Blackburn*, the court found: "the [computer-generated] report in this case was not kept in the course of a regularly conducted business activity, but rather was specially prepared at the behest of the FBI and with the knowledge that any information it supplied would be used in an ongoing criminal investigation… In finding this report inadmissible under Rule 803(6), we adhere to the well-established rule that documents made in anticipation of litigation are inadmissible under the business records exception."

It is the responsibility of the court to protect individuals' rights in this manner because it is possible for someone to alter computer records or logs. In fact, hackers regularly erase entries from computer logs to remove their trespass from plain sight.

Computer forensics is fast becoming a highly desirable field for top information security analysts. With the emergence of sophisticated monitoring devices and investigative tools, what was once an almost impossible science has become manageable and interesting. Forensic investigation needs to include two important components: the possibility to restore and examine deleted files, and the ability to replay and dissect attacks. By actually replaying an attack and examining deleted files that were originally created by the attacker, many clues as to the extent of damage done—and possibly the identity of the attacker—can be revealed.

As we have already seen, the IDSs available today have agents that capture statistics and flag suspicious activities. However, although this alert/response mechanism is important, it will not provide sufficient detail after a crime has been committed. The IDS and logging system help us establish the time line of activity and the sequencing of events. However, they often cannot provide proof a crime was committed.

Collecting and Analyzing Evidence

To obtain proof of a crime, forensic investigators often have to look no further than the information infrastructure of the attacker. Hackers create files as part of the attack process and delete them prior to exiting the system. Drug dealers, for example, have been known to fully automate their businesses, leaving key evidence on computer disks. Trusted insiders attempting information theft often collect and organize their materials electronically before making off with the goods. Identity theft is often conducted electronically with criminals collecting credit card or other identity information that is stored on electronic media. In all of these cases, the perpetrator may attempt to delete those files that could be used as evidence. What the perpetrator may not know is that simply deleting the information from the hard drive does not actually remove it.

When information is stored on a system, the record is assigned to open space on the disk. This space has an address. The file management system uses this address to reference the information. In other words, the file management system maintains a pointer to "used" space on the media and matches addresses and file names so that successful manipulation of the information can be achieved. When an authorized user instructs the file management system to delete a file, the file manager does not physically wipe the disk. Rather, it is a simpler operation to erase the pointer to the information, which for all intents and purposes makes the space on the disk free (i.e., it orphans the data). However, while we cannot reference the information by name because the pointer to it is gone, the configuration of bits that made up that information are still exactly where you left them. Even if you physically broke the hard drive and tried to destroy the media, there is a chance that the bit configuration would remain.

Through the use of sophisticated software, recovery of this information is very possible. Two tools for recovering and tracking deleted files are Guidance Software's EnCase (*http://www.guidancesoftware.com*) and Coroner's toolkit (*http://www.porcupine.org/forensics/tct.html*). These tools can be used on a variety of systems and provide the ability to recover all or parts of the information and the corresponding directory metadata.

Another useful class of tools is **network forensics analysis tools (NFATs)**. NFATs monitor network traffic and allow for the replay of attacks, tracking of information intruders back to their source, and isolation and playback of suspicious activity. Additionally, these tools can be used to test the vulnerability of an information security system by capturing an attack and then replaying it onto the network after adjustments have been made to the security posture to account for it. NFR Security's Network Flight Recorder (*http://www.nfr.com*) and SilentRunner (*http://www.silentrunner.com*) are network forensics tools that provide the capture capability for this type of analysis of attacks. These tools are often expensive and require extensive training to use. But for an organization that will pay a high price in the event of information theft or for law enforcement, it may be a worthwhile investment to track hackers and to counter attacks.

Crime Scene Management

Securing the crime scene is the next important investigative area of study. Often the electronic crime scene is badly disturbed before the computer forensics specialist has an opportunity to examine it. If your organization has been attacked, do not touch anything and report the incident to the proper authorities as soon as reasonably possible.

When encountering a crime scene, the investigator must be trained to understand where the possible evidence is and how to isolate it while preserving the context in which it was found. Hardware, software, removable drives, documentation, printers, trashed documents or media, notes, and the like are all potential sources of the information. As part of an initial investigation, crime scene investigators will usually

- Videotape the scene
- Not touch anything before the items have been cataloged and tested for physical evidence (e.g., fingerprints on a keyboard)
- Not power down systems except as a last resort to stop a rogue process from destroying evidence
- Work deliberately and methodically to preserve the chain of evidence
- Authenticate evidence by write protecting and sealing media used to collect evidence
- Write down everything they see and gather all of the handwritten notes and documentation available at the scene
- Make sure they do not exceed the limitations specified in the search warrant

This brief introduction to the investigative process should provide students with an indication of just how difficult it is to conduct such a tedious investigation. The process must be conducted without violating the preservation of evidence requirements, allowing too much time to pass, or being compromised by hacker automation (time bombs that destroy information during an investigative process).

In addition to the process described in this section, there are many more advanced investigative techniques. Investigators have access to an impressive array of technology enablers that both speed up and simplify the process. Further, investigators may utilize honeypots, an electronic dragnet, to catch criminals and further analyze hacker methods.

Creating a Honeypot

A **honeypot** is any configuration of an information system (systems, networks, applications, and information bases) placed in the public domain for the sole purpose of allowing attacks to be targeted against them. It can be a single networked system or an entire enterprise-sized information system. The honeypot is populated with interesting but useless data and is protected with just enough security measures to make the site appear real to a would-be hacker. The purpose of a honeypot is to

- Gather information on hacker techniques
- Distract a hacker from real and fruitful targets
- Convince the hacker they have penetrated a site undetected so you have time to conduct an investigation to learn the identity of the hacker and stop them

The only key component of a honeypot is the presence of significant monitoring systems (IDS) that can record and track the actions of the hacker. By learning new hacker tricks, an information security specialist will be able to modify the security regimen on real information systems to better harden them against a particular attack.

One flaw with honeypots is that a seasoned hacker can take over the honeypot and use it to launch springboard attacks against other sites. To prevent this attack, it is important to disable certain elements of the operating system (e.g., have the system reboot if the attacker changes mode to kernel) and install outbound network protections, which will effectively cage the attacker by not allowing any outward harmful network traffic. An alternative is to use software emulation honeypots, which act as a software decoy of a real information system. In this case, the hacker never really has control of anything other than a simulation. Good examples of honeypots are honeynet, Deception Toolkit, and the Honeypot Project.

What should you do if you catch the hacker online in a honeypot? It is important that you are prepared to monitor the attacker closely. You should log and record as much of what they do as possible. This will be of use when you sit down to analyze the style of attack. You should never confront the attacker or try to contact them. It is best that the honeypot work in stealth mode so that the hacker never knows he has been caught until the police arrive. Finally, in the event that the attacker does take control of the system, pull the plug on the operation before your system is used to launch other attacks.

Are honeypots illegal or unethical? It is possible to view the use of a honeypot as a form of entrapment. Under our federal guidelines in the United States, entrapment requires coercing a person to commit a crime that they would not otherwise have committed. Because a honeypot in no way entices anyone to do anything, it does not fall into that category. Hence, it is a legal form of catching and examining hackers. Keep in mind that the primary objective of a honeypot is to examine hacker techniques and to develop effective countermeasures against them.

The primary objective is not necessarily to catch the hacker. Evidence of a crime collected at a honeypot crime scene would probably be admissible against an attacker, but it is doubtful that law enforcement would use the information obtained in that way. An important piece of information that law enforcement can gain from a honeypot is the attacker's identity. Thus, the hacker is exposed and the agents can track the person and possibly catch him in the act of committing another crime (before he does any real damage to another party, but after law enforcement officials have had a chance to investigate the perpetrator to uncover clues of previous crime).

Russian Computer Hacker Sentenced to Three Years in Prison

John McKay, United States Attorney for the Western District of Washington, and Charles E. Mandigo, Special Agent in Charge, Seattle Division, Federal Bureau of Investigation, announced today that Chief United States District Judge John C. Coughenour has sentenced Vasiliy Gorshkov, age 27, of Chelyabinsk, Russia, to serve 36 months in prison for his convictions at trial last year on 20 counts of conspiracy, various computer crimes, and fraud committed against Speakeasy Network of Seattle, Washington; Nara Bank of Los Angeles, California; Central National Bank of Waco, Texas; and the online credit card payment company PayPal of Palo Alto, California. Gorshkov also was ordered to pay restitution of nearly $700,000 for the losses he caused to Speakeasy and PayPal.

Gorshkov was one of two men from Chelyabinsk, Russia, who were persuaded to travel to the United States as part of an FBI undercover operation. The operation arose out of a nationwide FBI investigation into Russian computer intrusions that were directed at Internet Service Providers, e-commerce sites, and online banks in the United States. The hackers used their unauthorized access to the victims' computers to steal credit card information and other personal financial information, and then often tried to extort money from the victims with threats to expose the sensitive data to the public or damage the victims' computers. The hackers also defrauded PayPal through a scheme in which stolen credit cards were used to generate cash and to pay for computer parts purchased from vendors in the United States. The FBI's undercover operation was established to entice persons responsible for these crimes to come to U.S. territory.

As part of the operation, the FBI created a start-up computer security company named "Invita" in Seattle, Washington. Posing as Invita personnel, the FBI communicated with Gorshkov and the other man, Alexey Ivanov, by e-mail and telephone during the summer and fall of 2000. The men agreed to a face-to-face meeting in Seattle. As a prelude to their trip to the United States, the FBI arranged a computer network for the two men to hack into and demonstrate their hacking skills. The men successfully broke into the test network.

Gorshkov and Ivanov arrived in Seattle, Washington, on November 10, 2000, and a meeting was held at the office of Invita. Unbeknownst to the Russian men, the participants in the meeting were undercover FBI agents and the meeting was recorded on audio and video tape. During the meeting, Gorshkov discussed their hacking prowess and took responsibility for various hacking incidents and activities. Gorshkov shrugged off any concern about the FBI, explaining that the FBI could not get them in Russia. When asked about their access to credit cards, Gorshkov declined to talk about it while they were in the United States and added that "this kind of question is better discussed in Russia."

A few days after the two men were arrested, the FBI obtained access via the Internet to two of the men's computers in Russia. The FBI copied voluminous data from the accounts of Gorshkov and Ivanov and examined the data pursuant to a search warrant issued by a United States Magistrate Judge. Gorshkov's pretrial challenge to the FBI's copying and search of the Russian data was denied by Chief Judge Coughenour in a written order dated May 23, 2001.

The data copied from the Russian computers provided a wealth of evidence of the men's computer hacking and fraud. They had large databases of credit card information that were stolen from Internet Service Providers like Lightrealm of Kirkland, Washington. More than 50,000 credit card numbers were found on the two Russian computers. The Russian computers also contained stolen bank account and other personal financial information of customers of online banking at Nara Bank and Central National Bank - Waco.

The data from the Russian computers revealed that the conspirators had gained unauthorized control over numerous computers - including computers of a school district in St. Clair County, Michigan - and then used those compromised computers to commit a massive fraud involving PayPal and the online auction company e-Bay. The fraud scheme consisted of using computer programs to establish thousands of anonymous e-mail accounts at e-mail web sites like Hotmail, Yahoo!, and MyOwnEmail. Gorshkov's programs then created associated accounts at PayPal with random identities and stolen credit cards. Additional computer programs allowed the conspirators to control and manipulate e-Bay auctions so that they could act as both seller and winning bidder in the same auction and then effectively pay themselves with stolen credit cards.

The above is an excerpt of a document contained at *http://www.cybercrime.gov/ gorshkovSent.htm.*

PROSECUTION

The prosecution of electronic crimes is a difficult process, in part because the prosecutor must overcome three separate learning curves: their own, the judge's, and the jury's. Probably the most difficult aspect of prosecuting a case involving the use of high technology is that it is hard to sometimes differentiate between criminal activity and noncriminal activity. The prosecution must not only provide compelling evidence and a clear motive, but it must provide a foundation and an education in technology so that the evidence and motive make sense to everyone listening. There are several real issues the prosecutor must overcome in order to provide such a foundation. First, the prosecutor needs to select jurors that are capable of understanding the material presented. Second, the prosecutor needs to find articulate expert witnesses who can present the information in an understandable, credible, and interesting way. Third, the prosecutor needs to keep the jurors from getting overwhelmed with this new information so they do not lose interest. Finally, the prosecution will have to persuade victims to testify.

Selecting a jury is not an easy process in a case that involves cybercrime. The prosecutor is going to want well-educated people to serve on the jury, preferably people with high-tech backgrounds. The defense will want just the opposite: people with no interest in technology who might not be well educated. Even one juror from either camp can cause a substantial problem for the whole jury. The way our justice works will probably result in a mix of both types of juror described. Therefore, it is imperative that the prosecution appeal to the least-common denominator among the group.

Providing expert witness testimony for the jury does bring a certain amount of credibility to the case. However, this works both ways. The defense attorneys will also bring in experts with opposite views who could influence the jury by providing reasonable doubt as to the reliability of methods, accuracy of the tools used by the forensic scientist, and by trying to overwhelm the jurors with technical minutia.

Expert witnesses are necessary to improve the worth of evidence. Sometimes just hearing a well-qualified person tell you that something in evidence is compelling and correct can be enough to formulate a verdict. Again, this works both ways. Therefore, it is important that the prosecution choose their witnesses carefully. The witness should obviously have a strong knowledge of the case and the evidence, impressive credentials and experience, but most importantly the ability to explain things clearly in layman's terms.

The presentation in the courtroom needs to flow well. Prosecutors are well served by adhering to the principle of simple, effective, and brief presentation. Courtroom presentation needs to be convincing without being overbearing and overly repetitive.

Finally, the prosecution has to be able to persuade victims to testify. This persuasion can be difficult. Many victims of white-collar crime in general, and cybercrime in particular, are concerned about making open-court statements on behalf of their organization. They may feel that by admitting there was a break-in, they might compromise their reputation or brand by exposing a weakness that could reduce consumer confidence. For example, imagine that you do business with a bank and use their automated home banking system. Let's say that the system is compromised by a hacker just one time and that only minimal damage was done. If that institution offers testimony in open court, consumer confidence would be shattered. The damage caused by the admission that the bank could be compromised in such a way might—and often does—make consumers nervous about exposing themselves to the same potential harm. Further, testimony might expose a business's technology weakness and create opportunity for others to create similar attacks against them.

The prosecution phase of our law enforcement model concludes with a postmortem of every case. Lessons are learned in every phase of the case from investigation through trial and sentencing. This is a new area of litigation; those tasked with the burden of prosecution are in many cases building the airplane while they are flying it.

INTERACTING WITH LAW ENFORCEMENT

Law enforcement is truly everyone's business. Each person and organization needs to be prepared to assist law enforcement in the investigation of cybercrime. Responsibilities of organizations and security staff include reporting cybercrime, keeping accurate records and logs of normal security analysis, understanding the best practices to use in the event you are victimized, having previously established law enforcement contacts, and having a security plan that includes a crisis-management strategy.

Communication between the victim and law enforcement should be honest and open. The victim should be prepared to provide documentation as needed. The law enforcement agents have a responsibility to the victim to be responsive and to minimize the impact of an investigation on the victim. Unlike other branches of law enforcement, where a crime scene investigation would normally be conducted on-site in a matter of hours or days and then moved into a laboratory environment, a cybercrime forensic investigation is almost always conduct ed on-site from start to finish. This can tie up the organization's resources and increase the financial damage already suffered.

We also have a responsibility to educate our users and leaders regarding risk, proper usage techniques, penalties imposed by law, and how to identify a problem. This can be an important step in preventing or curtailing an attack.

NIPC Recommendations for Victims

From the National Infrastructure Protection Center website: *http://www.nipc.gov.*

In addition to protecting your systems, consider taking the following actions to increase the chances of apprehending the perpetrator:

- Respond quickly. Contact law enforcement
- If unsure of what actions to take, DO NOT stop system processes or tamper with files. This may destroy traces of an intrusion
- Follow organization policies/procedures (your organization should have a computer incident response capability plan)
- Use the telephone to communicate. Attackers may be capable of monitoring e-mail
- Contact the incident response team for your organization. Quick technical expertise is crucial in preventing further damage and protecting potential evidence
- Consider activating caller identification on incoming lines. This information may help in leading to the identification of source/route of intrusion
- Establish points of contact with general counsel, emergency response staff, and law enforcement. Pre-established contacts will help in a quick response effort
- Make copies of files an intruder may have altered or left. If you have the technical expertise to copy files, this action will assist investigators as to when and how intrusions may have occurred
- Identify a primary point of contact to handle potential evidence and to work with law enforcement
- Establish chain-of-custody of evidence. Potential hardware/software evidence that is not properly controlled may lose its value
- DO NOT contact the suspected perpetrator

In addition to these points NIPC provides an incident report form, which can be found online at its Web site and in Appendix C of this text.

Reporting crimes is an important and valuable service we can perform. One of the primary problems with developing sound information security policies and effective countermeasures is that crime is underreported. Without the statistical data, it is hard to plan products, encourage organizations to participate in developing sound security plans and policies, and difficult to perform risk assessments (detailed statistics on crime probabilities are required to calculate the SLEs and ALEs described in Chapter 2).

THE LAW

As was mentioned earlier, the legislature plays an important role in helping curtail cybercrime. In general, lawmaking bodies have the ability (through the passage of meaningful laws) to set the tone of society with respect to cybercrime. They accomplish this by empowering law enforcement departments to conduct efficient and effective investigations, providing the penalties for information security crimes to act as a deterrent, and by enabling a framework through which individuals and organizations can protect their privacy and information assets.

Cyberlaw is a relatively new area of legislation, and several significant laws have emerged during the last ten years. For example, the Computer Fraud and Abuse Act of 1986 18 USC 1029 amended by the National Information Infrastructure Protection Act of 1996, and the **Electronic Communications and Privacy Act (ECPA)** represent the cornerstone of information security.

Working through the legislative process can be a time-consuming and daunting task. Just like the rest of us, our elected officials need to be educated on the nuances of information security concerns before they can act. Many of them do not have sufficient technical background to undertake such a mission. Subsequently, the investigative process is lengthened and many attempts fail to hit the mark.

Another by-product of our system of government is that, quite often, the needs of special interest groups are placed higher than the needs of society as a whole. For example, considerable effort was applied to the development of the Consumer Broadband and Digital Television Promotion Act, which was promoted as a security law. However, while this law has many relevant points, it lacks the technical details to enable its implementation. HIPAA legislation has been touted since the middle of the Clinton administration as providing significant strides regarding information security. HIPAA provides many important benefits to patients in the health care system. But while many hospitals have used this law to develop best practices for day-to-day patient care administration, this bill left out the majority of technical detail, making it difficult to implement in the electronic domain at this time. Although the government has taken many steps to resolve this problem, full implementation of HIPAA has been delayed by at least two years.

So what does the law enforcement and prosecutorial arms of government and the information security professional do while these laws continue to evolve? Use what resources already available and work toward improving upon them. The remainder of this chapter is used to examine the most important of these laws.

LEGISLATION WITH TEETH

Legislation concerning information security has evolved most significantly during the last ten years. Today, laws are on the books at the local, state, federal, and international levels. As with any branch of the law, it is not only the legislation that is important, but also the interpretation of the laws by the courts. In this section, we will review the most important of the federal laws and examine examples of each. It is important to stress that these laws in no way represent all of the legislation that exists. Rather, it is a beginning point for someone interested in cyberlaw. For those students that choose to pursue a career in computer forensic science, acquiring a base knowledge of the law in this area is essential.

The laws that we intend to study in this section break down into several groups:

- Laws that deal with protecting privacy.
- Laws that determine and protect ownership.
- Laws that protect information systems and information itself.
- Laws that empower technology and/or control its use.

The most important of the laws that we will study in this section are:

- Electronic Communications and Privacy Act (ECPA)
- Economic Espionage Act of 1996
- Freedom of Information Act

- National Health Insurance Portability and Accountability Act of 1996 (HIPAA)
- 1949 Arms Export Control Act (AECA)
- Export Administration Act (EAA)
- Wassenaar Arrangement
- The Electronic Signatures in Global and National Commerce Act
- Computer Fraud and Abuse Act of 1986 18 USC 1030—amended by the National Information Infrastructure Protection Act of 1996

Electronic Communications and Privacy Act (ECPA)

This law, also referred to as the Federal Wiretapping Act, was developed to restrict and regulate the interception and disclosure of electronic information. This legislation was set forth to limit the access of law enforcement to electronic information, whether in storage (residing on an electronic media device) or in transit (sent over the Net), without a warrant. This law specifically addresses how ISPs should respond to requests from law enforcement to examine Internet e-mail accounts and to monitor Internet communications. In many instances, ISPs want to cooperate with law enforcement to eradicate a hacker because ISPs are often victimized, but the law requires that they do not unless the requisite procedure is followed. According to a U.S. Attorney's Bulletin, "Tracking a Computer Hacker," by Daniel A. Morris (*www.usdoj.gov/criminal/cybercrime*):

> *Section 2073 of ECPA provides investigators with five mechanisms for compelling an Internet Service Provider to disclose information that might be useful in an investigation of a hacker. The mechanisms, in ascending order of the threshold showing required, are described below:*
>
> 1 *Subpoenas can be used by an investigator to obtain basic subscriber information from an Internet Service Provider, including the "name, address, local and long distance telephone billing records, telephone number or other subscriber number or identity, and length of service of a subscriber to or customer of such service and the types of service the subscriber or customer utilized."*
>
> 2 *Subpoenas also can be used to obtain opened e-mails, but only under certain conditions relating to notice to the subscriber..Subpoena s may be issued for e-mails that have been opened, but a search warrant is generally needed for unopened e-mails.*
>
> 3 *Court orders under 18 U.S.C. Section 2703(d) can be obtained by investigators for account logs and transactional records. Such orders are available if the agent can provide "articulable facts showing that there are reasonable grounds to believe the contents of a wire or electronic communication, or the records or other information sought, are relevant and material to an ongoing criminal investigation." The government must offer facts, rather than conclusory statements, in an application for a 2703 (d) order.*
>
> 4 *Investigators who obtain a court order under 18 U.S.C. Section 2703(d) can obtain the full contents of a subscriber's account (except for unopened e-mail stored with an ISP for 180 days or less and voicemail), if the order complies with a notice provision in the statute.*
>
> 5 *Search warrants obtained under Rule 41 of the Federal Rules of Criminal Procedure or an equivalent state warrant can be used to obtain the full contents of an account, except for voicemail in electronic storage (which requires a Title III order.) The ECPA does not require notification to the subscriber when the government obtains information from a provider using a search warrant.*
>
> *Voluntary disclosure by a provider whose services are available to the public is forbidden unless certain exceptions apply.*

Internet Service Provider Charged with Intercepting Customer Communications and Possessing Unauthorized Password Files

An Internet bookseller, which also operated an Internet communications service, was charged today in [a Boston] federal court with ten counts of unlawful interception of electronic mail messages ("e-mail") and one count of unauthorized possession of passwords with intent to defraud.

The information alleges that for periods of time between January and June 1998, the accused intercepted e-mail messages directed by online bookseller Amazon.com to accused bookseller's clients which had their e-mail addresses.

The information alleges that the purpose of the interception was, in part, to gain competitive commercial advantage for the accused's own online book-selling business by compiling a database of dealers' purchases and to analyze the book-selling market. In January 1998, the accused altered its e-mail service so that it automatically intercepted and stored e-mail addressed from Amazon.com to accused's book dealer customers. In a matter of weeks, accused intercepted and copied thousands of e-mail communications to which the accused was not a party and was not entitled.

The information also alleges that the accused obtained and retained unauthorized copies of the confidential and proprietary password files and customer lists of its competitor Internet service providers. As part of a plea agreement with the U.S. Attorney's Office, which must be approved by a U.S. District Court Judge, the accused has agreed to pay a total fine in the amount of $250,000.

The above is an excerpt of information contained at *www.cybercrime.gov*.

This legislation also limits the use of electronic wiretaps on the computer system, network connections, or other electronic communications pathways of a suspect during an investigation. As can be seen above, this tightly written legislation requires that the government apply for the appropriate subpoenas and warrants commensurate with the stipulations in this legislation.

This law is designed to protect the right to privacy of individuals with respect to their use of information systems for storing personal correspondence, ideas, and records, and for communicating them over a public infrastructure.

This law does not apply to private industry or interpersonal relationships. You cannot use these statutes to object to an invasion of privacy by an employer.

Another closely related privacy law is the **U.S. Privacy Act of 1974**. This law protects the right of individuals to restrict the use of personal information collected about them by the government.

Specialty Industry Privacy Law

Although there are particular laws regarding the right to privacy that apply to law enforcement and government officials, no such laws exist to protect people from having their privacy invaded by an employer, a coworker, or a hacker. Some laws do provide a legal remedy for criminal trespass onto your computer. Laws exist that protect your right to own intellectual property. There are even laws that protect against the fraudulent use of your identity. However, there are no laws that protect your privacy from a suspicious employer who wishes to monitor your Internet activity. There are no laws that prohibit Web sites from placing cookies on your machine (in fact, this is exactly how Web protocols function). Recently, the government has enacted two important pieces of legislation that are designed to protect the private information you share with health care professionals and financial institutions.

You will remember from Chapter 1 that HIPAA was enacted as part of broad-based legislation to protect the rights of individuals with respect to availability of health insurance and privacy of medical information. This legislation was initiated because of the unfair treatment of workers who may have developed serious medical problems during their tenure with a company that provided their health benefits. Prior to HIPAA, people in that situation may have found themselves living in fear of losing their benefits. This may have occurred if they lost their job and were then deemed too high of a risk to get health coverage through their next employer's insurance provider. It may also have been the case that their employer may have used this adverse health information to basically force employees to make concessions regarding compensation to stay with the company and maintain their benefits. Either way, HIPAA now states that employees have a right to medical coverage (portability) without exclusion for preexisting conditions if they find new benefits within sixty days of termination of previous employment. Along with these stipulations, the legislation also requires insurance providers, health care providers, pharmacies, hospitals, labs, clinics, testing facilities, outpatient care facilities, and health care billing organizations to maintain complete confidentiality of patient information (accountability.) This requirement is particularly important with respect to maintaining electronic patient information. There are many **transaction sets** that are considered routine in the insurance and health care industries. These transactions involve the transfer of patient information, billing information, diagnosis, hospitalization information, use of medications, use of prosthesis, or other confidential information that is used in the determination and payment of benefits. This information is considered sacred under HIPAA. There are serious penalties, including imprisonment, for breaches of HIPAA security. There is also a set of evolving standards known as X.12, which will outline the technological guidelines for attaining HIPAA compliancy. Health care providers currently have until October 2004 to become HIPAA compliant. It is estimated that the adaptation of HIPAA and X.12 standards will cost upwards of $30 billion in the next two years. This is an area ripe for information security professionals.

Likewise, we also provide much information to financial institutions that needs to be safeguarded. This information includes credit reports, financial statements, stock transactions, spending habits, and litigation. The **Graham-Leach-Bliley Act of 1999 (GLB)** forces financial institutions to disclose their privacy policies on sharing nonpublic information.

This law also provides for the disclosure of this information prior to a client initiating a business transaction with the institution. The law gives the client the right to prevent the sharing of personal, private information.

Intellectual Property Crimes

The concept of ownership of intellectual materials has been repeatedly addressed at the state and federal levels in significant detail. Concepts such as intellectual property, copyright, patents, and trade secrets have defined the ownership of everything from inventions to services to music to literature. Protecting the creativity and invention process is paramount in the advancement of our society through ingenuity. U.S. laws have long established intellectual property as a protected asset. Given the ease with which information can be gleamed from the Internet or subverted from a system, it is important that the government establish guidelines that address the use, representation, storage, and reproduction of intellectual property.

Music CDs, movies on DVD, licensed software, and other digital forms of entertainment and information can be copied and distributed with little effort. Most computer systems today have CD burners and readers capable of this activity. The illegal reproduction, use, and distribution of copyrighted materials is called **piracy**.

Most recently, extensive litigation between members of the music industry and Napster created significant news headlines (*The Recording Industry Association of America vs. Napster.*) Napster was a service that provided people with access to digitally stored versions of songs produced by thousands of artists. Napster never actually handled the copyrighted material. Instead, they created a user database of people who had digital representations of the music and linked them with people wanting to listen to them. The listeners would then electronically "borrow" the song from the owner of the original CD. At issue was the question of ownership. Napster contended that 1) they never actually distributed anything, they just provided a search engine of who owned what, and 2) by purchasing the CD, the user was free to lend the material (not to sell it) to anyone they wanted. This seems like a reasonable premise given that people often—and legally—give CDs, DVDs, or tapes to a friend to watch or to listen to. Napster contended that by not charging a fee for the movie or music, no royalties were stolen. The entertainment industry disagreed. They argued that the reproduction and distribution of digital music without a royalty fee being paid to the artist was an infringement of their rights because the digital representation of the music could be kept permanently, and therefore was not borrowed. The courts sided with the entertainment industry and ruled that there was an infringement of copyright. Napster was ordered to suspend this distribution channel or pay the required royalties. The courts further ruled that by purchasing a digital representation of copyrighted material, the user did not own anything other than the right to use the material. Therefore, any other person wanting to use the material was required to purchase the same right to use from the rightful owner (the production company). This ruling was an affirmation that existing copyright laws do extend into the electronic arena and cover intellectual properties. Losses as a result of copyright infringement cost the various entertainment and software industries tens of billions of dollars each year.

A **trade secret** is a legal brand that gives organizations the power to protect secrets from being divulged. Trade secrets are important to industry because once the secret is divulged, a corporate advantage may be compromised. Examples of trade secrets include the formula used to produce a food or chemical product, client lists, unreleased product information, algorithmic design of software products (remember you buy the executable, not the source code), internal processes and procedures detailing the provisioning of a service, and engineering specifications for products under development. It is important that this information be protected from industrial espionage or from the greed of an employee with whom you have shared the information as a matter of necessity such that they can perform their job. Foreign governments have also been known to spy on behalf of industries in their own countries to obtain these trade secrets.

Prior to 1996, no federal laws covered the protection of trade secrets. But given the needs of industry to protect these secrets, coupled with the need to maintain these secrets electronically (along with the once-strict rules governing the use of cryptography), the government was forced to act. The **Economic Espionage Act of 1996** was enacted to provide stronger penalties for anyone who revealed a trade secret, or fraudulently obtained (sold or bought) a trade secret to a foreign government, or conspired to commit such a crime or committed the theft of a trade secret. One important note: To establish something as a trade secret is a tedious process and requires extreme amounts of due diligence to maintain the designation once it is earned. For example, it is required that you not share the secret with anyone who is not on a need-to-know basis. Further, you must document the fact that you told the person who stole the secret that something is a trade secret. Any lapse on your organization's part could result in the loss of trade secret status and forfeiture of legal remedies.

Man Convicted of Trade Secret Violation

Say Lye Ow was sentenced today by U.S. District Judge Jeremy Fogel in San Jose, California, on his guilty plea to a felony charge of copying a trade secret in violation of the Economic Espionage Act of 1996. Judge Fogel sentenced Mr. Ow to a term of imprisonment of 24 months and a term of supervised release of two years to follow the prison term. Mr. Ow was ordered to surrender himself to begin serving his prison sentence on January 15, 2002.

Mr. Ow copied without authorization computer files relating to the design and testing of the Merced microprocessor (now known as the Itanium microprocessor). At the time, Mr. Ow knew that the materials contained trade secrets belonging to Intel Corporation. He copied the trade secret information with intent to convert it to his own economic benefit by using it at his then-new employment at Sun Microsystems. He also knew at the time that his act would injure Intel Corporation, in that he—as a former employee of Intel—possessed Intel's extremely valuable trade secret information without its knowledge. He also agreed that the information he copied was in fact a trade secret and that it was related to a product that was produced for and later placed in interstate and foreign commerce. The Itanium microprocessor was under joint development by Intel and Hewlett-Packard Co. since 1994 and was released earlier this year.

The above is a synopsis of the document contained at *http://www.cybercrime.gov/OwSent.htm.*

By contrast it is important that everyone be permitted equal access to information that has been developed or procured by the federal government using your tax dollars. The **Freedom of Information Act** governs obtaining information from the "public record." Naturally, this law does not apply to information that has been protected as a matter of national security. But under this law, a person or organization has the right to petition the court regarding the release of all information and its current designation.

If you recall from Chapter 1, information has certain properties that make it special and different from data or electronic signals. So while we can patent a hardware device or product and copyright intellectual and creative works, pure information still looms on the edge of legal protections. Information has value based on its use in an organization and the cost to develop and process it. Yet if information is damaged, it is difficult to quantify and exact that cost in court because the value of information varies from person to person and industry to industry. Further, it is entirely possible for two people to have acquired the same information independently of one another. It is analogous to building a new house and deciding to paint it the same exact colors as your neighbor. The neighbor may not like it, but he would have no legitimate claim to the exclusive use of that color. Therefore, there is a difference between intellectual property or trade secrets (such as a secret recipe) and information derived from the operation of your business (telephone or Internet usage statistics). The former is protected based on many well-established laws. The latter is protected from only illegal government searches. For this reason, important business items such as databases create difficult legal conundrums. Who owns the data in the database? Could the data be found somewhere else by chance? Who has the burden of proof that the database information is unique? These questions will make it difficult to exact a remedy from the courts in the event that someone breaks into your system and steals your "nonintellectual property information." In 1991, the Tenth Circuit Court decided in the case of the *United States vs. Brown*, 925 F.2d 1301, 1308 "that purely intangible intellectual property, such as a computer program, cannot constitute goods, wares, merchandise, securities or moneys which have been stolen, converted or taken within the meaning of Section 2313" (excerpt taken from Department of Justice report on the Structure of Title 18 Reform *http://www.usdoj.gov/criminal/cybercrime/1030_anal.html*). This ruling was a key reason that the Title 18 laws needed to be reviewed and reformed. It meant that since the information or intangible intellectual property had no directly assessable value, a crime had not been committed as interpreted strictly under Section 2313. This type of loophole requires us to more diligently than ever defend our information rigorously and not depend entirely on the wisdom of the courts.

THE LAW AND CRYPTOGRAPHY

The primary subject matter of Sections Two and Three of this text are concerned with the principles and applications of cryptography. It is appropriate, therefore, to present a detailed discussion of the evolution of legislation that applies to the use and export of this technology. Students may wish to revisit this material after completing Section Two of the text because this will seem more appropriate once the foundations of cryptography have been established.

The **1949 Arms Export Control Act (AECA)** was enacted to allow the government a way to control munitions manufactured in the private sector. The **International Traffic in U.S. Arms Regulations (ITAR)** determines which items are placed under these export controls. Cryptographic methods and encryption techniques have long been considered essential weapons of war. These regulations have been used for quite some time to regulate the exportation and use of cryptographic products. The ITAR falls under the jurisdiction of the Department of State. Through the **Export Administration Act (EAA)**, the Department of Commerce gained control of those items on the ITAR that are dual use (military and civilian), of which encryption and cryptography certainly are part.

During most of the four decades since that legislation passed, the U.S. government has applied extremely tight control over cryptographic methods. By way of example, the government (until quite recently) still kept the WWII Japanese and German cryptographic code machines and our code-breaking techniques classified as national secrets.

Beginning in 1992, the U.S. government began easing export controls because of significant industry pressure and lost product revenue in the private sector (especially the financial markets). Private industry was interested in utilizing encryption as part of international online transaction processing systems. The administration responded by allowing the export of cryptographic products with key sizes of less than fifty-six bits. As we shall see in Section Two of the text, by choosing relatively short key lengths, the government was able to guarantee the amount of time it would take to break the key it needed to execute a search warrant on the encrypted information. Essentially, the government wanted to guarantee they had a "way in."

While these moves were welcome by the industry, many still felt that the regulations were too restrictive. Government, in partnership with industry, then worked to establish a method that would allow for larger key sizes to be used and exported. In 1993, the Clinton administration supported the export of unlimited-sized key cryptography systems that used a **key recovery/escrow system**. Key escrow systems allow a user to create a key of any size, provided that a copy of the key is kept by a trusted third party who would surrender the key to authorities in the event a proper search warrant was served. Generally, as an extra privacy safeguard, the key is split between two trusted parties. Then, in the event of a request to surrender the key, both parties would have to agree to the validity of the search.

To promote this initiative, the government sponsored a new technology called the **clipper chip** created by the NSA (shown in Figure 3-2). The clipper chip utilizes the **skipjack encryption algorithm**. This algorithm utilizes 80-bit keys. An important feature of the clipper chip is its ability to create the **Law Enforcement Access Field (LEAF)**. The LEAF is a doubly encrypted copy of the message key. The encryption of the key is done using secure keys from two different sources that are trusted. In this case, the sources are the National Institute of Standards and Technology, and the Department of Treasury. The premise behind this method is that if a message were intercepted or obtained with a wiretap or search warrant, then the law enforcement agency conducting the investigation would obtain the keys from the two agencies mentioned to decode the LEAF. Once the LEAF were decoded, the original user-created encryption key would be revealed and the original message could be opened.

However, the skipjack algorithm and the clipper design were both withheld from public examination. As a result, this program never really gained momentum. Potential users wanted to test the strength of the cryptographic technique before they used it in a product design. Additionally, it was widely speculated that the criminal element this technology was meant to curtail would never use this technology anyway. It was also becoming increasingly obvious that the encryption technology the government was trying to protect was being made public through other foreign sources. The only real losers in this scenario were the businesses wishing to utilize strong cryptographic methods for the purpose of creating secure online business.

By 1996, even more easing of the regulations was in the works. In 1997 and 1998 unlimited key length encryption exemptions were granted to international financial institutions. This paved the way for further easing. In 1998, 56-bit encryption (or unlimited key length with key recovery) was available to all but seven countries with known terrorist affiliations.

The big step came in 1999 with the passage of the Security and Freedom Through Encryption Act. This law stipulated the following:

- The dropping of the requirement for escrow keys
- That the use of encryption is not probable cause to suspect criminal activity
- Relaxed EAA export restrictions
- Additional penalties for the use of encryption in the commission of a crime

In January 2000, the U.S. government relaxed the export control laws on cryptographic algorithms almost completely. U.S. companies can export to any end user in the United States or Canada, the European Union, Australia, Norway, the Czech Republic, Hungary, Poland, Japan, New Zealand, and Switzerland without a license.

As it stands today, according to an official U.S. Department of Commerce memo, "the Bureau of Industry and Security (BIS) is amending the Export Administration Regulations (EAR) to implement revisions to national security controls for microprocessors that were agreed upon in the February 2002 meeting of the **Wassenaar Arrangement** on Export Controls for Conventional Arms and Dual-Use Goods and Technologies (Wassenaar Arrangement)." This final rule removes license requirements for exports and reexports of general purpose microprocessors to most destinations to conform with changes in the List of Dual-Use Goods and Technologies maintained and agreed to by governments participating in the Wassenaar Arrangement. This rule does not change any of the existing restrictions on exports and re-exports of encryption items to designated terrorist supporting countries and nationals of such countries, and people designated in Part 744 of the EAR. The rule appears in the keypoint box titled, *The United States has Updated its Encryption Export Control Policy.*

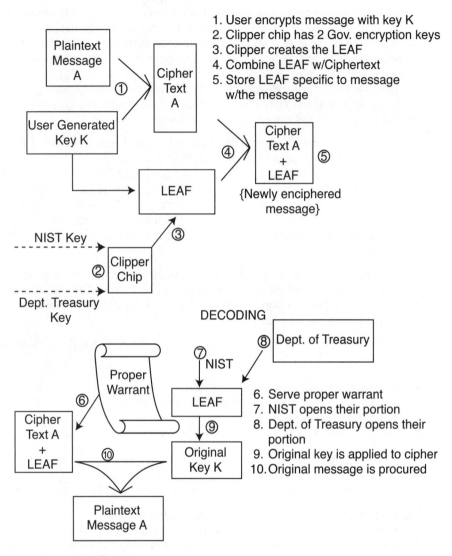

ENCODING

1. User encrypts message with key K
2. Clipper chip has 2 Gov. encryption keys
3. Clipper creates the LEAF
4. Combine LEAF w/Ciphertext
5. Store LEAF specific to message
   w/the message

Plaintext Message A

Cipher Text A

User Generated Key K

LEAF

Cipher Text A + LEAF ⑤

{Newly enciphered message}

NIST Key

Clipper Chip

Dept. Treasury Key

DECODING

Dept. of Treasury

NIST

Proper Warrant

LEAF

Cipher Text A + LEAF

Original Key K

Plaintext Message A

6. Serve proper warrant
7. NIST opens their portion
8. Dept. of Treasury opens their portion
9. Original key is applied to cipher
10. Original message is procured

Figure 3-2   Clipper.

 **The United States has Updated its Encryption Export Control Policy[1]**

The United States has updated its encryption export control policy to reflect changes made to the Wassenaar Arrangement list of dual-use items. This rule also clarifies existing provisions of the Export Administration Regulations (EAR) pertaining to encryption export controls. This policy update includes the following features:

Updated controls on "mass market" products with strong encryption features

For the first time, "mass market" encryption commodities and software with symmetric key lengths exceeding 64 bits may be exported and reexported under Export Control Classification Numbers (ECCNs) 5A992 and 5D992, following a thirty-day review by the Bureau of Industry and Security (BIS). Such "mass market" encryption products will no longer require post-export reporting or additional national security review for *de minimis* eligibility.

New review procedure for "mass market" encryption products

This rule amends the EAR by creating a new 30-day review procedure for "mass market" encryption commodities and software. The new "mass market" encryption review procedure is similar to the existing License Exception ENC review procedure for commodities and software controlled under ECCNs 5A002 and 5D002. To the European Union, Australia, the Czech Republic, Hungary, Japan, New Zealand, Norway, Poland, and Switzerland (except "code breaking" cryptanalytic products to government end users), you may immediately export your encryption products once your review request is registered with BIS and the ENC Encryption Request Coordinator. To other countries, unless you are otherwise notified by BIS, you may export your "mass market" encryption products 30 calendar days after your review request is registered, even if you have not yet received your official authorization response from BIS. Encryption products submitted for review under these "mass market" or License Exception ENC review procedures do not require independent commodity classification by BIS.

License Exception ENC eligibility for equipment controlled under ECCN 5B002

The new rule clarifies that test, inspection, and production equipment controlled under ECCN 5B002 is eligible for export and reexport to U.S. subsidiaries, government and nongovernment end users in the European Union (plus the eight additional countries) and nongovernment end users in all other countries (except in Cuba, Iran, Iraq, Libya, North Korea, Sudan, [and] Syria) under the provisions of License Exception ENC.

Certain encryption items may be exported and reexported without review or notification

This rule clarifies that, when a license is not otherwise required, no review or notification is required to export or reexport the following:

---

[1] This information is taken from the Bureau of Industry and Security website *http://www.bxa.doc.gov/encryption*.

- Encryption items (including technology and source code) to U.S. companies and their subsidiaries (except exports and reexports to subsidiaries located in designated terrorist supporting countries, and encryption technology or source code to foreign nationals of these countries) for internal company use, including the development of new products by employees, contractors and interns of U.S. companies. Exporters are referred to Section 734.2 of the EAR for applicable definitions of "export" and "reexport" that apply to encryption source code and technology. (The encryption products that are developed using these items are subject to the EAR and require review before they are sold or transferred outside the company.)
- Products that are only controlled as "Information Security" items because they incorporate parts and components with limited short-range wireless encryption capabilities (e.g., consumer products conforming to the Bluetooth, Home Radio Frequency—HomeRF or IEEE 802.11b—"WiFi" standards with operating range typically not exceeding 100 meters).
- Items with limited use of cryptography, such as for authentication, digital signature, execution of copy protected software, commercial civil cellular telephones not capable of end-to-end encryption and finance specific items specially designed and limited to banking use or money transactions.

It is important that manufacturers of products remain current regarding the import and export regulations of cryptographic algorithms (software and hardware logic). The following is meant to serve as a guide to those involved in this area.

The following chart is not all inclusive and is meant only as initial guidance for exporters. For additional information, please refer to Part 740 of the Export Administration Regulations for the complete set of license exception provisions, criteria, and restrictions that apply to encryption items.

License Exception	Types of Products	Class of End Users	Country Scope	Reporting Requirements	Restrictions
TMP - 740.9(a)(2)(i) "Temporary Exports - Tools of Trade"	Encryption products, including laptops with preloaded encryption	Exporters or employees of the exporter	Global, except Country Group E:2 countries and Sudan	No	Return in one year Must retain effective control and ownership
TMP - 740.9(a)(2)(iii) "Temporary exports - Exhibition and demonstration	Encryption products, including laptops with preloaded encryption	Exporters, employees or the exporter, or designated sales reps of the exporter	Global, except Country Group E:1[2] ("T-7")	No	Return in one year Must retain effective control and ownership No more than 120 days in one location Cannot be used for their intended purpose, except for minimum extend required for effective demonstration

BAG - 740.14	Encryption products for personal use, including laptops with preloaded encryption	U.S. citizens or permanent resident aliens	Global, except Country Group E:1[2] ("T-7")	No	Personal ownership Usual and reasonable quantities Not intended for sale Intended for a necessary and appropriate use of individuals or members of immediate family traveling with exporter
TMP - 740.9(c) "beta test software"	Beta test encryption software intended to be "mass marketed" to the general public after completion of beta testing	Certified testing consignees (see 740.9(c)(5))	For beta test encryption software: global, except Country Group E:1[2] ("T-7")	Yes—see 740/9(c)(8) for notification and reporting requirements specific to beta test encryption software	Refer to 740.9(c). There are a number of requirements and restrictions, and they apply to all beta test software (including beta test encryption software) subject to the EAR
TSU - 740.13(e)	Encryption source code that would be considered "publicly available" (e.g. "open source") and corresponding object code	All	Global, may not knowingly export to Country Group E:1[2] (:"T-7")	No	Notification or copy by time of export
ENC - 740.17(a)	Encryption items (including technology and "open cryptographic interface" items)	Government and nongovernment end users and subsidiaries	Located in Suplement 3 to Part 740 countries[3] ("EU+8"); subsidiaries not located in Country Group E:1[2] ("T-7")	Yes[4]	Requires review (immediate export upon registration of complete review request) Excludes cryptanalytic items to government end users

ENC - 740.17(b)(1)	Encryption items (includes source code, technology and "open cryptographic interface"—OCI items)	Foreign U.S. subsidiaries (includes foreign employees, contractors, and interns)	Global, except Country Group E:1[2] ("T-7")	No	No review for internal company use Developed products require review prior to reexport, resale, or transfer outside the company
TMP - 740.17(b)(2)	Encryption commodities, software and components; network infrastructure encryption products; commercial source code and general purpose toolkits	Nongovernment end users	Global, except Country Group E:1[2] ("T=7")	Yes[4,5]	Requires ENC review[6] Excludes OCI and technology items *Note: A license is required for government end users outside EU+8
ENC—"retail" products 740.13(b)(3)	Encryption commodities, software and components	Nongovernment and government end users	Global, except Country Group E:1[2] ("T=7")	Yes[4], except as described in 740.17(e)(4)	Requires ENC review6 and (to government end users outside the EU+8) specific authorization by BIS Excludes OCI items, network infrastructure products, source code, general purpose toolkits, cryptanalytic items and encryption items n.e.s. Product(s) must meet criteria in 740.17(b)(3)(ii)

Table Notes:

[1] See Supplement No. 1 to part 740 of the EAR for a complete list of country groups
[2] "T-7" = Cuba, Iran, Iraq, Libya, North Korea, Syria, and Sudan [Country Group E:1] — this includes exports and reexports (as defined in Section 734.2 of the EAR) of encryption source code and technology to nationals of these countries.
[3] "EU+8" = Austria, Australia, Belgium, the Czech Republic, Denmark, Finland, France, Germany, Greece, Hungary, Ireland, Italy, Japan, Luxembourg, Netherlands, New Zealand, Norway, Poland, Portugal, Spain, Sweden, Switzerland, and the United Kingdom [See Supplement No. 3 to Part 740]
[4] See §§740.17(e) for reporting requirements under License Exception ENC.

[5] Except foreign products developed from U.S. source code and items from or to a U.S. bank (or financial institution) for banking (or financial) operations.

[6] Exports and reexports to the EU+8 are authorized immediately upon registration of a complete review request (with BIS and the ENC Encryption Request Coordinator); 30 days after registration, exports and reexports to nongovernment endusers outside the EU+8 are authorized. Exports and reexports (of "retail" products) to government end users outside the EU+8 require specific authorization from BIS.

This information is taken from the Bureau of Industry and Security website: http://www.bxa.doc.gov/encryption.

Electronic Signatures

As we will see in later chapters, the use of cryptographic techniques to enable the process of digital signatures should play a significant role in the advancement of electronic commerce. **The Electronic Signatures in Global and National Commerce Act (ESIGN)** was formally signed into law on June 30, 2000. This law is an important adaptation of asymmetrical cryptography. The fundamental gist of the law is that it creates a framework in which electronic signatures (see Chapter 8 for a detailed description) can be accepted with the same validity as written signatures.

According to a prepared statement by the Federal Trade Commission made before the Committee on Financial Services United States House of Representatives on June 28, 2001:

> *"The Act's purpose is to facilitate the use of electronic records and signatures in interstate and foreign commerce by ensuring the validity and legal effect of contracts entered into electronically. In enacting this legislation, however, Congress was careful to preserve the underlying consumer protection laws governing consumers' rights to receive certain information in writing; thus, Congress imposed special requirements on businesses that want to use electronic records or signatures in consumer transactions. Section 101(c)(1) of ESIGN provides that information required by law to be in writing can be made available electronically to a consumer only if the consumer affirmatively consents to receive the information electronically and the business clearly and conspicuously discloses specified information to the consumer before obtaining the consumer's consent.*
>
> *Section 101(c)(1)(C)(ii) states that a consumer's consent to receive electronic records is valid only if the consumer consents electronically or confirms his or her consent electronically, in a manner that reasonably demonstrates that the consumer can access information in the electronic form that will be used to provide the information that is the subject of the consent. Section 101(c)(1)(C)(ii) overlays existing state and federal laws requiring that certain information be provided to consumers in writing. It also provides a framework for how businesses can comply electronically with the underlying statutory or regulatory requirement to provide written information to consumers—whether the information is a disclosure, a notice, or a statement of rights and obligations—within the context of a business-to-consumer transaction."*

The statement specifically goes on to address the need for protection against fraud and deception:

> *"Although measuring the consequences of omitting a provision like Section 101(c)(1)(C)(ii) is difficult, we believe that the inclusion of this provision helps prevent deception and fraud. The provision ensures that consumers who choose to enter the world of electronic transactions will have no less access to information and protection than those who engage in traditional paper*

transactions. Moreover, this provision reduces the risk that consumers will accept electronic disclosures or other records if they are not actually able to access those documents electronically. As a result, it diminishes the threat that electronic records will be used to circumvent state and federal laws that contain a writing requirement.

As enacted, ESIGN gives appropriate consideration to the threat that fraud and deception on the Internet pose to the growth and public acceptance of electronic commerce. Most laws protecting consumers against fraud and deception come into play after fraud has been committed and documented. ESIGN attempts to discourage fraud before it takes hold. ESIGN incorporates basic consumer protection principles that will help maintain the integrity and credibility of the electronic marketplace, bolster confidence among consumers that electronic records and signatures are safe and secure, and ensure that consumers continue to receive comprehensible written disclosures required by state or federal law."

CORNERSTONE CYBERCRIME LEGISLATION

The computer industry existed for decades with insufficient legislation to protect computer users from the abuse of hackers. This lack of legislation was primarily because in the early days of computer technology, cybercrime was rare because most computer operations were centrally controlled and tightly managed. Almost all communications services were of a private network nature and, as such, there was little if any intermingling of information via network multiplexing. In the early days of computing, most organizations, including the U.S. government, used single sources and vendors for procuring hardware, applications, and operating system software. As a result, the only real threat to a computer infrastructure came from well-placed trusted insiders. Security was more a matter of access control and physical security as opposed to the cryptographically-oriented information security requirements of today.

As true internetworking and vender interoperability evolved, it became easier for people to take advantage of the open platforms and operating system user-friendliness to commit crimes and cause disruption. By the mid 1980s, many of the traditional stances regarding single vendor, private networks, and low degrees of interoperability were changed to the more open approach. Organizations were able to achieve considerable savings by sharing public network facilities. Competitive advantage could more easily be gained through the use of the Internet for conducting research and sharing ideas. **Simple Mail Transfer Protocol (SMTP)** and the use of X.400 messaging interchanges created a ubiquitous Internet mail environment. At this same time, computer crime began to increase, which created a need for specific laws to protect the cyberworld and its elusive boundaries.

The Computer Fraud and Abuse Act of 1986 (18 USC 1030)—amended by the National Information Infrastructure Protection Act of 1996, was the most significant piece of legislation to ever be passed with respect to cyberlaw enforcement. This piece of legislation forms the cornerstone of the law enforcement process. It is the set of laws that both defines our electronic space and provides the mechanisms for prosecuting those that try to trample it. This law addresses protecting the confidentiality, integrity, and availability of the information and the information system. It is a multifaceted law that includes many parts that attempt to summarize cybercrime.

Subsection 1030(a)(1) states that a person who accesses a computer without authorization or exceeds authorized access for the purpose of obtaining or trying to obtain classified information "with the intent or reason to believe that such information so obtained is to be used to the injury of the United States, or to the advantage of any foreign nation" can be subject to fine and or imprisonment.

Former Federal Court Systems Administrator Sentenced for Hacking into Government Computer System

Anchorage, Alaska—Anchorage resident Scott Dennis, former computer system administrator for the U.S. District Court in Alaska, was sentenced January 19, 2001, for interfering with a government-owned communications system.

Dennis was sentenced to six months incarceration to be served by three months in jail and three months home confinement, followed by one year of supervised release. Dennis must also allow authorities to monitor his computer activity, and [he must] perform 240 hours of community service.

Dennis was charged with launching three denial-of-service attacks against the U.S. District Court for the Eastern District of New York. The prosecution contended Dennis was upset at plans to allow more users into a restricted e-mail list server. Dennis overwhelmed the Eastern District's server with e-mail messages to prove it was vulnerable to outside attacks. He repeated this [attack] twice because he thought his hacking went unnoticed.

Dennis has already paid $5,300 in restitution to the New York Federal Court System, GCI, and Internet Alaska. This case was investigated by the FBI and security officers at GCI and Internet Alaska.

Subsection 1030(a)(2) protects the confidentiality of computerized credit records and computerized information relating to customer relationships with financial institutions. This is important in that it is one of the first instances of protecting privacy in the commercial market. The GLB extends this law, as was previously described.

Section 1030 was revised to isolate many instances of information by type so that the law could be easily modified as the technology changes or different types of information emerge. In all instances of Section 1030, the law tries to differentiate between the mere possession of a particular type of information and the use of illegal trespass onto a particular computer to obtain the information.

We mentioned earlier that in the case of the *United States vs. Brown* 925 F.2d1301, 1308 (10th Circuit 1991), the court held that intangible intellectual property, such as a computer program, had no discernable value. One of the primary tenants of 1030 is to change the focus of the law from the information itself to "obtaining information." This means that any action, even reading information after a trespass, is a violation of the law regardless of the information content. Also, the law now stipulates that a crime becomes a felony if the trespass was committed for purposes of commercial advantage or private financial gain, or if the value of the information exceeds $5,000. This stipulation makes it a more serious crime if the trespass were committed for financial gain rather than just out of curiosity. This is a valid distinction that reflects the wide range of possible crimes involving information tampering. It separates simple trespass from fraud.

In 1030 (a)(5), the law addresses the integrity of the information system. It distinguishes between intentional damage (assessing maximum felony penalties), reckless damage (which, for a trespasser, is a felony but carries no penalty for an authorized user), and negligent damage (which for a trespasser is a misdemeanor and for an authorized user presents no penalty).

Subsection 7 covers interstate or international threats against information systems (e.g., an extortion demand based on the hacker's ability to reveal data or crash a system). The threat need not be placed via the computer network (it could come via a phone call, e-mail, or regular mail). Rather, it must be clearly directed at somehow destabilizing the information system.

In 2001, the **USA PATRIOT Act** further modified the National Infrastructure Information Protection Act by increasing penalties and giving law enforcement officials a broader range of options and greater latitude in tracking and prosecuting suspected terrorists.

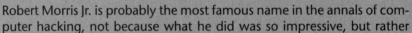

The First True Test of 18 USC 1030

Robert Morris Jr. is probably the most famous name in the annals of computer hacking, not because what he did was so impressive, but rather because he became the first person ever convicted under what at the time was the newest law in cybercrime fighting, 18 USC 1030. You will remember from Chapter 2 that Morris, the son of an Internet design engineer at Bell Labs, was a student at Cornell University who released what he believed was a slow-replicating worm onto the Net on November 2, 1988. The worm sought out vulnerable machines, infected them, searched out new targets, and spread. He originally sent the worm to MIT, the University of California Berkeley, and th e Rand Corporation. The worm spread rapidly, and thousands of machines were infected in a matter of hours. When system operators were able to gain access to their machines, they found that attempting to kill the rogue process caused the virus to spread faster. This was caused by a programming error that Morris had made. He claims that it was never his intention to cause such widespread chaos.

Sometime the next day, Morris realized what had happened; and, with the help of a friend at Harvard, sent an anonymous e-mail detailing how to stop the virus. Robert Morris Jr. was convicted under Title 18 USC 1030 and was sentenced to three years of probation, community service, and a substantial fine.

What makes this case important is that until a law has been tested in court, no one is really sure how it will be interpreted. In this particular case, the conviction was made—and eventually upheld on appeal. This case had two important outcomes. First, it established the new law as being viable. Second, it forever changed the attitudes of the media and the legislation with respect to cyberattacks.

For a more detailed review of Title 18 Reform, visit the Department of Justice website at *http://www.usdoj.gov/criminal/cybercrime/1030_anal.html*.

In addition to the aforementioned Title 18 subsections, Chapter 47, Section 1029 details the law with respect to fraud and related activities in connection with access devices, and Chapter 47, Section 1030 details fraud in connection with computers. These laws are important because they have become the focus of identity theft prosecutions.

As you can see, the laws are evolving. As the various legislative bodies gain more knowledge and insight into this arena, these laws will improve and be easier to enforce. The legislature is currently working on

Protecting Your Electronic Identity

Identity theft is a crime that is increasing in popularity among criminals. Identity theft is defined as the theft of identity information: name, address, social security number, student identification, date of birth, mother's maiden name, medical records, bank account numbers, credit or phone card number, etc.

The Internet was never designed to be secure. Contrary to popular belief, the Internet is based on relatively old technology and was originally conceived not as a vehicle for global commerce, but rather as a modern-day library. Only since the early 1990s has it been so easily accessible by individuals and corporations. This evolution of a ubiquitous communications infrastructure, combined with the increasing availability of high-tech financial and automated service applications, and electronic credit has given rise to a propensity toward identity theft. According to a 2001 Department of Justice document, "Identity Theft: The Crime of the New Millennium," by Sean Hoar: "It is estimated that identity theft has become the fastest-growing financial crime in America and perhaps the fastest-growing crime of any kind in our society."

Usually, victims of identity theft do not know the crime has even occurred for some time. People receive bills for items and services they never purchased (a common choice is phone services), suddenly have bad credit reports, or have cosigned for loans they know nothing about. According to the same report, "The Secret Service stated that actual losses to individuals and financial institutions which the Secret Service had tracked involving identity fraud totaled $442 million in fiscal year 1995, $450 million in fiscal year 1996, and $745 million in 1997... TransUnion Corporation, one of the three major national credit bureaus, stated that two-thirds of its consumer inquiries to its fraud victims department involved identity fraud." According to a recent Federal Trade Commission report, the number of reported cases of identity theft doubled between the years 2001 and 2002. This is a fast-growing problem of serious concern.

The methods of the identity fraud criminal range from simply examining the contents of someone's garbage (referred to as "dumpster diving") to sophisticated electronic eavesdropping and scanning. Social engineering techniques can be used to simply ask for and receive personal information. This is accomplished by people posing as representatives of a bank or a credit card company who are renewing or updating accounts. Some cybercriminals obtain access to systems and sift through your personal files looking for correspondence containing social security numbers, account numbers, and the like. The laws pertaining to this area are relatively new and somewhat difficult for the layperson to understand. In Hoar's report, he provides an excellent summation of the legislation: "There are a number of federal laws applicable to identity theft, some of which may be used for prosecution of identity theft offenses, and some of which exist to assist victims in repairing their credit history. The primary identity theft statute is 18 U.S.C. §1028(a)(7) and was enacted on October 30, 1998, as part of the Identity Theft and Assumption Deterrence Act (Identity Theft Act)."

He continues by quoting the statute:

"Section 1028(a)(7) provides that it is unlawful for anyone who: knowingly transfers or uses, without lawful authority, a means of identification of another person with the intent to commit, or to aid or abet, any unlawful activity that constitutes a violation of Federal law, or that constitutes a felony under

*any applicable State or local law... Section 1028(d)(3) defines 'means of identification' as used in §
1028(a)(7), to include 'any name or number that may be used, alone or in conjunction with any other
information, to identify a specific individual.' It covers several specific examples, such as name, social security number, date of birth, government-issued driver's license and other numbers; unique biometric data,
such as fingerprints, voice print, retina or iris image, or other physical representation; unique electronic
identification number; and telecommunication identifying information or access device... Section
1028(d)(1) modifies the definition of 'document-making implement' to include computers and software
specifically configured or primarily used for making identity documents. The Identity Theft Act is intended
to cover a variety of individual identification information that may be developed in the future and utilized
to commit identity theft crimes.*

*Identity theft is often committed to facilitate other crimes, although it is frequently the primary goal of the
offender. Schemes to commit identity theft may involve a number of other statutes including identification
fraud (18 U.S.C. §1028(a)(1) - (6)), credit card fraud (18 U.S.C. §1029), computer fraud (18 U.S.C.§
1030), mail fraud (18 U.S.C. §1341), wire fraud (18 U.S.C. §1343), financial institution fraud (18 U.S.C.
§1344), mail theft (18 U.S.C. §1708), and immigration document fraud (18 U.S.C. §1546). For example,
computer fraud may be facilitated by the theft of identity information when stolen identity is used to fraudulently obtain credit on the Internet. Computer fraud may also be the primary vehicle to obtain identity
information when the offender obtains unauthorized access to another computer or Web site to obtain
such information. These acts might result in the offender being charged with both identity theft under 18
U.S.C. §1028(a)(7) and computer fraud under 18 U.S.C. §1030(a)(4)."*

So how can you prevent identity fraud? The following is a brief list of precautions that people
and corporations should take to protect their electronic identity (these common practices will
discourage hackers from trying to perpetrate an identity theft crime on you):

- Guard your social security number. You should never e-mail your social security number and if you
  do, you should use encryption. A social security number opens many doors for identity thieves.
- Be careful about sharing identity information. When using credit card information over the Net, consider using products specifically designed by the credit card company to protect your privacy and
  number confidentiality.
- Do not carry unnecessary identity information when in public. If you lose your wallet, thieves will use
  this information online. This information includes social security numbers (which are best memorized), birth certificates, passports, even old credit card receipts. It has been documented that this
  may be the primary starting point of thieves who commit identity theft.
- Sign up for online alerts from credit card companies and credit reporting agencies so you know as
  soon as possible when inappropriate or suspicious activity begins.
- Consider adding identity theft insurance as part of your homeowners policy. This is a method of risk
  transfer.
- Properly secure your personal computer. Implement the latest software updates and be careful to not
  build files that contain important information (e.g., a family financial spreadsheet with account numbers and other personal information) and that remain on the hard drive.
- Install and use a personal firewall if connecting to the Internet.
- If you discard a computer, make sure to wipe the disk clean. Deleting files destroys only the pointers
  to the data but does not reclaim the space. The original data actually stays on the system until the
  disk is defragmented. There are many products available for cleaning a disk.

- Keep medical records secure. This material can be used to damage or threaten your reputation and privacy.
- Properly prepare your garbage. Be careful what is on the statements and mail that you discard. An old bank statement can be ripe with important information. Credit card application forms, instant credit offers, and the like are starting points for thieves. On the job, be careful what materials are left on the desk and in the garbage can. Use a shredder for all your sensitive waste.
- Clean cookies off your personal computer regularly. This will prevent an online attack that is focused on stealing passwords.
- Use virus protection software to protect against the insertion of software on your system, which may enable a hacker to access your personal files through a backdoor.
- Choose strong passwords for online accounts and change them regularly.
- Use encryption, secure Internet connections, and digital signatures to electronically protect your identity, authority, and information.

These common practices will discourage hackers from trying to perpetrate an identity theft crime on you.

all of the correct focus areas, but it needs to produce laws that have a more directed technology focus. The legislature also needs to better bridge the gap between a 227-year-old set of guiding principles and a technological capability our forefathers could never have ever imagined. The laws have to enable law enforcement officials to conduct their investigations and enforcement processes in cybertime. The laws also have to provide prosecutors with clear prosecutorial guidelines. The laws need to set reasonable limits on the export of advanced technology and the use of sophisticated cryptographic methods. But most important, the legislation must do all of this while protecting the rights of individuals to privacy and reasonable judgment. While the system currently in place is by no means perfect, it is usable. So we should take advantage of the available resources and remember what Confucius once said: "Better a diamond with a flaw than a pebble without."

SUMMARY

Information security legislation is being developed at a brisk pace. Prosecuting attorneys are faced with both technological and legal challenges. Every new case brings new interpretations of the law. Investigators face similar issues that are complicated by the requirement that computer forensic scientists complete a large part of their time-consuming work in the field and at the scene. Computer forensic scientists must be careful not to overstep the boundaries set forth in the warrant when sifting through a plethora of data. The current set of evolving laws are largely untested and may lack the technical detail required for judges to be precise in their interpretations.

One of the oldest prosecutorial tests, known as *mens rea*, still applies. This concept is still appropriate and is obvious in the revisions to Title 18 USC 1030. Under this cornerstone, legislation penalties vary based on the intent of the perpetrator, the type and amount of damage done, and the authorization level of the attacker.

Privacy is one of our most valued rights and is vigorously protected in the Constitution and Bill of Rights. Recent legislation does adequately protect individuals from any invasion of privacy by the government. The USA PATRIOT Act of 2001 does provide more leeway for investigators as they investigate people that are believed to have terrorist affiliations. In general, our privacy is not as well protected electronically in the private sector. It is commonplace for employees to be under electronic surveillance at work or to have information infiltrated while it may be in transit over the Net. For this reason, it is important that individuals protect their information with significant due diligence, vis-à-vis cryptography.

Some elements of industry, namely financial institutions and the health care industry, are regulated by relatively new laws, including GLB and HIPAA respectively. These laws represent a first attempt by government to guide specific industries in the protection of consumers' electronic privacy.

Students were presented a cybercrime fighter model, which includes three phases: prevention, investigation, and prosecution, as put forth by the FBI. The use of sophisticated tools, such as intrusion-detection systems, file regeneration tools, and network forensics analysis tools support the investigative process. IDSs are critical components that support law enforcement and crisis-management teams. These systems come in several varieties and have three primary components: agents, the director, and the notification agent. It is important that IDS and the logging system be active as a normal part of doing business. Failure to do so may result in the evidence collected being ruled hearsay and becoming inadmissible.

Investigators also utilize the honeypot concept to attempt to understand hacker methods and learn hacker identities. Honeypots are legal and are not a form of entrapment.

In this section we reviewed the following laws:

- Electronic Communications and Privacy Act (ECPA)
- Economic Espionage Act of 1996
- Freedom of Information Act
- National Health Insurance Portability and Accountability Act of 1996 (HIPAA)
- 1949 Arms Export Control Act (AECA)
- Export Administration Act (EAA)
- Wassenaar Arrangement
- The Electronic Signatures in Global and National Commerce Act
- Computer Fraud and Abuse Act of 1986 18 USC 1030—amended by the National Information Infrastructure Protection Act of 1996

While there are more laws being developed, including laws that are indirectly related to the study of information security, those listed above were chosen to represent the current state of legislation. Readers should pay particular attention to the history of cryptographic legislation and the Title 18 laws.

Title 18 was first tested in 1988 in the case of the *United States vs. Robert Morris Jr.* This case provided prosecutors with the precedent that real cases could be brought under this section of the legal code. Morris's conviction was upheld on appeal.

In conclusion, students should begin to understand the relationships between technology and the law. It is important that students understand the role of the computer forensic scientist and how the legislation defines the parameters of the tools that they use and the limits of their ability to discover. This is a significant and emerging field that requires all of the skills outlined in this text and more.

STUDY QUESTIONS

1 What piece of legislation allows computer records documenting criminal activity to be used in court? (choose one)

  a. Federal Rules of Evidence 803(6)

  b. Federal Computer Documents Rule 703(a)

  c. Digital Signature Bill

  d. National Infrastructure Protection Act

2 **True___ False___** A computer-generated log created by law enforcement for the sole purpose of being used as evidence is fully admissible as evidence.

3 What improves the worth of evidence? (choose one)

  a. A good prosecutor

  b. The hard drive of the system in question

  c. A printout of the information

  d. An expert witness

4 How should you **not** report computer crime? (choose one)

  a. Telephone

  b. E-mail

  c. Tell management in person

  d. Tell the IT department in person

5 What does the Economic Espionage Act of 1996 protect? (choose one)

  a. Employee rights when accused of a crime

  b. Product royalties

  c. Business computer systems

  d. Trade secrets

6 **True___ False___** You should have no expectation of privacy on your e-mail account from your ISP.

7 What has become a major Web problem with respect to security? (choose one)

  a. Mapping attacks

  b. Online surveys

  c. User ignorance

  d. Scripting errors

8 These are set up by organizations to encourage certain behaviors and prohibit others. (choose one)

   a. Privacy statements

   b. Preemployment agreements

   c. Usage policies

   d. Business contracts

9 **True___ False___** It is a crime to write malicious software.

10 What type of insurance should professional computer consultants carry? (choose one)

   a. Negligence

   b. Professional liability

   c. Programmer's warranty

   d. Errors and omissions

11 Which is not a problem with the misuse of information? (choose one)

   a. Duplication of information

   b. Untimely release of secret information

   c. Illegal sale of information

   d. Misrepresentation of information

12 What is most often overlooked when planning for information security? (choose one)

   a. Firewalls

   b. Education

   c. Virus scans

   d. Electronic surveillance

13 What helps focus a security plan? (choose one)

   a. A security budget

   b. Intrusion statistics analysis

   c. Threat analysis

   d. Government input

14 What one thing will a computer crime scene investigator will do (if possible)? (choose one)

   a. Keep all computers at the scene running

   b. Disconnect all computers from the network

   c. Remove all computers from the scene as soon as possible

   d. Send an e-mail from all computers that are running

15 True___ False___   The 1949 Arms Export Control Act (AECA) was put in place to allow the government a way to control munitions manufactured in the private sector.

16 Which of the following is not a reason for the difficulties in prosecutions of computer-related crimes? (choose one)

  a. The area of litigation is extremely technical and difficult to understand.

  b. Most crimes do not fall under any of the current laws.

  c. The laws themselves are relatively new and untested.

  d. The technology is dynamic and the tactics of the perpetrators are constantly changing.

17 The Digital Telephony Act of 1994 states that monitoring electronic transmissions is the same as _____ (choose one).

  a. Hacking

  b. Slander

  c. Wiretapping

  d. Stealing

18 The information that you supply _____ to websites is usually the most damaging. (choose one)

  a. Unknowingly

  b. Under duress

  c. During peak hours

  d. Voluntarily

19 What is authentication? (choose one)

  a. The act of binding an entity to a representation of identity

  b. The act of ensuring that information is being sent securely

  c. The act of ensuring that the receiver of information actually received it

  d. The act of binding a computer system to a network

20 When can negligence be punishable as a crime? (choose one)

  a. In all cases

  b. Never

  c. If it results in loss or harm to a person

  d. f it results in a breach of contract

21 What is not considered the misuse of information? (choose one)

  a. The deletion of information from a system

  b. The untimely release of secret information

  c. The illegal sale of information to rival companies

  d. The misrepresentation of information

22 True___ False___   It is important that a security plan be built from the outside in.

23 What type of organization is likely to have an open security stance? (choose one)

a. A university

b. A pharmaceutical firm

c. A research and development facility

d. A hospital patient information center

CASE STUDY

Back at Cureme Hospital you are now preparing for your meeting with Mr. Tobius Everything, the head of business administration, and his legal council, Frank N. Candid from the law firm of Dowee, Cheetum, and Howe. The purpose of this meeting is to brief the hospital council on your assessment of the hospital's potential to meet HIPAA. [NOTE: For the purpose of this exercise, assume that the hospital has no protections on information and is open to many attacks. This is not uncommon in the industry.]

Research and comment

■ What are the legal requirements for HIPAA?
■ What are the penalties if those requirements are not met?
■ Can the requirements be tested? How?
■ Can you express what the hospital position might be in terms of CAIN?
■ Why is it a good idea for the hospital to separate the information requirements from the information system requirements?
■ Write a brief on the requirements of Cureme Hospital in terms of the information gathered.

A Model for Information Security Planning

*A good plan violently executed now is better than a perfect plan
executed next week.*
—General George S. Patton, Jr.

By failing to prepare, you are preparing to fail.
—Benjamin Franklin

U.S. Secretary of Defense Donald Rumsfeld, in a memo ordering military sites to clean up the amount of unclassified information left available, wrote "An Al Qaeda training manual recovered in Afghanistan states, 'Using public sources openly and without resorting to illegal means, it is possible to gather at least eighty percent of information about the enemy.' One must conclude our enemies access DoD websites on a regular basis."

This is a shocking statement regarding the availability of unprotected information of the most highly sensitive nature. It also stresses the need for comprehensive **information security planning** and rigorous implementation of the same.

Now that we have looked at the composition of information, its properties, imminent threats and risks to it, quantification methods for defining an organization's information risk profile, the legislation that protects information, and the tools available to monitor and safeguard it, we are ready to develop comprehensive plans and policies that will lead to the implementation of a working security system.

In this chapter, we will introduce the concepts of

- A defensive, in-depth model of security
- Security plan components
- Policy creation
- Enforceability and understandability
- Industry standard policy development

This chapter should represent more than how to construct documents and create a workable plan; it should be about conveying an important message to the people who touch the information and information system. An important element of any security initiative is to realize that, for it to work, the people who use, operate, maintain, and manage the information and information system are perhaps the weakest link in the security chain. You can buy all the right products, write a great security plan, and have a policy for every imaginable contingency. However, if the people who are in contact with the information system do not support said policies, then you will have achieved little.

This chapter should also represent the need to establish a sense of urgency and constant vigilance regarding information security. Each person in the organization needs to feel empowered to do the right thing by being involved with security.

To successfully complete this chapter, students should pay particular attention to the following:

- Understanding the information security model concepts so that they can be effectively represented in the security plan
- Understanding the various industry standard formats that you will encounter in the industry
- Crafting a working information security plan by choosing the correct components, linking it to the vulnerability and risk assessment, and presenting it in the proper format
- Having students successfully apply the principles of least privilege, defense in depth, choke points, weakest link, fail-safe stance, universal participation, and simplicity of design to the security planning process
- Presenting a generic policy creation process, which can be adapted for use in specific industries and organizations
- Stressing the importance of educational and operational effort

The following key elements will contribute to each student's success:

- For students to have a firm grasp of the risk evaluation process and the theory of information presented in the first two chapters prior to undertaking this role
- For students to pay particular attention to learning the layers of the information security model and the concept of defense in depth
- Developing strong organizational skills to complement the skills acquired
- Realizing that developing this type of work in a large organizational environment is difficult and that educating staff and directing a large plan rollout is even more difficult

AN INFORMATION SECURITY MODEL

In Chapter 1, we presented a high-level overview of the information security model, as seen in Figure 4-1, which we will be utilizing in this text. During that discussion, students learned that the inner three layers will be stressed in this text, not because the other layers are not important, but because the outer layers work best when the layers closest to the information are implemented. The information security model that is presented in this text incorporates many ancillary skills that are beyond the scope of this text. Those skills are operating systems design and implementation, network design and configuration, Web development skills, and strong management skills. To become a leader in the information security field, it is important that you master those skills. Because this is a text focused on information security as opposed to cybersecurity, this approach is appropriate. However, for students to gain a fuller appreciation of the field, this chapter will cover each aspect of the planning process equally. Section Three of the text, while still maintaining a cryptographic focus, will extend this focus into the outer layers by discussing the application of cryptography to the information system.

A certain duality exists in our information security model. The model was designed from the inside out but tested from the outside in. By inside out, we mean that information is at the core of the model and

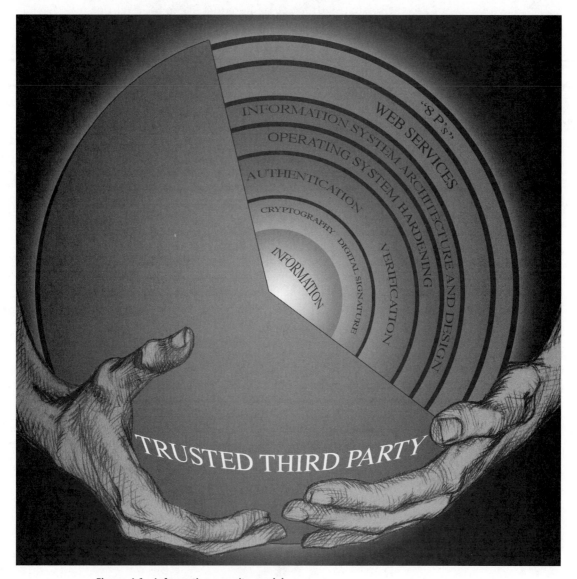

Figure 4-1 Information security model.

the most reliable protection elements of the plan are placed closest to it. As the model expands, the layers become more prone to successful penetration by the attacker. Essentially, this means that our security planning can be precise and highly reliable at the core, and it requires more planning and policy creation toward the outer edge.

KEY POINT

Having a multilayered model that is more difficult to penetrate as you move through the layers is advantageous. For example, it slows down a would-be attacker, it discourages and frustrates them, it gives us a better chance to identify the attacker, and it provides the crisis-management team with time to react.

Penetration by attackers occurs from the outside in. Attackers need to know certain information about the system before working their way through the layers of security to access the information. This is a concept known as **defense in depth**.

You may be wondering why an attacker would expend energy on the outer layers if they are more vulnerable. The answer is that the most successful information security plan is the one that discourages hackers before they ever get close enough to the information to do any real damage.

The benefits of this model are that it:

- Vigorously protects information
- Will slow down perpetrators as they attempt any attack
- Controls information access at multiple levels, making authorization and verification difficult for those without proper access credentials
- Should discourage would-be attackers by creating a sufficient number of hurdles for them
- Should assist in the identification of the hacker
- Can generally be implemented in a cost-effective fashion (cryptography is an inexpensive safeguard)
- Will foster participation and urgency on the part of users, staff, and management

INFORMATION AT THE CORE

As we stressed in Chapter 1, information will reside at the core of the model. This concept is logical because information is what we are trying to protect. Some would argue that the information system should be placed at the core. This would not be as effective based on the following four reasons:

- The information system is much too vast and cannot be narrowed sufficiently to take a single set of security actions that can have a one-to-one relationship with it. Information, however, is ideally suited to protection because cryptographic methods can be applied completely to each piece of information. Therefore, protecting information is manageable.
- Information has the mathematical properties that support the cryptographic countermeasures explicitly where the information system does not.

- The information system is better suited for adaptation to the outer layers of the model because the model and the information system have depth. Information is without such depth and, therefore, is more appropriately suited as a termination point.
- Because information can be replicated in a cost-effective manner and the information system cannot, information is best suited for backup and recovery processes (the ultimate defense).

As we demonstrated in Chapter 1 information has many interesting properties that make it easy to disguise, protect, authenticate, and test. These factors allow us to effectively manage information. Information also has the interesting quality of changing state and still retaining all of its semantic value. This might be information's single-most-important quality.

We can think of information at the bit, byte, field, record, or file level. Although most modern-day cryptography algorithms work at the bit level, the cryptographic applications normally work at the field, record, and most commonly file levels.

Even though we studied information in some detail in Chapter 1, and in fact whole areas of study are dedicated to it, information science is not a familiar subject to most people. Most people do not realize the semantic value of information to an organization and the need to protect it. Aligning information with value (the cost to the organization of a successful attack) will help users understand what is expected of them and the importance of the security plan and policies.

CRYPTOGRAPHIC METHODS LAYER

The second layer of the model is actually the most important from a security countermeasure standpoint. As we shall see in the next section, cryptography represents a formidable barrier that coats and protects information. Cryptography uses the information properties of changing state and retaining semantic value, and the property that all information can be manipulated mathematically to its advantage.

Cryptographic methods bind themselves with the information, providing a protective coating that stays with the information wherever it goes. Cryptography combines several important functions into one layer that enable a significant countermeasure:

- Cryptography disguises information so that even if the information were wrongly obtained, the attacker would not be able to read or use the information.
- Cryptographic methods are extremely complex and require significant time and cost to break. Information is considered protected only if either the time to break the cipher is longer than the useful life of the information, or if the cost to crack the cipher is greater than the worth of the information. These concepts are covered in detail in the next section.
- This layer of the model provides an elegant linkage to the authentication and verification layer above it. This is important because the interconnectedness of the innermost layers make them operate seamlessly, which makes them less prone to successful penetration.
- Cryptography methods are many and varied. Attackers not only have to devise a strategy for breaking through the coating, but they also have to identify which type of coating they are attacking.

Cryptographic methods are continually improving and changing. By isolating these methods within a single layer, the information security professional creates a situation where the substitution of one method for another improved method creates less impact to the organization.

KEY POINT

Cryptographic methods offer the most appropriate countermeasure to safeguard information. Encryption disguises information, digital signatures authenticate information, and checksums/hashes provide integrity for information.

In general, cryptography has four basic elements: **plain text** (the user-generated message devoid of any encryption), **ciphertext** (the disguised plain text produced as a result of encryption), **cryptographic algorithm** (the method used to encrypt the plain text), and **encryption key** (the secret shared between trusted parties for encryption and decryption application).

Cryptographic methods come in families. Within these families are a variety of algorithms that conform to the family method. Depending on a number of factors, information security managers may choose between members of the same family. The selections are generally based on the **cryptographic strength** of the algorithm and key, key length, symmetry required, speed of the algorithm, time value of the information, type of information, and cost value of the information. Some of the families that are available and studied later in the text are Data Encryption Standard (DES), triple DES (and other DES variants that use longer keys), RSA algorithms (RCx where x = 2, 4, or 5), Blowfish, TEA, IDEA, and Diffie-Hellman algorithms. Additionally, other cryptographic applications are S/Mime, PGP, SSL, SET, SSH, IPsec, and digital payment systems. (Each of these is addressed in Section Three.)

For the most part, users are largely unaware of the complexity of cryptography. This unawareness is because cryptography occurs behind the scenes and the cryptographic user interfaces (abstractions) are fashioned after the familiar. An example of this is the Microsoft Outlook and Outlook Express mail encryption and digital signature mechanisms.

As you can see in the icons shown in Appendix A, Lab 8: Using Asymmetrical Cryptography, the encryption and signature buttons are both obvious and easy to use. These abstractions are not at all intimidating, but they do enable a powerful set of cryptographic countermeasures.

The cryptographic methods layer of our model is analogous to a vault for each individual piece of information. As you will learn, cryptographic methods are extended into various applications and will show up throughout our model again and again. For now, however, we are considering cryptographic methods only as they apply to our compartmentalized information.

AUTHENTICATION AND VERIFICATION LAYER

As was previously mentioned, the verification and authentication layer of the model is closely related to the cryptographic methods layer. By capitalizing on the basic cryptographic mathematics and symmetries, we can create complex verification and authentication methods. These are both unique and difficult to circumvent. This layer has two distinct parts: 1) the inner authentication and verification piece that pertains to the information exclusively (e.g., digital signatures, code signing, etc.) and 2) the outer half, which provides an authentication and verification strategy for the information system (e.g. passwords, file management system access controls, VPN, etc.)

Authentication is the process of determining if the information presented is real (what the sender intended you to receive) or a fake (an altered, corrupt, or fabricated version.) Authentication can also be used at both the user and operator levels to identify imposters. Authentication schemes tie into both the cryptographic methods layer through the use of **hashing algorithms**, encryption, and **digital certificates**, as well as to the OS hardening and information systems design layers through the use of **X.509 v3 certificates**, passwords, pins, secret keys, and biometrics.

Authentication techniques usually take advantage of any of the following four factors to authenticate access to information, applications, networks, and systems:

- **Possession factor**—something you have that grants you access to information (e.g., a smart card, token, etc.)
- **Biometric factor**—something you are that identifies you uniquely (e.g., fingerprint, face print, DNA, etc.)
- **Knowledge factor**—something you know that is a secret (e.g., a password, username, or other shared secret)
- **Integrity factor**—something that allows the authentication routines to authenticate your actions after you are admitted access (i.e., **Message Authentication Codes (MACs)**)

KEY POINT

Authentication techniques can be used either directly with information or as part of the information system. With multilevel authentication, we can significantly decrease the chances of being successfully penetrated.

Verification is the one-to-one process of matching the user by name against an **authentication template**, maintained by a **trusted third party**, who tests the claim of identity (against previously confirmed authentication factors) and provides the authentication status. In section two, we will examine the **public key infrastructure (PKI)**, which makes provisions for verification of identity by a trusted third party via the application of X.509 v3 certificates.

By combining the cryptographic methods layer with the authentication and verification layer, both access control and decipherability of information are addressed. In most cases, given an appropriate set of certificate and encryption policies, the organization can be highly secured.

OS HARDENING LAYER

Operating systems are the basic **abstraction** that makes computer hardware useful. In the early days of computing, hardware systems were not easy to use because they had cumbersome interfaces, which required users to have intimate knowledge of the mechanics of the underlying infrastructure and circuit logic. Today, modern operating systems enable users with almost no computer savvy to run advanced applications in a variety of areas (e.g., word processing, automated spreadsheets, databases, entertainment applications, sophisticated drafting and engineering packages, etc.). By providing a significant abstraction between the complex underpinnings of the hardware and the intuitiveness of the **Graphical User Interface (GUI)**, this process is possible.

Abstraction means to hide detail. Hiding the detail requires the development of complex software that interprets the wishes of the users and converts those wishes to a complex set of base-level actions. Take, for example, the process of attaching to a remote file share. Today the user merely identifies the correct drive icon and clicks on it to initiate the action. That is the abstraction. Underneath the abstraction, the operating system interprets the request, and by using the **Network Extended Basic Input and Output System (NETBIOS)**, relays the request to the network sublayers. This sophisticated network interface converts the action into a series of bidirectional message exchanges between your client machine and the target server host. Upon completion of these protocol exchanges, the network sublayers return the requested output to the operating system that in turn presents it to you. You never see this series of intricate protocol exchanges, and based on the speed of the underlying hardware it seems almost instantaneous. This is where the danger lies. Hackers can be probing the operating system underpinnings without your ever noticing. The hacker can use the same logic as you to steal, corrupt, or divulge information that you have archived on remote servers.

Because hardware can execute software instructions so quickly, we may not notice that an attack ever took place. Additionally, the required complexity of the operating system often leads to inadvertent OS programming errors (e.g., special conditions that have been overlooked, or code that was improperly tested, or code that runs unnecessary services).

Layers within the OS can often conflict. For example, you may create an access control structure at the Windows level, thinking you have restricted access to a file (i.e., hiding the file from the user.) However, moments later an attacker might enter the system through the DOS layer where the files are completely visible to the hacker. Your method in this case has been circumvented.

Operating System Hardening (OS Hardening) is the process of closing programming holes, restricting access, and closing down unnecessary services. It involves the analysis of processes running on your system, monitoring performance characteristics of the system, and studying user patterns. By closing these holes, we can significantly limit the amount of entry points for the attacker to access the warehouses where data are stored. As can be seen by the overwhelming media attention that successful attacks can garner, it is obvious that there are a significant number of holes in major operating system production software, which can be exploited.

One important note is that OS hardening is the portion of operating system stabilization that you have control over. The operating system manufacturers really hold the keys to closing the majority system anomalies. They must perform due diligence in rigorously testing their software and distributing fixes to operating systems before the attackers find them. On your part, it is essential that you place all of the prescribed patches on your system that are suggested by the manufacturer. This relatively simple fix is probably the most important function you can perform to secure the information system.

Incorporating patches is important even if the manufacturer's patch is not documented as relating to security. Manufacturers often do not advertise that a patch is available to fix a security hole prior to a complete distribution of the patch to all affected users. If manufacturers did this, it would be like advertising that there is a problem, which would create opportunities for hackers to do damage.

KEY POINT

Incorporating vendor-recommended operating system patches is perhaps the most important function you can perform to increase the security of an operating system.

A significant number of scripts and tools are available for a variety of systems that can be useful in performing OS hardening processes.

These topics are dealt with in more detail in Section Three of the text. OS hardening involves a series of tasks that must be constantly performed to sufficiently lock down a system. At this layer, we can never guarantee that security will be airtight (short of locking the system in the closet with no network interface or foreign software ever being placed on it). This is the reason that the inner three layers are so important. It is likely that a breach will occur at this layer (especially because a good portion of the security countermeasures are outside of your control), so it is essential to protect the information in a completely independent way.

INFORMATION SYSTEM ARCHITECTURE AND DESIGN LAYER

The information system is the combination of systems, networks, ubiquitous service applications (e.g., e-mail, FTP, Web servers, proxy servers, directory services, etc.), and underlying telecommunication services. The way in which the underlying architecture is designed and implemented has a significant bearing on the overall information system's security.

In considering security with respect to information system architecture and design, we must remember that at this level we are generally operating in an open environment and that providing an airtight security seal is probably an unrealistic expectation. At this level, the information security specialist should be concerned with

- The creation of **choke points**. Choke points are those areas in a network where traffic must converge on a single, well-known gateway. These traffic funnels should be created so that screening of identity, content checking, and malicious signatures (virus, worm, or network-based attack) screening can be preformed. Choke points can be easily developed, as we shall see, through the use of routers.
- The screening of information for malicious content. Viruses and worms have long been the nemesis of information security professionals. Viruses and worms are software programs that can disrupt the operation of the information system or potentially destroy information itself. Virus scanners are available and should be used on server systems, firewalls, and end client systems to provide layers of protection. Virus scanners work by checking information content for a **malicious signature**. These signatures provide clues indicating that programs have been contaminated with a virus. As we shall see, the collection of these signatures is a time-consuming process and is most often reactive in nature.
- Maintaining a posture of **least privilege**. This is a simple idea that is often difficult to implement. Least privilege means that every user, process, or program should be able to operate by using the fewest amounts of system and network privileges possible. By doing this, the potential for accidental damage caused by legitimate use, as well as deliberate misuse of system resources, can be avoided. As we discussed previously, it is relatively simple for a hacker to take over or hijack a legitimate session. The idea behind the principle of least privilege is to minimize the attacker's potential.
- Understanding the security profile of third-party providers (e.g. ISPs, application service providers, telecommunications providers, etc.). One of the more difficult aspects of the information security professional's job is to estimate the security exposure that exists outside of the information system. Third-party providers are usually high-profile hacker targets. As such, if your site or information is warehoused within these locations, you

are exposing that information to the same risks. For this reason it is recommended that the information security specialist works with the service providers to understand their security issues and to take action to protect the organization's information. Here, again, is another good example of why applying cryptographic methods and authentication processes is important.

- Implementing event monitoring, intrusion detection, and logging systems. The implementation of each of these systems will be critical to the overall success of the security project. Event monitors can assist the security consultant in understanding hacker tactics by breaking down the attacks and actually replaying them. Through these systems, law enforcement officials may also benefit in the investigation of a crime.

  Intrusion-detection systems are a critical first step in making a crisis-management team functional. Finally, event logging needs to be established as part of the regular course of doing business.

- Developing a permission-based architecture (i.e., the base policy for systems and networks should be access-denied in most cases). As was previously discussed, establishing a fail-safe stance is one of the most important parts of extending security into the information system. Permission-based architectures are also known as closed architectures, meaning that, unless specifically permitted, you are denied access by default. In a network router, this architecture can be established when creating access control lists. This will be reviewed in some detail in Section Three.

- Extending the cryptographic methods for use at the network and system level (e.g. VPN, SSL, SET, IPsec, etc.). Cryptographic methods are the crux of this work. We have been focused on these systems as they relate to the protection of information. It is important to apply these same methods to the information access channels in the information system as well. Through the use of the above-mentioned network encryption services, it is possible to form secure tunnels through the open Internet, create mechanisms for the secure exchange of monetary transactions, provide secure Web access, and create digital currency. These important cryptographic applications have become critical to Web businesses as the use of the open network has increased.

- Securing the information system against both internal and external threats. (Remember, 70 percent of all computer crime originates from within the pool of trusted insiders.) Many security plans have failed by being too outwardly focused, assuming that the enemy lurks in the shadows of the Internet and is anonymous. But far too often, many security implementations fail because they are too trusting of insiders. It is the responsibility of the security management and corporate management to evolve a system that keeps a watchful eye both internally and externally.

- Creating system-, application-, and network-level tie-ins to the authentication and verification system. The information system has, by default, several access points to information. At the operating system layer (mentioned in the previous section), we try to disable as many of those access points as is reasonably possible without limiting service too extensively. At the information system architecture and design layer, it is important to account for each of these access points by tying them into the authentication and verification mechanisms presented earlier. It is possible to verify identity, legitimacy of software, access to systems, networks, applications, accounts, and files through this layer.

Each of these points will be discussed in detail in Section Three of the text.

WEB SERVICES PROTECTION LAYER

As the use of open systems and the Internet in particular continues to flourish, the need to secure that layer of services that has contact with the Web becomes crucial. Web services include browsing simple or complex information, file transfer, name and address resolution, secure funds transfer, transaction processing, and use of the Web for private communications. The Web service is different from proprietary information services in that users accept the risks that come with the open network when we initiate the activity. Also, from the Web server's perspective we are trying to make information public so the cryptographic methods have to be more difficult to break. We will see cryptographic methods at this layer to enable secure transactions. However, cryptography will not keep a Web site from being defaced or from being hacked.

With respect to this layer, we are trying to accomplish several specific goals that are layered on top of our previously mentioned goals:

- Client-side user privacy. As we have alluded to in previous sections, clients are at risk from a number of sources when using the Internet. They can inadvertently download malicious software, they can have their electronic identity stolen, they can be subject to break-ins, and they can have their actions monitored or privacy invaded. A primary function of the Web services layer in our security model is to prevent these attacks.
- Prevention of inappropriate release of secure content by clients. Given that many clients store confidential information on their personal computers, organizations must take extra steps to be sure that as clients become active on the Web, usage policies are followed and protective measures are taken to prevent this information from being compromised.
- Protection of the Web server from being accessed in an unauthorized way. This is perhaps the most difficult of the areas to protect against. Because we want people to visit our websites and to benefit from the information on them, we need to be as open as possible. Yet at the same time, we want to limit access to those servers to only those areas that are reasonable. As we have pointed out before, once attackers know about a software flaw or a loophole in a Web site, it is only a matter of time until they penetrate the system. This presents us with a significant dilemma. Fortunately, there are many methods available to secure those areas of the server that should be kept private. We can also use proxy services, which will isolate the traffic before it reaches the actual server, giving us a chance to inspect it in a controlled way.
- Prevention of document corruption. Web services are all about document access and control. For this system to work, we must make access to the documents open while protecting the integrity of the information enclosed within the document itself. In this case, we can use various cryptographic techniques such as digital signatures, code signing, and integrity checking to validate the integrity of the document.

The Web services layer does represent a shift in our security paradigm. It is the portion of the information system that must be open, yet secure—two concepts that are difficult to reconcile together. However, it is also a convenient layer because we can use it to our advantage. We can develop policies that limit all Web transactions to only those covered by this layer, meaning that the bulk of our information and information system is running in a more secure, closed environment elsewhere. Even though it is possible to disrupt the Web services that an organization provides, we need to realize that, for the most part, the server-side information made available is only a backup of the original, which is securely stored somewhere else.

KEY POINT

Web services security is becoming increasingly important as organizations utilize the Web to implement the distribution of information, develop brand, and reduce telecommunications costs. Having secure Web services is difficult because they exist in the public domain and often require high availability and open access.

At this layer, we are primarily concerned with attacks against the brand, infiltration of client-side systems, springboard attacks, denial-of-service attacks, and malware. We will focus on many of these topics in Section Three of the text.

THE EIGHT Ps OF SECURITY LAYER

Far too often, security consultants focus on developing the infrastructure, methods, and tools to foster increased security, and then they neglect those essential elements of security that concern people. It can be said with a high degree of certainty that people are by far the weakest link in the security chain. People would like to believe that they can buy security off the shelf. They want to purchase products and services, install them, and have information security. This is simply not possible. These products and services are a part of the chain, but if the people in the organization are not vigilant, do not know the correct actions to take, or ignore the policies and guideline set forth, disaster is almost a given.

Persuading people from all levels to buy into the security plan is difficult. Management needs to commit funding to security projects and promote participation. Employees need to adhere to policies and to be constantly reminded of their importance. Clients need to feel secure in the online access provided and need to have easy to follow procedures for successfully executing secure transactions. It takes only one person out of thousands to compromise the best of security efforts. For example, people fall victim to social engineering attacks, or use weak passwords, or do not follow a corporate guideline. Any of these breaches can lead to a significant attack.

Therefore, it is appropriate to have the outermost layer of the security model focus on incorporating those things that will encourage and direct people to take the correct actions with regard to security. These are called the 8 Ps of security. By spending time incorporating these thoughts into your security design, you will have a far greater chance of success.

KEY POINT

People represent the weakest link in the security chain and need to be well trained and prepared as to how to handle a variety of different situations. By incorporating the eight Ps layer of the model, we are able to address the circumstances under which people may be put to the test.

The eight Ps are:

- **People**—People need guidelines to direct their actions in the use of the information and the information system. Policies are written so that people can have a framework within which to operate. People need to understand the consequences of their actions, both technical and nontechnical. People should realize how easy it is to fall victim to social engineering attacks. They need to understand what those attacks are and how to prevent them. They also must realize that the use of personal portable computing devices (e.g., laptops and PDAs) require that they exercise extra caution when working outside the confines of the secure corporate network. The use of personal firewalls, virus scanners, and safe online habits can curtail hacker activity. People also need to be careful with how they store, use, and transmit information. The cryptographic methods layer works only if people apply the encryption to information requiring confidentiality. By keeping unprotected copies of information on a laptop, for example, and transmitting the information in the clear, people completely compromise the intent of the information security design.

- **Planning**—Another area where the information security designer needs to be diligent is in the preparation of a plan of security. Security design should not be considered a series of ad hoc steps taken independently of one another. Rather, the security professional needs to bring all of the elements of the planning process together as a single, well-thought-out, unified idea. The security plan, as we shall see, should start with the requirements of the organization, summary of the risk analysis, information on the cost benefit of a security design, and current vulnerabilities. The plan needs to continue with setting a direction and a strategy for the security design. This strategy needs to express the way in which the specific security requirements will be met. The strategy also needs to determine the actions that will be taken by the crisis-management team, users, and management in the event of an attack. The strategy need not be overly technical at this point. We can leave the implementation details for other related documents. The purpose of the plan is to educate and set direction. We should list products, services, methods, and strategies that will be deployed. We should also list the countermeasures that we plan to take. We need to use this section of the plan to build confidence in the strategy, not to develop the implementation strategy. Finally, the security plan should conclude with the policies that apply to each area of the security model. Policies should tell us what to do, when to do it, and why we are doing something.

- **Policy**—Policies are compartmentalized, high-level descriptions of the security controls put in place in an organization to express information confidentiality requirements, trade secrets requirements, legal notices regarding use/monitoring/trespass/and copyright of information or the information system, proper use of company resources, requirements for trusted third parties, e-mail/Web/other application access and usage, authenticity and verification procedures, and ownership of intellectual property. These policies need to be directed at the user community and should be specific and easy to follow. Policies generally define the rights of the employer, employee, user, and guest. They also should detail what actions are deemed inappropriate and the intent to prosecute those actions that result in harm or loss. The better defined the security policies are, the less the concern for legal liability, waste of corporate resources, or exposure of confidential information.

- **Procedure**—Procedures express the technical details of enacting a policy/process combination. A procedure should specify how something is implemented. (Note: The procedure statement is still not considered an implementation plan.) The procedure will, for example, detail how a choke point will be created in a network. The procedure would describe the insertion of a screening router, the details of constructing the access control list, and the fail-safe stance enabled. While the procedure does give us all this information, it does not outline the details of installing the router and developing an overall router configuration. However, the procedure does provide sufficient detail to make the person actually performing the actual router configuration fully aware of the security content of the implementation.
- **Process**—Process defines the actions that should be taken by the user community and security professionals to enable the workability of the security plan. These processes should complement the policies by instructing users, regarding the steps they need to perform to be compliant with the policy.
- **Product**—Products are the tools, hardware, and software that support the implementation and realization of the security implementation. Products need to be purchased commensurate with the requirements specified in the plan and the policy, not the other way around. It is important to specify the products being used, pros and cons of the product, product cost, operational specification, and the input/output process parameters. By clearly articulating the product functionality and limitations, we can better determine if the product meets the needs of the plan.
- **Perseverance**—Perseverance speaks to the drive and heart of the information security professional, the determination of management, and the spirit of the user community. Information security is a continual improvement process. Initially, a security plan may not be completely effective. That is expected and acceptable. You will still have accomplished quite a bit by implementing a workable plan. Information security takes a long time to "burn in" and settle. After the plan is in place, the information security analyst needs to begin monitoring and making adjustments accordingly. The user education process needs to kick in, and the users need to participate. Management should set realistic goals for achieving maximum security with reachable milestones for each area of the plan.
- **Pervasiveness**—Information security is everywhere in the organization, not just in the computer memory or at the network gateways. Information security success is measured by the combination of everyone's actions, the technology we use, the discipline we exert over our information categorization, the strength of our cryptographic methods, and the due diligence of the entire user community. It is just as important to apply cryptographic methods to protect our electronic information as it is to shred documents containing company-privileged information.

By working through the eight Ps, you will find that your plan will become more palatable to the user community. People will become more involved in security because you will have given them a role to play and goals to meet. By sharing the responsibility with the entire community of users, the probability of ubiquitous involvement goes up.

SECURITY PLANNING AND POLICY CREATION

Once you have completed the detailed risk and vulnerability analysis, and you have justified the need to implement a security infrastructure, the next step in the design process is to develop a blueprint for the information security system. This information security plan will provide the framework for the detailed implementation of the specified system. This section of the text outlines the concepts behind plan and policy creation.

As with any design effort, it is important to emphasize the need to articulate the development life cycle, shown in Figure 4-2.

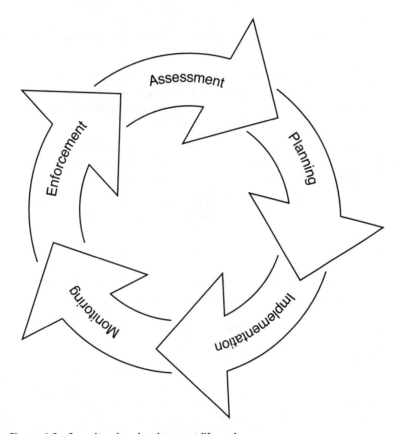

Figure 4-2 Security plan development life cycle.

In this five-stage life cycle, we first assess the needs of the organization and the requirements of each policy. It is important to develop goals that link the design to the stated need. The planning phase details how the goals will be addressed in the form of policy, process, and product. The implementation phase is the build out of the proposed countermeasure and its integration into the information system. This is a critical phase in the development cycle because it is critical that security countermeasures be tightly integrated into the information system. In the monitoring phase, the effectiveness of the countermeasure is observed.

It is at this time that we can tell if the products, procedures, and methods are having the anticipated effect. This is also the time during which actual penetration tests and vulnerability checks can be performed.

The enforcement phase is the period when the system is online. During the enforcement phase, the information security team works with the user community to be sure that the corresponding policies are being adhered to. At some point, the team may, for a variety of reasons, determine that it is necessary to start the process over again. By having adopted such a life-cycle planning strategy, information regarding the plan's acceptance and performance can be collected and used to refine the security plan/policy and affect an improvement in future cycles.

It is also important to emphasize the cascading relationship between a plan, the policies, processes, and procedures. As we can see from Figure 4-3, all of the information previously collected via the risk assessment process is expressed in terms of security requirements. These requirements, combined with the security intentions and posture of senior corporate management, are reflected in the mission statement of the security plan.

Each distinct area of activity that affects the access, use, storage, transference, manipulation, creation, or deletion of information requires a policy. The policy is the high-level definition of the risk, countermeasure, and impact. This statement should serve to set direction and should have the full support of upper management.

The process is the precise set of steps that the user community, management staff, and crisis-management team must follow to put the related policy into action. These steps may include both technical and nontechnical components.

Finally, the procedure is the set of technical details that can be derived from the policy and process as applied to a particular set of technology. These procedures are used to feed implementation plans.

The goals of a well-designed plan should be to:

- Provide clarity of purpose
- Gain the acceptance of management and the user community
- Reduce or eliminate liability to the user and the organization
- Protect information
- Reduce waste of corporate resources
- Minimize threats to information
- Define roles and responsibilities

One of the key components mentioned in Chapter 2 was the classification of information. Prior to designing an information security plan, it is essential that you understand all of the classifications of information and the security requirements of each. A well-structured plan will elaborate on the security requirements and policies corresponding to each classification. The plan should also present a strategy for the organization to actually perform the classification process.

PRINCIPLES

The following are underlying principles that can be gleaned from our information security model and from the industry standard models presented later in this chapter. It is important that the author of an information security plan include these principles while crafting planning and policy statements. Every policy and procedure developed should embody the following set of design principles:

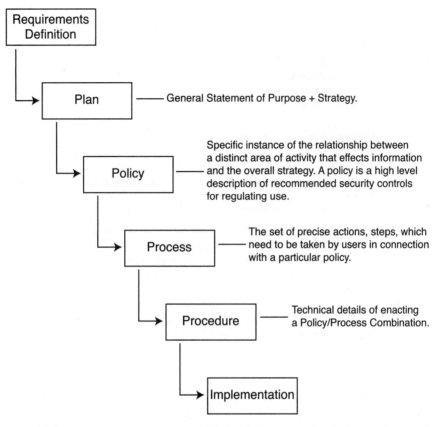

Figure 4-3   Plan, policy, process, procedure relationship diagram.

KEY POINT

Plans, policies, and processes are not implementation or how-to documents. They are better described as "why are we" and "what to do" documents. Procedures provide the linkage to the how-to implementation phase.

- Of all the principles involved in the development of an information security plan, the ability of the designer to keep the plan and policy simple is perhaps the most obvious, yet also the hardest to achieve. It is important for the plan's architect to remember whom the audience is and not to over complicate the messages that you are trying to send. By keeping the plan simple yet purposeful, the author can garner support and participation.

- Least privilege is a key concept in the development of information security policies. Each user service and application must be analyzed to determine only those privileges and permissions that are absolutely required to achieve usability. The requirement here is to isolate and remove instances of the unnecessary granting of privileges and permissions, either by the information system or the social structure of the organization. Those applications that do require the issuance of excessive user privileges should be investigated and potentially eliminated.

- The concept of defense-in-depth also plays an important role in the development of a security plan. As was previously mentioned, defense-in-depth corresponds to the notion of creating layers of security that must be penetrated to reach our information. This concept must transfer to the policy level as well as the strategic level of the plan. Each policy must consciously add to the depth of defense. It is important that the policy designer map the policy area to the precise layer of the model where the activity is taking place. Then the designer needs to construct a policy in keeping with the model. This is a key design point because it is easy to strategize about the defense in depth information security model and create policies, processes, and procedures that bypass it and effectively neutralize the concept. The designer should constantly test the policy against the model to see if each layer of the model is represented before information is accessed. Remember, it is the set of policies that the users follow.
- Consistent interpretation of the fail-safe stance should be reflected throughout the set of policies. By this, we mean that in the event a policy is compromised, a set of pre-planned actions should be detailed to determine exactly how the system will fail to the predetermined safe condition. For example, in a closed fail-safe stance, the condition would be to disconnect the local network from all outside connections.
- Encouraging universal participation is an important underlying principle. The designer needs to account for everyone when developing the plan and policies. It is inappropriate to alienate any group or individual because it leads to a disregard for policy, thus negating the security plan. Additionally, steps should be taken to encourage education and participation in the planning process.
- Two final principles are absolutely essential—enforcement and implementation. Every policy that the designer creates must be implementable and enforcable. Without meeting these criteria, the policy lacks merit. It is important to translate the requirements expressed by the organization into a workable and usable plan, and not a wish list of best-case but purely hypothetical activities. This plan needs to reflect real definable actions and procedures.

A Security Plan Outline

In constructing the security planning document, it is best to start with an outline. This section of the text should help you to create a framework for the construct of your plan. As we shall see later in the chapter, several formally recognized standards exist on the international level. These standards can also serve as a guide in developing your security plan and policies. Regardless of which security planning format you choose, it is important to minimally include the following items in the plan:

Suggested Table of Contents

I   Security Plan Document Approval and Control Sheet

II   Security Plan Mission Statement

III   Current State

IV   Roles and Responsibilities

    a) Senior management

    b) Crisis management

    c) Security planning

    d) Operations

    e) User groups

    f) Clients

    g) Third parties

V   Requirements

VI   Acceptable Usage Policy

VII   Information Confidentiality and Integrity Policy

VIII   Key Management Policy

IX   Certificate Policy

X   Information System Access Policy

XI   Account Management Policy

XII   Internet Connectivity and Usage Policy

XIII   Portable Computing Platform Policies

XIV   Other Corporate-Specific Policies

    E.g., physical security, confidential information, firewall management, lab policy, wireless network policy, customer policy, trusted third party policy, etc.

XV   Monitoring Policy

XVI   Logging Policy

XVII   Intrusion-Detection Policy

XVIII Enforcement and Violations

XIX   Implementation Time Tables

XX   Limits of Liability

Sections Two through Five of the plan provide background information so that the reader can understand the context of the plan. We should explain to the reader why the decisions outlined in the plan were made. To appreciate that detail, we must provide the requisite context. This information should be gathered during the discovery phase of the risk assessment detailed in Chapter 3.

The mission statement specifically tells us what the plan is about. It details the strategy of upper management with respect to the need for (and importance of) information security. It should outline organizational commitment to the plan. It should also specifically ask for the cooperation of all concerned parties.

The Roles and Responsibilities section of the plan specifically addresses ownership. Assigning ownership to a person or group for a particular section of the plan will foster a greater spirit of enthusiasm. It is also important to make security goals part of every person's job performance requirements. This section also defines the community of users that the plan addresses.

The Requirements section basically restates the departmental, organizational, managerial, application, client, partner, and user requirements for security. Again, this section is included so the reader of the plan can understand why decisions regarding security were made. This section also helps readers relate to groups other than their own in the organization.

Each of the following sections details specific policies pertaining to compartmentalized areas of information security. Every policy is to be crafted as a self-sustaining document that can be pulled out of the plan and judged on its own merit. Every policy should minimally include:

- A statement of purpose
- An appropriate use statement, which considers authorized access and prohibited use
- The precise wording of the policy and references to all related policies
- Any banners and statements that will be displayed to users online expressing the gist of the policy
- A policy control statement outlining the update schedule, the corporate sponsor of the policy, revision control information, review policy, suggestions and inputs, and an effective date

The Acceptable Usage Policy should detail the appropriate use of information system resources. It should outline the privacy expectations that users of the information system should have with respect to online storage, Web access, network usage, and application usage. This section will also detail the privileges and permissions that will be granted to the user on a normal basis.

The Information Confidentiality and Integrity Policy, Key Management Policy, and Certificate Policy are all closely related. The intent of these sections is to detail the cryptographic methods used in the implementation and requirements of the organizational members who will use cryptography. In these sections, it is not necessary to detail the specifics of encryption. Rather, they are intended to enable users to understand the requirements for the use of such facilities. Further, they are intended for security managers to understand the details of key distribution, key revocation, key recovery, and information system integration with cryptography. They are also intended to provide the basis for an X.509 v3 certificate system, which can be used for authentication and verification. These sections would outline the specifics of interactions with all trusted third parties.

The Information System Access Policy defines a collection of subpolicies that address the perimeter access control measures safeguarding the corporate information system. These documents will detail the use of access controls such as firewalls, DMZs, bastian hosts, Web interfaces, VPN access, and distributed system access control, among others. This section will also explain the security precautions incorporated into the file management system. Finally, this section will provide system and network policies defining allowable services and ports.

The Account Management Policy outlines requirements for using and maintaining user accounts. This policy should outline account access controls (knowledge, biometric, and possession factors). This policy should also address document control, ownership, and integrity.

The Internet Connectivity and Usage Policy will have the obvious implications as to what, when, how, why, and where a person may use the Internet for business and nonbusiness requirements. This set of statements also needs to address the reliability and copyright issues associated with research on the

Internet, the need to monitor for malware while connected, any monitoring of use by the organization, and the cost to the organization of frivolous Internet usage. Additionally, these policies should discuss the status of the corporation's own Web services, where they are maintained, and how they will be used, secured, and monitored.

Portable Computing Platform Policies are designed so that the user can understand the risks associated with removing a portable computing device (laptop or PDA) from the secure confines of the corporate information system. In essence, each time you take your laptop home and connect to the Internet, you are literally walking around the firewall and exposing the organization to viruses, Trojan horses, malware, logic bombs, and theft of information.

Other Corporate-Specific Policies as required should also be included in the security plan. Plans regarding physical security, confidential information, firewall management, lab policy, wireless network policy, customer policy, trusted third party policy, and more would all be useful if appropriate.

The Monitoring Policy, Logging Policy, and Intrusion Detection Policy are important for two reasons. First, it is important that the organizational parameters be stated so that all users are aware that their actions are being tracked. Second (and more important), to use any of these systems as evidence in court, they must be clearly stated and conducted as part of the normal course of doing business.

The Enforcement and Violations section of the plan should detail the methods and penalties that will be used to ensure compliance with policies and procedures. It is also important to make clear the extent to which people who perform criminal activities will be reported to the lawful authorities and prosecuted. This section must be clearly worded so there is no mistaking the organization's intention. It is also a section that must be carefully worded to avoid creating paranoia within the ranks.

The Implementation Time Tables section should detail the timeline for implementation of the plan, as well as the review and renewal dates for the plan. This section is especially important in a startup effort.

The Limits of Liability section should consist of a set of disclaimers. The organization will use this section to protect itself from the actions of rogue employees using information and information system resources for purposes other than those expressed in the Acceptable Usage section of the plan. This would include all unauthorized usage of which the organization has no knowledge or given no consent.

This outline should provide a good starting point in plan construction and development. The better constructed the plan, the better the chance that the information security system will withstand the tests of time and support.

KEY POINT

There are no right and wrong formats when developing a plan. Authors should simply choose one that they are comfortable with, one that makes sense for the organization, and one that reflects the requirements of government regulations, auditors, executive management, and third parties, and one that is easily interpreted by the user community.

FORMATS AND FRAMEWORKS

Although the previous section outlines a framework for a plan that closely parallels the information security model reviewed in this text, it is important to note that alternative frameworks are available. In particular, we will briefly review three other planning frameworks that are internationally recognized and supported:

- ISO 17799/BS7799
- NIST SP 800-18
- IEFT Security Architecture

The British standard BS7799 is the best-known internationally accepted security frameworks available. The International Standards Organization and International Electrotechnical Commission (IEC) adopted it as the de facto security standard for the international community. The formal name of the standard is ISO/IEC 17799, "Information Technology—Code Practice for Information Security Management." The formal materials for this standard are available for a fee. The intention of the document is to provide a basis for recommendations for security managers so international business partners can achieve similar security goals and be best prepared for secure interactions.

The plan covers ten primary areas:

- Security Organization Policy
- Organizational Security Infrastructure
- Asset Classification and Control
- Personnel Security
- Physical and Environmental Security
- Communications and Operations Management
- System Access Control
- System Development and Maintenance
- Business Continuity Planning
- Compliance

As you can most certainly tell from this list, the ISO document has an operational. It deals with the major components of the information system and the functionality of the information security and operations staff. This plan is not without its critics. The framework is not as comprehensive or complete as other standards. It is also not easily measured and, as an international standard, lacks the required granularity and acceptance. The United States, Germany, and Japan have not adopted this standard.

This resistance to accept ISO 17799 is not completely unanticipated, however. Acceptance takes time. Another possible approach that some have taken is the National Institute for Standards and Technology (NIST) SP 800-18, "Guide for Developing Security Plans." In fact, a series of documents are available for free that detail the setup, management, planning, assessment, and risk management of cybersecurity. SP 800-18 is the portion of the text that deals specifically with the development of the security plan.

This format is really more of a how-to-develop-the-plan package, which can be adjusted to organizations of any size. It is fundamentally an aid in the development of the plan and is highly recommended. This planning process takes the security professional through most of the steps presented thus far in this text. In fact, unlike the ISO 17799, SP 800-18 does separate the information from the information system. This separation provides an opportunity for us to implement the model presented in this text in conjunction with the NIST framework.

Specifically, the framework addresses authentication, cryptography, ownership, laws, people's behavior, auditing, integrity, crisis-management tie-ins, and physical security, among others.

One other group that warrants mention is the Internet Engineering Task Force (IETF). The IETF is the technical advisory board for Internet technology ideas. The Internet supports the RFC process, which is open and is meant to promote the open flow of ideas regarding the operation of the Internet. Because the Internet is now the de facto international network, it is important to monitor their suggestions. The IETF does not currently support a formalized framework, but it does endorse a series of important publications including the Site Security Handbook. The document, RFC 2196 ("Site Security Handbook"), although somewhat outdated, is still considered useful. It makes usage and security recommendations that should be accounted for in any plan.

A few other interesting (and more technical) RFCs that you may wish to review (especially if you use the Internet frequently) are:

- RFC 1825, "Security Architecture for the Internet Protocol," a discussion of IPv4 and IPv6 security mechanisms
- RFC 2222, "Simple Authentication and Security Layer," a method for adding authentication support to connection-based protocols
- RFC 2084 "Considerations for Web Transactions Security," which applies the CAIN principles to HTTP

These formats should be considered by organizations as alternatives to the outline presented earlier or in contrast to homegrown methods an organization may already use. When choosing a format for use in developing a plan, you should consider the following:

- The formats already familiar to the organization
- The formats preferred or required by third parties, clients, and government regulators (for certain business types)
- If the format is consistent with your security model
- If the format is easily readable and understandable
- If the format's sponsor offers any benefit to your organization (e.g., certification) for using the format, which can be considered a corporate asset

CRISIS-MANAGEMENT PLANNING

As was mentioned in Chapter 3, organizations need to develop a security crisis-management team. This team needs to represent all aspects of organizational security. As we analyze the aftermath of the attacks on the World Trade Center on 9/11, because many of the effected agencies, organizations, and private corporations had crisis-management teams, the reestablishment of services was handled at an effective pace. A crisis need not be that severe to warrant the establishment of a crisis-management team. Power outages, information security breaches, flooding, physical break-ins, earthquakes, storms, strikes, or the loss of key personnel can also be reasons to mobilize the team to ensure that the organization keeps running.

In developing the information security plan and policies, it is appropriate to define the precise role of the crisis-management team in the event of a breach in information security. What should the team do in response to theft of vital information? How should they respond to a defacement of the Web site? What actions should they take if the information system falls victim to a denial-of-service attack? These and many other questions should be thought through before, not during or after, a crisis.

The crisis-management team needs to be prepared to take the following actions:

- Determine possible alternative actions to gain control of the crisis or to guide the organization through the crisis with minimal impact.
- Involve law enforcement at the appropriate time and support its investigation as soon as possible.
- Assist law enforcement in the collection of evidence based on the logging, monitoring, and detection processes in place.
- Evaluate the impact of the crisis on the normal business operations.
- Create valuations of damage and accounting of lost assets.
- Notify key personnel and alert the appropriate technology and management resources of the crisis.
- Execute emergency management policies as determined appropriate to stop an intrusion, spread of viruses and worms, or to curtail the actions of rogue processes in the information system.
- Coordinate the activities required to maintain the information security posture during a crisis of greater proportion (i.e., maintaining information security during a hurricane or severe storm that may impact the availability of security countermeasures or processes).

DISASTER RECOVERY PLANNING

As has been mentioned repeatedly in this text, the ultimate security position is the organization's ability to recover from a disaster. Disasters are not all alike and will impact information in a variety of ways. Natural disasters may affect a significant portion of the nation, while a flood in the computer room may not even affect the whole organization. A strike by a service provider or a service provider outage can cause your business disruption of service without anything even being wrong. In any of these cases, the availability of information and the information system may be negatively impacted. In a small- or low-margin business, these disasters—even the minor ones—can cause businesses to fail.

Worse, breaches of information security can lead to silent disasters. For example, the organization can be under attack and not know it, may be damaged and not know where, or may be held in isolation (DOS attack) and not know by whom.

Having a disaster recovery plan is a key to overcoming these kinds of problems. A disaster recovery plan is different from the information security plan. The information security plan should reference the disaster recovery plan. The crisis-management team should have control of both documents.

A disaster recovery plan kicks in after the crisis is under control (via the crisis-management plan) and the reestablishment of normal service is possible. A disaster recovery plan should include:

- A business impact assessment. This assessment is important because management needs to understand the financial, workflow, and loss of functionality caused by a potential crisis. Additionally, the crisis-management team needs to know how to prepare proposals for the cost of the complete restoration of service. This policy will prepare the crisis-management team to be able to conduct this type of analysis under the stress of a crisis. Additionally, after the crisis-management team has used backup resources to overcome a crisis, the organization can be left with a new problem of being left for an extended period of time with no backup. Remember, there is no guarantee that a second crisis cannot hit while the first remains unresolved.

- Provisions for a long-term crisis. It is important that before a crisis hits, the organization has made arrangements for long-term backup sites (hot or warm sites depending on the failover timeframes of the organization), backup telecommunications facilities, backup computers, alternate communication methods for reaching key staff, possible housing accommodations for key resources, and availability of backup information at multiple locations. Further, the organization needs to be prepared to deal with personal tragedy involving its employees. It is important that especially small organizations consider "key man insurance," which would provide financial relief in the event of the death of a key person in the company.
- A plan for off-site information warehousing and backup (including a regular information backup plan). This plan should be constantly in use from the first day of normal business operations. It is important to back up data off-site at regular intervals. These intervals should be half the acceptable recovery time frame. So, if a business can be without its information for eight hours before it becomes problematic, information backup should be done at intervals of four hours or less. This cushion will give the organization enough time to recover the saved data and perform the required actions based on its contents.
- A plan for media types and access methods required at the standby sites. Make sure that the information is stored on a particular media that can be physically ported and installed on a hardware device in another location. Remember, in the event of a crisis, telecommunications can be impacted for extended periods of time and the communication of information during the transfer of control may have to be supplemented by direct media access.
- A reallocation of resources (people and objects) and the allocation of short-term personnel is necessary to continue operations during the relocation period.

EDUCATION AND MANAGEMENT

The management of an information security plan is the responsibility of the Chief Information Security Officer (CISO.) The CISO is required to develop the plan, present the plan to executive management along with a justification including a return on investment estimate, educate all concerned parties, act as the go-between with law enforcement agencies, and take charge of plan enforcement.

Of these responsibilities, one of the most difficult is education. The purpose of all this planning and policy design is to make sure that the crisis-management team, the executive management team, the staff, the users, the clients, and the business partners know how to interact in a secure way and how to prevent security breaches. However, it is unrealistic to assume that all of those people, especially in a large organization, are going to actually read all of that documentation.

It is important that the Chief Information Security Officer organize the requisite training activities to satisfy the requirement that everyone has:

- Appropriate exposure to the core components of the entire plan
- Awareness of the security measures that affect their job function and what actions are required of them
- A briefing on the penalties for breaching security, theft of information, and misuse of corporate resources

- Signed a security document indicating that they are aware of the plan and agree to abide by the policies and regulations contained therein
- An understanding of the importance of reporting security breaches and knowledge of the methods for doing so
- Been given examples of the real nature of the threats that exist to information and how they can directly impact the employee (e.g., loss of corporate revenue can cause the company to have to cutback in staff or benefits)

The CISO also should communicate the plan to law enforcement agencies that will likely be involved in the event of a breach of security or a potential crisis. The CISO needs to establish contacts within local, state, and federal agencies as required by the nature of the business that the firm conducts.

It is also strongly advised that the CISO adopt a strong incident reporting policy in conjunction with the National Infrastructure Protection Center (NIPC.) NIPC is a supportive organization that has an informative Web site filled with ideas for interacting with law enforcement, protecting your information, and gaining knowledge.

In Appendix C of this text is the NIPC Incident Reporting form that can be obtained online and utilized to report security breaches. The reporting of such information benefits everyone because a major weakness in the industry today is the lack of accurate statistics, as was discussed in Chapter 2.

In the event of a crisis or a breach of security, the CISO should work closely with the marketing and executive management teams in crafting the appropriate communications with the media. It is advisable to limit all initial comment as much as possible. This is a reasonable approach because you want to have an opportunity to understand the extent of damage, the impact on clients and third parties, and the needs of law enforcement. The CISO also should be careful in choosing early words regarding the situation; the wrong words can cause a loss of confidence in a business, question the integrity of information or services your organization provides, or cause a negative impact on stock performance. Making the right statement, at the right time, from the right person can make all the difference in creating a positive, thoughtful, and appropriate spin on the situation.

Finally, the CISO needs to constantly reevaluate the performance, effectiveness, and appropriateness of the plan and all of its subordinate policies. The organization should realize that the planning process is continual and requires a long-term commitment to achieve success. It is doubtful that the plan, policies, or implementation will be one hundred percent effective on the first pass. Most organizations have not even achieved a first pass at a plan. They have not even begun to evaluate weaknesses and concerns. By establishing a plan, your organization is taking an important first preventive step in protecting information. The commitment to the goal of corporate security and the determination to be vigilant will provide the best atmosphere for evolving your plan and safeguarding your organization.

SUMMARY

One of the most important tasks an information security team will execute is the development of a security plan. As a result of the data gathered during the risk analysis and vulnerability assessment process, the planning team should be fully aware of organizational weaknesses and deficiencies.

The first step in the planning process is to adopt a multilayered security model. Experts agree that a strategy of defense-in-depth provides the most benefit to an organization. A number of viable security models are available. A seven-layer model is presented in this text. This model was chosen because it covers both the security of the information itself as well as the security of the information system. The layers of the model are:

1 Information at the core

2 Cryptographic methods layer

3 Verification and authentication layer

4 OS hardening layer

5 Information system architecture and design layer

6 Web services layer

7 The 8 Ps of security layer

Of these layers, the cryptographic methods layer is perhaps the most important. It is strongly recommended that the planning team consider encouraging the use of cryptographic methods. Cryptographic methods capitalize on the mathematical representation of information. Cryptography can be used to coat the information and to protect it wherever it is. These same methods also allow us to satisfy the CAIN principles. These principles, when properly met, completely address information security.

The verification and authentication layer is another vital layer of the model. At this layer, the model bridges the information security with the security of the information system. The deployment of proper authentication and verification methods can be effective in controlling access to information. It is also important because it makes it much easier to detect unwanted intrusions. There are four factors upon which authentication can be based: possession, biometrics, knowledge, and integrity.

The OS hardening layer, information system architecture and design layer, and Web services layer specify the information system security measures. Through the creation of choke points and screening, content awareness can be established. Permission-based architectures combined with event monitoring and logging can be of tremendous benefit to the crisis-management team. It is at these layers that applications are secured. This is important because a significant part of what gives information value is the applications that process the data.

The eight Ps of information security are people, planning, process, procedure, policy, product, perseverance, and pervasiveness. They address the soft side of information security. If we revisit the statistics presented in Chapter 2, you should remember that information security breaches are most often caused by either human error or an inconsistency in the implementation of security procedures. By developing a plan that is concerned with the 8 Ps of information security, planners are likely to gain more cooperation and acceptance of the plan.

The most important part of the planning process is to develop a plan that is both implemented and enforced. Plans should be kept as simple as possible. Plans require structure. Information security plans are not how-to documents. Rather, they should address the questions of what to do and why do it.

Many planning document formats exist. There are various international standards to choose from. Whichever format is selected should be familiar, easy to understand, appropriate for the mission, and should provide a framework for consistency.

Once the plan is developed, the procedures that are outlined in it provide the linkage from the strategy planning to the specific implementation planning that is done next. Implementation plans explain the how-to information.

Crisis management and disaster recovery planning should be commensurate with information security planning. The development of a crisis-management team is closely tied into the implementation of intrusion detection, monitoring, and logging capabilities of the information system. Disaster recovery is the last line of defense in information security planning.

Education of the user population and management is a crucial step in developing a successful information security strategy. Through a comprehensive corporate education experience, cooperation and buy-in of the plan will follow.

Information security planning is not a one-time event. The risk assessment process should be continual. Management will require constant feedback regarding the return on investment and current vulnerability processes. It is important that the planning team be assigned a permanent role in the organization. The information security plan should include statements addressing the proliferation of the planning structure and the role of the team members as the plan evolves. Information security is a continual improvement process.

Chapter 4 ties together many of the themes presented earlier in this section of the text. Students need to practice the risk assessment planning presented in Chapter 2 and use the data developed in that exercise to attempt to develop a first draft information security plan.

Section One attempted to answer the "why" questions of information security. The remainder of this text deals with the questions of "what" and "how". This text is specifically focused on the use of cryptographic methods to successfully secure information.

STUDY QUESTIONS

1 What is defense-in-depth? (choose one)

  a. An abstraction

  b. A layering of progressive security strategies

  c. A method of invoking the IDS

  d. Both a and c

2 Where does information reside in our security model? (choose one)

  a. Outside the model

  b. Inside the OS hardening layer

  c. At the core

  d. In the systems

3 What is the second layer of the information security model? (choose one)

  a. Web services layer

  b. OS hardening layer

  c. Network architecture layer

  d. Cryptographic services layer

4 Which of the following is not a characteristic of a cryptography method? (choose one)

    a. Disguises the information

    b. Are few and limited

    c. Are extremely complex

    d. Are many and are varied

5 Ciphertext is _____? (choose one)

    a. Text that is visible

    b. Method used to encrypt plain text

    c. Disguised plain text produce as a result of encryption

    d. The secret shard between trusted parties

6 Authentication is a(n) _____ used for determining if the information presented is real or fake. (choose one)

    a. Process involving cryptographic methods and checksums

    b. System of hierarchical servers

    c. Application level user interface

    d. Information about information

7 Operating systems are the basic _____ that make computer hardware useful. (choose one)

    a. Processes

    b. Programs

    c. Requirements

    d. Abstractions

8 _____ are those areas in a network where traffic must converge on a single well-known gateway. (choose one)

    a. Content checking

    b. Malicious

    c. Choke points

    d. Least privilege

9 _____ are part of a critical first step in making a crisis-management team functional. (choose one)

    a. Logging systems

    b. Intrusion detection systems

    c. Event monitoring systems

    d. None of the above

10 What percentage of all computer crime originates from within the pool of trusted insiders? (choose one)

   a. 70 percent

   b. 45 percent

   c. 20 percent

   d. 5 percent

11 Which is not a part of the Web services protection layer? (choose one)

   a. File transfer

   b. Name and address resolution

   c. Access to systems

   d. Secure funds transfer

12 What is the primary concern of the Web services protection layer? (choose one)

   a. Code vulnerability protection

   b. Trojan horse protection and address spoofing

   c. Virus detection and prevention

   d. All of the above

13 _____ is/are the weakest link in the security chain. (choose one)

   a. Planning

   b. Policy

   c. People

   d. Hardware and software

14 Which one of the following is not part of the 8 Ps? (choose one)

   a. People/planning/pervasiveness

   b. Policy/process/procedures

   c. Programs/properties

   d. Products/perseverance

15 How many stages are in the security plan life cycle? (choose one)

   a. One

   b. Three

   c. Eight

   d. Five

16 In what phase is the effectiveness of the countermeasure observed? (choose one)

  a. Planning phase

  b. Monitoring phase

  c. Enforcement phase

  d. Assessment phase

17 What do Sections Two through Five of the security plan provide? (choose one)

  a. Background information to understand the context

  b. Certificate policy

  c. Logging policy

  d. Internet connectivity and usage policy

18 True___ False___   The ISO/IEC 17799, NIST SP 800-18, and IEFT Security Architecture are alternative frameworks.

19 Which one is not from the crisis-management plan? (choose one)

  a. Determine alternative actions possible to gain control of the crisis.

  b. Create valuations of damage and accounting of lost assets

  c. Execute emergency management policies as determined appropriate to stop an intrusion.

  d. Develop a plan for media types and access methods required at the standby sites.

20 In disaster recovery planning, all are true except _____. (choose one)

  a. A business has an impact assessment

  b. A business has provisions for long-term crisis

  c. A business has a plan for off-site information warehousing

  d. A business has requirements for system upgrades

21 All are in the relationship diagram except _____. (choose one)

  a. Design

  b. Plan

  c. Process

  d. Implementation

22 True___ False___   The information system is the combination of systems, networks, and ubiquitous service applications.

23 Which layer in the information security model has two distinct parts? (choose one)

  a. Web services protection layer

  b. Verification and authentication layer

  c. Information systems and design layer

  d. OS hardening layer

24 True___ False___   This chapter will not represent the need to establish a sense of urgency and constant vigilance regarding information security.

25 In which layer of the information security model do we use terms such as possession factor, biometrics factor, and knowledge factor?

    a. Cryptographic methods layer

    b. OS hardware

    c. Verification and authentication layer

    d. Web services protection layer

CASE STUDY

Back at Cureme Hospital, you are in the third week of your assignment and are beginning to pull together the beginnings of a plan. You have been requested to begin the assessment process of the information security plan. In this part of the exercise, assume that the hospital is working on a limited budget (less than $150,000 for services, software, and hardware) and has a reasonably capable technical staff (given your leadership).

Research and comment

- Given the information security model presented in this text, detail how you would address each layer of the model to the hospital information system. Assume that the hospital has Web capabilities and that physicians are experimenting with advanced technologies (e.g., imaging studies, clinical assessments, scheduling, automated patient records, etc.).
- Who would you want on a crisis-management team and what functions would you have them perform?
- What strategy might you want to employ for information disaster recovery and backup (keep in mind that some elements of the patient record, such as imaging data, can be quite large and complex)?
- Look up the functional specification for Dicom (*medical.nema.org/dicom.html*) imaging standard Part 15 (Dicom security). How do those standards map to parts of our information security plan?

SECTION II

Cryptographic Principles and Methods

OVERVIEW

As was demonstrated in Section One, information needs to be the focus of our security plan. In the case of a total system-wide failure, the preservation of information should be the primary goal of the information security professional. Information security implementations need to include two mechanisms that help us fully comply with the CAIN principles of information security, as well as our previously stated privacy requirements:

- The locking and safekeeping of information
- The development of trust mechanisms

We have already examined the properties of information, seen how to categorize the threats to information, learned how to develop policies for managing those risks, and understood how law enforcement can be included as part of our information security plan. Now it is time to concentrate our focus on the core of our information security model: cryptography, digital signatures, authentication, and verification. It is at these innermost levels of the model where we satisfy our privacy requirements.

Section Two divides this material across four focused chapters. Chapter 5 introduces the concepts of cryptography. In this chapter we will review the rich and interesting history of cryptography. Students will gain an appreciation for the complexities of character-based cryptography. Chapter 5 tells the story of the cryptanalysts who created the techniques to crack what, at the time, seemed to be insurmountable codes.

Chapter 5 will also review the use of passwords as a first line of defense in the protection of information and the information system. Popular password-cracking techniques will be demonstrated and detailed. The chapter continues with a review of the relationship between password length and the strength of the password in concrete mathematical terms. It is during this discussion that students will more fully appreciate the power of today's computers and the need for protections more substantial than passwords.

Chapter 5 concludes with a review of the CAIN principles and a discussion of how CAIN objectives are addressed through the use of modern cryptographic methods. CAIN objectives will be shown to be in concert with the inner core of our information security model.

Chapter 6 introduces the requisite mathematics for an introduction to cryptography. The majority of mathematics discussion has been largely isolated to this chapter of the text. Some students may already possess these skills and feel comfortable with only a brief review. Other students may wish to spend more time on this material because it is the key to unlocking the secrets of cryptography. The essential information presented in this chapter covers:

- Boolean arithmetic and base conversion
- Fundamentals of mathematical logic
- Hashing functions and checksums
- Special numbers that demonstrate unique qualities favoring encryption
- Simple probability
- Algorithmic application of cryptographic mathematics

Chapter 7 reviews the concept of symmetrical key cryptography. In this chapter, students are introduced to the concept of a key and its application to information. Chapter 7 then discusses the notion of symmetry and how it is achieved. Through the use of the TEA, students will achieve a complete grasp of what symmetrical encryption is and how the mathematics in Chapter 6 are applied through a real-world example. The TEA code is reviewed and working samples of the encryption routine and decryption routine are included on the CD accompanying this text. Students are encouraged to exercise these programs and play with the code to gain a fuller understanding of what is meant by the expression "applying a key."

A discussion of how a cryptanalyst might attack such algorithms will explain why we cannot just stop our security planning with the application of symmetrical key cryptography.

Chapter 7 concludes with an examination of other popular symmetrical key encryption schemes, operational issues likely to be encountered, and the applications of this technology to solve real-world problems.

Chapter 8 presents a discussion of the **Public Key Infrastructure (PKI).** PKI is achieved through the use of asymmetrical key cryptography. Students will explore this concept in detail and understand how it differs from the symmetrical key cryptography discussion of Chapter 7.

Chapter 8 also discusses building trust relationships using the digital signature concept in conjunction with the use of X.509 v3 certificates. This is also the point in the text where students should fully appreciate the need for a well-developed PKI. This section concludes with several examples of how we combine symmetrical key cryptography with PKI to achieve solutions to real-world problems.

SECTION GOALS

Upon completion of this section, students should be able to do the following:

- Describe the history of cryptography and present a strong argument for how it would be useful in the protection of information.
- Represent the inner core of our information security model in the context of privacy and CAIN.
- Describe the CAIN objectives.

- Demonstrate the relationship between the length of a password and its relative strength.
- Demonstrate the reversibility of key mathematical logic functions on binary operands.
- Discuss the need for special numbers in cryptography.
- Review the construction of hash functions.
- Describe what a software key is and how it could be applied to information using a reversibility function.
- Overview the TEA encryption algorithm and other symmetrical key products.
- Understand the strategies that a cryptanalyst might use to compromise symmetrical key encryption algorithms.
- Discuss the key rotation conditions that should be met to ensure information security.
- Describe the difference between symmetrical and asymmetrical keys.
- Draw the asymmetrical encryption process.
- Draw the asymmetrical digital signature process.
- Draw the combined asymmetrical encryption and signature process.
- Discuss how the topics listed above meet the privacy requirements of locking and trust.

KEY ELEMENTS TO SUCCESS IN MASTERING THIS SECTION

In order to master the topics in this section, students should:

- Review the mathematical principles provided in Chapter 6 and feel comfortable with bit-wise manipulations using mathematical logic functions.
- Spend time exercising the TEA code included on the CD in this book. Typically, this code helps students understand what encryption is and how it is done.
- Master the diagrams detailing the asymmetrical encryption and digital signatures procedures.
- Understand the progression of complexity as we move from passwords, to symmetrical keys, to asymmetrical keys, and how this complexity adds to the overall security.
- Go back and relate the information presented in this section to the threats outlined in Chapter 2 to gain an understanding of how these techniques can safeguard your information when faced with these threats.
- Complete the study guide and lab experiments presented at the end of the text.

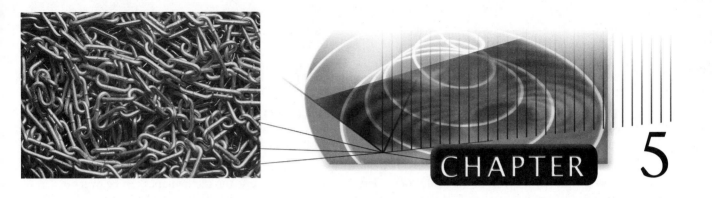

Cryptographic Philosophy

To know that one has a secret is to know half the secret itself.
—Henry Ward Beecher

Literally translated, cryptography means hidden writing. It is a fascinating and even intriguing science and has been the basis of many suspense thrillers. Keeping secrets is something that most people start doing at an early age: secret decoder rings, invisible ink, passing notes in secret code, or using a foreign language as a means of having a private conversation in a public forum. History books are filled with examples of military leaders utilizing cryptographic methods to keep information from their adversaries, while directing remote armies via courier.

In an attempt to understand the importance of the applications of cryptographic methods, it is crucial that we understand the history of how they evolved. From the time of early biblical writings, where evidence of simple substitution ciphers can be found, cryptographic methods were used to conceal meanings. These substitutions of characters with other characters are known as substitution ciphers. An early substitution cipher is named for Julius Caesar, who was the first to describe a shift cipher. A shift cipher is created by rotating the alphabet forward or back by a certain amount of letters. For example, a shift of one in our alphabet would produce the following substitutions: "A" becomes "B," "B" becomes "C," "C" becomes "D," and so forth. By World War II, the ciphers were constructed using complex electromechanical devices that performed the substitution and shifting algorithms on a large scale.

Today, we utilize complex bit-wise mathematical functions to disguise information. The first section of this chapter overviews the history of cryptography so the reader can gain an understanding of the evolution of the craft. To know where you are going is in part to understand where you have been.

Next we will focus on the importance of fulfilling the CAIN principles of information security described in Section One. These principles should always be the beacon of our plan. By satisfying CAIN requirements, we ensure success in protecting our information.

Next, the language of cryptography is presented so that the list of acronyms and crypto-terms do not turn into alphabet soup and cause confusion. Like any other science, cryptography has its own language and terms. One of the goals of an introductory-level text is to familiarize students with the terminology of the field. This goal is satisfied in this chapter.

Finally, the material in this chapter discusses the basics of modern cryptography. This section is meant to introduce the details presented in Chapters 7 and 8. This introduction enables students who read through the mathematics presentations in Chapter 6 to build mental bridges between these mathematical constructs and the basic methods discussed here.

Some people shy away from the details of modern cryptography because the mathematics can be overwhelming. One of the key goals of this book is to limit the mathematics to only the most basic required pieces. It is not necessary to understand all the mathematics in order to apply cryptography applications to our information and information system. It is useful to know the basic theory behind cryptography, which can be presented using reasonably easy mathematics. This understanding will help you better understand the risks, rewards, limitations, and benefits of various cryptographic methods. For those who are interested in developing cryptographic codes and cipher methods, it is necessary to set the mathematical bar much higher. But because this is an introductory text, the majority of presentation is kept mathematically simple. The approach taken in this book is equivalent to talking about electricity and its applications without describing the details of constructing a generator.

Cryptography is at the core of our model because it coats our information and remains with it. Cryptography costs little to implement and offers tremendous value to its user. As we shall see, cryptographic methods are extensible and its applications can prove both innovative and beneficial in supplementing information system security, as well as providing the core security of information.

 To successfully complete this chapter, students should pay particular attention to the following:

- The historical milestones presented and how every iteration of cryptography builds on the strengths of its predecessors
- The characteristics of language and how particular languages feature certain statistically predictable trends
- The CAIN principles. Students should be able to explain each in significant detail. Students should strive to adopt these principles as the basis for any information security strategy
- The use of key terms and acronyms. It is important to speak the language of cryptography if you wish to learn its principles
- The basic methods of substitution, transposition, shift ciphers, and block ciphers
- The differences between symmetrical and asymmetrical cryptography

CRYPTOGRAPHY EVOLVING

Cryptography is an old science. It has grown and changed over the last 2500 years[1] and is still growing and changing. Historically, the primary catalysts for this change have been wars and the need for secret

---

[1.] Some argue that evidence of cryptography can be traced back to 2000 B.C. to the writings on the tombs of the Pharaohs. However, evidence suggests that the caricatures were not designed to conceal meaning, but rather to create mystique. Thus, we will not include this period as part of the historical analysis.

communication. Today, much of the cryptographic enhancements have been developed out of a need for privacy and information authentication requirements.

In the field of cryptography are three primary roles for individuals to pursue: cryptographers, cryptanalysts, and cryptographic users. Cryptographers are people who create ciphers and devise methods for encoding information securely. Cryptanalysts are people who try to break codes of unknown origin. Cryptographic administrators are people who select and employ cryptographic methods as part of their daily work. Cryptographers are typically expert logicians, mathematicians, and computer scientists. They are people who have in-depth knowledge of cryptographic history and in-place methods. Cryptographers have a strong grasp on cryptographic theory.

Cryptanalysts are generally intuitive and resourceful mathematicians, logicians, and computer scientists who can be broadly categorized as expert puzzle solvers. The job of the cryptanalyst is hands-on and requires both diligence and a knack for detective work.

Cryptographic administrators are people with strong backgrounds in information science and information security. These are the field experts who create the information security strategies that are deployed in corporations and organizations worldwide. All three types of contributors are expected to be experts in their respective areas. Each type of participant needs to understand the details of the technology and track its success. Cryptographic administrators tend to be less theoretical and mathematical than their counterparts.

To become an expert in the field, it is necessary to understand what has been done to date. It is also important that we follow the research currently underway. As with any technology, advancements are generally in response to some stimulus. By understanding the impetus for, and outcomes of, a particular development effort, we are better prepared to form judgments regarding our own use of the technology. For example, as we saw in Section One, new laws and government regulations are driving a considerable amount of work in this area. Information security professionals will need to understand these new laws, examine the solution options available, and implement methods that best fit the needs of the organization and its legal requirements.

The field of cryptography is intellectually stimulating and has always been cloaked in mystery. From the 1940s through today, cryptanalysts have been locked away in secret, trying to decipher enemy codes. Code breakers, also known as cryptanalysts, are perhaps a government's greatest asset in a time of war. Today, people of the same ilk are creating revolutionary products to protect our electronic identity and our privacy. Cryptanalysts are constantly engaged in decryption analysis from a variety of sources. One of those sources is electronic correspondence over the Internet. This source was used by the terrorists that perpetrated the September 11th crimes. Those terrorists used encryption methodologies to obscure messages and transmit them over the public network. Currently, our government and many law enforcement agencies around the world scour the Internet for signs of criminal activity.

The work of the modern cryptanalyst is mostly computer driven and extremely complex. Using today's modern computers, the problem space generated by early ciphers is far too small to present much of a challenge (even to brute-force deciphering methods).

As we progress with this section, two terms will appear quite frequently: ciphertext and plain text. **Cipher** refers to the system that is used to create the secret message. These systems vary and change. **Plain text** refers to the native text prior to the application of any encryption. **Ciphertext** refers to the encrypted message generated by the specific cipher.

THE HISTORY OF CRYPTOGRAPHY

Cryptography can be viewed as developing in three phases:

- Early cryptography
- Cryptography of the world at war
- Modern cryptography

The contributions made in each of these phases enlightened those who carried the art forward. Each generation of cryptographic advances obscured the methods of the past.

Early works focused mainly on **transposition** (the mixing up of characters that retain their identity) and **substitution** (substitution of plain text characters with those from a cipher alphabet) cryptography. These methods were substantially complex to conceal secrets given the negligible technological advances over this 1800-year period.

The cryptography developed during the World Wars era was heavily influenced by both the invention of electromechanical signaling (telegraph and radio) and the advancement of precision machinery. During that time, warring nations were faced with the need to secure information being communicated over public telegraph lines and open radio frequencies. To accommodate these requirements, cryptographers had to assume that messages were frequently intercepted and that intense cryptanalysis was applied. Thus, there was a need to increase the complexity of the cipher methods. To accomplish this, they created enciphering machines that could apply iterations of cryptography. These machines were also capable of producing millions of potential cipher alphabets for substitution based on the implementation of cipher wheels. The manipulation of these wheels in machines such as Enigma (the German encryption device of WWII) created seemingly unbreakable codes. History reveals that while these machines were ingenious for their time, this period was owned by the cryptanalyst. The cryptanalyst's work was so remarkable that it altered the destiny of both world wars. The cryptologists of this time employed substantial mathematical prowess to crack codes. These code breakers created the mystique that even today surrounds the intelligence community. A significant source of historical detail regarding this period can be found on the Web site of the National Security Agency, the NSA's Center for Cryptographic History, and their Cryptographic Museum.

Modern cryptography has grown in parallel with the astonishing developments of computer hardware. The development of cryptography during the modern era has been significantly influenced by the parallel evolution of algorithmic methods. Today, cryptography is integrated into the fabric of most computer applications.

EARLY CRYPTOGRAPHY

Early cryptographic methods date back thousands of years. These methods enabled generals to control the actions of armies great distances away by creating a ciphertext message, giving it to a courier who had no knowledge of the cipher or the method, and delivering it to the remote camp. Once the message was received, it could be decoded using the proper decryption technique. The thought was that should the messenger be captured, the enemy would have gained no useful information because the courier had no knowledge of what he was carrying or how it was created. The enemy would simply be left with random information.

Around 500 B.C., the Spartan army used a cryptographic device known as a scytale. A rendition of this device is pictured in Figure 5-1. This device used a long strip of paper tape, which was wound around a cylindrical holder. With the tape firmly in place, a message was written across the bands of the tape as shown in the figure. Once the message was written, the tape was unwound and given to the messenger. When the tape was received at the destination, it was rewound around a similar device and the message could be read. Should the messenger be captured during the tape's transit, the tape, when reviewed linearly, would appear as a grouping of nonsensible characters. This technique is called a **transposition cipher**. In a transposition cipher, every letter of the original message changes position in the cipher but retains its own identity (alphabetically). The key to the Spartan scytale is that to read the message first, you would have to know what to do with the tape. More important, you would have to know the dimension of the roller that it was wound around. Using a roller of the wrong dimension misaligned the characters.

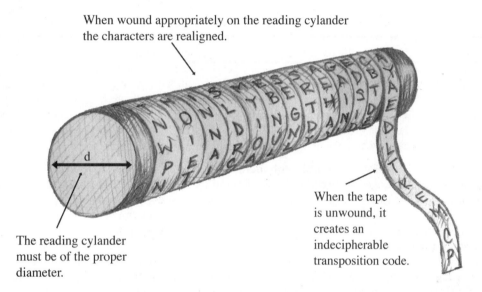

When wound appropriately on the reading cylander the characters are realigned.

The reading cylander must be of the proper diameter.

When the tape is unwound, it creates an indecipherable transposition code.

Figure 5-1   Spartan scytale used to create ciphertext by transposition of characters around 500 B.C.

In 50 B.C., the Caesar cipher was invented. The Caesar cipher is a **shift cipher**. A shift cipher uses an offset into the plain text alphabet to create the proper substitution sequence for creating the cipher code. For example, if we use a shift of four, the character "A" becomes "E", and "B" becomes "F" and so on. In this case, the word "CODE" is transformed into "GSHI."

During that time, ciphers were created and tattooed onto the shaved heads of slaves. Once some of the hair grew back the slaves were used as messengers to deliver the Roman codes. Upon arrival, the slaves' heads were once again shaved and the code read.

Shift ciphers are examples of **monoalphabetic ciphers**. In monoalphabetic ciphers, a substitution of one character in the plain text alphabet is made with a corresponding character in the ciphertext alphabet. In this case, the cipher alphabet is fixed throughout the encryption process.

Shift ciphers are generally regarded as weak ciphers because they can be figured out easily. Once the shift length is discovered, the cipher is easily broken. Some shift ciphers employ the concept of multiple shifts to make them more difficult to predict. However, even these can be discovered in a reasonable amount of time. It is important to remember that the cryptographic rationale of the time was to conceal the fact that there even was a secret. The ciphers were deliberately simplistic. It was important that the receiver not make a mistake in the decryption process because message verification (sending another slave back with confirmation) took so long. The Romans considered the discovery of the message to be unlikely anyway and the cipher was more or less a bonus. By today's standards, these simple shift ciphers are practically useless.

A monoalphabetic cipher that is considerably more difficult to break is known as a **substitution cipher**[2]. Substitution ciphers are similar in nature to shift ciphers except that they rely on a "codebook" structure that has a more random aspect to it than the shift cipher. Substitution ciphers match a plain text alphabet with an entirely new cipher alphabet and characters are simply substituted one for one during the encryption and decryption processes.

Combinations of substitution ciphers and shift ciphers can be significantly more difficult to break. Via modern methods, most monoalphabetic ciphers are easily attacked using brute-force methods with high-speed computers. The basic problem with monoalphabetic ciphers is that they do not create a large enough range of possible alternatives to classify the associated cipher problem as being difficult (given a brute-force computer algorithm). Another area of weakness is that monoalphabetic ciphers are subject to guessing based on the characteristics of the language of the plain text. For example, in the English language, certain characters (E, T, A, O, N, I, and S) occur more frequently in the normal plain text message. In a substitution cipher, this fact will also be present in the cipher code. Thus, by finding the high-frequency letters in a cryptanalysis process, one can have great success in breaking the code.

It was not until the mid-1400s that **polyalphabetic ciphers** were utilized. In a polyalphabetic cipher, the cipher alphabet changes throughout the encryption. Leon Battista Alberti, an Italian Renaissance man, is believed to be the first to demonstrate a device that creates polyalphabetic ciphers. The device, called the cipher wheel, had two concentric rings of letters. The sender and receiver had to agree by pre-arrangement on a secret letter, which would act as a synchronization spot for the inner wheel. The sender would then include as the first letter of the code a character from the outer wheel, to which the receiver should align the secret character of the inner wheel. At specified intervals throughout the message, the secret letter of the inner wheel could be realigned. This alignment was done by transmitting a new outer wheel alignment key at the designated intervals. Thus, the encryption alphabet would change as the code was developed. This promoted very secure coding.

Perhaps the most famous early example of a polyalphabetic code was created in 1585 by Blaise de Vigenere. The **Vigenere square** was developed to extend the idea of polyalphabetic ciphers to include the use of longer and stronger keys. The Vigenere square is a 26 x 26 matrix with the letters of the alphabet across the top and down the side as is shown in Figure 5-2.

Each column represents a shift cipher alphabet offset one from the column before. To use the square, you first must select a random key of some length. The fact that the key and the length are unknown to the person trying to decrypt the message creates a difficult problem to solve.

The operation of the square then becomes relatively trivial. Suppose that we wanted to encrypt the message "the quick brown fox jumps over the lazy dog."[3] Suppose that we choose the key "axyzbt." As seen

---

2. Most cryptographic texts regard a shift cipher as a primitive example of a substitution cipher. This is true because the shift or offset into the plain text alphabet creates a virtual cipher alphabet. However, in the classic example of a substitution cipher, it is likely that a completely random assignment of characters, including those that are not members of the plain text alphabet, will be used. For example, a random substitution of characters of one language can be made for those used in another.

Vigenere Square

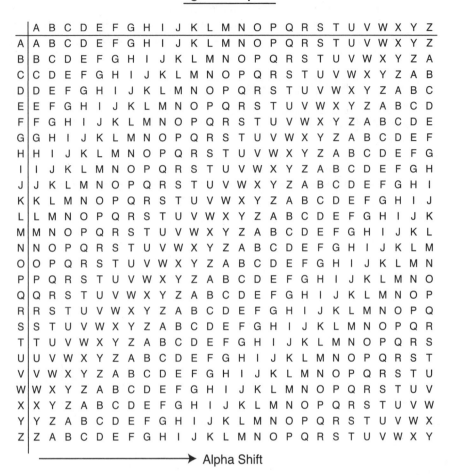

	A	B	C	D	E	F	G	H	I	J	K	L	M	N	O	P	Q	R	S	T	U	V	W	X	Y	Z
A	A	B	C	D	E	F	G	H	I	J	K	L	M	N	O	P	Q	R	S	T	U	V	W	X	Y	Z
B	B	C	D	E	F	G	H	I	J	K	L	M	N	O	P	Q	R	S	T	U	V	W	X	Y	Z	A
C	C	D	E	F	G	H	I	J	K	L	M	N	O	P	Q	R	S	T	U	V	W	X	Y	Z	A	B
D	D	E	F	G	H	I	J	K	L	M	N	O	P	Q	R	S	T	U	V	W	X	Y	Z	A	B	C
E	E	F	G	H	I	J	K	L	M	N	O	P	Q	R	S	T	U	V	W	X	Y	Z	A	B	C	D
F	F	G	H	I	J	K	L	M	N	O	P	Q	R	S	T	U	V	W	X	Y	Z	A	B	C	D	E
G	G	H	I	J	K	L	M	N	O	P	Q	R	S	T	U	V	W	X	Y	Z	A	B	C	D	E	F
H	H	I	J	K	L	M	N	O	P	Q	R	S	T	U	V	W	X	Y	Z	A	B	C	D	E	F	G
I	I	J	K	L	M	N	O	P	Q	R	S	T	U	V	W	X	Y	Z	A	B	C	D	E	F	G	H
J	J	K	L	M	N	O	P	Q	R	S	T	U	V	W	X	Y	Z	A	B	C	D	E	F	G	H	I
K	K	L	M	N	O	P	Q	R	S	T	U	V	W	X	Y	Z	A	B	C	D	E	F	G	H	I	J
L	L	M	N	O	P	Q	R	S	T	U	V	W	X	Y	Z	A	B	C	D	E	F	G	H	I	J	K
M	M	N	O	P	Q	R	S	T	U	V	W	X	Y	Z	A	B	C	D	E	F	G	H	I	J	K	L
N	N	O	P	Q	R	S	T	U	V	W	X	Y	Z	A	B	C	D	E	F	G	H	I	J	K	L	M
O	O	P	Q	R	S	T	U	V	W	X	Y	Z	A	B	C	D	E	F	G	H	I	J	K	L	M	N
P	P	Q	R	S	T	U	V	W	X	Y	Z	A	B	C	D	E	F	G	H	I	J	K	L	M	N	O
Q	Q	R	S	T	U	V	W	X	Y	Z	A	B	C	D	E	F	G	H	I	J	K	L	M	N	O	P
R	R	S	T	U	V	W	X	Y	Z	A	B	C	D	E	F	G	H	I	J	K	L	M	N	O	P	Q
S	S	T	U	V	W	X	Y	Z	A	B	C	D	E	F	G	H	I	J	K	L	M	N	O	P	Q	R
T	T	U	V	W	X	Y	Z	A	B	C	D	E	F	G	H	I	J	K	L	M	N	O	P	Q	R	S
U	U	V	W	X	Y	Z	A	B	C	D	E	F	G	H	I	J	K	L	M	N	O	P	Q	R	S	T
V	V	W	X	Y	Z	A	B	C	D	E	F	G	H	I	J	K	L	M	N	O	P	Q	R	S	T	U
W	W	X	Y	Z	A	B	C	D	E	F	G	H	I	J	K	L	M	N	O	P	Q	R	S	T	U	V
X	X	Y	Z	A	B	C	D	E	F	G	H	I	J	K	L	M	N	O	P	Q	R	S	T	U	V	W
Y	Y	Z	A	B	C	D	E	F	G	H	I	J	K	L	M	N	O	P	Q	R	S	T	U	V	W	X
Z	Z	A	B	C	D	E	F	G	H	I	J	K	L	M	N	O	P	Q	R	S	T	U	V	W	X	Y

⟶ Alpha Shift

Figure 5-2   Each row and column of the Vigenere square is a one-position-shift cipher alphabet of the row or column before.

KEY POINT

The variable-length secret key of the polyalphabetic Vigenere square creates a significantly complex problem for the cryptanalyst to solve. Many experts consider the Vigenere square to be the first "serious" cipher.

---

3. This message uses every character in the alphabet and is therefore a useful tool for cryptologists when studying the effects of a cipher on the alphabet.

in Figure 5-3, the first step is to map the key to the plain text message.[4] This step is done by repeating the key over and over under the letters of the plain text message until all of the plain text letters are exhausted. The next step is to go to the Vigenere square and find the column across the top with the corresponding plain text letter. Put your finger on that column. Next, go to the row on the left side of the Vigenere square that contains the character of the key that is being used to encrypt this particular plain

Plaintext:	T	H	E	Q	U	I	C	K	B	R	O	W	N	F	O	X	J	U	M	P	S	O	V	E	R	T	H	E	L	A	Z	Y	D	O	G
Key:	A	X	Y	Z	B	T	A	X	Y	Z	B	T	A	X	Y	Z	B	T	A	X	Y	Z	B	T	A	X	Y	Z	B	T	A	X	Y	Z	B
Ciphertext:	T	E	C	P	V	B	C	H	Z	Q	P	P	N	C	M	W	K	N	M	M	Q	M	W	X	R	Q	G	D	M	T	Z	V	C	N	H

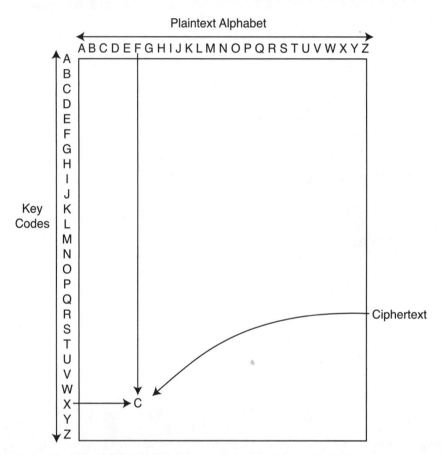

Figure 5-3   Vigenere square operation is simple. First you select the plain text letter to encrypt, then select the key value. The crossing point is the ciphertext. To decrypt, go to the row of the key value, move across to the cipher text letter, then go up to the column head for the value.

---

4. The keyword should consist of random characters to prevent a dictionary attack on the cryptosystem.

text character. Put another finger there. Now move your two fingers down the column and across the row to the intersection point. The character at this intersection is the ciphertext character. For example, to encrypt "F" with the key value of "X," we would intersect at the cipher character "C." By executing this process, we can create the ciphertext "TECPVBCHZQPPNCMWKNMMQMWXRQGDMTZVCNH."

The decryption operation simply reverses this process. First locate the row along the left side of the square that contains the appropriate key value. Next move across the row to the right until the cipher character to be decrypted is encountered. Finally, move up from that point to the top of the column to find the corresponding plain text character. It is strongly suggested that students attempt to code and decode several message using this method. As seen in the example provided, the letter "E" is used three times in the plain text. In the ciphertext, the corresponding cipher characters to each occurrence of "E" are "C," "X," and "D," respectively. Thus, true to its genre, the polyalphabetic cipher removes the statistical characteristics of the language. Additionally, by examining the ciphertext, you would see five occurrences of the letter "M." This pattern is purely coincidental and reveals nothing about the content of the plain text message.

It was widely thought that this type of cipher was unbreakable. However, in the 1920s, William Friedman created methods that proved that this cryptosystem was, in fact, vulnerable to an attack. This type of cipher ultimately drove Friedman to create mathematical and statistical proofs that could be used to predict cryptographic trends.

In 1790, Thomas Jefferson created another form of polyalphabetic cipher, the **wheel cipher**. Jefferson's device is relatively simple. There are thirty-six wooden wheels, numbered from 1 through 36. Each wheel has a scrambled alphabet around the outside. The wheels were placed on a metal spindle in an order previously agreed upon by the sender and receiver. This ordering was kept secret. The sender would take the plain text and break it into groups of thirty-six characters. The sender would create the message on the thirty-six wheels by aligning each of the plain text characters in a row. This meant that every other row on the wheel was a unique cipher. The sender can pick anyone of the other ciphered[5] lines and copy down the message. Once the entire message was ciphered, the ciphertext was aligned and sent to the receiver.

Upon receipt of the message, the receiver would break up the ciphertext up into blocks of thirty-six characters. The receiver would arrange the wheels in the predetermined order[6] and enter the first thirty-six cipher characters. Once they were in place, the decode process was simple; find the row on the wheel that had a proper sentence on it and copy it down. Once the first part of the cipher was decrypted, the receiver would move on until the next row of thirty-six characters was deciphered. This device is pictured in Figure 5-4.

This early period had numerous clever schemes for developing hard-to-break ciphers. Although many are interesting, they all display the same basic tactics, including character-oriented substitution or transposition cryptography using either monoalphabetic or polyalphabetic coding. As we have demonstrated, none of the cryptologists of this era had to combat computing like machinery, thus, brute-force attacks on any reasonably hard problems became impractical. People with strong language skills and a background in military strategy developed much of the work of this period. As we shall see, the period beginning in the late 1800s focused primarily on mathematics.

[5.] The cipher chosen could be picked randomly for each block of thirty-six letters. This created an additional level of complexity because each block of thirty-six characters could potentially correspond to a different block of letters.

[6.] The ordering could be randomized to coincide to the date, day of the week, or other clue.

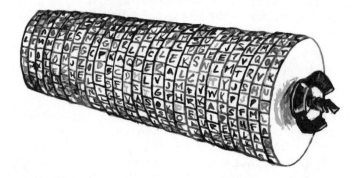

Figure 5-4   Thomas Jefferson cipher wheel.

CRYPTOGRAPHY OF THE WORLD WARS

The year 1917 was perhaps the most famous year in the history of cryptography. The Zimmerman telegram, the one-time pad, and William Friedman's theories all helped establish the first half of the twentieth century as a time of great advancement in the field of cryptography.

In 1917 the famous Zimmerman telegram—a secret German communication to Mexico in which the Germans offered Mexico territory for joining the war on Germany's side—was intercepted by British intelligence. The British encountered the message during their routine spying of American telegraph communications. British cryptographers had been able to read the German code for months. The problem was that the British needed to give the Americans the contents of the message without letting them know that British intelligence had been monitoring their trans-Atlantic telegraph services. The British did this by allowing the message to be sent to Mexico, and then seizing a copy of the message in printed form. This message was then decoded by the British. Shortly thereafter, the United States joined the British against the Germans in World War I. This example of the power of cryptanalysis caused this field to grow in importance throughout the era of World War I and World War II.

Gilbert S. Vernam of AT&T promoted the theory of the **one-time pad** around 1917. The one-time pad is a cipher that is considered perfectly secure. **Perfectly secure** is defined in cryptographic terms to mean that if an attacker has a copy of the ciphertext of a message, its content should yield no information regarding the content of the plain text message. In other words, there are no detectable patterns in the ciphertext that can reveal anything about the plain text. A one-time pad is created by using a cryptographic key that is the same length as the message to be decoded. Thus, this method is effective only for short messages, such as nuclear launch codes. For example, in the English language there are twenty-six letters in the alphabet. We will assign each letter a number ranging from one to twenty-six. For example, the plain text of the message "DINOSAUR" is 4,9,14,15,19,1,21,18. Because this is an eight-letter word, we need a predetermined eight-character key. It is best to use a randomly generated key and not another eight-letter word because the latter can be easily guessed. For this example, we shall use key 6,2,21,14,7,8,12,9. The cipher is created by shifting the original character by the number of spaces in the corresponding position in the key. Thus the "D" was shifted from a 4 to a 10, yielding the ciphertext "J." The "I" was shifted from a 9 to an 11, or a "K." The next character, "N," is 14. Mapping this to the key offset of 21 yields a 35. Because the one-time pad for English has a twenty-six-position maximum, we use modular arithmetic to realign the out-of-range number. Therefore, 35 mod 26 equals 1 with a remainder of 9. Thus we use an "I" as the correct character. Continuing with this method, we would get the one-time pad cipher for DINOASAUR = JKICZIGA. To decrypt the code, simply perform the reverse of the process using the same key. For example, the first "J" in the ciphertext is found in position 10 of the alphabet. By subtracting 6 from 10, we are left with the position of the fourth letter, or a "D."

Vernam's theory was later improved upon by Joseph Mauborgne, who proposed that the key not only be of the same length as the plain text, but that it also be completely random and nonrepeating. In theory, this was unbreakable. The one-time pad is a significant concept because it is a polyalphabetic cipher with every letter being subject to its own cipher alphabet. Therefore, if you successfully guess one character, it gives you no advantage in guessing the next. In practice, this theory is limited and impractical for three reasons:

- Very long messages would require the distribution of equally long keys, which is difficult
- The creation of a sufficient number of random, nonrepeating keys to keep up with the usage demands in a modern computing environment is impractical
- Securing the transmission of the secret keys is itself difficult

In 1917 William Friedman, known as the father of U.S. cryptography (see Figure 5-5), began the process of devising statistical methods of cracking ciphers. As we will see later in this chapter, there are important statistical patterns regarding letter use in any language. By studying these patterns, Friedman was able to create a test known as the Friedman Test (or the Index of Coincidence), which could be used by a cryptanalyst to determine the type of cipher that was being studied (monoalphabetic or polyalphabetic). Once the type of cipher is predicted, then the work of the cryptanalyst becomes much easier. Friedman's work set the tone. This work demonstrated the relationships between modern cryptography and mathematics, a theme that prevailed among the code breakers of the time and still is pervasive today. Because of this approach, many of the ciphers from the early days of cryptography were rendered too easily broken to be of any practical use.

One of the key statistics in the use of a language is one that tracks the frequency of groupings of letters. So-called **digrams** (groups of two) and **trigrams** (groups of three) are difficult to conceal and can tip a cryptanalyst as to the nature and behavior of the cipher. In 1929, Lester Hill addressed this issue in his famous **Hill cipher**. The Hill cipher is a multiletter cipher, which utilizes complex mathematics (specifically linear algebra) to help disguise frequency patterns that naturally occur in natural language from bleeding through into ciphertext. The method is sufficiently complex as to be beyond the scope of an introductory text on information security. However, it is appropriate to state that the method uses a system of matrix keys and matrix multiplication to encipher the information. The reversing process involves the use of determinants to create the proper decryption matrixes. This method can be effective in preventing attacks where the cryptanalyst has access to only the ciphertext. With this method, the larger the key matrix (2 x 2 v. 3 x 3 v. 4 x 4), the more multiletter frequencies can be disguised. For example, the 2 x 2 method hides single character frequencies. The 3 x 3 key hides both single character and digrams effectively. The problem with this method is that, for its time, it was considered computationally intensive.

Because of theories such as Hill's and Friedman's, it became necessary to automate such processes. During the Industrial Revolution, all of science became fascinated with the power and precision of mechanical devices. In 1927, this fascination finally brought automation to the science of cryptography in the **Enigma machine**. Enigma was created by German inventor Arthur Scherbius. This machine was originally thought to have significant commercial value. Its design was both unique and revolutionary for the time. Its primary goal was adding significant complexity to the solution space for character-based polyalphabetic substitution ciphers. In the case of the Enigma machine, the levels of complexity were increased to those never before realized. The machine's design is based on an electromechanical circuit that starts at a keyboard,

Figure 5-5   William Friedman.

passes through a complex series of rotors, and terminates at an indicator lamp showing the encrypted character. As seen in Figure 5-6, this machine was specifically designed with three rotors and a reversing drum that connected bidirectionally to a switchboard. The rotors had twenty-six electrical contacts on the front side. These contacts were randomly wired from the front side of the rotor through to the various spring-loaded contacts on the backside. Thus, each rotor changed the cipher alphabet. Every rotor could be started in one of twenty-six positions. After processing each character, the rotors would each rotate 1/26 of a revolution. To add even more complexity, the rotors could also be removed and interchanged in position before beginning the encryption. When the signal reached the reversing drum, it was then sent back through the routers and the switchboard via a different path.

Enigma Schematic

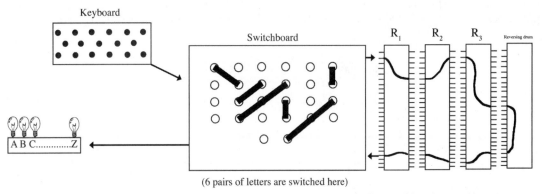

(6 pairs of letters are switched here)

3 removable and swappable rotors

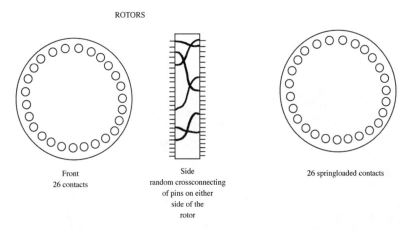

ROTORS

Front
26 contacts

Side
random crossconnecting
of pins on either
side of the
rotor

26 springloaded contacts

Figure 5-6   Enigma permits 26 ^3 or 17,576 rotor starting position combinations. It has six possible rotor configurations or 17,576 x 6 = 105456 possible rotor alpha-starting combinations. The switchboard adds 13! + 12! + 11! + 10! + 9! + 8! or 6,749,971,200 possible switch patches pairings.

Although this sounds quite complex, the operator simply typed the plain text letter into the keyboard. That act created an electronic signal that went into the switchboard. At the switchboard, up to six pairs of letters were swapped. The nonswapped letters were passed straight through. Each signal then was passed from rotor to rotor, being switched from one contact to another (changing its position in the cipher alphabet with each exchange) as it made its way through the three rotors. Upon reaching the reversing drum, the signal was sent back via a different path through the three rotors. Again the signal moved from contact to contact (continuing to scramble the cipher alphabet). Finally, the signal reached the front side of the wheel closest to the switchboard where it was passed through the switchboard and possibly subjected to the patch cord alpha-pair switching. The signal was then displayed on a lighted output device (see Figure 5-7), which indicated the cipher letter that corresponded to the plain character input.

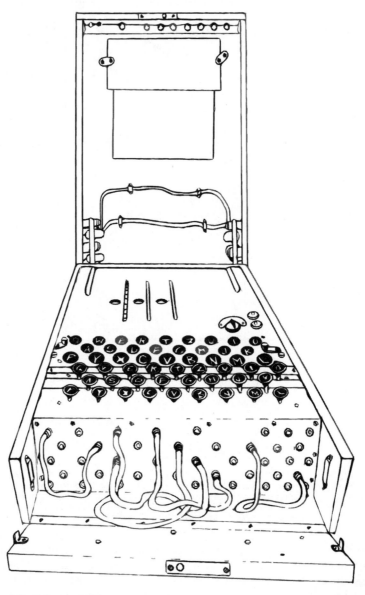

Figure 5-7   Enigma machine.

Field operatives using the device needed to know the correct order of the rotors, the manual patch configuration at the switchboard, and the correct starting position of each. The device yields the following statistics:

- $26^3 = 17,576$ starting positions of the rotors
- There are six possible orderings of the rotors themselves. This yields $6 \cdot 17,576 = 105,456$ possible pairings. Later in the war, the Germans distributed five possible rotors to fill the three slots, increasing the number of combinations to sixty and thus increasing the number of possible starting positions to 1,054,560 combinations
- At the switch board there are a possible $13! + 12! + 11! + 10! + 9! + 8! = 6,749,971,200$ ways of switching six pairs of characters on the switchboard
- An unknown complexity of being able to modify any of these settings at any time to avoid ongoing cryptanalysis

This device intrigued the Nazis, who later utilized this device in the war. Three Polish cryptanalysts, Marian Rejewski, Henryk Zygalski, and Jerzy Rozycki were able to break early versions of the Enigma code during the early 1930s. The Polish government passed on this cryptographic analysis to the British before the invasion of Poland by the Germans in 1939. The Germans made modifications to the Enigma machine by adding two extra rotors and a secret cryptographic key exchange, which was decoded first to allow the decryption operator to reset his rotors before decrypting the message that followed.

During 1939 the British began an effort to defeat the Enigma cryptography. This project was conducted at the Bletchley Park Wartime Cryptographic Headquarters of British Intelligence. During that time, the British engaged the services of Alan Turing (see Figure 5-8). Turing was a brilliant mathematician and logician who had been busy trying to answer questions about the completeness of mathematical theory[7]. At the time that Turing was brought into Bletchley Park, the Polish **Bombe machine** was being studied. Turing was instrumental in making the Bombe machine as sophisticated as it possibly could be. Turing was also responsible for assisting Britain in overcoming the Germans' later extensions of Enigma, which had temporarily rendered Allied code-breaking techniques ineffective. In achieving this latter feat, Turing created what many now consider the first electronic computing machine. With these devices, the Allies were able to decrypt German U-boat communications for the majority of the war from mid-1941 forward.

Again we see that cryptographic challenges were raised and met through the heroics of the cryptanalysts. The result was a significant impact on world events. In this particular instance, we also see the evolution of the modern computer with the origin of "Colossus," the computing device built by Turing, who is credited as being the father of computing.

In the Pacific theater, also in 1937, a cryptographic protocol known as **Purple** was being used to transmit Japanese diplomatic codes. Long before the war in the Pacific broke out, these codes were being transmitted to Japanese diplomats in Washington. William Friedman and his team of code breakers cracked the Japanese code. Information was available to U.S. diplomats throughout many negotiations during this time. Initially, they used information captured from this cryptanalysis to their significant advantage. The Japanese diplomats, unaware of the U.S. advantage, caved in to the predictably tough U.S. positions. This, in part, has been cited as a possible cause of Japanese aggression toward the United States.

About the time of the onset of hostilities, the United States became aware of a Japanese military cipher named **JN-25**. JN-25 was much tougher to break than Purple. During the initial phases of Pearl Harbor,

---

[7.] The question of completeness of mathematics can be expressed in layman's terms as 'Does there exist any method by which all mathematical questions can be answered?"

Figure 5-8   Alan Turing

JN-25 traffic increased. Unfortunately, at that time the United States did not know what that traffic increase meant. The Purple traffic, meanwhile, also increased but never made any direct mention of an invasion. U.S. diplomats were aware that the Japanese intended to break off relations on the day of the attack but had no idea why.

Just before the battle of Midway, a team of U.S. cryptanalysts, led by Lieutenant Commander Joseph Rochefort (see Figure 5-9), thought they had made some progress on JN-25, but they needed verification. Throughout the deciphering of the Japanese code, they believed that the term "AF" was being used to stand for Midway Island. Based on this information, they felt that the next target to be attacked by the Japanese was Midway. To test their theory, the team had a message couriered to Midway. This message was transmitted over a low-priority channel back to Pearl Harbor, stating that their freshwater system was broken. The U.S. cryptanalysts then started sifting through the Japanese traffic to see if they could find mention of this information. Within days they found it and gave the American fleet a decided advantage of surprise that turned the tide of the war in the United States's favor.

Figure 5-9   Lt. Cmdr. Joseph Rocheford

Cryptography Turns The Tide At Midway

Breaking the Japanese code known to Americans as JN-25 was daunting. It consisted of approximately 45,000 five-digit numbers, each number representing a word or phrase. For transmission, the five-digit numbers were super-enciphered using an additive table. Breaking the code meant using mathematical analysis to strip off the additive, then analyzing usage patterns over time, determining the meaning of the five-digit numbers. This complex process presented a challenge to the officers and men of Station Hypo, but Rochefort and his staff were able to make progress because the system called for the repetitive use of the additive tables. This increased the code's vulnerability. Even so, the work was painfully slow. Prior to the attack on Pearl Harbor, only 10% to 15% of the code was being read. By June of 1942, however, Rochefort's staff was able to make educated guesses regarding the Japanese Navy's crucial next move.

AF Is Short of Water

In the spring of 1942, Japanese intercepts began to make references to a pending operation in which the objective was designated as "AF." Rochefort and Captain Edwin Layton, Nimitz's Fleet Intelligence Officer, believed "AF" might be Midway since they had seen "A" designators assigned to locations in the Hawaiian Islands. Based on the information available, logic dictated that Midway would be the most probable place for the Japanese Navy to make its next move. Nimitz however, could not rely on educated guesses.

In an effort to alleviate any doubt, in mid-May the commanding officer of the Midway installation was instructed to send a message in the clear indicating that the installation's water distillation plant had suffered serious damage and that fresh water was needed immediately. Shortly after the transmission, an intercepted Japanese intelligence report indicated that "AF is short of water." Armed with this information, Nimitz began to draw up plans to move his aircraft carriers to a point northeast of Midway where they would lie in wait. Once positioned, they could stage a potentially decisive nautical ambush of Yamamoto's massive armada.

"The Battle"

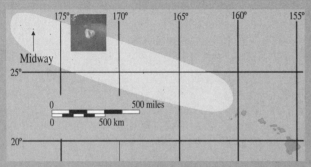

Due to the cryptologic achievements of Rochefort and his staff, Nimitz knew that the attack on Midway would commence on 3 June. Armed with this crucial information, he was able to get his outgunned but determined force in position in time. On 4 June the battle was finally joined. The early stages of the conflict consisted of several courageous but ineffective attacks by assorted Navy, Marine, and Army Air Corps units.

The tide turned however, at 10:20 a.m. when Lt. Commander Wayne McClusky's dauntless dive bombers from the USS Enterprise appeared over the main body of the Japanese invasion force. After a brief but effective attack, three of the four Japanese carriers, the Akagi, Soryu, and Kaga were on fire and about to sink. Later that day, Navy dive bombers located and attacked the Hiryu, the fourth and last major carrier in the invasion force, sending her, like the previous three, to the bottom.

Final Thoughts

As in any great endeavor, luck did indeed play a role, but Nimitz's "Incredible Victory" was no miracle. Gordon Prange, the distinguished historian, noted that "Midway was a positive American victory not merely the avoidance of defeat." General George Marshall, the U.S. Army Chief of Staff, in his comments on the victory, perhaps said it best, " as a result of Cryptanalysis we were able to concentrate our limited forces to meet their naval advance on Midway when we otherwise would have been 3,000 miles out of place."

By Patrick D. Weadon—*This information was adapted from an excerpt on the National Security Agency website at www.nsa.gov.*

MODERN CRYPTOGRAPHY

Each era of cryptography coincides with socioeconomic needs and developments. During the latter part of the twentieth century and into the new millennium, the socioeconomic drivers of cryptography have been the growth and power of computing platforms as well as the cryptographic needs of commercial business. The modern era starts concurrently with the advent of true computing technology. This technology minimizes the time required to conduct a brute-force examination of character-based cryptographic cipher. This trivializes the character cryptography problem space and requires cryptographic methods to once again increase in complexity. In order to be of any practical use, the cryptographic methods need to produce ciphers whose complexity requires the examination of an extremely large potential solution range. Over the course of the last fifty-five years, the requisite problem space has been forced to grow to practically infinite dimensions.

In 1949, Claude Shannon, a Bell Labs researcher (see Figure 5-10), accurately predicted this required cryptographic solution space behavior. Shannon is most famous for his work (along with William NyQuist) in data communications. His theories on exploiting the relationship between bandwidth (Hz) sampling

Figure 5-10   Claude Shannon.

rates and digital signal encoding, to increase information capacity on a digital circuit (expressed as $Cap = 2W_{Hz} \bullet \log_2 Signal$) created the basis for modems, digital telephony, and the telephone infrastructure.

In 1949, Shannon defined perfect security as requiring significant amounts of both diffusion and confusion. As we shall see in Chapter 6, these writings fostered the growth of bit-wise mathematical cryptographic algorithms. As had already been demonstrated by both Friedman and Hill, the use of complex mathematics could be used to strengthen the cryptographic methods. Shannon pushed this principle further by demonstrating that the problem space could be significantly enlarged through the use of bit-wise manipulations.[8]

Five factors have strongly influenced the growth of modern cryptography:

- The bit-wise manipulation of information and the availability of substantial computer memory capacity
- Extremely rapid development of super-high-speed processors
- High-speed networking and the convergence of voice, data, and video signaling onto a common open network
- Worldwide government sponsorship of privacy, industry, and fiduciary legislation targeted at electronic information
- Heightened intelligence gathering and cryptanalysis efforts on the part of communist nations required organizations, such as the NSA, to sponsor[9]

During the 1950s and 1960s, the worldwide fascination with computers began to grow. While only the largest corporations, universities, and government were in a financial position to own computers, commercial applications in telephony, banking, manufacturing, and research began to grow.

During this same cold war period, tensions between the United States and the former Soviet Union spawned the rapid development of advanced cryptographic and cryptanalysis methods. These methods were used for diplomatic and military exchanges on both sides. With the potential of quick-strike weapons of mass destruction, it was imperative that neither side gain any advantage over the other in the secret information intelligence war. This information intelligence also was active in the industrial space (both military and nonmilitary).

VENONA

On 1 February 1943, the U.S. Army's Signal Intelligence Service, a forerunner of the National Security Agency, began a small, very secret program, later codenamed VENONA. The object of the VENONA program was to examine and possibly exploit, encrypted Soviet diplomatic communications. These messages had been accumulated by the Signal Intelligence Service (later renamed the U.S. Army Signal Security Agency and commonly called "Arlington Hall" after the Virginia location of its headquarters) since 1939 but had

---

[8]. Because each character is worth eight bits and we can manipulate any bit in the pattern—and diffuse the technique by nonalignment with traditional byte-wise boundaries—the encipherment grows quickly in complexity. Thus, the solution space to any cryptographic problem should grow accordingly and the problem can then be considered hard.

[9]. NSA still pursues the brightest mathematical and computer science minds to continue these activities.

not been studied previously. Miss Gene Grabeel, a young Signal Intelligence Service employee, who had been a school teacher only weeks earlier, started the project.

The accumulated message traffic comprised an unsorted collection of thousands of Soviet diplomatic telegrams that had been sent from Moscow to certain of its diplomatic missions and from those missions to Moscow. During the first months of the project, Arlington Hall analysts sorted the traffic by diplomatic mission and by cryptographic system or subscriber.

The VENONA Breakthroughs

From the very beginning in February 1943, the analysis of the traffic proved slow and difficult. Then in October 1943, Lieutenant Richard. Hallock, a Signal Corps reserve officer who had been a peacetime archaeologist at the University of Chicago, discovered weaknesses in the cryptographic system of the Soviet trade traffic. This discovery provided a tool for further analytic progress on the other four cryptographic systems.

During 1944, the skills of other expert cryptanalysts were brought to bear on this Soviet message traffic to see if any of the encryption systems of the messages could be broken. One of these cryptanalysts, Cecil Phillips, made observations which led to a fundamental break into the cipher system used by the KGB, although he did not know at the time who used the system. The messages were double-encrypted and of enormous difficulty. In spite of Arlington Hall's extraordinary cryptanalytic breakthroughs, it was to take almost two more years before parts of any of these KGB messages could be read or even be recognized as KGB rather than standard diplomatic communications.

In the summer of 1946, Meredith Gardener, an Arlington Hall analyst, began to read portions of KGB messages that had been sent between the KGB Residency in New York and Moscow Center. On 31 July 1946, he extracted a phrase from a KGB New York message that had been sent to Moscow on 10 August 1944. This message, on later analysis, proved to be a discussion of clandestine KGB activity in Latin America. On 13 December Gardener was able to read a KGB message that discussed the U.S. presidential election campaign of 1944. A week later, on 20 December 1946, he broke into another KGB message that had been sent to Moscow Center two years earlier which contained a list of names of the leading scientists working on the Manhattan Project—the atomic bomb!

In late April or early May 1947, Gardner was able to read two KGB messages sent in December 1944 that showed that someone inside the War Department General Staff was providing highly classified information to the Soviets. These two messages are currently undergoing declassification review.

U.S. Army intelligence, G-2, became alarmed at the information that was coming out of Arlington Hall. An Arlington Hall report on 22 July 1947 showed that the Soviet message traffic contained dozens, probably hundreds, of cover names, many of KGB agents, including ANTENNA and LIBERAL (later identified as Julius Rosenberg). One message mentioned that LIBERAL's wife was named "Ethel."

General Carter W. Clarke, the assistant G-2, called the FBI liaison officer to G-2 and told him that the Army had begun to break into Soviet intelligence service traffic and that the traffic indicated a massive Soviet espionage effort in the U.S.

This information was adapted from an excerpt on the NSA Web site at http://www.nsa.gov.

By the early 1970s it became obvious that the confidentiality of commercial data needed to be addressed. The **National Bureau of Standards (NBS)** issued an industry-wide challenge to create a standard method of encrypting commercial data. IBM Corporation's research team at Watson Labs responded with a cipher called the **Lucifer cipher**. This cipher was a bit-wise symmetrical encryption coded to a 56-bit key. Given such a strong key[10], the government felt that making the encryption algorithm public would in no way compromise the security of the ciphers created with this method. In 1977 the NBS released the **Data Encryption Standard (DES)**. DES was a popular symmetrical encryption algorithm that is still widely used today.[11]

During this same period, it became obvious inside the cryptographic community that the use of symmetrical cryptography was becoming impractical because of the tremendous key management issue. As we will explore in detail in Chapter 8, key distribution to all potential computer users would require the management of an extremely large space. This is because for every pair of communicating parties, a secret key would need to exist.

In the years 1976 and 1977 three cryptologists, Diffie, Hellman, and Merkle pursued work on a so-called public key cryptography system. This system is based on the premise that algorithms exist so that creation of a two-key system was possible. Two-key systems permit the use of public (known to everyone) and private (secret) key pairs. This system would create an asymmetry in that messages encrypted with the public key could be opened with only the reciprocal private key of the pair. For example, if a message is encrypted with a public key, even that same public key could not open it. The message could be opened by only the corresponding private key. This method would significantly reduce the total number of keys in the system. This will be discussed in detail in latter parts of Section Two. Initially, there was a great interest in this work. In 1977, Rivest, Shamir, and Aldeman released the RSA encryption algorithm for public key transmission. This method is still widely used today. Because of a lack of industry-wide understanding of the technology and some unfortunate early trial results in 1976, most considered the method not secure.

During the last five years there has been a serious renewal of interest in this method. It turns out, as we shall see later, that asymmetrical cryptography can provide us with authentication, verification, non-repudiation, and a capability permitting the secret exchange of symmetrical keys. This method, which was virtually ignored for twenty-five years, has suddenly sparked the growth of a whole new industry.

One of the many applications of asymmetrical cryptography is e-mail. E-mail is one of the largest forms of communications known. Because it is possible to receive an e-mail message from unknown

---

[10]. Through the early 1990s, 56-bit keys were considered extremely strong because a brute-force attack against a properly constructed key remained outside the limits of practicality. The sheer number of combinations would take thousands of years of compute cycles given the technology of the time.

[11]. Today there are longer key variants of the protocol available. There are also algorithmic differences in later versions of the cipher.

sources, verification and authentication of the source and the message is necessary. In 1991 a method was created by Phil Zimmerman, who addressed these concerns. This method is **Pretty Good Privacy (PGP)**. PGP uses the RSA and Diffie-Hellman work at the core. This method presumes the existence of a widely distributed asymmetrical key infrastructure called a Public Key Infrastructure (PKI). As a member of the PKI, users would each be granted public and private key pairs. These pairs can then be used to provide authentication, confidentiality, and nonrepudiation services. The details of asymmetrical cryptography and methods such as PGP and S/MIME are addressed in Chapter 8.

In 1997, NIST determined that a replacement encryption standard was required for the DES standard adopted twenty years prior. DES (56-bit keys) and even triple-DES (128-bit keys) were believed to be vulnerable to attack. In particular, NIST was looking for an algorithm that was efficient, secure, flexible, free, publicly available, and easy to use. One of the primary considerations was that the algorithm had to support 128-, 192-, and 256-bit keys. To facilitate this development, NIST created a development contest. Of the fifteen submissions, five made the final list:

- RC6 from RSA Labs
- MARS from IBM
- Serpent by Anderson
- Twofish by Counterpane Security
- Rijndael by Daemen and Rijmen

These five algorithms were subjected to public testing. In 1998 the winning algorithm, Rijndael, was formally adopted by NIST as Federal Information Processing Standard 197. This algorithm is currently being phased in throughout industry as the new de facto standard. This algorithm is reviewed in more detail in Chapter 7.

An alternative approach to securing information is found in **steganography**. Steganography is the concept of hiding the existence of a message as opposed to cryptography, which acknowledges the existence of a message but is the science of hiding the meaning of the message.

Steganography is not a new idea. In 1623, Sir Francis Bacon produced early steganographic works. He created a method that hid encrypted messages inside a written text. Through the use of an early version of binary code (a and b rather than one and zero), a codebook, and steganography Bacon created these complex messages.

This concept of taking one piece of information and hiding it inside another has recently undergone a resurgence. Computer applications such as images, music, and movies contain many unused bits. These bits are necessary for padding the bit count or for providing informational codes. Steganography can take advantage of these areas and use them to hide encrypted messages. These minor bit variations will have little or no effect on the primary art form. These computer-created files can then be exchanged in the open without anyone seeing the hidden information. This modern implementation of steganography is quite impressive.

The future of cryptography appears to be taking a much different shape than the cryptographic methods presently used. Mathematically based cryptosystems nowadays rely on computational complexities to guarantee security. These methods are hard to create and slow to run. Experimentation is now under way with a new technique known as quantum cryptography. Quantum cryptography relies on the naturally occurring principles found in light as the device to achieving perfect or unconditional security. Quantum cryptography can be defined as a cryptographic technique based on the physics of light, not mathematics.

Sir Francis Bacon and Early Steganography

First, a message was encrypted using a binary-like code of lowercase a's and b's. The code was then laid out consecutively. Next, any random message was aligned with the code, character for character. If the random message character aligned with an "a," then the letter of the random message would appear in lowercase normal font. If the random message character aligned with a "b," then the letter of the random message would appear in uppercase special font.

Bacon's Bilateral Cipher

Bilateral Codes

A-aaaaa	H-aabbb	O-abbba	V-babab
B-aaaab	I-abaaa	P-abbbb	W-babba
C-aaaba	J-abaab	Q-baaaa	X-babbb
D-aaabb	K-ababa	R-baaab	Y-bbaaa
E-aabaa	L-ababb	S-baaba	Z-bbaab
F-aabab	M-abbaa	T-baabb	
G-aabba	N-abbab	U-babaa	

Method
1- Create plaintext, 2- Code plaintext, 3- Map the cipher text to some miscellanious, 4- Change the font or case of anyletter in the random message aligned with 'b'.

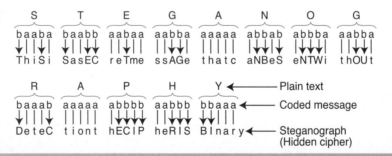

When people received the message:

"ThiS iS a sECreT messAGe that caN Be SeNT WithOUt DeteCtion thE CIPheR IS Binary,"

they would simply write a's under the lowercase regular font characters and b's under the uppercase special font characters. Then they could reverse the code. In this case, the plain text message passed is STEGANOGRAPHY.

The theory of quantum physics reveals that every light particle, a photon, has a specific orientation. For simplicity's sake, limit the orientation to only one of these four:

The sender and receiver predetermine which of these orientations are to be considered a 1 and which are to be considered a 0. The sender then transmits the bit stream using a laser that can change the orientation of each photon to match the 1 or 0 being transmitted. By using polarizing filters to screen the incoming photons, we can determine the orientation of the received photon and thus understand the stream. The reason this technique is secure is a direct result of Heisenberg's uncertainty principle. This principle states that by examining the photon, we will effect a change on it. This implies that if the message is viewed (eavesdropped) by a third party, the communicating parties will immediately know. Therefore, any message is 100 percent secure in that the first instance of eavesdropping will be noticed and appropriate action taken.

In theory this technique seems plausible. In practice, however, there are still many practical implementation problems including producing lasers that can transmit exactly one photon at a time in the proper orientation, reducing the significant numbers of retransmissions now thought to be necessary to invoke this method, and developing more discriminating filters for the receivers. This technology is still under development but appears promising.

HISTORICAL PERSPECTIVE

More than 1,800 patents are currently held on modern cryptographic methods. Given its long history and great advancement, cryptography can be thought of as both proven and sophisticated. In the annals of cryptographic history there are distinct break points in the timelines where major advancements took place. These break points normally coincide with related developments in the support technology.

We are rapidly approaching another of these break points: the development of sophisticated steganographic and quantum cryptographic methods and support technologies. Although it may take a considerable amount of time for these developments to become fully implemented and widely available, it is likely that they (or something equally as fascinating) will occur.

For these reasons it is safe to assume that cryptography will continue to be the primary mechanism utilized in the protection of information.

THE STUDY OF LANGUAGE

Information is normally communicated in the form of a proper language.[12] Each language has certain characteristics regarding what are known as usage statistics. Usage statistics represent information captured from the analysis of the literature of a language. Usage statistics supply the cryptanalyst with important information that can help decipher coded messages. A good cipher will attempt not only to disguise the message, but also to hide identifiable patterns that persist in the native language. Sometimes a cipher will permit these trends to pass through inadvertently. If this happens, the cryptanalyst generally uses usage statistics to assist in identifying these trends.

By examining a language, what can we learn that will help the cryptanalyst? Consider the English language and examine some of the trends that are normal in the written word.

[12.] Occasionally, information is represented in a pure numerical fashion, such as in machine-to-machine communications.

Take for example the complexity of a substitution cipher. We will substitute some character for every character of the alphabet. Essentially, we are building a codebook. To break a substitution cipher, we have to consider sixty-eight factorial possible different ciphers[13] (there are sixty-eight characters on the average keyboard) for a substitution cipher of the English keyboard (68 for A, 67 for B, 66 for C ... 1 for +). Notice that after each pairing of characters, we reduce the number of available choices for the next pair by one. Thus, there are $2.48 \cdot 10^{96}$ possible substitution ciphers to try. Obviously, this is too many ciphers to test on a trial-and-error basis (i.e. a brute-force strategy).

What is required, therefore, is a strategy. In fact, the English language usage statistics provide us with a basis for this strategy.

The most important character used in written English is the space character. We use the space character to separate words and sentences. The space character represents eighteen percent of all the characters used in the written text. The space character, then, presents a special problem for the cryptographer. If the cryptographer includes the space character in the cipher, it will appear in roughly eighteen percent of all the characters (even if the characters are scrambled). This will give the cryptanalyst a clue as to a plain text-ciphertext match. Once the cryptanalyst can determine a match, it is much easier to infer characteristics about the cryptographic method and encryption keys. Yet if the cryptographer decides not to encrypt the spaces, then we reveal characteristics about the structure of sentences and the length of words. These are also powerful decryption tools.

Another useful statistic is the predictability of letters of the alphabet in written text. Every letter in the alphabet is used with a certain predictable frequency. This predictability can help cryptanalyst structure guesses about the content of a message. Table 5-1 provides some approximations of frequency of character use.[14]

The cryptanalyst might use this information by examining the high-frequency characters of the ciphertext and attempt to match the letters E, T, O, A, N, I, or S as possible substitutions. It is wise to avoid the substitution of low-frequency characters in initial guesses. By using these frequencies, the cryptanalyst may be able to achieve some legitimate matches.

Table 5-1 Frequency of Character Use

E –12%	T –9.5%	O –8.2%	A –8%
N –7.5%	I –7.1%	S –6.5%	R –6.02%
H –4.75%	L –4.3%	D –3.4 %	U –3.21%
C –3.1%	M –2.6%	P –2.3%	F –2.25%
Y –2.2%	G –1.8%	W –1.69%	B –1.5%
V –1%	K - 0.75%	X - 0.25%	Q- 0.2%
J –0.17%	Z –0.08%		

[13.] This figure does not count the possibility of using both uppercase and lowercase characters or nonprintable characters.

[14.] Table 5-1 was created based on an empirical analysis of several large documents normalized against other industry averages. This table does not take uppercase versus lowercase into account.

Other less-obvious heuristics for trends in the English language include the following:

- The only single-letter words are in the English language are A and I. So stand-alone characters are likely to be one of those.
- The most common small words include the, and, to, of, is, in, it, on, as, at, are, but, if, my, so, or, do, no, me, an, by, we, all was, can, get, hi, etc., any, too, up, out, has, now, its, see, who, may, did, see, our, ill, two, one, use, that, have, this, with, will, some, your. These are statistically more common than any other stand-alone two-, three-, or four-character-word groupings.
- Digrams—pairs of letters appearing adjacent to one another—either stand-alone or are imbedded in a word. The total number of possible digrams is 27 x 27 = 729 combinations (including blanks) possible. The most common digrams are

TH –3%	HE –2.5%	AN –1.5%	IN –1.5%	ER –1.49%
RE –1.35%	ON –1.25%	AT –1.23%	OU –1.2%	OR –1.2%
ES –1.8%	HA –1.5%	TO –1.25%	TE - 1%	IS –1%

- Trigrams are triplets of letters that are adjacent to each other either stand alone or imbedded in a word. There are 26 x 26 x 26 = 17,576 possible adjacent triples (not counting blank spaces). The five most frequently used trigrams are THE, ING, AND, HAT, and THA.

PROTECTING INFORMATION

Information has natural links to cryptography. The properties of information that we reviewed in Chapter 1 provided us with the basis for this relationship. As we saw earlier in reviewing the history of cryptography, concealing information from an enemy or foe has long been the catalyst for applying cryptographic methods to information. During the growth of telecommunications during the twentieth century, integrity-checking mechanisms were included in the cryptographic suite in the form of checksums.

More recently, the rationale has been expanded to include authenticity and nonrepudiation as being important drivers of cryptographic applications for information.

For these and other reasons we shall explore, cryptographic methods, principles, and applications represent the core technology reviewed in the heart of this text. Students that can master this material are well on their way to developing a successful career in information security.

The remainder of this chapter will serve as a primer for the remaining chapters of this section. First, it is important to understand how the CAIN principles can be completely satisfied through the proper application of cryptographic methods.

We will then explore the language of cryptography. This exploration is important because so many terms and acronyms are widely misunderstood. This will also be used as an opportunity to review and consolidate what we have learned about cryptography from scattered sections in previous chapters.

Next, a review of the primitive types of security will be re viewed. These types can be thought of as the building blocks of current methods. Several of these have already been explored during our discussion of the history of cryptography.

Often, the term cryptographic strength is discussed. A brief discussion of strength is presented with specific reference to passwords and password cracking. This is an easy introduction to the topic that is familiar to most students.

Finally, a discussion is presented of why cryptography is placed so close to the core of our information security model. This again reviews and expands on some material that was presented earlier.

CAIN

As we have discussed as a main theme of this text, the basic principles of Confidentiality, Authenticity, Integrity and Non-repudiation (CAIN) should be considered the guiding principles of information security. We demonstrated in Section One of this text that the information and the information system are, indeed, separable. It is important to commit to information security at the core of our model as was demonstrated in Chapter 4.

Recently the CAIN principles were adopted as a guiding international principle. The X.800 Security Architecture for OSI by ITU-T (International Telecommunication Union Telecommunication Standardization Sector) uses and expands the CAIN principles in the discussion of telecommunications and data security. This CAIN-like structure has five categories that support fourteen specific services:

- Authentication—An assurance that the communicating entity is, in fact, the party that is communicating.
- Access Control—Restriction of unauthorized access.
- Data Confidentiality—Prevention of unauthorized disclosure of information.
- Data Integrity—The assurance that transmitted and received data are exactly the same.
- Nonrepudiation—Provides protection against one of the communicating parities denying participation in a communication that they in fact took part in.

If you read further in the standard, you will notice that the following methods are discussed for achieving success in the five categories mentioned above:

- Encryption
- Digital Signatures
- Access Control
- Data Integrity
- Authentication Exchange
- Traffic Padding
- Routing Control
- Notarization
- Trusted functionality
- Security labeling
- Event detection
- Audit Trail
- Security recovery

Throughout the remainder of this section of the text, we will focus on a good number of those categories as being crucial to our success in meeting CAIN from an information security standpoint. Encryption and cryptographic application, digital signatures, integrity checking, authentication, and notarization techniques—if applied to information correctly—can satisfy all of the CAIN requirements.

THE LANGUAGE OF CRYPTOGRAPHY

Cryptography is a blended science with roots in many different fields. As we saw earlier, cryptography was heavily used by warring armies. Cryptographers of the early era were artists, philosophers, and mathematicians. Scientists and inventors later became the dominant players in the field.

Today's work in this area is primarily done by mathematicians, logicians, computer scientists, and most recently (in quantum cryptosystems) by members of the natural science community. As a result of thousands of years of input, cryptography has developed its own rather unique language. Many of the words in this language are often misused or are used out of context in casual conversation.

Up to this point in the text, the language of cryptography has been introduced in various places. This part of the chapter recaps the many terms that were used—and introduces a few new ones that will be discussed in subsequent chapters—and helps to put them in context.

- **Algorithms** are step-wise, repeatable solutions to problems. Algorithms are opposed to **heuristics**, which are roughly defined as educated guesses. For example, the method for calculating a sum can be expressed algorithmically, whereas the choosing of a winning stock relies on the experience of the broker and is ,therefore, an informed judgment or a heuristic. Cryptographic methods are expressed algorithmically in a formal programming language
- **Cryptology** is the study of cryptographic methods
- **Cryptography** is the science dealing with the development of cryptographic methods.
- A **cryptanalyst** is a person that performs cryptanalysis of a message. **Cryptanalysis** is the science of converting ciphertext back into plain text without complete knowledge of all parts of the cipher
- A **cryptographer** is a person who develops ciphers
- A **cipher** is a method, expressed as an algorithm in programmatic terms, that can be used to transform an original message into an encrypted message. The cipher must also supply a method for converting the encrypted message back into the original message.
- **Plain text** is the original message without alteration or modification by a cryptographic method
- **Ciphertext** is the resulting output of a cipher, the encrypted message
- **Encryption** is the process of transforming plain text into ciphertext
- A **key** is a secret software code that is input into a cryptographic algorithm to enable encryption or decryption. This code causes or adjusts the behavior of the algorithm so that the results of encryption are unique. Keyed cryptographic methods are beneficial in that the algorithm can be made publicly available so long as the key is kept secret (more detail is provided in Chapters 6 and 7)
- **Decryption** is the process of turning ciphertext back into plain text
- **Encipher** is another term for encryption
- **Decipher** is another term for decryption

- A **symmetrical algorithm** is a keyed cryptographic technique that uses the same key for both the encryption algorithm and the decryption algorithm (more detail is provided in Chapter 7)
- An **asymmetrical algorithm** is a keyed cryptographic technique that uses one key for the encryption algorithm and another for the decryption algorithm (more detail is provided in Chapter 8)
- A **message digest**, **checksum**, or **hash** is a mapping function of the variable-length original plain text message to a fixed-length numerical code. The hash is calculated as a fixed-length value based on a certain mathematical interpretation of the bit-wise value of the original message (more detail is provided in Chapters 6 and 8)
- A **cryptographic checksum** is a message digest that is calculated for a message and is then encrypted with a secret key (more detail is provided in Chapter 8)
- A **digital signature** is a special case of a cryptographic checksum that is encrypted using a public key algorithm or asymmetric algorithm (more detail is provided in Chapter 8)
- **Unconditionally secure** means that no matter how much ciphertext cryptanalysts have, they cannot use it to understand the structure or content of the plain text or the encryption method. This term is sometimes called perfect security
- **Computationally secure** means that the information is secure if the time to break a cipher takes longer than the useful life of the information, or if the cost to break it is higher than the cost of the information
- **Steganography** is the concept of hiding the existence of a message. This concept is opposed to cryptography, which acknowledges the existence of a message but is the science of hiding the meaning of the message
- **Quantum cryptography** can be defined as a cryptographic technique based on the physics of light, not mathematics. This technique relies on **Heisenberg's uncertainty principle**, which states that by examining the photon, we will effect a change on it. This principle implies that if the message is viewed (eavesdropped) by a third party, the communicating parties will immediately know. This technology is still under development

KEY POINT

It is important for students to familiarize themselves with these terms. The language of cryptography is often misused and can be confusing.

In the study of cryptography, it has become necessary to use formal mathematical notation to express the outcomes of the methods that we wish to employ. Cryptographic methods always have the same form: a given plain text sample is exposed to a cryptographic technique which generates a specified ciphertext outcome. Given the complexities of some of these methods, the cryptographer requires a means to express these transitions succinctly. In the next chapter you will learn that the concept of a function (a process with specified inputs and output) is most appropriate for achieving this goal.

A symmetric cryptographic algorithm requires a common key to encrypt a plain text message and to decrypt the ciphertext. This process can be described quite clearly in mathematical terms as:

$$P = D(k, (E(k, P)))$$

This equation reads as follows: "Given a plain text *P* and a symmetrical key *k*, the encryption function *E* can be applied to those inputs to generate the corresponding ciphertext as expressed *E(k,P)*. This same ciphertext can be submitted to the decryption algorithm *D* with the identical key *k*, to regenerate the original plain text *P*."

The cryptographers' ability to express these relationships mathematically allows them to view the step-wise progress of an algorithm and thus understand and improve it.

Asymmetric cryptography can be expressed in much the same way. The following equation reads identically to the symmetrical equation except that the encryption is done with the encryption key K_e and the decryption routine uses the key K_d where the keys $K_e \neq K_d$.

$$P = D(K_d, (E(K_e, P))) \text{ where } K_e \neq K_d$$

Although this takes some getting used to, it is much easier and clearer. Throughout this text, a deliberate attempt to ease students into such nomenclature is made.

GENERALIZED CRYPTOGRAPHIC METHODS

The job of the cryptographer is to create methods that permit information to remain confidential, accurate, and authentic. As we have seen, many methods are available to the cryptographer to accomplish this goal. Another principle goal of the cryptographer is to be able to develop a problem that is complex enough so that the resulting ciphertext is difficult to reverse engineer. The job of the cryptanalyst is precisely to detect weaknesses in the cryptographic method and to exploit those weaknesses so that reengineering both the cryptographic method and the secret keys is possible.

The following methods are available to cryptographers:

- Substitution ciphers require minimally two alphabets: the plain text alphabet and the ciphertext alphabet. For each character in the plain text message, cryptographers find the corresponding secret code, which they then use in the corresponding position in the ciphertext message. Substitution ciphers require a predetermined coding strategy to be effective. Caesar ciphers use a simple shift coding strategy as described earlier. This shift strategy means that the sender and receiver needed to remember only the shift number. The secret cipher alphabet could then be automatically generated. Substitution ciphers are normally associated with codebooks. Substitution ciphers can be either monoalphabetic or polyalphabetic depending on the scheme employed. Substitution ciphers are usually vulnerable to brute-force computer attacks if they work at the character level. Substitution ciphers that work at the binary level provide a greater number of solutions for the cryptanalyst to consider, and are therefore still effective. A brute-force attack on a binary-level substitution cipher is considerably more difficult to break, especially if the substitution is based on a hard-to-solve mathematical problem. Modern substitution ciphers are generally keyed.
- Transposition ciphers are created by effectively scrambling the original message. Early forms of transposition ciphers were found in the Spartan scytales cipher shown earlier in this chapter. In a classic transposition cipher, the plain text alphabet is preserved; only the ordering of the characters is altered.
- Monoalphabetic substitution ciphers utilize a single-cipher alphabet in coding messages. This means that should the cryptanalyst guess correctly on several of the letter substitutions, the remaining coding scheme can be broken because all the characters

are related to the same cipher alphabet. Cryptanalysts have studied the statistics of language so they can make the best guesses possible in determining the cipher codes. One of the weaknesses of the monoalphabetic ciphers is that the cipher messages retain the language-usage characteristics of the original message and they are, therefore, prone to being compromised by this type of guessing strategy analysis.

- Polyalphabetic substitution ciphers are much more difficult to break. Polyalphabetic substitution ciphers require that the cipher alphabet changes throughout the encryption process. This allows for the normalization of language anomalies. As we saw in Thomas Jefferson's cipher wheel, all of the statistical language tendencies are removed from the message. This was because every thirty-sixth letter of the cipher had its own random cipher alphabet. Later we saw how the Hill cipher and the Vigenere cipher both could accomplish this same goal by a different means. Ultimately, the one-time pad was shown to be theoretically unbreakable if the key length and the message length were the same.

- Keyed cryptographic methods allow for flexibility in the cryptographic algorithm. The key influences the behavior of the algorithm. In early keyed cryptographic methods, the key was used to determine which cryptographic alphabet to use (such as in the one-time pad). In modern-day keyed algorithms, the key is used as part of complex mathematical computations to disguise the information. The concept of "applying a key" is difficult for most students to understand. In Chapter 7 we will examine the TEA to assist students in understanding this concept.

- Symmetrical cryptographic methods utilize a common key shared by the sender and the receiver of a message. Each of the communicating parties requires a set of reciprocal coding and decoding algorithms. The secret key is applied to both and enables the decode routines to undo the cryptography created by the coding routines. This methodology is covered in great detail in Chapter 6.

- Asymmetrical cryptographic methods require a key pair, one for the encryption routine and a separate one for the decryption routine. A special case of asymmetrical cryptography is public key cryptography, which is discussed in detail in Chapter 7.

- Block ciphers are symmetrical ciphers where large blocks of bits are transformed as a group into a ciphertext block of the same length. Block ciphers have two properties that are advantageous. First, they diffuse information from the plain text message across the corresponding ciphertext block. This best hides the relationship between the two. Second, by using a block cipher it is impossible for anyone to add information to the cipher (plant information). This is because the information added would change the block length and corrupt the encipherment. The guiding principle with respect to block ciphers is that the larger the block, the greater the security. However, this increased security does come at a price: sacrificed speed.

- Stream ciphers are ciphers that convert one plain text element into the corresponding ciphertext element without considering other elements in the message. Stream ciphers are less effective at concealing the method of encryption but are significantly faster than block ciphers.

STRENGTH OF METHOD

Throughout this introduction it has been emphasized that complex mathematical problems provide modern cryptographic methods with their strength. In the next chapter, we will review the underpinnings of the mathematics used to create these "hard" problems. From an introductory point of view, strength of cryptographic method can be thought of as being coincident with solution time: The longer it takes to crack a cryptographic method, the stronger that method is. Additionally, because most published cryptography standards require that the methods be publicly available, it is actually the key that provides the strength to the algorithm. In fact, it is accurate to say that the longer the key, the stronger the algorithm.

Table 5-2 suggests the relative strength of a symmetrical algorithm with various key lengths[15].

Table 5-2 Relative Strength

Key Size	Approximate Time to Crack
40 bits	< 2 Seconds
56 bits	< 35 hours
64 bits	< 11 Months
80 bits	< 10,000 years
128 bits	Approximately 10^{17} years Virtually Impossible!

It is important to note that brute-force attacks on cryptography can be divided among a group of computers. For example, if cryptanalysts suspect that they know the encryption algorithm type, they can make a guess at the key length. By doing so, they can assign ranges of keys to be tried by various computers available to them. Each computer then would have a manageable set of keys to test and thus, depending on the number of computers available, they could effectively reduce the time to crack the code. If we were trying to crack a 64-bit code with eleven computers, we might be able to complete the task in one month instead of eleven months.

Moore's law states that we achieve about a tenfold computing efficiency increase every five years. Thus, as every year passes, computers and networks provide us the ability to process information more effectively and to distribute brute-force attacks more efficiently. In 1997, RSA data security challenged the public to attempt to crack a variety of ciphers with key sizes ranging from 40 bits to 128 bits. Some of the results of this contest are shown in Table 5-3.

Although strictly measuring performance is a relative indicator of strength, other criteria should also be considered. In 1949, Claude Shannon published his thoughts on what is needed to make a "good" cryptographic method. In his work, "Communication Theory of Secrecy Systems," *Bell Systems Technical Journal*, v28, Oct 1949, he cited five criteria "that should be applied in estimating the value of a proposed secrecy system." His notes on this topic can be found in the section of the document entitled, "Valuations of Secrecy Systems." The following are the five principles outlined:

[15.] Estimates based on symmetrical cryptography running on average cost 2001 technology using a brute-force cryptanalysis program. This means that the algorithm will try every possible key in the solution range.

Table 5-3 RSA Challenge Test Results

Key Length	Time	Computers	Keys/Sec. Rate
40	3.5 hours	250	27 million keys/sec.
48	13 days	3,500	440 million keys/sec.
56	39 days	22,000 contributors (people, not computers)	34 billion keys/sec.

- **Amount of secrecy**—This principle refers to the amount of labor (measured in time) and the amount of material (captured ciphertext) requ ired to break a cryptosystem. The first of these, time, is consistent with the metrics discussed earlier relating key length and time to crack the system. Further, the time component of this principle also is closely related to the relative amounts of money our adversary will spend to attempt to crack our codes.

  The amount of material required to provide the cryptanalyst with enough clues as to the operation of the cipher is equally important, although much harder to quantify. This part of the first principle is related to the complexity of the cryptosystem. This principle yields drastically different results with every cryptosystem. For example, in a monoalphabetic system where the frequency characteristics of language are evident (consistent between the cipher alphabet and the plain text alphabet), the amount of material required to begin to infer the underlying strategy is relatively small. However, in a Hill cipher—which, by design, hides single-character frequency tendencies as well as those of digrams and trigrams—the complexity of the system requires substantially more intercepted data to yield similar results.

- **Size of Key**—Shannon stated that because the key must be secretly transmitted and possibly memorized, "it is therefore desirable to have the key as small as possible." This principle presents somewhat of a paradox. Throughout this part of the chapter (and even implied in the first principle), we have represented that a large key is preferable to a smaller one because a large key will represent the more difficult problem to solve. In fact, it is widely accepted that the one-time pad where the key is as long as the ciphertext is the de facto standard for perfect security.[16] Shannon's point can be best summarized by stating that all things being equal (e.g., same complexity of the problem), a short key is preferable to a long one. This criteria leaves us with the impression that Shannon was trying to urge us to choose the key size that best fits the job without excess.

- **Complexity of Enciphering and Deciphering Operations**—Shannon argued that for the sake of efficiency, the cryptographic algorithms need to be as simple as possible. Complexity leads to loss of time and errors in the process (manual or automated.) At the time of Shannon's writing, however, Shannon had no idea of the scale and cost effectiveness of today's modern computers. The principle (which was originally created for hand cryptographic methods), as a result, is somewhat less of a determinant as to

---

[16.] In a later section of the paper, "Incompa tibility of the Criteria for Good Systems," Shannon concludes that "perfect and ideal systems are excluded by condition 2...if the key is small, the system simple, and the errors do not propagate, probable word methods will generally solve the system fairly easily."

whether a particular system is of good value. It might be best to realize the modern-day equivalent of this principle as one of good program development practices. If the algorithm is simple in design (not necessarily in the complexity of the mathematics as we shall see in the TEA examples of Chapter 7), it can be more rigorously tested, more efficiently designed, and best understood.

- **Propagation of Errors**–The fewer errors anticipated in the enciphering process, the better. In hand-coded ciphers, the complexity of the process will generally lead to errors. These errors would then propagate throughout the message (especially in bit-wise polyalphabetic ciphers such as the Bacon or Hill ciphers.) Today, the established algorithm will yield reliability well beyond the expectations that Shannon ever imagined. This principle, however, was adopted by NIST in the establishment of the AES cipher by the requirement that the cipher be based on sound mathematics, be analyzed by experts, and can stand the test of time. In essence, these NIST criteria meet Shannon's intent.

- **Expansion of Message**—It is desirable for the ciphertext to be the same length as the original plain text message. Ciphers of the day would often pad the message with "garbage" characters to attempt to swamp and confuse cryptanalysts with more unnecessary information. In reality, this principle explains that the generation of too much information may actually be an advantage to cryptanalysts because it provides them with more opportunity to examine the cipher for a pattern. Additionally, because a large ciphertext message carries the same amount of data as the short ciphertext of the same plain text, it will be more prone to retransmission (based on either communication errors or cryptographic errors). This detail gives cryptanalysts even greater opportunity for review.

These five principles have been an underlying doctrine in the cryptographic industry for the last fifty-plus years. These principles represent the ideal state of the industry. They are generally regarded as addressing the philosophy of cryptography. They represent the ideal case (which even Shannon admitted may be unattainable), and that practical implementations of cryptography will trade the benefits of one principle against those of another. Later, we will examine Shannon's principles of confusion and diffusion, which detail the requirements of the complexities of the mathematical part of the ciphering process.

Example of Brute-force Attack on System Passwords

Password length and strength are related in much the same way as a cryptographic key is related to the cryptographic strength. Because most people are more familiar with the use of a password than the use of a cryptographic key, and because the system password usage is not complicated by difficult mathematics, it is easier to demonstrate the relationship of length to strength in this way.

The longer the system, file, or account password, the better protected that account, system, or file is. Similarly, passwords that are more difficult to guess or are random in nature are better choices than common words or proper names.

As we see in the password-cracking lab, password-cracking tools are readily available and relatively easy to use. Most of these tools provide dictionary attack and brute-force attack mechanisms. Dictionary attacks attempt to map passwords to common words or proper names.

For example, the NT password cracker demonstrated in the lab section of the text can crack the password "guest" or "password" in less than one second.

Likewise, a brute-force search of any random string of four characters can be done in less than one minute with the same tool. In either case, this efficiency is really just an exploitation of the power of modern computers. Searching 20 million combinations is a relatively trivial task for most computers. Even in combinations of random letters into the billions, this is a manageable task for a 2.2-Ghz processor.

By way of example, if we assume that there are sixty-eight characters on the normal ASCII keyboard (not differentiating between uppercase and lowercase characters), then the number of possible combinations of passwords of length z is 68^z. If we have a four character random password, we would need to conduct a worse-case brute-force attack of $68^4 = 21,381,376$ combinations. Table 5-4 demonstrates the relative cracking times of various-length passwords.[A]

[A.] *These estimates are based on the use of a 2.2-Ghz Pentium IV processor with 512-Mg memory attempting 320,000 password matches per second.*

Shannon's five criteria for a cryptographic system's success, combined with his thoughts on diffusion and confusion, are all focused on preventing cryptanalysts from having success. The five criteria also build systems that are functional, accurate, efficient, and cost effective. As we saw earlier, breaking large keys even with the use of thousands of computers can be difficult, if not impossible, using brute-force methods. Cryptanalysts need to be able to determine the following to be successful:

- Cryptanalysts must be able to determine if the method they are trying to break is a substitution cipher, transposition cipher, or a hybrid of the two
- Cryptanalysts need to be able to determine if the method is monoalphabetic or polyalphabetic (done through the use of the index of coincidence test developed by Friedman).
- Cryptanalysts need to guess the range of the key size (maximum size)
- Cryptanalysts need to have some form of captured information to begin work (ciphertext, plain text, both, or some form of directed encoding)
- Cryptanalysts need a sense of timing to determine how long it is taking their adversaries to encrypt or decrypt messages
- Cryptanalysts can utilize information regarding the language characteristics of their adversaries
- Cryptanalysts can utilize information regarding the length of message

For cryptanalyst to be successful, they need to pay close attention to clues. Clues are left in a variety of ways, primarily by people operating or utilizing the cryptographic methods and not necessarily by the methods themselves. It is for this reason that our model of information security includes the outermost layer—the 8 Ps of security. People require guidance and supervision so that the quality of the system can remain high. Off-the-cuff remarks, garbage carelessly discarded, or accounts left unattended can all provide clues that cryptanalysts need.

Table 5-4 Relative Cracking Times of Various Passwords

Password Length	Combinations	Time (worst case)
1	68	Instantly
2	4,624	< one second
3	314,432	<1 second
4	21,281,376	<1.1 minutes
5	1,453,933,568	< 1.2 hours
6	9.8×10^{10}	<3.5 days
7	6.7×10^{12}	<241 days
8	4.5×10^{14}	< 44 years

In general, three broad categories of cryptographic attacks can be carried out against an adversary:

- Ciphertext attacks are generally difficult given the polyalphabetic and complex mathematical nature of modern attacks. Ciphertext attacks generally look at text structure, wording, and syntactical analysis. This is done in, more or less, a brute-force way. In the ciphertext attack, the cryptanalyst looks for trends and then attempts to decipher the text (not necessarily to completely understand the underlying methods).
- Known plain text attacks occur when cryptanalysts capture a sample of the ciphertext and the plain text. In this case, it is possible to reverse engineer the cipher scheme and then be able to use the method against the adversary.
- Chosen plain text attacks occur when cryptanalysts have an opportunity to influence the adversary to encode something of choice. This gives cryptanalysts a chance to verify a suspicion, which can lead to the reverse engineering of a method. An example of this is seen in the United States's influencing the Japanese to use the term "AF" regarding the water system on Midway Island to verify their suspicions of the target of the impending battle.

SUMMARY

Information is positioned at the core of our information security model. We have analyzed the criteria for its safety and its behavior. The results of this investigation are compelling; information requires protection beyond those protections available at the system or network level (aka, the information system.) It requires protection that can be flexible, system independent, and actually coat or become integrated with the structure of information. Cryptography provides such a mechanism by exploiting the mathematical qualities of information.

Cryptography is an old science dating back at least 2,500 years. By studying the history of cryptography, we see that there are essentially three periods of historical significance:

- Early Cryptography
- Cryptography of the World Wars
- Modern Cryptography

Early cryptography focused on character-based substitution (such as the Caesar cipher) and transposition methods (such as the Spartan scytales). Generally, the methods were monoalphabetic. Much later in this period, Leon Battista Alberti created a polyalphabetic cipher, known as the cipher wheel. This creation significantly reduced the chances of cryptanalysis for the time. This concept was taken to an extreme with the creation of the one-time pad. The one-time pad is the only cryptosystem ever created that is proven to be perfectly secure.

During the period covering World War I and World War II, much of the focus of cryptosystems shifted to the mathematical analysis of these sys tems for the purpose of cryptanalysis. William Friedman is credited with starting this movement and was the first to create a test to decipher between the monoalphabetic and polyalphabetic ciphers.

This period, although relatively short, can be used to show the importance of strong cryptographic and cryptanalysis methods. The outcomes of both World War I and World War II were in large part swayed by discoveries of enemy intent by British and American cryptanalysts. The Zimmerman telegram, the undermining of the Japanese Purple, the Bombe machines that could decipher Enigma traffic, and the heroic effort to crack JN-25 just in time to defeat the Japanese at Midway Island are all significant examples of the sociopolitical implications of pursuing this technology.

Additionally, during this same period, Alan Turing, Alonzo Church (a contemporary of Turing's), and William Friedman heavily influenced the future of modern computing. Alan Turing used his time spent as a leading cryptanalyst for the British as an opportunity to explore the possibility of using electrical circuitry to process information. He eventually developed the first series of computing devices.

Claude Shannon's work at the end of the 1940s bridged the gap between the period between World War II and the start of the modern era of cryptography. Shannon's theories on the entropy of language and the valuation of secrecy systems became the underpinnings of modern cryptography. His work is still regarded as pertinent to the field some fifty years later.

A study of the English language is presented so that students can gain a sense of the tactics of the World War II cryptographers. By measuring language and letter usage, cryptanalysts could refine their attempts to guess cryptographic methods.

Modern cryptographic advances included the development of DES method, which provided the world with many security applications across a variety of industries. The establishment of asymmetrical cryptography as being possible revolutionized the thinking around public cryptographic methods. DES was eventually replaced by AES in the late 1990s. Current cryptographic methods are dominated by extremely complex mathematics involving large numbers that are computationally intensive.

The future of cryptography seems to be shifting away from the current complex problems space or "hard math space" into the realm of "impossible science." Steganography and quantum cryptography are on the forefront of experimentation and can potentially yield extremely productive results. The fact that these methods of cryptography rely on phenomenon other than mathematics means that they have the potential to be extremely effective and efficient.

The key point of the historical section is that the methods of cryptography evolve with respect to the availability of technology and to serve the needs of the population (primarily the military).

Cryptography is secure because it is beyond the intellectual and computational capabilities of most hackers. The X.800 standard embraces the CAIN principles stressed in Section One. This is yet a further indication of the promise of cryptography and confirmation that it belongs at the center of our model.

An analysis of cryptographic strength was presented so that students could grasp the reliability and trustworthiness of cryptography. This information will be expanded upon in subsequent chapters. Additionally, an introduction into the art of cryptanalysis was provided. These introductory concepts will be further built on in subsequent chapters.

The language of cryptography was reviewed to pull together the many references to cryptography mentioned thus far in the text. Students should familiarize themselves with the language of cryptography; this language is the basis for continued growth in the field.

This chapter serves as an introduction to cryptography, which is the primary focus of Section Two of this text. In Chapter 6 we will review the important mathematical concepts required to fully appreciate the science of cryptography. In Chapter 7 students will be immersed in the review of symmetrical cryptography. In Chapter 8 we shall examine the rapidly growing area of asymmetrical cryptography.

STUDY QUESTIONS

1 Shift ciphers and simple substitution ciphers are examples of _____.(choose one)
   a. Monoalphabetic ciphers
   b. Polyalphabetic ciphers
   c. Monosaccaridic shift ciphers
   d. Polypropenyl substitution ciphers

2 Historically, the primary reason for advances in cryptography have been_____: (choose one)
   a. Protecting business assets
   b. Wars
   c. The need for individual privacy
   d. Keeping diplomatic conversations secret

3 Literally translated, cryptography means: _____ (choose one)
   a. Coded letters
   b. Secret code
   c. Hidden writing
   d. Confusing pictures

4 What does a cryptographer do? (choose one)

   a. Break codes of unknown origin

   b. Study the history of cryptography

   c. Encode messages

   d. Devise methods for encoding information securely

5 Enigma was a machine used in World War II by: _____ (choose one)

   a. The Germans

   b. The Japanese

   c. The Italians

   d. The French

6 Purple was what? (choose one)

   a. A diplomatic code used by the Japanese

   b. A color used to indicate that a secret transmission had been intercepted

   c. A code used to deploy submarines

   d. A color armband worn by cryptanalysts

7 What happens in a transposition cipher? (choose one)

   a. Letters are substituted for other letters

   b. Letters are substituted for numbers

   c. Letters are combined with numbers

   d. Letters change position in the message

8 Which is not a weakness of a shift cipher? (choose one)

   a. Natural language letter frequency makes them easy to decode

   b. The number of letters in the alphabet makes them easy to decode

   c. Once the shift is determined, the message is decoded almost instantly

   d. Once you have the codebook, you can decode the message

9 What was considered the first "serious" cipher? (choose one)

   a. The Vigenere square

   b. The Spartan scytale

   c. The Caesar cipher

   d. The Waldorf circle

10 Approximately when were the first polyalphabetic ciphers utilized? (choose one)

   a. The mid-1600s

   b. The mid-1700s

   c. The mid-1400s

   d. The mid-1500s

11 Which past president developed a polyalphabetic encoding device? (choose one)

    a. George Washington

    b. Thomas Jefferson

    c. Abraham Lincoln

    d. Theodore Roosevelt

12 If an attacker has a copy of the ciphertext and its content yields no information at all with regard to the plain text message, the text is considered: _____ (choose one)

    a. Cipher perfect

    b. Perfectly secure

    c. Third-eye blind

    d. Third-party secure

13 **True___ False___**   The one-time pad is perfect for long messages.

14 The Hill cipher uses complex mathematics, specifically: _____ (choose one)

    a. Trigonometry

    b. Statistics

    c. Calculus

    d. Linear algebra

15 How did Claude Shannon define perfect security? (choose one)

    a. Requiring significant amounts of diffusion and confusion

    b. Requiring equal amounts of intent and effort

    c. Requiring significant amounts of contusion and explosion

    d. Requiring equal amounts of mechanization and computation

16 What is the Lucifer cipher? (choose one)

    a. A multishift asymmetrical encryption method developed by the government

    b. A geometric algorithm developed by NASA for satellite communication

    c. An encryption method requiring two dissimilar keys for decryption

    d. A symmetrical encryption coded to a 56-bit key developed by an IBM team at Watson Labs

17 **True___ False___**   The Data Encryption Standard (DES) developed in 1977 is still widely used today.

18 What is the main difference between steganography and cryptography? (choose one)

    a. Steganography attempts to hide the existence of the message

    b. Steganography uses graphics instead of letters to encode messages

    c. Steganography is not sent electronically

    d. Steganography must be done on a specific machine

19 True___ False___ Quantum cryptography is based on the physics of light.

20 Which algorithm was formally adopted by NIST in 1998? (choose one)

   a. RC6 from RSA labs

   b. MARS from IBM

   c. Twofish by Counterpane Security

   d. Rijndael by Daemen and Rijmen

21 The most common character in written English is: (choose one)

   a. E

   b. S

   c. Space

   d. N

22 Heuristics are _____ (choose one)

   a. Algorithmic methods

   b. Cryptographic Techniques

   c. Rules of thumb

   d. Decrypting techniques

23 Codebooks are normally associated with _____ (choose one)

   a. Substitution ciphers

   b. Caesar ciphers

   c. Spartan scytales

   d. Binary ciphers

24 A _____ requires that the cipher alphabet changes throughout the encryption process. (choose one)

   a. Monoalphabetic substitution cipher

   b. Polyalphabetic substitution cipher

   c. Quantum cipher

   d. Alphanumeric shift cipher

25 True___ False___ Block ciphers are symmetrical ciphers.

26 What defines the strength of a cryptographic method? (choose one)

   a. The number of shifts

   b. The need for a codebook

   c. The complexity of the algorithm

   d. The length of time needed to crack it

27 There are three broad categories of cryptographic attacks. Which of the following is NOT one of them: (choose one)

   a. Chosen plain text attacks

   b. Key analysis attacks

   c. Known plain text attacks

   d. Ciphertext only attacks

28 What is at the core of our security model? (choose one)

   a. Information

   b. Authentication

   c. The 8Ps of Security

   d. OS hardening

29 What did the Bombe machine do? (choose one)

   a. Encoded messages using a polyalphabetic method

   b. Decrypted Enigma traffic

   c. Decrypted JN-25 traffic

   d. Encoded messages using a binary substitution method

 **CASE STUDY**

This chapter presented many historical facts regarding the evolution of cryptography. It is an interesting exercise to research more of the details of the historical timeline of cryptography.

For this assignment, students should begin by going to the *http://www.nsa.gov/museum* website and researching the historical links provided. Construct a timeline with the advances and people mentioned.

Next, research the work of Alonzo Church and Alan Turing. Both of these innovators played a significant role in the advancement of cryptography.

Finally, no study of cryptography is complete without researching the founding fathers of U.S. cryptography: Friedman and Shannon. Shannon's career at Bell Labs is fascinating and is multifaceted.

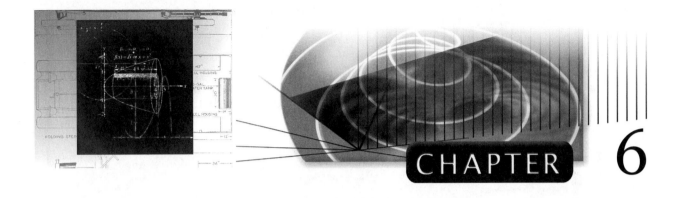

Mathematical Principles of Cryptography

Defendit Numerus: There Is Safety in Numbers
—JZ Newman, (ed.) *The World of Mathematics*, New York: Simon and Schuster, 1956

This quote is fortunately true in most security schemes. It is essential that we capitalize on the properties of information to best safeguard it. Information expressed as a cipher in a given language (character-based plain text) can have a certain predictability that, by its very nature, gives away critical information about its plain text counterpart. In just the same way that we would not want people to reveal pass codes to the enemy and give them the right of passage, we do not want to use cryptographic methods that tip off a potential attacker. Numbers, mathematics, ingenuity, and computing resources can be combined to achieve this goal.

Nearly anything can be represented using numbers. Surely, computer scientists must understand that concept, because it is the underlying nature of their work. Everything we do on a computer has roots in mathematics, bits being represented as binary digits zero and one, which electrically represent off and on, respectively. Cryptography has deep roots in mathematics. However, most students reading this book will be users of cryptography and not creators or decipherers of it. As we have mentioned before, most everyone understands how to use electricity to turn on a light, but few of us could build a generator. This analogy is appropriate. This text is set up so that this material need not be covered completely as part of an introductory class. However, it is a good idea for people intending to work in this field, or who wish to take more advanced courses, to work through this introductory-level mathematics of cryptography section.

For many people, mathematics represents a significant challenge. For this reason, the required mathematics necessary to gain a full appreciation of the inner workings of cryptography have been isolated (to a large extent) in this one chapter. The remainder of this book does require a basic knowledge of algebra, binary arithmetic, and minimal statistics. For those students who would like a review of those basic concepts, reading the first half of the chapter is recommended. For those students wishing to understand the nuances of cryptography and how it works on the inside, reading through this section is a must.[1]

---

[1] In addition, students interested in pursuing careers as cryptographers or cryptanalysts should review the materials suggested in the reference section to gain greater insight into this area.

The mathematics presented in this chapter has been kept as simple as possible by eliminating proofs and daunting mathematical formulas and derivations. Many of the textbooks on the market address the subject matter at the graduate level. However, cryptography plays such a fundamental role in the application of information security, it is best if students understand at least the basic mechanisms of how it works.

To successfully complete this chapter, students should pay particular attention to:

- Prime numbers and basic number theory
- Euclid's method for finding the greatest common divisor
- Confusion and diffusion
- Binary versus character-oriented cryptographic benefits
- Working with numbers in a base 2 system
- The ability to shift numbers from one base to another
- Fundamentals of mathematical logic
- Functions (and how those functions are used) in cryptography
- Why certain numbers with special properties (e.g., prime numbers) are important
- Complexity and probability

Elements of success for this material are concerned with basic mathematics. It is important that students review skills involving advanced algebraic methods, basic statistics, and the application of functions. Becoming strong in these areas will enable students to develop a deep understanding of this material.

MATHEMATICAL PROPERTIES OF INFORMATION

The mathematical properties of information provide a compelling basis upon which a large sector of information security is based. As we stated in Chapter 1, information is stored in the computer as sequences of ones and zeros. This representation, using binary arithmetic, provides three enablers of information security:

- First, treat all information the same (regardless of type) at the binary level. In other words, the type (integer, character, float, long, etc.) that the information represents to the corresponding application has no meaning at the bit level. This is important to cryptography because we can design cryptographic applications that are applied to the information ubiquitously without considering type
- Second, binding or blending cryptographic sequences (keys) with the information disguises the information. This binding can be removed via only the appropriate decryption routine. Failure to provide this routine and the requisite information (key or keys) will leave the cipher in place and render the information useless. The binding of the key and the plain text, therefore, transcends the bounds of the information system and extends the security afforded the information wherever it goes
- Third, apply all of the methods of number theory, described below, to our information to assist in the binding process

In the previous chapter, examples of cryptography were presented dating back to ancient times. Although, at the time, these ciphers were considered state of the art, they are no match for a cryptanalyst using a modern-day computer. Obviously, it was not until the mid–twentieth century that computers were available to assist in this process. Until recently, all encryption was performed at the character, symbol, or phrase level. Letters, integers, symbols, and phrases were manipulated to create cipher code. Even the mechanical encryption devices, (e.g., Enigma machines) used during World War II were complex, character-oriented encryption machines.

Given today's modern computers, encryption carried out at the character level would not generate a code complex enough to be considered a significant countermeasure. Because we can reduce our information to the bit level, and each character is minimally represented in eight bits, we can manipulate any bits of the information stream. Why is this important? As it turns out, cryptanalysts still employ methods that include capturing samples of ciphertext and plain text, comparing them, and analyzing the results. They try to find correlations between the two parts. This correlation can tip them off to a key or other clue, regarding what is happening in the encryption process. By forcing the encryption down one layer—to the bit rather than character layer—we can take advantage of the three previously mentioned enablers, making comparisons difficult.

For example, suppose that we have the characters "hello" represented as the ASCII codes "h" = "01101000," "e" = "01100101," "l" = "01101100", "l" = "01101100," and "o" = "01101111." By combining these parts, we can turn this pattern into the stream "0110100001100101011011000110110001101111," which is the word hello spelled out as ASCII code[2]. Now suppose that we decide to flip every fifth bit from 1 to 0 or 0 to 1. This would create the cipher "0110000000100111011111001110100001001110," or the (ASCII) printable character stream "`| $\Phi$ N". This would mean that the "`" = "h," "'" = "e," "|" = the first "l," " Φ " = the second "l," and the "N" = "o." By looking at the two l's, we can see that the encryption technique of manipulating every fifth bit tells us little or nothing at the character level. This is because the characters are made up of eight bits, and the manipulation is mapped to different bits within each of the characters eight-bit character streams. Although this is a relatively simple example for anyone to eventually break, it does illustrate the point.

KEY POINT

Bit-wise manipulation of information increases the complexity of the cipher over character manipulation, even though the total number of characters remains unchanged.

This example illustrates how using computers to create and break ciphers takes advantage of the fact that information can be represented as numbers to create more sophisticated ciphers or greater complexity. A worthy adversary in this process will likely have substantial computing resources and ample CPU cycles to analyze and decrypt our codes. It is, therefore, important that we take several precautions to neutralize this capability:

[2.] ASCII is an acronym for the American Standard Code for Information Interchange, which has specified the standard text representation that is implemented by almost every computer at the bit level worldwide.

- Encrypt at the bit level and ignore the information typing and logical character, integer, etc, boundaries. This will spread the encryption technique unevenly, increasing the difficulty in analysis
- Utilize complex mathematical techniques (at the bit level), which require the use of time-consuming and intensive computations processes to reverse
- Create as much confusion and diffusion (Shannon) as possible during the encryption process to limit the effectiveness of plain text attacks
- Apply the mathematics, substitutions, shifts, and transpositions during encryption in **rounds**, layer upon layer—encryption of encryption, so that the complexity is compounded and increased

These points, if adhered to, can significantly improve our cryptographic technique. With regard to the design principle of confusion and diffusion, Claude Shannon in the 1940s presented a principle that is still important today and continues to inspire cryptographers. As we saw in the previous chapter, every language has a certain statistical predictability that helps cryptanalysts with their mission. Shannon was addressing the best design techniques (character-oriented at the time, but extensible into the bit-oriented world) to reduce this predictability and enhance encryption efforts. Diffusion is defined as the action of spreading out the influence of a plain text element over many ciphertext elements. Through our previous discussion, we learned that by treating information at the bit level and disregarding the character (byte) boundaries, we have achieved this goal. In other words, we did not perform the same action to each byte; rather, we performed a similar action to every fifth bit, which divorced the predictability of the plain text message from the ciphertext message (the ls in this example did not use the same code). The statistical structure of the plain text was dissipated over a large group of ciphertext even through this simple technique. Thus we can increase the amount of **diffusion** and raise the complexity level of the code.

Confusion means that when we utilize a key to create ciphertext, we need to make the relationship between the key and the ciphertext as complex as possible. By ensuring this complexity, we have the best chance to hide local patterns in the language from cryptanalysts. As we shall see in Chapters 7 and 8, a great deal of effort is placed on achieving this goal.

What does all of this mean to students of information security? Because information is what we most value in our digitized world, then protecting it should be your first priority. Information's strongest property is that it can be reduced to numbers. Given that characteristic, cryptography is the most important tool at your disposal. As we shall observe throughout the rest of the book, cryptographic methods are affordable, balanced, and tamper resistant. However, the methods are complex. This places the burden on the security professional to understand the techniques (not necessarily create them) and to be able to choose and apply an appropriate solution.

NUMBER REPRESENTATION

One of the areas that many new students in the field of computer science struggle with is working with base 2 (binary), base 16 (hexadecimal), and base 8 (octal) numbers. Because we have already decided that, with respect to cryptography, it is best to work with information in its native binary representation, students should review and familiarize themselves with numbers in different bases.

In the United States, we teach students to count in decimal and that there are special numbers such as ten, eleven, twelve, and so on. In reality, that instruction is not true. "Special numbers" do not exist. In the decimal system (base 10), there are ten digits that we can work with: 0, 1, 2, 3, 4, 5, 6, 7, 8, and 9. When we use up these digits by performing the action of 9 + 1, we need to review exactly why we answer with 10. Instead of saying "ten," say "one zero," which is more appropriate. By definition, the units column of a decimal digit is a specific value between 0 and 9 and multiplied by 10^0, which is equal to one because any number other than zero, raised to the zero power, is one. Therefore, when we add 1 to ($9 \bullet 10^0$), we mean that we want to put a 1 in the 10^1 column and a 0 in the 10^0, or units, column. This process carries on for each column of the number system and the numbers continue to grow in an orderly fashion. For example, if we add 1 to 99, we yield the following: add 1 to ($9 \bullet 10^0$) and leave a zero in that column, and then carry a 1 to be added to ($9 \bullet 10^1$) column. We must leave a 0 in that column and carry a 1 to the next column [hundreds or ($1 \bullet 10^2$)].

If we can then rethink our counting vocabulary, we will significantly simplify working with numbers in other bases. Hence, we can think of counting in decimal as "… nine, one-zero, one-one, one-two, one-three, one-four, one-five, … ,one-nine, two-zero, two-one,…, nine-nine, one-zero-zero,…" etc.

Use of this procedure enables us to work in base two more efficiently. As seen in Figure 6-1, each of the digits in a binary number (a sequence of zeros and ones) represents 2 raised to the corresponding power of the place. These powers of two allow us to convert from decimal to binary quite easily.

Binary Numbers

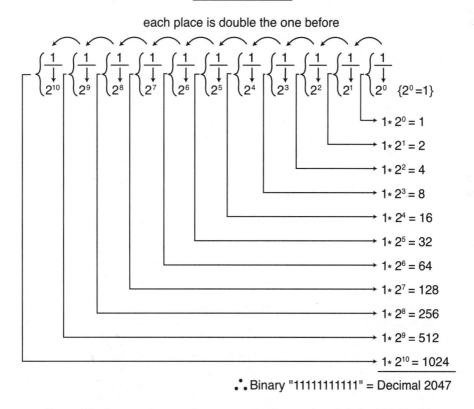

each place is double the one before

$1 * 2^0 = 1$
$1 * 2^1 = 2$
$1 * 2^2 = 4$
$1 * 2^3 = 8$
$1 * 2^4 = 16$
$1 * 2^5 = 32$
$1 * 2^6 = 64$
$1 * 2^7 = 128$
$1 * 2^8 = 256$
$1 * 2^9 = 512$
$1 * 2^{10} = 1024$

∴ Binary "11111111111" = Decimal 2047

Figure 6-1 Powers of two and representation/conversion of decimal 2047 as binary 11111111111.

It is often easiest to look at the composition of binary numbers in chart form:

Table 6-1 Powers of Two

Decimal Representation	Binary Representation	Powers of Two
0	0	$0 \bullet 2^0$
1	1	$1 \bullet 2^0$
2	10	$(1 \bullet 2^1) + (0 \bullet 2^0)$
3	11	$(1 \bullet 2^1) + (1 \bullet 2^0)$
4	100	$(1 \bullet 2^2) + (0 \bullet 2^1) + (0 \bullet 2^0)$
5	101	$(1 \bullet 2^2) + (0 \bullet 2^1) + (1 \bullet 2^0)$
6	110	$(1 \bullet 2^2) + (1 \bullet 2^1) + (0 \bullet 2^0)$
7	111	$(1 \bullet 2^2) + (1 \bullet 2^1) + (1 \bullet 2^0)$
8	1000	$(1 \bullet 2^3) + (0 \bullet 2^2) + (0 \bullet 2^1) + (0 \bullet 2^0)$
9	1001	$(1 \bullet 2^3) + (0 \bullet 2^2) + (0 \bullet 2^1) + (1 \bullet 2^0)$
10	1010	$(1 \bullet 2^3) + (0 \bullet 2^2) + (1 \bullet 2^1) + (0 \bullet 2^0)$
11	1011	$(1 \bullet 2^3) + (0 \bullet 2^2) + (1 \bullet 2^1) + (1 \bullet 2^0)$
12	1100	$(1 \bullet 2^3) + (1 \bullet 2^2) + (0 \bullet 2^1) + (0 \bullet 2^0)$
13	1101	$(1 \bullet 2^3) + (1 \bullet 2^2) + (0 \bullet 2^1) + (1 \bullet 2^0)$
14	1110	$(1 \bullet 2^3) + (1 \bullet 2^2) + (1 \bullet 2^1) + (0 \bullet 2^0)$
15	1111	$(1 \bullet 2^3) + (1 \bullet 2^2) + (1 \bullet 2^1) + (1 \bullet 2^0)$

We are essentially counting by one. Through this table, we can study how counting works in binary. Notice that as we progress through the table, we are simply adding 1 to the previous value. As seen in Figure 6-2, the process of adding in binary is not all that different from adding in decimal. In either case, we can perform simple addition so long as the number produced by the addition is less than the base of the system minus 1. With decimal, if we add 1 to 8, the result is 9, which is still within the limits of (base 10 – 1), so there is no carry. However, when we add 1 to 9, we need to carry. The process of a carry literally means to add 1 to the count associated with the next power of the base. Therefore, 9 + 1 requires a carry of 1 from the 10^0 column to the 10^1 column, producing a "one-zero" value.

The same is true in working with numbers in base 2. In this case, the possible values are 0 and 1 for each column representing a power of 2. In the case of 1 + 1, therefore, we need to carry a 1 from the 2^0 column to the 2^1 column, producing a "one-zero" value. Notice that in case (g), we wind up with a 1 + 1 + 1 in the 2^1 column as the result of a carry. In the binary system, 1 + 1 equals 10 and 10 + 1 equals 11. So in this case, we carry the 1 to the 2^2 column and leave a 1 (rather than a 0) in the 2^1 column as a part of the answer.

Subtracting in binary is somewhat more confusing because we need to learn to borrow in base 2. Figure 6-3 shows the borrowing process. This is much easier if you think of 1 plus 1 as being equal to one-zero. As you can see in Figure 6-3, one zero minus one is not difficult. First, borrow a 1 from the next column over. This reduces that column to 0. Then we proceed to perform the single-column subtraction. Because 1 + 1 = "one zero," then it makes sense that 10 – 1 = 1. Notice how this works for complex numbers.

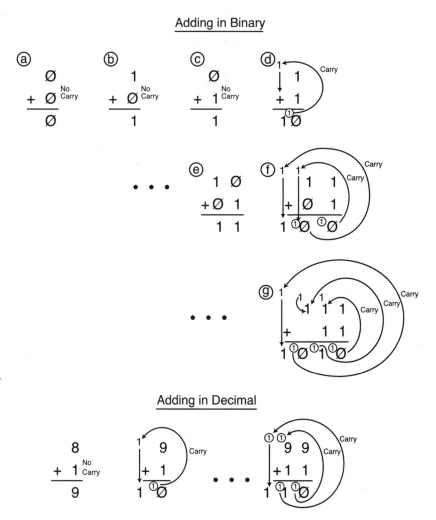

Figure 6-2   Anytime we use up all the numbers for a given power of 2 (0 or 1), we must perform a "carry." Notice the similarity to a ddition in decimal where we exceed 9.

Borrowing:

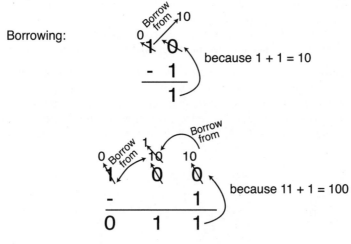

Example:

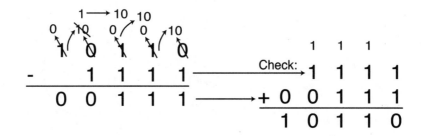

Figure 6-3 Binary Subtraction—Borrowing in binary is more complex than decimal because it tends to happen more frequently. In practice, it is really just as easy.

Binary addition and subtraction are useful to cryptographers because they are inverse operations—whatever can be done in addition can also be undone with subtraction.

Another bit-wise manipulation that is popular among computer programmers is **bit shifting**. Given a stream of bits, we can shift them left or right by any number of bits that we choose. As seen in Figure 6-4, when the binary number 1111 is shifted left one time, we wind up with 11110 (notice the insertion of the pad 0.) The base 2 number, 1111, is 15 in decimal, and the base 2 number, 11110, is 30 in decimal. Shifting left is equivalent to multiplication by 2. Bit shifting is a popular concept in cryptography because it increases diffusion. In many ciphers, such as TEA, bit shifting is an important part of the technique.

Choosing a numerical representation for our information is critical. Each representation offers advantages and disadvantages. Binary is quite advantageous because it is the natural representation of numbers in a computer. It is also convenient because bit-wise (power of two) manipulations (such as bit shifting) maximize diffusion. Most cryptographic algorithms manipulate data in a binary representation.

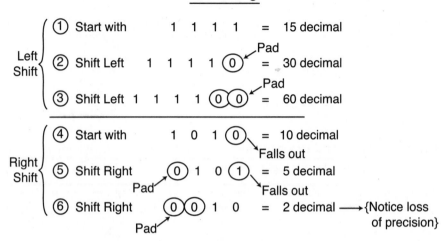

Figure 6-4   Bit shifting requires the insertion and deletion of bits into the stream. Shift left means multiply by 2. Shifting right is division (notice the loss of precision for odd numbers).

EXPONENTIATION AND LOGARITHMS

Exponentiation and logarithms are two important numerical methods that need to be understood. It is important to remember that exponentiation is an easy process to utilize, while logarithms are more difficult to calculate. These functions are inverses of one another. Thus, they can be used creatively with respect to developing difficult-to-crack cryptography. Exponentiation is computationally efficient, while logarithms are computationally expensive. Therefore, we can create large numbers by raising a number to a certain power quickly, but it takes a long time to reverse this process to find the original exponent (the log).

Exponentiation is simply repeated multiplication:

$a^n = a \bullet a \bullet ... \bullet a$ (repeated n times) This is read as "a to the power of n."

Exponents are easy to work with. Just to refresh the reader's memory, we will simply state some of the properties of exponents:

- $a^{m+n} = a^n \bullet a^m$ is so because a^{m+n} really means $(a_1 \bullet a_2 \bullet ... \bullet a_m) \bullet (a_1 \bullet a_2 \bullet ... \bullet a_n)$ or a times itself m times multiplied by a times itself n times
- $a^{n \bullet m} = (a^n)^m$ because in either case what you are really saying is take m groups of a times itself n times. For example: $2^{2 \bullet 3} = 2^6 = (2^2)^3 = 4^3 = 64$

- $a^{\frac{1}{n}} = \sqrt[n]{a}$ exponents expressed in fractional powers are expressed as roots. For example, $25^{\frac{1}{2}} = \sqrt[2]{25} = 5$, or more generally $a^{\frac{m}{n}} = \sqrt[n]{a^m}$, such as

$$2^{\frac{4}{2}} = \sqrt[2]{2^4} = \sqrt[2]{16} = 4$$

- $a^{-m} = \dfrac{1}{a^m}$ for negative powers

The logarithm is the inverse of the exponentiation process. For the exponentiation $a^m = R$, m is referred to as the logarithm of R base a. For example, the $\log_2 512 = 9$ because $2^9 = 512$.

One of the handy properties of logarithms is that the $\log_a (m * n) = \log_a m + \log_a n$. This is so because m and n each have their own relationship to a in terms of exponents. If $a^b = m$ and $a^c = n$, then $a^b * a^c = a^{b+c} = m * n$.

In the natural sciences, exponentiation is related to growth rates. Whatever grows exponentially grows quickly; whatever grows logarithmically grows slowly. In cryptography we are not concerned with the speed of growth. We are simply looking for reversible functions that are hard to compute in one direction and easy to compute in the other. Logarithms and exponentiation have this property.

MATHEMATICAL LOGIC

Another series of bit-wise manipulations that are popular among cryptographers involve the use of **mathematical logic**. Mathematical logic in its purest form is an analysis of the methods of reasoning. By this we mean math logic is more interested in the form of an argument than the contents of the argument. For example: "Robert is a rabbit. All rabbits like carrots. Hence, Robert likes carrots." This can be stated mathematically as the statement (proposition). "All A are B. R is an A. Hence, R is a B." We can then apply this form to any argument that fits it and test its truthfulness or falseness.

Truth can be represented in binary as a 1. Falseness in binary can be represented as a 0. Therefore, we can use what are known as the popular propositional connectives (and, or, not, exclusive-or) to construct arguments that resolve to either a 1 or a 0. These truth functions can therefore be used to manipulate bits by constructing an argument, applying the input bits to it (representing truthfulness or falseness), resolving the argument, and saving the result. To do this, we need to understand how truth tables relate to the propositional connectives.

Negation is the simplest of the connectives and is represented mathematically as the symbol "¬" and programmatically (using the C programming language notation) as the symbol "!".

A	¬A (read NOT A)
T	F
F	T

This table shows that whichever value is chosen for A is negated or reversed using the ¬ (not) function. Therefore, if A = 0 then ¬A = 1. We can use negation to switch ones and zeroes. It is also important to note that the negation function is reversible. This means that we can apply the function again and change the 1 back into a 0.

The propositional connective AND represented as ^ in mathematical logic terms and as && in the C programming language has the following truth table given the two variables (A,B):

A	B	A^B (A and B)
T	T	T
T	F	F
F	T	F
F	F	F

In this particular type of argument, both parts need to be true in order for the equation to evaluate as true. If either or both of the arguments are false, then the entire equation results in a false value. An example of this is an argument such as "If you are a registered student and you pay the tuition, then you can attend school."

If we say that A = "If you are a registered student," B = "you pay the tuition," and C = "you can attend school," we can state that A^B $\Rightarrow$C (read as A and B imply C). By using our truth table, if both A and B are true then we can imply that you may attend school. If either or both of these arguments are false, then we can state that we cannot imply C or you cannot attend school. Because we can see that the truth table covers all of the possible arguments, we can say that the logic statement can be satisfied.

Another commonly used propositional connective is OR expressed mathematically as v and programmatically in C as "|". The truth table for OR is written as:

A	B	AvB (A or B)
T	T	T
T	F	T
F	T	T
F	F	F

Notice that in this case, three of the four possibilities result in a T conclusion with only A = F, B = F resulting in AvB = F. If examined through the use of language:

"If your tuition is covered by financial aid OR you have private funding, then you can attend school." In this case, A = "your tuition is covered by financial aid," B = "you have private funding," and C = "you can attend school." Therefore, AvB $\Rightarrow$C can be validated by examining the possibilities. If you have a combination of some financial aid and some private funding, you may attend school. If you have financial aid and no funding, you may attend school. If you have no financial aid but do have private funding, you can attend school. However, if you have neither financial aid nor private funding, then you may not attend school.

Finally, we should cover the ***exclusive-or***, written $\oplus$ in mathematical language, or ^^ in the C programming language. The exclusive-or means either A or B is true, but not both. The truth table for the exclusive-or function is written as the following:

A	B	A ⊕ B
T	T	F
T	F	T
F	T	T
F	F	F

An example of this function can again be examined through language. "If you put chocolate syrup in your milk, or if you put strawberry syrup in your milk, then the milk tastes sweet and good." This is an example of the exclusive-or. Either choice—adding chocolate syrup or strawberry syrup—makes the milk taste sweet and good. But it would not taste good if you added both, and it would not be sweet if you added neither syrup.

The exclusive-or function is used heavily in symmetrical key cryptography because of its reversible nature. Plain text ⊕ key ⇒ciphertext can be reversed by ciphertext ⊕ key ⇒plain text. For example, if the plain text = "1010" and the key = "1100," then ciphertext = plain text ⊕ key = "0110." To reverse this, plain text = ciphertext ⊕ key = "0110" ⊕ "1100" = "1010."

It is important to point out that the AND function and the OR function do not share this characteristic. In fact, if you look at the truth tables from right to left instead of from left to right, you will notice that in both cases reversibility is impossible because a paradox exists. A paradox occurs when two sets of identical inputs applied to the same function are required to produce different outputs from one another. Look at the OR function truth table turned around.

AvB	A	B
T	T	T
T	T	F
T	F	T
F	F	F

Notice the first two rows. If we wanted to find a function to reverse the effect of the OR, it would require taking a T, T input pair and producing a T in the first row, while taking a T, T input pair and producing an F in the second row. Given that the function would need to be the same for all rows, that would be impossible and therefore would create a paradox.

It is also important to understand some of the fundamental mathematical relationships that exist in Boolean algebra. These relationships have long been used in electronics to simplify circuit design and can also be used to simplify and reverse cryptographic relationships.

Commutative Law: $A \lor B \Leftrightarrow B \land A$ also $A \land B \Leftrightarrow B \land A$

Associative Law: $(A \lor B) \lor C \Leftrightarrow A \lor (B \lor C)$ also $(A \land B) \land C \Leftrightarrow A \land (B \land C)$

Distributive Law: $A \land (B \lor C) \Leftrightarrow (A \land B) \lor (A \land C)$

Identity Law: $A \lor 0 \Rightarrow A$ also $A \land 1 \Rightarrow A$

DeMorgan's Law: $\neg(A \land B) \Leftrightarrow \neg A \lor \neg B$

BASIC NUMBER THEORY

Number theory provides us with insight into how numbers work. Number theory is primarily concerned with establishing the properties of integers. Remember that one of the key attributes of information is that it can be represented as a series of numbers. Because we can manipulate numbers through proven mathematical relationships, it is possible to disguise information via the application of mathematical properties and later restore it to the original form via related relationships to those properties. Basic number theory is useful in understanding those relationships. Users of cryptography should familiarize themselves with these concepts so they can understand the sophistication of the cryptographic methods described later. Much of this section will not be entirely new for students, but because of the fundamental importance of these principles to the study of cryptography, it is worth repeating.

Unfortunately, many people working in the information security field are unfamiliar with many of these principles and tend to underutilize cryptography as an essential part of the information security strategy. By building a confidence about, and appreciation of, the methods, readers can make better, more cost-effective judgments, regarding the appropriate application of cryptographic technology.

INTEGERS

Basic algebra provides us with **integers**, which are natural numbers, their opposites, and zero. The properties of integers are the primary focus of number theory. Using the basic principles of arithmetic, it can be demonstrated that integers carry on infinitely. The primary relationship between integers is that they are equally spaced; by adding 1, we can get to the next integer. This process of adding 1 to get to the next integer can obviously be used to prove that an infinite number of integers exist. This is done through contradiction. If we made the incorrect assumption that there is a finite set of N integers (0, 1, 2, 3, 4, …,N) and accepted the principle that we move to the right on the number line by using the add 1 process, then by adding 1 to N we would create a new set ending in N + 1. Therefore, we would have contradicted our original hypothesis, proving that integers continue infinitely. This point is important because we want to be sure that we can create cryptographic functions for any possible combinations of integer values representing information.

This process of adding 1 is also interesting because it has been demonstrated by Alonzo Church (lambda calculus) that by creating a function that adds 1 to 0, we can create the more complex functions of generalized addition, multiplication, and exponentiation through the repeated execution of this primary function.

Integers have many properties; two of the more important ones that we need to examine are

- Divisibility
- Modulo arithmetic or congruences

These basic principles of number theory are the building blocks of the sophisticated laws that form the basis for much of cryptography's so-called difficult problems.

Divisibility

Divisibility means that for any two integers x and y, $x \neq 0$, we can say that x divides y if there is an integer result of the division (i.e., no remainder.) There must, therefore, be a third number, z, such that $y = z \cdot x$. Another way of stating this relationship is that y is a multiple of x. For example, if we substitute 16 for y and 4 for x, then we know that 4 divides 16 because the result of the division is the whole number 4. We can conclude that 16 is a multiple of 4.

Conversely, if $y = 15$ and $x = 4$, then 4 does not divide 15 because the result of that division has a remainder and, therefore, can not be expressed as a whole number.

We say that b divides a if there exists an integer c such that $a = bc$, implying a remainder of 0. The mathematical notation for this relationship is $b \mid a$.

This principle is important because when one number is a multiple of another number, then those numbers have similar relationships to all other numbers (making them mathematically similar in their behavior). In cryptanalysis, a cipher can be more easily cracked if the seeds of the cryptographic algorithm contain multiples because the cryptanalyst can stumble upon a relationship using one of the multiples instead of the actual seed value. This is why we will focus so heavily on prime numbers later in this chapter because of their natural immunity to this problem.

Modulo Arithmetic—Congruences

In many computer science applications, the concept of modulo (mod) arithmetic is important. Modulo arithmetic is "clock arithmetic." For example, when we say in military time that it is 1300, hours we are really saying that it is 13 o'clock. According to the clock, this time equates to 1 P.M. (assuming that midnight is expressed as 0 o'clock). Essentially, it is $13 \div 12 = 1$ with a remainder of 1. The remainder is the offset into the next rotation of the clock that can be represented, thus we say 1 o'clock. This means that we can do arithmetic on the clock so that all the answers will be in the range of 0 to 11. For example, 7 + 6 = 13 mod 12 = 1, as just shown. 8 + 7 = 15 mod 12, which is 3 and so on. This continues to work even for large numbers. For example, 189 mod 12 = 9 because $189 \div 12 = 15$, with a remainder of 9.

Two numbers are said to be congruent if they produce the same remainder after the modulus division. For example, 13 and 25 are congruent because

13 ÷ 12 = 1 remainder of 1 and 25 ÷ 12 = 2 remainder of 1.

More formally, this concept can be summarized as follows:

For any integer a, divided by some other positive integer n, we get a quotient q and a remainder r, or a = qn + r. r must be greater than or equal to 0 but less than n. r is often referred to as the residue in formal mathematical terms. We then say that a mod n is defined to be the remainder portion of this division with the quotient being omitted.

If two different numbers a and b are each divided by n and produce the same remainder, they are said to be **congruent** modulo n. Formally, a and b are congruent modulo n if $\frac{a}{n} = q + r_1$ and $\frac{b}{n} = p + r_2$, where $r_1 = r_2$.

This relationship $(a \bmod n) = (b \bmod n)$ is written as $a \equiv b \bmod n$, where the special symbol $\equiv$ means "congruent to." Modulo arithmetic is a skill that students of cryptography are required to master.

SPECIAL NUMBERS

There are many instances where we require the use of a special number in our creation of hard or unsolvable problems. These numbers are considered special because either the number itself has an interesting characteristic or the method that is used to generate a special number is itself interesting. These special numbers are usually categorized into three distinct groups:

- Nonrepeating decimal numbers
- Truly random numbers
- Hashes

Each of these three types of special numbers can be found in many applications in computer science and are probably not new to students. Most people have used special numbers, such as pi, ever since they first learned elementary geometry. Random number generators play a big role in the development of computer games. Hashes or message digests are extremely important in data communications. All three of these special numbers play a crucial role in modern cryptography.

It is important that students develop an understanding of why these numbers are important and how to go about creating and using them.

Nonrepeating Decimal Numbers

Finding nonrepeating decimal numbers has long been a fascination of many mathematicians. Early mathematicians, such as Pythagoras and Euclid, were fascinated with these numbers. The trick is in proving that a number will not repeat after an extremely long sequence.

One use for these special numbers is in the generation of truly random numbers. We will address this topic in a subsequent section. Another useful application of these nonrepeating decimals is in their direct application to cryptography. To enable successful encryption of information, we need to make sure that as many bits as possible in the message are changed by our mathematical computation. If we, by chance, selected a key that was biased toward either mostly ones or mostly zeros, it is unlikely that the blending of this key (via some reversible mathematical operation) would produce the desired effect of significant bit pattern changes.

One way that has been used to introduce this kind of widespread change is to utilize nonrepeating decimal numbers as part of the mathematical process. Nonrepeating decimal numbers are rare and special. Three important nonrepeating decimal numbers are pi, e (natural logarithm), and the golden ratio (phi.) Aside from their value as nonrepeating decimals, these numbers are also special because they occur repeatedly in natural phenomena. For example, π is the ratio between a circle's circumference and a line running through its center, called the diameter. No matter how big the circle becomes, this ratio stays the same. Other places where these numbers show up include the theory of atoms, stellar cartography, geology, and structural engineering.

These special numbers are known as irrational numbers because they are nonrepeating and nonterminating. An irrational number is any number that cannot be written as M|N for any whole numbers M and N and whose fractional parts have no discernable repeating pattern in their digits.

The golden ratio, for example, is written as $\frac{(\sqrt{5}+1)}{2}$ or $\frac{(\sqrt{5}-1)}{2}$. In each, the repeating decimal is the same except that the former starts as 1.6... and the latter starts as 0.6...

Truly Random Numbers

A random event is unpredictable. An example of such an event is the location of the next lightning strike. Random events occur in nature all the time. Computers, on the other hand, tend to be quite predictable. A computer program is a script of action. Most computer actions are based on mathematics. To a large extent, mathematics is also quite predictable.

In the discussion that follows in later chapters, we will review the processes for generating keys for both symmetrical and asymmetrical cryptographic algorithms. As we saw in Chapter 5, when keys or passwords are common words or predictable sequences, they weaken the cryptographic effect because they are remarkably easy to guess. It would be best, then, if keys were completely random. By generating random

KEY POINT

The special numbers have an infinite range. These numbers are constantly being computed to determine more and more of the sequences. Obviously, this task will never be complete. For our purposes, we can use the following definitions of the numbers:

- The golden ratio starts out as 1.6180339887498948482045868343656381177203091798057628621354486227052…
- Pi can be written as 3.1415926536…
- The irrational number e can be written as $e = \lim_{n \to \infty} (1 + 1/n)^n$ and its value is approximately 2.718281828459045…

keys, we would maximize the effect of the cryptographic method and reduce guessing of keys to sheer brute-force methods. As we have demonstrated with keys even as short as 64 bits, brute-force guessing is such a time- and resource-consuming process that it is virtually useless.

To choose keys in a random fashion, we need to create truly random numbers. To say that a sequence of numbers is random, that sequence must display two necessary properties. First, the numbers must be independent of one another. That is, no number in the sequence can be guessed based on information gained from looking at either another part of the sequence or any other number in the sequence. Second, the distribution of the numbers must be uniform. This means that the frequency of occurrence of any one number should be approximately the same as that of any other number. These tests prove hard to pass for most random number applications.

Surely everyone has heard of computer random number generators. But many such programs were not really random at all. In fact, through detailed analysis many of these programs were found to leave traces of information that led researchers to be able to predict the next random number to be generated.

Guessing Random Numbers In Cryptanalysis

The SSL encryption protocol was introduced in 1994 as part of the Netscape Navigator Program. This cryptographic method represented one of the products major selling points at the time. SSL is still the predominant Web security method in the market, but it almost did not turn out that way. In the latter part of 1994, two Berkeley University students, Goldberg and Wagner, were able to devise a way to defeat the encryption, based on a flaw in the random number generator used in the UNIX version of the product at the time. It turned out that the random number generator was seeded through a combination of the process ID of the current process and that of the parent process, combined with the current value of the system clock. The two students were able to set up a program that could use the current values of these three inputs to guess the random numbers being generated.

Once these numbers were known, then guessing the randomly generated SSL keys (128 bits in length) was easy. This led to their being able to effectively defeat the SSL encryption in short periods of time. This defect was fixed in the product's version 1.3.

Effectively, the algorithms that generate random numbers are deterministic, meaning they produce sequences of random numbers that will eventually fail to pass the scrutiny of a statistical examination. However, the better algorithms are able to come close enough to meeting these criteria to be considered almost random. These algorithms are called **Pseudorandom Number Generators (PRNGs)**.

Currently, there are several approaches to creating PRNGs that are statistically acceptable as according to the previously mentioned criteria. One approach is the ANSI x 9.17 PRNG. This algorithm is seeded by the current time and date, and by a user-determined 64-bit seed value. Each of these values is updated throughout the encryption process. Because of the complex nature of the algorithm, this method produces random numbers and seed values that are virtually impossible to crack.

The **Blum Blum Shub** or BBS PRNG is a good alternative that does not rely on a clock value or other external stimulus to seed the generator. Instead, this method relies on the complexity of factoring prime numbers to protect its integrity. This method requires the initial input of two large prime numbers that both have a value of 3 (mod 4). Next, we choose a number s so that s has no common factors (is relatively prime) to our two large primes. Multiply the two primes together to form the value n. Once these values s and n are known, they are input into the algorithm:

$Seed_0 = s^2 \;(mod\;n)$ /* create the starting value */

for $i = 1$ **to** ∞ /* create an infinite pattern */

$Seed_0 = Seed_{i-1}^{2} \;(mod\;n)$ /* generate the next occurrence */

     $Next\_Bit = Seed_1 \;(mod\;2)$ /* take the low-order bit */

     call create_rand (Next_bit)   /* a function to collect the randomly generated bits and

                                        form the random number */

    next i /* loop again to get next bit */

This algorithm produces effective random numbers. The method has a statistical probability of near fifty percent that the next bit generated will be either a 1 or a 0. Because of the demonstrated randomness of the numbers and the formulation of the initial seed based on the product of two large primes, little information is available to cryptanalysts to allow them to compromise the method.

In conclusion, the use of random numbers is important to the study of cryptography. It is imperative that the cryptographer choose the random number generation method carefully, so as to not compromise the cipher.

Hashes

Hashes are special numbers that allow us to test the integrity of our information. Essentially, a hash is a mathematical function that maps an arbitrary length input string to a (usually) smaller fixed-length output string.

A good hash function is one that creates a one-to-one mapping between the source string and the output string. This property is called **collision resistant**. Given a message x and a hash value of H, it should be computationally infeasible to find a message y such that $H(x)=H(y)$. Hashes are considered strongly collision resistant if there is no overlap in the range of hash values for any two input messages to the hash function. It there is a potential of overlap in the range of hash values based on a weaker hash function, the hash is said to be weakly collision resistant.

A good hash should also be a **one-way hash**, meaning that nothing in the hash value or the hash function should allow anyone to reverse engineer the information. This is important because, for the hash function to be of any use, it must be a publicly known method.

Several methods exist that are widely endorsed for providing such hash values. These include the federal Secure Hash Standard (SHA RFC 3174) endorsed by NIST, PIREMD-160, HMAC (RFC 2104) and MD5 (RFC 1321).

Each of these hash functions is quite complex to implement. However, for learning purposes, take a look at a simple hash function presented in Figure 6-5. In this particular example, we will take advantage of mathematical logic to compute our function along with the rotation of bits to the left. The algorithm, while simple, is quite effective in providing integrity checking. In the algorithm, we first take a plain text message M. We then divide M in some equally sized block (in this case 16 bits per block) and number them B_1 thru B_n. We then create a checksum of 16 zeroed-out bits. Iteratively, take each of the n blocks and *exclusive-or* them one by one with the checksum. After each exclusive-or operation, we shift all the bits of the checksum left and rotate the low-order bit into the high-order position (or rotate the bits left). Once the nth block is included, the hash is complete and is then appended to the message.

FUNCTIONS

The concept of a function will be presented to students of computer science or mathematics many times during their education. Formally, a **function** is a rule that allows the mapping of elements of one **set** (the **domain**) to those of another set (the **range**). As seen in Figure 6-6, given a value x and a function f, we can map x to a value in the range that corresponds to the answer to $f(x)$ (read "f of x"). It is important to use the generalized mathematical notation of a function so you develop a proper math vocabulary. This vocabulary will enable you to easily read more detailed descriptions of the application of functions. An example of this is shown in Figure 6-6, where we have the domain of all integers and the range of all possible real numbers. The function, in this case, is the square root function. Any mathematical operator can be thought of as a function because it is represents a shorthand call for a complex action. In this case, the action is to perform the necessary steps of calculating the square root of a number. In the case listed $x=25$ is the selected value in the domain. The function f is represented by $\sqrt{25}$. The $\sqrt{25}$ maps to 5 in the range. This is a simple example and can certainly be expanded to incorporate more complex procedures.

Many people never appreciate the intrinsic value of the use of functions: they provide an important level of abstraction to our problem-solving methods. By using a function, we are providing the user of the function with an abstraction that hides or consolidates the details of a complex underlying process. In the example shown in Figure 6-6, the complex process was finding the square root. Do not be overly concerned about the details of *how* the function is carried out; rather it is important to know that it *can* be carried out. The use of functions promotes big-picture or strategic thinking.

We can see this more clearly by examining how functions are used in computer programming. In this context, a function can hide a complex series of steps (an **algorithm**) that performs some action (**process**), aligns it with some input data, and returns the effects (some change or analysis), resulting as **output**. Take, for example, a user-created function that sorts the elements of a list named "sort_it." We could then use this function to sort the contents of any list by executing the command

"sort_it(list1);"

Hashing

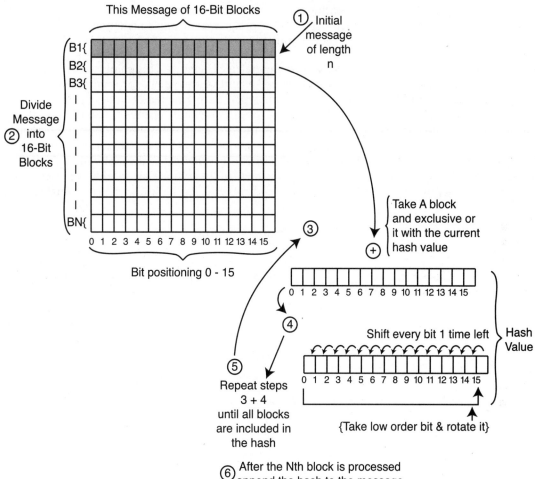

Figure 6-5 A simple but effective hashing function featuring the exclusive OR.

in the C programming language. The creation of this function provides the programmer/problem solver with four advantages:

- An abstraction to sort a list without needing to know the underlying details of the sort method
- An abstraction that can be applied to sort any list (*list1, list2, list3,., listn*)   providing that the content of the list (containing numbers or strings) meets the specified criteria of the sort routine

- A function whose method can be changed (say to a more effective one) without the strategist or problem solver caring about anything other than sorting the list
- A function is a separate piece of code from the main body of the program. This enables the problem solver to assign the creation of the function algorithm to another programmer, thus distributing the work by simply providing the input, output, and process specification. The details of the programmatic implementation are left to the programmer assigned to code that particular function

These are powerful advantages that clearly promote strategic thinking. This point is clearly demonstrated in Figure 6-7. Here we see three functions: get_plaintext, encrypt_it, and send_it. Each one specifies the required input and output values (including type). Each function describes the process and expected result. In this case, get_plaintext takes data from a previously opened file and returns it as a string to the main program. The main program takes the string and sends it to encrypt_it. Encrypt_it takes the string and the encryption key and creates cipher code. That code is then passed to send_it, along with a destination address. Send_it communicates the ciphertext to the destination. Notice that the main routine is simple and readable. It contains none of the complex algorithmic logic required to perform any of the three tasks. Aside from simple control logic, it is basically written in English.

Domain Range Mapping

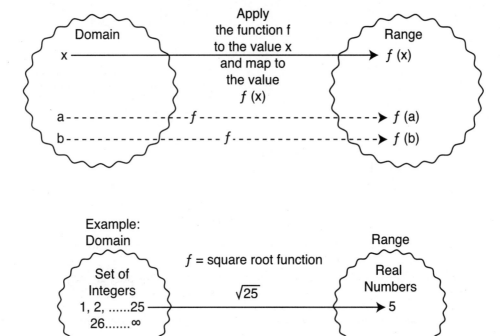

Figure 6-6   We use a function to map valves in our domain to corresponding valves in the range.

Functions in Computer Programming

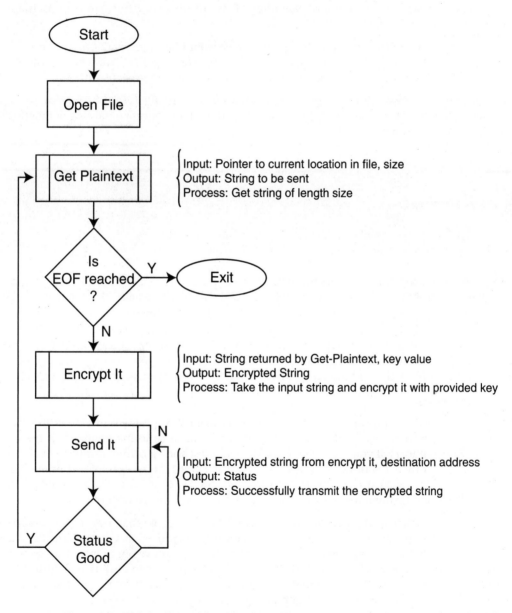

Figure 6-7   High-level set of functions to get information, encrypt it, and send it over a link.

The function allows us to remove the details and concentrate on high-level process. Functions themselves can call other functions to simplify their own work, thus we can legitimately have functions embedded in other functions. This is easiest when reviewed with basic mathematics. Remember that in any expression we evaluate the innermost parentheses first. This is always true of functions. In the case of the function,

$\sqrt{2^4}$, we have two functions. Written for the computer we would say (sqrt(exp(2,4)). In this case, we must first perform the calculation of raising 2 to the fourth power to get 16. We then substitute16 for exp(2,4) which leaves us with (sqrt(16)). This can then be evaluated to leave us with 4.

Expressed in general terms, this composition of functions is written $f_1(f_2(x))$. The result of $f_2(x)$ is then fed to $f_1(result)$ for the next stage of the calculation. This concept of nesting of functions can be carried on as many times as needed[3].

KEY POINT

It is important to remember that in the case of composite functions (nested functions), always resolve the innermost function first and use the result as the input to the next innermost function.

Cryptography is related to mathematics through the use of functions. For example, if we write a process that applies a shift cipher of 5 to the name "Bill," we might write: *shift₅cipher (Bill) = Gnqq*. By stating the process this way, we can see the effect of the function without dealing with the details of the process. From now on, we will refer to cryptographic functions in this format: *Cipher = Encrypt(Key, Plain)*. This function says, "use the function encrypt with the specified key to create ciphertext output from the plain text input provided." The reciprocal process is shown as *Plain = Decrypt(Key, Cipher)* read as "use the function decrypt with the specified key to create plain text output from the ciphertext input provided."

PRIME NUMBERS

As we work with cryptography and modern cryptographic algorithms, it is essential to utilize many of the concepts of number theory. Of those concepts, one of the most basic and important is the need to work with prime numbers. If you remember from elementary school, a **prime number** can be defined as an integer greater than 1 with no divisors other than itself and 1. Some examples of prime numbers include 2, 3, 5, 7, 11, 13, 17, 19, 23, 29, 31, 37, 41, 43, 47, 53, 59, 61, 67, 71, 73, 79, 83, 89, 97, ... and so on. Euclid's second theorem demonstrates that there are an infinite number of primes.

Euclid was a mathematician who lived in approximately 300 B.C. More than two thousand years ago, Euclid theorized that the number of possible primes is infinite. He proved this through the use of a principle called **contradiction**. Contradiction means that, rather than prove our point is true, we need to prove only that the opposing view is false. This is especially helpful when dealing with infinite sets of numbers. Therefore, if we want to prove that the set of possible primes is infinite, we need to prove only that it is not finite. Thus, if we have a list of primes $p1, p2, p3,..., p_n$, we can say that some number N exists such that $N = p_1 \bullet p_2 \bullet p_3 \bullet ... \bullet p_n + 1$ (the product of all of the primes multiplied together plus 1).

---

[3]. In the case of recursion, this process can be designed where a function calls itself over and over until a problem is solved. This topic is quite interesting but is beyond the scope of this text. Recursion is a powerful tool that can be applied to the study of cryptography.

N is definitely greater than 1, and if we divide N by any of the existing known primes, the result will be a number with a remainder of 1. It does not, therefore, divide evenly by a prime. The fundamental theorem of arithmetic states that any positive integer is the product of primes or it is prime. Because we know that axiom to be true, then N must be prime because it does not divide evenly by any of the list of known primes. Therefore, since N is larger than p_n, it is a new element to the prime list and this is the contradiction needed to prove the list of primes is infinite. For every N we develop, we find another prime—meaning the list is infinite. This theorem does not really tell us anything about the list of primes or how to find them, only that they are definitely endless.

Numbers other than 1 that are not prime are called composite numbers. The number 1 used to be considered prime but is no longer included in the list. The number 1 is a special case that is considered neither prime nor composite. For a larger subset of the prime numbers up to 5,000, see Appendix D. Any positive integer can be represented in exactly one way as a product of primes.

No one really knows how many large prime numbers exist. Among mathematicians is an ongoing search for the next large prime. George Woltman, a programmer from Orlando, Florida, created a program that is used worldwide by people to determine large primes. Recently it was used to determine that $2^{2,976,221} - 1$ is a prime number. This 895,932-digit prime is more than twice as long as the previously known longest prime. This calculation was done with a desktop computer and took fifteen days of compute time.

Prime numbers and divisibility share some interesting connections, which will help us in our discussion of finding large primes.

- A number is divisible by the prime 2 if the last digit of the number is even
- A number is divisible by the prime 3 if the sum of the digits in the number is divisible by 3 (e.g., 123393 can be shown as $1 + 2 + 3 + 3 + 9 + 3 = 21 \div 3 = 7$; therefore, $123393 \div 3 = 41131$ with no remainder)
- A number is divisible by the prime 5 if the last digit is a 0 or a 5

If we look at the entire set of numbers, n, it should be obvious that all even numbers (other than 2) and numbers ending in 5 (other than 5) cannot be prime. This is because even numbers are always divisible by 2 and all numbers ending in 5 are divisible by 5. This means that we have essentially eliminated six out of every ten numbers as possible primes. This leaves us with 40 percent of all numbers as "possibly" prime.

It can be demonstrated statistically that, given any large number y as a starting point, the occurrences of prime numbers around it will have a density of 1 in every $\ln(y)$. Given that we have already demonstrated that six of every ten numbers can be eliminated as possible primes, we can state that if we picked a large number y, and successively tested numbers around it for primality, we would find one prime number in $0.4(\ln(y))$ tests. That means that to find a large prime on the order of 3^{200} would require checking approximately eighty-eight integers (that are not even and do not end in five) around 3^{200}. Most of the encryption algorithms that require using large prime numbers deal with numbers of this magnitude or greater. Developing algorithms that test for primality is still an important focus of mathematics. Factoring large numbers into their prime factors is considered by most to be an exceptionally difficult problem. Some experts believe it is impossible given a large enough prime.

Another concept presented in more advanced number theorems is the concept of two numbers being **relatively prime** to each other. One number is said to be relatively prime to another if they have no prime factors in common. The only number that divides them both is 1.

As we go forward with our understanding of the mathematics of cryptography, you will learn that the use of primes can be used to create the necessary levels of complexity for our cryptographic techniques to succeed.

Unique Factorization

Earlier we spoke of important properties of integers. We covered congruence and divisibility in detail. We are all familiar with the basic mathematical operations of addition, subtraction, multiplication, and division. Laypeople think of the reverse of multiplication as division, and rightly so. However, remembering that we are concerned only with the mathematics of integers, it is more appropriate to think of the reverse of multiplication as the factoring process. Factoring means to divide a number into its multiplicative components (integers that can be multiplied together to create this number). From basic algebra, we learned how to find the factors of numbers and equations.

In keeping with our idea of creating hard problems, multiplication is easy and factoring is hard. Again, we have discovered a pair of reversible mathematical functions that is ideally suited for cryptography.

In the previous lesson, we reviewed the importance of prime numbers. Prime numbers are special because they can be factored into only the prime number itself, and into 1. Prime numbers are a core component of all fundamental mathematics. According to the fundamental theorem of arithmetic, "the standard factorization of every integer $>= 2$ is unique[4]." For this to be true, the factors need to be shown to be only powers of primes (because primes are unique in that they factor only to the prime and to 1.) Once a number is factored into primes, then this solution has to be unique because it cannot be reduced further in terms of whole integers.

For example, number 63 can be factored into 7 and 9. The number 7 is prime and cannot be factored. The number 9 can be further reduced to 3^2. Thus, 63 can be thought of as the product of $7^1 \cdot 3^2$, or the product of powers of primes. If you experiment, you will find that this is always the case. You will also realize that factoring large numbers into their primes is very difficult and extremely time consuming. From the cryptologists' point of view, this practice should be exploited.

Obviously, one could write a trivial computer program to find the prime factors of any number. This is done by starting at 2 and dividing the number, x, by each successive prime until the result of the division produces no remainder (or $prime|x$.) It is important to note that this program would stop at the closest prime to $\sqrt{x}$. This is obvious because if the $\sqrt{x}$ were a prime, then $\sqrt{x} \cdot \sqrt{x} = x$ making $\sqrt{x}$ the largest possible prime factor of x. This may seem trivial for small values of x. But as x grows (to greater than 100 places in length) the cryptanalyst is faced with two problems:

- The sheer number of divisions of primes would consume the computer
- Finding large primes is difficult (as demonstrated in the previous lesson)

Of all the reversible functions, therefore, this pair (multiplication and factoring) is frequently utilized.

ADVANCED NUMBER THEOREMS

Several important theorems are used to develop cryptographic methods or attacks. These theorems are somewhat advanced and require a significant bit of study to understand and appreciate. For those students who go on to develop cipher strategies, a sound understanding of these techniques is required. For those

---

[4.] We will not attempt to prove this here because the proof is somewhat confusing. This proof is standard in many mathematics books and can easily be found on the Web.

students who will use cryptographic solutions as part of the application of information security counter-measures, an understanding of these theorems will strengthen your conviction that, because of these methods, the underlying cryptographic algorithms need to be sufficiently complex to meet the challenges required of a strong cipher. These methods build on the concepts of number theory introduced earlier.

We shall examine three of these advanced number theorems: Euclid's method, Fermat's little theory, and Euler's theorem. (Students interested in more of these types of theories are encouraged to examine the literature for information on the Chinese remainder theory, multiplicative inverses, matrix multiplication, discrete logarithms, and tests for primality. These subjects are beyond the scope of this text). These three theories are important to understanding the nuances of many cryptographic methods. However, our purpose in this chapter is only to expose students to basic number theory. Presenting the core three advanced theories will allow for continuing this investigation through the literature.

Euclid's Method GCF

You were previously introduced to Euclid regarding his proof about an infinite number of prime numbers. Another of his famous works deals with finding the greatest common factor (GCF) of a pair of numbers (y, z). As we have alluded to throughout this section, cryptologists are constantly trying to define hard problems, specifically, hard problems to solve (or guess) and that are simple to create. Multiplying two numbers together is a simple process. However, factoring two numbers is really quite complex—especially if you are trying to find a specific pair of factors. For example, 100 can be factored into 10 x 10, or 25 x 4, or 20 x 5, or 50 x 2, and so on. Factoring is a tough problem because it requires us to think backward. Undoing things is an unnatural act. Trying to find a set of factors that generate numbers that can then be fit into a puzzle to reverse engineer a cryptographic method is part mechanical and part intuitive. Computers are quite good at mechanical and repetitive tasks, but they do not deal with heuristics and intuition well. As a result, factoring is hard for both humans and computers. Therefore we have designed a "hard" problem.

Euclid's method is truly genius and demonstrates the kind of thought that must be applied to cryptanalysis in order to not only crack a hard problem but to do so efficiently.

We will start with an example of brute-force testing when two numbers have a common factor. Given two numbers (A, B) and asked if they had a common factor, could you find out? I am quite sure that you could. Most people would start by determining if the numbers were both odd, both even, or one of each. If the numbers are even, then one answer is 2. If the numbers are both odd, we would suggest trying 3, 5, and 7 to start. If one is even and one is odd, the answer may be a bit trickier, but following a methodical trial-and-error pattern would yield a brute-force solution. A simple piece of pseudocode to accomplish this task is illustrated in Figure 6-8. Notice that the function tests if i is a factor of A or B based on a division with a remainder = 0.

If the numbers were quite large, would that make a difference? It would, in fact, make a difference. As the numbers grew in size, the brute-force method would become less and less useful because the algorithm would take too long to execute. This is often the case with any type of brute-force approach. In modern cryptography, numbers that need to be factored as part of a cryptanalysis are often quite large. Also, most often, the numbers that need to be factored are the product of large primes. Because large primes cannot be reduced, we have to change our fundamental approach. This means that our problem has essentially changed to finding the largest common denominator. How would that change the brute-force approach?

The brute-force approach could be modified to accommodate this request by simply counting backward from the smaller of the two inputs (A, B) by 1 (if the numbers are even), or by 2 from the closest odd number to the smaller of (A, B) if either of the numbers are odd. In general, finding the greatest common denominator is harder (than just finding a common factor) because numbers such as 2, 3, and 5 (which factor 60 percent of all numbers) cannot be tested until close to the end of the algorithm.

Again, supposing the numbers were quite large, how would that affect your method?

In this case, the problem will again take much too long and the brute-force method will not yield a reasonable response time.

Euclid saw this problem as a challenge and came up with a method that is really quite intuitive. In Figure 6-9, we see the algorithm for Euclid's method to find the greatest common factor (GCF). In the algorithm, A and B are compared to find the smaller of the two. In this case, let us assume that the smaller number is A. Our initial guess is that A is the GCF. To test this theory, we need to divide the bigger number by A, or GCF in this case. Because we are actually interested in seeing the remainder of the integer division, we will use the modulo function instead of a normal division. If the remainder of the division is 0, then the GCF is returned as set. If the remainder is not 0, then we set the bigger number

```
inputs A & B /* If A and B are even the solution is trivial */
    if (A and B) are both even
        then
            return (Common_Fact = 2);

/* if either A or B is odd then the
        common factor must be odd */

Small = min (A,B) /* use the smallest of the 2 inputs
        to gate the function */

        /* Brute Force test of all odd divisors */
for i: 3 to small
        {
            /* divides is a function x where True means no remainder */
                                      i


        if ((i divided (A)) and (i divides (B))
                then
                    return (common _Fact = i)
                else
                    i = i + 2 /* keep i odd */
                }
        /* it here no common factor */
            return (common fact = 1);
```

Figure 6-8 This algorithm will determine if A, B have a common factor. However, the method is inefficient.

Euclid's Method

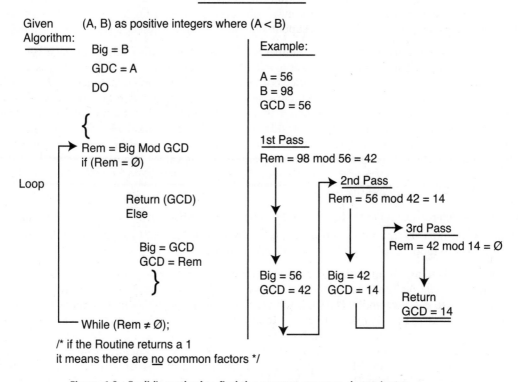

Given (A, B) as positive integers where (A < B)
Algorithm:

Big = B
GDC = A
DO

{
    Rem = Big Mod GCD
    if (Rem = Ø)

        Return (GCD)
    Else

        Big = GCD
        GCD = Rem
}

Loop

While (Rem ≠ Ø);

/* if the Routine returns a 1
it means there are no common factors */

Example:

A = 56
B = 98
GCD = 56

1st Pass
Rem = 98 mod 56 = 42

2nd Pass
Rem = 56 mod 42 = 14

3rd Pass
Rem = 42 mod 14 = Ø

Big = 56   Big = 42
GCD = 42   GCD = 14

Return
GCD = 14

Figure 6-9   Euclid's method to find the greatest common denominator.

equal to the GCF value we just tried, and we set the new GCF attempt to the remainder of the previous attempt. We then try this again, REM = Big mod (GCF). We continue this method until the remainder equals 0 or until the remainder is 1 (which implies that the only common factor is 1 or the two numbers have no common factor).

To better understand this, look at the example to the right of the algorithm in Figure 6-8. In this example, we will use A = 56 and B = 9 8. Here we see that the GCF can be found in three passes. In the first pass, we perform the operation REM = 98 mod(56) = 42. In the second pass, REM = 56 mod(42) = 14. Finally, in the third pass, REM = 42 mod(14) = 0. Therefore, the GCF is 14, and we found it in three passes.

Compare Euclid's algorithm with a brute-force approach. In the brute-force approach previously mentioned, we would count backward from 56 to 14 by 1 (because both of the numbers are even). In this case, we would have had to perform 42 divisions (compared to Euclid's 3) to accomplish the same goal.

This should help students understand that certain methods are more elegant and should be utilized to effectively reduce the time to crack cryptographic methods. One interesting byproduct of this discussion is that we can use this method to test if two numbers are relatively prime to one another. From now on, we shall say two numbers A and B are relatively prime to each other if GCF (A, B) =1.

Euler's Theorem and Fermat's Theorem

Euler's theorem and Fermat's theorem are critical components of asymmetrical cryptography. The relationships expressed in these theorems are not always obvious. For this reason, it is important that students experiment with them on a calculator that supports modulo arithmetic (especially for larger values).

Fermat's theorem states that for any prime number p, and any other number x, which is relatively prime to p, then $x^{p-1} \bmod p \equiv 1 \bmod p$ holds true. Let us examine this equation. This is read in English as "x to the p-1 mod p is congruent with 1 mod p (they both will produce the same remainder)." On the right side, 1 mod p is just a fancy way of saying 1, because 1 mod anything (other than 1 itself) is 1. This is because in integer division, when the 1 is being divided by a number bigger than itself, the answer will always be 0 with a remainder of 1. On the left side, we are saying is $x^{p-1} \bmod p = 1$ (this is the more commonly used). This, then, is at the heart of the theory. Let us try it out: If p is 17 and x is 4 (4 and 17 are relatively prime to each other since they have no common prime values), then we have $4^{17-1} \equiv 1 \bmod 17$. The first step is to check 1 mod 17 is 1. Then calculate $4^{16} = 4294967296$, and then from our theory it follows that 4294967296 mod 17 = 1.

From this, Fermat further states that $x^p \equiv x \bmod p$ (where p is a prime and x is any positive number). An example of this is $p = 17$ and $x = 6$. In this case, $6^{17} = 16926659444736$. Through integer division, 16926659444736 mod 17 = 6. Finally, 6 mod 17 also is equal to 6.

Euler introduced an important function in number theory known as Euler's totient function. This function is written as $Phi(n)$. The function Phi is defined as the number of positive integers less than n and relatively prime to n. For example, $Phi(10)$ is the set of 4 numbers (1, 3, 7, and 9) that are less than 10 and relatively prime to it, so $Phi(10) = 4$ because there are four numbers in the set. Notice that 2, 4, 5, 6, and 8 are not in the set because they each have a common factor with 10, other than the number 1. It is important to notice that for numbers that are prime, e.g., 59 by the very definition of a prime number, all of the numbers below it are relatively prime to it so the answer in this case, then, is 58. In general, for $Phi(p)$ where p is prime is $(p-1)$.

Using this information, Euler's theorem is as follows for two numbers x and n that are relatively prime to each other: $x^{Phi(n)} \bmod n = 1$. This is interesting because it states that x raised to the power of the number of relatively prime numbers less than n modulo n is equal to 1. You would not think that the number of relatively prime numbers less than some number would have any consistent effect on the number. But it does. Further, in cryptography we look for nonobvious relationships such as this one because we can exploit this relationship in building our algorithms. Then if the method falls victim to cryptanalysis, it is much harder to understand and hence harder to reverse engineer.

Let us try it and see. If we choose 7 for n, and 4 for x, then Phi of 7 is equal to 6 (since all of the numbers less than it are relatively prime to the prime 7). If 4 is raised to the sixth power, it equals 4,096. 4,096 modulo 7 = 1. It is important to note that with the exception of Phi of a prime, which is equal to the prime minus 1, there is no rule for determining Phi of any other kind of numbers.

The RSA algorithm for public key cryptography that we will review in Chapter 9 is based on exponentiation using modulo arithmetic. The details of this algorithm rely heavily on these two theorems.

COMPUTATIONAL COMPLEXITY

As we have mentioned, the cryptographer is always trying to create problems that are "hard" to solve. The cryptanalyst, on the other hand, is always trying to find innovative solutions to these hard problems that will cut down on the time it takes to crack a cryptographic method. This constant battle has been the primary driving force in the evolution of modern cryptography.

Most of us will not be in positions of either the cryptographer or the cryptanalyst. We will, instead, be the users of the cryptography and the owners of the information that is being protected. Consequently, it is most important that we be able to understand what makes a problem "hard," which, to some extent, we have already done. However, we also must be able to quantify the degrees of "hardness" of a problem. Determining problem's difficulty level is based on two areas of mathematics:

- The statistical analysis of the given problem space
- Complexity theory—the study of how hard a problem is to solve

Statistical analysis is an interesting area of mathematics that has a broad set of applications. In this text, we shall review the basics of statistics so that students can better understand comparisons of methods (made on a statistical basis) when opposing cryptographic algorithms are reviewed. Statistical analysis is used to determine the probability of finding a solution at all.

Complexity theory is broken into two parts:

- The complexity of algorithms (cryptographic or cryptanalysis) and the complexity of operations (multiplication, division, etc.)
- The determination of whether or not a problem is even solvable or how one type of problem compares to another

Understanding complexity helps us to better determine which operations fit best into a particular schema that is being engineered. Complexity theory is also important in determining the effectiveness of cryptanalysis algorithms. This part of the chapter is meant to serve as an introduction to both of these areas.

STATISTICAL ANALYSIS OF THE PROBLEM SPACE

Throughout much of cryptography, terms such as "the probability of" and "statistically speaking" are used. It is important that we better understand what these terms mean in order to better appreciate their meaning. One of the ways of determining the "hardness" of a problem is to compare the relative probabilities of events that will cause one to match a number from the domain with the proper target number in the range. By understanding how likely it will be for a hard problem to be solved, or how the range of one problem compares to another, is based on probability and statistics.

Statistics help us to understand the total number of combinations of outcomes there are in a closed system. The ability to list these outcomes is the key to determining the probability of an event. A key to probability is to understand the sample space well enough to correctly identify the numbers of both good and total outcomes in question. With these numbers, the determination of an event probability is relatively easy.

Let us start with the introduction of some basic statistical terms and build from there. As we saw earlier in the text when discussing the basics of Monte Carlo simulation, we realized that real-world events can occur with a certain frequency and pattern. This distribution can be charted on a graph to make it easier to understand. These distributions will form curves that can be measured. Some interesting measurements of these curves are the mean, mode, and median. The mean is the sum of the terms divided by the number of terms, and is usually referred to as the arithmetic average.

This is expressed mathematically as

$$\bar{x} = \frac{\sum_{i=1}^{n} x_i}{n}.$$

This calculation represents the statistical middle, or center, of the curve. However, this does not suggest that the center of the distribution is where most of the numbers occurred. For example, we can take the mean of test scores in which the grades were 70, 65, 60, 95, 99, 92 to be 80.16, yet no single person scored an 80 or anything close to it. In this case, we say that the distribution of events is polarized.

If we arrange the data points in size order (smallest to largest), we can find the measure of central tendency known as the median. The median is a calculation that divides this set of ordered points in half so that the value of the median is the one in the middle. In other words, fifty percent of the remaining values are equal to or less than the median, and fifty percent are greater than or equal to the median.

Another useful measurement is the mode. The mode of a distribution is the terms that occur most frequently in the list. The term with the highest frequency is the mode.

Although these values are important, they are somewhat misleading if the distribution is too small or skewed based on some outside influence (statistically called outliers). Often it is helpful to understand the variation or deviation between the mean and the rest of the data points. From a measurement such as this, we can tell how "tightly packed" the data points are with respect to the mean. This measurement of variation is called the standard deviation. It is calculated as:

$$\sigma_{n-1} = \sqrt{\frac{\sum_{i=1}^{n} (x_i - \bar{x})^2}{n-1}}$$

which is the square root of the sum of the square of the differences between all the data points and the mean, divided by n-1. A normal curve has a variance of within one standard deviation of the mean. Through the use of the standard deviation calculation, we can determine how "normal" our distribution is.

The study of probability allows us to understand how likely it is that something—called an event in statistical terms—will happen. The probability of an event happening is computed as the ratio of

$$\frac{favorable\_outcomes}{Total\_number\_of\_possible\_outcomes}.$$

The most important element, as seen in the formula, is to be able to identify and quantify all of the different outcomes that can occur and separate out the ones that meet your criteria as favorable. If all outcomes are equally likely to occur, then the given formula will suffice. For example, suppose that there are ten colored balls in a bin. Four of the balls are green and six of the balls are red. In this case, we see that the probability of randomly choosing a red ball from the bin is 6 ÷ 10 (because there are six potentially good outcomes out of ten total possible outcomes). This is computed as a percentage: there is a sixty percent probability of choosing a red ball.

Multiple events (e.g., choosing two red balls out of the ten balls in our bin) create a situation where each event becomes dependent on the others. For example, we have already shown that the probability of choosing one red ball is 60 percent. Suppose that we wanted to know the probability of drawing a red ball, not replacing it, and then drawing a green ball. We would figure out the probability of each and multiply them together. The probability of $6 \div 10$ for choosing a red ball remains the same. However, because the sample size is now nine (I just took out a ball and did not replace it), the probability of choosing a green ball increases to $4 \div 9$. Thus, the chances of both events happening is $6 \div 10 \times 4 \div 9 = 4 \div 15$ or 26.6 percent.

When we state that something has a zero percent chance of occurrence, it does not always mean that it will never occur. It can mean instead that it is extremely unlikely to ever occur. For example, given an infinite set of numbers, the chance that you will choose any particular number is 1/, which is essentially zero percent. Conversely, for an infinite quantity, if we say that there is 100 percent chance that you will not choose the number 81,884 out of infinity, it is still possible that you will. In fact, when you calculate the odds of winning the lottery, the probability will approach zero percent.

Calculating the odds of an event happening is not the same as probability. For example, if we bet that a baseball team has 5 to 3 odds of winning a game, it means

$$\frac{probability\_of\_our\_team\_not\_winning}{probabilitiy\_of\_our\_team\_winning} = \frac{5}{3}.$$

Odds are always expressed as the probability that an event will not occur to the probability that it will occur. If we want the probability of a win, we can convert the odds of A to B as

$$\Pr obability = \frac{B}{A+B}.$$

In the previous example, we can see that the probability of our team winning is $\frac{3}{5+3} = \frac{3}{8}$ or 37.5 percent.

COMPLEXITY THEORY

Complexity theory is the study of how difficult a problem is to solve. To calculate this difficulty, you have to understand the following three factors:

- **The classification of the problem itself**

  There are many types of problems that can be solved. Each problem type has a relative order of magnitude of work required to solve the problem. By studying this information, the cryptographer can decide if the type of problem created will create sufficient work for a cryptanalyst to break by just looking at the type. For example, multiplication of numbers is a much easier problem to solve than recognizing primes.

- **The efficiency of the algorithms available to crack a problem**

  By understanding the computational complexity required to break a code, a cryptographer can determine the useful life of the cryptography. This is important because the user of the cryptographic method can take action to reduce the effectiveness of an attack on cryptography. For example, if we suspect that a key can be compromised in ten days, then we can rotate keys every two days, thereby frustrating the efforts of the cryptanalyst.

■ **The language of complexity comparisons**

> By understanding how the analysis is conducted then a review of the available literature becomes easy enough.

The language of complexity comparisons is really quite simple. First, we have the operator O (some expression), read "the big O of some expression." Ultimately, we are trying to resolve all of our comparisons to an answer expressed in big O terms. The big O stands for the order of magnitude. Generally, big O numbers are compared based on a number n over the domain $n=0$ to infinity. As you can see from Figure 6-10, these comparisons are best expressed in graphical form. Notice how slowly the O(log n) function grows in comparison to a function of O(n^2). This representation can help us to understand the relationships between functions, especially as n gets large.

Big O Comparisons

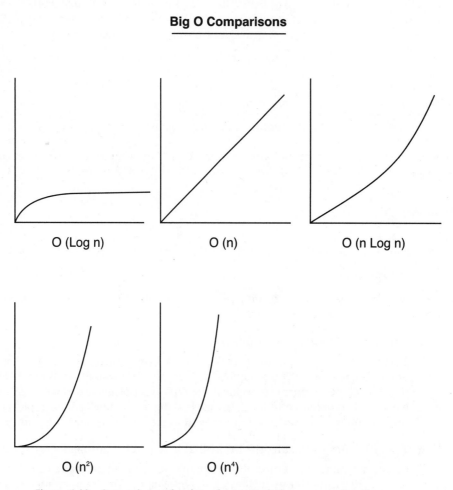

Figure 6-10 **Comparisons of orders of magnitude for common functions.**

The following are some common examples of big O comparisons:

Problem	Complexity
Multiplying n numbers	$O(n^2)$
Solving an n letter jumble	$O(26^n)$
Sorting a list using a bubble sort	$O(n^2)$
Searching a sorted list using binary search	$O(\log_2 n)$

The Knapsack Problem

The classic knapsack problem is a term used to define the class of problems known as NP-Complete. The knapsack problem was also the basis for the early asymmetrical encryption algorithms.

The problem can be stated as:

Given a set of items to be packed into a knapsack of a given size (s), is there a way to select some of the items to be packed to ensure that all of the space (s) of the knapsack is taken up? This problem is reasonably easy to state. In fact, it is even easier to restate in mathematical terms: Given a set of numbers $(a_1, a_2, ..., a_n)$ and a sum (S) is there a way to choose the numbers from the list such that

$$S = \sum_{i=1}^{n} (a_i * v_i)$$

where v_i is a selection vector (0 or 1) for each element i, that determines if the element a_i should be included.

For example, given the set of numbers (1, 4, 7, 10, 14) and S = 25, we can see that the subset (1, 10, 14) satisfies the equation. We can also see that for S = 16, there is no solution from this grouping of five numbers.

This problem is NP-Complete because we are computing the answer in a nondeterministic way, (that is, we are guessing). Without knowing the sum and the elements in the list, there is no way of predetermining how long it will take to solve the problem or declare it unsolvable.

There are four primary classes of problems that we can create: P, NP, NP-Complete, and EXP. A P problem means that for any problem in the class, there is a solution method that can be executed in polynomial time. Mathematically, we state this as $O(p(n))$, meaning that the time to solve a P problem is based on some polynomial p(n) that takes n as its input. As we showed above, the searching and sorting of lists can be done in polynomial time—$\log_2 n$, and n^2, respectively.

P problems are measurable and predictable. However, from the cryptographic standpoint, they are useful only if they take a long time to process (n is extremely large). Most of the problems from number theory are P problems. They tend to be useful because we choose n to be very large, which creates a large enough domain to minimize the effectiveness of most cryptanalysis.

A more interesting class of problems fall into the NP class. In this class, solution times are based on guessing and are, therefore, nondeterministic. A problem that is considered NP-Complete is in the class of NP problems and can represent the entire class. This is important because if it can be shown that if any one NP-Complete problem can be solved by any method in P, then all NP problems have a P solution. As a result, many researchers are looking for solutions to NP-Complete problems or conversely, proofs that NP-Complete problems are not solvable in P.

There is a final group of problems known as EXP for which a deterministic solution exists in exponential time, constant c^n. Our earlier example of solving a word jumble is a problem in the EXP space. EXP problems, while deterministic, are generally unsolvable in a reasonable time for large n.

We are not endorsing any type of problem as being the best type to use in a particular cryptographic algorithm. Doing so would represent a gross oversimplification of the theories presented. For example, NP-Complete problems are, in fact, solvable. We did solve one quite easily in the knapsack problem. Therefore, it is not always the best choice to try and utilize one of these problems as the basis for a cryptographic algorithm (as Merkle and Hellman did in proposing the knapsack algorithm as the basis of an early public key cryptosystem that was cracked).

From the cryptologist's perspective, tradeoffs need to be made so the methods are balanced:

- The problem must be hard to discover. That could be done with large P problems (based on the compute intensiveness of the method), NP problems, and certainly with EXP problems
- There must be an easy solution to allow the decrypt algorithm to execute it (of course, given the keys and necessary information that the cryptanalyst would not have). However, this easy solution or trick must be carefully hidden, or at least not obvious. This is the difficulty with NP problems. For many NP problems, if the domain and range is small enough, the problem can be guessed, or worse, a brute-force algorithmic approach might find the answer quickly. If NP problems are chosen, the problems must be large enough and chosen carefully enough to eliminate the potential of an easy solution
- The solution must be manageable for the decryption routine. For example, the one-time pad described in the Chapter 5 is of the EXP type. However, the necessity of moving a key as long as the message is unmanageable and unrealistic (which means that the method becomes unusable)
- The hardness of the problems need to be balanced against the duration of time that the cipher needs to remain valid. The longer the time, the harder the problem. It is also important to consider the worth of the information and balance that against the cost of cryptanalysis. The higher the cost, the harder the problem

CRYPTOGRAPHIC PRINCIPLES

As we progress through the remaining chapters in this section of the text, we will be examining cryptographic methods and strategies. As you have seen thus far, mathematics can be used to provide the underpinnings of many of these methods. The following are several cryptographic principles that are enabled through the application of many of the mathematical theorems and methods described in this section.

- A basic principle of cryptographic mathematics is to utilize operations and functions that make the creation of ciphers easy. These same operations and functions should also leave the cryptanalyst to reverse engineer extremely hard problems
- The cryptologist strives to create exceedingly large problem spaces. This is done primarily through the use of exceptionally large numbers, especially extremely large prime numbers. Problem domain ranges need to be large enough to withstand a distributed computer-enabled brute-force search
- Cryptologists need to incorporate reversibility into their algorithms. As we have seen, reversible functions, such as addition and subtraction, exponentiation and logarithms, multiplication and factoring, bit shifting, and logical exclusive-or, can all be used to accomplish this task
- Algorithms for implementing the encryption should attempt to utilize mathematics to cause as much "confusion and diffusion" (Claude Shannon 1949) as possible. Algorithms and methods need to be sufficiently complex to make it hard for the cryptanalyst to use the algorithm itself to find weaknesses in the cryptography that can lead to determining the key. Diffusion implies that a single instance of the application of the mathematical method will cause the maximum amount of change to the encrypted message as possible
- When combining functions and operations together to create the confusion and diffusion mentioned above, it is important that the operations be orthogonal so that one operation does not reverse or compromise the effect of the other operation. Orthogonal mathematics implies that the operations come from unrelated groups in mathematics. For example, if we utilize an exclusive-or operation in one line of the algorithm to cause confusion and diffusion, we want to use something like addition or multiplication or exponentiation as another operation to complement it in the next line. This is because the exclusive-or and the exponentiation do not have an obvious relationship that will offset one another
- Pseudorandom bit generation methods need to be carefully chosen so they are not compromised. Algorithms that utilize random numbers can easily be rendered ineffective should the seeding of the PRNG be determined
- Hash functions will be utilized as a key component of CAIN. Message digests are based on hashes and are utilized as part of the implementation of the authentication, integrity, and nonrepudiation schemes

SUMMARY

At the onset of this chapter, it was mentioned that not everyone enjoys or is skilled at complex mathematics. As such, the mathematics presented in this chapter has been tempered by this notion, resulting in only the necessary mathematics being presented. By now, you have probably noticed that modern cryptography is strongly linked to mathematics. Fortunately, mathematics that are deeply rooted in advanced algebra is a subject familiar to most college students.

Information is easily expressed in numbers. Information is stored in binary numbers as the native form on a computer. Binary numbers serve to sufficiently hide the meaning of information by obscuring the typing of information (e.g., character, integers, floating point numbers, etc.). Performing binary operations (addition, subtraction, and logical) are essential skills for students of cryptography. When working in the binary format, it becomes obvious that transposition ciphers can be effective in disguising information (e.g., flipping every third bit).

Cryptographic methods require the creation of hard problems. Problems can be categorized as P, NP, NP-Complete, and EXP. Hard problems exist in all three spaces. The cryptologist must decide which type of problem provides the proper degree of hardness to properly address the needs of the cryptographic method.

Number theory represents a branch of mathematics frequently utilized in creating hard problems. Most problems from number theory are in the P category of problems. However, given that the numbers used in the computations are large and often prime or relatively prime, the computations are often virtually endless. One of the most important characteristics of hard problems created through the mathematics of number theory is that the problems are easy to create but difficult to reverse engineer. The methods from number theory that are most often implemented involve reversible operations. Reversible operations can be found in addition and subtraction, multiplication and factoring, exponentiation and logarithms, the *exclusive-or* operation, and bit shifting (essentially multiplying and dividing by twos).

Another topic in mathematics that is often taken advantage of is the incorporation of special numbers into cryptographic algorithms. Special numbers include nonrepeating and nonterminating decimal numbers, hash values, pseudorandom numbers, and numbers such as Euler's totient function.

Mathematics is most effectively used in cryptography when applied algorithmically in rounds. That is, with each iteration of the algorithm, the complexities of the mathematics have a compounded effect on ciphering information.

Advanced algorithms, such as Euclid's GCF method, exist and must be accounted for in the cryptographic method. Euclid's GCF method is an example of a method that transforms the potentially huge algorithmic brute-force task of repeated division into an efficient method for finding the GCF.

In fact, we have pointed out that even problems in the NP space should not be considered sufficiently complex just for that reason. Many NP problems can be solved without too much trouble if the domain and range of the problem are sufficiently small.

The choosing of a hard problem and the development of cryptographic algorithms (and cryptanalysis methods for that matter) is, in large part, accomplished by applying the mathematics described in this chapter (along with many more advanced topics.) However, for students that are likely to be users of the cryptographic method, it should be said that developing even a cursory understanding of the mathematics in this chapter can only help in the selection and comparison of cryptographic methods, products, and services.

The final part of the chapter presented several of the basic concepts from complexity theory and statistics and probability. This information is useful when reviewing the literature in understanding the comparisons made in the analysis of cryptographic methods.

STUDY QUESTIONS

1 Claude Shannon presented the design principles of _____. (choose one)
   a. Multiplication and factoring
   b. Exponentiation and logarithms
   c. Perplexion and reflection
   d. Confusion and diffusion

2 Two numbers are said to be congruent if _____. (choose one)

   a. One is a multiple of the other

   b. They have the same prime number as a factor

   c. They are quotients of the same number

   d. They produce the same remainder after modulo division

3 What does the use of computers to create and break ciphers take advantage of? (choose one)

   a. The fact that the information can be represented as numbers

   b. The fact that human errors will not occur

   c. The speed of the processor

   d. The availability of more options

4 How do you enable successful encryption? (choose one)

   a. Use symmetrical algorithms

   b. Change as many bits as possible in the information

   c. Use a substitution cipher

   d. Use a digital signature when you send the message

5 Why is the *exclusive-or* function used heavily in symmetrical key cryptography? (choose one)

   a. Because it is easy to understand

   b. Because it works well in binary

   c. Because of its reversible nature

   d. Because it is difficult to understand

6 Mathematical logic is more interested in the _____ of an argument than its _____. (choose one)

   a. Reasoning/ mathematical function

   b. Form/contents

   c. Contents/ cryptographic method

   d. Factors/result

7 Number theory is concerned with establishing the properties of _____. (choose one)

   a. Integers

   b. Functions

   c. Fractions

   d. Logarithms

8 Which pseudorandom number generator relies on the complexity of factoring prime numbers to protect its integrity? (choose one)

a. Barr Cohen Barr

b. Rivest Shamir, Adelman

c. McCoy Bashir Zimmerman

d. Blum Blum Shub

9 A good hash function creates _____ mapping between the source string and the output string. (choose one)

a. Complex

b. One-to-many

c. One-to-one

d. Divisional

10 NP problems have solution times that are: _____ (choose one)

a. Based on guessing and are not predictable

b. Always quadratic and are predictable

c. Linear

d. Based on the number of prime factors

11 The function defined as "The set of positive integers less than n and relatively prime to n" is _____. (choose one)

a. Pi(n)

b. Phi(n)

c. Theta(n)

d. Epsilon(n)

12 Cryptologists need to incorporate _____ into their algorithms. (choose one)

a. Bit mapping

b. Reversibility

c. Large numbers

d. Variability

13 Cryptography is related to mathematics because _____. (choose one)

a. The functions of mathematics have cryptographic properties

b. Logarithms can cause convergence of numbers

c. Mathematics is simple and easy to use

d. Information can be represented as numbers and manipulated mathematically

14 True___ False___ The median and the mean are the same thing.

15 Complexity theory is the study of_____. (choose one)
  a. How many bits the encryption algorithm utilizes
  b. The number of primes used to create the message
  c. How many rounds are used to encrypt the information
  d. How difficult a problem is to solve

16 A number is relatively prime to another if _____. (choose one)
  a. They have only each other as factors
  b. They have no prime factors in common
  c. They have only one prime factor in common
  d. They are both divisible by 7

17 The fundamental theorem of arithmetic states that any positive integer is _____. (choose one)
  a. The product of primes or is prime
  b. Not divisible by primes unless it is prime
  c. Easily made into a nonrepeating decimal
  d. Divisible by at least three numbers

18 Binary numbers obscure the _____ of information. (choose one)
  a. Word distribution
  b. Meaning
  c. Typing
  d. Identity

19 Message digests are based on _____. (choose one)
  a. Hashes
  b. Multiplication
  c. Shift ciphers
  d. Random numbers

20 When one math operation does not reverse or compromise the effect of another operation, the operations are _____. (choose one)
  a. Secure
  b. Polynomial
  c. Logarithmic
  d. Orthogonal

CASE STUDY

Working With Numbers—Crypto Style

I)

a) Using the 8-bit ASCII character code for each letter, write a binary representation of the word "MEET." (This should result in a binary string of 32 bits.)

b) Now flip every third bit of the binary string, starting at the bit that is third from the leftmost bit. [NOTE: If the new string has a 1 bit in the highest bit of any byte, flip it back to a zero. The ASCII code does not use that highest bit.]

c) Then, convert the new (encrypted) binary string to characters. What is the new, encrypted string? How does it compare to the original? What do you notice about what happened to the 'double E' from the original string?

d) If you used this technique to encrypt a long message, and the "enemy" was trying to decode it by looking at the frequency of certain letters, would this encryption technique foil that attempt?

e) Now take the encrypted string and shift every bit to the left one place, wrapping the left-most bit around so that it becomes the rightmost bit. (Again, if the new string has a 1 bit in the highest bit of any character, flip it back to a zero.)

f) Convert this binary string back to characters—what is the new string?

g) When you create the algorithm to decrypt this string back to the original string (and you had better, if you want anyone to be able to read your message!), what two operations must be performed, and in what order?

h) List the cryptographic concepts that are illustrated by this problem.

i) Does this example illustrate the use of a key?

II)

a) Write the number 7 as a binary number.

b) Now write the number 1 as a binary number having the same number of bits as the binary number 7.

c) Add these two numbers together using binary addition. What binary number do you get? How many bits does it have?

d.) Does this problem require any "carry" operations? What about "borrow"

e) List the reverse (or inverse) of the following operations:

- Addition
- Subtraction
- Multiplication
- Division
- Shift left, then wrap
- Raise to the power of 3

f) In which of the above cases was the reverse operation harder to perform than the original?

g) Without using a pen and paper or a calculator, multiply 5 by 17. Then, divide 102 by 17. Which of these two operations is more difficult? Why?

h) If you were to use these two operations (multiplication and division) as part of a cryptographic technique, which one would you use for encryption, and which for decryption? Explain your answer.

III)

Complete the following Truth Table:

A	B	A or B	A *exclusive-or* B
F	F		
F	T		
T	T		
T	F		

IV)

a) Calculate the following:

- 41 mod 17
- 58 mod 17

b) Are 41 and 58 "congruent modulo 17"?

V)

a) Suppose your spy colleague wanted to send you messages that you could be sure came from him (and not an enemy trying to pretend to be him). Your colleague tells you: "Whenever I send you a message, the last thing in the message will be a number. That number will be a count of the number of letter E's in the message. If you get a message, and the number at the end is NOT an accurate count of the number of letter E's, that message is from an imposter."

b) This number, put at the end of each message, is an example of what cryptographic item?

c) Does it have the characteristic of being one way?

d) Is it collision resistant?

VI)

a) Is 101 a prime number?

b) What is the next prime number AFTER 101? (without looking in the tables).

c) Consider the number 101 and the answer to b). Are these two numbers relatively prime?

d) Are the numbers 34 and 57 relatively prime?

e) If you have two primary numbers, can you make a generalization about whether they are relatively prime?

f) If you have two odd numbers, can you make a generalization about whether they are relatively prime?

g) If you have two even numbers, can you make a generalization about whether they are relatively prime?

h) Any number can be expressed as a product of its prime factors, raised to their respective powers (e.g., $56 = 2^3 * 7^1$; $100 = 2^2 * 5^2$). Express the following numbers as products of prime factors:

- 34
- 76
- 900

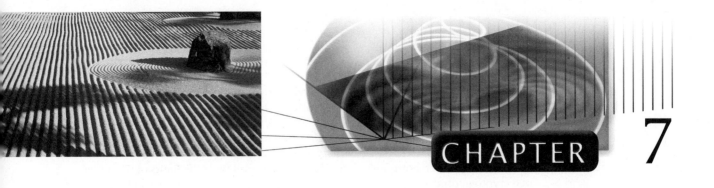

CHAPTER 7

Symmetrical Key Cryptography

The shaft of the arrow had been feathered with one of the eagle's own plumes.
We often give our enemies the means of our own destruction.
—Aesop (620 B.C.–560 B.C.)

Thus far we have looked at cryptography historically, mathematically, and conceptually. We have examined the theories of great minds such as Claude Shannon, William Friedman, Euclid, and Alan Turing. These pioneers in modern cryptography set the standards by which all modern cryptography is currently measured.

Mathematically, we have explored many options for effecting the desired changes on plain text in the creation of ciphertext. We have studied the reversibility of operations and we have demonstrated this technique in a number of ways. A primary reason for including the chapter on mathematics is that mathematics is extremely useful in creating "hard" problems. These hard problems form the basis for almost all modern cryptography (barring quantum cryptography).

Transposition ciphers and substitution ciphers are two styles of ciphering that have been widely used and modified throughout the history of cryptography. Today we use computers to generate our codes, but we still rely on many of these same concepts at the core of our field. In fact, today most ciphers represent combinations of the two techniques. The primary difference between the cryptography of today and the cryptography of a mere sixty years ago is that today's cryptographic methods rely almost exclusively on computers. We have shown that computers bring us two considerable advantages over the methods utilized throughout the balance of history:

- Computers represent information as bits, while we prefer to think of information as characters and various forms of numbers. Bit-wise representations provide an extra degree of freedom in the creation of either substitution or transposition ciphers. As we have shown, a bit change in every byte of a piece of information will allow for us to inflict significantly more changes to the information than manipulation at the character level. This is because a bit change in every byte affects each piece of information differently. For example, one bit change in an ASCII character changes the character. One bit change per byte in a long integer changes that number in four different places. Further, we have demonstrated that making the changes every third or fourth bit makes tracking the transposition almost impossible.

- Even the most modest computer available today provides the ability to perform extraordinarily large calculations. This allows algorithms to utilize keys that are very strong. This also makes the computations required to break a cipher extremely time consuming. Unfortunately, this also allows the average hacker tremendous computing power to run distributed brute-force attacks against cryptography. Because of this mutual availability of computing power, both sides continue to escalate and push the limits of computerized cryptographic enhancements. Normally, increases in computing power benefit cryptographers more than cryptanalysts, as we will see later in this chapter.

Symmetrical key cryptography is the workhorse of the industry. Algorithms such as DES have faithfully served the user community for almost thirty-five years. AES, the DES replacement, promises to be equally capable. Symmetrical key cryptography is used as the basis for many important security applications, including secure financial transactions, government encryption, VPN, and other forms of secure tunneling protocols, to name a few.

Symmetrical cryptography is regarded as efficient and has a wide spectrum of applications. We begin our exploration of this area with a generalized discussion regarding the structure of symmetrical algorithms. Next, the concepts of key creation and management are explored. This material should lay the groundwork for a more detailed discussion of the topic.

Usually these algorithms are complex and difficult to understand. It is a primary goal of this chapter to expose students to the inner workings of symmetrical cryptography through a comprehensive exploration of the **Tiny Encryption Algorithm** (**TEA**, pronounced Tee-uh). TEA is a compact and efficient piece of software that utilizes many of the features found in other symmetrical cryptographic methods. TEA is an easy-to-read and easy-to-understand piece of code. Through this discussion in the text and the examples provided on the CD included with this text, students should be able to develop a real understanding of what cryptography is all about. Students are encouraged to play with the code, modify it, and experiment with the various parameters. While developing this part of the text, David Wheeler, one of the authors of the TEA code, was consulted regarding the development of the TEA algorithms. It is hoped that this learning experience solidifies the concepts presented thus far on cryptography.

The chapter concludes with a generalized discussion of several other popular symmetrical routines.

Prior to beginning this chapter, it is essential that students minimally review the use of the exclusive-or statement and the basic concepts of programmatic iteration. Students should also review the CD-based TEA examples. This chapter is one of the most crucial chapters. Grasping this material is an essential step in becoming an information security professional.

SYMMETRICAL CRYPTOGRAPHY BASICS

As we saw in Chapter 5, symmetrical cryptography is not new. In fact, the cryptographic ideas conceived 2500 years ago employed many of the same general schemes that we see in practice today. The most basic element of symmetrical cryptography is that the sender and receiver need to have established a prearranged method of encoding and decoding messages with a shared secret. For example, the Caesar cipher required that both the sender and receiver agree by prior arrangement that the coding method would be a shift of the alphabet. Further, they needed to agree on the amount of the shift employed (the secret or the key). It is in this prior arrangement that symmetrical cryptography gets its strength. The private

 To successfully complete this chapter, students should pay particular attention to the following:

- The concepts behind symmetrical cryptography, including operational philosophy and key generation
- How a key is "applied." This is often an area where students become confused. Through the TEA algorithm, this concept should become quite clear
- How TEA is constructed and the concepts of rounds, confusion, and diffusion
- The symmetry of the algorithm. By utilizing the TEA examples on the CD, students should be able to appreciate the workings and symmetry between the encryption and the decryption routines.
- The way that TEA expands the requirements of necessary information for the cryptanalyst, making cracking the cipher more difficult
- The relatively convenient size and speed of the TEA algorithm
- The design of other important symmetrical algorithms including DES and AES

secret (if in fact it is kept private) means that the cryptanalyst would be required to guess both the secret and the method employed. Even today this is a difficult task.

Unlike those early days of cryptography, today the modern cryptographer almost always uses a secret software key. Keys correspond to coding and decoding algorithms (software programs)that were specifically designed to use the key and encode and decode the message. These keys must still be a well-guarded secret of the sender and receiver. They are also so complex in construct that any form of simple guessing by the cryptanalyst would be a waste of effort.

The basic symmetrical key cryptography system has the following parts:

- The plain text, which is the message to be coded in a natural language format
- The ciphertext, which is the converted plain text created as a result of the application of the encryption method
- The encryption algorithm, which is a software program that executes the cryptographic strategy and produces the ciphertext. The encryption algorithm takes both the plain text and the key as input
- The decryption algorithm, which is a reciprocal software program to the encryption software that decodes the ciphertext and returns the plain text. The decryption algorithm takes both the ciphertext and the key as input
- The secret key, which corresponds to both the encryption and decryption algorithms and controls their actions. The key value must have no relationship to the plain text. The encryption and decryption algorithms will create varied output as a result of the key entered
- The communications environment is the transport medium that will be used to move the coded message

These parts work together as illustrated in Figure 7-1. The plain text is created and fed into the encryption algorithm along with the symmetrical key. The encryption algorithm in turn generates the ciphertext. The ciphertext is then communicated to the intended recipient[1], who inputs it into the decryption

---

[1] Or until it is stored until the recipient picks it up.

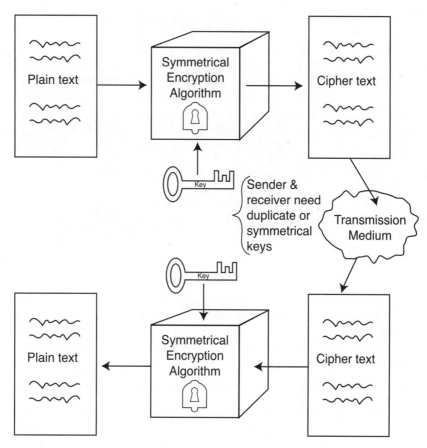

Figure 7-1   Symmetrical key cryptography system components.

algorithm along with the same symmetrical key that was used during the encryption process. This key is usually exchanged by some prearranged, out-of-band method. For this symmetrical system to work, the secret key must be exchanged prior to the transmission of any ciphertext. Usually this is done via a different public key exchange method (discussed in the next chapter), It could just as easily be accomplished via the regular mail, in person, or over the telephone. Today there are even key-generating devices that can be physically possessed by both the sender and the receiver of information. When the next key is needed, both devices can produce the next key for each party without any communication between them at all. The decryption routine then generates the plain text as it was originally entered.

As was stated earlier in the text, the mathematical equivalent of Figure 7-1 can be expressed mathematically as $P = D(k,(E(k,P)))$. This expression allows us to view the encryption and decryption services as programmatic or algorithmic functions, which use the key and the plain text or the key and the ciphertext [$E(k,P)$] as their inputs, respectively.

As we shall see, in modern cryptography it is rare, if ever, that a given cipher can be classified explicitly as either a substitution cipher or as a transposition cipher. Most of the modern ciphers affect both kinds of changes on the information for maximum diffusion and confusion.

Symmetrical ciphers can work on either blocks of information or on a continuous stream of information (arriving as bits). Blocks are basically same-sized chunks of information. Streams represent a continuous flow of bits that are processed on an as-arrived basis.

Streams are encrypted by manipulating the bits as they arrive. This can be done in a variety of ways. For example, we can flip every fifth bit. More comprehensive stream encryption can take the form of both a bit-wise transposition and a group-wise substitution. In the case of blocks, the encryption and decryption routines work by applying their respective algorithms to all of the bits in the block. Once the block is ciphered, the next block is encrypted.

Chaining is the process of cryptographically linking every block together with the previous blocks. In effect, this process can be thought of as encrypting streaming blocks. This is perhaps the most common method of block ciphers. While this seems difficult to envision and appears it would cause great difficulty for the human cryptographer to implement, it is really no problem for a computer. We use the ciphertext created in one block as part of the encryption of the next. This method is useful because it forces the cryptanalyst to have complete copies of the ciphertext in order to decode a message. This method is shown in Figure 7-2. If the encryption of a block is independent of the previous block, it is synchronous. If the encryption of a block is dependent on the previous block, it is asynchronous, as in Figure 7-2.

Using a cryptographic system implies that there is a trust between the sender and the receiver of the messages. This trust allows us to share a secret and to utilize the cryptographic method as it was intended. For example, this trust implies that senders and receivers will not leave keys unguarded or share them with others. It implies that partners in a cryptographic method will be careful with the trusted information once it has been successfully received. Obviously, if there is a breakdown in the trust mechanism, any cryptographic method will fail.

We do not need or want to keep the cryptographic algorithms private. That would prevent widespread use of the technique. In fact, DES and AES (reviewed later in the chapter) were created so that the algorithms could be made public. By making these algorithms public, we are creating ubiquitous availability of the cryptographic technique. This means that all the users of the technique need to do is agree upon the secret key, exchange it, and begin using the method. In fact, financial institutions do this all the time. Banks and securities firms have been using DES-based information exchanges for quite some time.

This is the part of cryptography that confuses many people. It is hard to understand why you would be willing to allow cryptanalysts to have access to the method. Are we not giving them too much insight into the decryption requirements? No, not really. As long as the key is sufficiently strong, making the technique public is really not a worry. As we saw earlier in Section Two, making a key strong is normally a product of two functions:

- The length of the key. We have already shown that key lengths of sizes greater than 64 bits cannot normally be guessed in any reasonable amount of time using any brute-force method[2]

[2.] The subdivision of the key space can be managed in a distributed attack against encryption. In fact, this is how some of the earliest attempts to crack the 56-bit DES were accomplished.

Chaining

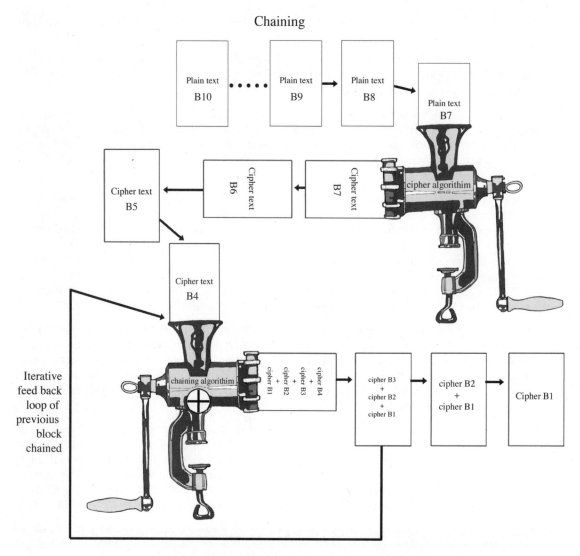

Figure 7-2 Chaining a stream of blocks. Decrypting this requires all the previous blocks of ciphertext. Each chained block is composed of a piece of all the previous blocks through the system. The exclusive-or function works well for the chaining mechanism.

■ Key strength is also a function of how the key is constructed. As we saw in Chapter 6, sometimes the cryptanalyst need not find the exact key. Rather, it is often possible to crack an algorithm by finding multiples of the key. This is one of the primary reasons that we strive to build keys from very large prime factors. By doing so, we strengthen the keys because the primes will have no multiples less than the primes themselves. This reduces the chances that the cryptographic attack will be successful

Once the key is constructed, it is important to establish an estimate of the useful life of the key. Once this is known, symmetrical cryptography usually will enhance security by establishing a key rotation policy. A key rotation is the act of deactivating an in-use key and replacing it with a new one. This act preserves the integrity of a cryptographic system. As we will see in Chapter 9, VPNs establish cryptographic tunnels through the Internet using symmetrical cryptography. By periodically rotating the symmetrical session keys, we can prevent a hacker from discovering the key identity and deciphering our messages.

Awareness of cryptanalysis methods is important for both the cryptographer and the user of cryptography. Many cryptanalysis techniques currently exist. One of the weaknesses of the symmetrical method is that the systems are used repeatedly without changing anything other than the key. This gives the cryptanalyst the opportunity to look at and experiment with captured ciphertext. Also, as we mentioned earlier, it is often possible to influence the transmission of a known plain text message (similar to the technique used in breaking JN-25 "AF has a water problem"). These captured messages can reveal qualities about the key and the decryption technique. We should be aware of the following realities and take the proper action dictated by each to preserve the encryption:

- The attacker can use a brute-force or distributed brute-force attack. These attacks, as mentioned earlier, can be effective if the selected key length is too short. Therefore, it is always best to select the maximum key length supported by the algorithm
- Intuitive cryptanalysis methods can be created from time to time. These methods can reduce the effectiveness of a particular method. For example, earlier we sighted the case of the SSL pseudorandom number generator being compromised. It is likely that these compromises will happen because so much effort is placed on cracking codes. Users of a particular cryptographic method need to continually review the literature to see if the technique has in any way been compromised or weakened. Often the vendors of products using these methods will provide software updates shortly after a breach has occurred[3]
- Mathematical analysis is often a concern. For example, in the previous chapter we saw how Merkle and Hellman failed in an early attempt at a public cryptographic method based on the knapsack problem, once a flaw in the method was discovered. Modern cryptographic methods are generally mathematically intensive. However, the strength of this mode of cryptography may also be a weakness. In one sense as we have seen that the potential for hiding a secret among the confusion of sophisticated mathematics is very impressive. However, it is often equally difficult for every principle to be positively proven to be as resilient as we initially anticipate. Such is the problem with all NP-Complete problems. Once one falls, they all fall. Further, as was discussed in Chapter 5, just because something is NP does not mean that it can never be solved. In fact, NP problems are usually trivial to state and to solve when the domain and range are relatively small. So it is often not just a matter of using sophisticated mathematics, but also using sufficiently hard problems
- We should be aware of what cryptanalysts have to work with and what they seek. Cryptanalysts will most often start with ciphertext and attempt to reverse engineer both the method (or at least guess which method it is) and the key. Obviously, we do not want to give away the key because that would be disastrous. We have already conceded that

---

[3.] This is a primary reason to always apply all vendor patches for systems, networks, and applications. Often, to prevent widespread abuse of the breach by hackers, a vendor will not reveal that a breach has been discovered. The downside of this is often bug fixes are buried in other nonsecurity-related upgrades. To receive the benefits of these patches, therefore, the user should apply all patches regardless of how obscure they may seem.

we can utilize publicly available cryptographic methods, which we can be sure our adversary has and has analyzed. Some cryptographic algorithms (such as TEA) allow us to manipulate the operating parameters of the algorithm. One such parameter is the number of rounds (or iterations) the algorithm will execute. In the case of TEA, that quantity needs to be known before the decryption process can begin

By ensuring that we know what the analyst has, or may get, we can make a decision on how strong the cryptography must be. Using excessive cryptography can be problematic because cryptography is a conversion, another step along the way to using the information.

Cryptography, even in the best case, increases access time. Symmetrical cryptography tends to be more efficient in processing than asymmetrical cryptography. Yet unnecessarily wasting processing time can never be justified, especially if there is no added value to the user.

Designing a proper cryptographic algorithm (or choosing one for that matter) requires a considerable amount of strategy and planning. Shannon's five principles for creating an ideal cipher really do sum up the design principles behind most symmetrical ciphers:[4]

- Evaluating the amount of secrecy required
- Determining an appropriate key size
- Controlling the complexity of the encryption and decryption routines
- Controlling the propagation of errors
- Regulating the expansion of the message

The creation of symmetrical ciphers is as much about the creation of the key as it is about the execution of the algorithm.

SOFTWARE KEYS

Almost all modern cryptographic systems utilize software keys. Keyless methods such as the transposition method (e.g., the rail fence) are relatively easy to compromise. Keys allow systems to be public, meaning that the algorithms can be widely publicized without fear of compromising the cipher developed by it. The idea of a secret key and a public algorithm is known as Kerckhoff's principle. The complexity of the key is a function of length, its primality, and the randomness with which it is created.

Keys in a symmetrical system are shared. However, because they are computerized and stored digitally, we can essentially eliminate the Shannon principle of optimizing key length[5]. Instead, we shall utilize the maximum key lengths supported in the various algorithms. In the TEA algorithm, which we will explore in detail, the predefined key length is 128 characters.

Keys effectively cause (by way of the encryption algorithm) unique permutations of the original information. The key controls the actions of the algorithm so that the information changes according to the rules of the algorithm, but as influenced by the bits in the key. It is important for students to realize that in most algorithms, "applying" a key should be thought of as "blending the key with the information" in some way.

[4.] These principles are more fully detailed in Chapter 5.

[5.] Remember that at the time Shannon wrote the paper, keys were generally committed to memory; unusually long and random keys were considered fallible because we might forget them.

Take this example: The information stream is 11111 and the first key is 10101. If the cryptographic algorithm is a simple exclusive-or function, then the encryption is 01010 (reversing this with the exclusive-or and the same key gives back the 11111). Now change the key to 00011. If we use the same exclusive-or function and the same original information 11111, our cipher code is 11100. Notice the algorithm (exclusive-or) did not change, but the key "blends" differently in each case, thus influencing the outcome of the encryption.

Key creation is a task that should be done with great care. For keys to be of maximum benefit, they should be crafted as large as possible. Depending on the algorithm, the keys can be hundreds of bits long. For years, the de facto standard was 56 bits. It is now far more common to see keys of 128 bits. The sheer size of the key is enough to stagger any brute-force attack. However, if we think of the 128 bits expressed as characters, the bits form only 16 characters. Therefore, it is best to avoid creating keys that are translated into a 16-character word or phrase. It is optimal to create the keys as random events and avoid obvious pitfalls such as a key of all ones or all zeros. In the next chapter, students will learn that asymmetrical keys are created through a much more rigorous process involving the combining of large primes. In the case of symmetrical keys, most algorithms rely on randomness and size to create the proper complexity.

Two other important components of key selection are key rotation and reuse. As we mentioned earlier, keys have a useful life. This life is measured by a best-case estimate of the time and computer resources required to compromise the key. It is imperative that the key be rotated long before that time. In the case of the theoretical one-time pad, each message is encrypted with a different key. Obviously, this is an unreasonable requirement for most applications. Instead, it is appropriate to rotate the key inside the window of usability. It is also essential to limit or eliminate reuse of a key. Given the extremely large number of combinations of bits in a 128-bit key, this should not be difficult. If keys are generated randomly, there is a small probability that the same key will occur often. Thus, randomly selected keys do satisfy these requirements.

With this method, it is possible for a particular random key to be relatively weak. A weak key is defined as a key that is at the edges of the range of possible keys or has a substantial number of nonprime factors. As we mentioned earlier, it is not always necessary to guess the exact key; sometimes a multiple of the key can provide similar results.

Key strength was discussed in the previous chapter. In that discussion we concluded that longer keys created from the multiplication of two relatively prime numbers would represent the best choice. Here again we are faced with a tradeoff. We can make strong keys that are not random (or are random within a much smaller domain—relatively prime numbers) with key rotation/nonreuse, or we can use key rotation/nonreuse and random selection (which could occasionally leave us with a weak key). These choices are made on an individual basis.

Key scheduling is a term that describes how a key is used in each round (iteration) of the cryptographic algorithm. Inside the encryption algorithm, it is not necessary to utilize the entire key as presented. In the TEA example, the key is split into four parts and applied to the plain text in a manner that blends the first and third parts with elements of the plain text, and the second and fourth with a different element of plain text. In the DES algorithm, the key schedule splits the key in half, shifts it left one or two bits depending on the round number, then the shifted 56 bits are mapped to a 48-bit pattern by a **compression permutation**. Either of these methods illustrates that by taking a key apart and using it, we further complicate any possibility of reverse engineering the key.

One of the drawbacks of a symmetrical key cryptography system is that the number of keys in a large system can grow to significant numbers, which are difficult to manage. In general, one key is needed for every two parties sharing information. In a system with n users, this number is: $\frac{n \bullet (n-1)}{2}$.

This system, combined with the previously mentioned guidelines for key creation, nonreuse, and key rotation makes key distribution and key management important considerations in a large system.

Key management is a fascinating area of cryptography. This part of the craft has long been a problem for cryptographers to solve. It is not simply the handing out of keys that is problematic; rather it is the issue of communicating the new key in a confidential manner that is interesting. In many early cryptosystems, the system could be compromised if a key or codebook were captured. Such was the case with Enigma. In modern cryptosystems, symmetrical key rotation requires a successful and secure exchange of symmetrical keys. As we shall see in the next chapter, the Diffie-Hellman algorithm for asymmetrical cryptography is a good possibility for accomplishing this task. Another significant method is known as **Kerberos.**

Kerberos, a project that originated at MIT, is utilized for the secure key exchanges between users in a network. The Kerberos method is named for the three-headed dog in Greek mythology that guarded the gates of Hades. When you look at Figure 7-3, notice that the client must face the three-headed guard comprised of the trusted authority, the ticket-generating authority, and the server in order to access the information.

The method is based on two primary concepts. First, the system must be small enough so that the trusted authority has a unique symmetrical key to share with each member. Second, all of the cryptography is symmetrical and tickets are required with valid time stamps (an issue unto itself).

In the Figure 7-3, the following are the steps that summarize the action:

1 The client sends the trusted authority a request for a session key with the ticket-generating authority. All requests for sessions are actually requests for a symmetrical session key and a request for a validation ticket, which is time-stamped.

2 The server checks the validity of the client and (assuming that the validity checks out) sends the client an encrypted response using the preestablished client/trusted authority session key. Inside the message is a symmetrical session key to be used with the ticket-generating server and a ticket to permit a session with the ticket-generating server.

3 The client decrypts that message and extracts the ticket and the new symmetrical key. The first of the three checks is completed (a validation of identity).

4 The client next encrypts a message to the ticket-generating server using the key just obtained in the previous step. Inside this message, the client requests a ticket and session key to enable a session with the server required. The ticket-generating server first validates the ticket presented by the client (obtained in Step 2), checks that this client is authorized for the request, and validates that the time stamp is within a certain time of the time it was issued. If these three items are verified, the ticket-generating server proceeds.

5 The ticket-generating server returns an encrypted message to the client with the server session key and server ticket.

6 The client decrypts the message and proceeds to the final stage of the tests. The client has now passed the second test (eligibility of service).

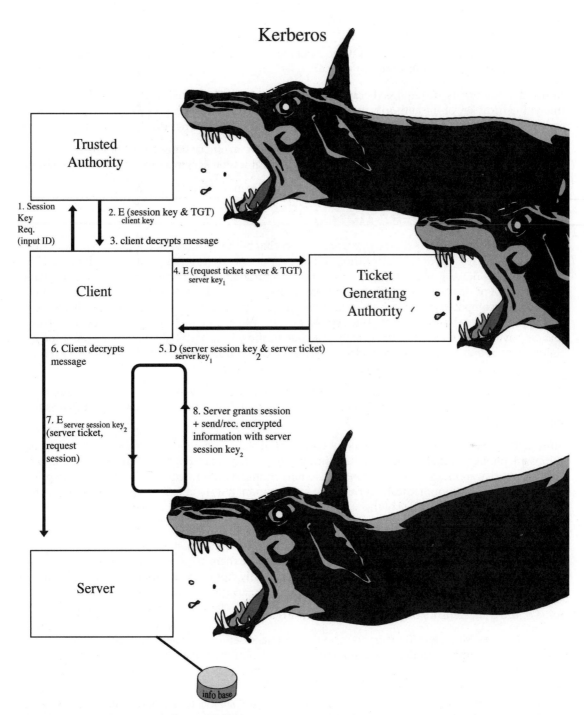

Figure 7-3 Kerberos method.

7 The client now encrypts the server ticket and specific request to the server using the server session key.

8 The server accepts the ticket and continues the session with the client until complete. The third test is complete (access to service).

Notice that the tickets are required because once you have communicated with a server the first time, the symmetrical key of the authority or server is known to you. The ticket prevents unauthorized server reuse. Hence, the ticket prevents the client from skipping the triple authentication process in the future.

This method does work but is difficult to administer. It requires an official time-stamping procedure that cannot be forged. It will allow for the distribution of symmetrical session keys in a very secure manner, however.

The Diffie-Hellman algorithm is easier to implement and is more secure.

SYMMETRICAL OPERATIONS

Symmetrical algorithms take their name from the fact that both the encryption and decryption routines utilize the same key. (Hence the algorithms for encryption and decryption need to be symmetrical in operation to work.) Additionally, if you review the TEA tutorials and experiments on the CD (explained in appendix A of this text), you will also notice that the symmetry is the same in how the cipher is composed and decomposed in a step–by-step fashion. In the experiment, you are provided with a working TEA algorithm that shows a six-round encryption process. When you run this experiment you will notice that we have imbedded print statements in the code to show how both halves of the information are changing by round. Notice the symmetry between the encryption rounds as they compare with the decryption rounds. They are exactly reversed, just as we would expect.

What this proves is that symmetrical algorithms must be based on reversible operations. These operations were discussed in detail in the last chapter. The reversibility of the operation is what makes the shared secret (key) work for us.

Although there is great similarity in the way symmetrical algorithms work, a number of choices of algorithms are publicly available. There are significantly more that are not public. Nonpublic symmetrical algorithms are warranted for applications where maximum security is required in a completely private user base. Nonpublic symmetrical algorithms require cryptanalysts to attempt to break the code without the key and without knowledge of the underlying method[6]. This custom cryptography can be built into homegrown applications.

Regardless of choice (public or private implementation), there is no shortage of cryptographic algorithms. In fact, this is a great strength of the industry. Because there are so many algorithms and variants of algorithms in the public domain, a cryptanalyst with only ciphertext would have to search out both the key (a hard problem unto itself) and also try the key in a variety of algorithms.

Some of the characteristics of symmetrical algorithms are:

- Most algorithms try to meet the criteria as set forth by Shannon in 1949. These are important design considerations and blend the right amount of security with the appropriate usability of the cryptosystem

---

[6.] There is reason for concern when an algorithm is available for use without your having access to the code. One concern is that you can never be sure how secure your algorithm is because you cannot study it. Another concern is that the algorithm may provide key escrow capabilities that allow others to open your encrypted messages and files.

- Algorithmic strategy influences the outcomes and the relative security of the cipher. As we shall see, designers will have to choose from a number of algorithmic alternatives in confirming their designs. These choices include block versus stream, using the key as presented or in a split (Feistel) fashion, lengths of keys, selection of mathematical methods, fixed-size output versus variable-size output, and the number of rounds or iterations of the algorithm

- Algorithms have traditionally fallen into either the transposition or the substitution categories. Most of today's symmetrical algorithms utilize both techniques to maximize the diffusion of the cipher

- The concepts of monoalphabetic and polyalphabetic ciphers were presented in Chapter 5 because it was a major consideration of classic ciphers. The use of polyalphabetic ciphers obviously produces the maximum effect on the cipher. In modern cryptography, we perform encryption beneath the character level, at the bit level. This produces an effect similar to polyalphabetic ciphers. The concept of the polyalphabetic cipher is to hide the predictable letter-usage frequencies that are measurable in the language of the cipher. Working with bit-wise manipulations produces that effect as demonstrated in Chapter 6

- **Stream ciphers** present one alternative in symmetrical cryptography. Stream ciphers take one bit of plain text at a time and submit it to an encryption algorithm. Based on the bits fro m a key that are "applied to the stream," the bits of plain text are converted into ciphertext. Ron Rivest's RC4 is a stream cipher that is commonly used. Other stream ciphers are auto-keyed Vigenere ciphers and Vernam ciphers. Stream ciphers need the capability of creating long streams with nonrepeating bit patterns. If the recurring pattern of bit manipulation is too short, the cryptanalyst will find it and the cryptographic method can become vulnerable

- **Block ciphers** are far more popular and usually represent a stronger cryptographic method than stream ciphers. Significantly more time and effort has been spent on developing these types of algorithms. DES is perhaps the oldest and best known of the block ciphers. We will examine DES in more detail later in the chapter. The replacement for DES—AES—is also a block cipher that we will examine.

  Block ciphers take a fixed-length block of text as input to an encryption algorithm along with the symmetrical key. This encryption algorithm applies the encryption method to the block of plain text in an iterative fashion. Once the algorithm is complete, the resulting ciphertext is produced. The ciphertext is of the same length as the plain text block. Figure 7-4 illustrates the primitives of the stream and block styles of encryption.

  A problem with block ciphers is that they require a large sample of text. Therefore, anytime we use the same plain text message multiple times, we will generate identical blocks of ciphertext. As we learned in Chapter 5, whenever you give an attacker multiple looks at the same cipher output, it gives away certain qualities regarding the method

- **Modes** are used in block ciphers to help prevent the problem of repeating ciphertext for highly structured, lengthy, and possibly repetitive blocks of plain text. Four modes are defined in the DES cipher, perhaps the most popular block cipher.

  Electronic codebook mode (ECM) is essentially a pass-through mode. In this mode, the encryption routine simply calculates the cipher one block at a time until it is done. This encryption is done without concern about duplication of cipher blocks. This mode

Stream v. Block Cipher

Blocks...

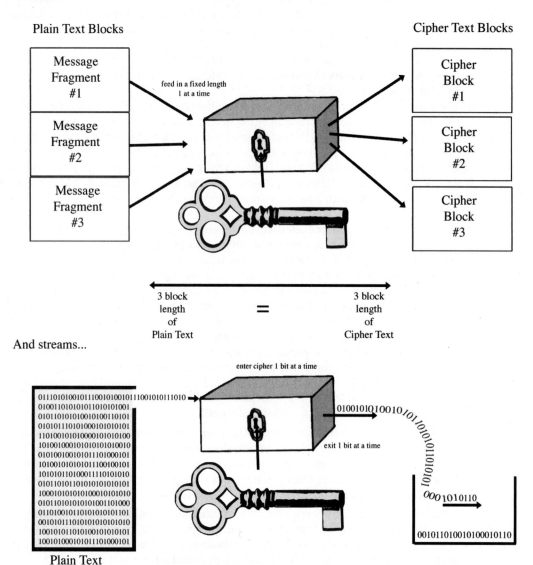

Figure 7-4 Block ciphers encrypt plain text one block after another. Stream ciphers, one bit at a time, enter the encryption algorithm. That bit is manipulated based on a key value and output. Both ciphers usually produce fixed-length outputs.

is available for short messages with low probabilities of repeating blocks. This method obviously adds speed to the encryption algorithm because it imposes no additional computing cycles

Cipher block chaining (CBC) is perhaps the most common mode available. The CBC mode is diagramed in Figure 7-5. In this mode, the algorithm starts by performing an exclusive-or operation on the first block of plain text and an arbitrary initialization vector[7]. The resulting output is run through the encryption algorithm (with the key) to produce the first block of ciphertext. This block of ciphertext is then combined with the second block of plain text via another exclusive-or operation. The output of this operation is then encrypted to create the second block of ciphertext. This process continues until the nth block of plain text is incorporated into the cipher. To decrypt the message, the process is exactly reversed. This process makes the cipher stronger because 1) there is no chance of a repeat cipher block, even if there is a repeat plain text block, 2) The initialization vector is another thing an attacker would have to know to successfully defeat the cryptography, and 3) By chaining everything together, the attacker needs to capture the complete ciphertext to reverse the process.

Cipher feedback and **output feedback** are two additional modes available to the designer. These modes are similar to the chaining mode because they combine the cipher and plain text. However, instead of operating at a pure block level, these variants treat the blocks as streams of bytes. These methods are not as common as CBC

- **Rounds** are common in Feistel ciphers. A round is a single iteration in the encryption or decryption process. In programmatic terms, it is the number of cycles in a FOR loop. During each round, the encryption is applied a certain number of times depending on the number of iterations (rounds) in the loop. When the specified number of rounds of encryption is complete, the plain, text-to-ciphertext conversion is considered complete. Rounds add additional complexity to the algorithm and become another variable that the attacker needs to consider

- **Feistel ciphers** are algorithms that allow us to define our own complex reversible functions. The idea of a Feistel cipher is to obscure the statistical relationships that exist between keys and ciphertext. In a normal symmetrical algorithm, the key and the ciphertext are strongly related. Given enough time (in some cases an eternity) these relationships can be discovered. In Feistel ciphers, these relationships are blurred by a process of mixing parts of a key with parts of plain text to create the ciphertext. This mixing, combined with a complex mathematical function, can maximize the amount of confusion and diffusion. These are applied to block ciphers and can be used in the various modes.

  Feistel ciphers require these components: n bits of data, $2n$ bits of key k, i iterations (rounds), a key schedule, and an arbitrary mathematical function (which we will call f, which applies the scheduled key to parts of the data iteratively through rounds i and reduces the output MOD 2, it puts the output back in a binary form). The basic Feistel

---

[7.] The initialization vector is required by both the encryption and decryption routines in advance. Just like the key, the attacker needs to know this to successfully attack the algorithm. This adds another layer of complication to the algorithm.

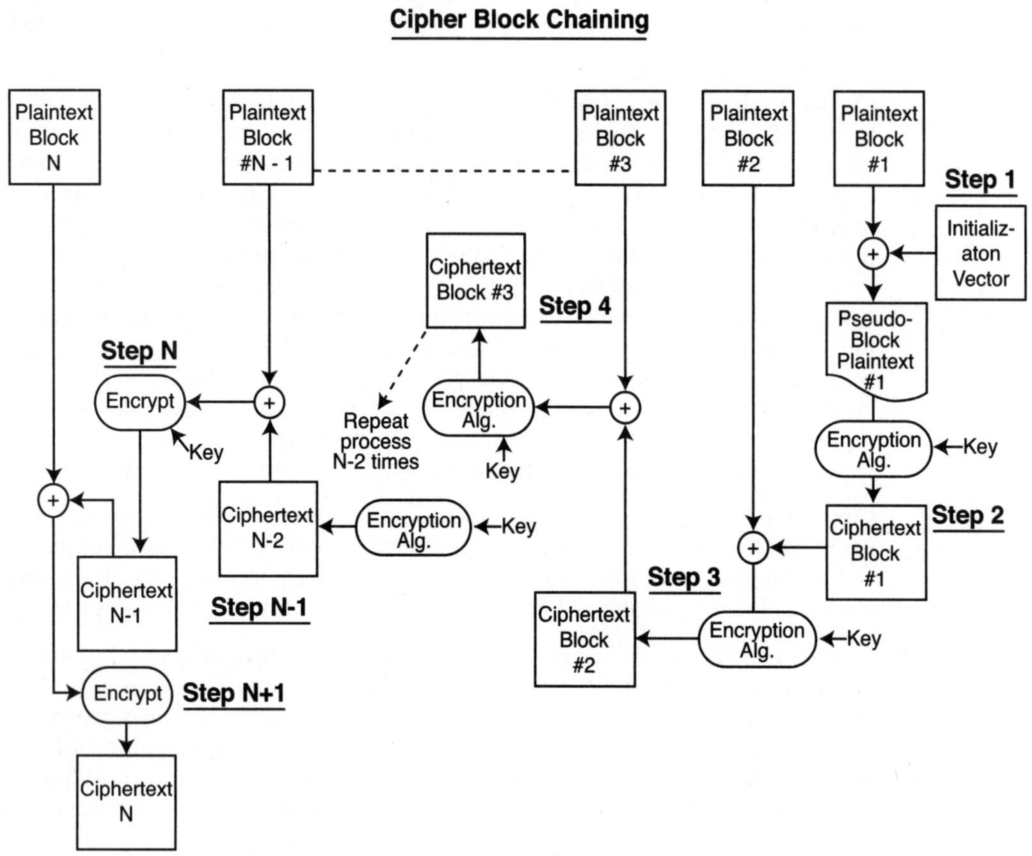

Cipher Block Chaining

Figure 7-5 Chaining of blocks links all plain text and ciphertext together.

structure requires that we take the n bits of data and divide them in half (L and R). The Feistel mechanism F is then stated as $F_f(k,L,R) = (L \oplus f(k,R),R)$.

The key characteristic of the Feistel mechanism is that if we apply $F_f(F_f(k,L,R)$ (or if we apply the Feistel function to the same function twice), we get back the original (L,R), therefore, it is reversible. This idea for encryption is shown in Figure 7-6.

The concept is not nearly as intimidating as it appears. As we saw in Chapter 6, the logical binary operator exclusive-or is reversible in repeated steps on the same data. In this particular method, the use of exclusive-or accounts for the reversibility. Whatever function is chosen for f is irrelevant as long as it leaves us with the same number of bits we started with (hence the mod 2) and is chosen from the reversible math described in the previous chapter. By mixing the right and left halves of the plain text (and ciphertext on the decryption side), we are requiring that an entire block of ciphertext be obtained to attack the cipher.

The Feistel mechanism is frequently applied concurrently with the CBC method described above. This method increases the protective qualities of the cryptography.

Feistel Functions

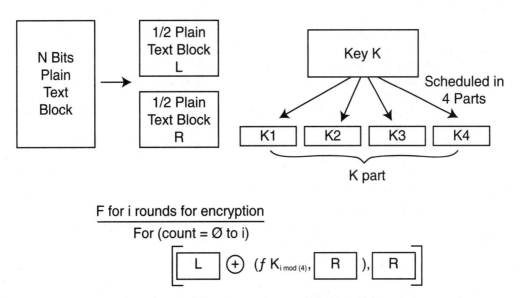

Figure 7-6   By breaking blocks of data in half and creating our own reversible functions, Feistel ciphers allow us to maximize confusion and diffusion.

A final design consideration and the enabler of the symmetry are the reversible mathematical functions that are required. As we saw in Chapter 6, many reversible mathematical functions can be applied to create symmetrical cryptographic methods. The simplest of these is a table translation, which matches plain text to ciphertext and ciphertext to plain text. Addition and subtraction are reversible, as are multiplication and factoring. Exponentiation and logarithms are reversible. The exclusive-or function is reversible. Any of these, and combinations of these, and other more interesting functions can produce the desired effect of symmetry.

In designing symmetrical algorithms, all of these items must be considered. However, it is equally important that the designer also take into account the requisite balance between complexity, usability, speed, and security that are required to best fit the application.

TEA: A TINY ENCRYPTION ALGORITHM

Many students have difficulty envisioning how a symmetrical encryption algorithm really works. The concept of applying a key, explained earlier, is often misunderstood. As you can see from the description above, encryption techniques can be very complicated and confusing (this is partially deliberate). Far too often, students never really gets a sense of the inner workings of an encryption algorithm because they are too hard to follow. But TEA represents an elegant and easy-to-follow cryptographic algorithm that makes it easy to follow the encryption process.

Symmetrical algorithms come in many different varieties. Some use complex mathematics to enable the encryption. Others use translation tables to compute the cipher. However, as we have discussed, in the modern era of cryptography, almost all of them have a few points in common. The following is a brief recap of these points:

- Most of the ciphers are computed algorithmically using an iterative process, which we call rounds. During each round, the mechanism of cryptography is applied such that a cumulative effect (over the course of all rounds) is realized
- Most ciphers attempt to adhere to Shannon's rationale for producing a quality cipher. Most cipher authors emphasize confusion and diffusion
- Most cryptographic methods attempt to maximize the diffusion of the encryption in each round
- Most cryptologists attempt to create algorithms that utilize large keys to reduce or eliminate the possibility that the key may be guessed
- Symmetrical encryption requires maximum secrecy of the shared key
- In systems that involve a large number of users, key distribution and management are problematic
- Symmetrical algorithms tend to be fast

At this point in the text we are ready to explore one of the many publicly available cryptographic algorithms. By way of example, we will study an extraordinary algorithm developed by David Wheeler and Roger Needham in November 1994 at the Computer Laboratory at Cambridge University in England. This algorithm demonstrates most of the above-mentioned bulleted points quite well in compact and elegant pieces of code.

Students are encouraged to work along with the text and experiment on the code (provided on the CD). A C++ compiler is all you need to experiment with the cipher. Students should practice with the code. By focusing on this material, students will get a firm grasp of cryptography.

What makes this algorithm so special and of particular interest to us is that it is so small and easy to review, yet it is extremely powerful. It is a fast and efficient algorithm, which is very secure. Because of its especially compact nature, a comprehensive review of the code will be possible. Three important points follow regarding symmetrical key cryptography:

- The openness (public nature) of the algorithm in no way compromises our ability to use it. The nature of the algorithm and how it applies a key (even the simple one we have imbedded in the code) makes the code secure
- The algorithm exploits the arithmetic properties of information. In the TEA algorithm, the bit-wise manipulations are intensely applied in two lines of code. They are interesting from two perspectives: First, the mathematical manipulations cause significant diffusion with each round (that is, although the authors call for a 32-round cipher, it has been demonstrated that complete diffusion can be achieved in a mere 6-round cipher); Second, this cipher's use of mathematics is interesting because although the code is brief, it generates enough confusion to make backtracking through the ciphertext difficult
- The nature of the symmetry of the encode and decode routines is fascinating. As with all pieces of symmetrical code, the mechanisms described earlier will produce the required reversibility. In this case, the algorithm is a Feistel cipher that uses addition and subtraction as the reversible operators (rather than the exclusive-or that is more the norm in the Feistel routine). What is more appreciable in the TEA algorithm than in most is that students can follow the complex relationships involving split keys and data elements without becoming lost in the code

The f (complex mathematical function) prescribed (as per the Feistel method) in this algorithm uses operations from orthogonal algebraic groups. By orthogonal, we mean that they are mutually independent or are nonoverlapping. In the specific case of TEA, the orthogonal algebraic groups of additions, exclusive-ors, and bit shifting in the c commands (z<<4) + k[0]^z + sum^(z>>5) + k[1] or (y<<4) + k[2]^y + sum^(y>>5) + k[3] (where ^ is the c operator for the exclusive-or, and >> and << are the right and left shift operators) from the routines do not interfere with each other.

TEA is cryptographically strong, encrypting 64 bits of data using a 128-bit key. Because it is a Feistel cipher, the data are split into a left and a right half. To further increase the diffusion and confusion, the key is also split into four parts (key scheduling) and applied in an alternating fashion.

In keeping with the classic definition of Shannon's diffusion and confusion, the f needs to be designed to maximize the impact of the key over the widest possible range of bits. It is also important that the function be able to compensate for inherently weak keys (as we utilize in the TEA learning tool on the CD). Wheeler and Needham include several mechanisms in this algorithm to accomplish these goals:

- The splitting of the key into four parts and then applying the key in a mixed order can potentially strengthen the weakest (most predictable) of keys. This strengthens the key by increasing confusion at the ciphertext level
- The use of the nonrepeating decimal (in this case the golden ratio) (see Chapter 6 for an explanation) at 32 bits of length. By using not only the nonrepeating decimal but also by shifting it (via addition to itself—which causes the same effect as a left shift) at each successive pass of the algorithm, they ensure bit changes in every portion of the data during the exclusive-or operation. This by definition increases diffusion
- Bit shifting of the data portion of the encryption (of distances 4 left and 5 right respectively) was chosen via experimentation to increase confusion and thus strengthen the cipher
- The Feistel method itself enhances an algorithm by blending the key with part of the data and through the use of rounds

The following is the C code for the encode routine that is diagrammed in Figure 7-7:

```
void code(long* v, long* k)
 {
unsigned long y=v[0],z=v[1], sum=0,    /* set up */
 delta=0x9e3779b9, n=32 ;              /* a key schedule constant */
while (n-->0) {                        /* basic cycle start */
  sum += delta ;
    y += (z<<4)+k[0] ^ z+sum ^ (z>>5)+k[1] ;
    z += (y<<4)+k[2] ^ y+sum ^ (y>>5)+k[3] ;    /* end cycle */
              }
v[0]=y ; v[1]=z ;
 }
```

The code begins with an initialization of the parameters of the routine. 64 bits of data and a 128-bit key are passed into the encryption routine. The data are split into a left and a right half. The key is split into four parts k[0]. k[1], k[2], and k[3]. The number of rounds is set to 32 in the routine.[8]

TEA Encryption

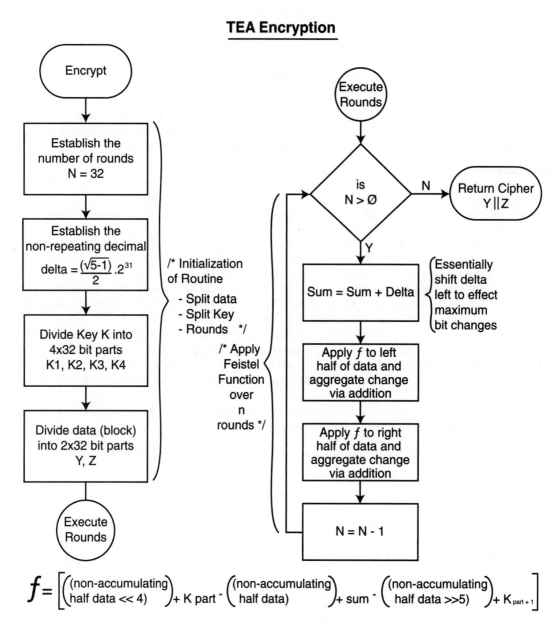

$$f = \left[\left(\begin{array}{c} \text{(non-accumulating)} \\ \text{half data} << 4 \end{array} \right) + K \text{ part } \widehat{} \left(\begin{array}{c} \text{(non-accumulating)} \\ \text{half data} \end{array} \right) + \text{sum } \widehat{} \left(\begin{array}{c} \text{(non-accumulating)} \\ \text{half data} >>5 \end{array} \right) + K_{\text{part}+1} \right]$$

Figure 7-7   TEA can be diagrammed as showing all the necessary parts of a Feistel cipher.

---

8. Bit shifting to the left 5 places is the same as multiplying the number by 32 because each position shifted in a base 2 system produces a doubling effect.

Once these parameters are configured correctly, then the algorithm begins the round-by-round encryption process on the first block. Note that the TEA algorithm presented on the CD is presented in electronic codebook mode. The calls to this encryption function could easily be processed in a CBC design at a higher level.

Each round is performed as per the Feistel method (substituting additions for the exclusive-ors). During each round, delta is effectively shifted left 1 bit through the operation sum = sum + delta. The round count is decremented at the end of each pass. When the rounds have all been executed, the accumulated ciphertext is reassembled (left half placed next to the right half) and returned to the calling function.

The following is the code for the decode routine:

```
void decode(long* v,long* k)
{
 unsigned long n=32, sum, y=v[0], z=v[1],
 delta=0x9e3779b9 ;
sum=delta<<5 ;
                         /* start cycle */
 while (n-->0) {
     z-= (y<<4)+k[2] ^ y+sum ^ (y>>5)+k[3] ;
     y-= (z<<4)+k[0] ^ z+sum ^ (z>>5)+k[1] ;
    sum-=delta ;  }
                         /* end cycle */
 v[0]=y ; v[1]=z ;
 }
```

The decode routine is similar to the encoding process, with a few notable exceptions. As seen in the flow-chart of the routine presented in Figure 7-8, two separate phases occur (as was the case during encryption): initialization and iteration. During the initialization process, the algorithm begins by first establishing $n = 32$ as the number of rounds. It is important that this number be set to the same value as the encryption phase. This number can be customized to a particular implementation of the algorithm. This customization adds an additional degree of difficulty for would-be cryptanalysts to overcome.

One of the key parts of the initialization routine is the setting of delta. In this case, the symmetry plays a role because everything has to work exactly backward from the end of the encryption process. To accomplish this initialization, we must reestablish delta to be in the same bit positions as it was when the encryption routine ended. We effectively need to multiply delta by n. However, the authors chose to bit shift because this is a faster process.[9]

In the final step, the initialization phase divides the key into four 32-bit parts and splits the ciphertext into a left and a right half (as would be consistent with the Feistel method). It is essential that the halves of ciphertext and the splitting of keys be consistent with the position of those elements at the end of the encryption routine.

We are now ready to begin the round-by-round application of the decode method. Remember that the authors chose to use addition and subtraction as the reversible operators in this implementation of a

---

[9.] The *f* function is set up with the proper key parts and the proper alternating halves of ciphertext.

TEA Decryption

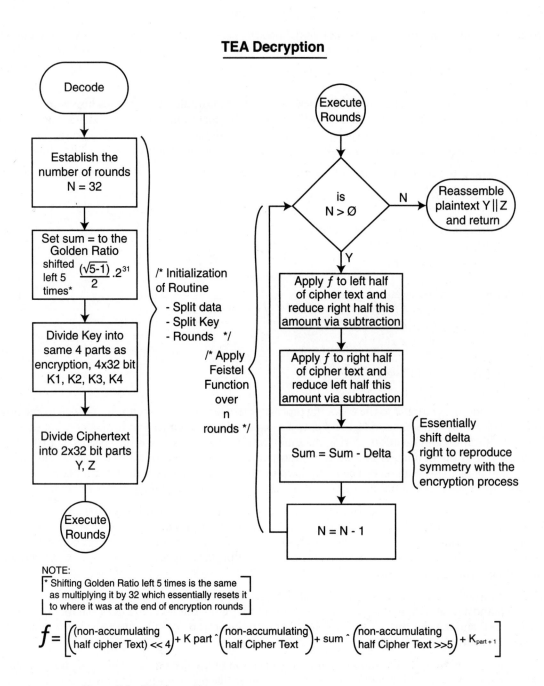

Figure 7-8   TEA decryption.

Feistel cipher. During each round of the decryption process, we subtract the effect of the properly appointed mathematical function *f* from each half of the ciphertext.[10]

Notice that delta is reduced at the end of each round rather than at the beginning. This reduction is again necessary to maintain the symmetry of the design. We then subtract 1 from the value of *n* and retest the state of the iterative mechanism. Once the loop is satisfied, the algorithm reassembles the two halves of what is now plain text and returns that value to the calling routine.

Notice that TEA decryption is also presented in electronic codebook mode. If you use TEA in CBC mode, this reassembly would be handled at the level of the routines that are calling TEA. Because it is public, small, fast, and secure, it is a reasonable choice for many applications.

As was noted earlier, complete diffusion was realized at six iterations. The use of a 128-bit key by itself would all but eliminate the potential for a successful brute-force attack. As with any cipher, the creation of the key needs to be done so that guessing the key is unlikely. The topic of key construction is handled in more detail in the next chapter. We can conclude, therefore, that TEA (given a reasonable distinct set of keys of high quality) is computationally secure.

Additionally, without knowing the number of rounds in advance, it is impossible to set delta in the decode routine correctly. Furthermore, the nature of a Feistel cipher in CBC mode requires a complete version of the ciphertext, complicating the cryptanalyst's job.

The original TEA paper written by Wheeler and Needham can be found online at *http://www.ftp.cl.cam.ac.uk/papers/djw-rmn/djw-rmn-tea.html*.

Two additional algorithms that are the most important in the industry and deserve extra attention are DES and AES. These algorithms will be presented in somewhat strategic terms because their programmatic details and fundamental mathematical inner workings are beyond the scope of this text. However, because these are the de facto industry standards for symmetrical cryptography, we will review their concept and design.

DES

The **Data Encryption Standard (DES)** block cipher is perhaps the best known of all the modern ciphers. DES is a block cipher that uses 64-bit data blocks and a 56-bit key. This cipher, as was discussed in Chapter 5, evolved from the Lucifer cipher developed by Horst Feistel's team at IBM in the early 1970s. The DES algorithm had become a commercial standard for financial applications and was widespread in its application. In fact, DES was adopted by NIST (then the National Bureau of Standards) as Federal Information Processing Standard 46.

Today it has been demonstrated that DES can be attacked attacked because the key space of the standard algorithm is so small. Essentially, the computational effectiveness of modern processors can be harnessed to crack keys of the 56-bit length. As a result, DES can no longer be considered computationally secure.

An alternative implementation of DES, known as triple DES, has since taken over as the de facto industry standard. Triple DES applies the base cipher three times in a row (encryption—decryption—encryption) using larger keys (2 x 56) of either 112 or 168 bits. Because of this repeated application of the DES cipher, the triple DES implementation, although secure, is considerably slower. This is a major drawback to the

---

[10.] In the original algorithm, this is set to 32; however, the number is adjustable and can be effective even at settings as low as 6. The value of *n* does affect the value of delta. Thus the setting of delta in the decryption routine must be initialized to the multiple of the golden ratio commensurate with the number of rounds in the routine. Also, the encryption and decryption routines must use the same number of rounds.

triple DES algorithm. However, by implementing the DES algorithm in hardware, these problems can be mitigated to a large extent. Unfortunately, hardware implementations have their own set of limitations.

The DES routines are extremely complex and hard to follow. The routines contain so many details that tracing through the routines becomes confusing. The basic routine is obviously a Feistel cipher (because it was created by Horst Feistel). In this case there are sixteen rounds. During the initialization phase, the key is input as 64 bits. In fact, the algorithm uses a 64-bit key but eight of the bits are reserved for parity. As seen in Figure 7-9, immediately after receiving the key, the algorithm strips out every eighth bit, leaving only the 56-bit key.

The algorithm then subjects the remaining key to an original permutation. The permutation routines are what make following the algorithm difficult. Thus, for the purpose of this text, we will eliminate the details of the various permutations. The permutation is a highly precise rearrangement of the bits.

Next, as we can see from the flowchart, the algorithm receives the block of data to be manipulated. This data are then sent through a similar initial permutation phase. Again this function uses a precise set of manipulations to rearrange the data. The permuted data is then split into two 32-bit halves, which we will call L and R (for left and right).

DES is now properly initiated and is ready to begin the encryption process. Like the TEA algorithm, the left and right halves of the data and the current key value are sent to the Feistel routine. However, the DES implementation of the encryption process (and likewise the decryption process) is not nearly as elegant or compact as TEA.

The routine begins by establishing an iteration control variable $n = 16$. Each round of the encryption will perform a significant manipulation of the right half of the data, using both the key and the left half, and then conclude the round by swapping the right and left halves. This concept is illustrated in Figure 7-10. Notice that in this diagram, we use four functions known as the expansion permutation function, key compression permutation function, the key scheduling function, and the substitution box function. Like the initialization permutation function, these functions are essentially mappings of old bit locations to new bit locations. In the case of the compression and substitution functions, several bits are mapped to the same location or are eliminated (causing a reduction in the number of bits). In the case of the expansion function, the function causes the number of bits to increase.

Of the four functions, the two most interesting are the round-by-round manipulation of the key as controlled by the key scheduling function and the key compression function. The key scheduling function takes the key and shifts it left with a wrap a number of places determined by round. In the DES key schedule shown in Table 7-1, the number of places to shift is connected through this table to the round number.

Once the key is shifted, it is then reduced in size from the original 56 bits to the 48 bits necessary for the algorithm. If you look at the flow chart diagram, you will notice that the right half of the data is then expanded from its current 32-bit length to a 48-bit length via an expansion permutation. Now that the key length and the data length are the same, the reversible exclusive-or function can be applied. Upon conclusion of this manipulation, the algorithm applies a substitution function that remaps the 48-bit output back to the original 32-bit length. At this time the L value is exclusive-or'd with the new R value, and the new L value is then updated to the old R value (swapping in anticipation of the next round). When the sixteen rounds have been completed as detailed above, the encryption routine returns the final ciphertext, which is then subjected to a final permutation.

The algorithm is then further complicated by its own incorporation into one of the four modes previously discussed. Normally, the CBC mode is selected. Like all of the other symmetrical methods that are

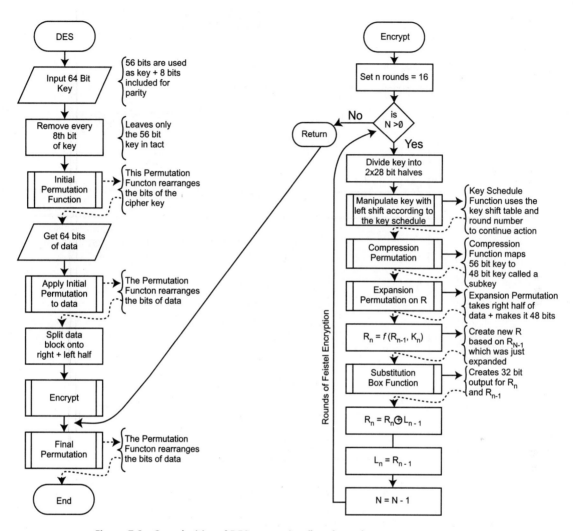

Figure 7-9   Complexities of DES encryption flowcharted.

generally endorsed, DES is publicly available and requires that only the key be guarded. The resulting ciphertext blocks are the same size (64 bits) as the plain text inputs. This detail is important in block ciphers because it actually makes it harder to attack the cipher.

As was mentioned earlier, the DES cipher is no longer considered computationally secure. However, the concept is considered usable in the triple DES implementation, which utilizes a much longer key (actually 2 x 56-bit keys). Even still, in 1998 the cost of the first machine capable of breaking DES cost $100,000.

Triple DES actually repeats the DES algorithm three times with different keys and is extremely secure. However, because the DES algorithm is complex and the permutation mapping processes are computationally

1 Round of DES Feistel Encryption

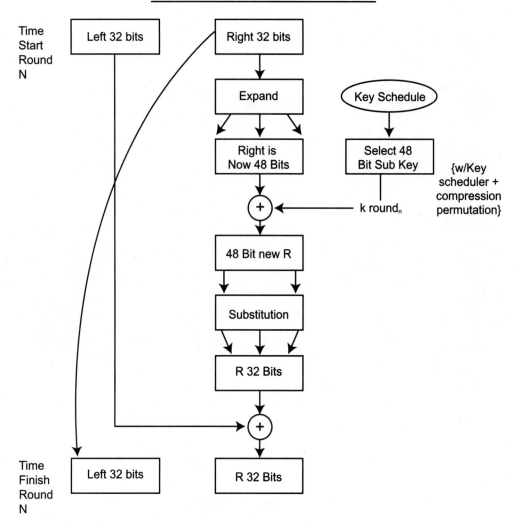

Time
Start
Round
N

Left 32 bits

Right 32 bits

Expand

Key Schedule

Right is
Now 48 Bits

Select 48
Bit Sub Key

{w/Key
scheduler +
compression
permutation}

+

k round$_n$

48 Bit new R

Substitution

R 32 Bits

+

Time
Finish
Round
N

Left 32 bits

R 32 Bits

Figure 7-10   How the classic Feistel cipher is used in DES.

Table 7-1 DES Key Schedule

Round	1	2	3	4	5	6	7	8	9	10	11	12	13	14	15	16
Shift	1	1	2	2	2	2	2	2	1	2	2	2	2	2	2	1

expensive, the algorithm tends to be very slow. This is problematic because the idea of symmetrical cryptography is to handle the bulk encryption work, which requires fast and efficient processing capabilities.

AES

As was discussed in Chapter 5, with the compromise of DES came a call to the cryptographic community to develop a replacement algorithm for DES. NIST established guidelines for the final product's requirements. The product had to support larger keys, larger block sizes, a range of key sizes, and was required to be faster than the DES implementation. AES was essentially an open competition. The round-two finalists were MARS from IBM, RC6 from RSA Labs, Serpent by Andersen, TWOFISH by CounterPane Security, and Rijndael by Daemen and Rijmen. Rijndael was the winner.

This algorithm, or FIPS Pub 197, is a symmetrical block cipher that can utilize 128-, 192-, and 256-bit keys. This specification mandates the use of this algorithm by the government to protect those documents that it considers classified when stored electronically.

The algorithm transforms data using two-dimensional matrices (called vectors) and matrix multiplication. Algorithms of this type are known as **Affine ciphers**. The basic unit for processing is at the byte level. The blocks are input as arrays of bytes and the manipulation is done at this level. The math associated with this type of cipher deals with finite fields. That level of mathematics is well beyond the scope of this book. The cipher uses rounds of length 10, 12, or 14 depending on key length. The algorithm also uses substitution boxes at the byte level.

AES is faster than DES and is more secure based on the longer key lengths. For more information on DES, triple DES, and AES, go to the NIST Web site's cryptographer's tool kit at *http://www.nist.gov/cryptotoolkit*. This site has a significant amount of information, specifications, usage suggestions, software implementations, and other helpful items that is useful when implementing symmetrical cryptography. Additionally, the site can be used to keep you up-to-date with the latest vulnerabilities and improvements in the code.

OTHER SYMMETRICAL ALGORITHMS

As we mentioned earlier, many symmetrical cryptography algorithms are available. Although TEA is an interesting algorithm, it is not as widely used as many of the others. DES (also double and triple DES) and AES are more commonly found in production applications. Other algorithms are available and have been shown to be reliable as well. A brief summary of those algorithms follows:

- RC2 , RC4, RC5 and RC6 are all RSA symmetrical algorithms were developed by Ron Rivest. The "RC" in the names stands for "Ron's Code." RSA is an important company in the industry and it provides a worthwhile site for reviewing its contributions. The site can be found at *http://www.rsasecurity.com*
- IDEA is a 64-bit, 8-round block cipher with a 128-bit key. This algorithm, like TEA, also uses mathematical functions from orthogonal algebraic groups. This algorithm is found in many applications such as PGP and SSH
- Double DES and triple DES are the expanded—and more secure—versions of the DES family of algorithms. They still rely on the same base DES concepts but with larger keys distributed over various iterations of sequential DES application
- Blowfish is a 64-bit, 16-round Feistel cipher. This is a public cipher found in SSH and is designed for use in encryption of large amounts of data

- TWOFISH was an AES competition finalist designed by CounterPane. This algorithm allows a 128-bit block, and a choice of 128-, 192-, and 256-bit keys. It is a block cipher and supports all standard modes. It uses 16 rounds
- MARS is also an AES semi-finalist submitted by IBM. The algorithm utilizes a 128-bit block length and a variable key length. It is faster than DES
- Serpent was another AES candidate and in fact received the second-highest number of votes. It is a 128-bit block cipher that works similarly to Rijndael

Another interesting site that can help you further direct your exploration of symmetrical encryption algorithms can be found at *http://www.mandala.co.uk/links/cryptography/*.

The evolution of modern symmetrical cryptography has been outstanding during the last fifty years. What began with the Shannon, Turing, and Friedman in the 1940s has become complex and competitive beyond anyone's ideas. This field continues to evolve and faces many interesting challenges, including the ever-increasing speed and agility of the modern computer. With this increased capacity to test the limits of key strength, thoughts about modern cryptographers have taken two distinct paths.

The first of these paths is toward more and more complex mathematics and longer keys. These algorithms are increasingly difficult and are setting an upper bound for complexity. The second path is toward cryptography through the use of emerging science. The use of quantum cryptography will revolutionize the industry if the science can be stabilized and made usable.

Safe for Now

Moore's law states that periodically, computing power will double. This means that the ability of hackers to successfully accomplish a brute-force attack can occur twice as fast.

The cryptographer can double the search space of an encipherment by simply adding one bit to the length of the key 2^{n+1} is double 2^n. Based on this logic, it appears that the advances in computing power really do not help cryptanalysts as much as it might seem.

At this time, a 128-bit key is considered secure because a brute-force attack is computationally unfeasible. However, cryptographers agree that even a linear increase in the complexity of cryptographic algorithms to accommodate the extra key bits will eventually force the field to look in different directions.

The need for continued growth in this field continues and the proliferation of these symmetrical techniques throughout the popular applications being used is paramount. For Internet businesses to flourish and to protect our privacy, symmetrical cryptography needs to become more manageable, commonplace, and standards based.

SUMMARY

Modern symmetrical cryptography is important for the confidentiality of information. Normally, symmetrical methods of cryptography are fast and secure. Symmetrical cryptography means that the sender and the receiver of the information share a secret. This secret dictates how the encryption method will perform. In early cryptography, the secrets were such things as how many letters to shift an alphabet or the diameter of the Spartan scytale roller. During World War I and World War II, cryptographic secrets were usually kept in codebooks.

Modern cryptography creates software keys, which are long strings of binary numbers. These secret software keys are plugged into symmetrical algorithms that "apply," or blend, these keys with the data. This concept of blending or applying keys is done through reversible mathematical operations such as the exclusive-or function.

Symmetrical key cryptography has several basic parts:

- Plain text
- Ciphertext
- Encryption algorithm
- Decryption algorithm
- Secret key
- Communication medium

Mathematically, the relationship between these items is expressed as $P = D(k,(E(k,P)))$. This relationship shows the symmetry between the encryption and decryption function. The decryption function plus the symmetrical key undoes whatever the encryption function plus the symmetrical key does.

Keys must be carefully constructed to avoid being subject to guessing. In general, the longer the key, the better. Key sizes of 56 bits are currently no longer considered to be computationally secure. Modern algorithms use minimum key sizes of 128 bits. Longer keys can often mean slower processing. This is a tradeoff that must be considered.

Another important key design principle concerns the use of prime numbers (especially large primes). Large primes (200-plus decimal places) are very hard to calculate, hard to guess, and cannot be factored. The use of these numbers prevents many sophisticated mathematical guessing mechanisms.

Given enough time, a cryptanalyst may be able to break a key. For this very reason, a key rotation policy should be put in place. Given the number of symmetrical keys required to manage a large key infrastructure and the key rotation issue, key management is a big concern.

Most symmetrical algorithms adhere to Shannon's principles for a good-quality cipher. These five principles should guide cryptographers in their design.

Symmetrical algorithms rely on the reversibility or invertability of operations. In Chapter 6 we learned that a number of mathematical operations are inherently reversible when paired with their composite function (e.g., addition and subtraction). The use of the exclusive-or function is perhaps the most well known of these functions.

Key scheduling is a mechanism used in many symmetrical algorithms. Key scheduling is how the cryptographic method utilizes the key. In the DES cryptographic method, the key schedule is specified in a table and dictates the number of bit places to shift the key, depending on the round number.

Kerberos, a method developed at MIT, allows the exchange of symmetrical keys. Kerberos works by establishing a number of secret keys that allow for secure transmission between the trusted server and all the clients. The clients contact the trusted server to request access to the ticket-generating server. The ticket-generating server then generates a permission ticket with which a client can contact the server of choice.

By obtaining this ticket and the appropriate key from the ticket-generating server, the client is able to communicate with the requisite application server.

Symmetrical ciphers can be either block ciphers or stream ciphers. Stream ciphers operate on a bit at a time, presented in a stream. These algorithms are not commonly used. Block ciphers operate on blocks of data at a time. A block is normally 64 to 256 bits. Most block ciphers support modes. There are four common modes: electronic codebook mode, cipher block chaining mode, cipher feedback mode, and cipher output mode. Modes (other than electronic codebook mode, which is essentially the absence of a mode) add complexity and confusion to a cipher.

Rounds are another important element of a symmetrical cipher. Rounds are the number of iterations that a piece of plain text is subjected to in the cryptographic method. When the number of iterations is satisfied, the encryption of that particular block is complete.

Feistel ciphers are a method created by Horst Feistel in the early 1970s as part of the IBM Lucifer project. The Feistel cipher is a popular method that allows cryptographers to design their own complex reversible functions. This type of cipher is recognizable because the data are split in halves, which are exchanged and blended on an alternating basis during the iterations. These methods normally make use of the exclusive-or mechanism. The DES encryption method is based on this strategy.

TEA, designed by Wheeler and Needham in 1994, is an elegant and interesting cipher. This cipher demonstrates all of the classic Feistel block cipher cryptographic principles. Students can learn much from a detailed review of this fast yet small set of codes.

The DES cryptographic algorithm represented the principle encryption method of the last decade. DES is based on a 56-bit key and encrypts 64-bit data blocks at a time. This method supports the four popular modes. In 1998, the method was compromised because it was proven that 56-bit keys were no longer computationally secure.

Double and triple DES are considered computationally secure. They use longer keys (actually two 56-bit keys) than DES and apply them during consecutive applications of the DES algorithm. DES is a highly complex algorithm with many parts. These parts include all of the parts of a classic Feistel cipher, plus permutations of keys and data, expansion and contraction permutation, substitution permutations, and bit shifting. Once the DES algorithm was deemed obsolete, NIST sponsored a contest to encourage the brightest talent in the industry to develop a powerful publicly available alternative. AES is the new standard that is used. This cipher is strong, fast, and complex. It is based on a technique known as an Affine cipher, which implies that the algorithm applies matrixes of keys to matrixes of plain text using matrix multiplication.

Many other symmetrical ciphers exist and are popular in the industry. Most recently, the science of cryptography has begun looking in new directions for ways of creating durable and strong ciphers. As the power of computers grows, the potential for failure of an older (such as DES) cryptographic method increases. New technology is based in science. Methods such as quantum cryptography and steganography represent the best alternative possibilities to mathematically intensive methods at this time.

STUDY QUESTIONS

1 The primary difference between today's cryptographic methods and those of sixty years ago is our _____. (choose one)

    a. Use of substitution ciphers

    b. Use of symmetric keys

    c. Reliance on computers and complex mathematics

    d. Reliance on transposition ciphers

2 For a symmetric key system to work, the keys must be exchanged _____ the transmission of ciphertext. (choose one)

    a. Prior to

    b. During

    c. After

    d. Within

3 Symmetrical ciphers work on _____ of information. (choose one)

    a. Blocks or continuous streams

    b. Bits or bytes

    c. Packets

    d. Sectors or rounds

4 _____ is used for secure key exchanges between users in a network. (choose one)

    a. Chimera

    b. Kerberos

    c. Horta

    d. Grendel

5 **True___ False___**   Symmetric cryptography is usually more efficient than asymmetrical cryptography.

6 A drawback of a symmetrical key system is that_____. (choose one)

    a. The number of keys can grow very large

    b. The keys can be discovered easily

    c. The keys are nonchanging

    d. The keys are public

7 A key that is at the edges of the range of possible keys or has a substantial number of non-prime factors is _____. (choose one)

   a. A strong key

   b. An acceptable key

   c. A weak key

   d. An unusable key

8 Today the most common key length is _____. (choose one)

   a. 56 bits

   b. 64 bits

   c. 96 bits

   d. 128 bits

9 **True___ False___** Block ciphers are weaker than stream ciphers.

10 Using TEA, complete diffusion can be attained in as few as ___ rounds. (choose one)

   a. 6

   b. 8

   c. 16

   d. 32

11 _____ mix parts of the key with parts of the plain text to create ciphertext. (choose one)

   a. Electronic codebook modes

   b. Shannon ciphers

   c. Feistel ciphers

   d. Polyalphabetic shift ciphers

12 In a long integer, one bit change per byte changes the number in ___ different places. (choose one)

   a. 2

   b. 4

   c. 8

   d. 16

13 In symmetrical key cryptography, the decryption algorithm _____ to the encryption algorithm. (choose one)

   a. Has no relationship

   b. Uses a separate key

   c. Is reciprocal

   d. Is identical

14 An encrypted block dependent upon the previous block is said to be _____. (choose one)

   a. Asynchronous

   b. Synchronous

   c. Interdependent

   d. Symbiotic

15 **True___ False___**   It is necessary to keep cryptographic algorithms private.

16 The idea of a public algorithm and a secret key is known as _____. (choose one)

   a. Shannon's principle

   b. Kerberos

   c. Kerckhoff's principle

   d. Diffie-Hellman algorithm

17 The _____ controls the action of the algorithm. (choose one)

   a. User

   b. Plain text

   c. Ciphertext

   d. Key

18 The term describing how a key is used in each iteration of a cryptographic algorithm is _____. (choose one)

   a. Key fractioning

   b. Key division

   c. Key rotation

   d. Key scheduling

19 Because the key space of the algorithm is so small, _____ is no longer considered computationally secure. (choose one)

   a. DES

   b. RSA

   c. TEA

   d. Diffie-Hellman

20 Affine ciphers process information at the _____ level. (choose one)

   a. Bit

   b. Byte

   c. Block

   d. Word

CASE STUDY

In reviewing the material in this chapter, you should have noticed that the algorithms for creating symmetrical cryptography have progressed significantly over time. You should complete the TEA lab in Appendix A. Given that experience and the discussion of symmetrical algorithms, what do you suppose is a weakness of TEA? How might TEA be made more secure? How much easier is TEA to crack after one round as opposed to six? Why?

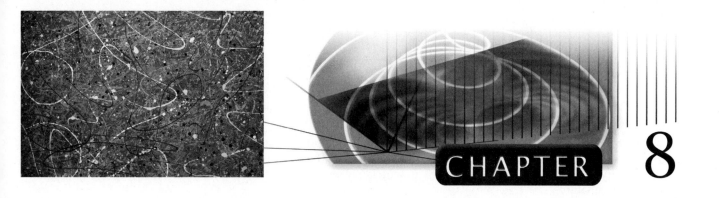

CHAPTER 8

Public Key Infrastructure

> *It is an equal failing to trust everybody and to trust nobody.*
> —Eighteenth-Century English Proverb

Developing a widespread "trust" between users is of paramount importance in the evolution of a digital marketplace. Developing such a trust in an electronic medium where users cannot physically meet is a substantial challenge. Through the use of asymmetrical algorithms, this goal can be accomplished.

The mathematics of information allows us to incorporate checksums and hashes into information metadata to verify its integrity. The same mathematical nature of information also allows us to utilize cryptographic methods to disguise the information and thereby keep it confidential. These are two of the most important components of the CAIN principle. Thus far, we have focused on the use of symmetrical key cryptography, meaning that the sender and receiver of the message both need to have the same key and cryptographic algorithm to encrypt and decrypt the information. While this is a very workable scenario in current widespread use, it does have several limitations:

- It does not account for the possibility that senders might wish to communicate secure information to recipients they have never made contact with before, thus, precluding the possibility that they (sender and receiver) could have exchanged secret keys prior to the communication
- Symmetrical cryptography does not address the issues of authenticity and non-repudiation
- Symmetrical algorithms require a periodic recycling of keys to minimize the potential of a successful key discovery by an attacker. This secret key exchange cannot be done in band because it must be assumed at the time of the key renewal exchange that the current session key is known to a possible attacker. This assumption is necessary because to assume otherwise would leave us in a situation where we could never regain a secure channel if the original key were somehow compromised

Asymmetrical cryptographic methods can be useful in addressing all three of these issues. The asymmetrical relationship between public and private keys, *Plain = Decrypt (Key$_{priv}$, Encrypt(Key$_{pub}$, Plain))*, is exploited to provide a unique and interesting scheme of encryption. This scheme is also useful for providing confidentiality signatures and for establishing ownership.

This asymmetrical set of keys involves the use of special algorithms that utilize modular arithmetic and are computationally slow. Therefore, asymmetrical algorithms are usually reserved for low-volume specialty applications such as encrypted symmetrical key exchange, e-mail encryption, code signing, or digital signatures.

However, it is these relatively low-frequency, infrequent, and slow transactions that make the whole cryptographic method layer, and the authentication and verification layer of our model, work. We will study the underpinnings of asymmetrical cryptography, key relationships, digital signatures, and the development of a PKI.

Once we have demonstrated that the CAIN principles can be successfully, effectively, and efficiently addressed through the use of combinations of symmetrical and asymmetrical encryption algorithms, hash functions, a variety of keys, and various applications, it is necessary to make it widely available in a standard form for it to be of real use. There is a definite need for a public key infrastructure that will make available key providers, verification, and authentication agents, provide a standard of implementation, and foster a requisite spirit of trust.

Trust is required for the authentication and verification piece to work. By allowing a person's electronic signature to be verified by an independent third party, we acquire a trust relationship. This relationship provides the basis for many sophisticated transactions where it is necessary to have formal verification before the transaction can be executed (i.e., digital cash.) The PKI needs to be standards based. There are several significant standards available. We will study two sets, PKCS 1 through 12 and the X.509 standards. We will study the trust requirements, the need for a PKI, and the operational issues of the PKI.

 To successfully complete this chapter, students should pay particular attention to the following:

- The appropriate application of public and private keys to enable the asymmetric encryption
- The necessity for a mathematically complex key definition and computationally intensive encryption /decryption algorithms so this method is hacker resistant
- The diagrams of asymmetric encryption and digital signatures
- The need for trust, the definition of trust, and how a trusted third party works
- The construction of the X.509 v3 certificate
- The components of the PKI
- The standards for a PKI
- Operational issues that arise in the management of a PKI

Elements of Success

Students reading this section may become easily confused by the asymmetrical nature of the cryptographic relationship. For this reason, it is important for readers to practice the reproduction of the schematics in this section. Once readers understand why a public or private key is applied at a particular time, the scheme becomes manageable. This is important because in Section Three of the text, these methods are extended to enable important security applications, which are where the real benefits of asymmetrical cryptography and PKI are realized.

ASYMMETRICAL KEY CRYPTOGRAPHY

Symmetrical key cryptography took advantage of algorithms that were principally based on the concept that by "applying" a **shared secret** to information (usually in a mathematical way), we could disguise information. These enciphering algorithms then had mirror-image algorithmic counterparts that could reverse the process by applying the same shared secret, decoding the cipher, and reproducing the original information. These shared secrets, or keys, need to be exchanged by previous arrangement for this method to be successful. Until 1975 the only cryptographic algorithms available were symmetrical.

After the development efforts of Ralph Merkle in 1976, Martin Hellman and Whitfield Diffie first proposed the idea of asymmetrical cryptography in the form of a public key cipher. This idea, although brilliant, has taken nearly three decades to become widely used.

Asymmetrical cryptography can be defined as a cryptographic method that uses a split secret (rather than a shared secret), where knowledge of the encryption secret by the cryptanalyst provides the cryptanalyst with very little (if any) useful information about the decryption secret. As opposed to symmetrical cryptography, asymmetrical cryptography does not rely on a "shared" secret. Instead the method works by "splitting" the secret into two parts.

The two parts of the **split secret**, as seen in Figure 8-1, work inversely to one another. This means that what is encrypted with one part can be decrypted by using only the other part. This is an important point because it means that something encrypted with one half of the secret cannot be opened again with the same half.

This ability to split a secret allows us greater flexibility in encrypting information than shared secrets do. The "public" part of the split secret can be openly distributed and considered common knowledge. The would-be receiver of any information always keeps the other half of the secret private and never shares it with anyone. By doing so, the senders of information can be confident that no matter who else has the receiver's public secret, only the receiver can decipher the information with the private part of the secret. If the person with the private part of the secret keeps it completely private (does not share it with anyone), then only that person can decipher any of the publicly ciphered messages with corresponding public key. This is the most important benefit of asymmetrical cryptography.

Asymmetrical cryptography allows many senders to encrypt information to a single recipient with a complete expectation of privacy. These two secrets are commonly referred to as a key pair. Any one of these keys has a similar function to a symmetrical key, as was the case in the last chapter when discussing symmetrical cryptography. A major difference between asymmetrical and symmetrical cryptography is that the keys in the asymmetrical pair have special and powerful relationships to each other.

In the case of asymmetrical cryptography, we have two keys: a private key (retained and kept private) and a public key, which is purposely made public. Therefore, all potential senders of information need access to every other participant's public key. While this sounds like a lot to keep track of, it turns out that it is a far smaller number of total keys than would be required in a symmetrical cryptographic method addressing the same number of users and sessions. Asymmetrical cryptography takes advantage of this one-to-many relationship to reduce the number of total keys required in the system.

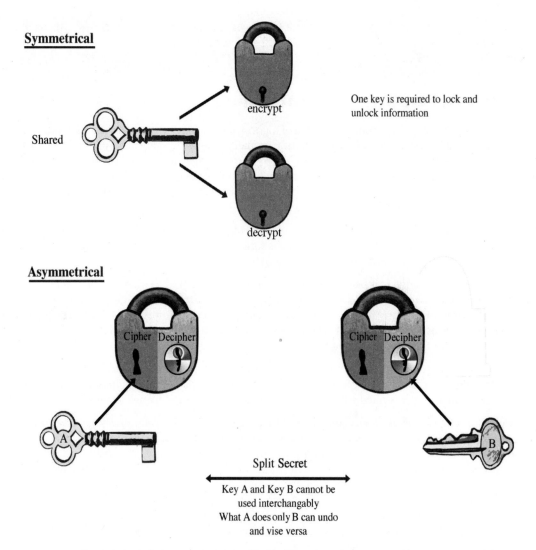

Figure 8-1   Splitting a secret: Instead of using a shared secret, asymmetrical crytography splits the secret. Each half can be used either to encrypt a message or to decrypt a message. However, once the half has been used for encryption, only the other part can undo the encryption.

Remember that in a symmetrical encryption system, if there are n users of the system, then there is a need for

$$\frac{n \bullet (n-1)}{2}$$

keys in the system if everyone wants to exchange information secretly with everyone else. This is obviously a lot of keys to manage and remember.

KEY POINT

By using asymmetrical cryptographic methods, senders can encrypt information with the receiver's public key without concern that others with the receiver's public key can view their encrypted information. This is because access to the receiver's private key is required to decrypt the information, and because access is restricted to only the receiver. As we shall see when discussing the PKI, the ability to publish a common encryption key among all possible senders is a powerful benefit. This method allows people to exchange encrypted information even if they have never previously met and had the opportunity to exchange a common secret, as seen in Figure 8-2.

Using asymmetrical cryptography, the same n users of the system each require only a public key for each user. In addition, users need to maintain their own private key. This is a total of n public keys plus n private keys in the entire system, or $2n$ keys. As is shown in Figure 8-3, 100 symmetrical sessions require 4,950 keys to manage, while an asymmetric method would require managing only 200 total keys.

Normally, we express this asymmetrical relationship mathematically, as

$$Plain = Decrypt \ (Key_{priv}, \ Encrypt(Key_{pub}, \ Plain)).$$

Using this mathematical notation, it is easy to see that the Encrypt function takes as input the public key and the plain text and returns ciphertext. Thus, we can say

$$Cipher\_text = Encrypt \ (Key_{pub}, \ Plain).$$

This means that we can substitute as follows:

$$Plain = Decrypt \ (Key_{priv}, \ Cipher\_text).$$

This equation shows that to open the ciphertext, you run the decrypt function, which takes as input the ciphertext and the receiver's private key.

Asymmetrical cryptography offers many outstanding benefits in developing information security strategies that are not available via symmetrical cryptography alone. We have already seen that asymmetrical cryptography offers the benefits of secure encryption, reduced key management responsibilities, and a publishable encryption key that can be used to form an encryption key directory. Additionally, we will see how asymmetric cryptography can be used to sign code, exchange symmetrical session keys securely, and provide digital signatures.

HOW IT WORKS

Students of cryptography struggle with two issues concerning asymmetrical cryptography. The first is remembering which key is used for which purpose, and the second is understanding exactly how this all works. This section of the chapter addresses both of these issues.

As was previously stated, in somewhat more general terms, asymmetrical cryptography requires that the sender and the receiver of information split a secret. That means that we create one key pair for each user of the cryptography system. The key pair consists of a **public key** and a **private key**. The private key must be kept very secure and never shared for this to system to work. The public key is meant to be open to anyone with a need to send you encrypted information. Typically, the exchange of encrypted information using an asymmetrical algorithm is graphically illustrated as shown in Figure 8-4.

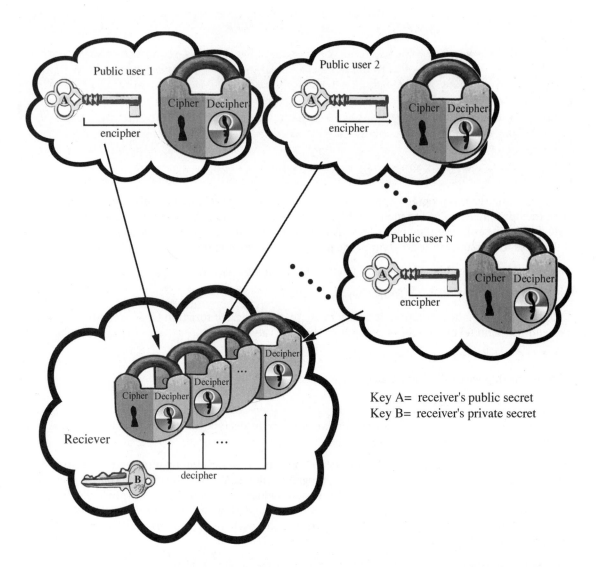

Figure 8-2   Many to One: Notice that asymmetrical cryptography provides a many-to-one relationship m:1 between potential senders and the receiver. Also notice that because the receiver is the only one with the private part of the secret. No one else can view the encrypted information of others.

For example, Bob wants to send an encrypted message to Alice. (Bob and Alice are the industry choice as king and queen of the encryption prom; they are in every textbook ever written on the subject.) Bob decides to use an asymmetric algorithm for encryption. First, he creates a plain text message to give to Alice. Next, he goes to his public key ring, where he stores all of his friend's public keys and selects Alice's public key. He then uses Alice's public key together with the asymmetrical algorithm (symbolized by the lock itself) and

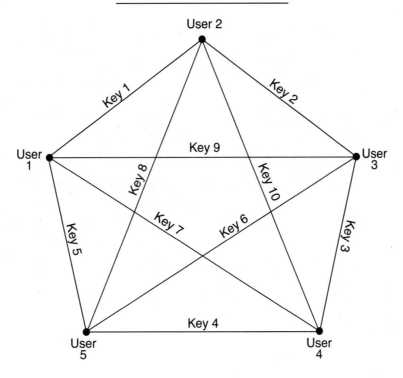

Symmetrical Key Proliferation

For n = 5 users requires $\dfrac{5 * (5-1)}{2} = \dfrac{5 * 4}{2} = \dfrac{20}{2} = 10$ Keys

For n = 100 users requires $\dfrac{100 * (99)}{2} = 4950$ Keys

As n gets larger this becomes difficult to manage

Figure 8-3   **For *n* users to exchange secrets using symmetrical cryptography, each user needs one secret key for each of the sessions they wish to have. Because the keys are used in pairs, we need n*(n-1)/2 keys systemwide.**

creates the ciphertext representation of the plain text message. In essence, we can say that the ciphertext is the "locked" version of the plain text. Thus far, we have reviewed the encryption procedure.

Bob now sends the ciphertext to Alice. This communication can be made via any network connection, including the Internet. Remember that along the way, if the message is intercepted by an attacker who might also have Alice's public key, we do not have to be concerned. Because Alice is the only person with access to her private key, only she can decrypt the message. The attacker sees only the ciphertext, which is meaningless to him.

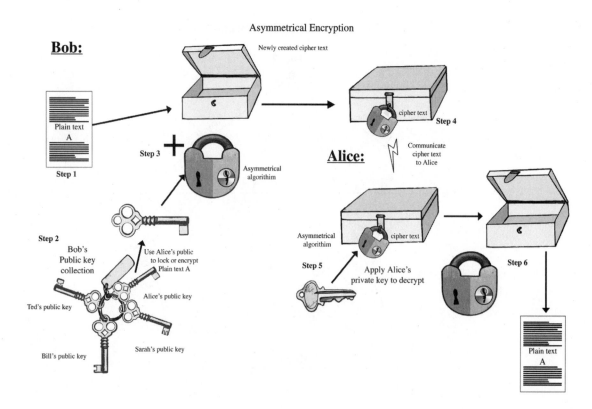

Figure 8-4 Bob sends Alice an encrypted message and she eventually decodes it.

When Alice receives the ciphertext, she uses her private key together with the decryption algorithm and unlocks the cipher. This process requires that she have both the corresponding private key to the public key Bob encrypted with and the corresponding decryption algorithm to Bob's encryption algorithm. Assuming that she does, she unlocks the cipher and is able to view the plain text that Bob originally sent. This is the decryption procedure.

It is useful for students to practice reproducing Figures 8-2 and 8-4. It is important to pay particular attention to the process. Equally important is to recognize whose key, Bob's or Alice's, and of which type, private or public, is being used in which part of that process.

Asymmetrical Encryption Details

The second difficulty that many students experience is understanding how asymmetrical encryption works. In the previous chapter, we detailed the use of TEA as an illustration of how a symmetrical encryption algorithm is applied to information. Unfortunately, no straightforward, elegant, easy–to- understand example exists for asymmetrical cryptography.

Asymmetrical cryptography is necessarily complex and requires a significant familiarity with number theory to understand fully. It needs to be complex because of the open nature of the method. The idea in most encryption schemes is to keep both the keys and the algorithms secret. By keeping this secret, the cryptanalyst has a significantly reduced chance of cracking the cipher and gaining access to the information. This also allows for simpler implementations of cryptography, including mathematical manipulations, PADs, and other easily conceived plans. In an asymmetrical cryptography system, the private part of the secret is the only component of the system kept confidential. The public keys, as well as the encryption and decryption algorithms are made public by necessity. For this system to work, it is important for all the potential users to be able to easily access the components of the cryptosystem and implement them. This fact requires that the key creation process be both mathematically sophisticated and complex.

> **KEY POINT**
>
> In an asymmetric cryptosystem, all of the underlying components of that cryptosystem, except the private key, need to be made public for the system to work. That cryptosystem includes the public keys, encryption algorithm, and the decryption algorithm. The private key is the only component that should be kept extremely confidential.

There are seven required parts of an asymmetrical cryptosystem:

- The plain text message
- The key-generation system
- The private key
- The public key
- The encryption algorithm
- The ciphertext
- The decryption algorithm

The mathematics behind key generation may vary slightly depending on which implementation is chosen. However, the general scheme usually involves algebraic manipulations of numbers to generate keys so that the generation process of the two keys is relatively simple but whose relationship is difficult to discover. This process is often referred to as **practical irreversibility** or a **trapdoor**.

An example of practical irreversibility can be found in combinations of extremely large prime numbers. It is obviously easy to take two large primes, p and q, and multiply them together, $n = p*q$, to obtain a very large integer, $n = 10^{200}$. However, to reverse this process requires factoring n into its component parts, and more specifically to factor it into its prime parts p and q. Factoring as a mathematical process is considered very difficult. Factoring an integer into its largest prime components presents the attacker with two problems: First, the attacker must factor the integer, which is a hard problem; second, the attacker must identify the large factors as prime numbers. Determining large primes is a computer-intensive task. There is no simple or efficient means of accomplishing this task. The test for primality, according to the prime number theorem, states that primes are found approximately 1 in every $(.4 * ln\ n)$ integers. To find a large prime on the order of 3^{2000}, for example, requires approximately 88 passes of the algorithm used to test for primality. If you then figure that you need the product of two such primes as factors, the required number of computations becomes quite large. This ensures that the factoring process required to break the keys is impossibly difficult.

Another example of practical irreversibility is the relationship between exponentiation and logarithms. Exponentiation is easy, simple multiplication. Calculating logarithms is more difficult. When combined with a modulation function, we create a difficult mathematical problem for the attacker to solve[1].

Once the keys are created, users require access to the encryption and decryption algorithms. Several popular algorithmic implementations of asymmetrical key cryptography are available. The entire user community must agree on a single set of algorithms and standards for this to work. This is one of the difficulties in developing a widespread application of this technology. In the next part of this chapter, we will explore three such algorithms to give the reader a flavor for their construct.

The seven required components and associated mathematics can be applied to successfully achieve a working asymmetrical cryptographic method. This method has many advantages over symmetrical cryptography. One of the primary drawbacks of asymmetrical cryptography, however, is that all of the necessary complexity tends to make it slow. This means that asymmetrical cryptography is not the best-suited algorithm for large blocks of information.

ASYMMETRICAL ALGORITHMS

The previous section detailed the required components of an asymmetrical cryptographic system. In this section, we shall take a closer look at two such systems, their similarities, and what makes them unique. The major components of the system are the key-generation process and the relative security of the system. The two most popular systems that we need to review are RSA and Diffie-Hellman.

Other systems do exist and offer various pros and cons as compared with these two base systems. One system, known as the **El Gamal** system, is available and is relatively easy to learn if you already know the Diffie-Hellman algorithm. This system is endorsed by NIST and is simply a more complex variant of the Diffie-Hillman method.

There are also **Elliptic Curve Cipher (ECC)** algorithms. These ciphers are relatively new and much more complex than the previously mentioned three algorithms. (Variants of the El Gamal and Diffie-Hellman are available in ECC form.) ECC algorithms take advantage of geometric properties of certain curves. These algorithms work by mapping plain text to points on a curve and then using elliptical mathematical methods on those points to create the desired cryptography. These ECC ciphers offer advantages over other asymmetrical methods. One important improvement is the ability to use shorter key lengths with the same strength as significantly longer ones in other methods. Finally, new asymmetrical methods such as the **NTRU cipher** are becoming available and are currently under investigation.

All of the newer more advanced methods are excessively mathematical and complex. Therefore, they are beyond the scope of an introductory text. Given so many choices available, it is possible to write a whole text dedicated to them (and in fact there are!). However, for our purposes it is important to understand the two most popular and widespread of these methods: RSA and Diffie-Hellman. These two algorithms represent a great starting point in understanding the tenants of asymmetrical cryptography and do not overemphasize complex mathematics. To master these methods, it is necessary to review some of the number theory basics covered in Chapter 6 (especially working with primes, exponentiation, logarithms, and Eulers totient function).

---

[1] For more information of the mathematics of cryptography please refer to Chapter 6.

RSA

RSA is perhaps the best known of the three methods. It is also the most widely accepted in practice. It was proposed by Rivest, Shamir, and Adleman in 1977. This method generates keys based on the combining of large primes. Thus, its relative security is proportional to the cryptanalyst's ability to factor large primes.

The key pair is represented as (private (d), public(e)). Each of the keys in the system consists of two parts: the calculated component and the multiple of two large primes, which relates e and d.

In the RSA system, the key-generation process represents a series of steps that capitalize on a good portion of the mathematics discussed in the Chapter 6. The steps are as follows:

1 Select two prime numbers p, q such that $p \neq q$. These numbers are normally large prime values generally at least 100 digits. These numbers must be kept secret.

2 $n = p*q$ It is not necessary to keep n private because the factoring of large primes is quite difficult.

3 Phi(n) = $(p-1)(q-1)$ This is an extension of Euler's totient function (because n is the product of the primes p and q).

4 Select an integer e *(the encryption key)* so that e is relatively prime to Phi(n). The greatest common devisor of e and Phi(n) is 1. Also, e must be less than Phi(n).

5 Calculate d <i *(the decryption key)* as being congruent with e^{-1} mod($Phi(n)$).

6 The public key is then stated as $K_{public} = \{e,n\}$.

7 The private key is then stated as $K_{private} = \{d,n\}$.

8 Encryption of a message M to obtain ciphertext C is calculated as $C = M^e$ mod(n).

   M is equal to the calculated decimal value of the bits in the block of the plain text message. It is important that $M < n$ so that after the encryption, the block can be expressed in the same number of bits.

9 Decryption of the ciphertext C is $M = C^d$ mod(n).

Given that the best-case scenarios for factoring large primes are not very impressive[2] (for n of size 155 the time to factor would be 8,000 MIPS-years[3]), the factoring process is reduced to guessing. It has been determined that for several conditions (particular values or ranges of p and q), finding the decryption key is relatively easy. Also, there are tables that are kept with factors of large primes already in them. However, given that the key-generation process is carefully done and that the designers of the algorithms follow industry best practices, the RSA algorithm is very safe.

Diffie-Hellman

Diffie-Hellman is the oldest of the asymmetrical cryptosystems. It is still in use today and is based on primes, exponentiation, and logarithms. It is mostly used as a method of exchanging secret keys, for reasons that will become obvious as we further our discussion. In the Diffie-Hellman system, all of the users

---

[2.] Not very impressive in terms of the practicality of attacking an asymmetrical algorithm such as RSA with any hope of defeating the cryptography within the useful life of a message. The factoring capabilities are impressive in terms of progress made in the general mathematical techniques. As modern computers get faster, these methods will eventually be a threat to all algorithms of this type.

[3.] According to the RSA challenge results.

share a common secret. The users share two numbers: a large prime p and a second number, which is called x (where x cannot be 0, 1, or (p-1)).

Every user in the Diffie-Hellman system then selects a private secret number. In the case of user A exchanging cryptographic methods with user B, we will use the numbers A and B respectively to indicate these secret numbers. The users now calculate their respective public key as

$$a_{public} = x^A \, mod(p)$$

and

$$b_{public} = x^B \, mod(p).$$

Both parties then exchange public keys.

To exchange messages they compute a shared secret key using their own private key and the other's public key as follows:

$$shared_{A \rightarrow B} = b_{public}{}^A \, mod(p) \text{ and } shared_{B \rightarrow A} = A_{public}{}^B \, mod(p).$$

Notice that they are actually the same because at the base, we see that through substitution

$$(x^B)^A \, mod(p) = (x^A)^B \, mod(p).$$

Thus through this elaborate scheme, we have managed for both sides to essentially exchange a symmetrical key (shared secret) that is private only to them, based on a public key concept. In this case A never knows B's secret, only B's public key and visa versa. If the prime and the secrets are extremely large, then the message is deemed safe. This method is really a hybrid between the pure asymmetrical and the wholly symmetrical. But it is effective and it does work.

The El Gamal cipher is a variant of the Diffie-Hillman algorithm and is also similar to the RSA algorithm with its encryption and decryption steps. The El Gamal algorithm is refined to present less cryptographic weaknesses than either of the other two, and it is endorsed by NIST.

DIGITAL SIGNATURES

So far we have seen many compelling reasons to use asymmetrical cryptography. Although it is usually characterized as a slow process (which becomes somewhat less of a problem as processor power and memory continue to improve), the reduced key management, many-to-one relationships, and ability to send encrypted messages without prior establishment of session credentials is motivation enough for most people to try it.

However, asymmetrical cryptography is not without its own share of problems. First, there is the problem of destroyed messages. While this problem can exist in any cryptographic scheme, it is more prevalent in asymmetric public key cryptography because this style of cryptography is most often used over public networks, rather than secure or private networks. One of the many attacks that we discussed in Section One was the denial-of–service attack. Any time a hacker can deny access to information, they have achieved a hacker milestone. With asymmetrical encryption, it is difficult to crack the codes, yet it is easy to access the ciphertext. The countermeasure to this flaw is to uniquely identify a message through either a number or an algorithm so that the receiver will realize that something in the information stream is missing. In many military applications, a single plain text message is divided into several ciphertext messages and sent. This is done so that if a single message is intercepted and decoded, only a part of the message is obtained and not the whole message. This technique can also be employed to safeguard against the opposition destroying the message. If the parts were numbered, the receiver would notice the missing part and ask that it be retransmitted.

Second, if we accept that destruction of messages and information is a problem in the public domain, then we must also acknowledge the threat of message damage. This has been addressed in the symmetrical encryption section of the text through the use of checksums, which can define the integrity of information for us. It is recommended that in the context of asymmetrical cryptography, users continue to implement this best practice.

Third, **message substitution** is a serious issue. Message substitution can be problematic when the sender and receiver communicate over a public network. In this scenario the attacker intercepts an encrypted transmission from Bob to Alice. He then removes it from the network so that Alice never receives it. Thus far the attacker has stolen only a message he cannot use. (It is encrypted, therefore we assume the attacker would have trouble opening it.) However, assuming that the attacker has some idea of what Bob and Alice might be talking about in their correspondence, he might consider creating a fake message with fake content from Bob to Alice. Because the attacker also has Alice's public, key he can take the fake plain text, encrypt it with Alice's public key as shown in Figure 8-5, and send it to replace the original message from Bob. Alice would then receive the message, decrypt it, read it, believe it is from Bob, and be in receipt of false information without realizing that it is not authentic.

For a long time this consideration caused considerable consternation among the supporters of asymmetrical encryption and public key cryptography. Substituting a message for an original making its way through the public network undermines the required principles of trust that asymmetrical cryptography hoped to foster.

This problem can be successfully addressed through the use of **cryptographic checksums**, otherwise known as **Message Authentication Codes (MACs).** MACs can be constructed as part of the asymmetric cryptographic method to create a digital signature. This process is described below.

Once we have the message digest, we can encrypt it to keep it secret. To check the integrity (the fact that the original content is unchanged) of the message, in theory, all that needs to be done is decrypt the checksum, recalculate the message digest on the original message, and compare the old checksum now decrypted with the new one just calculated.

Message authentication codes can be constructed using a symmetrical encryption method. For this to work, both the sender and receiver must have the secret key. For maximum security, the encrypted message digest should be sent separately from the encrypted message. Once the receiver has both the encrypted message and the encrypted message digest, they can begin the recovery and comparison process. If the MACs are equal, then the integrity of the message is good. Also, if Bob and Alice keep their shared key secret, then only Bob could have created the message because only he and Alice share the secret. This method, shown in Figure 8-6, is known as challenge/response and is subject to a reflection attack. This procedure provides a measure of authenticity.

This method of integrity checking and authentication should work in concept. The requirement for all pairs of communicants to have a symmetrical MAC key would be prohibitively difficult to manage in an open and public implementation where it would be most useful. Likewise, the use of cryptographic checksums in a private communication environment has only limited application. Using encrypted checksums as part of a file integrity checking system is a valid implementation of using the concept locally. MACs in the symmetrical world have limited applicability, but they can be effective in the limiting of integrity problems.

Message Substitution

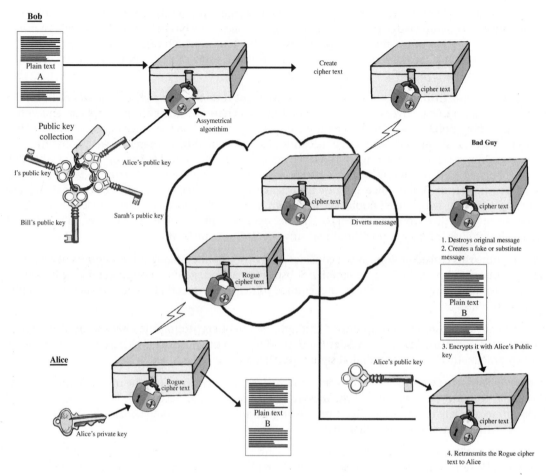

Figure 8-5 Bob sends Alice a message that is intercepted, discarded, and replaced with a fake.

Using asymmetric encryption, MACs, private keys, and public keys, we can create authentication devices that are highly reliable. These authentication devices are known as digital signatures. Digital signatures are constructed by computing a message digest of the plain text message, as was done in the symmetrical version. This message digest gives us a strong indication of the integrity of the message. In fact, checksums have been utilized for generations in computer networking protocols to assist network engineers in determining if line problems corrupted data. When utilizing message digests as part of a security package, however, we hope to achieve integrity, authentication and nonrepudiation.

As was shown in the discussion of symmetrical implementations of MACs, by applying a shared secret to the MAC, we create a cryptographic checksum. This cryptographic checksum can prove that the message is authentic because only the other person that shares the secret could encrypt the checksum in this

Constructing MACs Using Symmetric Encryption

A **checksum** is a function that takes a long sequence of data and represents it in a significantly smaller one. This checksum value can be constructed so that there is a low probability that two random pieces of data will generate the checksum or **message digest** value. By using an appropriate mathematical value, we can compute the message digest, which reflects the integrity of the longer plain text. It is easy to conceptualize a message digest through analogy. Your fingerprint or a sample of your DNA is a message digest of you. While it is within the realm of possibility that two people could have the exact same fingerprint, in reality it is so highly unlikely as to boarder on absurd. This is true with message digests of long plain text messages as well (for details of how to compute a checksum, please see Chapter 6). Several guidelines should apply to the creation of the message digest:

- Given the plaintext *P*, then the message digest of *P* should be efficiently (quickly) created
- The message digest of *P* (call it *d*)should be constructed to not reveal any information about the original message *P*. Therefore, the message digest function should not be reversible. This is known as a **one-way hash**
- The hash function used to create the digest needs to be simple to create yet significantly complex to calculate in reverse. For example, calculating $y = x^5$ is easy, but computing $\sqrt[5]{y}$ is difficult (this example is not difficult with a computer but serves the purpose regarding degrees of difficulty; factoring is another example)
- The function should be created so that given two messages *P* and *Q*, the chances of the *MessageDigest(P) = MessageDigest(Q)* are remote at best. This means that the set of message digests for any messages *P* and *Q* should not intersect, or should only minimally intersect

way. If an attacker attempted to substitute the message, he would be unable to re-create the proper checksum and thus the message would stand out as a fake.

If we choose to pursue this strategy with symmetrical keys, we are left with two rather cumbersome problems. First, every pair of potential users would require a predetermined secret symmetrical session key to support the exchange. Second, users would all have had to predetermine in advance that they needed to share a secret for authentication purposes. This is somewhat of a contradiction because the whole point of authenticity is to allow for a first-time transmission between two parties to be judged as unique. The analogy is similar to receiving a bank draft from an institution other than your own. You need to be able to authenticate the validity of the check and the authenticity of the person signing it. The same is true with information.

A solution to these two issues is to execute a similar procedure as was discussed previously for cryptographic checksums. The difference is that this time we will use asymmetrical key cryptography. As shown in Figure 8-7, we can see that we can use a process where we sign or create a cryptographic checksum with our own private key, which can then be verified with our public key by people who receive the message. This not only provides the recipient with the integrity checking that was so important, but it also provides a strong authentication mechanism.

In Figure 8-7, Bob wishes to send a message to Alice. The message requires authentication and integrity assurance. (For ease of understanding, we do not show Bob also encrypting the plain text. But under many

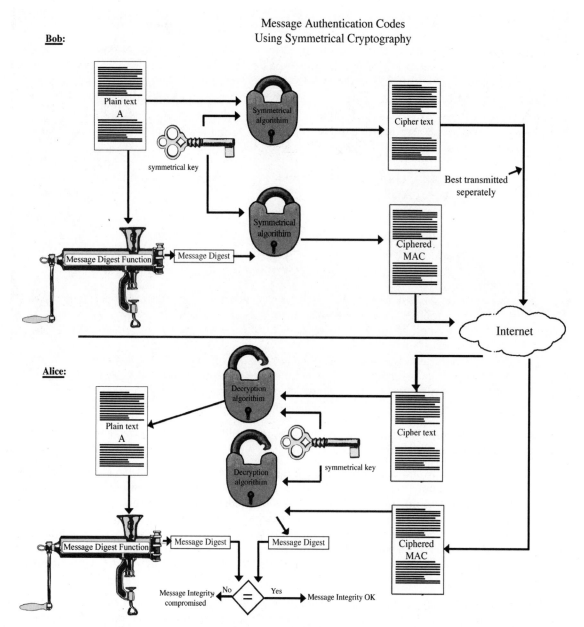

Figure 8-6 Using MACs symmetrical encryption and a shared secret key, Alice can verify the integrity of Bob's message.

circumstances the sender would sign and encrypt the message. But for this example, Bob sends the plain text in the clear.) Bob first computes the message digest of the plain text. Then Bob "signs" the message digest by applying his private key and the asymmetrical encryption algorithm to the MAC. Once the MAC is encrypted, Bob transmits the encrypted MAC and the plain text message to Alice. Note that Bob signed

Digital Signatures

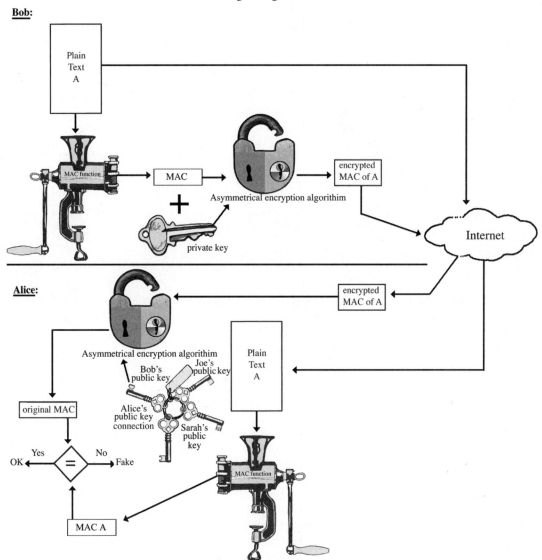

Figure 8-7   Digital signatures utilize asymmetrical cryptography to authenticate messages. Notice Bob signs the message with his private key. This validates the message because he is the only person with access to that key. Alice opens the message with Bob's public key.

the message with Bob's private key. This is different from the standard encryption mechanism described earlier in which Bob encrypted the plain text with Alice's public key. In the case of a cryptographic check-sum (aka digital signature), Bob needs to show that only he created the message digest. By signing with his private key, Bob fulfills this requirement. Because Bob is the only person with access to Bob's private key, no one else could possibly sign the message and produce the same encrypted hash as Bob.

Bob then transmits the plain text and the encrypted message digest to Alice over the public Net. Even if an attacker intercepts the message and modifies it and recalculates the hash, the attacker would need Bob's private key to sign it. Because the attacker does not have this key, any attempt would fail to conceal the forgery.

When Alice receives the message, she then uses Bob's public key and the asymmetrical decryption routing to decipher the message digest. It is important to reiterate that because the message digest was encrypted with Bob's private key, only Bob's public key can undo the encryption. The public and private keys can be applied reciprocally to each other in the encryption and decryption process. Once Alice decrypts the message digest, she sets it aside and recalculates a new message digest on the plain text message. She then compares the newly calculated message digest to the one that Bob had sent. If they are the same, then the message is authenticated and the integrity is validated. If they are different, it means either that the message is a fake or that a transmission error changed something in the plain text, thereby compromising the integrity. In either case, Alice should contact Bob to obtain another copy of the message.

> **KEY POINT**
>
> Message digests are turned into digital signatures when we apply the sender's private key to the message digest through the asymmetrical encryption algorithm. Because only senders have access to their own private keys, they are the only party that can generate such an encrypted hash. When receivers receive the messages, they decode the encrypted hash with the sender's public key. This public key reverses the encryption and returns to the receiver the original has value calculated by the sender. By recalculating the hash on the plain text message, the receiver can verify the authenticity and the integrity of the message.

Students should notice that the signature can be read by anyone (not just Alice in this case) with access to Bob's public key. This is not a problem; rather, it is a feature. Because we are authenticating the signature and the integrity of the message, it is important that any party should be able to do this. If Alice forwarded the information to someone else, this signature process also demonstrates to the party that the original message was from Bob. This important step provides us with the final piece of the puzzle, nonrepudiation of the information. By this we mean that since Bob signed the information, he can never deny that it is his information. This is analogous to going to the store and purchasing an item with a credit card. By using the card, authenticating yourself to the clerk, and signing the slip, you agree to the purchase. The merchant then sends the slip to the credit card company, which also can authenticate your signature as a means of preventing you from later claiming that you never made the purchase. This process provides the necessary checks and balances that make the credit card system work. The digital signature provides the same benefit by binding the signer of information, thereby demonstrating ownership.

As with the schematics detailing the asymmetric encryption process, it is equally important to commit the digital signature process to memory. It is recommended that students be able to reproduce this figure as part of the learning process. Pay particular attention to which key (and of which type) is applied to each step of the process. Also be mindful to not confuse the encryption process and corresponding key selection with the signature process and its corresponding use of the public and private keys.

The proper use of a MAC provides the authentication necessary to separate fake messages from real ones. This digital signature mechanism has been so successful that in 1998 it was adopted into law through the Electronic Signature Bill. This law endorses and validates the use of digital signatures in lieu of a written signature in almost all cases.

ATTACKS AGAINST ENCRYPTION

Just as we demonstrated with symmetrical algorithms, it is possible to successfully attack asymmetrical cryptography as well. In the late 1970s, early versions of asymmetrical encryption were successfully compromised[4]. These demonstrations caused many to distance themselves from asymmetrical methods. Although those early problems were fixed and the algorithms made sufficiently complex, attacks can still be run against them. These attacks are extremely complex and require significant energy, time, and money to execute effectively. These methods are presented at a relatively high level to give the reader a sense of warranted caution. The fact that these methods exist in no way suggests that asymmetrical methods are any less effective than their symmetrical counterparts. Remember, all cryptography is subject to attack and, so long as we maintain the principles of making the encryption strong enough to cost more than the information is worth to crack, or take longer than the information is valid to crack, the fact that a compromise can be devised is insignificant.

In general, there are two broad categories of attacks: 1) brute force and 2) using the public key to compute the private key or a mathematical attack. Brute-force attacks are successful when the prime number component of the cipher is small. It is always wise, then, to use extremely large primes to reduce the effectiveness of the attacks. The mathematical attacks are most likely computationally infeasible (from our discussion of NP problems in Chapter 6). However, if one of these problems falls, then they all fall. To date no one has solved one or proven that they cannot be solved in polynomial time.

The attack types include the following:

- Brute-force attacks—Brute-force attacks represent an attempt to try every possible combination of key. In this case we can use a brute-force attack to attempt to factor the large combinations of primes used as the base of the RSA algorithm
- Small decryption exponent attack—If the RSA d component is less than $n^{1/4}$, then it is possible to recover d
- Small public exponent attack—In this method, it is possible to send the same message to a distribution list of persons using each of their public keys in determining the shared secret. If we choose e in the RSA equation to be small and the number of messages on the distribution list is greater than e, then it becomes mathematically possible to recover the message
- Logarithm computation attacks—As we discussed earlier, it is possible to use mathematical attacks to recover exponents
- Timing attacks—An adversary times the computation, thereby figuring out the number of exponentiations occurring in the decryption, and thus understanding the decryption exponent

---

4. The knapsack problem was the basis of the Merkle-Hellman algorithm that was compromised.

THE NEED FOR A PUBLIC KEY INFRASTRUCTURE

At this point, we have reviewed asymmetric cryptography and digital signatures in some detail. Through the use of these mechanisms, a manageable public infrastructure of encryption and message signing should be possible. The vision that is created is one in which all users have the ability to correspond with one another in a confidential fashion. Through the use of digital signatures, we can establish sophisticated online financial transactions, including digital currency, secure message exchange, personal authentication, and code signing.

For the information presented in this chapter to achieve its full potential, it must be able to be managed as part of a large-scale public application. This is very difficult to achieve because it requires not only an effective implementation of the methods, but also education of the public, a standard that all vendors agree to, operating policies and procedures that can withstand the volume of interactions possible, third-party verification and authentication authorities willing to participate, meticulous key management plans, and most important, a widespread trust of the system.

The remainder of this chapter deals with the requirements and the design of this kind of public system. This system that we are trying to implement is a PKI. This PKI is in place today and has been developing over the last decade. Several well-known companies, such as VeriSign, Baltimore, and Entrust have developed product and service offerings in this space. Recent legislation, such as HIPAA, also has begun to generate interest in this area of security. A widely accepted PKI could provide much-needed confidence in the management and distribution of information.

These companies, laws (including the Electronic Signature Bill), and developing business requirements are slowly pushing our public information infrastructure into requiring this type of system. Currently, many private implementations of public key infrastructures exist. Each of these is important because the technology exists to chain these implementations to a true public provider and integrate them into the public domain.

This evolution is not unlike the one that was witnessed with the advent of the telephone or the Internet. In both of these cases, it took time for the populous to understand the offering, garner the required components of the solution (phone numbers, Internet addresses, key pairs), and find applications that are useful to them where the new technology comes into play. There was a time when not everyone had a telephone; even if you had one, you might not be able to call everyone you want. There was a time when most people did not have a public e-mail address or an Internet address, so what purpose did connectivity serve?

Today, enabling trust in a business to business (B2B) and business to customer (B2C) application requires a catalyst to make the business use of the Internet regain momentum. Part of the catalyst can be found in applications such as digital currency and digital signatures. Developing the PKI (or something remarkably close to it) is an important step in the evolution of our national information infrastructure.

DEVELOPING TRUST

For us to establish this public system, we need to address the principle missing ingredient, trust. Trust is defined as "confidence in or reliance on some quality or attribute of a person or thing, or the truth of a statement."[5] Trust is inversely proportional to risk. That is, as the trustworthiness of a system increases, our risk exposure decreases. When we deploy a PKI that is trustworthy, important applications (e.g., digital currency) can begin to flourish.

[5.] Oxford English Dictionary, Second Edition.

Trust is important if any meaningful exchanges of information are to take place. As an example, look at a national monetary system. For such a system to work, a considerable amount of trust needs to be built into the system. What is a dollar? Without the backing of, or our trust in, the government, it is merely a piece of paper. What about checks? Would you accept one if you had no trust in our banking system?

The same principle is true for our information system. Without the proper trust, applications are unable to function in the public domain. We need to be assured that keys, information, users, and other authenticated entities are who they claim to be. We need to be sure that information is unaltered. We need to have confidence that the accountability for electronic transactions of any kind is reliable and provable. Trust is measured by our adherence to the CAIN principles defined earlier.

One difficulty that exists in the creation of cybertrust is that, in the electronic world, the parties participating in a trust relationship have little or no knowledge of one another. You cannot proverbially look someone in the eye to determine if they are trustworthy. In fact, you may not even be in the same legal jurisdiction so that contracts and agreements can be enforced. Trust, therefore, is definable in terms of the strength and integrity of the in-place cryptographic authentication systems. Cryptographic authentication systems must be backed by authorities whose trust is beyond question. These entities are known as **trusted authorities** or **trusted third parties.**

If we can agree that trust is earned, then to become a trusted third party an organization needs to have earned that position. A trusted authority can be described as a company that is trusted by others to provide verifiable information about its members. The trust from one trusted authority, then, is transferable to any other authority it deems trustworthy.

This concept is, of course, then extended to the trusted authorities members (all of whom has had their identity verified and validated by the trusted third party). This passing of trust is known as a **trust relationship.** These relationships are used to pass trust from what is known as the **trust anchor** to all of the subordinate members of the group. As is shown in Figure 8-8, this trust relationship can be either hierarchical or networked in nature.

In the hierarchical model, the trust emanates downward from the trust anchor or root authority to subordinate authorities and then on to the members. The root authority can be a government body, a financial institution, or other organizational types that "can be trusted." The root authority may transfer trust to a tier-two or local authority. The local authority then can transfer trust to the member community. This process is known as chaining. In the hierarchical model, the higher the position of the entity, the more trust authority the entity has. The lower the entity, the more the entity seeks assurance.

The networked trust relationship is less formal and models the individual trust relationships that most people enjoy. Each trust relationship that people enjoy can be transferred to those people that they know. Those people can then continue to proliferate that trust exchange. In this model, the flow of trust is controlled. You may trust me, but I may not necessarily trust you.

In general, the hierarchical model is more controllable and is best suited for addressing the internal trust between members of a PKI. For the purposes of this discussion, we will assume that, internally, a PKI is hierarchical. We can further assume that the relationships between competing PKIs will be networked. This is familiar because this is the organizational construct of most telephone companies. In practice, trusted authorities could exist in both public and private domains, and on the local, national, and international levels. These authorities create a network by forming alliances with other authorities. This allows users to communicate securely with every user of every authority with whom their authority has

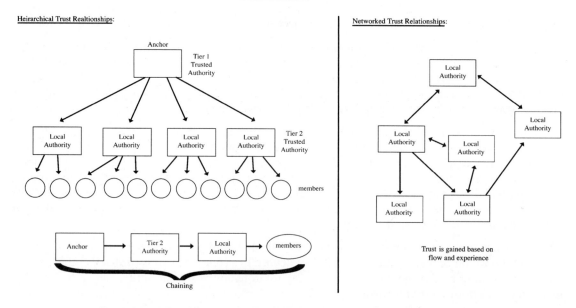

Figure 8-8 Cybertrust relationships are based on these models, which can be formal hierarchical or causal based on networking (your experience and the experience of others).

an agreement. Once these relationships are forged, the trusted authority becomes the organization(s) that issues the asymmetrical keys and digital certificates that accompany them to its own members.

How do we establish trust? Trust is established between the trusted authority and the PKI member by taking the following steps:

1 The trusted authority must establish a unified certificate format that minimally identifies the certificate authority issuing it, names or identifies the member, contains the member's public key, identifies the useful life of the key, and is digitally signed by the issuing authority.

2 The certificates must be used in conjunction with a **certificate policy**. The certificate policy determines the operating parameters regarding the generation, distribution, and management of key pairs. This includes key revocation, key issuance, identity verification, and the administration of **digital certificates**.

3 Establishment of an identity verification process. For the trusted authority to maintain a high degree of integrity, the identity verification process must be rigorous and comprehensive. The verification process is often outsourced by the trusted authority to a **certification authority**. The certification authority addresses this process but does not issue certificates.

4 As a result of a successful verification, the trusted authority must bind the distinguished name of the user (certificate subject name) and identity of the member.

5 The trusted authority then creates a public/private key pair for the member. At this point, the trusted authority binds the public key to the distinguished name of the member in the certificate.

What Kind of Existing Company Would Make a Good Fit as a Certificate Authority?

To perform the verification process with the rigor required by the trusted authority, the certificate authority generally needs to be already in possession of some of a perspective member's personal information. The reason for this is that if I already have some of your personal information (things that only you should know,) I should be able to use it to verify your identity. For example, the companies that conduct credit investigations and issue credit reports have very large repositories of information about you that only you should know. For example, assuming that you have a credit card or have applied for a home loan, the various credit bureaus have your credit history. Thus, if you applied for membership in a PKI, they would be able to verify your identity by asking you questions such as, What is your mortgage company and account number? What is the outstanding balance on a particular account? Government bodies (e.g., a division of motor vehicles) can also be a good source of information, and anyone with access to that information can use it also to verify your identity.

Current government proposals are concerned with the establishment of formal guidelines for such verification processes and with protecting the privacy of individuals.

6 The trusted authority then issues the key pair to the member. The trusted authority retains a copy of the member's public key and the member's certificate only. No copy of the member's private key should be retained by the trusted authority.

KEY POINT

When a trusted authority issues a key pair for a member, the trusted authority should retain a copy of the member's public key. The trusted authority should not retain a copy of the member's private key because that would actually decrease the integrity and degrade trust (because the private key is used as part of the digital signature process and the decryption process). It is imperative that no third party (including the trusted authority) be in a position to wield the power of a member's private key. To do so is equivalent to granting power of attorney to a third party.

7 Once the certification and key issuance process is in place, the trusted authority must send the new member a copy of the trusted authority's public key. This allows any correspondence from the trusted authority to the member to be verified by the member via the digital signature process describer above. In other words, the trusted authority signs all of its correspondence to the membership so that the membership can rely on the correspondence's authenticity.

8 Through a cryptographic mutual authentication process (described next), two communicating members can verify each other's identity. This is done by requesting verification of a binding between an entity and their public key from the trusted authority.

As we have seen, the trusted authorities need to work in concert much the way that phone companies allow for the interconnection of their users. If the PKI is to work, this requirement must be realized. Because the sheer number of members is overwhelming, no single trusted third party can manage the entire process. Rather, as discussed earlier, certain trusted authorities act as trust anchors. This means that they are the root of the trust hierarchy, a place where all members have a common trust. Because many members are already part of some other hierarchical structure (belonging to their university, a company, the government, etc.) the hierarchy of that organization can be used as the distribution mechanism of trust. This is done by making that organization a local authority that inherits trust from the trust anchor. This process is the chaining of trust to local authorities.

In practice, the local authority generally uses its own means to verify identity, create keys, distribute keys, and manage the local membership key space. The trusted authority is responsible only for imparting trust to the local authority and servicing authorization requests outside the local domain. This means that the trusted authority represents the local authority's members to outside sources. The local authority handles the authentication requests between local members. As we bring this together in a global PKI, we begin to see why the distribution of trust and the kinds of trust relationships are so important. A way of seeing how the distribution of trust is realized is shown in Figure 8-9.

USING DIGITAL SIGNATURES AND CERTIFICATES AS INSTRUMENTS OF TRUST

In the previous sections, the cryptographic checksum was presented as a guaranteed way to address the integrity and authentication parts of the CAIN principle. As discussed, when senders keep their private keys confidential, we are able to authenticate the sender of the message (because they would be the only party with access to the private portion of the secret). Unfortunately, there is a set of circumstances by which our digital signature strategy can be compromised and rendered useless.

In Figure 8-10, we can see how an attacker can steal our electronic identity by substituting their private/public keys for ours. In this example, Bob creates and signs a message destined for Alice. Along its route, the attacker hijacks the message and destroys the original message sent by Bob. The attacker then creates a fake replacement message. The problem is that this message needs to be signed with Bob's private key. However, it is customary to send your public key along with any message that you sign in case the recipient does not have it. The attacker in this example uses this to his advantage by signing the fake message with his private key and including his valid public key as a replacement for Bob's. In the case where this communication represents the first between Bob and Alice, or if it is one of a few infrequent exchanges between Bob and Alice, this attack will probably work.

The reason it will work is that Alice may or may not have retained Bob's public key. She may also reason that Bob may have changed his public key.[6] Remember that in the real world, the PKI is quite large. If users receive a large number of signed messages, they will probably purge their public keys occasionally. Thus, the substitution of identities may go unnoticed in the large application of this technology. Once this substitution of identity is made, Alice will accept the fake message without question.

This problem of identity substitution is the last hurdle that must be cleared before we can place our trust in our PKI. The underlying problem is that because this potential masquerade can occur, we find that our trust in the system wanes. So what can we do?

[6.] Changing asymmetrical keys is not as common as rotating symmetrical session keys, but it is good key management practice to occasionally refresh user keys. Therefore, it would not be all that out of the ordinary to see someone's keys change occasionally.

Trust in a PKI

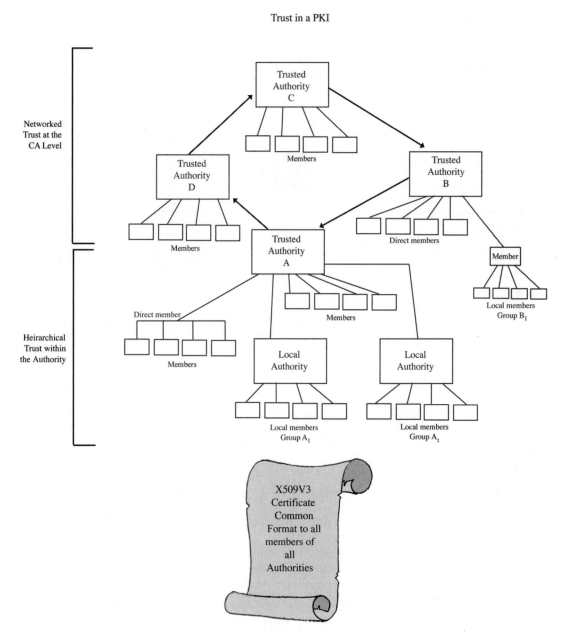

Figure 8-9   Trust relationships in a widespread PKI-each member is issued a certificate that verifies signature.

Compromising Digital Signatures

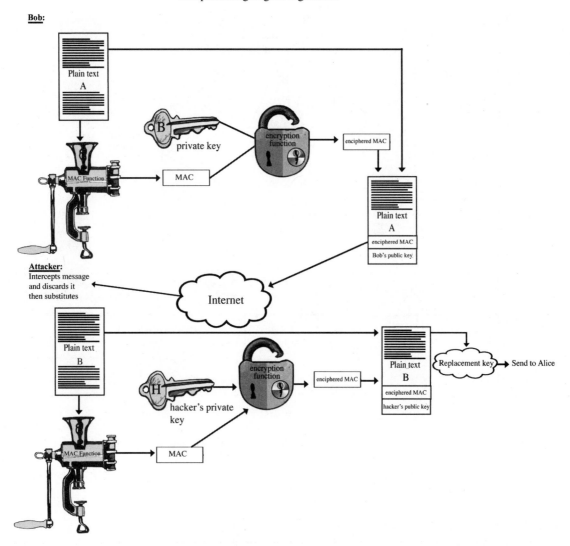

Figure 8-10   Attackers can defeat our asymmetrical method if they hijack Bob's message, destroy it, create and sign a new message with the attacker's private key, pose as Bob, and send along a new public substitute key that Alice will think is legitimate.

The answer to this identity issue is not all that different from the problem of identity verification that banking institutions have had solved for years. Simply put, if we can verify that the public key accompanying the message and the cryptographic checksum is really Bob's, then we can accept the message. The PKI provides a mechanism for this validation and authentication service. It is the trusted third party and the digital certificate.

In the PKI, the trusted third party is responsible for key generation, key distribution, and maintaining digital certificates. This type of tight control enables the PKI to ensure that trust relationships will be valid. An improved method of using digital signatures combines the signature with the verification through digital certificates. This removes the possibility of identity fraud from our PKI. In this case, Bob generates the plain text, MAC, and digital signature with his private key as before. He attaches a copy of his public key and transmits the message to Alice. After receiving the message, Alice strips off the digital signature. She then recomputes a MAC based on the original plain text. She takes the digital signature and the public key sent by Bob and applies the decryption algorithm to them. The result of this is the original MAC calculated by Bob. If the two message digests do not match, then obviously the message is a fake.

However, if they do match, she still cannot be sure that the message is authentic until she verifies the signature. To accomplish this verification, she requests a copy of Bob's digital certificate from the trusted third party or certificate authority that sponsored Bob. The trusted third party creates a digital certificate including Bob's identification information, a copy of his public key, and other information about Bob's relationship with them. The **Certificate Authority (CA)** then computes a message digest of the certificate information. The CA then encrypts this message digest using their own private key to create a digital signature of the certificate about Bob. The CA then transmit the signed certificate back to Alice.

Because there are fewer CAs than users, it is reasonable to require the PKI users to retain copies of the CA's public keys. Alice would then use the CA's public key that she knows is valid to decrypt the signature on the certificate. She then recomputes the message digest of the certificate. If the message digest that she computed matches the one that the CA sent, then she knows that the certificate is authentic. She then compares the public key that Bob sent to the key that is included in the certificate. If they do not match, the message is a fake. If they do match, then she has authenticated that the message was in fact from Bob. This process is shown in Figure 8-11.

Certificate signing is the process by which the trusted authority applies its own private key to the message digest of each member's certificate to produce a digital signature on the certificate. This signature authenticates the certificate by binding it to the trust anchor via the signature process. Thus, when the certificate authority sends a copy of the certificate to the requesting verifying party, that party can use the authority's known public key to check the authenticity of the certificate. Once the authenticity of the certificate is verified, then the public key of the sender of a message can be used to verify the authenticity of the received message.

Although this information sounds complex, in reality it is not any more complex, from the user's point of view, than making a long distance phone call, or transmitting an e-mail. Either of those applications has an extremely complex series of behind-the-scenes actions or enablers. However, they are all transparent from the user. The same is true with verifying digital signatures using digital certificates.

The applications that support the use of a PKI for digital signatures and encryption provide the necessary abstractions that make user involvement as easy as the press of a button (see the lab exercises at the end of the text).

NIST endorses several algorithms for creating and verifying digital signature. These include RSA, DSA, and ECDSA.

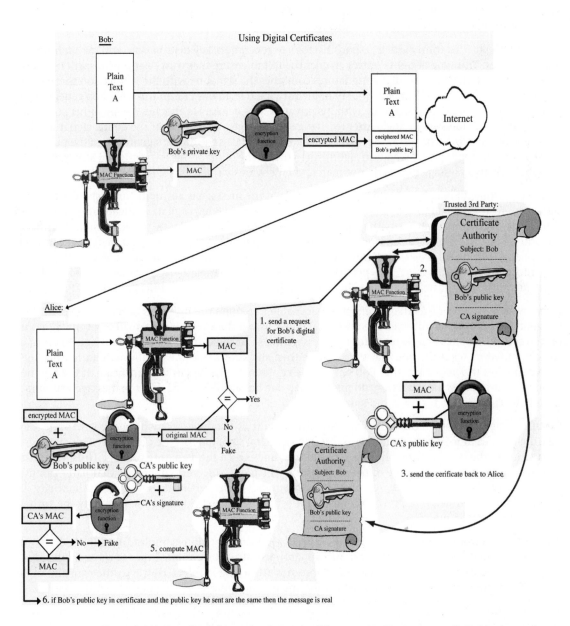

Figure 8-11 By using information from a certificate authority, we can verify Bob's electronic identity.

X.509 V3 CERTIFICATES

X.509 v3 certificates and policy constructs can be used to model trust relationships in cyberspace. The use of a standard is extremely important in the world of online business.

The X.509 specification is a part of the X.500 series of specifications. X.500 represents a set of standards for the implementation of a unified directory service on the net. **Lightweight Directory Access Protocol (LDAP)** is one of the X.500 protocols used to create such a directory service. By participating in the LDAP protocol, PKIs can share certificates and obtain authentication of identity through a convenient and widespread mechanism as shown in Figure 8-12.

In the LDAP environment, directory servers (represented as the squares) are distributed throughout particular domains. All members have their certificates stored at the directory of their PKI trusted authority (usually at the local authority level[7]). When a relying party requests an authentication, they utilize the LDAP request/response protocol to first find the correct server that has the certificate. If the server that the relying party contacts does not have a copy of the certificate in question, then that server responds with a referral to another server that may have the information in question. This referral process continues until the correct server is found. The server with the requested information then responds to the relying party with the certification requested.

Certificates are stored as objects in the directory. Each object has a particular type and an associated set of attributes. The X.509 certificate components are shown in Figure 8-13.

- **Version**—The version number needs to be specified to distinguish between the version of this certificate and other X.509 version certificates available. The default is 1. For a version 3 certificate, this needs to be specified in this field
- **Serial number**—The serial number is a unique integer value assigned by the trusted authority that created this certificate. The serial number is unique to this certificate
- **Signature algorithm identifier**—This field specifies the algorithm and parameters used to sign this certificate. This information must be consistent with the information specified in the CA signature field at the end of the certificate
- **Issuer's distinguished name**—This is the X.500 distinguished name of the trusted authority that is signing this certificate
- **Validity interval**—The validity interval is the duration of time, starting at a particular time and ending at a particular time, for which this certificate is valid. This information is tied to the certificate revocation list for the purpose of canceling and updating certificates
- **Subject's distinguished name**—The X.500 name of the entity whose key is being certified
- **Subject's public key information**—This is the field used for the authenticity checking process. This is a copy of the subject's public key, the algorithm that they use, and the parameter list associated with the algorithm
- **Issuer's unique identifier**—This field is used for further clarification of the unique identity of the issuer of this certificate
- **Subject's unique identifier**—This is an optional field used to further clarify the subject's unique identified
- **Extensions**—These are optional fields used to communicate policy, create a mapping between trusted authorities, and communicate certificate practice statements

---

[7.] Multiple entries can be stored at both the local authority level and at the root authority level.

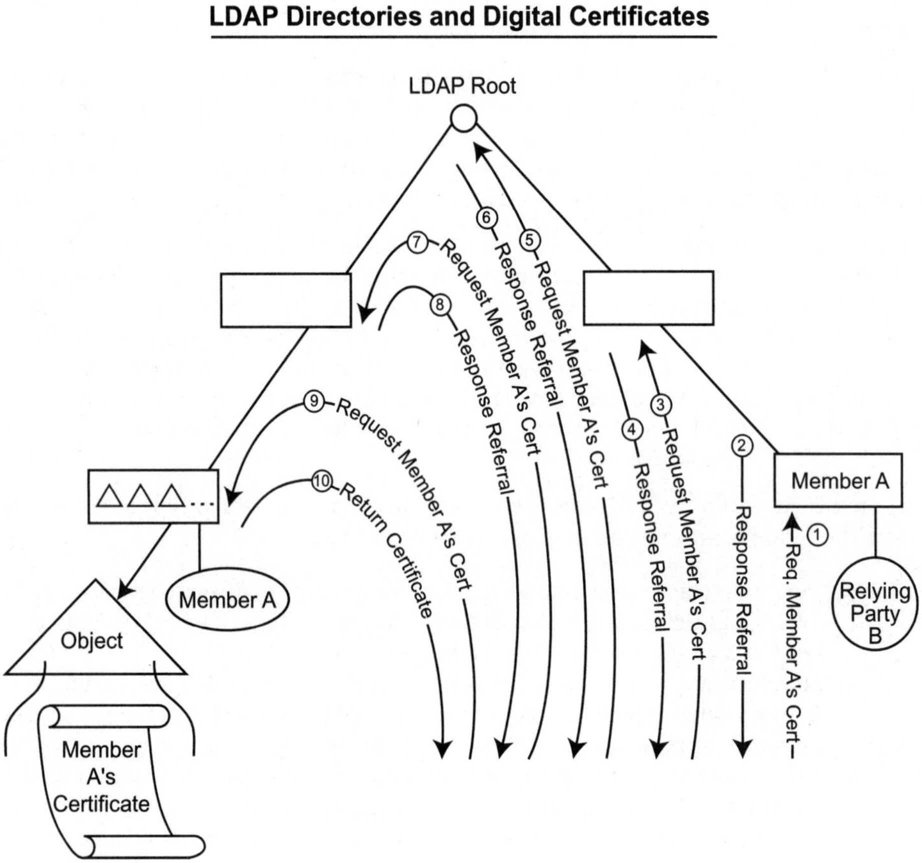

LDAP Directories and Digital Certificates

Figure 8-12 By using information from a certificate authority, we can verify Bob's electronic identity.

- **Signature**—This is the signature of the certificate authority based on the message digest of the other fields in this certificate

Certificate policies and certificate practice statements are used to define the certificate processes employed by a trusted authority. They are also used to communicate to the **relying party** (the members) what the particular certificates are for, how they were created, and how much trust you should have in them. Certificate policies also are used to define the limits of liability of the certificate authority. The following are some examples of various types of certificates:

- **Base trusted authority (CA) certificates**, described above, can be used as the basis for establishing trust between the CA and members, and thus extend trust to all of the member-to-member relationships

X.509 v3 Certificate

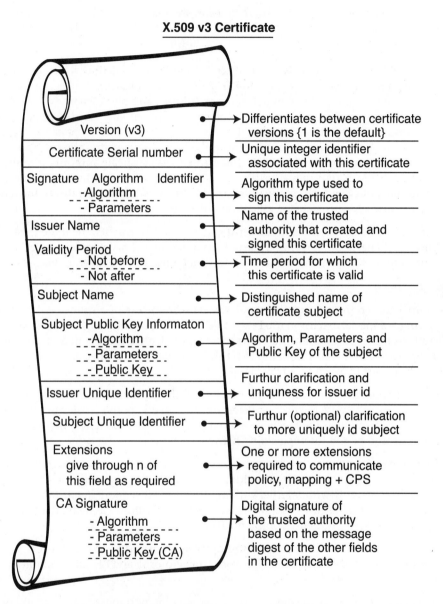

Version (v3)	Differientiates between certificate versions {1 is the default}
Certificate Serial number	Unique integer identifier associated with this certificate
Signature Algorithm Identifier -Algorithm - Parameters	Algorithm type used to sign this certificate
Issuer Name	Name of the trusted authority that created and signed this certificate
Validity Period - Not before - Not after	Time period for which this certificate is valid
Subject Name	Distinguished name of certificate subject
Subject Public Key Informaton -Algorithm - Parameters - Public Key	Algorithm, Parameters and Public Key of the subject
Issuer Unique Identifier	Furthur clarification and uniquness for issuer id
Subject Unique Identifier	Furthur (optional) clarification to more uniquely id subject
Extensions give through n of this field as required	One or more extensions required to communicate policy, mapping + CPS
CA Signature - Algorithm - Parameters - Public Key (CA)	Digital signature of the trusted authority based on the message digest of the other fields in the certificate

Figure 8-13 X.509 v3 certificate binds a user-distinguished name to a public key and a PKI identity.

- **Secure/Multipurpose Internet Mail Extension (S/MIME) certificates** are designed to support e-mail applications. These can be used to sign and encrypt e-mail and are the basis for single sign-on applications. This technology is addressed in detail in Section Three of the text

- **Secure Socket Layer (SSL)** certificates are used in many Web-based applications for secure client server access over the Net. This technology is also discussed in detail in Chapter 3

The extensions field of the certificate is where the certificate authority defines which policies (aka paths) are valid for the given certificate. According to RFC 2459, the certificate authority can use a policy qualifier field (part of the extensions field) to point to a certificate practice statement (via a URI). According to the American Bar Association: "A certification practice statement may take the form of a declaration by the certification authority of the details of its trustworthy system and the practices it employs in its operations and in support of issuance of a certificate…It may also be part of the contract between the certification authority and the subscriber." As you can see, the certificate authority formulates the use and extent of the certificate type in the certificate policy. The certificate authority then describes how it will implement that policy and the specifics of its contract with either the member or the relying party— the person requesting the certificate for validation purposes.

The stronger the certificate policies and the certificate practice statements, the more trustworthy the trusted authority will be. In other words, these policies and statements define how much confidence the certificate authority has in itself as a measure of how much risk it is prepared to take.

PKI STANDARDS

Interoperability between trusted authorities relies heavily on the use of certificate practice statements. **Policy mapping** is a special extension used exclusively between certificate authorities. This is the mechanism that allows the trusted authorities to work in concert. Unlike the hierarchical trust relationships discussed earlier between members and the PKI, this mechanism is designed as part of the networked trust that needs to exist between peer trust providers.

Through policy mapping, one CA can indicate that the policies of another CA can be considered equivalent. This is important because the policies determine the validity of the certificate for use in particular applications. Policy mapping is the mechanism used to smooth out differences between competing certificate authorities and permit interoperability between them.

As with all evolving technologies, it is best when, as an industry, we can observe certain standards for interoperability. This has long been the case with the worldwide telephone network, broadcast radio and television, and more recently with internetworking. Today, most vendors support the X.500 standards for directory services. There is growing support for X.509 v3 certificates as being the basis of trust relationships (part of the X.509 authentication framework).

Other standards include the **Public Key Cryptography Standards (PKCS)** for syntax and interfaces for deploying certificates, S/MIME[8], RFC 1305 Network Time Protocol, and RFC 2030 Simple Network Time Protocol.

PKCS standards are a good place to continue your investigation of standardization of PKI development and deployment. The standards were first distributed by RSA laboratories; some of these standards have since been adopted as the industry standard. Numbers 2 and 4 of the original draft are no longer active because they both have been incorporated into standard PKCS # 1. The following are the PKCS standards as they now exist:

[8.] Reviewed in Section Three of the text.

- PKCS #1: RSA Encryption Standard. This standard describes the RSA encryption process to be used in the digital signature and digital enveloping process. It utilizes the MD5 message digest algorithm and the RSA encryption techniques to form the standard
- PKCS #3: Diffie-Hellman Key Agreement Standard. This standard describes the Diffie-Hellman process so that two parties can, without prior arrangement, exchange secret keys
- PKCS #5: Password-Based Encryption Standard. This standard is designed to allow for the exchange of private keys from the trusted authority to the member based on a one-octet encryption technique
- PKCS #6: Extended Certificate Syntax Standard. This standard describes the use of the extensions fields of the X.509 certificate
- PKCS #7: Cryptographic Message Syntax Standard. This standard describes a standard for the data that may have cryptography applied to it
- PKCS #8: Private Key Information Standard. This standard describes syntax for private key information including the key itself, the identity of the algorithm, and a set of attributes defined in PKCS #9
- PKCS #9: Selected Attribute Types. This standard defines the attributes used in PKCS #6 and PKCS #7
- PKCS #10: Certification Request Standard. This standard defines how a request to the trusted authority for a digital certificate is made and responded to

Message digest algorithms MD2 and MD5 are also included in the RSA standards as being the hash algorithms of choice for all digital signature hashes.

As we can see in Figure 8-14, the PKI system has many parts. The trusted authority is the central player in this system and is also responsible for accommodating membership requests, such as enrolling new members and handling authentication requests. The trusted authority works with third parties to conduct verification procedures. Based on the successful results of this verification, the trusted authority creates and issues the keys and certificates for the membership.

The trusted authority needs to establish the X.500 directory services to promote the use and proliferation of digital certificates. The authority also issues certificate practice statements and certificate policies that determine the operation of the authorities. The trusted authority also reviews the policies, mapping, and statements of other trusted authorities to ensure interoperability.

It is important to note that in the event your organization wishes to become its own local authority, it will have to adhere to and provide these same mechanisms for the local membership. While this is not terribly hard to accomplish in technical terms, it can be a rather large and time-consuming process that requires significant project management (especially for a large organization).

As a result of all of this effort, the membership enjoys trust and is CAIN ready. The standards mentioned in this part of the chapter are not considered binding in any way. However, it is only through the use of and adherence to standards that these methods will become the trust fabric that we are hoping it will become.

OPERATIONAL ISSUES

The operation of a PKI is rather complex. As we mentioned earlier, the basis of the X.509 certificates is so that they fit into the X.500 directory access scheme. The LDAP directory access protocol significantly improves the operation of certificate exchange and authority checking. Directories make deploying and managing the PKI easier. Certificates are stored in the directory.

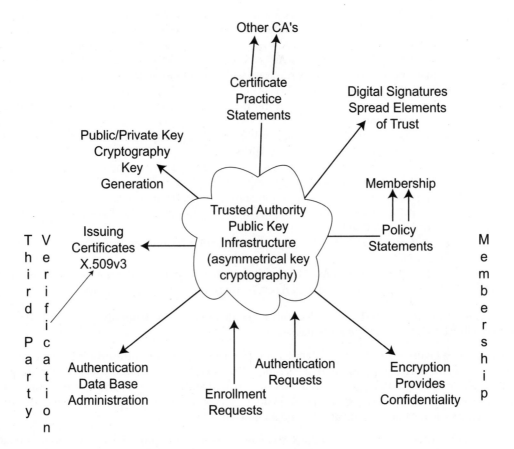

Figure 8-14   PKI system.

All of the operational issues of the PKI are described in policy statements and certificate practice statements. A certificate policy is "a named set of rules that indicates the applicability of a certificate to a particular community and/or class of application with common security requirements."[9] Certificate policies specify the key generation process, the key recovery process, certificate generation and distribution processes, certificate storage and archiving, and certificate revocation/renewal/update processes.

Key management is of vital concern in any PKI. As we stated earlier, while symmetrical algorithms are strong, they are definitely difficult to organize from a widespread use perspective. This is one of the strength areas of PKI and asymmetrical cryptography.

Several issues should be examined in more detail from the key management perspective:

- Key generation and distribution
- Key storage
- Key revocation

---

[9] Information Technology—Open System Interconnection: the Directory: Authentication Framework

- Key recovery
- Secret key exchange

Key generation and distribution can be done in a number of ways. First the PKI needs to select a key generation method. Most PKIs use the RSA algorithm. Then a second method must be chosen for private key distribution. A possible choice is the Diffie-Hellman method for key distribution. This is known as a key exchange.

Key storage must be looked at from two perspectives. The first is the storage and availability of the public keys. From this perspective the matter is one of establishing an X.500 directory service (LDAP implementation) and populating the servers with the public keys and certificates as described earlier in this chapter.

Key storage, from the point of view of the private keys, is more philosophically complex. In this case we need to consider the consequences of the PKI or any other governing body retaining copies of the private keys of the membership. For the most part, this is a really bad idea. In fact, it can degrade the trust of the organization because if the PKI trusted authority retains your private key, it is possible for the trusted authority to use it or give it to the government for search of your private files and correspondence. Worse yet, it might be possible for someone to penetrate the trusted authority's defenses, access your key, and use it to create your forged digital signature.

There is one instance where the PKI's retaining a copy of the private key makes sense: key recovery. Suppose you lose your key and cannot open important documents. As we have already described, the possibility of cracking the RSA keys is remote at best (computationally infeasible). For this purpose, it would be helpful to have access to a copy of your private key. This process is known as a **key escrow**. A key escrow means that the PKI has a means of reconstituting the key. This is done through a regeneration process based on information used at the key generation. This concept is generally used to allow law enforcement personnel to conduct a lawful search (with a warrant). Once a key has been recovered, the key is compromised and the information needs to be reencrypted with a new private key.

Key revocation in the X.509 system is controlled by a key revocation list. This list is maintained by the trusted authority and is tied to the validity field of the certificate. Once those dates have expired, the keys are revoked, updated, or replaced as per the policy of the PKI.

Secret key exchange **(digital enveloping)** is a primary use of the Diffie-Hellman algorithm. This secret key exchange is generally used to send a symmetrical key (sometimes called a session key) along with the ciphertext it will eventually decrypt. In this case we are using an asymmetrical algorithm to transmit the symmetrical key.

CAIN Revisited

Early on in the text we examined the CAIN principles of information security. At that time, the statement was made that if the CAIN principles were met, then our information could be considered secure. Throughout the last few chapters, we have been introducing topics that can be combined to form a cohesive security infrastructure aimed at meeting the CAIN challenge.

The PKI model discussed previously is a powerful infrastructure that can be utilized to ensure that our information retains its integrity and authenticity. Through the use of a well-established PKI, asymmetrical key cryptography can flourish. Through a combination of PKI, asymmetrical key cryptography, symmetrical cryptography, and digital signatures, we can completely secure our information.

As is shown in Figure 8-15, we can use asymmetrical cryptography to both encrypt and to sign messages. This forms the basis of many of the applications we will examine in Section Three.

It is important to be able to reproduce the process detailed in Figure 8-15. Mastery of this combination asymmetrical cryptography figure is essential for the information security practitioner.

After having studied both symmetrical and asymmetrical algorithms, we can see how the CAIN principles are addressed. As has been demonstrated, asymmetrical algorithms are quite reliable and can be very difficult to penetrate (providing the underlying primes are chosen to be very large). However, these algorithms are slow by comparison to their symmetrical counterparts. Thus, it is necessary to utilize both styles of encryptions in tandem to make realize all the benefits of CAIN.

CAIN can be addressed in the following way:

- Confidentiality is realized through symmetrical encryption. This is the fastest and easiest way to encrypt/decrypt bulk data. The confidentiality scheme will require the frequent rotation of symmetrical session keys. This key rotation is enabled using the PKI mechanisms described in this chapter
- Authenticity is realized through the PKI digital certificate process. It is important to note that not only people can benefit from certificates. The certificate process is extensible and can become the basis for applications such as code signing, secure e-mail, secure symmetrical key exchange for applications such as VPN, and single sign-on. The certificate is put into operation through the digital signature and authentication process. It is important that the certificates be accessible on the Net. This is why this process is so closely tied to the LDAP services of X.500
- Integrity is realized through the use of message digest functions and hashes. These same ingredients, which we use to produce a digital signature, are also used to perform integrity checking of a block of data
- Nonrepudiation is inherent in a strong PKI. If the PKI maintains rigorous discipline regarding the maintenance and administration of certificates, then only a particular member will have access to his or her private key. Thus, anything that is signed with that key represents the original signature of that member

These CAIN benefits are all derived from the principles of cryptography. For the most part, these benefits are available to organizations at little or no cost and obviously go a long way to meeting information security goals. This is why cryptography and authentication are wrapped so tightly around the core (information) of our model.

A PKI is complex to build and has many parts. There are trusted authorities, relying parties and members, directories of certificates, the certificates themselves, verification partners, keys, and competing authorities. These are all blended together to form a trust.

A number of standards can be followed to help this process work properly. The most important of these are X.500, X.509, LDAP, PKCSs, the RSA, Diffie-Hellman, and El Gamal algorithms.

PKIs have many operational issues, including key management, key generation, key revocation, key recovery, member verification, certificate creation, authentication, and management of directory services.

Through the use of asymmetrical cryptography, symmetrical cryptography, and hashing, we can satisfy the CAIN principles. The CAIN principles provide us with a solid foundation and verification of information security.

As this section of the text concludes, students should understand the important role cryptography plays in any information security plan. Through the combination of the security mechanisms described in this section, the CAIN principles can be realized. Through our cryptographic strategies and tactics, we can confirm that our information is secured.

In Section Three of the text, we will turn our attention to the security of the much broader (and much more difficult to secure) information system. Students will observe how much of the knowledge gained in Section Two will be incorporated into the securing of the information system. Many of the products and services utilized to secure systems, networks, websites, and applications have deep roots in cryptography.

STUDY QUESTIONS

1 **True____ False____**   Modular arithmetic is computationally fast.

2 Asymmetrical encryption is commonly used for all of the following EXCEPT ____. (choose one)
   a. E-mail encryption
   b. Digital signatures
   c. Online purchases
   d. Code signing

3 Until what year were only symmetrical cryptographic methods available? (choose one)
   a. 1972
   b. 1975
   c. 1981
   d. 1983

4 Asymmetrical cryptography uses a _____ secret. (choose one)
   a. Split
   b. Shared
   c. Mirrored
   d. Reversible

5 What is the most important benefit of asymmetrical encryption? (choose one)

    a. It speeds up the encryption process

    b. It makes e-mail easier to encode

    c. Only the sender knows to whom the information is going

    d. Messages can be transmitted openly and only the receiver can decrypt the information

6 **True____ False____** Asymmetrical cryptography requires more total keys than symmetrical cryptography.

7 What is the unique quality of asymmetric encryption? (choose one)

    a. The encryption key and algorithm are public

    b. The message can be sent only via a secure channel

    c. Only the sender and receiver can send encrypted messages to each other

    d. Keys are very short

8 ECC algorithms take advantage of_____. (choose one)

    a. Reversible mathematics

    b. Geometric properties of certain curves

    c. Polynomial qualities of large primes

    d. The limits of human memory

9 The oldest of the asymmetrical cryptosystems is_____. (choose one)

    a. RSA

    b. PKI

    c. El Gamal

    d. Diffie-Hellman

10 _____ can be defined as the strength and integrity of the in-place cryptographic authentication system. (choose one)

    a. Trust

    b. PKI

    c. Integrity

    d. Nonrepudiation

11 **True____ False____** The trusted authority normally destroys the private key of a member after issuance.

12 What permits interoperability between certificate authorities? (choose one)

    a. Content filtering

    b. Policy mapping

    c. Trust distribution

    d. Exchange authentication

13 A key generation process that is simple but produces keys whose relationship is difficult to discover has the characteristic called _____. (choose one)

   a. Confusion

   b. Practical irreversibility

   c. Impractical reversibility

   d. Production complexion

14 **True___ False___**   Asymmetrical cryptography is best suited for large blocks of information.

15 Which problem of public key cryptography is solved by the use of cryptographic checksums? (choose one)

   a. Destroyed messages

   b. Secure key exchange

   c. Verification of recipient

   d. Message substitution

16 To create a digital signature, a sender needs the plain text, the asymmetrical encryption algorithm, and _____. (choose one)

   a. The sender's public key

   b. The receiver's public key

   c. The sender's private key

   d. The receiver's private key

17 As the trustworthiness of a system increases, our _____ decreases. (choose one)

   a. Demand for keys

   b. Confidence

   c. Risk exposure

   d. Need for security

18 What determines the operating parameters regarding the generation, distribution, and management of key pairs? (choose one)

   a. The certificate policy

   b. The key policy

   c. The hierarchical policy

   d. The trust policy

19 S/MIME certificates are designed to support _____. (choose one)

   a. Client-server access

   b. E-mail applications

   c. Directory services

   d. Digital addressing

20 The algorithms of choice for all signature hashes in the RSA standard are _____. (choose one)

    a. MD1 and MD2

    b. MD3 and MD5

    c. MD3 and MD4

    d. MD2 and MD5

21 Which part of CAIN is realized through the use of message digest functions and hashes? (choose one)

    a. Confidentiality

    b. Authenticity

    c. Integrity

    d. Nonrepudiation

CASE STUDY

Back at Cureme Hospital, you are proceeding nicely at your assignment. One day, Dr. Looksee, the head of physician services, asks your opinion on how physicians might be able to electronically sign off on hospital orders and reports. He also wants to know if it might be possible to verify the identity of a communicating physician online so that physicians can gain access to confidential information. He figures that as technology grows, the lifestyle of physicians will change and they will want to work away from the hospital and have access to their patient data and the appropriate applications for using it.

Research and Comment

What do you think of the good doctor's comments? Given what we have learned in Section Two, what are some suggestions you might offer? Draw a diagram of the process that a physician might go through to work away from the office, maintain confidentiality, and digitally sign a hospital order for one of the doctor's patients.

Write a brief for Dr. Looksee explaining this technology in layman's terms. How can you convince him that the solution is realistic and workable? How can you convince him it is secure?

SECTION III

Information System Security

OVERVIEW

Section One described for us the difference between information and the information system. We needed to make this distinction because, as we saw in Section Two, securing the information itself is a completely separate process from securing the information system. We learned how to use various cryptographic methods to meet CAIN and privacy objectives for information security. We also observed that these cryptographic applications are used to encapsulate the information in a hardened barrier that can be penetrated only by those with the proper privilege and keys. This information security coating stays with the information wherever it goes—inside or outside the information system.

The information system, on the other hand, is large and difficult to completely secure. The information system includes the hardware systems, operating systems software, networks and network infrastructure, accounts, and applications of various kinds. Each of these components of the information system may have extremely complex operating parameters and may be more or less vulnerable to a security breech. Security for the information system needs to be planned both at the system-wide level and at each of the subsystem levels.

A difficulty with securing the information system is it typically is part of an open network and can be attacked from countless sources, both internal and external to your organization. The access potential to any system on the Net is enormous and can be difficult to predict.

Finally, the information system is made up of a combination of older proven software applications, operating systems, networks and protocols, as well as newer software components. In the case of older software, most of it was designed at a time when security was not a high priority. Systems and networks tended to be mostly private. It was often the case that a software designer was more trusting of their peer applications and the design was focused more on interoperability than on security. Newer applications probably were designed with more of a security focus, but because they are new and have not had a sufficient burn-in period, they may not be as reliable as the older stalwarts. In either case, there are usually more security concerns than solutions regarding information system components, thus making the possibility of an information system security failure always possible.

As was stated previously, the possibility of accounting for all of the possible holes in the information system, let alone closing them all, is unlikely. Combine this with the vulnerabilities and unpredictable behavior of the people using and operating the information system, and it becomes almost a certainty that the IS will be compromised at some point. This may occur as the direct result of a system or network attack (e.g., DDOS) or as the result of a virus or Web-directed attack.

The layering of the information system is why our security model itself has so many layers. We need to invoke a model that forces the hacker to penetrate layer upon layer of the information system before getting close to information at the core. This technique is known as defense-in-depth. The information system is addressed at the outer layers of the information security model. Via these outer layers, we address the areas where network and security managers should remain vigilant. Unlike our cryptographically oriented core, security implementations of the outer layers of the model cannot be quickly planned and implemented. Rather, addressing security at these layers is more of a continuous improvement process. OS hardening, information systems architecture and design, utilizing cryptographic methods for network encryption, Web services security, and the eight Ps of security (people, perseverance, pervasiveness, product, policy, planning, procedure, and process) need to be addressed, planned for, constantly monitored, and continuously improved (as described in Chapter 4).

This text has two purposes: First, it serves as an introductory text on the topic of information security and the application of cryptographic methods; second, it is meant to provide a survey of the state of the art of information system security. The first of these purposes was served in Sections One and Two. The state-of-the-art security survey for information systems is addressed in this section.

This section addresses four of the most significant topics:

- Access control to our information, systems, files, applications, networks, and physical premises
- Improving IS security through enhanced network design using cryptographic methods, system security, and OS hardening
- Understanding malware
- Securing Web services

Section Three concludes with a comparative analysis of all the techniques discussed in the text. This discussion will effectively position students to make informed choices when planning and deploying information and information security strategies and products.

SECTION GOALS

Upon completion of this section, students should be able to do the following:

- Discuss the application of Access Control Lists (ACLs)
- Detail the use of various file-level protections
- Demonstrate how to check for changes in system application and file content
- Describe a content-aware application
- List the four-step OS hardening process
- Detail the IPsec and SSL secure cipher methods for network cryptography
- Draft a design of a totally secure VPN pathway across the Internet
- Illustrate a network design including a firewall, DMZ, screening router, choke points, bastian host, and proxy server

- Understand the various security methods that an be applied to client server configurations
- Discuss the anatomies of viruses and worms
- Present an effective strategy and product regiment for combating malware attacks
- Conclude the course by effectively solving the case study questions in a clever and creative manner by utilizing the tactics described in this text

KEY ELEMENTS TO SUCCESS IN MASTERING THIS SECTION

To master the topics in this section, students should

- Pay particular attention to the discussion of application, file, and system-level security suggestions, because these represent the next layer in the information security model beyond the core
- Devote time to understanding the VPN secure tunneling methods, because these are increasing in popularity. By having command of these services and procedures, security professionals will be well positioned to provide immediate impact to their organizations in this high-profile area
- Concentrate on the development of a strategy to combat malware attacks because these are fast becoming the largest drain on information security resources
- Complete the case study projects throughout the text to gain practical experience in the design of an information security system
- Take the CD-based course self-test to increase confidence and test skills

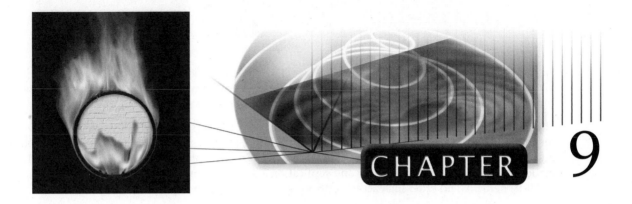

CHAPTER 9

Securing the Information System

Any sufficiently advanced technology is indistinguishable from magic.
—Arthur C. Clarke from *Technology and the Future*

Up to this point in the text, we have focused on the security of information. The idea is that information could be completely secured by the application of methods that satisfy the CAIN principles. In Section Two of the book, it was demonstrated that all the parts of CAIN could be effectively realized through the application of symmetrical cryptography, asymmetrical cryptography, digital signatures (cryptographic checksums), and the evolution of PKIs. Given that all of these are readily available, easy to use, and inexpensive, it is safe to say that we have satisfied the requirements of the inner three layers of our model.

At this time it is important to begin to expand our discussion to the protection of the information system. As we have already determined, information systems are difficult to completely secure. However, we really do not need them completely secure because our information is now protected in its own right. The idea of information system security is really to create barriers to entry, which make trespass difficult for would-be attackers. By taking this approach, we are able to control the pace of intrusion. Through the use of intrusion-detection systems, we are able to isolate and possibly track the attacker.

As is suggested in the quote at the beginning of this chapter, much of technology applied to the security of the information system appears magical. It is important for the reader of this text to have an understanding of the nature of these devices and techniques as well as their applications.

This chapter presents an overview of information security techniques, which address security of the following:

- The physical premise that the information system is located on
- The control of access to the premise and applications
- The applications themselves
- Systems
- Networks

Please note that in this section of the text, we overview a great number of technologies. Although we will take a somewhat high-level view of these technologies, we will endeavor to take a more in-depth look at those technologies that expand the use of cryptographic methods to secure the information system.

The information security model proposed in Chapter 1 addressed the security of the information system at the four outermost layers. Authentication and verification, Layer Three, has a dual purpose. With respect to information security, Layer Three is addressed through the implementation of a PKI. With respect to information system security, authentication and verification is addressed through the use of explicate access control lists, Kerberos and other such access controls, screening routers, and physical security.

Level Four, OS hardening, addresses the steps that can and should be taken to maintain the integrity of the operating system. Many of these techniques may seem rather simple, but they are essential to stabilizing the operating environment.

Level Five, information system architecture and design, addresses the placement of strategic network resources, security software, and intrusion-detection mechanisms. This level is normally the focus of many security plans.

Level Six, web security services, addresses the security of the open internetworking business environment. In this layer, we once again see a focus on cryptographic methods as the basis for secure transactions.

The outermost layer, the eight Ps of security, was addressed to a large extent in Chapter 4. This layer is specifically designed to address the user community. As mentioned earlier, design should occur from the core out. The outermost layer reflects the policies and procedures that communicates how the other six layers work, why they are there, and how the users should interact with them. This layer is of vital importance because it links the user to the security plan.

Chapter 9 focuses on Levels Three (from an information system security perspective), Four, and Five of the information security model. It provides students a feel for the breadth of technologies and strategies that can be used to implement information system security deployments. We conclude with a discussion regarding strategic placement of IDS system components, content scanning software, virus protection software, and Internet security measures.

 To successfully complete this chapter, students should pay particular attention to the following:

- The concepts of physical security and the various factors that are considered essential to properly validate information system access
- The use of access control lists for both file access and network access
- The concept of hiding and encrypting files on a system
- OS hardening procedures
- Integrity checking of information
- Techniques for creating network chokepoints
- Incorporating intrusion-detection systems in the architectural plan
- The use of VPNs for secure connectivity across the Internet
- The concepts of network cryptography

The material in this chapter presumes that the reader has had introductory exposure to concepts of networking and operating systems. Information security specialists generally have expert knowledge in these areas. This chapter provides some of the details behind the networking and system technologies, but it should not be considered a substitute for formal training in this area.

PHYSICAL SECURITY

Physical security of the information system may be perhaps the most underappreciated aspect of security planning. Thus far, we have spent two-thirds of the text considering how to best isolate and protect the electronic representation of information. We have concluded that the implementation of rigorous cryptographic methods will ensure that the CAIN principles are satisfied. However, what about information that is simply left in a file cabinet or on a desk overnight? Is this information at risk? What about the computer system in your office, or your laptop? Do improper security procedures leave you vulnerable? How well do you check the background of people working in your office complex? Do you monitor access to sensitive areas in the company, where primary information stores are located? How much do you really know about your business partners? Are they allies or foes?

As was discussed in Section One, the majority of information security breaches occur from within the community of trusted insiders. This community consists of employees, business partners, clients, and management. But what about the cleaning people? Are they to be trusted? And how about the other tenants in your building? Are they trustworthy?

A popular tactic for gaining access to information and to information systems over the years has been to use social engineering techniques to gain unauthorized access. The first attempt at a security breach should be to simply ask for what you want. If you call people and tell them that you are from the IT department and that you need to work with them to conduct a routine audit of their system, they will probably believe you. Simply ask the people to temporarily change their passwords so that you can gain access, or give them a disk (which contains a Trojan of course) and a set of instructions that will perform an auto audit of the system, and most users will run it with no questions asked. These kinds of problems can compromise the most secure information security plans. Obviously, education of the user community is a key ingredient to thwarting this behavior. Another way to avoid becoming victim to unsavory characters is to deny them access to the organization to start with.

The same philosophy holds true for your garbage. A significant portion of identity theft starts in the dumpster. Throwing away receipts with credit card numbers, bank statements, medical records, and the like can lead to serious trouble. It is important that organizations control access to all of their information, both online and on paper.

An organization that allows a cleaning crew in after hours without proper background checks is taking a significant risk. What better way to get information than to vacuum a few rugs in the middle of the night and have the next few hours to crack systems?

Physical security can be broken down into three parts:

- Access control
- Environmental control
- Premise security and waste management

The information system security plan and the user policies and procedures need to be closely aligned on these issues. It is important that the plan balance these measures appropriately against the amount of online information security to be taken. These measures are equally as important as those taken to secure information in the electronic realm.

ACCESS CONTROL

Access control applies to many parts of the information system. This includes access to files, the systems themselves, the networks, and the physical premises. **Access control** is defined as the control of admission of a user to a trusted area of the organization (physical or electronic) based on the implementation of an access control policy using products, procedures, access control lists, and an authentication information base.

It is advisable to establish access control policies for each part of the information system considered a high-security area. Policies should be conceived to reflect who has ultimate control of the information. For example, in the government environment, information classified as secret or above falls under the control of a central authority. Even the author of the information looses control of the information once it becomes part of the system. This is known as **mandatory access control**.

Discretionary access control policies give the owner of the resource control of access. In this case the author of the information or the owner of the system determines the access requirements.

Once it has been decided who controls the information or resource, the policy should stipulate the required authentication level. This can range from a user simply being part of an access control list, to subjecting the user to a comprehensive identity check. The level of authentication and identity verification required will dictate the products and specific procedures that must be followed.

In general, every user of the information system needs to be enrolled in the authentication information base. The enrollment process will have minimally three phases:

- The application phase
- The verification phase
- The establishment phase

The application phase is initiated by the user (or some agent of the user, e.g., personnel) requesting permission for the user to be included into the access control system. The user will request access to information, resources, and physical locations based on a number of criteria:

- Job code or position
- Project requirement
- User group
- Work location
- Other specific need

The verification phase requires the organization to check the validity of the request itself with management or other parties who have a detailed knowledge of the user's requirement. The verification phase is also the time in the process to verify the identity of the user. Often a comprehensive background check of employees is made during the hiring phase. All that is required is confirmation of identity via an internal resource (e.g., personnel).

The enrollment of the individual concludes with the establishment phase. During this phase, users are granted access to the requested resource and have their identity matched to the specific authentication factors being utilized. The access control process is shown in Figure 9-1.

Once the enrollment of users into the access control system is complete, users can begin to exercise the access privileges for which they have been approved. This use of the system occurs when the **authentication factors** that have been validated during the enrollment process are presented by the user to gain access.

Authentication factors are methods that allow the organization to verify the user's identity based on information stored in the authentication information base. These factors include **knowledge factors**, **possession factors**, and **biometric factors**.

Knowledge Factors

Knowledge factors can be thought of as information only the user knows. The most common example of a knowledge factor is a password. Most systems require that users log in with a simple password. These

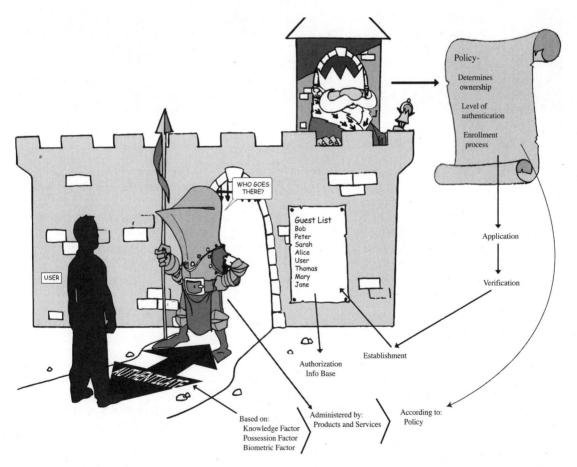

Figure 9-1   Access control.

passwords are created by the user and are refreshed from time to time. The user should not share the password and should choose a password of significant strength so that it resists cracking. As Chapter 5 demonstrated, password cracking becomes computationally infeasible when the number of characters in the password exceeds seven, is of mixed type (alpha, numeric, symbols), and avoids the use of common words. Other examples of knowledge factors are Personal Identification Numbers (PINs), personal information (e.g., your bank account number), and information about your personal relationships (e.g., your mother's maiden name).

Creating Strong and Useful Passwords

Password creation must be done with a great deal of care. If the passwords are too short or contain too many common words or phrases, the password is weak and easy to crack. Conversely, by making the password too obscure, the user cannot remember it.

The solution is a method that is easy to use, complex enough to be useful, and is easy for the user to remember. We will construct a password as a phrase of at least eight characters. We will substitute the number zero for any "o" in a wo rd, the exclamation point for the letter "l," the "&" for the word "and," and the "%" for a "p." Obviously, you can modify this scheme to fit your personal use. Given the phrase, "I ate pizza and soda" as a potential password, we would use "I8%!zza&s0da" as the pass word. This meets all of the criteria for a strong password.

Some of the strengths of knowledge factors are as follows:

- They are ubiquitous. They are in your memory, so that they go wherever you are. This also means that wherever you are when you access the system, the knowledge factor is right there with you
- They are inexpensive. Passwords are an inherent part of most systems and can be implemented with little or no additional cost
- They are easy to use. Knowledge factors are commonplace and familiar to the users making them intuitively obvious
- They are reliable (given they are chosen correctly). Password-choosing criteria need to be incorporated into the policies of the organization

Unfortunately, knowledge factors have some glaring weaknesses, which most of us are all too familiar with, such as:

- Being subject to memory loss. It is important to stress in the policies we develop that the strength of knowledge factors is found in the fact that they are committed to our memory. This prevents inadvertent thievery of the factor. We do not want to write the knowledge factor down, which exposes it to theft. This unfortunately means that certain knowledge factors (especially those that we do not access frequently) are subject to memory loss, e.g., we forget a password. Memory loss shows up in maintenance of the system
- Being subject to guessing (especially if we are not careful in how we choose a PIN or a password). Again, by design we would prefer for the knowledge factor to be chosen

randomly, which all but eliminates brute-force attacks. This, however, will increase the probability of forgetting the secret. On the other hand, by utilizing more common terms and sequences of characters or numbers, we open the secret up to more creative attacks which involve guessing. We need to employ a balanced approach to solving this problem

- Being subject to social engineering tactics. People can be easily tricked into revealing their passwords. This is a common attack in which the hacker simply asks for the password under the guise of performing an installation, or upgrading the person's account in some way. Other tactics involve asking a person to temporarily change a password to a known string (last name and a number) so that work can be done in the next ten minutes and then the password can be reset.

Additionally, the tactic of **shoulder surfing** involves watching someone key in their password and memorizing the keystroke pattern. This was a major source of phone card theft cases in the early 1990s. This threat can be minimized by using longer passwords. The sheer number of keystrokes makes it difficult to memorize the pattern.

Cracking passwords using tools or intuitive guessing is becoming a relatively easy attack. If a person uses too short a password, brute-force guessing becomes very easy. If a person uses a common name, tools running dictionary attacks can be effectively utilized. An exhaustive search of the entire English dictionary can be done in seconds. Using the NT Password Cracking Utility, demonstrated in the password-cracking lab included in Appendix A, you can see that a common dictionary attack can be executed in a matter of a minute or so.

The weakest link in this chain is, again, the user. Guessing of passwords often coincides with guessing the obvious: names, pet's names, children's names, names spelled backward, parts of phone numbers, birthdays, etc. It is imperative that these types of codes be avoided entirely

- Being subject to poor administration. The knowledge factor policies should reflect the need to change passwords (update them) frequently. The time of refresh and the length of the password are tightly coupled as was demonstrated in Chapter 5. A password of five characters may be useful for only a couple of hours, six characters for a week, seven characters for a month, and eight or more characters for months. The refresh time needs to coincide with these guidelines.[1]

Additionally, administrators need to be sure that the password registry is secure and encrypted, preventing any attacks on the server itself. As is demonstrated by the password-cracking experiment, an entire registry can be discovered and attacked in minimal time

Knowledge factors represent a secure access control mechanism. They are by far the most popular of the methods and are easily implemented. They also integrate well into most product sets.

Possession Factors

Possession factors are something that only the user has. Possession factors are very common. Access cards, keys, credit cards, tokens, and the like are all examples of possession factors. Possession factors

---

[1] These guidelines are constantly changing based on the computing resources and effectiveness of the attack strategy. It is recommended that the refresh policies be less than one half the predicted cracking time of the password.

should be kept private and not be shared with or borrowed to others in the organization. Possession factors possess the following strengths:

- They are common and familiar. People use possession factors all the time and trust that they are secure
- They are reliable. Cards, rings, pins, and smart devices are engineered to be virtually indestructible. Possession factors have been well established in the industry for some time and have been engineered to endure. The readers that accommodate the devices are also very reliable and common at this time
- They are cost effective. Most of the items in this product set have become commoditized and are affordable to make and purchase. The readers are also affordable and have become reliable

Some of the weaknesses associated with possession factors are as follows:

- The reading devices are sometimes difficult to use or become soiled and operate ineffectively
- The possession factor itself is something that can be lost or stolen
- The possession factor is subject to duplication. However, smart chips and other advances can help render the factor inoperable after it has been stolen or it can force an identity check on usage
- Certainly possession factors are subject to social engineering. People ask to borrow or inspect a possession factor and then they use it to gain unauthorized access
- Possession factors are normally part of a system including the readers, wiring, and the factors themselves. This means that there is a larger management burden than either of the other two factors (knowledge or biometric). This is the only one of the three methods that requires actual asset management of the factor itself

Possession factors are useful because they solve multiple problems. For example, by including a bar code, personal description, organizational description, and a picture on a card, the factor can serve multiple uses such as an employee ID card, an entry card to a building, and system access. It can be used as a charge card for on-campus purchases. Despite its weaknesses, its flexibility makes possession factors popular.

Biometric Factors

Biometric factors are something that the user is or does. Biometric factors can include retinal scans, fingerprints, voice prints, facial geometry, signatures, and palm prints. In recent years, the technology that enables the use of biometric factors has become reasonably priced and far more reliable than the equipment of even five years ago. This technology is growing rapidly and has become widely accepted in the industry.

The recognition characteristics shown in Figure 9-2 should give the reader some idea of how these technologies work. In general, most of these devices are constructed to scan an image and store minutiae, or localized points of reference, for future comparisons. These files are encrypted and stored. When the person presents the factor and challenges the system, the readers scan the body image again and compare the localized reference points to determine a match. It has been shown that this technique of not storing the entire image can be done quite effectively.

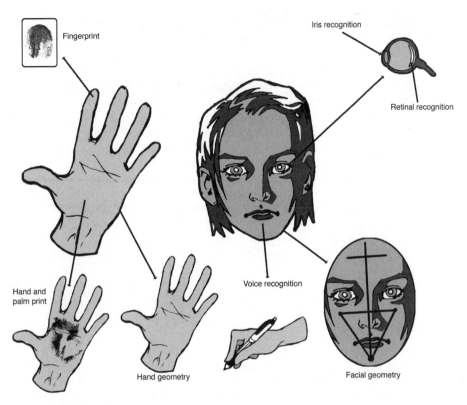

Figure 9-2 Recognition characteristics.

The following are the strengths of biometric factors:

- The costs associated with the use of biometric products has become moderate and affordable. The devices that scan and compare the factor presented used to be cost prohibitive. That is no longer the case
- The products are remarkably simple to use
- The factor cannot be lost or stolen
- The factors are difficult to forge and counterfeit
- The user cannot lend or give someone else the use of their factor. This is an important component of the biometric factor because it significantly reduces the potential for a user to compromise the system while attempting to be accommodating

The following are some of the weaknesses of the technology:

- These devices are still considered part of a niche market. Therefore, most firms that are creating and manufacturing this equipment are scattered and economically vulnerable. Most of the large firms OEM this equipment and resell it under their label. This leaves the client vulnerable for service and product support

- False enrollments are a weakness of many of the technologies that are associated with biometric factors. These errors occur because the enrollment process is complex. First are normal enrollment issues associated with erroneous data entry on the part of the operator setting up the account. Next are the problems of the scanner misrepresenting the image, which will cause the enrollment to be invalid. Then the possibility that a person can alter the biometric (intentionally or inadvertently) exists. This can occur if, for example, the person gains or loses too much weight (in the case of facial geometry), or a burn can alter a person's fingerprints. All of these issues can create a false enrollment, which later on translates into false negatives and false positives during operation
- False positives or false acceptances occur when the person is permitted into the system fraudulently. In other words, a person gains entry to the system because the reader or identification method is faulty. False positives are the one type of error that is most dangerous to the information system. In the case of the false enrollment of the false negative, the user can be locked out. This situation can be easily corrected via a reactivation or reenrollment. The false positive can, however, create a situation where an attacker is granted access
- False negatives or false rejections occur when the person that should be permitted into the system is rejected because the pattern matching algorithm or the scanner are not working correctly. This can also occur as a result of false enrollment. False negatives are not generally regarded as serious errors; rather, they are considered an inconvenience

Combining Factors

Studies indicate that any one of these factors used alone can be defeated or return false results. These same studies have also shown that security increases dramatically when any two of the factors are combined. In fact, the studies indicate it really does not matter which two are combined because all pairs yield similar results. Most banking applications, for example, rely on a possession factor (the ATM card) and a knowledge factor (the PIN). This combination is currently the most popular.

More and more, we are seeing the biometric factor combined with the knowledge factor. Many of the inexpensive thumbprint scanners used to control access to a PC also come with a password option. Thus, when people log on, they first scan their thumbprint into the system and then enter a password. Both must be correct for the user to gain access. This type of biometric/knowledge factor combination helps to reduce (almost eliminate) the possibility that the geometry of the thumbprint could be inaccurate or create a false positive.

Finally, these studies indicate that there is not much difference between using combinations of two factors and combinations of three factors. It appears that the benefit of using all three factors does not provide enough benefit to offset the additional cost.

While all of the access control methods described above can help organizations in maintaining discipline and order with respect to enforcing asset permissions, it should be stressed that a strong access control policy is required to make physical security work. As was addressed in Chapter 4, users represent the weak link in the security enforcement chain. People are susceptible to social engineering techniques, but machines are not. Generally, this is because the users try to be polite and accommodating, and that can get in the way of effective security. For example, **tailgating** or opening the door with your security pass and allowing someone else to follow you into a restricted area without presenting their authentication credentials, is a major user problem. While this may seem polite, it is a major breach of policy and can lead to trouble. Strong policies need to complement strong physical security measures.

ENVIRONMENTAL CONTROL

Security of the information system takes many forms. As we have seen in Chapter 1, the information system is large and many factors dictate its security. Up until now, we have focused our discussions on security risks that involve an overt attack on the information or information system by a hacker. However, in planning the security of the information system, other problems can compromise the system integrity. Environmental complications can compromise the integrity of the information system. Integrity is an important part of security. The environment in which systems, networks, and information stores operate must be secured.

Twenty years ago, most computers were warehoused in large computer rooms. These computing facilities were designed to meet stringent fire, heating, ventilation, air-conditioning, power conditioning, and antistatic guidelines. Many facilities in place today still require this type of planning diligence. More recently, information system manufacturers have improved the engineering of their equipment so that the need for these special rooms would be significantly reduced. Much of computing equipment in use today requires minimal HVAC, power, fire, or antistatic preparation. Still, it is wise for us to review some of the important concerns regarding the planning of a secure environment, for completeness' sake.

Fire Protection

Fire safety is a primary concern in any security plan. Fires in office complexes can be serious, life-threatening problems if the fire accelerates quickly. Planning for fire prevention involves detection of a fire, alert of emergency response, and automatic suppression of the fire.

Fire-detection devices range from manual user-operated alarms to sensitive ionization sensors that react automatically to the chemical compounds in smoke. Some detection systems measure the temperature in a room or the rate of change (rise) of the temperature in a room. Flame detectors react to the infrared light given off by a flame. Whichever detection method is chosen, it is important that the devices be installed liberally throughout the facility. A major concern for information security planners is that much of the equipment that makes up the information system resides in closets and confined spots. These locations are usually out of the normal pathway of the user community and as a result are largely unmonitored. Locations of this type most definitely require fire alert devices.

Once a fire has been detected in the facility, several steps need to occur. First, the alarm system in the facility needs to be triggered. Second, as the evacuation of the facility is under way, the alert needs to be relayed to the fire department and the crisis-management team.

The alert should also trigger the automated suppression system that exists in the secure area. Because most of the fires in which components of the information system are involved are electrical fires (Class C by code), the agents that douse the fire must be nonconducting. Until 1994, the most common fire-suppression agent for Class C fires was halon. Under the Clean Air Act, halon products were banned from production. Existing halon systems could continue to be used, but eventually the systems would need to be recharged and eventually replaced. Halon is harmful to the ozone layer of the atmosphere. Several new products are approved substitutes for halon: HCFC-123 and -124, carbon dioxide, trifluromthane, FE-13, FM-200, PyroGen, Dynameco, and Phirex+, among others.

Flood Protection

Flooding caused by natural disasters or plumbing system malfunctions can also be a threat to the information system. This is especially true because many facilities maintain their computer operations centers in the basements of buildings. As most insurance companies will attest, damage from flooding results in more claims per year than any other threat to property. Unfortunately, unlike fire-suppression systems, pumping and drainage facilities are only minimally effective in dealing with rapidly rising water levels. The destructive power of water is especially damaging to computer equipment. It is important that information security planners check with local authorities to determine the flood planning for the community and the history of flooding in the area. In areas where flooding is likely, it is important to plan computer facilities on the upper floors.

Disaster Strikes New Jersey Phones

In September 1999, Hurricane Floyd struck the East Coast of the United States and caused tremendous flooding. One of the communities hard-hit by this disaster was Rochelle Park, New Jersey. This small town located in northern New Jersey was home to a key Verizon Communications telephone switching center. A significant amount of the information system owned by Verizon was located in underground facilities. As the floodwaters rose, the center fell victim to the devastation. A significant part of northern New Jersey was abruptly left without phone service (including cellular service and emergency services phone services) as it attempted to recover from one of the state's most widespread disasters.

Air-Conditioning Power Conditioning

Heating, ventilation, and air-conditioning (HVAC) concerns are also key environmental factors that need to be considered. HVAC planning is a major concern in three areas: the common work area, the computer operations centers, and satellite facilities (e.g., wiring closets and satellite equipment rooms). HVAC technology is used to monitor and control the temperature, humidity, air exchange, and static electricity in an environment.

Computer equipment can generate a significant amount of heat. This same heat can seriously damage media or the computer equipment itself. For this reason, it is important that the temperature inside facilities be regulated so they never exceed eighty-five degrees Fahrenheit. Protection of this type is administered through two systems. Rooms must be sized and fit for air-conditioning platforms. It is important to have a qualified HVAC mechanic review the power consumption requirements of your systems and properly size an air-conditioning system to meet those specific demands.

This AC system needs to be backed up with an emergency shutoff system that will trigger automatically if the room temperature climbs above 110 degrees. These systems are relatively inexpensive and easy to retrofit into an existing site. They can be tied into system management systems and can be triggered to gracefully shut down the systems in the affected areas. A hard stop should be applied if temperatures in the room continue to rise beyond 120 degrees.

Humidity is another environmental factor that needs to be managed. As the amount of humidity in a room is reduced, the amount of static charge in the environment increases. While static electricity is harmless to humans, it can kill computers. Electrostatic discharge precautions are a must for preventing damage to computer circuitry. Humidity levels of between forty and sixty percent are optimal for computing environments.

Another HVAC concern is maintaining a positive pressure environment in the computer facility. This means that when opening a door to the facility, the air pushes out of the room. This act will keep dust particles from entering the facility in large quantities.

Power management systems and **uninterruptible power supplies (UPS)** are also very important in organizations where near 100 percent uptime is critical. These systems essentially monitor the power flow to the facility and in case of a power outage, they provide backup power. These systems are generally battery fed. However, propane and gas generators are also available. Power management systems also provide power conditioning services to monitor and normalize power spikes and fluctuations.

Another significant electrical concern is proper grounding. Grounding electrical circuits has the primary benefit of making the service safe. Improperly grounded systems do not provide the electrical service with the proper return path to ground. The user can inadvertently become the return path, resulting in injury or death. Grounding is also important to information system networking technology (LANs) because the ground provides the reference point for network signaling.

PREMISE SECURITY AND WASTE MANAGEMENT

The final component of physical security is managing the security of the premise and its contents. Much time and effort is spent building significant electronic barriers around information. That time and effort can be wasted if the very information we are trying to protect is exposed to attackers in its paper form. While paper records are certainly being consolidated in this era of computerization, in many industries the paper backup of electronic information is mandated. Thus, it is important to take the following precautions in securing the facility and managing corporate waste:

- Using physical barriers, mantraps, electronic surveillance, and security checkpoints as is warranted by the nature of your business creates a solid perimeter defense, cuts down on social engineering attacks, and creates the feeling of strong security. With the attention received by precautions that many federal and state agencies are required to take, many industries are following suit. The **American Society for Industrial Security (ASIS)** is an organization that focuses on this technology and offers training and education in this area. The Office of Homeland Security is another source that can provide organizations with direction and information about deployment of these capabilities. These sources also are good for recommendations on appropriate precautions for particular scenarios

- Shredding old or unwanted documents that contain sensitive information is another critical step that can be taken in the fight against social engineering attacks. From all accounts, information obtained from discarded documents is the number-one cause of identity theft. A careful program of shredding documents, document control, and screening waste management resources can significantly curtail dumpster diving attacks

- Locking portable devices is a must in organizations that have made the change from desktop to laptop devices. Cable locks that plug into the side of the laptop in a predetermined lock port and then can be attached to a nonremovable part of the desk unit are very useful

- Impedance checkers are also useful in a corporate-wide physical security plan. Impedance checkers measure the impedance on the line of a device connected to the network. If the device becomes disconnected from the network, a change in the impedance on the line triggers an alarm in the measuring device. This device can then alert premise security, which can immediately lock down that part of the facility and search for the missing device

- The act of tailgating occurs when a person opens a door or passage using an approved method of entry. The tailgater follows behind the person and enters at the same time. One way to prevent this is to place guards at the entry point. Other ways include the use of passcard-activated turnstiles that limit entry or exit to one person at a time
- Video surveillance has become much more affordable. The quality of recognition software available has improved considerably and can be used to simultaneously monitor an entrance and to identify those passing through the field of view of the camera. Video surveillance systems can also be taped so that law enforcement officials can replay activity to determine who was in a particular place at a particular time
- **Electromagnetic radiation (EMR)** is given off by electrical pulses conducted inside a wire. It is also possible to obtain this same phenomenon from LED devices. These emissions can be analyzed to determine the data traveling down the wire or appearing on the screen. **TEMPEST** is a technology that can be used to monitor EMR and actually reconstruct screen shots and data streams from the EMR patterns
- Physical network security can be obtained through a variety of methods. One method is through the use of a pressurized conduit. This method would only be used in a maximum-security environment, but it illustrates the lengths to which methods can be taken.

    Wireless LANs have grown in popularity because of their convenience and portability. The 802.11b wireless standard provides wireless connectivity of 11 megabits per second to minimum distances of 300 feet. For personal LANs, there is the 802.15 variant known as Bluetooth. Bluetooth provides wireless connectivity of 750 kbps with minimum distances of 30 feet. It is important to take precautions against **war driving** when exacting physical security on the LAN. War driving is the modern-day equivalent to the war-dialing scenarios of the 1970s and 1980s ("dial for a modem"). War driving is simple: take your portable device with an 802.11b-compliant NIC in promiscuous mode and roam the streets of your city in the car. As you pass facilities with wireless 802.11b running in an unprotected mode, you will be included as part of their network. Then through the use of packet sniffing equipment, you can eavesdrop on conversations

- Secure server areas and satellite equipment rooms can be secured with programmable/mechanical door locks or through the use of electronic password locks. All entrances to these facilities should be secured because this can be a source of a physical attack
- Perhaps the most important consideration in any physical security plan is to devise a method to report crime. Through the reporting of suspicious persons or activity, crime can be prevented or reduced

APPLICATION AND FILE PROTECTION

Information is composed of two parts: the processed data (which normally resides in files) and the applications that process and retrieve data. The files are generally controlled either through the operating system or the database management system. The applications that access files can be homegrown (custom applications), part of the database management system, or off-the-shelf specialty products (e.g., Word, Excel, etc.). Security of the applications and files is a level above security of the information (CAIN principles). At this next layer up, we are generally more concerned with access controls, sign-ons, privileges and rights, format control, change control management, and usage monitoring.

War Driver's Toolkit

War drivers will normally be able to utilize 802.11b NICs running in promiscuous mode up to one-fifth of a mile from the target. Several studies have shown that in major metropolitan settings, war drivers were able to get connections to servers six blocks from the source.

A war driver will typically use a toolkit. The toolkit contains a mobile computing device, an 802.11b NIC, additional antenna when required, and network sniffing software. War drivers can supplement their toolkits with GPS devices to help them map the networks they find. They can also use smartware such as Network Stumbler (PC), MAC Stumbler (Macintosh), or Wave Stumbler (UNIX) that can help detect and track signals, monitor signal strength, and provide other information about the connection. A war driver will obviously want to use a network packet sniffer to be able to decode the information gathered. Examples of these are Ethereal and Air Magnet.

Most war driving can be prevented by turning on the proper encryption protocols. Cryptography should be used to hide the content of information transmitted on the Net and to authenticate the users. The **Wired Equivalent Privacy (WEP)** encryption protocol uses cryptography to encrypt the frames and hide information. WEP encrypts wireless communications using a symmetrical key algorithm that encrypts data between the broadcast point and the device. The standard does not discuss how the symmetrical keys are exchanged; this is left up to vendor implementation. **802.11i Temporal Key Integrity Protocol (TKIP)** provides for enhanced encryption that is superior to WEP.

The **802.1X** uses the **Extensible Authentication Protocol (EAP)** to authenticate users joining the wireless LAN (WLAN). In order to participate in a wireless session, the user must first pass the authentication test at the EAP server. Then the EAP server issues the new user a symmetrical session key that is valid for the current wireless session only. Cisco Systems has a version of this known as **Lightweight EAP (LEAP),** which is available although it is not a full-blown implementation of the EAP protocol and is somewhat less secure than proposed in the standard EAP recommendations.

It is advisable that all wireless connectivity be done outside the boundaries of the traditional corporate LAN on a **Demilitarized Zone (DMZ)**. The DMZ is a spot on the corporate network where all users can be screened and authenticated. Once validated, the user can access the corporate LAN via access services that are provided, such as the proxy server.

Finally, it is important to write proper WLAN policies. These policies should cover the use of wireless security protocols, the use of wireless Hot Spots (public wireless access points), and the isolation of wireless access services.

Access to systems that warehouse information obviously should be controlled. This is primarily done through the use of usernames and passwords. These mechanisms need to be regulated so that the passwords and usernames are not easy to crack.

A simple way to control what a person can do with data in a system is to restrict all user access to read-only data to diskless workstations. This restriction would allow the user to see information but be unable to copy, print, or redirect the output information. However, in the age of networked everything, this method is not very practical.

Organizations with large databases and access issues need to be prepared to control access via software methods. Access to the data stores can be controlled via operating system or the **Database Management System (DBMS)**. Access protection can be either access permit or access deny list via system or file **Access Control Lists (ACLs)**. Additionally, access control can be linked to the rights of a user to perform certain functions on the file. For example, one user may access the file with privileges to read, write, delete, and modify a file. A second user may have the right only to read the file (known as read-only access). Database management systems control similar rights. On a DBMS, a user may create, update, delete, read, modify, etc. These actions may govern actions of the database user regarding the access to files, reports, queries, tables, and views.

Structured Query Language (SQL) is a standards-based database query language that is common to most relational databases. SQL permits users to create tables, manipulate the data in the tables, perform data administration, and create queries (aka select statements) that can be used to extract information from the database. Through the use of the SQL GRANT and REVOKE statements, database administrators can control the privileges of users to access data and use certain commands.

Through the use of the NTFS file system, users can have password controls applied to files. In this system, files can also be encrypted and stored. NTFS is a replacement for the FATS and FATS 32 file systems commonly found on most Microsoft operating systems. NTFS enables local file security.

In both operating system and database-level access control schemes, it is possible to establish work groups. Work groups allow for common information to be shared between members of a common group. This access is determined on a need-to-know basis.

There are many other important application and file-level controls and security precautions that can be taken:

- Patching and code revision keeps software up to date with the latest revisions and patches. It is one of the most important steps an information security specialist can take in securing the information system. Management of the code levels and keeping the latest versions online ensures that the user is afforded all of the protections known to the manufacturer
- Application-level passwords and encryption are becoming more commonplace than ever before. The only drawback to this level of password protection or encryption is that it is offered on a case-by-case basis by various vendors and is not centrally coordinated. Although it is responsible to use such mechanisms, it also can be a source of frustration if the passwords or keys are lost. For organizations or groups planning to use these product features, it is a good idea to implement password control and key-recovery policies
- Assigning users privileges is an important system and application security precaution. The idea of least privilege was presented in the first section of the text. Essentially, it means that users will not be granted more permissions than is required for them to accomplish their particular tasks
- The type of file format can increase the amount of protection afforded by the system. Under the FATS and FATS 32 file systems, very little security protection is available to

the end user. Under NTFS, users can encrypt data and add passwords. In the UNIX environment the *des* command is available to encrypt data under the DES encryption standard. Under UNIX there is also the *crypt* command that allows for files to be encrypted. The method, however, is not nearly as secure

- Hiding files under Windows keeps files or directories from appearing in the explorer screens. Although this is an effective way to keep a casual intruder from finding files and directories, it does not stop someone from searching through the DOS-level directory trees and finding the files
- Checking for unauthorized changes to information or integrity checking of files is a good way to monitor what is perhaps the most difficult and dangerous of hacks: the unknown changing of information. These systems monitor the files on a system as well as the system registry for changes and modifications. The software is generally operating system type. Some of these products are free and others are available for a fee. Most have a notification agent (usually e-mail) that allows for the designated resource to be notified in the event of an unauthorized action. Most of these products also log events as determined by a profile established by the system manager. The following are just a few of the products that address this need:
  - GFI LANguard System Integrity Monitor from GFI software is freeware that can be used on Windows 2000 and NT systems. Visit *http://www.gfisoftware.com* for more information
  - Data Sentinel is a more high-powered and versatile product that can address many different file integrity monitoring needs. Visit *http://www.ionx.co.uk* for more information
  - Tripwire for UNIX and NT is perhaps the most established product of the group. This product can monitor up to twenty-four system and registry attributes. Visit *http://www.sales@tripwire.com* for more information
  - Intact from pedestal software is a system-monitoring tool that is multifunctional and monitors systems for changes and integrity. Visit *www.pedastal.com* for more information

SYSTEM SECURITY

Host-based operating system security addresses weakness in the default operating system. Operating systems are the part of the system responsible for creating the ease-of-use abstractions that hide from us the details of program execution, network access, memory management, file access, peripheral control, and user administration. Every operating system is configured and constructed somewhat differently. There are many types of operating systems, operating system vendors, and versions of operating systems in the same family. Keeping track of and addressing the needs of all of these disparate systems are perhaps the most difficult parts of managing the security of systems. In order for system security measures to be effective, the security policy must be applied ubiquitously across the enterprise. This can be difficult if some operating systems afford the organization more or less security measures than others.

In large organizations, with a mobile workforce and lots of systems, scaling the system security implementation can be difficult. In some organizations, simply accessing all of the machines is difficult because they are not all online and accessible in a stationary spot. Thus, most organizations have to resort to automation of system security policies so they can be enforced and monitored.

OS hardening is the process of locking down a system to ensure it is not providing too much access or too many unnecessary services. Many system administrators take an unbalanced approach to system management and security posturing. By this we mean that the system is either too open or too secure. Systems that are too open generally are systems that have too many unused services enabled and have lax provisions for access control. Systems that are too secure can become unusable. It is important that the system manager start the hardening process by assessing the needs of the organization and by matching those needs to a system security policy on a system-by-system basis.

OS hardening is generally done via a five-step process:

1 Tighten all directory and file permissions.

2 Remove all unnecessary services (network and system).

3 Set accurate user permissions.

4 Apply all vendor patches.

5 Monitor system integrity.

The removal of unnecessary services is an important aspect of system hardening. Most system managers overlook this simple step and expose the systems to unwanted intrusions. On many systems, for example, after the new operating system is installed, the system enables all protocols on the network. This is risky because if your organization does not use a specific protocol, it may not take precautions against it at the routers. (It is easy to forget to deny a particular protocol type.) Thus, all services that are not being used, or accounts that are inactive, should be disabled. You will also want to turn off all NetBios file- and print-sharing capabilities because these can be vulnerable access portals for a hacker.

Of these five steps the application of all system patches and upgrades is perhaps the most important. You should make it policy to apply all vendor patches regardless of the schedule of listed improvements. For example, do not assume that a particular software upgrade for a print driver does not affect you because you do not use the printer, or that a small patch should not be applied because it affects a service you do not use. In fact, these very patches can contain valuable security upgrades that are important for the firm.

For example, suppose a vendor becomes aware of a security hole in the system that it produces either as the result of a customer finding a problem or through internal testing. If the vendor makes a public statement regarding the problem, this will alert the hacker community that such a problem exists. The hacker community can discover the nature of the bug and exploit it before a vendor can distribute the patch to the installed base. (Remember, some users never upgrade or are slow to react.) Instead, the vendor can "slip" the patch into regularly scheduled release upgrades or upgrades that address niche problems of an unrelated nature.

KEY POINT

Performing all system upgrades is essential in the successful management of system security.

Systems should also be monitored by system integrity checkers (similar to those mentioned above for files) that can monitor the OS for changes to configurations, settings, accounts, passwords, files, software versions, and registry entries. These products essentially create hashes of files, objects, and registries after an approved change. These hashes are periodically recalculated and compared to determine if anything changed. Depending on the sophistication of the system, these comparisons can be very precise. One particular product from WetStone Technologies, SMART Watch, is a capable product that can be used to conduct this analysis. This particular tool is proactive and can restore and reverse changes after they have been discovered.

License management and auditing is the next area of system monitoring that affects security. It is a criminal and civil offense to steal intellectual property or to use that property without the proper license. It does not matter whether the offense was deliberate or not. The fines can be substantial. Courts have ruled that it is the responsibility of the organization to check to be sure that the licenses for software products running on their machines are accurate and up to date. There are a number of software products that perform this type of service.

Install a personal firewall on each of your systems, especially portable devices. These systems can regulate and monitor access to your system and also perform other integrity-checking functions. Personal firewalls often include virus protection software and perform Trojan detection as well. You should check your system for viruses and Trojan horses on a regular basis. You also need to update your virus definition files regularly. Check the McAfee (PC) and Virex (Macintosh) websites at least once a month for updates if you are using those particular products.

SYSTEM ACCESS CONTROL

Access control on the system level is usually done through a username and password. These security measures are effective only if the password policy is sound. The passwords must be at least eight characters and should not include common words or names. Passwords must include other nonalpha characters such as numbers or punctuation. Passwords such as *1ht0*3q are considered strong. One of the main problems with these types of passwords is that they are difficult to remember. Another problem is that most of us have more than one account and, thus, can have multiple usernames and passwords to track. Given that these passwords need to be reset often, keeping them all current and memorized is difficult.

More sophisticated access control mechanisms can be created using what is known as **Single Sign-On (SSO)**. SSO is considered the ultimate login process. A user logs into a requisite security server and performs the normal login and verification procedure. From that point, all client server login requirements are handled automatically for the user without the need to log in to each service the client wishes to use along the way. Microsoft began providing the Microsoft SSO under the Windows 2000 platform. This system is based on a combination of Kerberos and SSL security applications. Novell makes a product known as Secure Login, which is based on similar technology. A problem with SSOs is they have to share a common security server, protocol infrastructure, and policy definitions. This is currently difficult because many of the applications we use and systems we run are based on many small market niche products that are developed outside the scrutiny of major software providers. There are many who argue as to whether true SSO actually exists.

Plans are currently under way for the standardization of the **Security Assertion Markup Language (SAML)** as a potential solution to this problem. SAML is a language that will be used to send security information across Web sites. This language is based on three kinds of assertions about users: security assertions, decision assertions, and attribute assertions. Security assertions of the user are based on the assertion of identity. Once a user is validated, these assertions remain in effect. Decision assertions describe what the user can do for one instance of an interaction (not indefinitely). Attribute assertions are primarily aimed at determining the privilege of the user or level of authority the user has. Through the use of a standards-based language, true multivendor interactions can be realized much the same way that HTML has enabled the creation of platform-independent applications for the Web. To provide this same level of seamless integration, SAML will provide for binding of assertions across platforms.

The RSA ClearTrust application is a Web-based access management solution. RSA is the creator of SAML and many other security technologies. ClearTrust enables SSO, authentication policy management, identity management, and security across multiple applications.

An alternative to SSO is the concept of **password synchronization**. Password synchronization is based on an inexpensive concept of a server that essentially manages all of our passwords and usernames. Every application and user is managed through a central server. Accounts are established and access rights to applications and systems is granted through the password synchronization server. This alternative manages the amount of passwords in a typical user-operating environment, but it does not economize the number of user keystrokes. In this system, the user must still log in to each application and system and enter all requisite information. The difference is that the synchronization maps the username and passwords so that they are all the same. One major drawback to either of these systems is that if attackers get into the system, they are in every application and secure area to which the user has access.

NETWORK SECURITY

Network security planning is currently in vogue. During the last ten years, the area of network security has overshadowed the majority of other security areas. This is a result of the expanded role that the Internet plays in both our personal and business lives. It is unheard of for an organization not to be connected to the Net. Companies are constantly reminded of the dangers of Internet connectivity by the ISPs, news media, and the very companies that sold them the network connectivity gear in the first place. These players have created network security hysteria in the market. This overemphasis has led to confusion in planning for information security.

Another reason that this area of security has become so predominant is because it offers us a logical place to watch for our adversaries—outside the system. The view of many security specialists is that the network is the common ground where hackers can be confronted before they gain access to the system and, ultimately, the information. This philosophy is centered around the concept of creating **choke points**. Choke points are the place where all inbound and outbound network traffic to an organization can be examined. Choke points are established through the use of network architecture and design techniques.

Because of this increased attention, vendors have created many methods that can be applied to create layers of security inside the network. These techniques, products, and services are easy to deploy. Although the word "firewall" has become synonymous with comprehensive information security, it is a common myth that this means your network is completely safe. Network security is a part—albeit a large and important part—but only a part, of the overall security plan.

Precautions with respect to network access need to be taken seriously. Companies need to protect themselves from the unknown adversaries that lurk in the shadows of the anonymous Internet. In no way should anyone try and take anything away from the many fine products and services available that afford us network security, but it is important to view security as an overall strategy and not just one product. Many companies sacrifice proper information security planning because their network vendor sold them a network security solution under the guise of a total solution. Organizations have purchased several highly redundant solutions, which overemphasize one aspect of network security at the expense of others. And worse yet, some organizations have expended excessive amounts of capital on network security and have had to make cost-cutting sacrifices in other equally important areas.

By taking appropriate steps at each layer of the information security model, and by avoiding redundant countermeasures, organizations can achieve balance in their plans. Network security is the second-most-important area of cybersecurity next to securing the information itself, but it is also the most expensive security solution area. It is important to make the right choices in deploying network security measures. The balance of this chapter is aimed at highlighting some of the most effective network security choices that will complement the overall information security posture.

KEY POINT

For students who need to review some TCP/IP basics, Appendix B provides a TCP/IP cheat sheet and pointers to sites and resources that may be helpful.

NETWORK ARCHITECTURE

Most network architectures today are based on TCP/IP. TCP/IP is a relatively old networking technology and includes little in the way of native security functionality. However, based on the success of the Internet and its astronomical rate of growth, this old and underpowered protocol has become the basis for the second-largest form of communication on the planet (next to the worldwide telephone network).

In the late 1960s and early 1970s, the ARPANet ran on a protocol known as **Network Control Protocol (NCP)**. This protocol was limited and required that communicating hosts be of the same type. While this concept is inappropriate given today's technology, in the 1970s that technology was sufficient. Networking was considered an extension of the operating system, and the computer giants were unwilling to comply with open standards. However, given that the Net was small and of little or no commercial value, this was an acceptable posture.

In 1983, TCP/IP was introduced as the replacement for NCP. Within two years of its introduction, TCP/IP was powering the Internet, which at the time consisted of approximately 1,950 hosts. The Net, however, continued to grow at an exponential rate. By 1990, approximately 100,000 network hosts were on the Net. With the commercialization of the World Wide Web and the advent of inexpensive personal computers and network connectivity gear, the Internet growth accelerated further. By January 1997, more than 16 million servers were connected. (This number did not account for the number of dynamically addressed clients connecting through ISPs.) As we saw in Section One of the text, current projections suggest that there are in excess of 500 million interconnected users at this time and more than 100 million domain names. The initial designers of the 1983 TCP/IP could not have predicted these staggering numbers.

Three points should be made to properly outline our discussion of network security:

- TCP/IP was never intended as a protocol for the primary interconnection between hundreds of millions of users and millions of hosts
- At the time of TCP/IP's conception, most networks were interconnecting trusted users over semiprivate and completely private facilities. The user base was primarily from academia and government. Computer crime was not a concern at the time
- The number of network connectivity devices in the Internet are vast. These devices form a "living" network that is constantly changing, making it impossible to map the Net. Subsequently, most everything running on the Internet is outside of our control

Thus, we have to implement network security on the TCP/IP-driven Internet on two levels: First, network security architectures need to implement the segment of (RFC-based) suggestions on improving TCP/IP security that are commensurate with the organization's usage; Second, network security architectures need to implement those products, configurations, and services that influence the strong management of Internet traffic and thus permit tighter security control. In other words, because we cannot control much of what goes on inside the Internet, we really need to take control of network access and screening at our own sites.

Students of information security should be well schooled on the inner workings of networks. In particular, students should have a sound understanding of IP addressing, the use of TCP ports, the structure of TCP and IP packets, an understanding of UDP, an understanding of IP version 6, and the operating parameters of the TCP and IP protocols[2].

KEY POINT

The Internet as we know it today is significantly different in terms of size and scope from what it was originally designed to do. TCP/IP has an addressing upper bound of 3,758,096,384 possible addresses (assuming no wasted address space). There are currently more than 500 million users, 100 million domain names, 16 million known servers, and countless numbers of internetworking routers that need addresses. Given these numbers and the poor address utilization characteristics of TCP/IP networks, that address space (under v.4 of TCP/IP) is all but used up. IP version 6 has addressed this problem in large part but is still not widely understood or implemented. Thus we are operating in an environment that is overutilized, underpowered, and not security focused.

Screening Routers

The basic network security technique found in most networks involves the creation of network choke points. Most of today's corporate networks are designed to accommodate open interaction between clients and servers. Most of the LAN technologies used today support peer-to-peer communications. In general, networks are designed so that inside the trusted domain of the corporate backbone, communication transactions occur openly. Unfortunately, this trust can be violated and networks can be compromised in a number of ways. Internally, trusted insiders can take advantage of that trust and access services for which they are not authorized. Externally, our networks can be easily penetrated by hackers in a variety of ways if the designs are too lax. Choke points are network architecture designs that force traffic to or from restricted (high-security) or suspect areas to funnel through a particular set of devices. These devices (normally routers and firewalls) can be configured to inspect the traffic for various anomalies. As can be seen in Figure 9-3, choke points are a natural consequence of network architecture choices.

There are many ways to implement choke points. **Screening routers** are perhaps the most well-known method of creating choke points. A screening router is a router that sits between the corporate entity and the Internet. The router acts like a guardian or sentry protecting the entrance to the private areas. The screening router filters traffic via ACLs that check the protocol headers based on **ACL rules** that

---

[2] TCP and IP are actually two different (related) protocols. IP operates at the OSI layer 3 or routing layer. TCP is a transport (layer 4) protocol that provides end-to-end services.

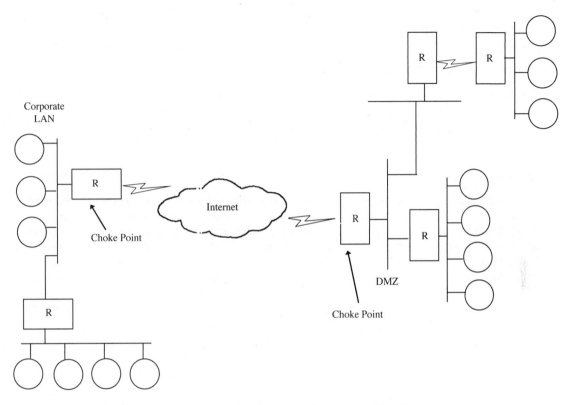

Figure 9-3   Choke points are important architectural considerations.

are established by the network administrator. Most router operating systems (known as the IOS) supply commands that can be used to create the ACLs. These commands are normally of the following form:

> *LIST # n ACCESS {permit or deny} protocol, source address, source port, destination address, destination port*

These commands form a script that dictates the action of the screening router. The commands in the script add to the functionality defined by the previous commands. Thus, the effect of the script is cumulative. These actions define the security posture of that portion of the network. For example, suppose that an organization had a need to connect to the Internet and wanted that interconnectivity to be screened and secure. In this case, the script might look like this:

> *List #1 deny tcpip all all*

> *List #2 permit tcpip 112.111.12.23 all 81.99.101.11 80*

The first of these two commands essentially tells the screening router to close the port to every one in both directions. This means that everything is denied unless explicitly permitted. This is called a closed posture. The second command opens only Port 80 on node 81.99.101.11 to all ports from node 112.111.12.23. All else is denied.

Conversely, we could adopt a more open posture by creating an ACL that looks like this:

> *List #1 permit tcpip all all*
>
> *List #2 deny tcpip 111.12.21.10 all*

This combination creates a situation where everything is allowed unless explicitly denied.

Depending on which posture you start with dictates how extensive the ACL will be. These commands allow us to monitor which source addresses, contained in the IP packets, are permitted in and which ones are not. They tell the router which destinations packets can flow to, and which type of protocol to use. This is considered to be a very basic form of screening and is generally regarded as the basis of a more evolved network security plan.

Demilitarized Zones

The next step that has evolved in the creation of choke points is the addition of a buffer zone or **Demilitarized Zone (DMZ)**. A DMZ is an intermediate LAN that sits between the two screening routers and is a neutral portion of the network. By this we mean that whatever is on the buffer LAN is open to the public (or nonrestricted user group permitted by the ACL defined on the outermost router). The backend screening router will have a more tightly controlled ACL, which will restrict access and thus be harder to penetrate. As Figure 9-4 shows, this is a good solution for keeping a secure organizational network and an open Web server.

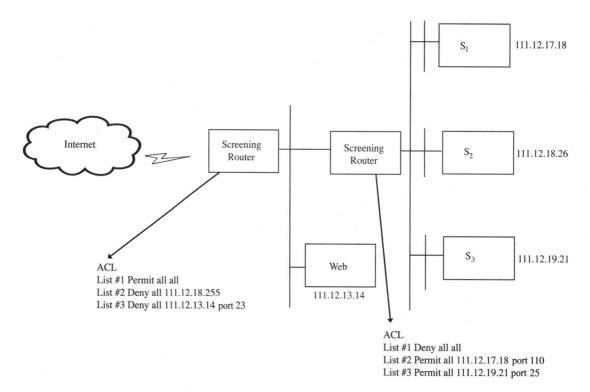

Figure 9-4   An example of a DMZ.

In this example, the first screening router permits all traffic as a base posture. It then explicitly denies traffic to the center private subnet and the telnet port (23) on the Web server. The backend router takes a closed initial posture and explicitly permits access where warranted. The backend router permits the flow of information to only those ports (110—POP 3 and 25—SMTP) where the mail servers are, but no other systems or ports. Further development of the idea would need to be constructed for outbound traffic and systems. Specialty devices such as the SonicWALL are specifically designed for the purpose of creating this DMZ. This particular is shown in Figure 9-5.

Bastian hosts are systems that reside on the DMZ buffer. These hosts are atypical in their design. Primarily, these hosts have most of the standard services normally provided on a host turned off. All network protocols are disabled except the one (usually TCP/IP) that is used for primary access. All ports within the TCP environment are closed. All files on the system are provisioned as read-only. Other unnecessary access mechanisms (accounts, authentication services, etc.) are turned off. Because a Bastian host is considered compromised from the very start, it is not considered trustworthy.

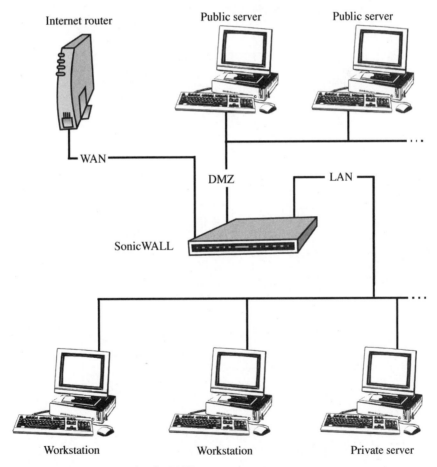

Figure 9-5 An example of a DMZ.

Proxy Servers

Proxy servers are servers that act as intermediaries between the public network and the private servers. Proxy servers are sometimes called **application-level gateways**. If we think of the function of the proxy server in terms of the OSI model, the proxy server strips away all of the protocol encapsulation and gets to the raw data (the service request or message). This message is then redirected to the server by the proxy server using the proxy's network address and trust. The server then responds to the proxy appropriately and the proxy, in turn, resubmits the information through the network to the client (in the nontrusted space). This process is computationally expensive and slows the transaction process down. But as you can see in Figure 9-6, this security precaution allows for four controls that would otherwise be difficult or impossible to implement:

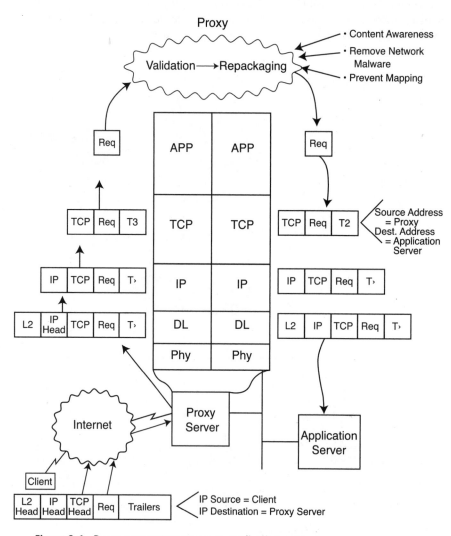

Figure 9-6 Proxy server operates as an application gateway.

- **Content checking:** Content checking is possible in the proxy because the packets are resolved back to the data level. Data can be examined for appropriateness and malware before reassembly
- **Header replacement:** Removal of harmful protocol attacks occurs because the packets are stripped off and new protocol headers are applied
- **Authentication:** Authentication of the client for access to information based on the request is possible because the proxy can have access to information data bases that can correlate the request to an authentication level. Further, the use of digital signatures can provide an alternative method of authentication
- **Hidden addressing:** This method, like network address translation, prevents mapping of the network. This is accomplished because clients connect to the proxy and only the proxy knows the location and address of the application server

Network Address Translation

Network Address Translation (NAT) is a useful add-on to prevent the mapping of the network. NAT devices convert between the real Internet addresses assigned to an organization and an internal-only set of proprietary addresses. NAT devices work by simply pooling valid IP addresses and temporarily assigning them to entities that need to communicate via the Internet. The internals of the device simply maintain a translation table for the duration of the connection. At the logical conclusion of the connection, the valid Internet address is simply recycled. This tactic maintains privacy of the internal addresses because users from the suspect Net never learn the real identification of the internal system. Further, by constantly changing the addresses (rotation as a result of recycling), an attacker never has a clear picture of what is where. This technique is shown in Figure 9-7. Proxies need to be set up in accordance with access security policies. There should be procedures in place for denying service requests in addition to the accept-and-pass strategy mentioned above.

According to RFC 1918, NAT is most often used to map from legitimate (sanctioned) IP addresses to the nonroutable private address space allocated as:

CLASS A:	10.0.0.0	...	10.255.255.255
CLASS B:	172.16.0.0	...	172.31.255.255
CLASS C:	192.168.0.0	...	192.168.255.255

Firewalls

Firewalls by definition are combination products that provide the functions of screening routers, proxy servers, network address translation, plus stateful inspection. **Stateful inspection,** or dynamic packet filtering, is an advanced form of filtering based on the state of the enterprise application environment, the state of the network, and the policies of the security plan. Firewalls perform stateful inspection at level three of the OSI model. This inspection creates a table of active sessions and the applications driving them (either internally or externally).

For example, suppose that a client requests an FTP session with a server. When the server generates the upload connection (transmits the requested information) using a particular port, the firewall grabs that port number and monitors the actions that follow.

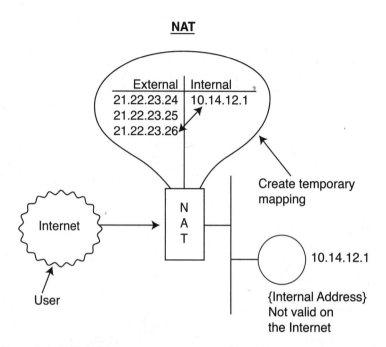

NAT

Figure 9-7   NAT devices create a temporary mapping between an internal address and an Internet address.

First, it temporarily enables the port and grants the access (if the policy allows for it). Once the session is under way, the firewall makes sure that the use of the session is legitimate. Once the session is terminated, and the transmission fulfilled, the port is once again closed. Thus, we have a more secure environment than can be achieved through simple packet filtering. This method prevents rogue processes (Trojans) from establishing unauthorized network connections. It prevents someone from utilizing a port inadvertently left open or unguarded for attacking the system. Through the use of the proxy and NAT capabilities, the firewall can also hide servers, examine content, and rewrite packets.

It is easy to see from this example how organizations may believe that with a properly configured firewall, their security requirements and policies can be satisfied. It is important to realize that this discussion can lead one to believe that the firewall is easy to use and that the coverage is everywhere. In reality, firewalls are expensive, need to be replicated at every entrance to the network, and require significant (and well-coordinated) scripting and configuration management to maximize their effectiveness.

Another important concern with the use of this technology is that it needs to be applied discriminatingly. It is easy to overuse this technology. Given a large organization, thousands of connections can pass through the firewall. This can lead to overexamination of the information, which can slow down performance.

Virtual Private Networks

VPNs are a significant and somewhat recent advance in network technology. VPN provides both secure and cost-effective networking. Until recently, most networking needed to be private to be secure. In other words, organizations made significant investments in private leased lines from service providers and integrated those lines with routers and switches to form a private network infrastructure. Because the facilities were private, the network was considered totally within the span of the trusted environment.

Today, organizations really do not require the building of a private infrastructure considering the amount of public connectivity available on the Internet. Using the public facility's organizations can dramatically decrease telecommunications budgets and increase the number of services available to the user community. The problem is that public solutions increase the risk to information and to the information systems that we are trying to protect.

VPNs utilize a technology known as private tunneling to provide a secure pathway over a public network. A tunnel is virtual, meaning that it is not actually a private connection. Rather, the privacy is created through the symmetrical encryption of the source/destination network traffic. When two entities (servers and clients) are connected via a VPN connection, all the information exchanged between them is encrypted. If an attacker sees the information on the Net, it would be unreadable. This differs somewhat from the application-level symmetrical cryptography discussed in Section Two of the book; VPN applies to all users of a system or network, not just a particular user or session.

Two modes of VPN can be deployed:

- **Transport mode:** Transport mode uses encryption on the data part of the packet only. In transport mode the original packet headers are left unencrypted
- **Tunnel mode:** In tunnel mode everything gets encrypted (headers and information sections of the packet). Because the original headers are encrypted, the entire packet needs to be encapsulated in a new packet. When the tunneled packet reaches a safe area at the destination, the encapsulation is removed and the packet (including the header) is decrypted. Tunneled traffic needs to make an extra decryption stop along the way

As we can see from Figure 9-8, VPN can be deployed in three possible ways:

- **Host-to-host:** In this case the VPN connections reside on the hosts and offer exclusive privacy between all traffic flowing between the two systems. All of the users and applications on these two systems are afforded the benefit of this tunnel. In this case, you need to use the transport mode because these are end-node systems
- **Site-to-site:** In this case, the VPN exists between two routers (one at site A, and one at site B) that are connected to the Internet. In this case, all traffic on the Internet sides of these two routers are protected by the tunnel. All traffic on the LAN sides of these routers is open within the organization. In this case, the user is more likely to use the tunnel mode to hide the source host addresses of the communicating systems from any would be hacker. Site-to-site configurations imply that the local environment is trustworthy
- **Host-to-site:** In this configuration, the client computer has a host-based VPN application that is connecting that client to a router at the boundary between the organization and the Internet. This allows the client to behave exactly as if it were locally attached to the LAN. In other words, on the WAN part of the connection, the traffic is in a cipher or private form, and on the LAN side it is exposed

With VPN—as with any symmetrical cryptographic method—it is important to recognize and address the key management issues. The more tunnels created, the greater the key management problem becomes. Therefore, this may not be the best solution for organizations that require large quantities of private sessions on the Net. To maximize the effect of the VPN while minimizing the management effort, site-to-site configurations are recommended with client-to-site and host-to-host configurations mixed in sparingly.

VPNs also require a mechanism to update the symmetrical session keys on an as-needed basis. Perhaps the best method to address this problem is to encrypt the keys in an asymmetrical cryptographic application and exchange them using this method. This has become an increasingly popular mechanism to effect this type of symmetrical key exchange.

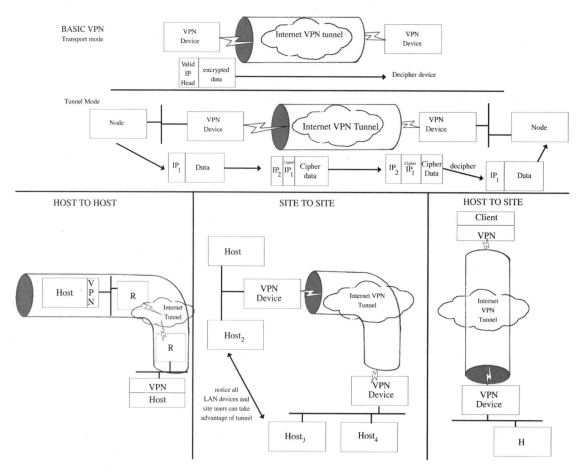

Figure 9-8   Possible configurations of VPN.

Three primary VPN protocols can be used in any of the three configurations described previously:

- **Point-to-point tunneling protocol (PPTP)** is the Microsoft version of VPN. It is inherently supported by the operating system. This protocol is not well regarded as being the most secure
- **L2TP** is the creation of a joint development effort between Cisco and Microsoft. L2TP is a minimal security tunneling protocol. It is recommended that L2TP be used in conjunction with IPSec, which provides encryption. The Internet Engineering Task Force (IETF) recommends this combination

- **IP Security or IPSec** is the industry standard protocol used for implementing VPN. IPSec is focused on encrypting the IP packets (in either transport or tunnel modes). IPSec does not handle multiprotocol tunneling, and it is required to be combined with additional multiprotocol tunneling applications such as L2TP. Most VPN products on the market are IPSec capable

One of the primary drawbacks of VPNs is that, during a VPN session while all traffic in the tunnel is considered secure, Trojans can become very dangerous. Suppose that a tunnel had been established on a system that has been infiltrated with a Trojan. If the Trojan becomes active while the VPN is in place, it will have the same destructive access as if the Trojan were fired up on a system inside either end of the connection. Remember that the VPN makes the remote client or network appear as though they are connected in a private fashion (i.e., behind the firewall).

Virtual Local Area Networks

Virtual Local Area Networks or VLANs are useful architectural constructs, which can be used to enhance security and to promote user work groups in large LAN environments. Prior to VLANs, it was usually necessary for workers sharing information to be working in the same physical proximity to one another. The reason for this was that by connecting to the same LAN segment, the users could maintain privacy, and share servers/information without having to place the data onto common LAN backbones, which were less secure. In fact, the only way to logically isolate work groups was by bridging or routing off their segments from the rest of the network. Through the use of firewalls and screening systems, the LAN could manage security quite effectively. The problems arose when someone needed to move or was required to be part of two different work groups.

VLANs solve these problems by tagging the ethernet frames (802.1Q) with VLAN IDs. These IDs allow VLAN switches to effectively keep packets with particular IDs to stay on only those ports that share that ID. Essentially, a user system is assigned to a switch port as shown in Figure 9-9. These switch ports are then tagged with a particular VLAN ID. Thus, that port can communicate with all other similar ports (tagged with the same ID) anywhere in the switch fabric.

The distribution of these switches can form an elaborate set of virtual LANs that can span an entire campus. This distribution is done by allowing the switches to share VLAN IDs between them, as shown in Figure 9-10.

The VLAN technology is fast and can be used to efficiently partition work groups. This technology is one of the few network security technologies designed specifically for the LAN environment.

INTRUSION DETECTION

Intrusion-detection systems are a critical element required in securing the information system. Crisis-management teams rely on the alerts generated by these systems to set their actions in motion. Many intrusion-detection systems can be proactive and take steps to drop or reset TCP/IP sessions and to lock out attackers before problems arise.

Intrusion-detection systems come in a wide variety of types and costs. Some of these systems can be closely integrated with operating systems, networks, and information storage devices. These devices can be heavily scripted and tailored such that the actions they take or do not take can be customized to fit your organization's security plan.

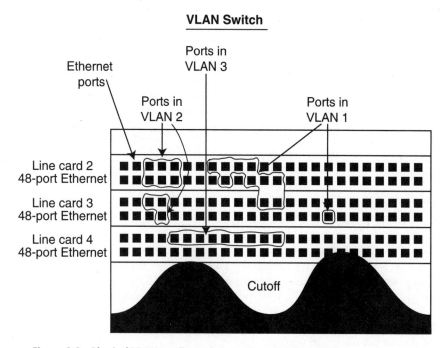

Figure 9-9 Physical VLAN configuration on Cisco Catalyst 6509.

Intrusion-detection systems, also known as IDSs, essentially function by determining when inappropriate actions have been taken within the information system and notifying the proper authority of the anomaly. This can be done either by comparing current activities to the statistically derived normal actions on a host or network **(statistical analysis/anomaly models)** , or by performing a **signature analysis (misuse models),** which compares sequences of actions with those known to cause harm. Additionally, IDSs can examine the state of the information itself to look for changes where there should not be any **(integrity analysis).**

Dorothy Denning suggests in *An Intrusion-Detection Model*, IEEE Transactions on Software Engineering 13 (2), pp. 222–232 (Feb 1987) that information systems not under attack take statistically predictable actions on information. Additionally, systems not under attack do not execute commands that undermine the stability of the system or they have a normal signature. These are important findings because they represent the backdrop against which all unwanted activities are judged.

Intrusion-detection systems have three primary components:

- **Agents,** whose job is to sit on the information system entities, collect information, and report it back to a central repository
- A **director,** whose job is to take the collected information and analyze it according to the IDS method deployed (statistical or misuse)
- A **notification agent,** which is the IDS alert interface and is programmed to take required actions commensurate with certain preestablished criteria

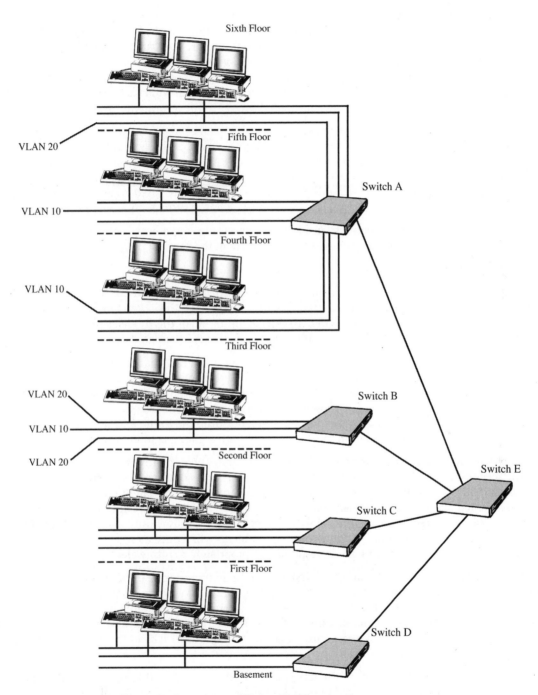

Figure 9-10   Assigning ports to different VLANs.

In a statistical analysis model of an IDS, the director of the system collects information on statistically measurable activities with respect to time intervals $(T_1, T_2,..., T_n)$. Subsequently, the IDS determines if the current set of behaviors at any time T_n is of statistically low probability compared to the norm. If so, this anomaly is reported through the notification agent according to the information security plan. As you can see, this type of model has the benefit of **aging**. Aging is the process of allowing the system to evolve its statistical database over time. The longer the system runs, the better it will characterize the normal set of behaviors and the easier it will be to notice unwanted actions in the information system.

Statistical analysis models have several drawbacks. First, they take a relatively long time to burn in and become reliable. Second, a proficient hacker, with patience, can trick the system by introducing unwanted behaviors slowly and repeatedly (without causing any eye-catching damage at first) such that the IDS grows accustomed to them. Later, these actions will not flag any anomaly and then the hacker has a safe haven inside your computer. Additionally, these statistically based systems can cause a significant number of false alarms, which can reduce confidence in the system, especially in the early stages.

Misuse models are rule-based expert systems. Rules are knowledge representations based on expert interpretations of the desired behavior patterns. These rules are of the form:

> "If (condition) then (action)."

These systems capture the rules of the information security plan (as understood by the security expert) and monitor the information system either for cases where the rules have been violated or for instances of known abnormal signatures (patterns of behavior). A limitation of this model is that each time a well-known new attack is determined, the system needs to have the rule base updated.

Finally, integrity detection IDSs are available, which look for unwanted changes in the information base itself. By this we mean that if information has been modified, deleted, or added without authorization, the IDS will recognize the change and take the appropriate actions. Generally, these systems characterize the state of the information based on known valid checksums. Any unauthorized changes to the information would invalidate the checksum, indicate a variance from the norm, and cause the notification agent to execute. The major limitation to this type of system is that it is totally reactive.

Each of these models has significant pluses and minuses. One way to improve the odds of a system meeting the specified needs of the organization is to find a system that combines the methods discussed into a single system with less faults. There is currently much debate over the extent to which IDS systems should be relied upon. Because of their complex logic, a problem with IDSs tends to be that they can produce false results (reporting an intrusion when there is none—a false positive—or not recognizing an attack in progress—a false negative). Either of these problems will reduce confidence in the system and can cause the crisis-management team to respond inappropriately to future alerts.

Yet these limitations not withstanding, IDS systems can be an important part of our crisis-management process. They can be programmed to take either proactive or reactive action and can be fairly reliable. A key to maximizing the potential of the IDS is to be sure that the IDS is a well-integrated part of the whole strategy and not used in a stand-alone fashion. An IDS is not a cure-all for information security, rather it is the part of the information system security plan that interfaces with all of the devices and the crisis-management team.

The placement of the components of the IDS system is extremely critical in the information system security design. Normally, probes need to be placed at all of the network choke points. This will allow for the monitoring of traffic in and out of the organization. The network choke points can also be very busy places and the amount of content sifting can degrade network performance. In order to avoid this problem, be sure that the functionality of the IDS (e.g., signature analysis of viruses) is not being duplicated in a firewall or proxy server.

Other strategic places where intrusion-detection system components may be placed include the network interface of information stores and sensitive servers, at branch or remote office facilities, and inside each router domain. As can be seen in Figure 9-11, Cisco systems manufactures a suite of products that can be used together to form a network-based IDS and firewall system.

One of the main criticisms of IDSs is that even in proactive systems, the attack has already taken place and the damage may be done before the system has had a chance to react. This is often the case in real-world applications of IDSs. This leaves organizations with the problem of cleaning up after an attack, a process that can be tedious and expensive.

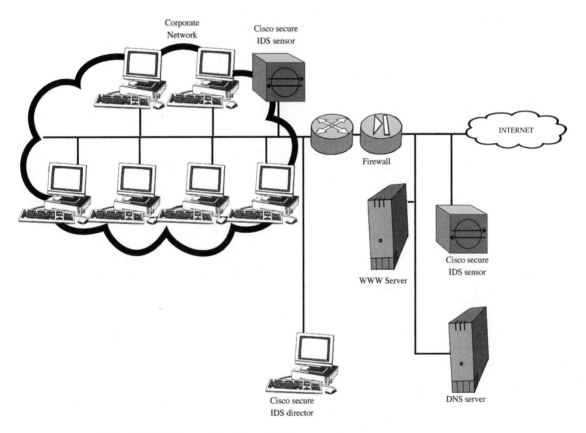

Figure 9-11   A Cisco network-based IDS.

SUMMARY

This chapter has been focused on security issues that apply to the information system. The security of the information system is different from the security of information itself. Information security can be accomplished with a high success rate by embracing the CAIN principles. Information system security is, by far, more complex. One of the primary complexities is that it is not entirely under your control.

Information system security plans need to address the following:

- Physical security
- Application access
- System security
- Network security
- Intrusion-detection systems

Physical security can be broken into several parts:

- Access control
- Environmental security
- Premise security and waste management

Access controls are generally built around certain validity factors. These factors are knowledge factors (things that we know), possession factors (things we have), and biometric factors (things that we are). These factors can be incorporated into the authentication schemes through hardware and software applications that can enroll users, validate them, and authenticate them.

Environmental services include fire protection, HVAC considerations, power management, and flood management. The environmental security considerations are often overlooked in the grand scheme of information system security planning, but they are extremely important.

Access to files and applications is another important and often overlooked part of information system security. Products such as databases have many security controls built into the system (e.g., SQL GRANT and REVOKE commands.) Through these application-level security controls, we can encrypt files, control access, and determine the appropriate level of access (read or write or both) on a per-user basis.

Systems are essentially secured through the processes of secure access and OS hardening. Password controls can be effective if a strong password management policy is in place in the organization. Weak passwords are a major concern of most organizations.

OS hardening can be thought of as being decomposed into the following activities:

- Tighten all directory and file permissions
- Remove all unnecessary services (network and system)
- Set accurate user permissions
- Apply all vendor patches
- Monitor system integrity

Of these, applying all vendor patches and upgrades is without a doubt the most important of the group.

Network security is primarily focused on architectural design. The concept of creating choke points or funnels through which all information must pass is useful. This concept can be combined with DMZs, screening routers, NAT devices, proxy servers, and firewalls to form a secure perimeter in the information system. Other network security provisions include content-aware network strategies, VPNs, VLANs, and 802.11B WEP security measures.

Finally, it is important to monitor and coordinate the activities of the various components protecting the parts of the information system. This is the job of the IDS. The IDS monitors the various parts of the information system to determine if the system is under attack. If it is under attack, the IDS uses a combination of alert and scripted response mechanisms to minimize damage from the attack.

STUDY QUESTIONS

1 One should establish access control policies for each part of the information system that is _____. (choose one)

   a. A high-traffic area

   b. A high-security area

   c. A high-maintenance area

   d. Accessible to the public

2 Access control policies that give the owner of the resource control of access are called _____. (choose one)

   a. Discretionary

   b. Indiscriminate

   c. Mandatory

   d. Owner driven

3 In which part of the enrollment process is the identity of the user verified? (choose one)

   a. The authentication phase

   b. The identification phase

   c. The establishment phase

   d. The verification phase

4 The weakest link in the security chain of any information system is _____. (choose one)

   a. Windows operating systems

   b. Linux operating systems

   c. People

   d. Improperly configured firewalls

5 The best method for authenticating a user to a system is the use of _____.(choose one)

   a. Knowledge and biometric factors

   b. Knowledge and possession factors

   c. Possession and biometric factors

   d. Any of the above

6 The emergency system should_____ if the room temperature reaches 110 degrees. (choose one)

   a. Begin a backup

   b. Reboot

   c. Gracefully shut down

   d. Initiate a hard stop

7 7. What is one practical method to protect sensitive documents against social engineering attacks? (choose one)

   a. Black out all sensitive information

   b. Shred documents containing sensitive data

   c. Keep all documents for forty years

   d. Print no documents with sensitive data

8 Searching through cities and other areas looking for wireless access points is called _____. (choose one)

   a. Signal sniffing

   b. War driving

   c. Wave running

   d. Radio reaping

9 If you are attempting to gain access to restricted information, what is the first action you should take? (choose one)

   a. Kidnap an employee

   b. Ask for what you want

   c. Spoof the server

   d. Disable the alarm system

10 What is the most important security feature of biometric factors? (choose one)

   a. They are not subject to memory loss

   b. They are unique to each user

   c. The systems are very accurate

   d. Both a and b

11 Mantraps discourage _____. (choose one)

   a. Hacking

   b. Shoulder surfing

   c. Tailgating

   d. Bioengineering

12 Why are impedance checkers important in maintaining physical security? (choose one)

    a. You will be alerted when a device is disconnected

    b. You will be alerted to power surges

    c. You will be protected from power outages

    d. They have nothing to do with physical security

13 What should be included in all physical security plans? (choose one)

    a. Authentication methods

    b. Computer locks

    c. Lock codes for doors

    d. A method to report crime

14 One of the most important steps an information security specialist can take to secure the information system is _____. (choose one)

    a. Keeping the software up to date

    b. Ensuring users change their passwords

    c. Using a proxy server

    d. Using biometrics to control access

15 Security assertions of the user are based on the_____. (choose one)

    a. Privilege level of the user

    b. Ability of the user

    c. Assertion of identity

    d. User applications

16 SAML is an acronym for _____. (choose one)

    a. Security assertion markup language

    b. Secure access markup language

    c. Securely accessible migration language

    d. Secret access markup language

17 Most network architecture is based upon _____. (choose one)

    a. Novell

    b. Microsoft

    c. TCP/IP

    d. NCP

18 _____ are devices that are normally configured as choke points. (choose one)

   a. Modems and switches

   b. Firewalls and routers

   c. Routers and switches

   d. Firewalls and modems

19 Screening routers filter traffic via _____. (choose one)

   a. Access control lists

   b. Accountability control lists

   c. Control filter lists

   d. Script control lists

20 Intrusion-detection systems have the following three components: (choose one)

   a. Agents, directors, and actors

   b. Agents, directors, and notification agents

   c. Actors, agents, and administrators

   d. Directors, administrators, and clients

21 Another name for an application-level gateway is a _____. (choose one)

   a. Demilitarized zone

   b. Choke point

   c. Bastian host

   d. Proxy server

CASE STUDY

At this point at Cureme Hospital, you have decided on a plan for protecting critical information. You have embraced a strategy that includes symmetrical and asymmetrical cryptography, as well as an innovative use of X.509 v3 certificates for authentication (digital signatures).

You turn your attention to the details of the security plan for the hospital information system itself. The hospital is fairly large, has two thousand users (operating at various access levels), has many physical security requirements, enjoys high-speed Internet connectivity, and has in the past fallen victim to many virus outbreaks. What will your information system security recommendations include?

- How will you create choke points for the Internet connectivity?
- What physical security will you put in place and how will access be controlled?
- What OS hardening tactics will you use? Assume that the systems are running a variety of Microsoft OS products and applications.
- How will you authenticate users for access to information and the associated applications?
- What will your password creation policy be?
- How will you monitor security events in your network?

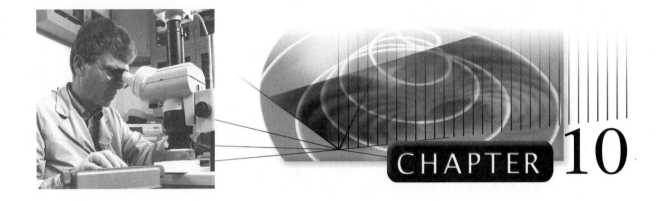

Viruses, Worms, and Malicious Software

*I cannot imagine any condition which would cause this ship to founder.
Modern ship building has gone beyond that.*
—E.I. Smith, Captain of the Titanic

Perhaps the item of greatest concern in the development of an information system's security plan is the threat presented by malicious software. For years, the computer industry has struggled with the task of managing software development efforts so that they produced quality products. Even with the most stringent of management practices, software bugs have been released into the general population. These bugs can cause problems with application effectiveness, data storage and retrieval, and potentially even the crashing of systems. This type of software, while destructive, is not necessarily malicious in nature.

Computer programmers have learned from these inadvertent mishaps. Some people use this knowledge to create stronger and more effective software development control methods. Others have used this knowledge to create software that can deliberately be written and distributed to cause harm and disruption. This type of malicious software is becoming a high security concern and has recently become the topic of many news headlines. We have already examined one particular instance of malicious software in the Morris worm. In that case, what started as a prank wound up causing a two-day major disruption of service throughout the academic Internet community.

Morris was, of course, caught and prosecuted for his actions, but this was only the beginning of what has become a worldwide problem. Viruses, worms, rats, Trojans, bombs, scanners, and trapdoors are just a few of the names used to describe the various types of malware.

In any case, whether the harm was done with malicious intent or not, we need to prepare ourselves, and our sites, for the possibility of these kinds of attacks. With the growth of the Internet and the free exchange of information on the Web comes an increased likeliness that you will be negatively impacted by malicious software. The attackers of today have devised so many delivery mechanisms for the malicious code that it is almost impossible to keep up with. In fact, as was pointed out in Chapter 3, over ninety percent of Internet users will fall victim to a virus or worm at some time.

right
387

This problem has spawned a multibillion-dollar industry of companies that are actively engaged in the study of the malicious software problem, the development of detection methods, and the administration of virus aftermath cleanup activities. While this industry is absolutely paramount in combating malicious software threats, it is a largely reactive industry that produces little in the way of lasting security strategies and products. Unfortunately, as we shall see, there are far more problems in this area of information security than there are solutions.

The chapter examines each of the categories of potentially harmful software. Each category is described and addressed so that the student can differentiate between the different software issues.

The chapter then focuses on the anatomy of viruses and worms. These two categories of malicious software are largely misunderstood. It is necessary for students to develop a broad-based understanding of how these two categories are similar and how they differ. Once we understand the nature of the beast, we can begin to develop methods and strategies for dealing with it.

The chapter concludes with recommendations for addressing this very serious threat to the security and stability of our information system. In many ways this problem is exactly analogous to the problems faced by people who work at the Centers for Disease Control and Prevention in combating human viruses.

To successfully complete this chapter, students should pay particular attention to the following:

- The types of problems that can be caused by programmer errors. These are generally mistakes that attackers learn and then exploit
- The distribution mechanisms of malicious software. By understanding these, we can be more proactive about preventing the spread of malicious software
- The ways that a virus or a worm can attach itself to files on our systems
- The different types of viruses
- The general categories of defenses that can be deployed to combat the problem of malicious software

HARMFUL CODE

After the release of the Code Red worm, the U.S. government published a report entitled "Malicious Software Still Threatens, but Crisis Avoided," which can be found on *http://www.usinfo.state.gov/topical/pol/terror/ecom*. This document is a series of papers regarding the increasing numbers of harmful computer viruses and worms being distributed. In one of the subdocuments released by *http://www.NIPC.gov* entitled "Code Red—The Aftermath and Behind the Scenes Look at the Worm" dated August 3, 2001, it was stated that:

> *"Over the course of the past week, government an d industry groups worked together to address the threat of the Code Red Internet Worm and to warn the public to take the necessary preventative measures to combat its further spread. What is not well known is the 'behind the scenes' efforts by technical security experts who did everything from monitor the spread of the worm to personally answering questions from concerned users on how to protect their computers.*

> *After a new and stronger version of the Code Red Worm appeared in mid-July, industry and government organizations realized that the next outbreak could have much more impact on the Internet if users did not download the software patch to inoculate their system. Going public was not an easy decision, but the impact of not going to the public to ask users for help could have had even worse ramifications."*

The article goes on to state:

> *"[S]elf propagating worms that exploit vulnerabilities in commonly used software platforms will be a vector of choice by hackers as we move forward. These worms require no social engineering and require no action on the part of the users, like opening an attachment. As we saw with Code Red, they can hurt us in two ways: they can consume Internet bandwidth during their propagation phase if the numbers are big enough and can carry harmful payloads, like the instructions to launch against a chosen target."*

This article is interesting for several reasons: First, it shows a deep concern on the part of the government for what might come next in this area of security. Obviously, the sentiment that you get from reading the paper is that the situation could have been and probably will get worse.

Second, if you read between the lines, so to speak, you realize that the government and industry does not always tell us about the whole story. The line "the decision to go public…" (which they did) implies that there are times when they do not go public. This is not surprising because sound information security practices dictate that, by telling the user community about pending problems, vendors can cause the hacker community to attack before the fix can be put in place.

Third, the government is concerned about the delivery method of the self-propagating worm because it requires us to do nothing to receive it or trigger it. The creation and delivery of malicious software is varied and tricky to understand. This is a huge industry-wide problem because varied delivery mechanisms also make any defense scenario prone to failure.

An old adage says, "The chain is only as strong as its weakest link." That link for information system security is undoubtedly malicious software. Since the time that the first program was ever written, the potential for a piece of software to cause system-wide problems has existed. In this chapter we will review the most likely sources of trouble. As we can see in Figure 10-1, there are many forms of harmful code, including malicious and nonmalicious types. Of the nonmalicious types, validation errors and buffer overflows are bugs that can easily occur and have been adapted by hackers in many of the early network attacks. Every software design effort results in some bugs getting into the code. Nonmalicious software problems are usually the result of poor software project planning and testing. To eliminate these types of bugs, it is important to build sufficient testing time into the security plan implementation.

Malicious software is written with intent to be harmful. A variety of attacks can occur and they all have somewhat different characteristics. Trojans, viruses, worms, and port scanners are the most common types.

The idea behind this chapter is to learn what the various types of harmful code are so that students will recognize them and prepare to defeat them in the workplace. Better products are evolving that can screen out harmful code and prevent the problem.

NONMALICIOUS CODE

All programmers make mistakes. We will use some examples from the C programming language to illustrate the point. C is a fairly old language developed by Kernighan and Ritchie at Bell Labs. The purpose of

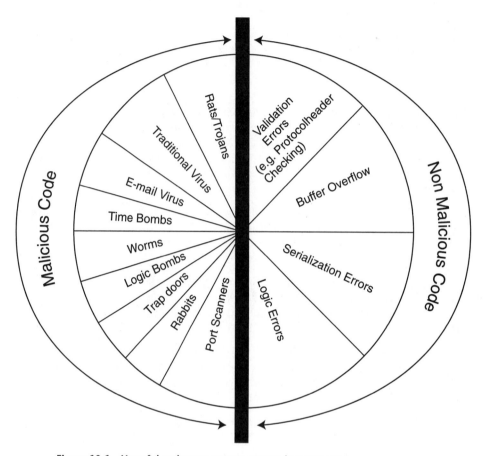

Figure 10-1 Harmful codes can enter a system in many ways.

the language was to provide a powerful, high-level programming language that could be used across multiple computing platforms. One of the interesting characteristics of C is that the language provides significant direct memory access and control. Two important C commands allow us to directly access memory:

    &   ...meaning the address of a variable

    *   ...meaning the value at the address

For example, if variable X is created as an integer type, &(X) provides the address in memory where X is located. *(&(X)) returns the value at the address of X or the value of X. Used correctly, these operators are powerful enablers of programming creativity.

A simple but devastating problem that can occur with the language happens when an operation attempts to write to memory and is mistakenly pointed to the wrong place. In Figure 10-2, we see the normal use of the *scanf* function. *Scanf* is a function that takes input from the keyboard and converts it to a particular data type, and then writes it to memory at a specified location. In the example, the correct form of the command to input an integer and place it in location X is scanf("%i", &X). The %i is a switch

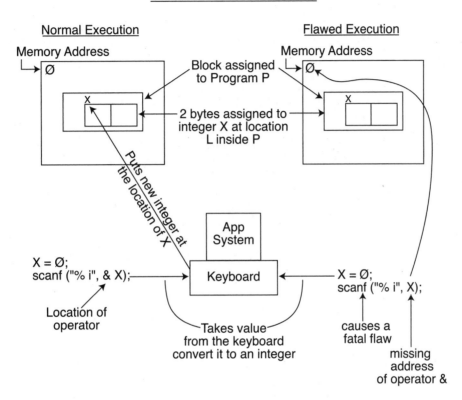

Figure 10-2 By inadvertently forgetting the address - of operator, a significant memory access violation can occur.

that tells the function to take the input from the keyboard and turn it into a 16-bit integer. The &X tells the function to place that integer value at the location in memory of the variable X.

In the flawed program, we forgot to put the & sign in and instead wrote the command *scanf("%i", X)*. This command is flawed because the function is expecting the second input argument to be a legal memory address. Because in this example we initially assigned X the value of zero and omitted the address of operator &, the command attempts to assign the new integer to memory location zero. This is out of bounds for the program and thus will kill the program (in most cases).

Another function that is harmful is the system function. In C, the system ("command") function lets you execute operating system commands in a running C program. Suppose you issued the following command:

    system("dir");

This command would execute the DOS-level directory command under a Windows operating system. This is a useful function for programmers with a need to exercise various parts of the operating system.

These commands are not limited to the simple DOS commands. You can also pass the name of an executable file, and that executable will be run.

Although this seems harmless, what happens if someone executes a malware program from inside the system command? Further, consider the following command:

System("delete c:*.*");

This command will delete all the files and directories found in the root C drive.

These are just a few examples of the simplest of C statements that can lead to trouble. It is easy to see how a hacker might attempt to exploit these errors when building malicious software.

Buffer overflows are another serious problem having to do with memory. A buffer is a predetermined area where a specified amount of data is to be stored. In C, we can specify what is known as an array of characters (a string of contiguous characters) that acts like a buffer. The C command

Char array1[10];

establishes 10 bytes in memory of the type character. If we say

array1[0] = 'd';

array1[1] = 'i';

array [2] = 'c';

array [3] = 't';

array [4] = 'i';

array [5] = 'o';

array [6] = 'n';

array [7] = 'a';

array [8] = 'r';

array [9] = 'y';

we have entered the word 'dictionary' into the string. Notice that the index 9 is used to represent the tenth item in the list because it is standard practice in computer science to begin the indexing of arrays at position 0. This may seem trivial, but making a mistake in the indexing could inadvertently cause a buffer overflow. For example, the command array1[i] = 'h'; where i=10 will overflow the bounds of the array and cause the h to overwrite the item in that byte of memory. This will not be picked up at compile time because the index was specified in the variable i, which, at the time of the compile, had no value. This is another example of the type of error hackers frequently exploit.

To see how a hacker can take advantage of this type of bug, see what happens when a programmer creates a validation error in a networking program and a hacker uses a buffer overflow to exploit it.

As we can see in Figure 10-3, the normal IP header specifies a total length field as part of the header. This field represents the total length of the packet that the receiver of the packet is parsing. This field is important because the receiver uses it to create and utilize buffer space to store the packet during examination.

In early versions of IP programs, programmers often took the specified length at face value. In other words, they never bothered to check the length by actually counting the bytes in the packet.

When hackers became aware of the validation deficiency, they immediately began causing deliberate buffer overflows. Hackers placed malicious code at the end of the packet and made the length field smaller than the actual packet (including the malicious software). The program then took the entire packet and copied it to the buffer in memory. The malicious code overwrote the end of the buffer and was able to sit in memory. If a process came along and accessed that particular part of memory to read it (say during a memory cleanup operation), the malicious code triggers and executes.

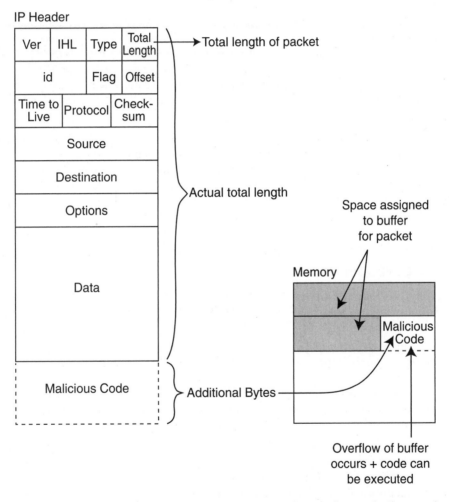

Figure 10-3   By not verifying the length of the packet by actually counting bytes and comparing the total to the length field, dangerous overflows can occur.

Logic errors provide an additional source of problems that are very difficult to trace. In designing pieces of code, programmers need to check their logic to make sure that the code is actually doing what they had intended. Faulty logic can result in many difficulties for the user of the application. For example, suppose that a programmer wrote a program that was scheduled to do some activity repetitively until some value changed which would create a stop condition. This could be written in C as:

```
while (X == TRUE)
        {
                do some actions
                get the next instance of X
        }
```

This programmatic structure examines the contents of X to see if X is the same as the value of TRUE (presumably a 1). If they are equal, then the actions specified in between the brackets will occur again. If X is not equal to true, then the looping stops and the program continues. A logic error that would be hard to detect could occur if something in between the brackets kept changing X to be TRUE, when in fact you thought it would become false. This would cause the loop to continue indefinitely. This situation is bad enough, but if the commands inside the brackets were consuming system resources, this kind of logic bug could cripple the system.

A final instance of a nonmalicious code problem concerns Web scripting. CGI scripting errors can cause serious problems for Web users. In one instance, a programmer used the wrong commands in posting a form to a database and inadvertently caused a user's financial information to be disclosed to every other person that visited the site until the error was found. Fortunately in this instance, no harm was done. Other common problems with CGI scripts include unauthorized access to change the contents of existing files, unauthorized privileges being granted to users, and the ability for users to access system resources without authorization. These programmatic holes were not created deliberately and were certainly not meant to be malicious.

SOFTWARE DEVELOPMENT PRACTICES

A great deal of these programming errors result from poorly planned or poorly executed software development practices. To reduce errors and improve product quality, software manufacturers need to improve the rigors of their software development practices.

Software development is not a trivial task. Many development managers make the mistake of not leaving themselves enough time to properly plan, develop, test, and document the system before it is shipped. This is often a result of overly ambitious project goals and unrealistic vendor-client agreements. One rule of thumb is that the time spent actually coding the project should be the shortest interval in the project development cycle compared to all the others. More time needs to be spent in the planning, specification, scoping, definition, architectural design, documentation, and testing phases.

Far too often these steps in the process are hurried, and the emphasis is shifted to writing lines of code. Then companies begin to cut short the testing process. Instead of testing the entire product, shortcuts are taken, and product designers test only the core functions of the product under ideal conditions. This leaves many uncertainties when the products are finally delivered to market. So the first and most important of the general product improvement guidelines is to have a methodology that emphasizes development planning and testing. The second is to leave enough time in the schedule for all of the tasks involved in the development model to be executed properly. The third guideline is to develop the test plan before the product is actually in the programming phase. The time to think of all the test scenarios under which the program might fail is during the specification phase.

> **KEY POINT**
>
> Budgeting enough time to complete the proper software development life cycle is perhaps the single most important consideration you can make to enhance quality in software products. Another key to success is to build a comprehensive test plan, starting long before the first line of code is written. This is how logic errors can be detected.

Another way to improve product performance is through the use of alpha and beta test sites. These sites are actual live operating environments in which clients understand the risks associated with new program burn-in and are willing to take them. Through this closely monitored burn-in period, the designers of the code can get feedback on the current status of problems and fix them before a general release of the product. This is one of the best ways to cut down on holes in the software.

MALICIOUS SOFTWARE

Malicious software is a broad classification. To fit in the class, the software has to have been created and distributed with the sole purpose of intending to do harm or cause disruption. The following are examples of harm:

- The destruction of property (information)
- The defacement of a Web site
- The corruption of an operating system configuration
- The complete consumption of system resources leading to system-wide failure

The following are some examples of disruption of service:

- The denial of service through the network interface
- Lockouts at the operating system
- Excessive consumption of CPU cycles and memory
- Introduction of rogue processes into the operating environment
- Nuisance messages and pop-up windows

People who create this type of software are usually skilled and innovative. The users of this type of software are usually unskilled and trying to experiment. You should remember from Chapter 3 that the design of malicious software is not illegal. It is the use of the software that is against the law. People that build hacker tools and malicious software are not breaking any laws until they attempt to use the software for illegal purposes.

One question frequently asked is whether there any legitimate uses of this software. The answer is yes. One example is to write destructive software to test virus protection products or to test the vulnerability of systems. Another reason to write software that might consume excessive system resources is to try and stress-test a system. But do not be fooled by these rare legitimate instances of creating malware. Most often hackers create the software because they can. The code designer's intent to commit a crime is somewhat nebulous. The user of the software would have no motive when using malware other than to cause either harm or disruption of services or both.

This area of information security has a concise vocabulary associated with it. The following is a review of several important terms:

- **Trojan**—A piece of software that appears to serve a useful purpose (and often does), but also has hidden components that perform unexpected and unwanted actions. **Remote administrative tools (RATs)** are Trojans that, once enabled, let the attacker take control of the remote site
- **Virus**—A piece of code that replicates by attaching itself to other executables in the operating system. When that subsequent executable instance of the virus runs, the virus is activated again and continues to replicate
- **Worm**—A piece of code that replicates itself and activates all subsequent copies causing exponential consumption of the system resources
- **Network worm**—A worm that uses network connectivity to spread to other systems where it continues to spread on and from that system
- **Scanners**—Software that detects weaknesses in a system or network
- **Payload**—The set of program instructions that form the malicious software
- **Time bomb**—Malicious software that remains dormant until a particular time or date has passed
- **Logic bomb**—Malicious software that remains dormant until a specific condition (e.g., the presence of a file on the system, a particular type of network connection is activated, etc) is met

RATS AND TROJANS

RATs and Trojans are popular malware programs that are placed on systems via seemingly legitimate means. A Trojan or a RAT has the basic characteristic of being seemingly useful. In most instances, the Trojan is a desired program or file such as a Web cookie, game program, video file, or wav file that is loaded onto the system. Once the Trojan is on your system, some event **triggers** the dormant malware. For instance, the Trojan may be a time bomb in which a particular time has to pass before the malware launches. Another trigger for these covert programs is a communication from another system or a network event (such as the running of a communications program.) Whatever the trigger, the malware is activated and the system is then under attack.

In Figure 10-4, we see an example of how a Trojan can have a delayed effect. In the example, the Trojan is downloaded as a seemingly routine and harmless program—an e-mail, cookie, game, etc. The system processes receipt of the message and stores it appropriately. At some point, the trigger fires and the Trojan releases some kind of malware.

KEY POINT

Trojans are a delivery mechanism of malware.

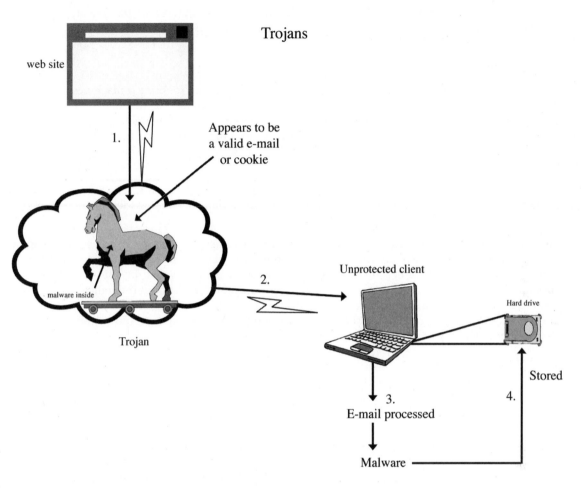

Figure 10-4   A Trojan gets on a system and waits for a trigger to activate it.

The malware can be a virus, password cracker/sender, key logger, destructive program, or an FTP Trojan. Each of these (and many others) Trojans can be self-replicating. This is similar in function to a virus in that it can make copies of itself.

ANATOMY OF A VIRUS

The first known virus was the Elk Cloner virus, which was indigenous to Apple II machines in 1981. In these early years, viruses traditionally targeted systems of a particular ilk. The first IBM PC virus was the Brain virus in 1986, a type of **boot-sector virus.** Boot-sector viruses inject themselves into the boot sector of the disk. The first time the disk is accessed, the bootstrap is run. In this case, the virus executes on startup. The virus then activates code that runs anytime a new disk is added to the floppy drive and replicates itself on the boot sector of that disk.

Viruses typically infect an .exe- or .com-type file. When that file is run, the virus spreads to other files of the same type. When the virus is activated, it could take any number of countless actions, depending on the virus writer's intentions.

Viruses have grown and mutated at an alarming rate. Several rather early viruses are still active on many systems today. One of the reasons viruses have grown in such a prolific fashion is that users tend to exchange executable code rather than source code because the platforms that run the executables are virtually all the same type and no compiling and linking are required. Without the source code, it is difficult to tell if there is a virus in the executable. Given the ever-increasing number of clone systems, it is unlikely that this growth rate will stabilize any time soon. Viruses can replicate but require the executable program that they are hosted on to run before they are activated.

Viruses have five basic parts:

- **The infector** is the part of the code whose primary job is to seek out new targets and form the necessary attachments to proliferate the existence of the virus
- **The concealer** is responsible for hiding the virus from anti-virus programs. This could be a mutation engine in the case of a polymorphic virus
- **The payload** of the virus, as we have stated, can be almost anything
- **The trigger** is used for delayed-action payloads that are transported with the virus
- **The signature byte** is used to mark host files so that the virus knows if the file has already been infected. This is important because the file needs to replicate; infecting the same files over and over is counterproductive

Figure 10-5 shows several schemes for how viruses can reside on your system. In example one, we show the normal disposition of the file directory and the media as they relate to each other. In Example 2a, the legitimate file pointer remains the same but the virus actually overwrites the file. When a user activates file A the virus is actually run because it is pointed to by A's pointer. In Example 2b, the virus causes the directory access pointer to be changed. This is a different method that has the same effect as 2a. In Example 3, the virus is integrated with a particular file. The virus occupies certain parts of the file. This helps the virus avoid detection. Finally, in Example 4, the virus is appended to the end of the file.

As we mentioned, viruses spread by attaching themselves (in one of the ways just listed) to other files. When the file is run, it is spread to the next file. In the case of removable media, the traditional virus can be distributed to other systems. This is shown in Figure 10-6. An infected file is placed on removable media, which is placed in a foreign system. The infected file is then run on the local system and the virus is spread.

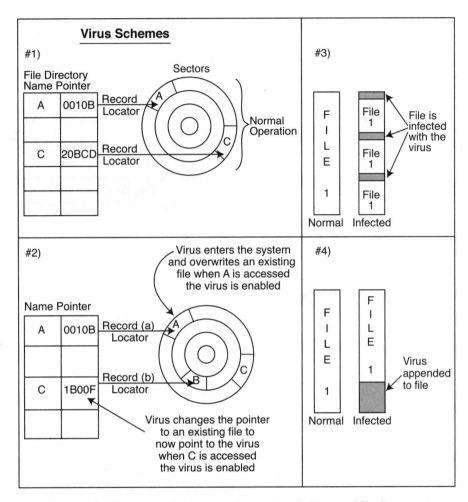

Figure 10-5   Viruses can attack systems in many ways: 1) normal file directory structure, 2) a. virus file replaces or overwrites legitimate file, b. virus redirects the access locator to point to the virus, 3) virus blends with an existing file, 4) virus is appended to an existing file.

Figure 10-7 illustrates that once the host system is infected, the virus can begin to spread rapidly. This happens because the virus is resident in computer memory and continues the attachment process until the computer is powered off and the memory is cleared. Although a shutdown does remove the virus from memory, it does not remove it from previously infected files.

A variant of these traditional viruses is the newer and more established **e-mail virus**. E-mail viruses work by taking advantage of the macros or scripts that can be run in attached files from such programs as Word, Excel, PowerPoint, and Access. These scripts can be set to run when the mail message is opened.

Polymorphic viruses change form each time they are attached to a new host. This helps to conceal the fact that a virus is passing through a signature filter on a firewall or virus scanner. This virus alteration is

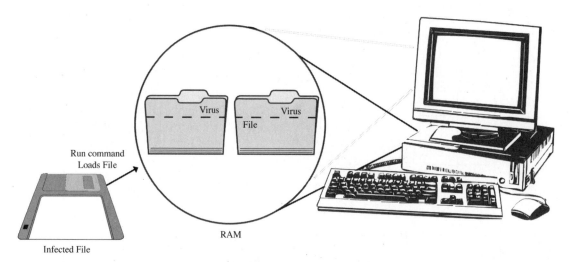

Figure 10-6 The virus copies itself into memory.

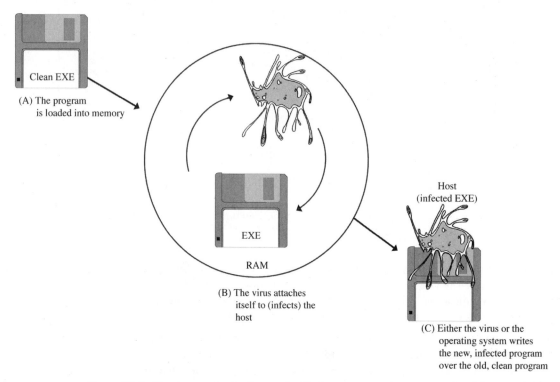

Figure 10-7 The virus copies itself onto the file in memory and saves over the disk copy of the file.

done programmatically with the help of a **mutation engine**. A mutation engine, shown in Figure 10-8, is a program that uses one of many different methods to alter the signature of the virus.

For viruses to be useful they have to grow and replicate over long periods of time. To do this, the creators usually keep the payloads somewhat innocuous or, at the very least, time delayed. The sooner the detection software realizes that the attack is on, the sooner it will begin to search for and eliminate the virus.

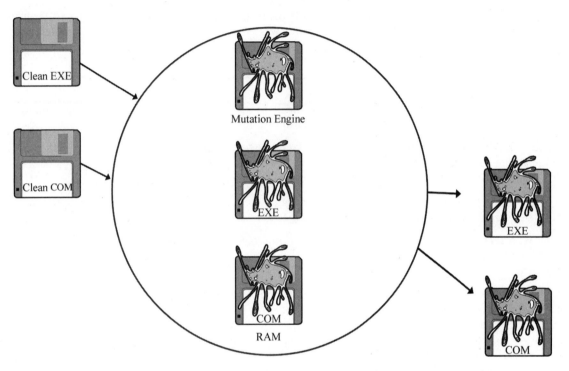

Figure 10-8   The polymorphic virus changes its signature from infection to infection.

WORMS

We have already studied worms in general terms in Chapter 3. Robert Morris in 1988 created the Morris worm, which successfully churned its way through most of the academic community, replicating as is went. The Morris worm was the first instance of a virus or a worm receiving worldwide media coverage. It was also the first instance of a person being prosecuted for such an offense.

A worm, by definition, is a self-replicating and self-activating piece of code. The worm is self-contained, and, unlike a virus, a worm does not attach itself to other files. Worms can be designed to grow on a particular system, constantly recreating themselves and consuming all the system resources, or they can move from system to system.

Also, unlike viruses, the worm is fast-acting. Worms spread rapidly from system to system and replicate as many times as possible in the shortest possible time. The desired effect of the worm is to consume the resources of the system or the network and essentially such it down. Because the worm becomes known quickly, it also is contained rapidly. The problem with worms is that they spread at alarmingly fast rates and can cause all kinds of outages. This, as we mentioned in the introduction, has the infrastructure protection people on edge. Given the right worm, with the right amount of destructive power, significant portions of the World Wide Web could fail. Code Red, Nimda, Ramen, Loveletter, and the most recent, Blaster, are all worms that spread on a worldwide basis at alarming rates. Code Red is perhaps the best known of the worms. First released on July 19, 2001, the Code Red worm infected nearly 250,000 Microsoft Internet Information Servers (IIS) worldwide in only nine hours. The now-famous "Hacked by Chinese!" message displayed by Code Red was only the beginning of the devastation, estimated at more than $2 billion. The overall infection from the code was estimated to be 750,000 machines. The virus concluded its aggression by launching a worldwide distributed denial-of-service attack against the White House website.

OTHER FORMS OF MALWARE

Although worms and viruses are the most noteworthy of the malicious software group, other equally capable pieces of malware can do damage and harm systems.

Rabbits are programs that are loaded and executed on a given system that are purposely designed to consume all the resources of a particular type (e.g., memory) on a particular host. The purpose of a rabbit is to either crash the system or to create a denial-of-service attack.

Trapdoors are programs that can be accessed through secret entry points. The object of these programs is to allow unauthorized access for people wanting to gain entry onto the system.

Port scanners provide attackers information on unprotected ports in a system. By procuring this information, attackers can attempt to gain access into a particular port and then continue working their way into the system.

Social engineering software is directed at getting the user to perform some action on the attacker's behalf. For example, the attacker sends the user an e-mail under the guise of coming from the IT department. The attacker asks the user to delete a particular file on the user's system (usually an important system file). Or, the attack may request that a user send a particular piece of information or load a program on their system. These kinds of attacks can be the launch points for rabbits, trapdoors, viruses, and worms.

Logic bombs are programs that stand alone or are part of a Trojan. They are programs that wait for particular events to trigger them. **Time bombs** are similar in that their event is connected to the system clock.

Keystroke monitors are programs that, once activated, monitor the keystrokes of the users. This information is logged and all sensitive user information is collected. At some point, the monitor may dump the capture file to a designated location for pickup. These types of programs can yield information such as passwords, correspondence, usernames, and other valuable secrets.

Password crackers are programs that enable the attacker to procure usernames and passwords, which are then used to gain access. These programs can be found almost anywhere. There are many versions of these programs and they can have all kinds of automatic features, such as reporting capabilities.

There are many other kinds of malicious software, including all of the software that enables various denial-of-service attacks and network attacks. As we demonstrated in the nonmalicious code section of this chapter, any possible programmatic error or activity can be turned into a potential attack.

The use of these tools is a violation of federal law and offenders can be prosecuted. It is also important to point out that many of the sites that warehouse this information are potential places where visitors can be infected.

MALWARE DEFENSES

As we have previously stated, there is no end to the creative variations that can be applied to the development of malicious code. Thus, we have an ever-evolving problem to deal with. For every virus or worm detected, five new ones are created. Some malware is eradicated quickly; others linger.

A huge part of the problem of malicious software is that the hardware platforms of the users are all similar (as are the operating systems—more importantly). This similarity means that the software can move quickly from one system to another without barrier. This is an unfortunate by-product of the well-intentioned move to open systems. Additionally, the eradication of malware depends to a large extent on the speed with which the user community responds to the call to action. Further, viruses and worms do not actually behave out of the norm on the system if the activity is looked at on a one-time basis. This is problematic because it makes detection difficult. (It is easy to find rule breakers, but not tricksters.)

The field of malware defenses is largely reactive, in part because it is impossible to predict the next virus. While there are tools available to detect malware, perhaps the best method of prevention lies in user education. Strong policies regarding visiting dangerous sites and the use of untested software can curtail problems.

There are several basic tools that can help in reducing this type of activity:

- Detection tools or vulnerability assessment monitors are tools that watch the normal activity of the system. If there is a perceptible change in the status of the system, the tools immediately begins searching for the source of the change. These tools also safeguard the innermost operation of the operating system at the interrupt level

  Integrity-checking programs can also be used to find out if a file has been changed. The change is detectable because the presence of the virus in the file will change the checksum associated with the known working file

- Identification tools or scanners primarily look for signatures of various known malware. (The emphasis is on the word *known*.) If a new virus is created, the signature may not be recognized as part of a family, and therefore the scanner will not detect the malware. Further, with the advent of mutation engines, the virus signatures change, making the scanner's job more difficult

- Removal or cleaning tools are necessary to track and reverse the effects of malware after the fact. This is a reasonable and prudent precaution because it is likely that your system will be infected and compromised

- Antivirus software is important because it usually comprises many of the tools mentioned above. It is important to keep the software current by downloading a new signature file from the vendor as often as is required. Generally these files are updated on a weekly basis

- Patching the operating system can plug many holes and decrease the number of vulnerabilities. Installing inoculation software and updates serves a similar purpose

- Establish best practices policies for your organization regarding installing and using software, copying data files, use of anti-virus safeguards, and software licensing

No matter which method you choose, make sure that the method is activated and policies enforced. In this case prevention is the best medicine.

Figure 10-9 illustrates a number of safeguards that can be included in the corporate antimalware policy and used to prevent the spread of malware. The safeguards can be summarized as follows:

- Do not preview e-mail. If an e-mail virus is script- or macro–enabled, the preview is enough of an action to trigger the script
- Do not leave any network path unprotected
- Scan all downloaded files to be sure they are not infected before they get on your system.
- Scan the entire hard drive at least two times per month
- Write-protect media that you normally use when it is installed on other systems. This prevents the other system from writing on your drive
- Remove all external media while booting
- Make sure that the bios boots from the C drive first

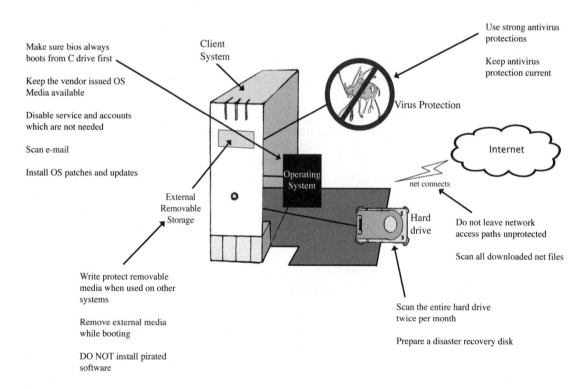

Figure 10-9   Examples of safeguards to protect systems against malicious code.

SUMMARY

Harmful software can be either malicious or nonmalicious. It is perhaps the single most-uncontrolled element of information system security. By all accounts, this is the fastest-growing attack area. The devastating power of these software-based attacks is stunning and can be overwhelming for the average IT manager.

It was demonstrated that simple coding mistakes can create serious problems for an application user. Many undetected application programming errors are the result of poor software development practices. By allocating more time to the entire life-cycle development effort, fewer mistakes would occur.

Many of the programming glitches that have plagued the industry have been incorporated into the malicious software. Malicious software can be delivered in a variety of ways. The Trojan horse is a deceptive method for downloading malware. The Trojan horse has a useful part and a covert part. The covert part can be activated based on a trigger once inside the host system.

Viruses are malware programs that attach themselves to .exe files every time that particular .exe file runs. This means that viruses spread based on the intervention of users or systems that run the software. Viruses have core parts including the infector, the concealer, and the payload. Viruses are generally less overtly destructive than other malware.

Worms are self–replicating, self-activating software that do not need host files. Worms attempt to spread with maximum speed. They attempt to consume as many resources as possible during the replication process. In the case of the Code Red worm, once the worm had spread substantially, it launched a worldwide denial-of-service attack.

Other types of malware exist that can be used to do harm to systems. These pieces of software include rabbits, port scanners, logic bombs, time bombs, and trapdoors, as well as other variants.

The defenses against malware are largely reactive and require significant planning. Perhaps the best defense is found in strong policies and combined with the use of virus-scanning software. Policies should minimize the import of software from unknown sources, prevent the screening of e-mail, and detail what to do with e-mail from unknown sources.

The industry and the government recognize the seriousness of this problem and through the diligent and creative efforts of both the situation should improve. Unfortunately, the number of hackers has also grown and the amount of knowledge required to build a virus is significantly reduced.

STUDY QUESTIONS

1 Approximately what percentage of Internet users will fall victim to a worm or virus at some time? (choose one)

a. 60 percent

b. 70 percent

c. 80 percent

d. 90 percent

2 Which of the following is NOT a programming error that has been exploited by hackers? (choose one)

   a. Buffer overflows

   b. Logic errors

   c. Math errors

   d. CGI scripting errors

3 **True**___ **False**___   In software development, code writing should be the shortest phase of the project.

4 Which types of viruses come into a system disguised as something harmless? (choose one)

   a. Trojans and RATs

   b. Buffer overflows

   c. Denial-of-service attacks

   d. Worms

5 What part of the virus is primarily responsible for seeking out targets so that it may proliferate itself? (choose one)

   a. Payload

   b. Infector

   c. Concealer

   d. Trigger

6 **True**___ **False**___   The anti-virus software industry is reactive in nature.

7 The function that lets you execute operating system commands in a running C program is _____. (choose one)

   a. System ("command")

   b. Execute ("command")

   c. Operate ("command")

   d. Run ("command")

8 Which C command(s) allow(s) us to directly access memory? (choose one)

   a. &

   b. *

   c. Neither a nor b

   d. Both a and b

9 What type of deficiency do hackers take advantage of to cause buffer overflows? (choose one)

    a. Validation

    b. Error checking

    c. Size

    d. Packing

10 _____ are Trojans that, once enabled, let the attacker take control of the remote site. (choose one)

    a. Worms

    b. Time bombs

    c. RATs

    d. ROACHes

11 Viruses typically infect a _____ file. (choose one)

    a. .bat or .dll

    b. .com or .exe

    c. .jpg or .bmp

    d. .png or .wma

12 One of the best ways to reduce problems with software performance is through the _____. (choose one)

    a. Testing of core functions only

    b. Use of shortcuts

    c. Use of alpha/beta test sites

    d. Testing under ideal conditions

13 **True___ False___** Worms attach themselves to files.

14 A virus uses a _____ to mark files it has already infected. (choose one)

    a. Tagged bit

    b. Signature byte

    c. Flagged byte

    d. Germ tag

15 A worm's goal, once in a system, is to _____. (choose one)

    a. Hide

    b. Alter file extensions

    c. Infect programs

    d. Consume resources

16 _____ look for signatures of known malware. (choose one)

    a. Scanners

    b. Integrity checkers

    c. Keystroke monitors

    d. Vulnerability assessment tools

17 There is often a delay in informing users of software vulnerabilities because it causes _____. (choose one)

    a. Users to flood help lines

    b. Hackers to attack before a fix is in place

    c. Lack of faith in a company

    d. Both b & c

18 _____ are programs that can stand alone or be part of a Trojan. (choose one)

    a. Trapdoors

    b. Logic bombs

    c. Keystroke monitors

    d. Rabbits

19 For antivirus software to remain effective, the _____ must be kept up to date. (choose one)

    a. Inoculation files

    b. Operating system patches

    c. Virus engines

    d. Signature files

20 **True___ False___** There are legitimate uses for malware.

CASE STUDY

Discussion and Comment

For this exercise, students should go to the McAfee Web site at *http://us.mcafee.com/virusinfo* to view the latest virus information as of the day of the exercise. Click on antivirus tips and read the suggestions. Do these seem likely to secure a corporate system from a virus attack? Can you think of other countermeasures?

Next, click on the virus map and check out the current known outbreaks of viruses. Why do you suppose that the viruses are geographically clustered? What does this tell us about the nature of the virus and its creators?

Finally, click on the virus-removal tools. Which tools do you currently run on your systems? What are your thoughts on adding to the current protections based on what you have read.

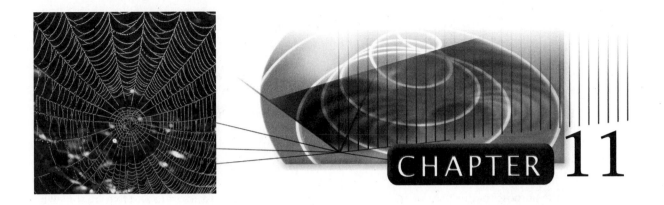

CHAPTER 11

Securing the Digital Marketplace

Don't find a fault. Find a remedy.
—Henry Ford

Throughout much of the 1990s and into the early part of the new millennium, a great deal of the focus of computer technologies has been on the Web. Along with the commercialization of the Web, we have witnessed tremendous growth in Web-based applications and Web-based businesses. Web-based business had an immediate rise to prominence during the late 1990s. The vision of a comprehensive set of online applications that allowed online shopping, online banking, Internet-wide e-mail, online access to personal information, complete access to a plethora of online knowledge banks, personal and business online management tools, and online entertainment applications carried us into a new age. Unfortunately (with the exception of e-mail), progress slowed as many entrepreneurs realized that several issues were undermining their ability to make profits on their Web-based businesses. These are currently being addressed and a resurgence of these Web-based businesses is anticipated. Remedies lie in evolving trust and information security.

The first, and probably most important, issue that faces Web-based business owners is that people generally do not trust online services. Users who regularly use credit cards in traditional retail environments feel uncomfortable about making purchases on the Web.

Second, there is a need to create "digital currency" so that transactions between merchants and clients can occur in an atmosphere of trust that does not extend beyond the bounds of that particular transaction. In other words, clients should not have to worry about merchants using their credit cards inappropriately or revealing the credit card information (e.g., revealing the credit card information to others either deliberately or by accident). Likewise, the merchant should not have to worry that they will not get paid.

Third, users are concerned about their Internet privacy. Who can see what they have been doing? Can someone watch which sites you visited? Is your e-mail really private? These are all valid concerns that need to be addressed to foster the growth of trust.

Fourth, the quality of information found on Internet sites is not always reliable. In fact, many sites provide suspect information. Many universities are rethinking their positions about encouraging students to rely on the Internet as the source of their information. Several research universities have begun to pull together a "trusted Internet" for sharing information that is monitored and regulated.

Fifth, performance expectations of Internet users need to be met. The Internet community is faced with the challenge of providing an environment in which true quality of service can be guaranteed to users of various applications on the Net by service providers. With the true integration of voice, data, and video, the Internet needs to actively manage this traffic so that the packets move through the network at the best possible speed.

For the purposes of this text, we will focus on the first three of these issues (four and five are somewhat outside the scope of the text). Our emphasis will be on how to use the information presented thus far in the text to design a Web environment built on trust, one that has a digital currency, and that provides privacy for the users.

Throughout the text we have emphasized the many parts of information and the information system security: system security, network security, physical security, and of course the security of the information itself. Our model outlined in Chapter 1 has a layer dedicated to securing the Web. This is an important and relatively new layer of the model. At this layer, many of the individual tactics described throughout the text need to come together to create a trusted Web environment.

In this layer of the model, we begin by examining parts of the Web. This includes the Web-specific protocols, services, and architectures that are commonly used. Next, the chapter links the integration of cryptographic protocols with the base Web transaction sets. Digital currency is an emerging technology that will be examined. The remote administration and authoring of the Web is another topic that needs to be carefully evaluated. Finally, there is a need to compare and contrast the many technology choices available to provide client-side and server-side security.

The chapter concludes with a review of the many technologies presented throughout the entire text and attempts to provide a careful analysis and comparison of the technologies. This review is meant to demonstrate the overlap between these technologies. It is also meant to help students gain an appreciation of the appropriate use of particular technologies. This part of the text should help students pull all the pieces of the model back together and begin to think of the information security and information system security as a unified security solution.

 To successfully complete this chapter, students should pay particular attention to the following:

- The requirements for trust on the Web
- The traditional Web technologies (HTTP and HTML)
- The use of encryption to establish privacy on the Web
- The use of encryption to establish trust on the Web
- The client-side security measures
- The server-side security measures
- Remote administration and authoring on the Web
- The comparison of technologies that are available to build comprehensive security solutions, which need to come together to provide Web security

WEB BUSINESSES AND SECURITY REQUIREMENTS

Web business transactions and interactions have many security requirements. These requirements form the basis for how our security plans and policies develop. Obviously, these requirements are based on the risks that a Web-based business will face. As we discussed in Section One, risk needs to be measured through a carefully crafted analysis of the organization. Web-based businesses are no exception. We need to conduct a risk analysis and collect security information about the site, the organization, the clients, and the threats that the information transacted on the site will face. Because the Web is an open environment, one advantage over private information systems is that there is likely to be publicly available information regarding the security and operation of similar sites for us to review.

For most Web-based e-business systems, at least the basic security requirements should be obvious. There are six basic requirements in a Web-based e-business security implementation, as shown in Figure 11-1. It would be wise to start with these six and then continue to customize the Web security requirements definition based on the results of an in-depth risk analysis.

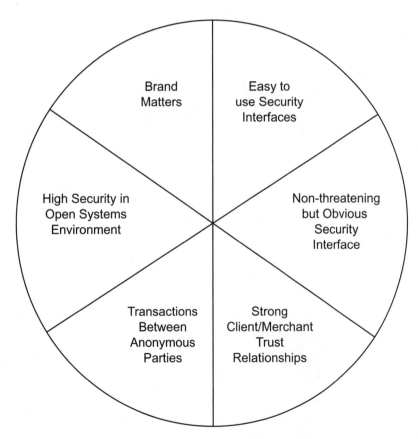

Figure 11-1   Six major requirements for an e-business Web security system.

Web-based businesses face the ultimate security challenge. For a Web-based business to succeed, we need to provide plans that allow for high levels of security for systems and transactions operating in the open environment of the Internet. This is almost a contradiction in terms. The challenge is that the very protocols and technological advances that make the open Internet possible logically preclude the notion of maximum security. Until recently, securing a Web transaction was difficult at best. Sites offering only minimal security were being touted as "safe" sites. Accounts regarding the divulgence of personal information, the misuse of trusted materials, the unauthorized access to private networks, and malicious code downloads from servers to unwitting clients have begun to erode the trust that is necessary for Web businesses to flourish.

As with any business, Internet-based businesses need to be based on a trust relationship between the clients and the merchants. This trust is more difficult to establish than the trust that normally exists in the traditional marketplace, because in the digital marketplace, there is no real opportunity to establish a personal, or face-to–face, relationship. Most of the business conducted on the Internet is done anonymously, giving the transaction a different look and feel than business conducted in the standard marketplace.

The CAIN principles, discussed earlier in the text, form the basis for developing a trust in the Web business environment. Cryptographic solutions such as digital signatures, asymmetrical cryptography, VPNs, and other symmetrical methods can help us cast the secure environment that is necessary.

KEY POINT

Cryptographic methods and the CAIN principles are strongly connected to Web security. The use of cryptography as part of the transaction sets for Web-based businesses can offer trust to anonymous business partners.

A second concern for the Web security planner is that transactions must not be threatening for either party and the security of the transaction should be obvious. In other words, the application interface that uses the cryptography must not be overbearing and riddled with detail, yet at the same time it must be obvious to the user that the security actions are being taken. A perfect example of this type of transactional interface can be found in Microsoft's Outlook and Outlook Express mail agent's S/MIME implementation. The Microsoft mail agents allow for the users to implement asymmetrical cryptography to encrypt and sign e-mail messages. As can be seen in the e-mail security lab in Appendix A, the interface to the sender of the mail is obvious (two security icons on the toolbar—one for signatures and one for encryption) but not threatening. On the receiver side, the message authenticity is verified and the receiver is notified of either a valid signature (which breeds confidence) or that the message is suspect. In the case of a suspect notification, the results are obvious and the rationale for the decision is spelled out. The user of this system is well informed about what is happening without being overburdened with confusing, misleading, or threatening information.

For Web businesses to succeed, the interfaces to these complex cryptographic systems need to be easy to use. It is important to recognize that the target audience of Web-based commercial business is largely nontechnical. People who are either not skilled or are uninterested in technology can be threatened and turned off by complicated interfaces. It is important that the interfaces be of the plug-and-play variety and that they be no more complicated to operate than a standard radio, television, or microwave. Again, we can look to the Microsoft Outlook and Outlook Express S/MIME interfaces as a good example. The icons associated with encryption and digital signatures are easily identifiable, and the technology is invoked through a click of the appropriate icon. Unfortunately, as is demonstrated in the lab, the mail security interface is a bit of a chore to set up. Luckily, this is a once-and-done process.

Finally, Web businesses must understand that corporate image or brand is communicated through the websites that an organization establishes. These sites convey strong messages to the user community. Through the unauthorized changing (defacing) of a website, corporate brands can be disparaged. Think for a moment of the amount of advertising dollars that a mid-sized, publicly traded company might spend on advertising between commercials (radio and television), newspaper advertisements, direct mail, and their website. If any one of those is compromised, the entire brand can be placed in jeopardy. Thus, securing the website is equivalent to protecting the brand, and brand matters.

Now that we have thought through at least the basic requirements for a Web-based business, we must now turn our attention to the various security options currently available on the Web.

WEB TECHNOLOGY BASICS

How does the Web work? What are the core technologies that make Web sites accessible and usable? What is it exactly that we are trying to protect when we invoke the term "Web security?" These are good questions, the answers to which are not always obvious. However, to better understand our security mission at this level, it is important to describe some of the details of the Web architecture and operation.

The **World Wide Web (WWW)** is often simply referred to as the Web. The Web is a system or collection of electronic documents that are hyperlinked to other documents, forming a network of interconnected documents. These documents are called **Web pages** and are generally based on the **Hypertext Markup Language (HTML)**. HTML is a simple programming language. HTML is designed to be used with a **Web browser**, a special application program that runs on a client for the sole purpose of interpreting HTML documents. HTML is essentially a formatting language that tells the browser how to display its contents. HTML does this through a series of tags that convey the formatting information. Other forms of Web-based information also exist. These can be loosely categorized as electronic mail documents, online transaction processing documents, and forms.

This interconnected collection of electronic documents uses the facilities and mechanisms of the Internet for transport. The links in the HTML document are **Uniform Resource Locators (URLs)** that can be translated into actual IP addresses via the domain name server. Once the names are known, the client can contact the server warehousing the Web pages of interest via the **Hypertext Transfer Protocol (HTTP)**. This basic Web architecture is shown in Figure 11-2.

Essentially there are two types of systems on the Web: the client and the server. The client is the user system that runs the Web browser software and requests the information to be displayed via the HTTP protocol. Servers are the recipients of these HTTP requests and are the systems that maintain the information stores of the HTML (Web) pages. The servers issue HTTP responses to fulfill HTTP requests that have been issued to them.

The basic set of Web transactions is shown in Figure 11-3. In this figure, we see that the user requests the page by entering a URL into the browser. The browser then passes the URL to the client network protocol stack. The client then needs to find out the IP address associated with this URL. To do this, the client sends a message to the **Domain Name Server (DNS)** nearest to it. A DNS can be based on many technologies. DNS, essentially, is a hierarchy of servers containing information in a logical sub-tree of the overall domain. Once the name has been resolved, it is sent back to the client. The client

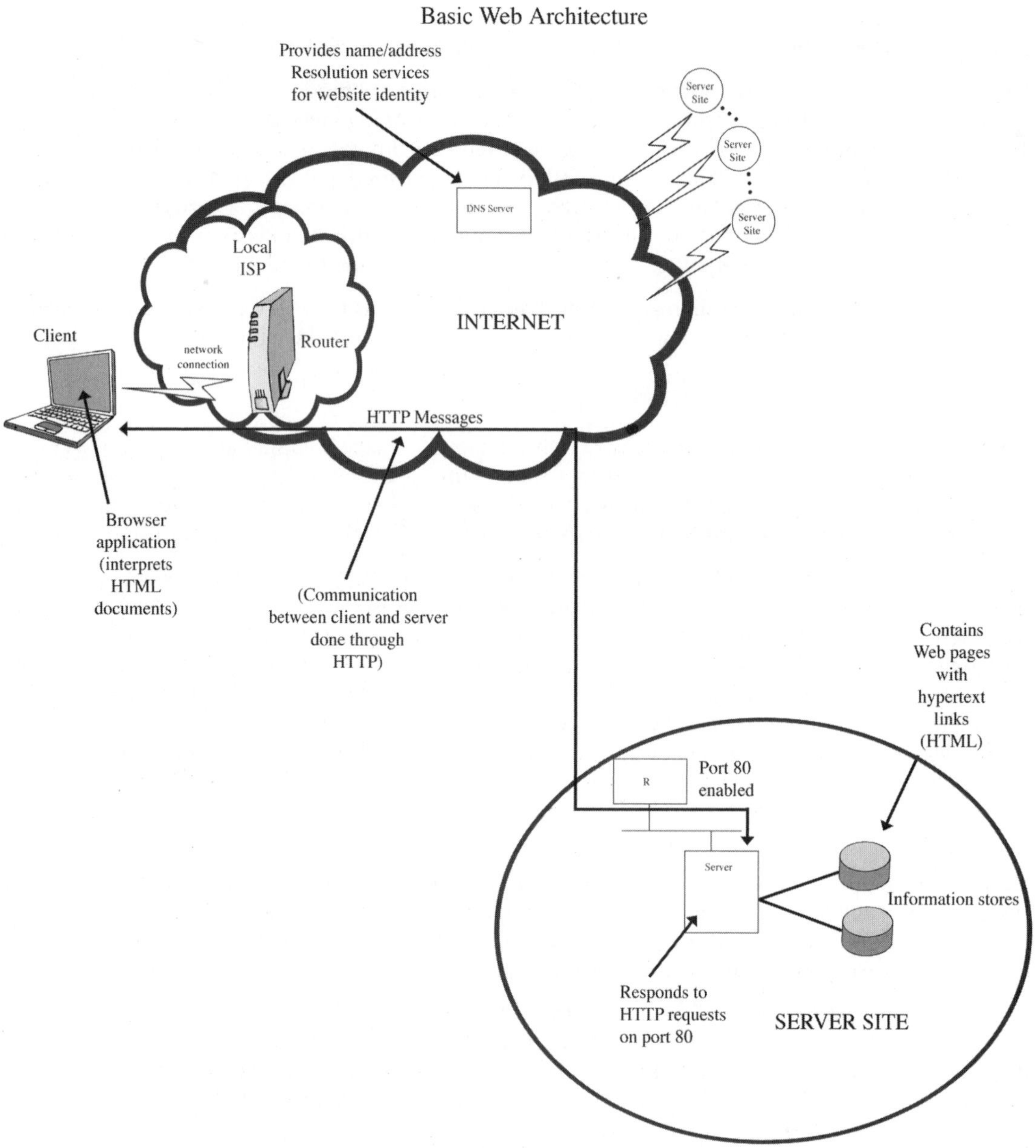

Basic Web Architecture

Provides name/address
Resolution services
for website identity

Server
Site

Server
Site

Server
Site

DNS Server

Local
ISP

INTERNET

Client

network
connection

Router

HTTP Messages

Browser
application
(interprets
HTML
documents)

(Communication
between client and server
done through
HTTP)

Contains
Web pages
with
hypertext
links
(HTML)

R

Port 80
enabled

Server

Information stores

Responds to
HTTP requests
on port 80

SERVER SITE

Figure 11-2   Basic Web architecture.

then uses this IP address to send an HTTP request for the page to TCP PORT 80 (HTTP port on the server). The server then receives this request. The server and the client can exchange operating parameters with each other. Once the session parameters are finalized, the server responds to the browser's

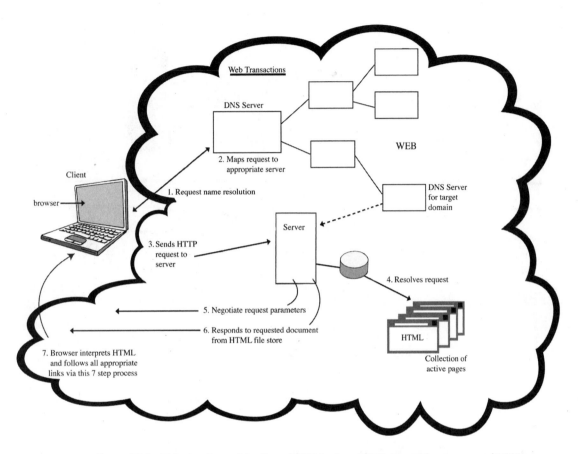

Figure 11-3   **This simple combination of DNS lookup, HTTP request/response, and HTML document translation and interpretation drive Web performance.**

request. The browser then interprets the HTML file. Based on the content of that file, the browser may initiate additional HTTP requests for resources specified inside the HTML page.

As is shown in Figure 11-4, the complete HTTP connection is exactly one transaction long. The HTTP protocol is stateless, meaning that each session is independent of the next. The entire process of working with Web pages has context from only the user's point of view. From the network point of view, these exchanges are without continuity (stateless). The messages exchanged contain headers along with the requested content. These headers are used to convey important metadata about the page, its properties, the page's security, and connection error messages and codes.

On the server side of the connection, Web servers usually run special server software. This software enables the server to handle multiple inbound requests for information, all from the TCP port 80 interface. This software can also be the base for managing the security policy of the server. Generally, these servers are fast systems with large amounts of memory and high-speed network connections. These systems run the minimum of necessary system services and have unnecessary services turned off. It is advisable to place the Web server on the DMZ of the site so that everyone can access it, yet it is isolated from

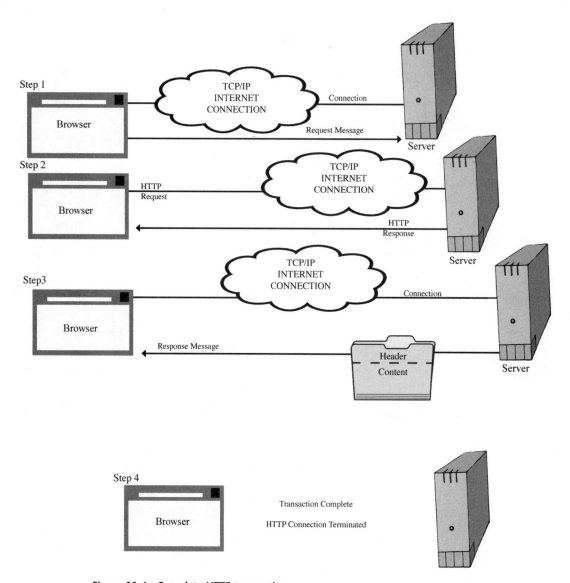

Figure 11-4   Complete HTTP transaction.

the corporate backbone. Server files should be write-protected and the server operating system hardened. Servers run many back end applications such as databases. Through these back-end applications, Web servers can provide advanced Web services.

Because the HTTP sessions are stateless and the servers often require a stateful connection with the client to satisfy backend applications, Netscape invented the cookie protocol. The cookie protocol is a part of HTTP v1.1. Essentially, the first time a client and a server connect, the server sends the client information back about the context of the session in a cookie (a small file). The content of the cookie varies and is determined by the server, based on its needs. An example of where a cookie is useful is in the case of filling out an online application. Because the HTTP sessions are one transaction long each, we cannot realistically complete a long application without cookies. First, the user begins the session and invokes the client to request the form. The server then delivers the form and opens up a back-end database application to capture the information on the form. The server gives the client a cookie with the information necessary for the server to, from time to time, get back to the database record just established as the user progresses with the session. Each time the user updates the database, the user passes the cookie back to the server. This enables the server to track the context of the conversation.

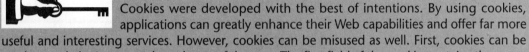

These Cookies Are Not Any Good

Cookies were developed with the best of intentions. By using cookies, applications can greatly enhance their Web capabilities and offer far more useful and interesting services. However, cookies can be misused as well. First, cookies can be used to track the Internet whereabouts of the user. The first field of the cookie contains the name of the site that issued the cookie. This information is always in the same place, so the process of extracting it can be automated. Anyone that has one of the user's cookies can formulate a template of that user's favorite sites. At the very least, this is clearly an invasion of privacy.

Second, the cookie can be used to deliver malware. The cookie protocol is nonspecific with respect to cookie content and, thus, it can become a perfect avenue to deliver malicious code that can slip through normal detection methods.

Third, the site that creates the cookie can share information about you and your interests with other sites. Lately this type of information has been used to create "customized advertising" directed at you. This customization is done through the exchange and monitoring of cookies from sites you visited. Through the use of tagged cookies, called persistent user ID cookies, you can then be tracked as you browse from site to site. Then when you log into a site that is part of the system of marketer's network, you are inundated with "directed advertisement."

Worst of all, there is really no easy way to discriminate between good cookies and bad ones. One way to address this concern is through the use of **cookie cutters**. Cookie cutters are software (separate or part of the browser) that offer you the choice of accepting or rejecting a cookie. One word of caution is that if you refuse a cookie, some sites may not operate correctly. Additionally, some sites will continue to offer the cookie over and over again even if they are continually refused.

The client systems can be made up of any computer and operating system that supports TCP/IP, the HTTP protocol, and an HTML browser. The client would also need to be able to reach the DNS server and have available user TCP ports.

USING CRYPTOGRAPHY TO BUILD A WEB TRUST

As you can see, the use of the Web is not extremely complex. In fact, the transactions are relatively simple. The complexities of the Web are handled through the specialized browser and server software applications. Thus, we are left with several security concerns that need to be addressed in the context of the client/server-oriented Web environment:

- How to provide confidentiality
- How to build trusted e-business relationships
- How to provide secure e-mail
- How to remotely manage the Web server and its contents

Because we have already defined the Web as a collection of interconnected pieces of hyperlinked documents, it logically follows that those documents are information. As was mentioned in Section Two, the cryptographic methods used to secure our information created from traditional on-system sources can be extended into other system and application areas. E-mail, online transactions, Web pages, and back-end application data are all forms of information. Thus, it is wise to proceed with the security of the Web by invoking cryptographic methods to protect this information.

The application of cryptographic methods to the Web environment is suitable. Just as we saw in the application of cryptography to network privacy in VPNs, this same extensibility exists in the Web space.

One difference between network information applications of cryptography and the Web-based application of cryptography is that, in the former, the information was exclusively under our control. On the Web it is not. With respect to Web services, the information is not really under any single entity's control and is, in some ways, linked to other elements of the system, which in turn can be linked to other elements of the system, and so on. This means that because it is difficult to predict in advance who will use the information and where it will travel, Web security cryptographic measures must employ extended strategies to be useful. The Web security level of the model is part of the information system security subset because it is not under the control of any one entity. Users of the Web, therefore, have little control over the extended security planning. We must protect ourselves by implementing strong security policies regarding Web usage. We must verify that merchants with whom we choose to engage in electronic commerce comply with our standards.

In the subsections of this chapter, presentations will be made regarding the most popular of these protocols and their applications. Then we will take a more detailed look at four of the protocols: **Secure Socket Layer (SSL)**, **Secure Electronic Transaction (SET)**, **Secure Shell (SSH)**, and **IPSec**. Each of these four protocols has a special purpose and is part of a comprehensive set of Internet protocols that can be integrated to form a Web security implementation.

SECURE WEB PROTOCOLS

Many protocols have been developed over the years to enhance the security capabilities of TCP/IP. Most of these protocols are based on one of the cryptographic strategies detailed in Section Two of the text. As can be seen in Table 11-1, a number of protocols can be used to enhance Internet (and Web) security. IPSec is perhaps the most fundamental of the group. IPSec operates at level three of the network model and can be used to provide secure tunneling (described in Chapter 9), authentication services, confidentiality services, and integrity services. IPSec is a standard feature in IP version 6.0.

SSL and **Transport Layer Security (TLS)** are two protocols designed to secure the exchange of information at the TCP level between clients and servers. SSL interacts with the applications and the TCP port. SSL is designed to allow for first-time communicating parties to share a trust without having any prearranged exchange of secure keys.

Table 11-1 Protocols that Enhance Internet Security

Applied Cryptographic Method	Secured Service
SSL (Secure Socket Layer) or TLS (Transport Layer Security –under development as Internet Standard version of SSL)	TCP Level -4 encryption (port 443)
SET (Secure Electronic Transactions)	Funds Transfers
SSH (Secure Shell)	Secure Login
S-HTTP (Secure Hypertext Transfer Protocol)	Secure Web Transactions
IPSec (IPv6)	Secure Level 3 (IP)
PGP (Pretty Good Privacy)	Secure E-mail
S/MIME (Secure Multipurpose Internet Mail Extensions)	Secure E-mail

Secure Hypertext Transfer Protocol (S-HTTP) is an extension of the HTTP service explained earlier. Although this service provides attractive security options, it is declining in popularity now that SSL is in place. S-HTTP, while somewhat of a legacy protocol, is available on a great number of Web servers.

SET is an application-layer architecture. SET integrates public key cryptography and digital signatures into a scheme of interconnecting customers to merchants to financial institutions. SET provides a mechanism for secure credit card usage on the Web. This strategy enables merchants and customers to exchange order and payment information electronically. It provides complete privacy of the credit card number and prevents credit authorization reuse.

Secure e-mail can be addressed utilizing the application layer–protocols S/MIME or PGP encryption. These protocols enable the CAIN principles for e-mail.

SSH is freeware developed in Finland that was designed to replace many of the remote administrative services developed previously (e.g., rlogin, TELNET). This package provides strong encryption for the establishment of secure communications pathways between administrators and remote systems. This method can be convenient for organizations with remote Web services.

In Figure 11-5, we see these protocols in relation to the TCP/IP model. Notice how the various security protocols show up at different layers of the model. This provides users with tremendous flexibility in addressing their Web-based security needs. In other ways, this creates confusion and can potentially cause implementation errors by network administrators who inadvertently forget a piece or cause conflicts in the configurations of complimentary products.

We will examine several of these protocols in more detail. It is important for readers to consult Appendix B to refresh their TCP/IP knowledge before proceeding.

Internet Protocol Security

Internet Protocol Security (IPsec) is an add-on technology to supplement the base IP protocol to enhance security. IPSec is optional in version 4.0 of IP but becomes a fully integrated part of the IP suite

Relating the Network Model to Web Security

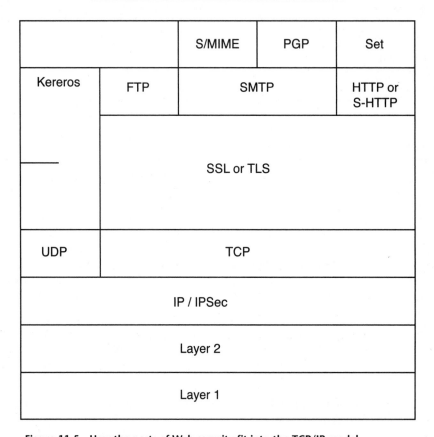

Figure 11-5   How the parts of Web security fit into the TCP/IP model.

in version 6.0. IPSec is specified in RFC 2401 (Overview of a Security Architecture), RFC 2402 (Description of a Packet Authentication Extension to IPv4 and IPv6), and RFC 2406 (Description of a Packet Encryption Extension to IPv4 and IPv6).

IPSec provides a flexible security process. It can be configured to be either extremely secure or minimally secure. IPSec ties the organization's security policy to the IPSec security controls. The basis for choosing between the security options is the use of a security association database. This database contains information regarding the type of cryptography, authentication algorithm, key values, key life, time interval of the security association, mode, and negotiable protocol parameters. Each piece of outbound traffic has its security parameter index matched to the particular security association. After the match is found, the proper method can be applied and the traffic can proceed along its way with the appropriate level of security.

IPSec comprises two different methods designed for different security applications:

- **Authentication Header (AH)**
- **Encapsulated Security Packet (ESP)**

The AH method is most often used when all that is required is the verification of the identity of the user or application that sent a packet. This method was devised to reduce the likeliness of IP spoofing and replay attacks. Essentially, each packet has both a MAC and a sequence number to protect against impersonation and reuse respectively. The MAC is tied to the security association and is therefore connected to keys that only the sender and receiver know. This provides authentication. The sequence numbers are unique in a session and therefore prevent the replay of a packet sequence.

The AH method can run in either tunnel or transport mode. AH does not support a mechanism for confidentiality of information. Figure 11-6 shows the variation in packet format between the two modes.

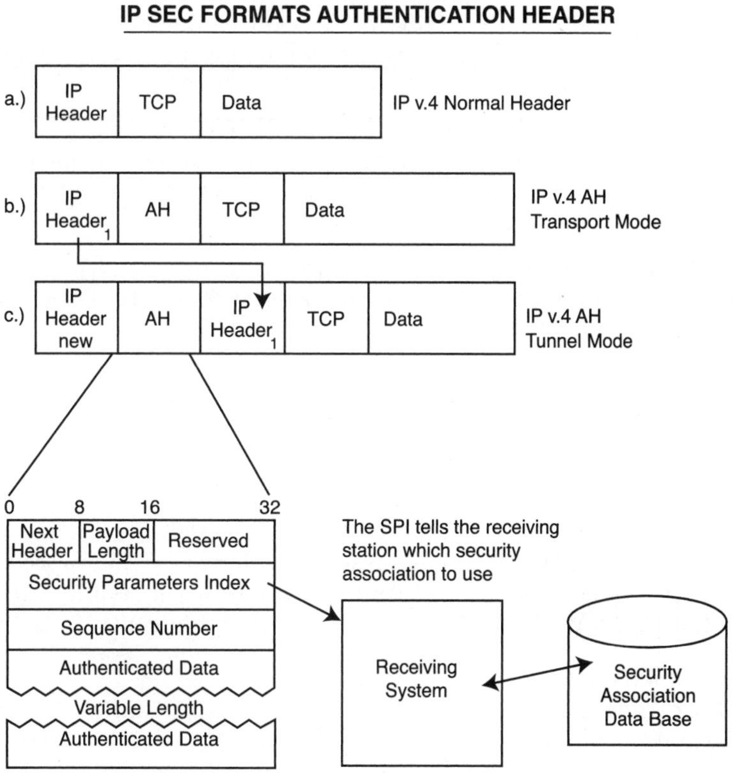

IP SEC FORMATS AUTHENTICATION HEADER

Figure 11-6 **Authentication header allows for a receiver to authenticate the user or application. This protects against IP spoofing and replay attacks.**

Notice that in tunnel mode, the AH includes the IP header; in transport mode it does not. It is also important to point out that the MAC is included in the authentication data field.

Earlier in the text we discussed the use of VPNs for the creation of cryptographic tunnels that can guarantee privacy while communicating through the Internet. We established that while there are several competing protocols (L2TP and PPTP), IPSec has now become the de facto industry standard. The other protocols are endorsed by technology giants Microsoft and Cisco. But IPSec has gained user community and Internet Engineering Task Force support. With the advent of IPv6, IPSec will be the principle VPN tunneling protocol.

The IPSec standard that is used for this purpose is the ESP method. This method provides confidentiality through your choice of rigorous cryptographic methods. It also provides optional authentication services. Like the AH method described previously, ESP is flexible. Each outbound packet is inspected by the IPSec router and the SPI is mapped to the corresponding security association. In this case, the SA will determine the type of encryption to use and the proper key to encrypt with. ESP also has a sequence number to prevent replay attacks.

The complete set of ESP packets for IPv4 is shown in Figure 11-7. Notice the difference between the tunnel mode and the transport mode. In the transport mode, the original user IP header is left intact and is not encrypted. In the tunnel mode, the original IP header is included in the encryption for maximum privacy. The original header is then replaced with the header from the source of the tunnel to the destination of the tunnel. This way, for site–to-site communications, the sending and receiving host addresses remain secret while the packet is on the Internet. This secrecy eliminates the possibility of the hacker mapping the network.

As in the case of AH, the ESP method can be configured to permit authentication of a user or an application through the inclusion of the MAC. If this is the case, ESP will add an optional authentication trailer to the message, as shown in Figure 11-7.

IPsec is a major milestone in the development of IP security. This protocol has profound implications for secure Web transactions because the IPSec protocol runs at level three of the OSI model and thus can be applied to any of the upper-level Web services.

S-HTTP

S-HTTP is a replacement service for HTTP when secure Web transactions are required. S-HTTP was a popular service at one time. The widespread acceptance of SSL, however, has reduced the need for the less-effective S-HTTP.

S-HTTP is a relatively simple extension of the HTTP protocol. Essentially, S-HTTP uses asymmetrical cryptography to initiate the service. This process begins with the client requesting a secure communication from the server. The user stipulates in the S-HTTP message header which security key lengths it supports and which encryption algorithms it uses. The server responds to this request with three items:

- Its public key
- The corresponding key length
- Algorithm information choices that correspond to the initial client request

The client then chooses a symmetrical session key that it wishes to use for the transaction. This key is temporary and because it is exclusively determined by the client, it is deemed to be as strong as the client key creation process permits. This is important because the use of weak keys can be problematic (see Chapter 7). Using the process described in PKCS #7 (Cryptographic Message Syntax Standard), the session key is determined. This key is then asymmetrically encrypted using the server's public key and sent to the server in the digital envelope. Upon receipt of the encrypted message, the server uses its private key and decrypts the digital envelope. This gives the server access to the symmetrical session key to be used during the upcoming exchange. The server then sends an encrypted message to the client using the symmetrical session key. This is shown in Figure 11-8.

The client can now decrypt the message and read the secure contents, as shown in Figure 11-9. Notice that the client is not required to identify itself. It is also not necessary for the client to participate in the PKI.

IP SEC FORMATS ENCAPSULATED SECURITY PACKET

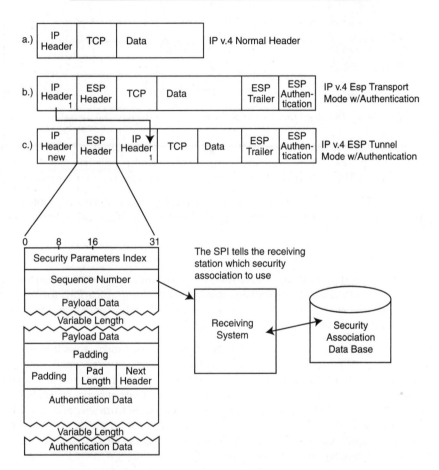

Figure 11-7 **ESP provides confidentiality through encryption and can optionally provide authentication services.**

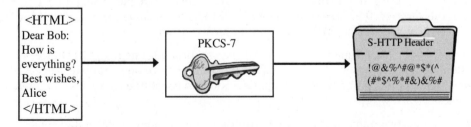

Figure 11-8 **The server encrypts the plain text message and wraps it within S-HTTP.**

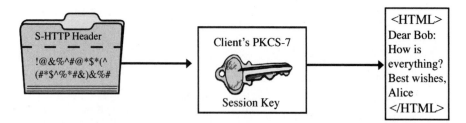

Figure 11-9   The client uses its PKCS-7 session key to decrypt the message.

This process is extremely inefficient because of the high setup time required to perform one transaction. (By definition the HTTP protocol is stateless and treats events asynchronously—one HTTP transaction is limited to one exchange.) This repetitive setup per transaction process is a major problem with S-HTTP.

Another objection to S-HTTP is that it works with Web transactions only. This is problematic because more and more Web applications extend beyond the traditional Web boundaries. For these reasons, SSL has become dominant.

Secure Socket Layer

SSL was originally developed by Netscape to provide secure communications between Web clients and servers. It has since grown to take on a prominent role in secure communications for Web transactions, FTP exchanges, and secure e-mail. SSL not only provides security functions but also acts as a compression agent. Because of its greater flexibility, it has replaced S-HTTP.

SSL operates at a level below the application with respect to the OSI model, thus it is able to support a variety of applications. Those applications include SSL-capable Web servers, e-mail, news, TELNET, or any TCP/IP port/socket application modified for this purpose. SSL requires the use of a port/socket interface (normally port 443). It allows a variety of key lengths and a choice of symmetrical encryption methods, including DES, Triple-DES, RC2 and RC4 methods, which range from secure to **crippled** (lax). Because the SSL session is at the TCP level, everything occurring at the application level is encrypted and confidential. This includes all information contained on the page, the particular URL that the session is accessing, cookies, HTTP header contents, and more.

The cryptographic technique is complex. The majority of that complexity is found in session establishment procedure. The steps to establishing an SSL session are shown in Figure 11-10.

In Step One of the process, the client initiates the secure connection request using the SSL client "hello" message. In this message, the client stipulates its desire to have a secure session and transmits its preference for encryption method, key size, and compression algorithm.

The server responds to this request in Step Two with an acknowledgement and its choice of cipher and compression methods. If for some reason the two sides cannot agree on a mutually agreeable set of parameters, the session fails at this point. Steps One and Two constitute a logical set of interconnected instructions.

Step Three has the server transmit its X509 v.3 certificate. This includes a copy of the server's public key, which is required by the client for use in Step Eight. At this time, the client has the option to verify the authenticity of the server through contact with the PKI trusted authority, Step Four. This is an important

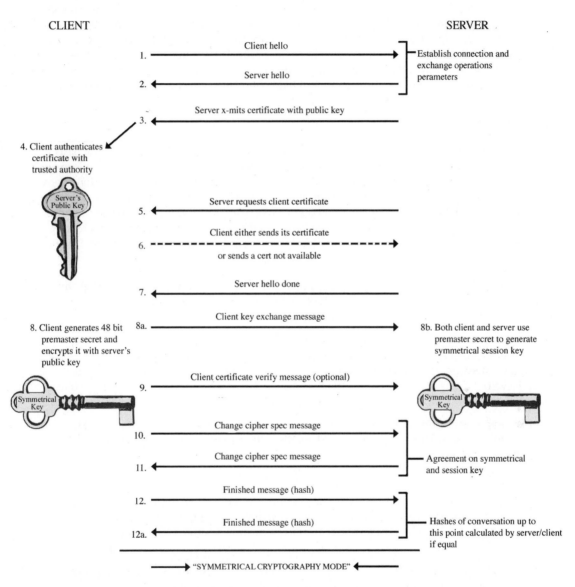

Figure 11-10   **The SSL handshake allows for building secure trusted relationships on a temporary basis.**

part of SSL because this is the step that enables trust between communicating parties. So often, clients are deceived by fraudulent Web sites and wind up conceding valuable personal information to an attacker.

Step Five of the process is the server request for a client certificate. This step and Step Six (the client response to this request) are both optional. The idea behind making these steps optional is that in some applications the client may not want to share identity information and therefore choose to remain anonymous. Because it was the client that initiated the connection, this is reasonable in some cases. However, for those cases where verifiability and authentication of the client are required, the mechanism is available. Steps Three through Six are the next logical block of related server actions, which conclude with the server "hello done" message.

Step Eight has three parts:

- Initially, the client calculates a 48-bit premaster secret. This secret is the basis for formulating the symmetrical session key later.
- This secret is encrypted with the server's public key, thus placing it in a digital envelope. This envelope is then transmitted to the server in the client key exchange message
- The server decrypts the digital envelope using its private key, revealing the premaster secret. At this time, both the client and the server use the premaster secret to generate the symmetrical session key (the process for doing this depends on the symmetrical algorithm chosen)

Step Nine is optional and is used only if the client authentication option is invoked. If Step Nine is used, it is the symmetrical key generated in step eight that is used to generate a secret that demonstrates that the client knows what the key is without revealing the key.

Steps Ten and Eleven are a mutual exchange of the "change cipher spec messages." This exchange confirms that both sides are in agreement as to the cipher arrangement. This is followed by each side sending the other a finish message. These messages contain a hash of the complete handshake (starting from Step One to Step Eleven). When both sides see that their respective checksums are equal, the two sides move to symmetrical cryptography mode, which begins the transmission of application data and transactions.

SSL provides a trusted and flexible relationship built on a temporary basis with no prior knowledge of the recipient necessary. Once in place, the SSL relationship can exist for all corresponding applications and multiple HTTP exchanges.

Secure E-Mail

Because e-mail is recognized as the number-one application used on the Internet today, it should be highly secured. Ironically, people that are weary of placing their credit card information on the Net are not the least bit concerned about sending personal and business correspondence via e-mail.

E-mail spoofing is a serious problem on the Net that can compromise a person's integrity and can cause major disruption to business operations. As can be seen from the simple e-mail spoofing lab in Appendix A, the ability to substitute a name into the from field of an arbitrary e-mail message is trivial. Even though the e-mail header information can be used to verify that the message did not in fact come from the person identified in the from field, how many people know how to check? For example, suppose someone sends a message to you that your bank is going out of business. It was stated in the message that you might wish to consider reallocating your funds to another recommended bank. If the message looked official enough, you just might take it seriously.

Authenticity is perhaps the single-most-important quality that e-mail has to have to continue to be accepted in a widespread fashion. Authenticity can be achieved through the use of digital signatures in conjunction with a trusted PKI.

Integrity of e-mail messages is equally important. Mail systems are essentially store-and-forward systems. Message stores are usually made at systems under the control of your employer or ISP. How do you know that no one has compromised the integrity of the e-mail? Changed content can lead to confusion. Subtle changes to messages can go unnoticed and be taken at face value. Integrity can also be addressed through the use of digital signatures.

Confidentiality or the expectation of mail privacy is something that most people take for granted. It is important that confidentiality be regarded as a high-priority item. Confidentiality is accomplished through encryption. However, since we do not always know the people we correspond with, it is unlikely that we will be able to secure a one-time symmetrical secret key from them. (Even using methods such as SSL are limited because they may not be set up for it.) Thus, even though asymmetrical cryptography is not well-suited for bulk-rate encryption of data (it is best suited for the exchange of symmetrical session keys—digital enveloping—as is the case in S-HTTP or SSL), we may be forced to use it for the confidentiality of secure e-mail. Of course, this presumes that the recipient of the e-mail is a member of a PKI and has a public key that you can use for encryption.

The two competing standards for e-mail security are the PGP method and the S/MIME method. Many similarities exist between the two methods. However, while the PGP method is more widely used, the S/MIME method is the Internet standard for secure e-mail transmission. This is because the S/MIME standard requires the use of X.509 v.3 certificates, which are verifiable through a trusted third party. PGP keys are issued by the parties themselves and the trust relationship is implied at the participant level. The trust is networked, meaning that if you trust me, then you will trust my friends. While that sounds nice, it is not the best of models to build a business around.

As can be seen in Figure 11-11, secure mail gateways can be used to convert messages from one format to the other. This should not be mistaken for increased trustworthiness, but it does provide a unification strategy that could potentially evolve into a ubiquitous trust.

In either case, as the figure shows, the digital signature is the essence of creating the authentication and integrity checking required. Of course the digital signature, in the presence of a PKI, can extend the principle of nonrepudiation into the mix.

Secure Electronic Transaction

SET was developed by Microsoft, Visa/MasterCard, and Netscape in order to promote secure credit card transactions on the Web. SET is a method of applying various cryptographic techniques to solve the problems associated with authentication and confidentiality of financial information within the realm of online businesses.

Unlike all of the other protocols that we have reviewed thus far—which are communications between client and server pairs—electronic business transactions are generally forged between three parties or more. In the SET model, are a minimum of four primary participants in a transaction: the customer, the merchant, the merchant's bank, and the customer's bank (issuer of the credit card).

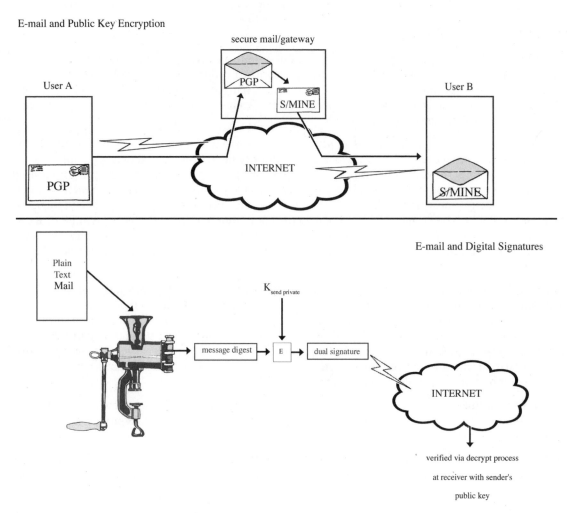

E-mail and Public Key Encryption

secure mail/gateway

User A

PGP

S/MINE

INTERNET

User B

PGP

S/MINE

E-mail and Digital Signatures

Plain
Text
Mail

$K_{send\ private}$

message digest

E

dual signature

INTERNET

verified via decrypt process

at receiver with sender's

public key

Figure 11-11   E-mail security.

Electronic financial transactions introduce the following complications that are not as prevalent in other Web communications:

- There are always more than two participants in the transaction. For the transaction between merchant and customer to be consummated, both the merchant's bank and the customer's bank needs to be involved

- Not all parts of the secure transmission should be accessible to all parties. The merchant does not need to see the customer payment information. From the merchant's point of view, what is needed is verification that the transaction was completed successfully. Verification from the merchant's bank, which has received verification from the customer's bank, should be more than sufficient. Likewise, there is no reason that the bank should be privy to the details of the customer's order information

- The payment information needs to be valid for one transaction only. This is perhaps the most important element of the SET transaction. If the customer provides the merchant with valid payment information (even though it is encrypted so the merchant cannot see it), what is to keep the merchant from resubmitting the payment information with false orders? SET has a strategy that handles exactly that scenario

As seen in Figure 11-12, the SET process is a synthesis of cryptography, specialty digital signatures, digital certificates, and best business practices. This figure shows the SET process as consisting of twelve steps:

1 After the customers have found the items they wish to purchase from a particular online merchant and procure the proper ordering form and certificate of the merchant's bank, the customers construct the order. On the order, clients specify the item identifiers, quantity, and cost.

2 The client prepares the payment information in a separate document. This information will include the name, number, and expiration of the credit card. This information is then tied to the order through a special dual-document digital signature.

3 The client then creates an encrypted version of the payment information and the dual-document digital signature. This encrypted Payment Information (PI) is coupled with the Order Information (OI) to form the outbound message.

4 SET then sends the information to the merchant.

5 The merchant takes the message apart and sends the PI on to the merchant's bank.

6 The bank receives the PI and decrypts the message. The merchant verifies the authenticity of the customer's bank with the trusted authority.

7 The merchant's bank sends an interbank request to the customer's bank for authorization.

8 The customer's bank responds with the authorization code.

9 The merchant's bank then sends the merchant the payment authorization.

10 1The merchant verifies the order with the customer and completes the transaction.

11 The merchant completes the transaction by confirming the completion of the transaction with the merchant's bank.

12 The customer's bank bills the customer and subsequently settles all accounts.

As you can see from this strategic level, the SET transaction satisfies the special requirements set forth earlier. Figure 11-13 details the two most important parts of the transaction: the construction of a confidential payment instrument, and the creation of the dual-document signature.

The creation of the dual-document signature is important because it limits the usefulness of this PI to this particular transmission. Because of the dual-document signature, the PI is tied to the order that is presented to the merchant. The signature process is quite simple. A message digest is calculated for each of the two documents: the OI and the PI. Those message digests are then concatenated to form the dual-document hash. The hash is then signed with the customer's private key. This generates the dual-document digital signature. It is important to realize that the signature is created using the customer's private key. This means that only the customer could have created it. This is important for two reasons.

First, the customer has taken responsibility for the purchase and the nonrepudiation aspect of the financial transaction is satisfied. Second, the order and the payment information are linked. Because no one else has the customer's private key, no one else can use the payment information for any other purchase (they would have to generate a new dual-document digital signature).

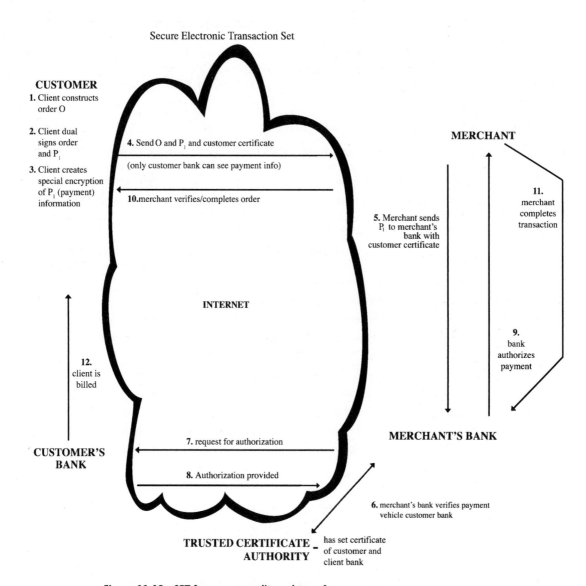

Figure 11-12   SET for secure credit card transfers.

The confidential payment instrument is important because it allows the customer to give the merchant the PI without the merchant being able to see what is in it. The process is somewhat more complicated that the normal encryption process and is shown in Figure 11-13. In the case of SET, the PI, dual-document digital signature, and the OI message digest are encrypted symmetrically with a customer-chosen symmetrical key.

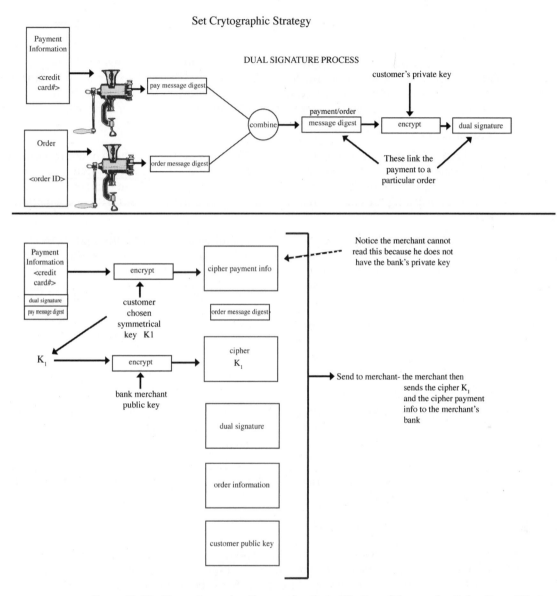

Figure 11-13 The customer has the merchant's certificate and the merchant's bank's certificate. By using these, the customer can send private and confidential payment information to the merchant's bank that the merchant cannot see.

The customer-chosen symmetrical key is then encrypted with the bank's public key. This forms a digital envelope for the bank to be able to retrieve the symmetrical key later. The cipher PI, order message digest, cipher key, dual-document digital signature, OI, and the customer's public key are then sent to the merchant.

The merchant can verify that the message came from the customer with the customer's public key and a digital certificate supplied by the PKI trusted authority. The merchant cannot read the PI because the merchant does not have the bank's private key.

The merchant then sends the cipher PI, the cipher symmetrical key, and the customer's public key on to the bank to get a payment verification from the financial institution. This payment method is actually more secure than a traditional in-person credit card transaction. Because the method has been engineered to restrict the reuse of the payment information, it is superior to any other method in use.

Remote Administration of Websites

Thus far we have been totally focused on the transactions that occur during the course of doing business on the Web and the special security requirements that make each unique. It is also important to consider the need for remote access to websites for page updates, collection of accumulated data, or to enable additional services. Considering how many organizations outsource their Web sites, there is a definite need to work remotely.

In the past, working remotely was difficult because the standard remote login facilities (RLOGIN, TELNET, etc.) were not equipped with security features. The SSH service was created for just that purpose. The program is freeware (for UNIX users)[1] that presupposes no existing affiliation with a PKI for the interaction. The program is a blend of both asymmetrical and symmetrical cryptography. Essentially, a secure login can be requested through the command:

```
User> ssh -L5555:www.yoursite.com:80
         Password: ********
```

Through these sessions, the administrator can run secure HTTP and FTP transmissions.

If this facility is not available, the next best thing is to use authenticated FTP services. Authenticated FTP services are standard on most Web server platforms. The problem with this approach is that the session is not encrypted (unless it is run over an SSL or IPSec session). The other issue that confronts users of this system is that the interface is susceptible to password cracking.

One last note regarding site management is that there is no replacement for a well-organized backup and recovery scenario. Assuming that your site is successfully hacked and defaced, it is critical that you be able to restore it as quickly as possible.

MAKING THE RIGHT CHOICE

During the course of reading this book, you have been exposed to many plausible security solutions. These solutions were presented in relative isolation of one another. This technique encourages focus. However, in the field, the practicing professional needs to choose between these various technologies. These solutions can overlap and cause confusion. It is important to note that not every technology is appropriate for every organization. In most large organizations, you will see almost all of these solutions in some form or another. In small organizations, you may see only one or two deployed.

In general, one can compare the effectiveness of a product based on eight criteria:

[1.] Commercial equivalents are available for Microsoft platforms.

- **The degree of security provided.** This area of study is dedicated to increasing overall security. Solutions need to incorporate this as their primary mission. This can be done either directly, such as through the use of cryptographic methods, or indirectly, by performing essential support services (i.e., IDS)
- **How easy or simple the solution is to use as a part of normal business operations.** Ideally, users should not feel the impact of the solution. The higher the degree of transparency to the user, the more likely the effect on security will be positive. This includes, but is not limited to, minimizing extra required actions by the user, limiting unnecessary planning or scheduling by the user, and avoiding the creation of new services
- **Focusing the solution on securing information.** As has been stressed throughout this text, securing the information we use should be the primary goal of any information security plan. Organizations must be sure to include products and services in the solution portfolio that enable the achievement of this goal
- **The degree of focus the solution has on the information system.** In the text we have repeatedly stressed the necessity of separation between the information and the information system. While the primary goal is to secure the information, the next-most-important series of actions needs to be securing the information system. Although we realize that this task is far more difficult, it is necessary to slow down intrusions, catch intruders, and discourage attack. The solidifying of the information system buffers the information from harm and maintains a high degree of trust in the system
- **The extent to which a product is internally focused with respect to the organization.** As was mentioned early in the text, a good number of attacks originate inside the perimeter of an organization. Most products and services are externally focused and offer little protection against inside jobs
- **The effectiveness of the solution at encouraging openness.** An underlying motivation for increasing information security is to promote openness. Security promotes trust, and trust promotes openness. Solutions that are offered should encourage applications that can be used to provide open services and the use of public transmission facilities
- **The affordability of the solution.** Many organizations today are finding themselves in economically difficult circumstances. Often, security will suffer as organizations choose to deploy the bulk of dollars elsewhere. The information security professional should be prepared for this. Choose solutions that provide the necessary coverage and security at an affordable price
- **Ease of implementation.** As with all technology, there is often a tradeoff between ease of use and ease of implementation. Many organizations do not maintain sufficient technical staff to engage in the deployment and maintenance of complex solutions. Ways to enhance ease of implementation should include configuration automation, rules-based systems, enhanced management and monitoring tools, and convenient scripting facilities

Throughout this work, we have discussed a number of the most common security technologies. Although generalizing at the category level can ignore certain isolated vendor adaptations, it is generally true that the products in the category measure similarly to the criteria posed. To that end a presentation of seven classes of security countermeasures are compared based on the eight criteria listed above. This presentation is made so that students can begin to understand the relationship and overlap of various products and strategies. This overlap is meant to illustrate the need for multiple countermeasures to be included in a solution. It is not meant to suggest, however, that any of the solutions presented should be displaced or avoided.

The eight criteria have been represented in a spider chart (Web diagram). These diagrams are useful in comparing attributes of a solution that are measured using multidimensional criteria. Charts that show a polarized set of measurements (skewed to one side) reflect more of a niche solution. This type of solution is generally good at accomplishing limited goals. Charts that reflect a more circular series of results elicit thoughts of balance and pervasiveness. The more rounded the chart and the more it covers the graph area, the more balanced and effective the solution is respectively.

The solutions that are compared include the following:

- Symmetrical cryptography
- Asymmetrical cryptography
- Antivirus countermeasures
- Firewall technology
- OS hardening solutions
- Screening router, demilitarized zones with address translation capabilities solutions
- Intrusion-detection systems

As seen in Figure 11-14, symmetrical cryptography fairs well. It is a good choice for providing overall security. It obviously provides the necessary information-security focus mandated by our model. Symmetrical cryptography is affordable, relatively easy to implement and secure. It is a technology that meshes well with other technologies that secure the information system such as VPN, SSL, and the like. Thus, we rate it highly. This technology provides security coverage with both an internal and an external effectiveness. Through the use of symmetrical encryption, information can be safe wherever it resides. Several burdens are placed on users of the technology, such as remembering to take the encryption action, rotation of keys, and secrecy requirements. The system also introduces additional work for system and network administrators. Symmetrical cryptography is most effective when used in conjunction with other solutions. This includes the network encryption packages discussed earlier and asymmetrical cryptography for secure automation of secret session key exchange.

Figure 11-15 illustrates the spider chart representing the asymmetrical encryption security profile. This solution is information-centric and secure. This may be one of the most affordable ways to protect information. It is extremely easy to use and requires little training. However, the product is complex to implement, especially in large environments, because it requires a significant project management effort to coordinate the multiple PKI vendors that source the information, build the required key distribution and management infrastructure, and to bring the system online. The system requires a great deal of continued management. This countermeasure does little to support the security of the information system. The strongest point of this solution is that it encourages open applications and online commerce better than any other strategy. This solution is an appealing complement to other solutions. It can be used with symmetrical cryptography to proliferate the secure exchange of symmetrical session keys. It can be used as part of authentication and verification systems. It can be used to sign code for distribution. It is an essential element in almost any public application.

Figure 11-16 illustrates the antivirus protection solution security profile. Antivirus countermeasures are a necessity in today's modern security implementation portfolios. By looking at the spider chart, we see a well-rounded solution that provides moderate levels of security throughout all aspects of the security implementation. This solution is provided at midrange pricing levels and is important in the security of

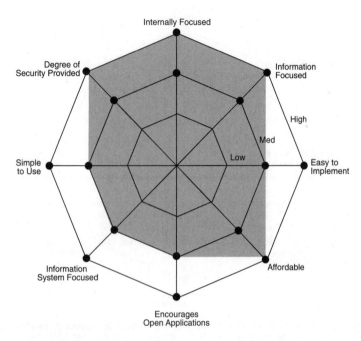

Figure 11-14   Symmetrical encryption has perhaps the most balanced security profile. It offers affordable, secure, and easy-to-use protection for both internal and external coverage.

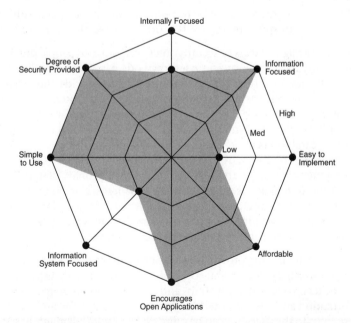

Figure 11-15   Asymmetrical cryptography protects information and encourages openness in a secure way. Its affordability offsets its apparent lack of contribution to information system security.

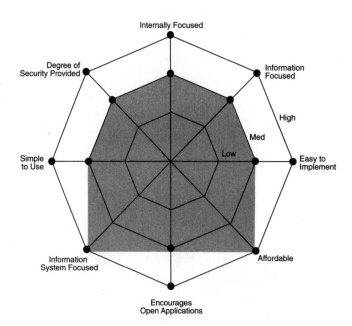

Figure 11-16 Antivirus countermeasures are a necessity in today's modern security implementation portfolio. It offers moderate yet balanced security across all areas of the organization at midrange pricing. The single drawback is that it is primarily reactive in nature.

the information system. The single drawback of this class of products is that they require a signature file to function properly. This signature file must be refreshed from time to time. This product uses the signature file to identify malicious software threats. It is primarily reactive in nature.

Firewalls are regarded as the flagship class of security solutions. Most laypeople quickly identify cybersecurity with firewalls and many individual Internet users own one. However, as is illustrated in Figure 11-17, firewalls are actually quite skewed in their application. Firewalls do provide enhanced information system security focus. They also encourage the opening of our systems to the Internet in a secure fashion. These products are transparent and offer good levels of security. However, they are primarily externally focused and offer little to no protection against internal attacks. They really do not focus on the security of the information directly and can be expensive and difficult to configure and use. The latter of these is especially true in a large corporate environment. Firewalls offer the best protection for the information system that is connected to the Internet because that is the intent of their primary design. They attempt to secure the area of the information system that is subjected to the broadest spectrum of attacks. Therefore, the firewall can never be totally secure. There are varying levels of firewall products ranging from limited personal firewalls to impressive corporate security management firewalls. Firewalls, when combined with symmetrical encryption, can create a formidable entry-level security blanket.

As seen in Figure 11-18, OS hardening provides much of the internally focused security required by our model. OS hardening is broken up into several components: best practices (especially performing system updates), integrity checkers, system analysis tools, and configuration management tools. OS hardening affects both the information and the information systems. Generally, the applications of OS hardening techniques are transparent to the users but can be quite difficult to implement. Based on the broad range

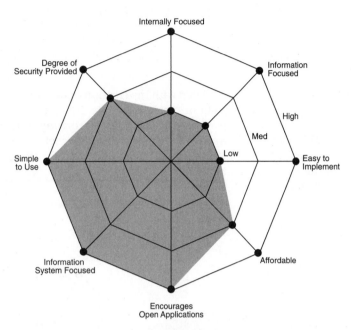

Figure 11-17 Firewalls address a focused part of information security with intense accuracy. Firewall products are generally considered complex and outwardly focused.

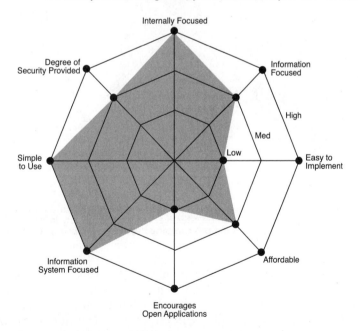

Figure 11-18 OS hardening provides important coverage of the internal information system. Essentially, these tools, methods, and software "keep our house in order" and lay the groundwork for other security measures.

of possible attacks against operating systems, these solutions can never achieve the highest levels of security. Attacks against operating systems are constantly evolving, making them difficult to defend against. These OS hardening solutions do help us effectively "keep our house in order". One of the noticeable deficiencies is that OS hardening provides little noticeable benefit to encouraging openness. Actually, the harder the OS, the less open the system becomes.

Figure 11-19 depicts the security profile associated with the creation of network choke points, otherwise known as demilitarized zones. These DMZs utilize screening routers, LAN technologies, and address-translation devices to isolate public from private portions of the information system. The creation of the DMZ can be used as an alternative to firewalls or for a most secure Internet access point in conjunction with firewalls. Notice the similarity in profile between this solution and the firewall solution. The DMZ accomplishes many of the same goals but is somewhat more limited in scope. Again, this is a specialty solution and is outwardly focused.

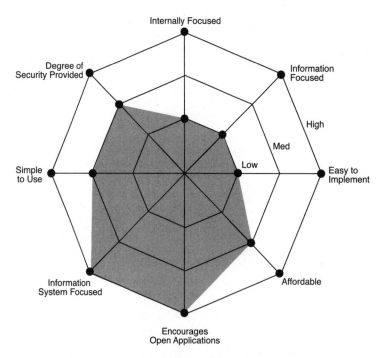

Figure 11-19 The creation of a DMZ provides an alternative to the firewall. Both are niche products that can be effective. The DMZ lacks any internal focus. It can be (and in some cases should be) combined with firewall products to form a considerable perimeter defense.

Finally, in Figure 11-20, we examine the security profile of the intrusion-detection system. The IDS profile is also skewed. This time the skew favors internal protections and the information system. Notice that this diagram illustrates that the IDS is moderately tough to use and can impact users (depending on implementation tactics). IDSs can be expensive, and are generally work intensive to install and make useable. IDSs are primarily reactive and serve in more of a support role to other defense measures. IDSs are necessary in today's security portfolios. They align technology with crisis-management operations and

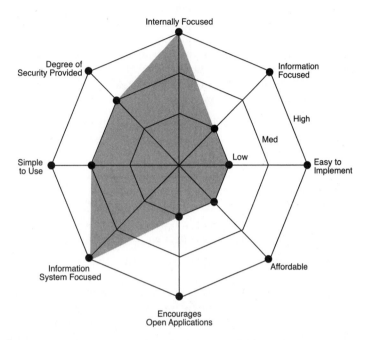

Figure 11-20   IDSs are a necessary complement to other security countermeasures. The generally reactive products provide the necessary internal focus to trigger action. They are generally regarded as the intermediary between technology and crisis-management teams.

provide the necessary interface between them. IDSs also can be used to trigger appropriate responses to minimize ongoing damage from various continuing attacks. IDSs complement most of the other aforementioned technologies.

These classes of solutions represent a broad survey of the industry. They are included to illustrate the type of analysis that should be conducted in the security design process. The object is to combine as many of these solutions as are required (to the appropriate degree) so that a graph of your complete security solution covers the entire graph area. Notice how several of the solutions are complementary and feed nicely off each other. Some of the solutions are internally focused, others are externally focused. Some of the solutions emphasize information security, while others are aimed at the security of the information system.

WHERE TO FROM HERE?

Having completed the material in this text, you should now have a firm understanding of information security concepts. The most important of these concepts is the integration of cryptography into security planning and implementation, which can be achieved in a variety of ways. Cryptographic methods are used for safe storage of information. They can be used to provide digital signatures, network tunneling, and Web transaction security. They are also useful agents of authentication and verification protocols. Cryptographic methods help us to satisfy the essential CAIN requirements for information security. It is essential to become involved in surveying the literature for new advancements in cryptographic methods.

Complementary material to this text includes a broader course in information system security. It is clear that it is necessary to separate the information security requirements from the information system security requirements. Students should have a firm understanding of how to effectively and directly protect information. Therefore, it is now necessary to focus on the security of the networks and systems, which create the information system. Students should keep in mind the overlap between securing the information and securing the information system. Securing the information system is a much more daunting task. It can almost assuredly never be complete. Information system security is a continual improvement process.

Students that aspire to work in this field should also take courses in cyberlaw and computer forensics. These courses will build on many of the concepts presented in this text. Their particular focus is on law enforcement technique. This information can lead to many interesting career opportunities. These courses also provide the necessary background to work with other branches of corporate security.

Those students wishing to pursue careers in the development or cracking of cryptographic methods will require the advanced study of cryptography. Many courses and texts address this subject. Most of these require an understanding of advanced mathematics. It is essential that students wishing to work in this area take the requisite mathematics courses as part of their preparation.

Looking ahead, the practicing professional should be associated with organizations that provide security and technology updates. They should also become collectors of information security statistics. They should become regular reviewers of the Web sites listed in the reference section of this book. They must possess strong project management skills. Practicing professionals require highly developed technical skills. These skills should be in the areas of network design, information management, and systems administration. They need to be visionaries who can adapt quickly to change. The essence of the subject matter is that it will be continually evolving and improving.

SUMMARY

This chapter was constructed to address the extended security needs associated with the Web-based business use of the Internet. The use of the Web for business transactions create a variety of requirements that are more complicated than the simple exchange of messages between two parties.

All of the exchanges are conducted primarily over the open Internet. Some exchanges are simply informational (e.g. requesting a Web document). Other exchanges (financial transactions) involve sensitive information and may include multiple concerned parties. Still other transactions may include the need for bulk transfer of encrypted information between nonacquainted parties. All of these requirements need to be addressed using the TCP/IP protocol, which was not originally intended to perform these types of security functions.

Cryptography plays a substantial role in the satisfaction of these advanced Web-based requirements. During the last decade, a significant number of security protocols and security methods have been integrated into the TCP/IP architecture to accommodate these needs.

The most basic of these is the IPSec method. IPSec runs at Level 3 of the OSI model and thus can be used as a security blanket for all traffic leaving a protected site or host. The problem with IPSec is that it cannot directly touch the application and, thus, does not offer complete end-to-end security.

S-HTTP was at one time considered the best security option for Web-based document transfer. This method was replaced with SSL, which offers more flexibility and versatility. The SSL session, once established, can address the needs of many Web-based applications simultaneously.

S/MIME and PGP can be used to provide confidentiality, authenticity, integrity, and nonrepudiation (in the case of S/MIME) for e-mail traffic. S/MIME is the Internet standard because it adheres to the hierarchical trust network utilizing X.509 v3 certificates. PGP does not offer the same level of trust. Although PGP is popular, it is not as formally accepted.

SET was created to allow for the secure exchange of financial information between multiple parties. This protocol is a set of special digital signatures, symmetrical and asymmetrical cryptography, digital certificates, and best business practices, which form the unified secure payment network.

SSH is a program that uses a combination of cryptographic methods to allow for the remote administration of servers. This program allows for a secure login and subsequent secure sessions (also FTP and HTTP) with a server.

Authenticated FTP is an alternative solution to SSH. FTP has some limitations, yet it offers reasonable authentication control. It is also important that all servers utilize best practice disaster recovery and backup plans.

The chapter concluded with an analysis and comparison of all the general categories of methods described in the text. This information is presented to give students a perspective on the amount of overlap between methods. It should also help reinforce the absolutely essential need for cryptographic solutions to protect information. This information also points out that no single technology can address all of the requirements of information and information system security.

STUDY QUESTIONS

1 For Web-based businesses to be successful, it is essential that the interfaces to the cryptographic systems are_____. (choose one)

   a. Easy to decipher

   b. Extremely complicated for the user

   c. Easy to use

   d. Based on SSL

2 What is the name for the group of applications whose sole purpose is to interpret HTML documents? (choose one)

   a. Search engines

   b. Web browsers

   c. Tag interpreters

   d. Web clients

3 How does a client machine find the Web address associated with a particular URL? (choose one)

   a. It uses translation software in the interpreter

   b. It sends a message to the nearest DNS

   c. It uses hashing to translate the address

   d. It sends a message to the URL server

4 **True___ False___**   HTTP is a stateful protocol.

5 What does the first field of a cookie contain? (choose one)
   a. Chocolate chips
   b. The encryption algorithm
   c. The public key for the site
   d. The name of the issuing site

6 At which level of the network model does IPsec operate? (choose one)
   a. Level 6
   b. Level 4
   c. Level 3
   d. Level 2

7 **True___ False___**   In a successful SSL transaction, it is necessary for the client to grant the certificate request of the server.

8 The best security method for the transmission of secure e-mail is_____. (choose one)
   a. Symmetrical encryption
   b. Asymmetrical encryption
   c. IPSec
   d. SSL

9 In the SET model, what is the minimum number of primary participants in a transaction? (choose one)
   a. Two
   b. Three
   c. Four
   d. Five

10 Which security solution is best for protecting the information system connected to the Internet? (choose one)
   a. Virus scanning software
   b. Encryption
   c. Biometric authentication
   d. Firewalls

11 AH and ESP are two security methods of _____. (choose one)

   a. SSL

   b. SET

   c. PPTP

   d. IPSec

12 Most of the business conducted on the Internet is done _____. (choose one)

   a. Anonymously

   b. Using eBay

   c. Through banks

   d. Via e-mail

13 Cookies can NOT be used to _____. (choose one)

   a. Track Internet whereabouts

   b. Track context of a session

   c. Send e-mail

   d. Deliver malware

14 _____ invented the cookie protocol. (choose one)

   a. Microsoft

   b. Netscape

   c. AT&T

   d. Apple

15 SSL and TLS secure the exchange of information at the _____ level. (choose one)

   a. TCP

   b. IP

   c. Network

   d. Session

16 A(n) _____ accomplishes many of the same goals as a firewall but is more limited in scope. (choose one)

   a. Proxy server

   b. Screening router

   c. IDS

   d. ICQ

17 _____ favor internal protection and the information system. (choose one)

    a. PKIs

    b. IDSs

    c. Screening routers

    d. DMZs

18 SET is a(n) _____ layer architecture. (choose one)

    a. IP

    b. TCP

    c. Session

    d. Application

19 **True___ False___** OS hardening makes a system more open.

20 The HTTP port on a server is TCP port ____. (choose one)

    a. 21

    b. 23

    c. 80

    d. 84

ESSAY QUESTION

Given that the IPSec protocol is emerging as a ubiquitous standard for encryption, how will this network-based protocol provide more secure Web transactions? How can this protocol affect the information stored on the Web site? How will this protocol affect system performance?

What do you suspect will happen to S-HTTP in the next three years? Why?

CASE STUDY

Back at Cureme Hospital, you are almost complete with your assignment and the hospital administration is pleased with your progress. However, Phil Memory has asked that you perform one additional task before you leave. He is working with Tobias Everything on an electronic pharmacy and an online bill payment system for the hospital. He wants your opinion on how to create secure and private transactions. He would also like to know how doctors from various practices can communicate patient referrals online (including sending patient case files on the Internet from doctor to doctor confidentially).

What do you propose? Break the problem up into three parts: (1) currency transactions, (2) Internet privacy, and (3) authentication and verification. Look at the use of SET, IPSec, and SSL. Do any of these fit the need? What else might you propose?

Finally, collect all of the information from the seven case studies that you have completed and compile a final project summary document. This document should be made as professional as possible. If you are working in a group, create a paper and a PowerPoint presentation for the class on your project's highlights.

GLOSSARY

abstraction
Programmatic enhancement intended to hide the details of complex sublayers of the system. An example of this is Windows Explorer, which hides the details of the more complex file-management subsystem.

ACC
Annual Cost of the Countermeasure. The ACC is the yearly cost of methods used to ensure information security.

access control
The control of admission of a user to a trusted area of the information system (physical or electronic) based on the implementation of an access control policy using products, procedures, access control lists, and an authentication information base.

ACL
Access Control List. A means by which the identity of a user is mapped to a resource for the purpose of authentication and granting of access and use privileges.

ACL router rules
Rules allowing or denying access based on protocol headers. The rules are established by the network administrator.

active attack
Overt action taken by someone to disrupt, manipulate, corrupt, or access a system.

agent
Part of the IDS, whose job is to reside on information system entities, collect information, and report it back to a central repository.

aging
The process of allowing the IDS to evolve its statistical database over time.

anomaly models	An IDS model that compares current activities to the statistically derived normal actions on a host or network and reports those activities that deviate from that norm.
application-level gateways	Servers that act as intermediaries between the public network and the private servers. These gateways force the complete stripping of all protocol headers from the information in transit, reauthenticating the user, verifying content, and repackaging the information in local protocols. Application-level gateways are also known as proxy servers.
Arms Export Control Act (1949)	Law put in place to allow the government a way to control munitions manufactured in the private sector.
ARP cache poisoning	Also known as ARP spoofing. Method of session hijacking. Attacker assumes the IP host identity of a trusted host while substituting the attacker's MAC address for that of the attacker.
asymmetrical algorithm	A keyed cryptographic technique that uses one key for the encryption algorithm and another, different key for the decryption algorithm.
attack probability	Calculation of the likelihood of an attack based on historical data, broad-based data sources, and the information security professional's instincts.
authentication	The act of binding an entity (information/person) to a representation of identity.
authentication factors	Methods that allow the organization to verify the user's identity based on information stored in the authentication information base.
authenticity	The ability to determine whether the information accessed is the original information as it was intended to be presented.
backdoor	Application entry points purposely left unclosed so developers or hackers can gain unobstructed access at their convenience.
bastian hosts	Systems that reside on the DMZ buffer. These hosts have most of the standard services normally provided on a host turned off. They are typically used to preauthenticate users prior to actually granting access to the desired service.
bind	Process of associating the distinguished name of the certificate user and the identity of the member, via a certificate policy.

biometric factors — Authentication factors based on a physical characteristic or a means of physical expression that only the owner can reproduce. Signatures, voice prints, and fingerprints are examples.

bit shifting — Moving the position of a set of binary bits right or left. Shifting left is equivalent to multiplication.

bits — Single binary digits. The smallest addressable computer data unit represented as a one or a zero.

block cipher — An encryption method taking a fixed-length block of text as input to an encryption algorithm along with the symmetrical key.

boot sector viruses — Viruses that inject themselves into the boot sector of the disk

brand — Name recognition and name association used by a company linking the company image to its products. It is one of the most important elements of a company's commercial success. Brand value is difficult to quantify.

buffer overflow — Memory bounds violation caused by a faulty application or system program, which allows a communications program or other user program to input more data to the fixed-size buffer than it was designed to handle.

bytes — Groups of eight bits.

CAIN — Confidentiality, Authenticity, Integrity, and Nonrepudiation.

CBA — Cost Benefit Analysis. This compares the annual loss expectancy prior to implementation of security measures with the Annual Loss Expectancy (ALE) after the countermeasure deployment plus the Annual Cost of the Countermeasure (ACC).

certificate — An electronic document that identifies a party and that party's public encryption algorithm, parameters, and key. The certificate also includes, among other things, the identity and a digital signature from the entity that created the certificate. The content and format of a certificate are defined by ITU-T Recommendation X.509.

certificate policy — The certificate policy determines the operating parameters regarding the generation, distribution, and management of key pairs.

certificate practice statement	Interauthority policies used to define the certificate processes employed by a trusted authority. These statements provide the foundation for interauthority cooperation.
certification authority	Entity who verifies the identity of a party applying for a digital certificate and manages the administration of certificates.
chaining	Process of cryptographically linking every block of a message together with the previous blocks.
checksum	A function that takes a long sequence of data and represents it in a significantly smaller one via a mathematical mapping process. See Hash.
choke points	The place that all inbound and outbound network traffic to an organization's private network is forced to travel through so it can be examined.
chosen plain text attack	An attacker forces the source to generate a cryptographic message containing a specific known term or phrase.
cipher	A method, expressed as an algorithm in programmatic terms, that can be used to transform an original message into an encrypted message. The cipher must also supply a method for converting the encrypted message back into the original message.
cipher block chaining (CBC)	Mode of block encryption that makes use of an arbitrary initialization vector and the exclusive-or function. After the first block of text is encoded, the cipher is used to create the second block of text. This process continues until the nth block of plain text is incorporated into the cipher.
cipher feedback	Mode of block encryption similar to the chaining mode of combining the ciphertext and plain text.
ciphertext	Resulting output of a cipher; the encrypted message.
clipper chip	NSA chip that utilizes the 80-bit skipjack encryption algorithm and has the ability to create a double-encrypted copy of the message key (see LEAF).
closed architecture	See permission-based architecture.

code vulnerabilities	Identification of coding flaws that can be exploited.
collision resistant	Property of a hash function that creates a one-to-one mapping between the source string and the output string, ensuring that another message using the same hash function would not result in the same hash value.
computational linguistics algorithms	Programs that use heuristic methods to express language relationships programmatically.
computationally secure	Term meaning that if the time to break a cipher takes longer than the useful life of the information, or if the cost to break the cipher is higher than the cost of the information, the information is secure.
computer forensic science	The science of acquiring, preserving, retrieving, and presenting data that have been processed electronically and stored on computer media.
confidentiality	The concept that information is not made available or disclosed to unauthorized individuals, entities, or processes.
confusion	Utilizing encryption keys to create a relationship between the key and the ciphertext that is as complex as possible for the purpose of hiding language patterns.
congruent	Two different numbers, each divided by the same number and producing the same remainder.
content checking	Screening information for malicious data.
cookie cutters	Software (separate or part of the browser) that offers you the choice of accepting or rejecting a cookie.
cracker	Person who breaks into computer systems with malicious intent. Crackers often damage information, create disruptions in service, and/or execute denial-of-service attacks.
crippled	Information security term for an encryption method that is lax, weak, or has been compromised.
critical information failure	Failure of a business to retrieve, produce, or modify information critical to serving customer needs that results in a partial, ongoing, or total loss in revenue.

cross-scripting   See poison cookies.

cryptanalysis   The science of converting ciphertext back into plain text without complete knowledge of all parts of the cipher.

cryptanalyst   A person that performs cryptanalysis of a message; a code breaker.

cryptographer   A person who develops ciphers.

cryptographic algorithm   The method used to encrypt plain text.

cryptographic checksum   A message digest that is calculated for a message and is then encrypted with a secret key. See Message Authentication Codes (MACs).

cryptographic strength   Measurement of the average time it would take for an encryption code to be broken, based on algorithm, key, key length, etc.

cryptography   The art of protecting information by making it unreadable (encrypting information).

cyberterrorists   Those who manipulate systems in the worldwide computer community for the purpose of causing mass confusion, disruption of critical infrastructure, destabilization of financial mechanisms, obtaining false documents, conducting covert operations, or, in extreme cases, to actually cause harm or death.

Data Encryption Standard   See DES.

data integrity   The concept that data have not been altered or destroyed in an unauthorized manner.

data origin authentication   The corroboration that the source of data received is as claimed.

DDOS attack   Distributed Denial-Of-Service attack is the coordinated effort of simultaneous DOS attacks, usually initiated from unsuspecting hosts (zombies).

decryption   The process of turning ciphertext back into plain text.

defense-in-depth	Concept of layering security defenses so that the outer layers of the security model discourage or block hackers before they ever get close enough to the information to do any real damage.
DES	Data Encryption Standard. Popular symmetrical encryption algorithm that is still widely used today. It was released by NBS in 1977.
diffusion	Dissipating the statistical structure of the plain text alphabetic patterns so they are nonexistent in the ciphertext.
digital enveloping	Also known as secret key exchange. An asymmetrical algorithm (primarily Diffie-Hellman) used to transmit a symmetrical key.
digital signature	A special case of a cryptographic checksum that is encrypted using a public key algorithm or asymmetric algorithm. It allows a recipient of the data unit to prove the source and integrity of that unit and protect against forgery by the recipient.
digrams	Groups of two letters appearing with a predictable frequency in the plain text message.
director	Part of an Intrusion-Detection System (IDS), whose job is to take the collected information and analyze it according to the IDS method deployed (statistical or misuse).
discretionary access control	The author of the information or the owner of the system determines the access requirements.
DMZ	Demilitarized Zone. A DMZ is an intermediate LAN that sits between the two screening routers that is a neutral portion of the network for visitors and owners of the site.
DNS	Domain Name Server. A hierarchy of servers, each containing information in a logical subtree of the overall domain for the purpose of identifying network entities.
DNS spoofing	Method of session hijacking. Attacker directly manipulates the DNS server entry, redirecting connection requests to the attacker who is posing as the trusted host.

DOS attack   Denial-Of-Service attack occurs when an attacker sends a large number of connection requests, information requests, or synchronization messages that overwhelm the host, rendering it impossible for legitimate requests to be processed.

dumpster diving   Hackers search the garbage or desk of the victim in an effort to find access codes, file names, information itself, or other important items that can be used to compromise security.

dynamic packet filtering   An advanced form of packet filtering based on the state of the enterprise application environment, the state of the network, and the policies of the security plan. Also called stateful inspection.

EAA   Export Administration Act. Controls items on the ITAR which are dual-use (military and civilian) and is part of the Department of Commerce.

Economic Espionage Act of 1996   Enacted to provide stronger penalties for anyone who reveals a trade secret or fraudulently obtains a trade secret to a foreign government, conspired to commit such a crime, or committed the theft of a trade secret.

El Gamal algorithm   Asymmetrical key generation algorithm.

EMR   Electromagnetic Radiation. Energy given off by electrical pulses conducted inside a wire, screen, or other electrical device.

ECM   Electronic Codebook Mode. Block cipher method where the encryption routine simply calculates the cipher, one block at a time, until it is done without concern about duplication of cipher blocks.

elliptic curve cipher   Asymmetrical key generation algorithm that takes advantage of the geometric properties of certain curves. The algorithm maps plain text to points on a curve, then use elliptical mathematical methods to create the cryptography.

e-mail flood   Attack rendering a user's e-mail system unmanageable by filling it with huge amounts of unsolicited e-mail messages.

e-mail spoofing   Sending a message using a different person's name in the sender field so as to impersonate the actual legitimate user.

e-mail virus   Viruses that work by taking advantage of the macros or scripts that can be run in attached files (e.g., Word, Excel, PowerPoint, Access). These scripts can be set to run when the mail message is opened.

encrypt   Process of cloaking or encoding information so it is not easily identifiable.

encryption key   A secret software code that is input into a cryptographic algorithm to enable encryption or decryption. This code adjusts the behavior of the algorithm so the results of encryption are unique.

Enigma machine   Encryption machine created by German inventor Arthur Scherbius. The machine uses a keyboard that feeds into a complex series of rotors, terminating at an indicator lamp that shows the encrypted character.

entity   An entity can be a person, computer, piece of information, file, software package, network component, or other principal that can be uniquely labeled inside the information system.

ESIGN   Electronic Signatures in Global and National Commerce Act. Signed on June 30, 2000, this law creates a framework in which electronic signatures can be accepted with the same validity as written signatures.

eavesdropping   Social and electronic methods with the ability to record content of network messages that can be reviewed to reveal information.

Feistel ciphers   Encryption algorithms that allow us to define our own complex reversible functions. These algorithms mix parts of an encryption key with parts of plain text to create the ciphertext. Feistel ciphers have the general properties of using rounds, chaining, reversibility, and operating on blocks in various modes.

Financial Services Modernization Act   See GLB.

firewalls   Combination products that provide the functions of screening routers, proxy servers, network address translation, plus stateful inspection. Guardian devices that are meant to block network-based attacks from infiltrating into the private network.

flooding   Overloading a system or host with an unreasonable amount of legitimate messages requiring action.

forecasting	Predicting the outcomes of events where certain (isolated) situational inputs are unknown, based on highly evolved historical data or experimentation.
Freedom of Information Act	Under this law, a person or organization has the right to obtain information developed or procured by the federal government from the public record.
function	A rule that allows the mapping of elements of one set (the domain) to those of another set (the range).
GLB	Graham-Leach-Bliey Act of 1999 articulates the privacy requirements of banks, insurance companies, and securities firms with regard to the disclosure of personal information. Also known as The Financial Services Modernization Act.
hackers	People who break into computer systems; they are usually more interested in the technological challenges than causing harm (no malicious intent).
hash	Function of the original plain text message calculated as a fixed-length value, based on certain mathematical interpretation of the bit-wise value of the original message.
hearsay	Legal term implying unreliability of any statement made outside of court and without the benefit of either cross-examination or corroborating evidence that clearly connects the statements to the context in which they were made.
Heisenberg's uncertainty principle	A quantum physics term from 1927: " The more precisely the position is determined, the less precisely the momentum is known in this instant, and vice versa." Paraphrased for modern times, "To observe something is to change it."
heuristics	Educated guesses and methods based upon experience. "Rules of thumb."
hijacking	Act in which a hacker monitors the electronic conversation between two communicating hosts in order to assume control of the communication path. Also called man-in-the-middle attack.
Hill cipher	Multi-letter cipher that utilizes complex mathematics, specifically linear algebra, to help disguise frequency patterns that naturally occur in language from bleeding through into ciphertext.

HIPAA Health Insurance Portability and Accountability Act. Legislation that details the privacy requirements with which medical records and patient information must be handled.

hoax Warning of a nonexistent malware threat.

hoax attack Attack by which the warning of a nonexistent malware threat is spread. The false information may include real malware in the warning message.

honeypot Any configuration of an information system placed in the public network domain for the sole purpose of allowing attacks to be targeted against it so that the perpetrator of the attack can be tracked, observed, and identified.

HTML Hypertext Markup Language. A simple programming language used to create Web pages.

HTTP Hypertext Transfer Protocol.

HTTPD bypass Attacks in which the attacker alters the content of a Web page in an undetectable fashion.

HTTPD overflow Attacks that target the HTTPD protocol that manages the ports and buffers used by Web servers. Buffers are intentionally overflowed; an attacker causes the overflow data to be executed, thereby providing access to the system.

HVAC Heating, Ventilation, and Air Conditioning.

idempodent Mathematical term meaning that the same answer is obtained every time an operation is performed.

identity theft When attackers obtain personal information from victims and use it to falsely represent themselves.

Identity Theft Act This act protects a variety of individual identification information that may be developed in the future and utilized to commit identify theft crimes.

IDS Intrusion Detection System. Inspects all inbound and outbound network traffic, system activity, and information access requests for the purpose of identifying suspicious patterns that may indicate an attack on a system. It can be either proactive or reactive.

image flood	See URL flood.
information	Processed data, along with the associated application(s) used to create and reproduce the data.
input	As a noun, the data entered into a computer. As a verb, to enter the data into a computer.
integrity	The property of the information being complete and uncorrupted, retaining its original and intended form.
integrity analysis	Examining the state of the information itself to look for changes where there should be none. This is usually done via the inspection of information checksums.
intrusion attack	Deliberate attempt by an attacker to penetrate the defenses of the information security system and gain unrestricted access to information.
involuntary risk	Risk that we take based on events that we cannot control or which are affected by more variables than those for which we can account.
IPSec	Internet Protocol Security. Used for implementing VPN and standard in IP v6. IPSec is focused on encrypting the IP packets (in either transport or tunnel modes). IPSec defines both encryption and authentication mechanisms associated with TCP/IP transactions.
isochronous	Time-dependent, networked, data-delivery method.
ISP	Internet Service Provider. A company providing Internet access to customers via dial-up, cable, DSL, or other means.
ITAR	International Traffic in U.S. Arms Regulations. An agency that determines items to be placed under the Arms Export Control Act and falls under the jurisdiction of the Department of State.
JN-25	World War II Japanese military cipher that was more difficult to break than the cipher Purple.
Kerberos method	System utilized for secure access between users in a network, ticketing authorities, and destination servers.

key escrow   A means for reconstituting a private key. It is done through a regeneration process based on information used at the key generation.

key management   The generation, storage, distribution, deletion, archiving, and application of keys in accordance with a security policy.

key recovery/escrow system   Systems that allow a user to create a key of any size, provided that a copy of the key is kept by a trusted third party who would surrender the key to authorities if a proper search warrant were served.

key rotation policy   Policy based on the estimated useful life of a key, establishing a period of time when a symmetrical key is deactivated and replaced with a new one.

keystroke monitors   Software or software/hardware combinations that record every keystroke made by a particular computer.

knowledge factor   Authentication factor based on something that only the user knows. A password is an example of a knowledge factor.

L2TP   Level 2 Tunneling Protocol. The creation of a joint development effort between Cisco and Microsoft, L2TP is a minimal-security tunneling protocol.

LDAP   Lightweight Directory Access Protocol. One of the X.500 protocols used to manage directory services and entries.

LEAF   Law Enforcement Access Field. A double-encrypted copy of the message key. The encryption is accomplished by using secure keys from two trusted sources that are part of a key recovery system.

least privilege   Every user, process, or program should be able to operate by using the fewest number of system and network privileges possible.

lockout   Attack resulting in the legitimate user being unable to access the system.

logging   The act of tracking system/network activities.

logic bomb   Piece of code that causes the operating system to lock up and subsequently fail using a buffer overflow, database deadlock, or excessive consumption of resources.

Lucifer cipher   A bit-wise symmetrical encryption coded to a 56-bit key.

MAC	Message Authentication Code. A cryptographic checksum or message digest constructed as part of the asymmetric cryptographic method used to create a digital signature.
mail bombing	See e-mail flood.
malformed commands	Legitimate network commands (ICMP packets) that are purposely malformed, resulting in a programmatic confusion caused by incorrect error-handling logic.
malicious code	See malware.
malicious signatures	Malware patterns recognizable by various programs (e.g., virus scanners), the presence of which may indicate that the data may be contaminated.
malware	Malicious software. Software developed for the purpose of causing harm. Viruses, worms, and Trojans all fall into this category.
man-in-the-middle attack	See hijacking.
mandatory access control	Policy where the author of the information looses control of the information once it becomes part of the system.
mapping	Passive attack technique that monitors network connections for the sole purpose of determining the network map of the targeted organization.
mathematical attack	Given that the cryptographic algorithm is known, the attacker can mathematically produce a list of valid keys and use a brute-force approach to determine which one is in use.
mean	Mathematical average of all values given.
mens rea	A prosecutorial test under which penalties vary, based on the intent of the perpetrator to do harm, the type and amount of damage caused, and the authorization level of the attacker. A qualitative measurement of the intent to do harm.
message digest	See hash.
message substitution	A type of man-in-the-middle attack where an actual message is removed and a replacement message is sent in its place.

metadata Literally translated as "data about the data." Metadata may contain information regarding when the data was developed, by whom, and/or how it is formatted.

misuse models Intrusion-detection method that compares sequences of actions with those known to cause harm.

modes Various methods used in block ciphers to attempt to prevent the problem of repeating ciphertext.

monoalphabetic ciphers Ciphers where a substitution of one character in the plain text alphabet is made with a corresponding character in the ciphertext alphabet.

mutation engine A program that uses one of many different methods to alter the signature of the virus in each successive generation/application of the virus.

name spoofing Use of the name of the attacked party (person, machine, or software) to falsely represent oneself as that party.

NAT Network Address Translation. NAT devices convert between the real Internet addresses assigned to an organization and an internal-only set of proprietary addresses.

NBS National Bureau of Standards.

negligence Willful disregard of potential bad outcomes in completing or failing to complete a task.

network mapping attacks Attackers monitor the flow of traffic into and out of a site for the sole purpose of capturing IP addresses and identifying key hosts and TCP ports of services they wish to compromise.

network worm A worm that uses network connectivity to spread to other systems where it continues to spread on and from that system.

NFAT Network Forensics Analysis Tools. Tools that monitor network traffic and allow for the replay of attacks, tracking of intruders back to their source, isolation and playback of suspicious activity, and vulnerability testing.

nonrepudiation Undisputed participant in an information transaction.

notification agent	Part of an IDS alert interface, programmed to take required actions commensurate with certain preestablished criteria.
NTRU cipher	Asymmetrical encryption method.
one-way-hash	Method of constructing a message digest so that no information about the original message is revealed. Nothing in the hash value or the hash function should allow anyone to reverse-engineer the information.
one-time pad	Cryptographic method in which the key is the length of the message. This cryptographic method is considered unbreakable. It is also highly inefficient.
OS hardening	Operating System hardening. The process of locking down a system to ensure that it is not providing too much access or too many unnecessary services.
OSI model	Model depicting seven distinct layers controlling various functions of the communications architecture.
passive attack	Nonintrusive attacks on the information system. In passive attacks, the perpetrators monitor elements of the information system to glean information that will be useful in compromising the system. Eavesdropping or spying on the exchange or processing of information and access routines are examples of passive attacks.
password cracking	Attack aimed at discovering passwords to gain access. Brute-force and dictionary attacks are two of the most common password-cracking methods.
password synchronization	A system where a server manages all of our passwords and usernames. In this system, the user must still log in to each application and system and enter all requisite information. The synchronization maps the username and passwords so they are all the same across application platforms and systems for a given user.
payload	The set of program instructions that form the malicious software.
perfectly secure	Cryptographic term meaning that, if an attacker has a copy of the ciphertext of a message, its content should yield no information at all regarding the content of the plain text message.

permission-based architecture

Also known as closed architecture. System construct that denies access by default. Access to resources is granted only by specific permission.

PGP

Pretty Good Privacy. Asymmetrical encryption method created by Phil Zimmerman in 1991 using RSA and Diffie-Hellman at the core.

phreaker

Person who has detailed knowledge of how the phone system works and exploits that knowledge to gain unauthorized access.

ping of death

Hacker-created attack using an oversized ping request that forces the network to fragment the packet. The reassembled fragment's total is greater than the maximum allowable packet size, which, when placed into the input buffer, causes an overflow and subsequent crash of the system.

piracy

The illegal reproduction, use, and distribution of copyrighted materials.

PKCS

Public Key Cryptography Standards govern the syntax and interfaces for deploying certificates and implementing the PKI.

PKI

Public Key Infrastructure. A system of registration authorities that issue digital certificates and authenticates the identity of those involved in certificate-based transactions. The PKI provides a means of verification of identity by a trusted third party via the application of X.509 v3 certificates.

plain text

The original clear text message without alteration or modification by a cryptographic method.

plain text attack

Attacker having access to a piece of ciphertext and a corresponding piece of plain text uses cryptanalysis to attempt to discover the key and algorithm from which the message was originally coded.

point-to-point tunneling protocol

See PPTP.

poison cookies

Attacks utilizing a script planted in the cookie as the vehicle for the attack that can change the appearance of a Web site or cause login information to be divulged.

policy mapping

A mechanism designed to ensure interoperability between equivalent, competing certificate authorities.

polyalphabetic ciphers Cipher in which the cipher alphabet changes throughout the encryption.

polymorphic viruses Viruses that change form each time they are attached to a new host.

port scanners Equipment that provides attackers information on unprotected ports in a system.

possession factor Something you have that grants you access to information (e.g., smart card, token, etc.).

power management systems These systems essentially monitor the power flow to the facility and, in case of a power outage, provide backup power.

PPTP Point-To-Point Tunneling Protocol. Microsoft version of VPN.

practical irreversibility Process of generating keys, usually involving algebraic manipulations of numbers so that the generation process of the two keys is relatively simple but whose relationship is difficult to discover.

prime number An integer greater than 1 with no divisors other than itself and 1.

Privacy Act of 1974 This law protects the right of individuals to restrict the use of personal information collected about them by the government.

private key Used in asymmetrical cryptography to decode messages encoded using the individual's public key or to encode digital signatures. Only the owner possesses this key.

PRNG Pseudorandom Number Generator. Algorithms able to pass the scrutiny of a statistical examination.

process An executing computer program.

protocols Communication formats allowing data transmission between devices.

proxy servers Servers that act as intermediaries between the public network and the private servers. They are also known as application-level gateways.

pseudorandom numbers Numbers generated by a computer algorithm started with a random seed that have a generation pattern imperceptible to the average person.

public key Used in asymmetrical cryptography to encode messages to a particular individual. This key is available to all.

quantum cryptography Cryptographic technique based on the physics of light, not mathematics. The technique relies on Heisenberg's uncertainty principle and states that by examining the photon, we will affect a change on it. This principle implies that if the message is viewed (eavesdropped) by a third party, the communicating parties will immediately know because by observing the transmission, the hacker will have changed the message.

rabbits Programs that are loaded and executed on a given system that are purposely designed to consume all the resources of a particular type (e.g., memory) on a particular host. The purpose of a rabbit is either to crash the system or to create a denial-of-service attack.

range Set of all values attained by a given function throughout its domain.

RATs Remote Administrative Tools. Trojans that, once enabled, let the attacker take control of the remote site.

relatively prime A number is said to be relatively prime to another if it has no prime factors in common (i.e., the only number that divides them both is 1).

release of message content Distribution of information intended to be kept private.

relying party One who is depending upon the information supplied by a trusted authority for validation purposes.

replay attack When a hacker captures information (regardless of its encryption status) and replays it in order to gain access or trigger an event.

risk Potential of loss or harm associated with the uncertainty of particular events or outcomes.

risk analysis Qualitative and quantitative measurement of risk.

risk entities Valued things that are at risk.

risk factors Threats that pose a potential risk.

risk identification Applying the information security model to identify potential risks.

risk minimization   Applying successful countermeasures once risks have been identified.

risk mitigation   Reducing the impact of an attack once a breach has occurred.

risk transference   Ensuring information or outsourcing information management when methods of stopping a perpetrator are unlikely to remain successful or when the recovery value of assets is prohibitively high.

rounds   In encryption, refers to the number of loops an encryption algorithm uses to increase the complexity of the encryption itself. Commonly used in Feistel ciphers.

S/MIME certificates   Secure/multipurpose Internet mail extension certificates are used to sign and encrypt e-mail and are the basis for single sign-on applications.

sabotage   Unwanted modifications, deletions, or unintended release of information.

SAM   Security Acceptability Metric. An index of security posture.

SAML   Security Assertion Markup Language. A language used to send security information across Web sites. This language is based on assertions about a user.

SANs   Storage Area Networks. Network of machines that store data.

scanners   Software that detects weaknesses in a system or network.

screening routers   A screening router is a router that sits between the corporate entity and the Internet.

script kiddies   Youthful offenders who utilize previously scripted hacks written by accomplished and skilled hackers. Generally, their attacks are mere nuisances or experiments to test their abilities.

SSL certificates   Certificates used in many Web-based applications for secure client server access over the Internet.

security context   Security information that represents, or will represent, a security association to an initiator or acceptor that has formed, or is attempting to form, such an association.

sequence number prediction	Method of session hijacking. Attackers attempt to gain control of an ongoing session in place of the trusted client in order to access a server.
secure electronic transaction (SET)	Developed by Microsoft, Visa/MasterCard, and Netscape to promote secure credit card transactions on the Web. SET is a method of applying various cryptographic techniques to solve the problems associated with authentication and confidentiality of financial information within the realm of online businesses.
shift cipher	Encoding method using an offset into the plain text alphabet to create the proper substitution sequence for creating the cipher code.
shoulder surfing	When an attacker watches the keystrokes of a user to determine usernames, passwords, and other private information.
S-HTTP	Secure Hypertext Transfer Protocol works as a replacement service for HTTP when secure Web transactions are required.
SMTP	Simple Mmail Transfer Protocol. One of the most common protocols used to send e-mail messages between servers.
Smurf attack	Exploit of TCP/IP. A ping command that is sent to the network broadcast address, causing all nodes to attempt to respond at the same time. The attacker also fakes the source address of the packet to be that of the victim, causing all responses to converge simultaneously. This type of attack slows network performance and locks the network interface of the target.
sniffer	Electronic device used to monitor network activity.
social engineer	Person who uses deception to manipulate the social structure in an organization to gain computer passwords, critical phone numbers, configuration files, and the trust of an organization.
springboard attack	A hacker uses a hacked site for the purpose of launching attacks as part of a widespread offensive against the actual target site.
SSL	Secure Sockets Layer.
SSO	Single Sign-On. A system by which a user logs into a security server and performs the normal login and verification procedure. From that point, all client server login requirements are handled automatically for the user without the need to log in to each service the client wishes to use.

state	A way of maintaining context and flow to a session.
stateful inspection	An advanced form of filtering, based on the state of the enterprise application environment, the state of the network, and the policies of the security plan. Also called dynamic packet filtering.
steganography	Concept of hiding the existence of a message. This is opposed to cryptography, which acknowledges the existence of a message but is the science of hiding the meaning of the message.
stream cipher	An encryption method that takes one bit of plain text at a time and submits it to an encryption algorithm. Based on the bits from a key that are "applied to the stream," the bits of plain text are converted into ciphertext.
substitution	Switching plain text characters with those from a cipher alphabet.
symmetrical algorithm	A keyed cryptographic technique that uses the same key for both the encryption algorithm and the decryption algorithm.
SYN flood	Exploit of the handshake part of the TCP/IP protocol. A number of connect requests in excess of what a system can handle is submitted, shutting out legitimate user connection requests.
teardrop attack	Exploit of the IP sequencing strategy. Long IP packets are broken down and reassembled in order. A teardrop attack is constructed by sending a series of fragments with a confusing offset in the second or latter packet(s). The server may have trouble dealing with the numbering sequence and crash or fail in some way, creating a denial of service to other users.
TEMPEST	A technology that can be used to monitor EMR and actually reconstruct screen shots and data streams from the EMR patterns.
threat agent	Potential perpetrator of threats, ranging from mischievous to malicious and calculated.
threats	Risk events that can endanger the information system.
time bomb	Malicious software that remains dormant until a particular time or date has passed.

timing attacks	Exploit of the availability of cached information on the Web browser that can expose information regarding Internet usage, password, and account information, or to create and deposit poison cookies on a victim's system.
transport mode	Mode of VPN. Transport mode uses encryption on the data part of the packet only. In transport mode, the original packet headers are left unencrypted.
transposition cipher	Encryption method that mixes up characters in the ciphertext while allowing them to retain their identity.
trapdoor	A secret way into a piece of code deliberately left open by the designer.
triggers	Programs set to release a coordinated set of attacks. Triggers are usually set up on multiple sites used as part of a springboard attack.
trigrams	Groups of three letters appearing with a predictable frequency in English.
Trojan horse	An innocent-looking file planted on a victim's system that is actually a malicious software package activated at a later time, based on a predetermined trigger.
trust anchor	The originating trusted third party in a trust relationship.
trusted authority	Authority whose trust is beyond question and who endorses cryptographic authentication systems.
tunnel mode	Mode of VPN transport. In tunnel mode, everything is encrypted (headers and information sections of the packet).
unconditionally secure	Term used to mean that no matter how much ciphertext cryptanalysts have, they could not use it to understand the structure or content of the plain text or the encryption method. This term is sometimes called perfect security.
uninterruptible power supplies (UPS)	These devices provide protection from power outages and often monitor and normalize power spikes and fluctuations. These systems are generally battery fed. However, propane and gas generators are also available.
unrealized threats	Unsubstantiated rumors regarding the vulnerability of an online service or software product

URL flood   Attack meant to cause a denial of service. These occur anytime port 80 becomes inundated with repeated rapid reload requests.

URLs   Uniform Resource Locators. Web address names that can be translated into actual IP addresses via the domain name server.

usage policies   Expectations set by the organization to encourage certain behavior and to prohibit other behaviors.

variance   Reflection of the dispersion of input values around the mean value of the solution set for these random variables.

verification   The one-to-one process of matching the user by name against an authentication template maintained by a trusted third party who tests the claim of identity and provides the authentication status.

Vigenere square   A 26×26 matrix with the letters of the alphabet across the top and down the side. The alphabet is filled from the starting letter of the column or row. Each column and row is a one-position-shift cipher alphabet of the row or column before.

virus   Software that attaches itself to another program on a user's system. It is activated when the known application is invoked.

voluntary risk   Known risk that we decide to take.

VPN   Virtual Private Network. A virtual network utilizing a technology known as private tunneling to provide a secure pathway over a public network.

vulnerabilities   Weaknesses in the operating system that may allow access to someone who wishes to harm a system.

war driving   Taking your portable device with an 802.11b-compliant NIC in promiscuous mode and roaming the streets seeking network connectivity. As you pass facilities with wireless 802.11b running in an unprotected mode, you will be included as part of their network.

weak key   Encryption key whose numerical properties cause the encryption algorithm to falter or diminish.

WEP   Wired equivalent privacy. Method of wireless security that encrypts wireless communications using a symmetrical key algorithm that encrypts data between the broadcast point and the device.

worm   Software that replicates itself, spreading from host to host over a network.

zombie   Host of a springboard or DDOS attack.

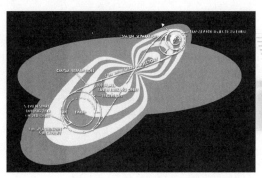

APPENDIX a

Labs and Experiments

A course in information security can be an interesting and stimulating experience for students. Few courses can raise the interest level of computer or information science students in so many varied areas of the discipline through a single experience. Information security as a profession is fast developing into a key component of every IS department. For students to be best prepared for one of these positions, it is important to gain practical, hands-on knowledge. The use of hands-on experimentation is a must for this course. Included with the text is a CD that contains several interesting programs that can be run, tested, and modified to learn more about information security.

This appendix includes lab experiments that have been tested, are easy to build, and do not require much more than access to a network and a host system. It is important to stress that some of these labs teach some hacking techniques. It is illegal to run these experiments outside of the controlled lab environment. Other labs focus on running cryptographic experiments that are interesting and not at all harmful. However, remember that if you use this software (or change the format of a disk) and employ encryption, you should back up the information that is being encrypted and develop a strategy for key recovery. Otherwise you may not be able to open your own data files if you inadvertently lose the key.

CAUTIONARY NOTE

It is illegal to carry out an attack on any site, computer, source of information, person, network, or computer entity, for any reason. Not even as a joke! Perpetrators of hacks, attacks, and pranks are subject to prosecution under the law and can be fined or imprisoned. This information is provided exclusively for the instructional use of students. Please take this warning seriously.

It is recommended that course instructors utilize "safe labs" (see next page) for conducting experiments with various attacks. It is also important to note that many of the Web sites available for gathering prepackaged attacks are booby-trapped and can infect the target systems and networks requesting the download. Using a safe lab can isolate problems and minimize exposure to problems.

BUILDING A SAFE LAB

Running information security experiments can make school lab administrators nervous. A good way to provide this expertise while minimizing or eliminating risk to the school is to build a safe lab.

A safe lab is an environment completely isolated from the school infrastructure where attacks and defenses can be simulated, mock viruses can be used and detected, and information systems can be configured repeatedly without any disruption of service to the school infrastructure.

Students utilizing this facility will gain knowledge in system management, network architecture and configuration management, programming, use of tools, and exposure to the most common threats that face the security expert.

Building the lab minimally requires the following hardware:

- One desktop Windows XP–based client station per student
- One low-end router (capable of handling router ACLs) per four students
- A centralized switch to simulate the Internet
- A UNIX server to simulate Web sites, DNS servers, and mail servers
- An NT server to simulate other server platforms and to be used as the instructor console

The following software is required for optimal lab performance:

- Windows XP professional edition
- A C/C++ language compiler
- Router IOS compatible with a current release of the Cisco IOS. This software must be able to administer ACLs and basic firewall commands.
- SMTP mail agent
- Windows Active Director
- UNIX
- Windows NT
- Other software as required for your particular configuration
- Ethereal
- BadCopy Pro v 3.65a

You can find the following malware and hacker tools on the Net:

- Elite attack software
- NetBrute from Raw Logic
- ANTex NT hash dumper and password cracker
- Doom IGMP flooder
- AGP free antivirus program
- Other products listed throughout this text

It is best to organize the lab in teams. Each team should be segmented in a subnet with a private router and ethernet. The instructor should keep the mail, TFTP server, FTP server, and course files. The instructor should also have a LAN segment with a private subnet. The switch will simulate the Internet. The real Internet should be attached via a separate connection, not part of the safe lab, to a single machine equipped with a CD burner and the following security configuration as specified in Figures A-1, A-2, and A-3.

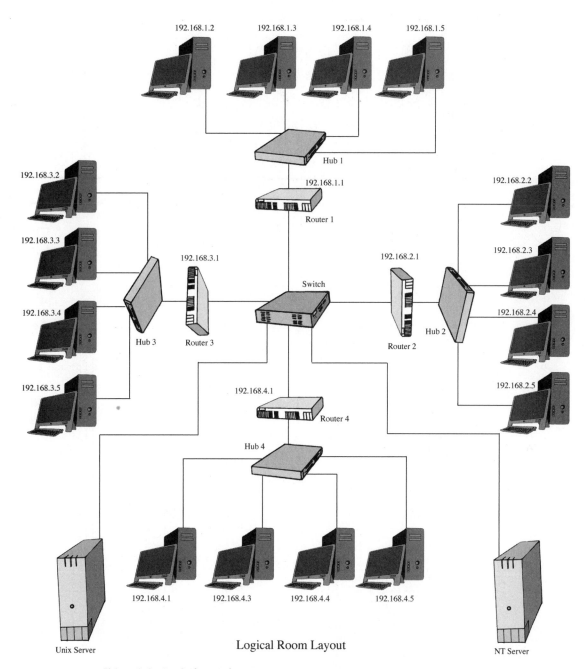

Figure A-1   Logical room layout.

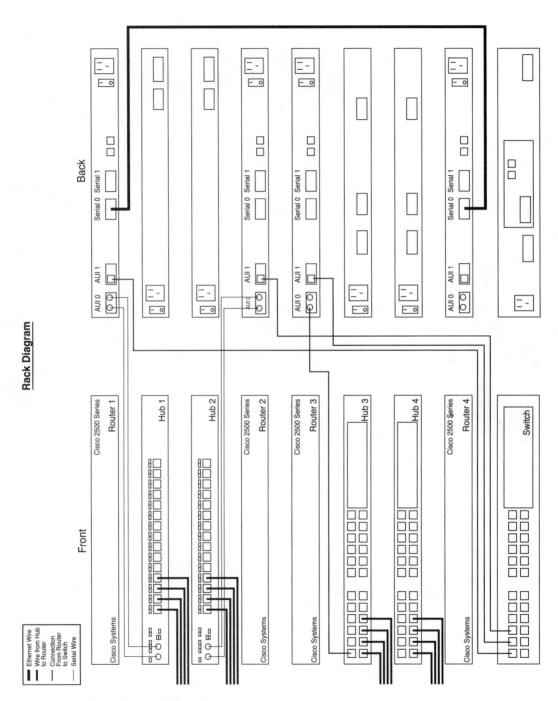

Figure A-2 Rack diagram.

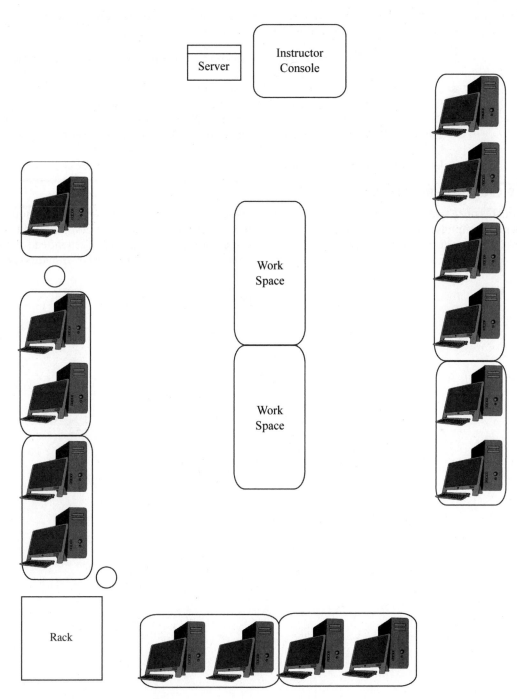

Figure A-3   Lab floor plan.

You can develop this or similar labs for use in the classroom. The author encourages instructors to pursue this endeavor and to be mindful of the following precautions:

- Disconnect the lab from the campus backbone and stringently firewall all Internet connections
- Set up and utilize mock accounts for every student
- Refrain from storing important data and information on these systems
- Reiterate to the students not to attempt these labs in a live environment and to exercise caution with the use of encryption (so as not to lock out information in the event of key loss)
- Use private Internet addresses

THE LAB EXPERIMENTS

Confucius once said, "I hear and I forget, I see and I remember, I do and I understand." Throughout this appendix, emphasis will be placed on hands-on experiences for the student. It is recommended that these labs be performed on systems allocated for experimentation rather than those intended for production purposes. Some labs in this section can permanently alter file structure and information access.

Lab 1: Creating NTFS Files

FATs 32 File Systems versus NTFS

FATs 32

The FATs 32 file system allows users to utilize space more efficiently within their own PC. This file structure was introduced to free up hard drive resources on the machine. Using the FAT partitioning system creates 4k clusters on the hard drive for data storage, allowing for small files to occupy limited amounts of clusters.

The limitations of the FAT32 file system includes the inability to communicate with any version of Windows older than the OSR2 version of Windows 95. Another drawback of this system is that privacy protection and encryption were not available features.

New Technology File System

NTFS is a relatively new file system that has been introduced to enhance security, control, fault management, and compression. Options such as granting privileged access to files is available on NTFS modified machines. This option allows the user to set permissions to grant or deny access to particular files. Once these options are set, the NTFS will protect the system remotely and locally.

NTFS also allows the creation of log files within the system so that data can be restored to earlier points with ease. Once files are stored to the hard disk, the NTFS records all changes that have been made to that file in a log that can be accessed in the event of a catastrophe.

NTFS allows the user to compress individual files and directories. This benefits the user because files used infrequently can be compressed to save storage space. It will also allow for the user to pack files that have to be copied to remote storage devices allowing storing of much more data.

File System Conversion Exercise

This lab will introduce you to the NTFS offered by Windows. Currently, most users are using **File Allocation Tables (FATs)** file systems for storing files on disk drives and removable storage devices.

Enabling the NTFS on Windows XP machines allows for greater functionality for the user regarding the manipulation of files. The NTFS concentrates on localized security needs for the computer. With NTFS, Windows XP will allow for the encryption and compression of files with ease.

 Before you decide to convert your hard drive to the new NTFS, you should be absolutely sure that this file system will suit your needs. Once implemented, it is difficult to convert back to your original file system.

In the exercise below, you will be converting a standard FAT32-formatted Zip disk to the new NTFS.

Lab Objectives

- Determine whether a disk drive or removable storage device is configured under FAT or NTFS
- Successfully convert a FAT partition to NTFS

Resources Needed for Lab 1 and Lab 2 Exercises

- A computer running Windows XP
- A partitioned drive or removable storage device with FAT or FAT 32 file systems running
- A blank Zip disk

Let's Try It!

1 Click **Start**

2 Click **Run**

3 Under Run, type "CMD"

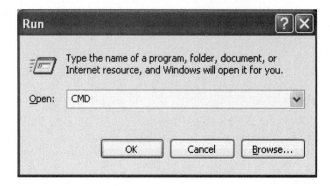

Figure A-4

4 At the command line, enter the command **chkntfs e:**
This step will verify which file system is currently being used on the machine. It will also determine whether any corruption exists on the drive.

(You may have to change the drive letter to suit your machine.)

NOTE: If the drive is not dirty, then no corruption exists*

5 To convert the FAT partition to NTFS, enter

```
"convert e:/fs:ntfs" at the command line.
```

Notice the detailed information shown before the file system conversion takes place (see Figure A-5).

NOTE: If the current drive has a volume label, enter it when prompted.
You will also have to restart the machine for the conversion to take place.

6 At the command line, enter **chkntfs e:** to determine the successful conversion from FAT to NTFS. This step will also check to make sure the disk or removable drive is free of corruption (see Figure A-6).

Figure A-5

Figure A-6

7 Close all windows and log off.

Lab 2: File Encryption Using NTFS

NTFS allows users to encrypt files and folders locally to protect them from being read or modified. This is important when working with confidential information. Having the ability to control who can view your files locally (from your own machine) is an advantage not possible prior to NTFS.

Encryption Files in Windows XP Professional NTFS

For this exercise, you will need the following:

- Two user accounts (both accounts need access to one shared file)
- Notepad

Let's Try It!

1 Open My Computer.

2 Double-click on Shared Documents.

3 Right-click on New/Folder.

4 Rename the folder Private Documents.

5 Minimize the window.

6 Create a text document in Notepad that says "This is a confidential document."

7 Save the document in Shared Documents/Private Documents as private.txt (see Figure A-7).

8 Restore Private Documents.

9 Right-click private.txt and click on Properties. Then, click Advanced.

10 Click the Encrypt Contents checkbox to secure data. Then, click Ok (see Figure A-8).

11 Click Apply.

12 Click Encrypt the file only radio button (see Figure A-9).

The file has now been encrypted. To verify that other users cannot view the document, we are going to log on to the machine under another username and attempt to open the document. This is where access to the folder becomes an issue.

13 Log off current user.

14 Log on as different user.

15 Click My Documents/Shared Documents/Private Documents.

16 Double-click on private.txt. Notice that the document cannot be opened (see Figure A-10).

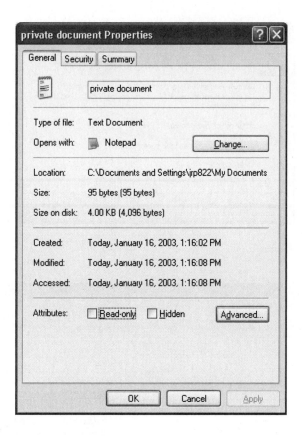

Figure A-7

Figure A-8

Figure A-9

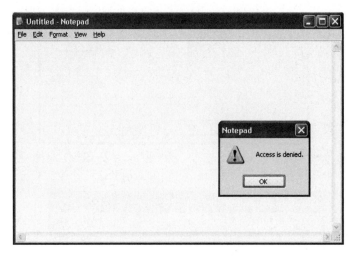

Figure A-10

Lab 3: Password Vulnerability

A hacker technique that has deep roots is password cracking. Password cracking involves breaking the encryption of passwords stored on a system. To do this, a password-cracking program generates encrypted passwords using the same algorithm that the system uses. It then compares the generated password to the stored password and looks for a match. If it finds one, it informs the user of the plain text password.

Another method password cracking programs use is to repeatedly try different passwords until it finds one that works—password guessing. The two most popular varieties of either method are brute-force attacks and dictionary attacks. Brute-force attacks try every possible combination of letters, numbers, and special characters within the limits set by the attacker. Dictionary attacks use a dictionary file (a word list) to determine which character combinations to attempt.

To protect a system from password cracking, an administrator can lock out a user after a set number of incorrect password attempts. The administrator should also develop a password policy (minimum number of characters, types of words to not use, etc.) and inform the users of the policy.

Lab Objectives

- Test the vulnerabilities and weaknesses of passwords
- Understand the outcomes associated with having weak passwords
- Learn how you can better protect yourself regarding passwords

Resources Needed for Lab 3 Exercises

- A computer running Windows XP, NT, or 2000
- A running version of Advanced NT Security Explorer (obtainable at *www.elcom-soft.com/antexp.html*)

Let's Try It!

1 Run the software by going to Start→ Programs→ Advanced NT Security Explorer→ Advanced NT Security Program.

2 The screen in Figure A-11 should be present, which will familiarize you with the software.

3 The next step will be to click on the "Dump Password Hashes from Memory" icon located in the center of the screen.

4 A save-as screen will be summoned (see Figure A-12). Save the file as Test and click Ok.

5 Select the user by marking the check box to the left of the user name you wish to attack.

6 Choose a type of attack located at the top left of the screen. Select the dictionary attack method.

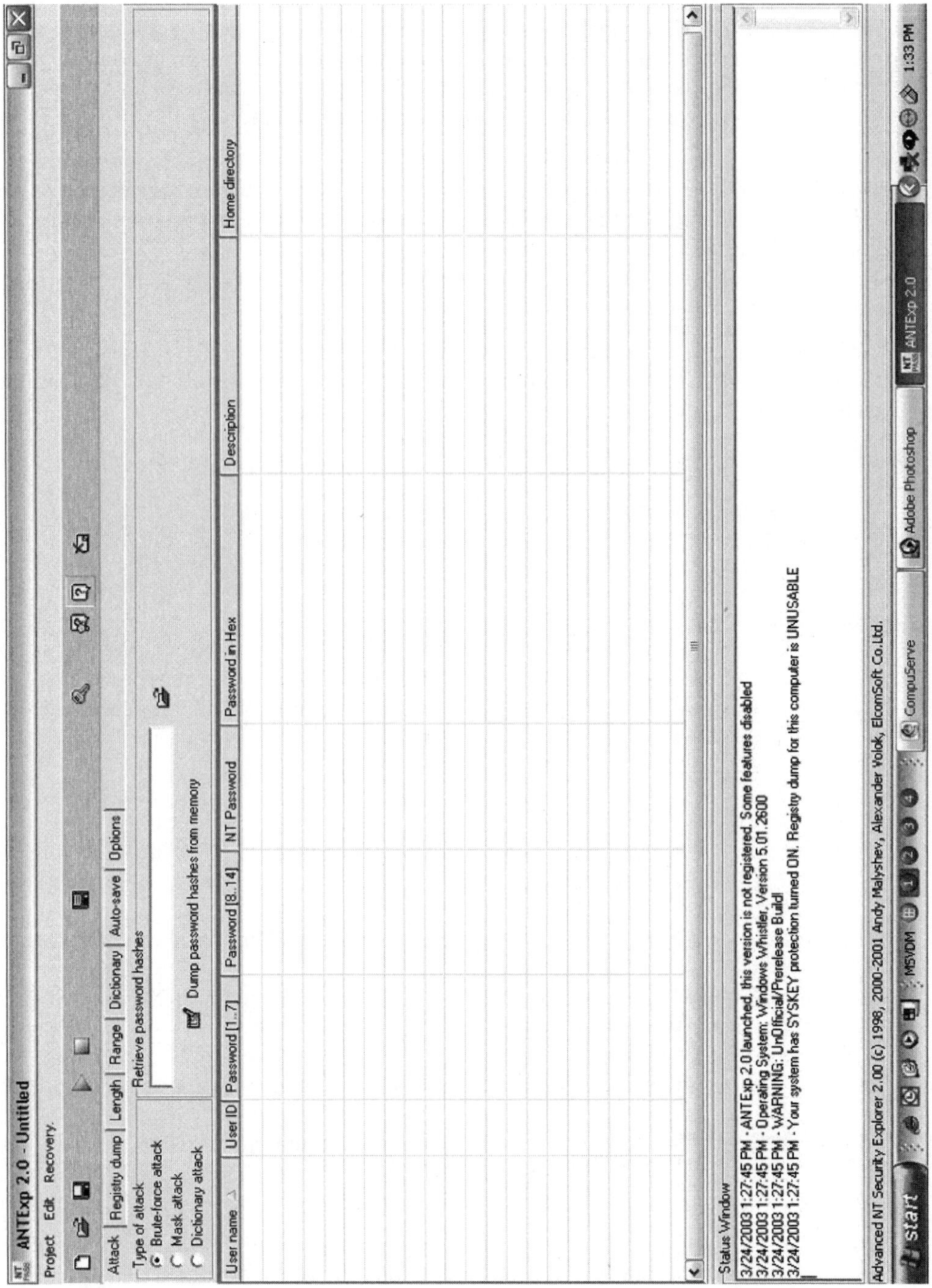
ANTExp 2.0 - Untitled
Project Edit Recovery
Attack Registry dump Length Range Dictionary Auto-save Options
Type of attack
Brute-force attack
Mask attack
Dictionary attack
Retrieve password hashes
Dump password hashes from memory
User name User ID Password [1..7] Password [8..14] NT Password Password in Hex Description Home directory
Status Window
3/24/2003 1:27:45 PM - ANTExp 2.0 launched, this version is not registered. Some features disabled
3/24/2003 1:27:45 PM - Operating System: Windows Whistler, Version 5.01.2600
3/24/2003 1:27:45 PM - WARNING: UnOfficial/Prerelease Build
3/24/2003 1:27:45 PM - Your system has SYSKEY protection turned ON. Registry dump for this computer is UNUSABLE
Advanced NT Security Explorer 2.00 (c) 1998, 2000-2001 Andy Malyshev, Alexander Volok, ElcomSoft Co.Ltd.
start
MSVDM
CompuServe
Adobe Photoshop
ANTExp 2.0
1:33 PM

Figure A-11

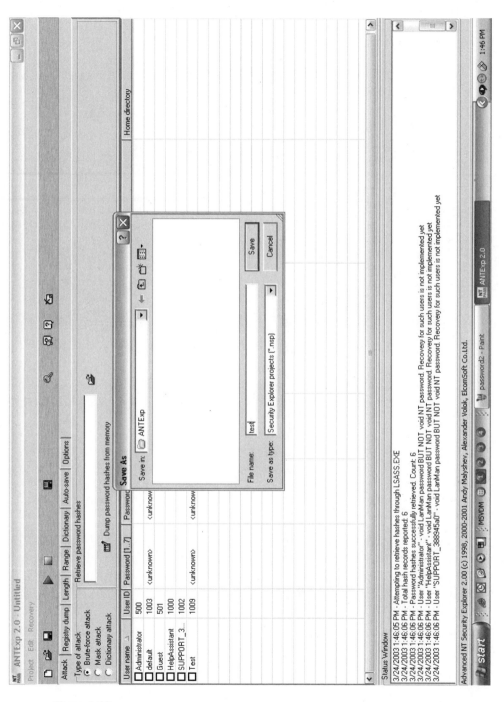

Figure A-12

7 Click the Play button located on the top center of the screen.

NOTE: For illustration purposes a test account name has been set up for you to view the demonstration.

8 The password for the illustration has been successfully broken (see Figure A-13), and the password is "dinosaur."

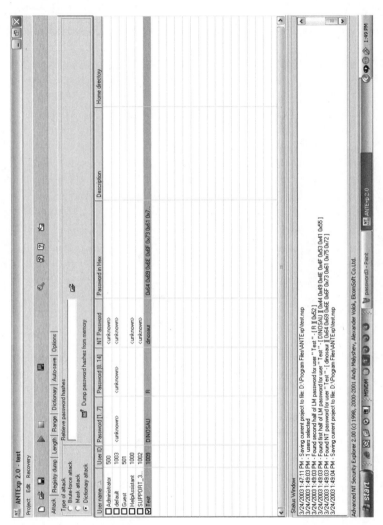

Figure A-13

Lab 4: Network Forensics

Network Forensics File Recovery

This lab will serve to demonstrate a file recovery tool for Windows. This particular software is called Bad-Copy Pro (version 3.65a) from JufSoft. The software can be downloaded at *http://download.jufsoft.com/ download/badcopy3.exe* free of charge. The software is a trial version and will not actually save the recovered file, but it will display the files it finds. To recover the data, the full version must be purchased.

For the purpose of this lab, however, the trial version is adequate because it shows you that erasing a file and doing a quick formatting of a diskette does not necessarily eliminate the existence of the file, nor does it prevent the data from being recovered.

The easiest way to demonstrate the tool is with the use of a floppy disk.

1 Download and install the trial version of BadCopy Pro.

2 Save some files on a blank floppy disk. The idea is to create a number of files of different types (Word, PowerPoint, images, etc.).

3 Go to My Computer, highlight the floppy disk drive, and right-click. From the drop-down menu, select Format. This not only destroys the data on the disk but also reformats the data so that one would think it is totally inaccessible.

4 From the Format menu (see Figure A-14), check the Quick Format box, then click Start.

5 When the formatting is complete, keep the diskette in the drive and start BadCopy Pro (see Figure A-15).

6 From the icons on the left frame, select the floppy disk. From the Recovery Mode drop-down menu, select Rescue Lost Files—Mode #1. If it recovers nothing, select Mode #2 (see Figure A-16).

Even though the file names are different (because of how the program works), the tool recovered the file that you thought had been erased when you performed a Quick Format of the disk (see Figure A-17).

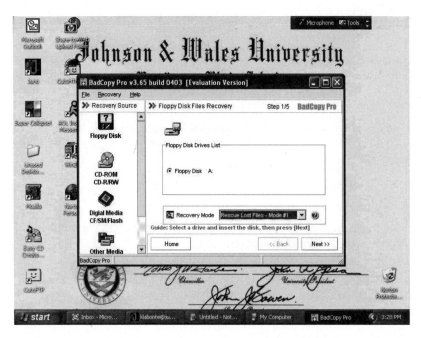

Figure A-14

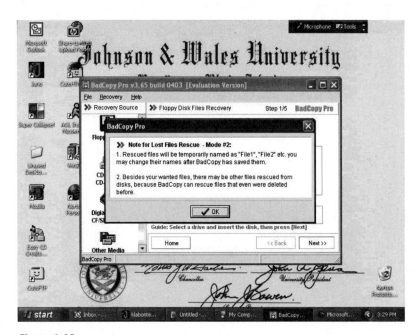

Figure A-15

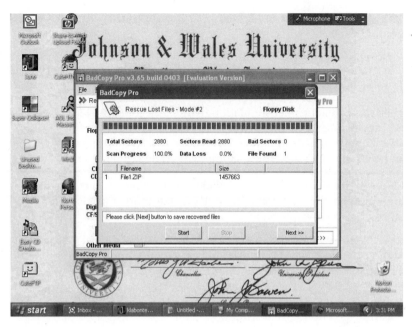

Figure A-16

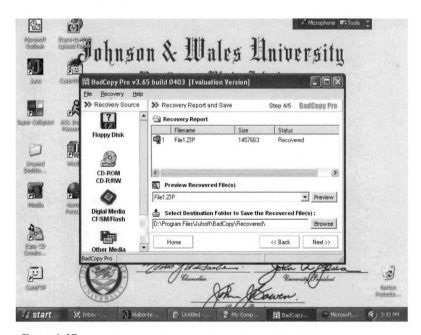

Figure A-17

Lab 5: Cryptographic Methods

Early Cryptographic Analysis

In studying Chapters 5 and 7 of the text, student learned many of the early cryptographic methods that have been used in the last 2,500 years. We reviewed four very famous ciphers, which have been simulated on the CD in the back of this text:

- Bacon's binary cipher simulation (written by Louis Pittsley Jr.)
- Caesar cipher simulation (written by Sanaa Kerroumi)
- Rail fence cipher simulation (written by William Robsky)
- Jefferson cipher wheel simulation (written by Jason Cabral)

Students should run all of these ciphers. They should use the same plain text message for each of the cipher algorithms. Compare the output and the styles to one another (transposition versus substitution and monoalphabetic versus polyalphabetic).

The second part of this lab involves comparing and modifying the code that is provided with the ciphers. Because none of these methods were ever meant to be run on a computer, it is interesting to review the algorithms and compare the complexities of each.

Lab 6: Tiny Encryption Algorithm

TEA was the focus of much of the discussion in Chapter 7 of this text. This lab is designed to help students understand how TEA and other similar algorithms work. On the CD included with this text is a section entitled "TEA Lab."

In this part of the CD there are three tabs:

- Source C++ code
- Message translator
- Execute TEA

Resources Needed for Lab 6 Exercises

- A PC running Windows 98 or greater operating system
- A C++ (or a C) compiler

This lab will take approximately one hour to complete.

Let's Try It!

1 Insert the CD into the reader; it should auto start. Once the menu is displayed, click on TEA Experiments.

2 Review the salient points of the TEA method discussed in Chapter 7. Student should have read Chapter 7 in its entirety prior to beginning this lab.

3 Click on the Source C++ tag. This will open the Notepad application and allow students to view the TEA source code. Notice that the code is set up with N (the number of rounds) set equal to 5 (one less than is needed—according to the author for total diffusion). Click the Execute screen to see the screen shot of the code executed.

4 Analyze the executed code. Notice the symmetry between the rounds of encryption and rounds of decryption. Work through the code and match the lines of code to the flowcharts shown in the text.

5 Student should recompile the code with the N set to the 32 rounds originally specified by the authors. Rerun the code (from your own environment) and observe the greater complexity. In order to set N = 32 in the encryption, all that is required is a trivial replacement of the 5 with a 32 for N. Certain file adjustments (e.g., headers) to get this code to run under a new C compiler (e.g., .Net).

In the decryption routing, notice that the required changes include the same substitution of 32 for 5 in N, but also a recalculation of delta to reflect the encryption with 32 rounds. This means that SUM must be set equal to N × 32 (or delta is shifted left 5 times).

The diffusion will increase as the rounds progress. Focus on rounds 5 and 6, which should demonstrate a vast difference in the amount of diffusion.

The shifts of 4 to 5 were chosen to maximize the rate of diffusion by trial and error. The greater shift is to the right because addition propagates a little to the left. Experiment with different shifts or equal shifts. What is the difference in the output? The authors used experiments to determine the required shifts in the original algorithm. A rejected complication by the authors was to have different shifts for y and z. See if you can find the optimal 4 shifts and see how many rounds can be omitted and still offer the same amount of diffusion.

6 On the CD, click on the tag Message Translator. This piece of software developed by Chris Veness (TEA javascript Implementation © Chris Veness, Movable Type Ltd.) allows student to input variable-length keys and data to encrypt. This code is written in Javascript and is interesting to play with. Students should compare this style of encryption with the cryptographic methods covered in the previous experiment.

Lab 7: Viruses

This lab is meant to familiarize students with one of the many products on the market that can be used to detect and deal with viruses. The student will learn to use Anti-Virus Guard (AVG) and use it to detect viruses.

Resources Needed for Lab 7 Exercises

- Make sure every PC has an e-mail account set up with Outlook
- All students (or teams if there are multiple students per PC) need a Zip or floppy disk for the viruses
- Systems may need to be checked for the viruses after the lab exercises are completed. They should be present only in the Desktop→Attacks→Virii folder

The viruses used in this exercise are not real. They appear to be viruses to most antivirus programs, but they will not actually damage a computer.

Let's Try It !

1 Download the virus software from *http://www.grisoft.com/html/us_downl.htm?session=15616f6c7cbab10a7de9706d84e7c2cc#FREE*. By filling out a simple questionnaire, you can download a trial version of the software (complete with dummy nonharmful viruses).

2 Cut and paste the three viruses onto a Zip or floppy disk. (Go to Desktop→Attacks→Virii.) It is important that you remove them from your hard drive completely and put them on a disk or your results will not match those expected.

3 Open Outlook and compose a new e-mail message. The message text can be anything you want.

4 Attach the three viruses to the message and send it to your partner.

5 When you receive the message, download the three files to your hard drive. Put them in Desktop→Attacks→Virii folder.

6 Open AVG. Desktop→Attacks→Anti-Virus.

7 In the top menu bar, click on Tests and choose Custom Test.

8 AVG asks you to select which folders you want to scan. Select the entire hard drive (C), and check the box next it.

9 Click Start to begin the test.

Lab 8: Using Asymmetrical Cryptography

This experiment will show students how to utilize PKI with Outlook Express. We will use Outlook Express to encrypt and digitally sign e-mails to guarantee their source and validity. We will apply for a sixty-day digital certificate from VeriSign, a leading certificate authority. We will digitally sign an e-mail and transfer digital certificates.

Resources Needed for Lab 8 Exercises

- Outlook Express 6 (preconfigured to receive e-mail)
- Internet access
- Personal e-mail address or one created at Hotmail for this experiment

Signing Up for a Digital ID

1 Open Outlook Express (usually found under Start, Programs).

2 Left-click Tools and move the mouse pointer to Options (see Figure A-18). This will bring up the Options box in Figure A-19.

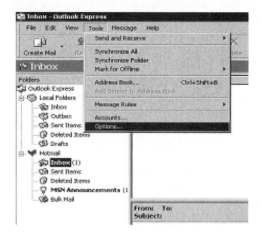

Figure A-18

3 Left-click the Security tab.

4 Left-click the Get Digital ID button. This will open your Web browser to Office Assistance Center (see Figure A-20).

5 Locate the VeriSign, Inc. link on this page and left-click on it. This will open the Digital ID Center at VeriSign (see Figure A-21).

6 At the bottom of the page, left-click on Click here for the 60-day free trial. The enrollment for a VeriSign Class1 Digital ID page will appear (see Figure A-22).

Figure A-19

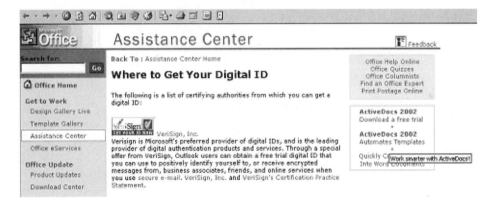

Figure A-20

7 Fill out the page with your corresponding information. Leave the Microsoft Base Crypto-graphic Provider v1.0. Read through the document as you go to be sure you understand what the page is asking you for.

8 When you are done with the enrollment, click Accept. It will ask you if you want to accept the certificate from the provider (see Figure A-23). Click Yes.

9 VeriSign will then prompt you that it is creating a new RSA exchange key (see Figure A-24). Leave the security level at Medium, and click Ok.

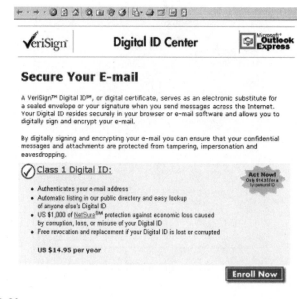

Figure A-21

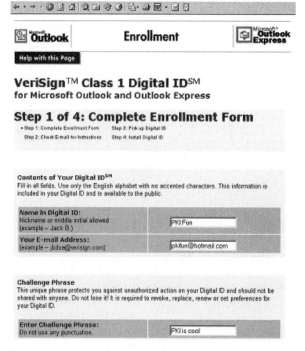

Figure A-22

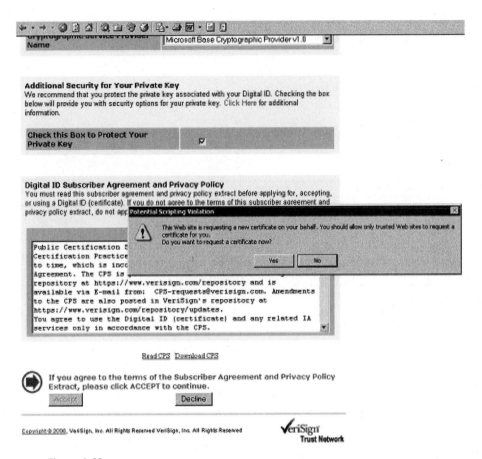

Figure A-23

10 We are done applying for our certificate (see Figure A-25). Now we have to wait for Veri-Sign to send it to us. It is automated and should not take long.

Setting Up the ID to be Used with Outlook Express

1 Close any open Internet browsers that are open.

2 Open your Outlook Express e-mail (see Figure A-26). Soon you should receive an e-mail from the VeriSign Customer Support Department.

3 Open the e-mail and confirm the information you typed on the enrollment.

4 Click Continue to open a browser to get your certificate (if you receive a message about nonsecure/ secure items, click Yes. A page with Step 4 will open and allow you to install the certificate).

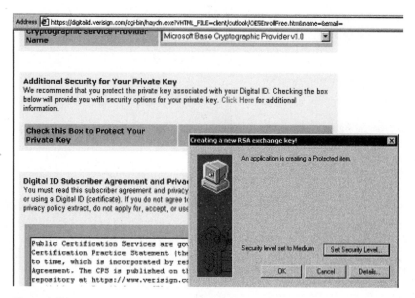

Figure A-24

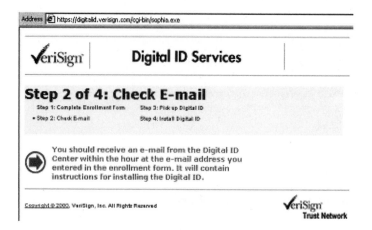

Figure A-25

5 Click Install (see Figure A-27).

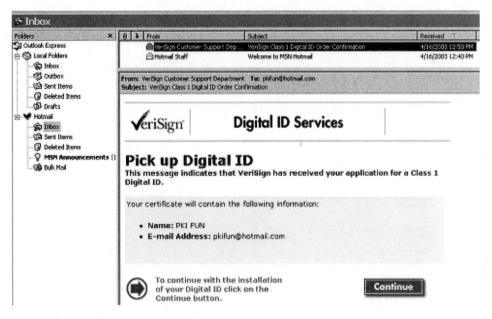

Figure A-26

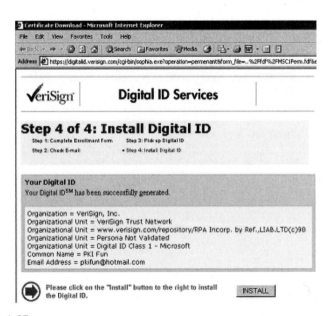

Figure A-27

6 The page will then ask you if you wish to add the certificates now (see Figure A-28). Click Yes.

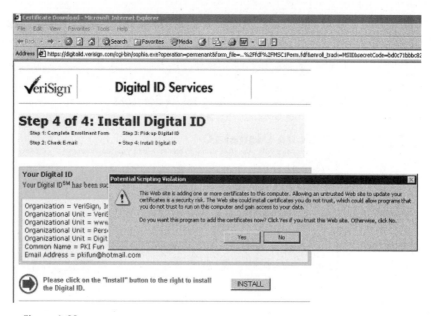

Figure A-28

7 A final page will appear (see Figure A-29): What do you do next?

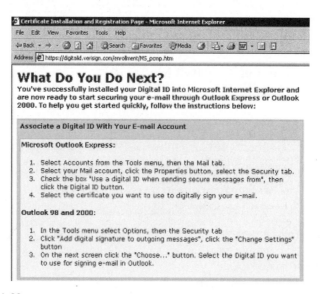

Figure A-29

Now that we have the certificate, we must attach it to our Outlook Express client, using the following steps:

1 Open Outlook Express, left-click Tools, and move the mouse down to Accounts (see Figure A-30).

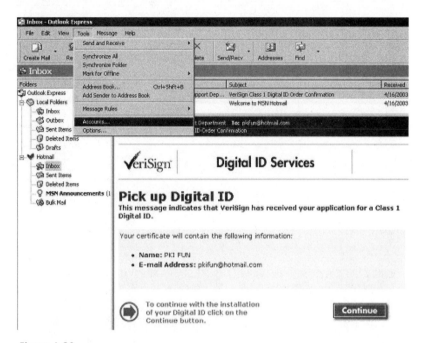

Figure A-30

2 Click the Mail tab and highlight your e-mail account (see Figure A-31).

3 Click Properties, which will open the properties box. Click on Security (see Figure A-32).

4 Click Select under Signing Certificate and the Select Default Account Digital ID box will appear (see Figure A-33).

5 Click your Digital Certificate, and press Ok.

6 Click Select under Encrypting Preferences and click on your certificate there also.

Now we are ready to send e-mails that are digitally signed and encrypted, using the following steps.

1 Close the Accounts box, and click Create Mail. Two new icons will be available on the toolbar: Sign and Encrypt.

2 Type in a fellow student's e-mail name and click Sign (see Figure A-34). Type a subject and a message in the e-mail and send it.

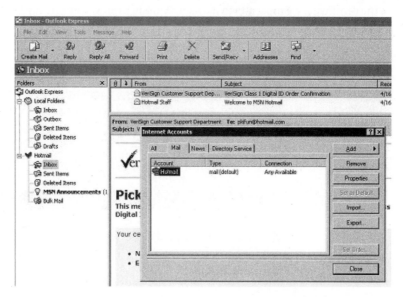

Figure A-31

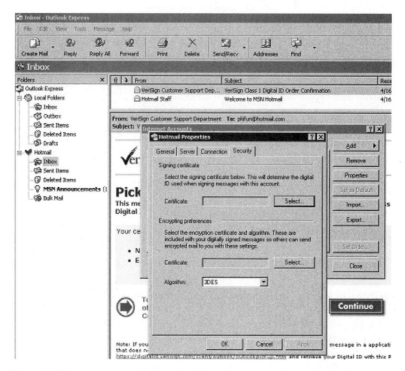

Figure A-32

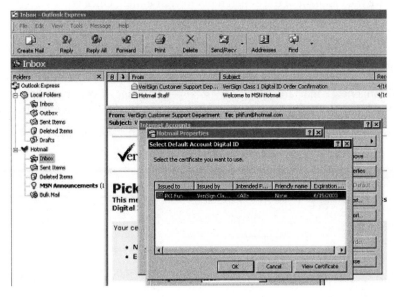

Figure A-33

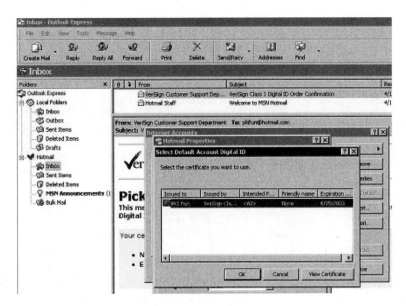

Figure A-34

3 Have the recipient of the e-mail reply to your e-mail. Once you have both digitally signed and traded e-mails (see Figure A-35), you can both encrypt your e-mails.

4 Now that we have sent each other signed e-mails to trade certificates, we can encrypt the e-mails.

5 Try sending encrypted e-mail to each other.

6 Open a new e-mail and click Encrypt. Type a message. If you try to send an e-mail to someone with whom you have not traded certificates, you will receive an error (see Figure A-36).

7 Now that we have sent each other signed e-mails to trade certificates, we can encrypt them.

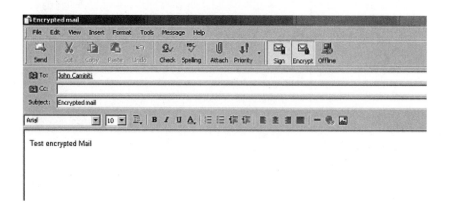

Figure A-35

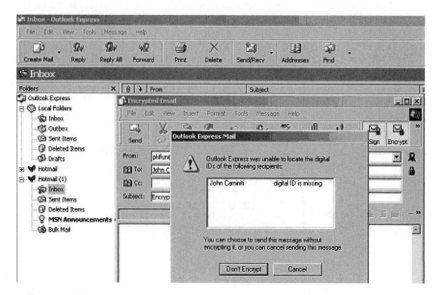

Figure A-36

Lab 9: Denial-of-Service Attacks

Malicious software is readily available throughout the Internet. These types of software applications can wreak havoc on PCs. By rule, if one computer is pinged by another, it must respond. Using this law to a hacker's advantage, it allows for software to be created that generates multiple pings to occur until all of the computer's resources are diverted to responding to pings. Eventually the computer will seize up and need to reboot.

In this lab you will learn how to crash a computer using multiple ping software. You will also be able to view in detail the traffic that is generated over the network by using the software program Ethereal. This software application will allow you to examine the detailed type of traffic that is generated over the network. This will demonstrate the dangers that can be utilized in this type of malicious software.

Lab Objectives

- Demonstrate the dangerous of malicious software that is readily available on the Internet
- Demonstrate that exploiting standard machine vulnerabilities can be devastating

Resources Needed for Lab 9 Exercises:

- Three computers running Windows XP, NT, or 2000. These computers must utilize LAN technology
- A copy of Ethereal running on one computer (obtainable at *http://www.ethereal.com*)
- A copy of ICMP for Windows (obtainable at *http://iraniancracker.8m.com/Download/*)

CAUTIONARY NOTE

Downloading hacker software is dangerous because of its malicious nature. Software intended for malicious use often contains viruses and Trojan horses. Please exercise caution!

Let's Try It!

To start Ethereal:

1 Start Ethereal to capture the network traffic. Click Start-> Programs-> Ethereal-> Ethereal (see Figure A-37).

2 Select your correct capture settings and click Ok (see Figure A-38).

3 You should be able to see normal network traffic on Ethereal (see Figure A-39).

4 Open ICMP by clicking Start-> Programs-> Attacks-> ICMP (see Figure A-40).

5 You will need to enter the IP address of the computer you wish to attack. Enter this address into the Host field and click Start (see Figure A-41). Now you will see the malicious software attacking the victim computer (see Figure A-42).

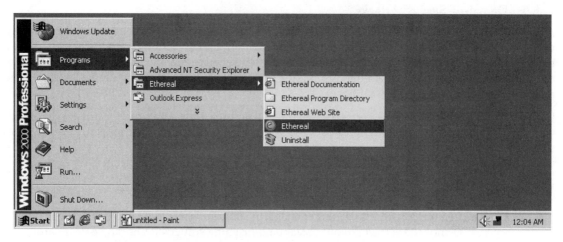

Figure A-37

Figure A-38

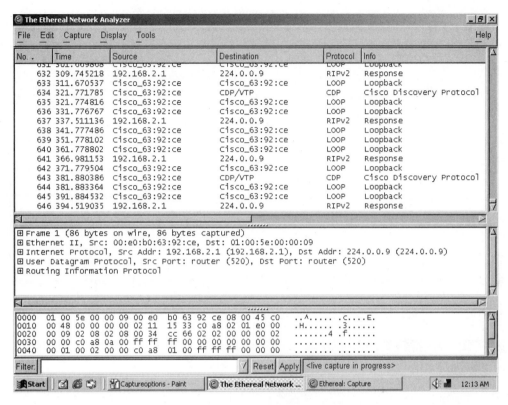

Figure A-39

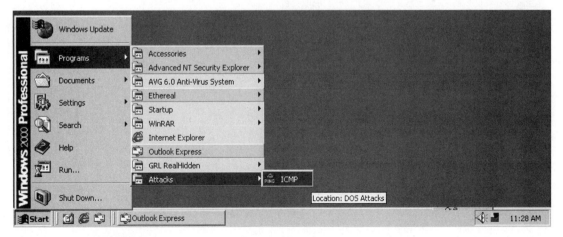

Figure A-40

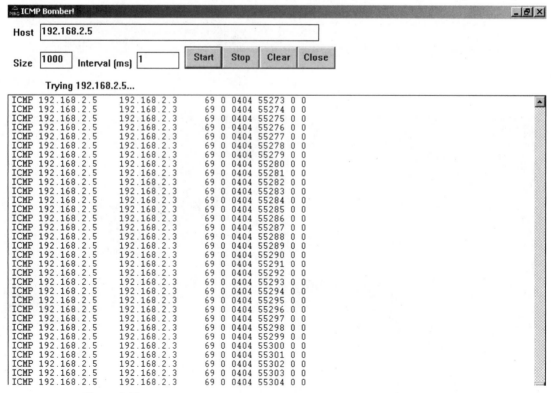

Figure A-41

Figure A-42

View the Effects

1 Look carefully at the traffic on the network that Ethereal has captured (see Figure A-43). You can see in detail the computer being pinged repeatedly.

2 Here you can view the target computer responding to the numerous computer attacks repeatedly, causing it to crash (see Figure A-44) .

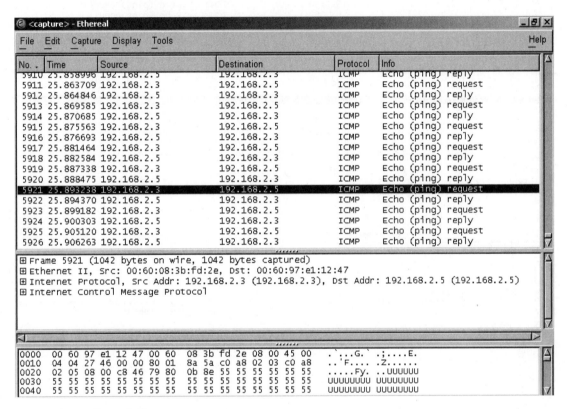

Figure A-43

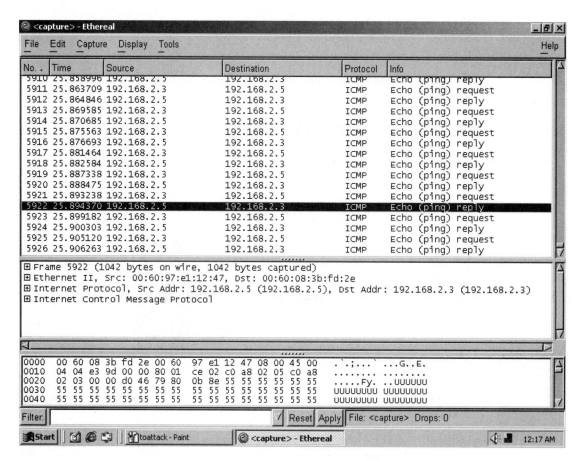

Figure A-44

Lab 10: E-mail Spoofing

Introduction

Although e-mail is among the most popular and most frequently used forms of communication, it is surprisingly nonsecure. Nearly everyone who uses a major online service, such as America Online, or a free e-mail account such as Hotmail, has experienced e-mail spoofing. E-mail spoofing is mail that has an incorrect e-mail address or possibly no e-mail address at all. The sender's identity is masked, and it is seemingly impossible (we will discuss this later) for the receiver to identify the e-mail's source.

The techniques behind the spoofing of e-mail vary, depending on mainly the operating system of the sender. In a UNIX/Linux environment for example, the techniques are quite different than from a Windows 9x/NT environment. Despite the difference in the actual technique, however, the same result is achieved.

Lab Objectives

- Understand the dangers of spoofed e-mails
- Learn how to spoof e-mails
- Understand the importance of digital signatures in the workplace
- Determine if an e-mail is unauthentic or spoofed

Resources Needed for Lab 10 Exercises

- A working internal e-mail system
- At least two working e-mail addresses
- Operable version of Outlook or Outlook Express

Let's Try It!

1 For your convenience, two e-mail accounts have been set up for demonstration purposes. First we will send an actual authentic e-mail from **Server@securitylab.com** to **Student5@securitylab.com**. Example: Server@securitylab.com will send an actual e-mail to the other e-mail account (see Figure A-45).

2 Once the e-mail has been sent, click on the Send/Receive button located on the top center of the screen. This step will allow the e-mail to be transmitted over the network.

3 Now check the e-mail located at the Student5@securitylab.com account. Again, click the Send/Receive button located in the top center of the screen. You will now see the actual e-mail from Server@securitylab.com (see Figure A-46).

4 Double-click on the e-mail.

Note that the From portion of the e-mail states that it is from Server. You have now sent an actual authentic e-mail. We will now spoof an e-mail from the Server@securitylab.com e-mail account. To spoof an e-mail, follow these steps:

5 Click Accounts under the Tools drop-down menu (see Figure A-47).

6 Select the e-mail account system you are currently using and click Properties (see Figure A-48).

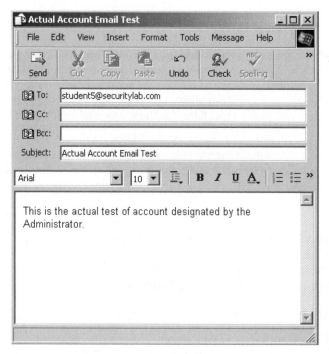

Figure A-45

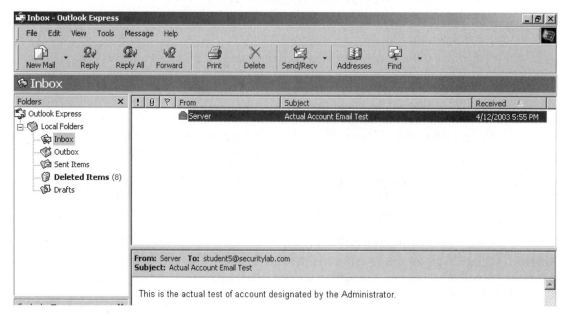

Figure A-46

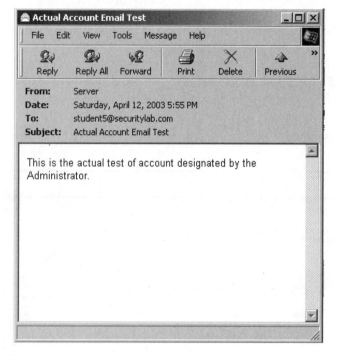

Figure A-47

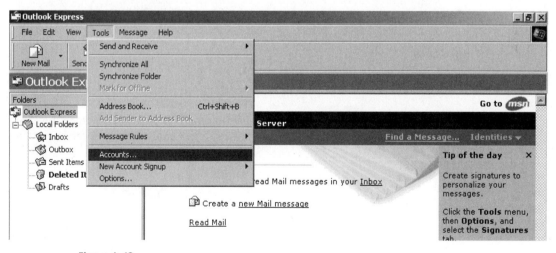

Figure A-48

7 Now we will have to change the Name category (see Figure A-49).

8 Change the name to anything you would like (see Figures A-50 and A-51).

9 Click Ok.

NOTE: For demonstration purposes, we have changed the name Category to Mr_Spoofed_E-mail.

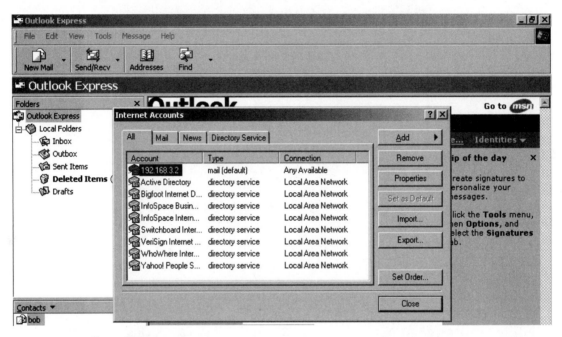

Figure A-49

10 Construct another e-mail to Student5@securitylab.com. Once completed, click Send.

11 Click the Send/Receive button located at the top center of your screen. Once the e-mail message has traveled throughout the network, read the e-mail from the receiver's account.

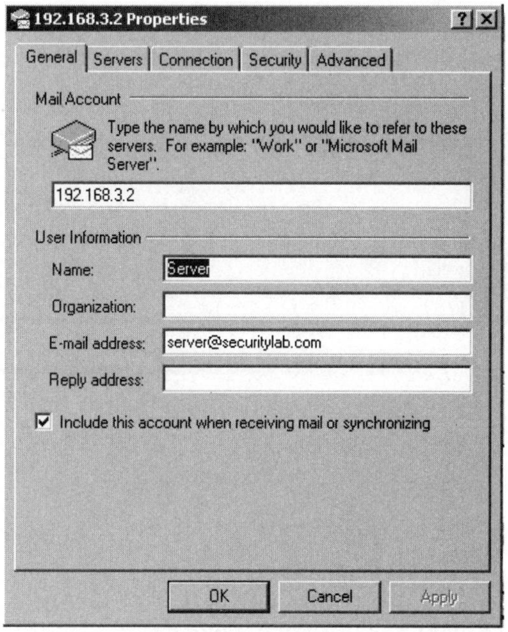

Figure A-50

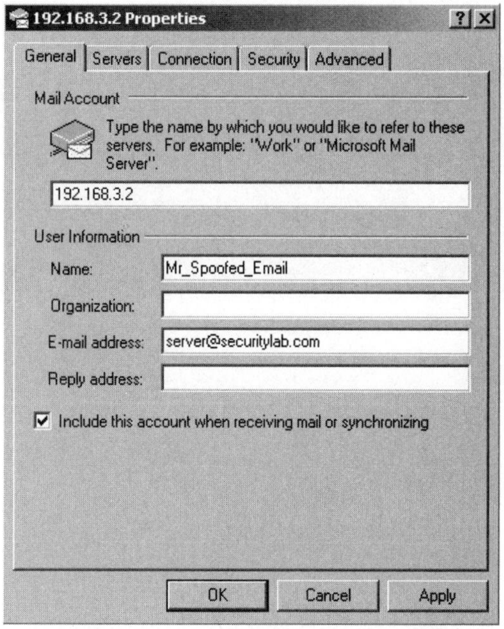

Figure A-51

12 Click the Send/Receive button located at the top center of your screen. You will now see both received e-mails (see Figure A-52).

NOTE: One e-mail shown is from Server and one e-mail is from Mr_Spoofed_E-mail.

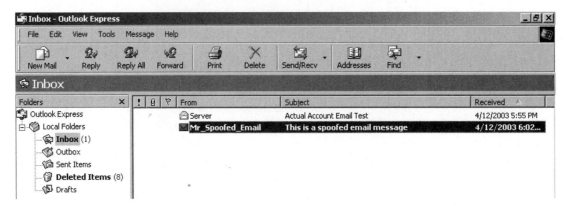

Figure A-52

13 Double-click the e-mail from Mr_Spoofed_E-mail. This will show you that the e-mail that was sent by Mr_Spoofed_E-mail (see Figure A-53).

NOTE: The From category has now changed from Server to Mr_Spoofed_E-mail. You are currently viewing a spoofed e-mail.

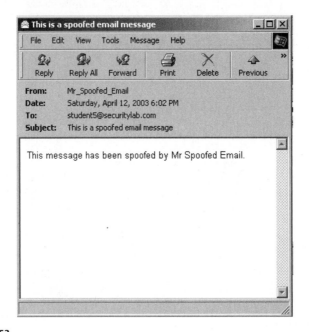

Figure A-53

How to Determine IF an E-mail Is Authentic or Spoofed

14 Now that the spoofed e-mail is currently open under the File drop-down menu, click Properties (see Figure A-54).

15 Click on the Details tab. This will allow you to determine the authenticity and origin of the e-mail. Note that the e-mail has originated from Server@securitylab.com even though the name has been changed form Server to Mr_Spoofed_E-mail (see Figure A-55).

16 Please change all settings back to their original state.

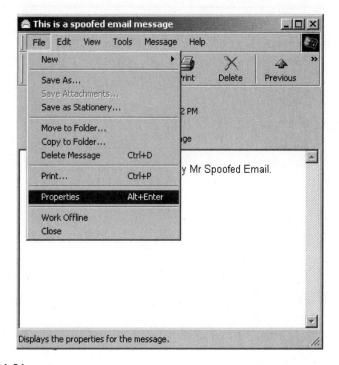

Figure A-54

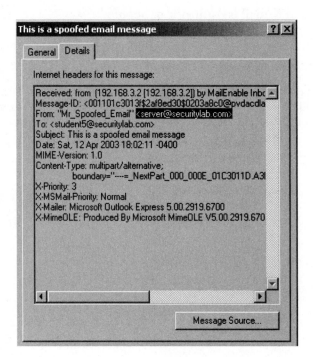

Figure A-55

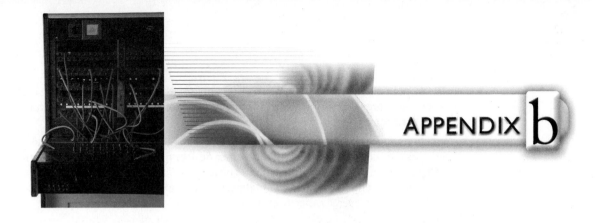

TCP/IP Fundamentals

The following information is meant to serve as a network primer for students that need to refresh their network skills. It is primarily focused on the Transmission Control Protocol/Internet Protocol (TCP/IP), the predominant protocol used in the Internet and the focus of much of the discussion presented regarding networks in this book. The field of networking is vast; a significant number of additional topics and methods need to be understood by the information security professional. This information is in no way meant to replace or be a substitute for a substantial course or text on networking. This information should be used by students to measure whether their networking background is sufficient for grasping the network security material presented in this text.

DEFINITIONS

The following are important networking terms and definitions.

> **LAN** (Local Area Network)—Point-to-point level two–type connections between hosts in the same local network structure.
>
> **WAN** (Wide Area Network)—Connections between computers in remote locations over the public communications network.
>
> **MAC address**—The hardware address of the level-two device that connects the computer to the level-two medium.
>
> **NIC** (Network Interface Card)—The physical layer interconnecting the computer to the LAN. These cards have predefined MAC addresses and must be purchased according to the media type of the LAN.
>
> **Repeater**—Regenerates and retimes a signal on a wire. This device also extends the segments beyond the limitations of the permitted cable lengths.
>
> **Bridge**—A level-two device for interconnecting two LANs. This device is used instead of a repeater to segment LAN traffic.
>
> **Router**—Used to interconnect WAN locations. These devices route packets through the network to remote destinations. Routers support the IP protocol and use special internal protocols to exchange routing updates. These devices reduce broadcast storms. Routers

play an integral role in designing network security solutions because they can be used to inspect level-three addressing, protocol, and length information, and they apply rules that dictate actions to be taken as a result of the inspection.

Switch—Switches can be purchased as level-two, level-three, and level-four devices. A switch performs the actions associated with the other devices normally found at these same layers (bridges, routers, hubs). However, switches increase performance to the end station as they isolate communicating pairs and allow multiple pairs of nodes to communicate at the same time. This increases the overall capacity of the network.

Proxy server—Used to isolate internal computers on the LAN from people entering the network from untrusted sources. The proxy server can perform enhanced security inspections at each level of the OSI model, address translation, and other proxy functions.

Firewall—Used to prevent unauthorized access to the hosts it protects from sources outside of the trusted area. Firewalls can perform screening functions, content aware inspections, proxy functions, and they can implement effective attack countermeasures.

TCP (Transmission Control Protocol)—Effectively establishes connections (via ports) across the network, so that applications on a local machine can communicate with applications on a remote machine. Applications connect to the local port via a socket. This port / socket relationship forms the basis of all distributed applications in the TCP/IP environment. TCP guarantees data delivery.

UDP—Provides nonguaranteed connectionless communications between two applications across the network.

DHCP—Dynamically allocates an IP address to a host on power-up. This facility allows organizations to use IP addresses most efficiently. V4 IP addresses are in short supply.

DNS (Directory Naming Service)—Used to resolve computer names such as www.myhost.com to IP addresses such as 114.12.75.111.

Active directory—Microsoft's version of an X.500 directory service.

ARP (Address Resolution Protocol)—The protocol that a host uses to map an IP address to a LAN hardware address. This is a broadcast protocol from the host to which the target system replies.

Cable modem—A modem used to connect a computer to the broadband network used to provide cable television.

Destination address—The address in an IP packet that specifies the end node that the packet has been sent to. This address must be a unique IP address.

Source address—The address in the IP packet that specifies the node that originated the transmission of the packet. This address must be a unique IP address.

Domain—The Internet can be thought of as a tree structure. End users are at the leaves of the tree structure. All leaves are members of various subtrees of the network (such as the .com subtree, the .org subtree, or the .edu subtree). Through this structured domain directory service, protocols can identify and resolve addresses.

IP tunneling—The process of encapsulating the packets of a nonroutable protocol inside an IP packet for transport across the Net.

internet (with a lowercase "i")—A set of interconnected computers that use routers and TCP/IP as the base protocol. These systems are networked using private lines and are not part of the public network infrastructure.

Internet (with an uppercase "I")—The global (lowercase "i") internet that connects computers on a worldwide basis.

Intranet—A private internet that uses the public Internet (uppercase "I") privately via secure tunneling protocols (IP from the private Net encapsulated inside the IP used on the public Net with applied cryptography) to communicate between remote branches of that organization.

IP version 4—The current version of IP that uses 32-bit addresses. This version of the protocol is more than twenty years old and dangerously low on available space. It also has limited built-in provisions for security.

IP version 6—The successor to the older IP version 4 protocol. This protocol features 128-bit addresses that will solve the address shortage problems of version 4.

NAT (Network Address Translation)—These devices allow organizations to map their internal (usually nonofficial IP addresses) to valid IP addresses that are recognized on the Internet. NAT devices serve two important purposes: First, they conserve Internet address space by allowing private organizations to use nonauthorized IP addresses inside their private networks. Second, they reduce the chances of network mapping.

Ping—A service provided in the TCP/IP suite that allows for the testing of communications paths across the network (a network echo service).

SNMP (Simple Network Management Protocol) —Allows us to check the health of the network and remotely manage network components via a set of simple commands.

POP3—A service that delivers electronic mail between the mail server and the client.

FTP (File Transfer Protocol)—A service that allows for the transfer of files and file management services between information on remote hosts.

HTTP (Hypertext Transfer Protocol)—The Web-enabling protocol that establishes connections between browsers and servers to establish Web site connectivity. This is a simple request/response protocol that transfers HTTP-style documents.

INTERNET PROTOCOL

The basic function of the Internet Protocol (IP) is to interconnect systems across the WAN so that they can communicate in either a connection- or connectionless-oriented fashion and exchange data. This protocol defines both the form of the IP packets and the mechanisms for communication using the level three of the network.

The IP header is shown in Figure B-1.

FIELD DEFINITIONS

Version—This is the IP version number (currently this is 4)

IHL—Internet Header Length

Flags—Fragmentation switches

Type of service—Flags to specify operational parameters (e.g., precedence, delay, throughput, and reliability)

Version 4 IP Header

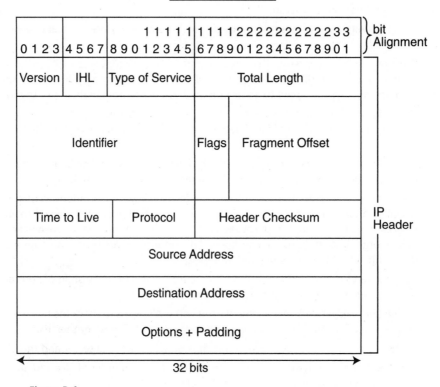

Figure B-1

Total length—Total length of the IP packet (min → 576 max → 65,535)

Identifier—Provides a unique identifier for this packet

Fragment offset—Where in the entire block does this packet belong (measured in 64-bit units from the beginning of the block)

Time to live—Hops allowed while in the network before mandatory removal

Protocol—Identifies the protocol at the next level above IP included in the data field of this packet

Header checksum—A validity identifier included in the packet

Transmission Control Protocol

The basic function of TCP is to establish and manage connections across the Internet. This is the first level from the bottom where a message using the protocol is meant for the destination system and not an intermediate station (end-to-end connectivity). The TCP header is shown in Figure B-2:

The fields in this header are the following:

> **Source port**—The number of the calling port
>
> **Destination port**—The number of the destination port

TCP Header

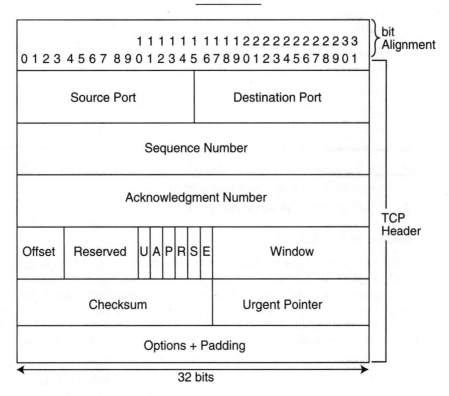

Figure B-2

Sequence number—The number of this part of the message so that the entire message can be reassembled in order

Offset—The number of 32-bit words in the header before the data

Reserved—Set to zero

Flags—Control functions for the session (e.g., set up, termination, reset)

Window—The receive window size

Checksum—A check of packet integrity

Ports are the connection points between the applications and the network. Private ports are defined at the local system and well-known ports are reserved for standard network services. There are many well-known ports:

7:	ECHO
9:	DISCARD
11:	Active users
13:	Time and date service

15:     NETSTAT

17:     Quote of the day

20:     FTP data

21:     FTP

23:     Telnet

25:     SMTP

53:     DNS

69:     TFTP

80:     HTTP

110:    POP3

119:    NNTP (network news transfer protocol)

137:    NetBIOS-NS (naming service for NetBIOS)

220:    IMAP3 (Internet mail access protocol 3)

IP ADDRESSING BASICS

IP uses classes of addresses that form a network hierarchy. These addresses are 32 bits long in the IP v4 scheme. The address is divided into two parts: network and host. Depending on the class of the address, the amount of bits assigned to each part varies. Class A addresses contain 8 bits (one-bit identifier) in the network and 24 bits in the host. Class B addresses contain 16 bits (two-bit identifier) in both the network and the host. Class C addresses contain 24 bits (three-bit identifier) in the network and 8 bits in the host. Class D addresses are used for multicast addresses and class E addresses are reserved for future use.

Class	Number of Networks	Number of Hosts
A (0 through 127 in the first byte)	128	16,777,216
B (128 through 191 in the first byte)	16,384	65,536
C (192 through 223 in the first byte)	2,097,152	256

The decodes of the bits that identify the classes of addresses are shown in Figure B-3.

IP addresses are expressed in dot-decimal notation by translating each of the four bytes in the 32-bit address into a decimal equivalent. For example, addresses take the form 123.11.125.232. The range of addresses is from 000.000.000.000 to 255.255.255.255. Internet addresses must be unique in the network and are therefore assigned by a central governing authority, the Internet Assigned Number Authority.

Subnet masking provides a mechanism to avoid network address misuse and thus conserve network addresses. Subnetting allows the organization assigned a particular range of addresses to subdivide them and to create an abstraction that allows routers to subdivide the single space across parts of the organization. Routers determine subnets based on the establishment of subnet masks.

IP Address Class Decodes

```
Ø 1 2 3 4 5 6 7 8          16          24          31
┌─┬─────────────┬──────────────────────────────────────┐
│0│  Network    │               Host                   │
└─┴─────────────┴──────────────────────────────────────┘
Class A

┌─┬─┬───────────────────────┬──────────────────────────┐
│1│0│    Network            │           Host           │
└─┴─┴───────────────────────┴──────────────────────────┘
Class B

┌─┬─┬─┬───────────────────────────────┬─────────────────┐
│1│1│0│    Network                    │       Host      │
└─┴─┴─┴───────────────────────────────┴─────────────────┘
Class C

┌─┬─┬─┬─┬───────────────────────────────────────────────┐
│1│1│1│0│          Multicast Addresses                  │
└─┴─┴─┴─┴───────────────────────────────────────────────┘
Class D

┌─┬─┬─┬─┬───────────────────────────────────────────────┐
│1│1│1│1│          Reserved for Future Use              │
└─┴─┴─┴─┴───────────────────────────────────────────────┘
Class E
```

Figure B-3

ROUTER CONFIGURATION AND CONTROL BASICS

Control of IP is done through the use of routers and router configurations. One of the most basic router configuration parameters is the use of access control lists. Normally these lists are of this form:

> *List # Access {deny or permit}protocol, source address, source port, destination address, destination port*

These commands can control the flow of information into and out of an organization through preestablished choke points. These commands also form the basis of screening routers.

For example, the command

> *List #1 access deny al*

postures the interface closed to all traffic. Subsequently, issuing the command

> *List #2 access permit TCP/IP 110.23.35.255 all 255.255.255.255 port 80*

would permit all of the class c addresses from segment 110.23.35.xxx to enter into any HTTP session with all Web servers behind the router.

NIPC Cybercrime Reporting Form

[rev. 07/17/2002]

NATIONAL INFRASTRUCTURE PROTECTION CENTER

CYBERTHREAT AND COMPUTER INTRUSION INCIDENT REPORTING GUIDELINES

This form may be used as a guide or vehicle for reporting cyberthreat and computer intrusion incident information to the NIPC or other law enforcement organizations. It is recommended that these Cyber Incident Reporting Guidelines be used when submitting a report to a local FBI field office.

Do NOT include **classified** information on this form unless you adhere to applicable procedures for proper marking, handling, and transmission of classified information. Please contact NIPC Watch Operations Center at 1-888-585-9078 to arrange secure means to submit classified information. Information concerning the identity of the reporting agency, department, company, or individual(s) will be treated on a confidential basis. If additional information is required, you will be contacted directly.

Report Date/Time: _____

When completed, fax to NIPC WWU (202) 323-2079/2082.

SECTION 1

Point of Contact (POC) Information

Name: _____

Title: _____

Telephone/Fax Number: _____

E-mail: _____

Organization: _____

Address: _____

Street: _____

City, State, Zip Code: _____

Country: _____

SECTION 2

Incident Information

Name of Organization: (if same as above, enter "SAME") _____

❑   (Check here if Federal Government Agency)

Organization's contact information: _____

Telephone number: _____

Address: (if same as above, enter "SAME")

Street: _____

City, State, Zip Code: _____

Country: _____

E-mail: _____

Physical location(s) of victim's computer system/network (Be Specific): _____

Date/Time and duration of incident:

_____

Is the affected system/network critical to the organization's mission?

❑   Yes   ❑   No

Which critical infrastructure sector was affected? (Check only **one**)

❑ Power

❑ Banking and Finance

❑ Government Operations

❑ Gas & Oil Storage and Delivery

❑ Telecommunications

❑ Transportation

❑ Emergency Services

❑ Water Supply Systems

❑ Other (Provide details in remarks)

❑ Not Applicable

Nature of problem. (Check only **one**)

❑ Intrusion

❑ Unauthorized root access

❑ Compromise of system integrity

❑ Theft

❑ Unknown

❑ System impairment/denial of resources

❑ Web site defacement

❑ Hoax

❑ Damage

❑ Other (Provide details in remarks)

Has this problem been experienced before? (If yes, please explain in the remarks section):

❑ Yes

❑ No

Suspected method of intrusion/attack (Check only **one**)

❑ Virus (provide name if known)

❑ Denial of Service

❑ Distributed Denial of Service

❑ Unknown

❑ Vulnerability exploited (explain)

❑ Trojan horse

❑ Trapdoor

❑ Other (Provide details in remarks)

Suspected perpetrator(s) or possible motivation(s) of the attack (Check only **one**)

❑ Insider/disgruntled employee

❑ Competitor

❑ Unknown

❑ Former employee

❑ Other (Explain in remarks)

The apparent source (IP address) of the intrusion/attack: _____

Evidence of spoofing?

❑ Yes

❑ Unknown

❑ No

What computer system (hardware and/or software) was affected (e.g., operating system, version)? (Check only **one**)

- ☐ Unix
- ☐ Linux
- ☐ NT
- ☐ Sun OS/Solaris

- ☐ OS2
- ☐ VAX/VMS
- ☐ Windows
- ☐ Other (Specify in remarks)

What security infrastructure was in place? (Check all that apply)

- ☐ Incident/Emergency Response Team
- ☐ Firewall
- ☐ Intrusion Detection System
- ☐ Security Auditing Tools
- ☐ Secure Remote Access/Authorization tools

- ☐ Packet filtering
- ☐ Encryption
- ☐ Banners
- ☐ Access Control Lists

Did the intrusion/attack result in a loss/compromise of sensitive, classified or proprietary information?

- ☐ Yes (provide details in remarks)
- ☐ Unknown

- ☐ No

Did the intrusion/attack result in damage to system(s) or data?

- ☐ Yes (Provide details in remarks)
- ☐ No

What actions and/or technical mitigation have been taken?

- ☐ Backup of affected system(s)
- ☐ Log files examined
- ☐ System(s) disconnected from the network
- ☐ Other (Please provide details in remarks)

- ☐ System binaries checked
- ☐ No action(s) taken

Has the local FBI field office been informed?

- ☐ Yes (which office)
- ☐ No

Has another agency/organization been informed? If so, please provide name and phone number.

- ☐ Yes
- ☐ State/local police
- ☐ CERT-CC
- ☐ JTF-CNO

- ☐ No
- ☐ Inspector General
- ☐ FedCIRC
- ☐ Other (incident response, law enforcement, etc.)

When was the last time your system was modified or updated?

Date: _____

Company/Organization that did the work (address, phone number, POC information):

_____

_____

_____

Is the System Administrator a contractor?

❑ Yes (Provide POC information)   ❑ No

In addition to being used for law enforcement or national security purposes, the intrusion-related information I reported may be shared with:

❑ The public   ❑ InfraGard members with secure access

Additional Remarks (please limit to 500 characters—amplifying information may be submitted separately):

_____

_____

_____

_____

_____

_____

_____

_____

_____

If the reported incident is determined to be a criminal matter, you may be contacted by an agent in your location for additional information.

Table of Primes up to 5,000

2	3	5	7	11	13	17	19	23	29
31	37	41	43	47	53	59	61	67	71
73	79	83	89	97	101	103	107	109	113
127	131	137	139	149	151	157	163	167	173
179	181	191	193	197	199	211	223	227	229
233	239	241	251	257	263	269	271	277	281
283	293	307	311	313	317	331	337	347	349
353	359	367	373	379	383	389	397	401	409
419	421	431	433	439	443	449	457	461	463
467	479	487	491	499	503	509	521	523	541
547	557	563	569	571	577	587	593	599	601
607	613	617	619	631	641	643	647	653	659
661	673	677	683	691	701	709	719	727	733
739	743	751	757	761	769	773	787	797	809
811	821	823	827	829	839	853	857	859	863
877	881	883	887	907	911	919	929	937	941
947	953	967	971	977	983	991	997	1,009	1,013
1,019	1,021	1,031	1,033	1,039	1,049	1,051	1,061	1,063	1,069
1,087	1,091	1,093	1,097	1,103	1,109	1,117	1,123	1,129	1,151
1,153	1,163	1,171	1,181	1,187	1,193	1,201	1,213	1,217	1,223

1,229	1,231	1,237	1,249	1,259	1,277	1,279	1,283	1,289	1,291
1,297	1,301	1,303	1,307	1,319	1,321	1,327	1,361	1,367	1,373
1,381	1,399	1,409	1,423	1,427	1,429	1,433	1,439	1,447	1,451
1,453	1,459	1,471	1,481	1,483	1,487	1,489	1,493	1,499	1,511
1,523	1,531	1,543	1,549	1,553	1,559	1,567	1,571	1,579	1,583
1,597	1,601	1,607	1,609	1,613	1,619	1,621	1,627	1,637	1,657
1,663	1,667	1,669	1,693	1,697	1,699	1,709	1,721	1,723	1,733
1,741	1,747	1,753	1,759	1,777	1,783	1,787	1,789	1,801	1,811
1,823	1,831	1,847	1,861	1,867	1,871	1,873	1,877	1,879	1,889
1,901	1,907	1,913	1,931	1,933	1,949	1,951	1,973	1,979	1,987
1,993	1,997	1,999	2,003	2,011	2,017	2,027	2,029	2,039	2,053
2,063	2,069	2,081	2,083	2,087	2,089	2,099	2,111	2,113	2,129
2,131	2,137	2,141	2,143	2,153	2,161	2,179	2,203	2,207	2,213
2,221	2,237	2,239	2,243	2,251	2,267	2,269	2,273	2,281	2,287
2,293	2,297	2,309	2,311	2,333	2,339	2,341	2,347	2,351	2,357
2,371	2,377	2,381	2,383	2,389	2,393	2,399	2,411	2,417	2,423
2,437	2,441	2,447	2,459	2,467	2,473	2,477	2,503	2,521	2,531
2,539	2,543	2,549	2,551	2,557	2,579	2,591	2,593	2,609	2,617
2,621	2,633	2,647	2,657	2,659	2,663	2,671	2,677	2,683	2,687
2,689	2,693	2,699	2,707	2,711	2,713	2,719	2,729	2,731	2,741
2,749	2,753	2,767	2,777	2,789	2,791	2,797	2,801	2,803	2,819
2,833	2,837	2,843	2,851	2,857	2,861	2,879	2,887	2,897	2,903
2,909	2,917	2,927	2,939	2,953	2,957	2,963	2,969	2,971	2,999
3,001	3,011	3,019	3,023	3,037	3,041	3,049	3,061	3,067	3,079
3,083	3,089	3,109	3,119	3,121	3,137	3,163	3,167	3,169	3,181
3,187	3,191	3,203	3,209	3,217	3,221	3,229	3,251	3,253	3,257
3,259	3,271	3,299	3,301	3,307	3,313	3,319	3,323	3,329	3,331
3,343	3,347	3,359	3,361	3,371	3,373	3,389	3,391	3,407	3,413
3,433	3,449	3,457	3,461	3,463	3,467	3,469	3,491	3,499	3,511
3,517	3,527	3,529	3,533	3,539	3,541	3,547	3,557	3,559	3,571
3,581	3,583	3,593	3,607	3,613	3,617	3,623	3,631	3,637	3,643

3,659	3,671	3,673	3,677	3,691	3,697	3,701	3,709	3,719	3,727
3,733	3,739	3,761	3,767	3,769	3,779	3,793	3,797	3,803	3,821
3,823	3,833	3,847	3,851	3,853	3,863	3,877	3,881	3,889	3,907
3,911	3,917	3,919	3,923	3,929	3,931	3,943	3,947	3,967	3,989
4,001	4,003	4,007	4,013	4,019	4,021	4,027	4,049	4,051	4,057
4,073	4,079	4,091	4,093	4,099	4,111	4,127	4,129	4,133	4,139
4,153	4,157	4,159	4,177	4,201	4,211	4,217	4,219	4,229	4,231
4,241	4,243	4,253	4,259	4,261	4,271	4,273	4,283	4,289	4,297
4,327	4,337	4,339	4,349	4,357	4,363	4,373	4,391	4,397	4,409
4,421	4,423	4,441	4,447	4,451	4,457	4,463	4,481	4,483	4,493
4,507	4,513	4,517	4,519	4,523	4,547	4,549	4,561	4,567	4,583
4,591	4,597	4,603	4,621	4,637	4,639	4,643	4,649	4,651	4,657
4,663	4,673	4,679	4,691	4,703	4,721	4,723	4,729	4,733	4,751
4,759	4,783	4,787	4,789	4,793	4,799	4,801	4,813	4,817	4,831
4,861	4,871	4,877	4,889	4,903	4,909	4,919	4,931	4,933	4,937
4,943	4,951	4,957	4,967	4,969	4,973	4,987	4,993	4,999	

BIBLIOGRAPHY

"About Virtual Private Networks," *http://www.wkmn.com/newsite/vpn.html* [25 March 2003].

Aitken, Peter and Bradley L. Jones. *Teach Yourself C in 21 Days*, 4th ed. Indianapolis: Sams Publishing, 1997.

Austin, Tom. *PKI: A Wiley Tech Brief*, New York: John Wiley & Sons, Inc., 2001.

Baase, Sara. *Computer Algorithms: Introduction to Design and Analysis*, 2nd ed. Reading: Addison-Wesley Publishing Company, 1991.

Barr, Thomas H. *Invitation to Cryptology.* Upper Saddle River: Prentice Hall, 2002.

Bergquist, Carl. *Guide to Electronic Surveillance Devices.* Clifton Park: Delmar Learning, 2002.

Bishop, Matt. *Computer Security: Art and Science.* Boston: Addison-Wesley, 2003.

Brown, Lawrie. "Introduction to Number Theory." *http://www1.Shore.net/~ws/security-notes/lecture/publickey.html* [22 January 1998].

Campbell, Paul, Ben Calvert, and Steven Boswell. *Security + Guide to Network Security Fundamentals.* Boston: Course Technology, 2003.

Cohen, Fred. "A Short History of Cryptography." *http://www.All.net/books/ip/Chap 2-1.html* [25 March 2003].

Cretaro, Paul. *Lab Manual For Security & Guide to Network Security Fundamentals.* Boston: Course Technology, 2003.

"Cryptographic Timeline." *http://library.thinkquest.org/28005/flashed/timemachine/timeline.shtml* [16 July 2002].

Denning, Dorothy E. *Information Warfare and Security.* Reading: Addison-Wesley, 1999.

Dormann, Henry O., Comp. *The Speaker's Book of Quotations*, Rev. ed. New York: Ballantine Books, 2000.

Fisher, Dennis. "Security Encryption: Turning the Key on Data." *eWeek* **89** (November 2002).

Garrett, Paul B. *Making, Breaking Codes: An Introduction to Cryptology.* Upper Saddle River: Prentice Hall, 2002.

Granger, Sarah. "Social Engineering Fundamentals, Part I: Hacker Tactics." *http://www.securityfocus.com/infocus/1527* [27 March 2003].

Hazlewood, Donald and Carol Hazlewood. "Divisibility." *http://www.Math.swt.edu/~haz/prob_sets/notes/node3.html* [11 April 2003].

Hodges, Andrew. "The Turing Machine." *http://www. wadham.Ox.ac.uk/~ahodges/t-machine.html* [26 April 1997].

Householder, Allen, Kevin Houle, and Chad Dougherty. "Computer Attack Trends Challenge Internet Security." *Security & Privacy,* 2002, 5-7.

Icove, David, Karl Seger, and William VonStorch. *Computer Crime: A Crimefighter's Handbook.* Sebastopol: O'Reilly & Associates, Inc., 1995.

Jamsa, Kris. *Hacker Proof: The Ultimate Guide to Network Security,* 2nd ed. Albany:Thomson Learning, Inc., 2002.

Knott, Ron. "The Golden Section—The Number and Its Geometry." *http://www.mcs.surrey.ac.uk/Personal/R.Knott/Fibonacci/phi.html* [8 January 2002].

Kong, Jeijun. "Valuations of Secrecy System." *http://netlab3.cs.ucla.edu/Shannon1949/node5.html* [6 April 2003].

Kramer, Arthur D. *Mathematics for Electricity & Electronics,* 2nd ed. Albany: Thomson Learning, Inc., 2002.

Mendelson, Elliott. *Introduction to Mathematical Logic,* 3rd ed. New York: Chapman & Hall, 1987.

Northcutt, Stephen, Judy Novak, and Donald McLachlan. *Network Intrusion Detection: An Analyst's Handbook,* 2nd ed. Indianapolis: New Riders, 2001.

Parker, Allan. "Why Use Statistics?" *http://www.math.swt.edu/~haz/prob_sets/notes/node3.html* [15 April 2003].

Pfleeger, Charles P. and Shari Lawrence Pfleeger. *Security in Computing,* 3rd ed. Upper Saddle River: Prentice Hall, 2003.

Skoudis, Ed. "Infosec's Worst Nightmares." *Information Security,* 5 (2002) p. 38–49.

SooHoo, Kevin J. "How Much Is Enough?" *http://216.239.51.100/Search?q=cache:_gK9Xvdvpyuc.www.sims.berkeley.edu/resources/...* [2 January 2003].

Stallings, William. *Cryptography and Network Security: Principles and Practices,* 3rd ed. Upper Saddle River: Pearson Education, Inc., 2003.

Stallings, William. *Network Security Essentials: Applications and Standards,* 2nd ed. Upper Saddle River: Pearson Education, Inc., 2003.

"StegoArchive.Com." *http://steganography.tripod.com/stego.html* [25 March 2003].

Stein, Lincoln D. *Web Security: A Step-by-Step Reference Guide.* Boston: Addison-Wesley, 1998.

Taber, Mark, ed. *Maximum Security: A Hacker's Guide to Protecting Your Internet Site and Network,* 2nd ed. Indianapolis: Sams Publishing, 1998.

Trappe, Wade and Lawrence C. Washington. *Introduction to Cryptography With Coding Theory.* Upper Saddle River: Prentice Hall, 2002.

United States. National Institute of Standards and Technology. "Advanced Encryption Standard (AES)." November 2001.

United States. Department of Justice. Federal Bureau of Investigation. "Los Angeles Man Sentenced to Prison for Role in International Computer Hacking and Internet Fraud Scheme." *http://www.usdoj.gov/criminal/Cybercrime/paesent.htm* [28 February, 2003, 9 March 2003].

United States. Department of Justice. "United States Code Annotated Title 18. Crimes and Criminal Procedure." *http://www.usdoj.gov/criminal/cybercrime/1030NEW.htm* [9 March 2003].

United States. Department of Justice. "Ex-employee of Airport Transportation Company Arrested for Allegedly Hacking Into Computer, Destroying Data." *http://www.usdoj.gov/criminal/cybercrime/ tranArrest.htm* [20 February 2003, 9 March 2003].

United States. Department of Justice. "Computer Crime and Intellectual Property Section (CCIPS)." *http://www. cybercrime.gov/PatriotAct.htm* [9 March 2003].

United States. Department of Justice. "Pair From Cupertino and San Jose, California, Indicted for Economic Espionage and Theft of Trade Secrets From Silicon Valley Companies." *http://www.cybercrime.gov// yeIndict.htm* [4 December 2002, 9 March 2003].

United States. Department of Justice. "Los Angeles Man Indicted For Theft of Trade Secrets For Stealing Information Pertaining to DirecTV's Most Advanced Conditional Access Card." *http://www. cybercrime.gov/serebryanyIndict.htm* [16 January 2002, 9 March 2003].

United States. Department of Justice. Office of the Attorney General "Renewal of Approval Requirement Under The Economic Espionage Act of 1996." Mar. 1, 2002. [9 March 2003].

United States. Department of Justice. "Wire and Electronic Communications Interception and Interception of Oral Communications." *http://www.usdoj.gov/criminal/cybercrime/18usc2510.htm* [9 March 2003].

United States. Dept. of Justice. "Searches and Seizures by Government Officers." *http://www.usdoj.gov/criminal/cybercrime/42usc2000aa.htm* [9 March 2003].

Walsh, Lawrence M. "Standard Practice." *Information Security*, 2002, p. 62–68.

Wells, Nicholas. *Guide to Linux Networking and Security.* Boston: Course Technology, 2003.

Wheeler, David and Roger Needham. "TEA, A Tiny Encryption Algorithm." *ftp://ftp.cl.cam.ac.uk/papers/djw-rmn/djw-rmn-tea.html* [7 January 2002].

Whitman, Michael E. and Herbert J. Mattord. *Principles of Information Security.* Boston: Course Technology, 2003.

ADDITIONAL USEFUL SITES/READING

Computer. October 2001.

Information Security. July 2002.

www.rsasecurity.com/rsalabs/faq

http://www.sei.cmu.edu/str/descriptions/

http://www.techweb.com/encyclopedia/

http://www.cryptography.com

http://www.verisign.com

http://www.zdnet.com/filters/zdhelp/

http://world.std.com/~franl/crypto.html

http://axion.physics.ubc.ca/crypt.html

http://www.pacific-pages.com/support.contrib.pgp

ftp://ftp.prairienet.org/pub/providers/pgp/pgpfaq.txt

http://www.cypherspace.org/~adam/timeline

http://axion.physics.ubc.ca/crypt.html

http://www.pgpi.com

http://www.pgp.com

http://www.rsasecurity.com/rsalabs/faq3-2.html

http://www.abisoft.net/des.html

http://crypteon.eon-solutions.co.uk/des-file-encryption-dll.htm

http://www.axion.physics.ubc.ca/crypt.html

http://www.tropsoft.com/strongenc/des3.html

http://www.cisco.com/univercd/cc/td/doc/product/software/ios120/120newft/120t/120t/3desips.htm

http://csrc.nist.gov/cryptval/des/tripledesal.html

http://www.abisoft.net/des.html

http://developer.netscape.com/docs/manuals/security/sslin/contents.htm

http://wp.netscape.com/security/techbriefs/ssl.html

http://www.rsasecurity.com/standards/ssl/

http://www.ssl.com

http://www.comsoc.org/livepubs/surveys/public4q98issue/stallings.html

http://www.snmp.com/

http://hunnysoft.com/mime/

http://www.rsasecurity.com/standards/smime/

http://www.bacus.pt/Net_SSLeay/smime.html

http://www.oac.uci.edu/indiv/ehood/MIME/MIME.html

http://www.davidreilly.com/topics/electronic_commerce/essays/secure_electronic transactions.html

http://www-3.ibm.com/software/webservers/commerce/payment/support/overview.html

http://www.aibn.com/help/Advisories/set.html

http://www.netbsd.org/Documentation/network/ipsec/

http://www.intel.com/network/connectivity/resources/doc_library/white_papers/products/ipsecurity/index.htm

http://www.commweb.com/article/COM20000912S0009

http://www.freenet.edmonton.ab.ca/~jsavard/crypto/co0406.htm

http://www.counterpane.com/bfsvverlag.html

http://www.counterpane.com/blowfish.html

http://www.bsn.ch/Lasse/bfacs.htm

http://www.rsasecurity.com/rsalabs/pkcs/index.html

http://citeseer.nj.nec.com/rivest95rc.html

http://saturn.hut.fi/~helger/cryto/link/block/rc5.html

INDEX

A

abstraction 16–18, 149, 447
ACC (annual cost of countermeasure) 447
access control 348–354, 447
   biometric factors 352–354
   discretionary 348
   knowledge factors 349–351
   mandatory 348
   possession factors 351–352
   system 363–364
ACL (access control list) 447
ACL router rules 447
active attacks 61, 447
active directory 522
actuarial formulas 74
AECA (Arms Export Control Act) 124, 448
Affine ciphers 291
agents 376, 447
aging 378, 447
AH (authentication header) 421
Alberti, Leon Battista 184
algorithms 207
American Society for Industrial Security (ASIS) 357
annual loss expectancy (ALE) 82
anomaly models 448
ANTex 81
Anti-Virus Guard (AVG) 495
application and file protection 358–361
application layer 27
application service providers (ASPs) 46
application-level gateways 370, 448

Arms Export Control Act (AECA) 124, 448
ARP cache poisoning 69, 448
ARP spoofing 69
ARPANet 365
ASIS (American Society for Industrial Security) 357
asymmetrical algorithm 208, 308, 448
asymmetrical key cryptography 301–310, 506
   asymmetrical algorithms 308
   Diffie-Helman algorithm 309–310
   encryption 306–308
   keys 303–306
   RSA encryption algorithm 309
   shared secret 301
   split secrets 301
   See also cryptography
   See also symmetrical key cryptography
attacks 8
   active 61
   against encryption 71
   buffer overflows 66, 449
   DOS (denial-of-service) 63–66
   e-mail flood 65, 454
   e-mail spoofing 31, 426, 454, 513–519
   flooding 64, 455
   frequency 58
   intrusion 66–69, 458
   mail bombing 65, 460
   malicious codes 70
   man-in-the-middle 69, 460
   name spoofing 67, 461
   passive 61, 72–73

attacks (continued)
  perpetrators 51–55
  ping of death 66, 463
  port scanning 68–69
  probability 58, 448
  release of message content 465
  replay 69, 465
  session hijacking 69
  springboard 43
  statistics 50–51
  SYN Flood 64, 468
  timing 72, 317, 469
  Web-based 72
audits trails 110–111
authentication 102, 149, 371, 448
authentication factors 448
  biometric factors 352–354
  combining 354
  knowledge factors 349–351
  possession factors 351–352
  See also access control
authentication header (AH) 421
authenticity 334, 448

B

backdoors 70, 448
Bacon, Francis 201
BadCopy Pro 489
bastian hosts 369, 448
biometric factor 149, 352–354, 449
bit shifting 449
Blaster worm 402
block cipher 210, 277, 449
Blowfish encryption 291
Bombe machine 193
boot sector viruses 398, 449
Brain virus 398
brand 449
bridges 521
browser 413
brute-force attacks 317
buffer 66
buffer overflows 66, 449
bytes 18, 449

C

cable modems 522
cache 24
Caesar cipher 183, 209
CAIN (Confidentiality, Authenticity,
    Integrity, and Nonrepudiation) 13,
    21, 206–207, 333–334, 449
certificate policy 320, 328, 449
certificate practice statement 450
certificates 449
certification authority 320, 450
chaining 269, 319, 450
checksum 208, 450
Chief Information Security Officer (CISO)
    167–168
choke points 151, 364, 450
chosen plain text attack 71, 215, 450
cipher wheel 210
ciphers 181, 450
  block chaining 279, 450
  definition of 207
  feedback 279, 450
  simulation 492
  See also cryptography
ciphertext 148, 181, 207, 450
ciphertext attacks 215
clipper chip 125, 450
closed architecture 450
Code Red virus 7, 402
code vulnerabilities 70, 72, 451
collision-resistant hashes 451
Colossus computing device 193
compression permutation 273
computational linguistic algorithms 109,
    451
computationally secure 208, 451
computer crimes 8
  cornerstone legislation 132–134
  identification of 103–105
  intrusion incident reporting guidelines
      529–533
  investigation of 109–112
  and law enforcement 116–117
  laws 117–137
  perpetrators 51–55

prevention of 105–109
prosecution of 95–96, 115–116
statistics 49–51
computer forensic science 109, 451
Computer Fraud and Abuse Act of 1986 118, 132–134
concealer 398
confidentiality 334, 451
confusion 451
congruent 451
content checking 371, 451
cookie cutters 417, 451
cookies 101, 416–417
copyright infringement 8, 104, 121–122
Coroner's toolkit 111
cost benefit analysis (CBA) 84, 449
Courtney 81
CPU (central processing unit) 18
crackers 52, 451
credit card fraud 7
crime scene management 112
crippled 451
crisis management team 107–108, 166
critical information failure 56, 451
cross scripting 72, 452
cross-site scripting 101
cryptanalysis 207, 452
cryptanalysts 181, 207, 214, 452
cryptographers 181, 207, 452
cryptographic administrators 181
cryptographic algorithm 148, 452
cryptographic checksum 208, 311, 452
cryptographic strength 148, 452
cryptography 452
    asymmetrical 301–310
    ciphers 492
    computers in 265–266
    English language in 203–205
    history of 182–203
        early period 182–187
        modern period 197–203
        World Wars 188–194
    in information security model 147–148
    language of 207–209
    and laws 124–128

methods 209–210
quantum 201
strength of method 210–215
substitution 182
transposition 182
in Web security 417–432
cryptology 207
cyberterrorism 54
cyberterrorists 54, 452

D

data 15–16
data abstraction 18–20
data encryption standard (DES) 200, 287–291, 453
data integrity 452
data link layer 29
data origin authentication 452
Data Sentinel 361
data warehouses 26
DDOS (distributed denial-of-service) attack 63, 452
decryption 207, 452
defense in depth 146, 453
demilitarized zone (DMZ) 359, 368–369, 438, 453
DES (data encryption standard) 200, 287–291, 453
DHCP (Dynamic Host Configuration Protocol) 522
Diffie, Whitfield 301
Diffie-Helman algorithm 309–310
diffusion 453
digital certificates 149, 320
digital currency 409–410
digital enveloping 453
digital ID 496–506
digital signature 208, 310–317, 322–325, 453
Digital Telephony Act of 1994 98
digrams 189, 453
director 376, 453
disaster recovery 34, 166–167
DISCARD 525
discretionary access control 348, 453

DMZ (demilitarized zone) 359, 368–369, 438, 453
DNS (domain name server) 413, 453
DNS spoofing 69, 453
domain 522
DOS (denial-of-service) attacks 63–66, 454, 507–511
double DES encryption 291
Draper, John 53
dumpster diving 68, 454
Dynamic Host Configuration Protocol (DHCP) 522
dynamic packet filtering 371, 454

E

EAA (Export Administration Act) 124, 454
EAP (Extensible Authentication Protocol) 359
eavesdropping 73, 455
ECHO 525
ECM (electronic codebook mode) 277, 454
Economic Espionage Act of 1996 122, 454
El Gamal algorithm 308, 454
electromagnetic radiation (EMR) 358, 454
electronic codebook mode (ECM) 277
Electronic Communications and Privacy Act (ECPA) 119–120
electronic identity 100, 135–137
electronic signatures 131–132
Electronic Signatures in Global and National Commerce Act (ESIGN) 131–132, 455
elliptic curve cipher 308, 454
e-mail 31, 426–427
e-mail flood 65, 454
e-mail spoofing 31, 426, 454, 513–519
e-mail virus 399, 455
EMR (electromagnetic radiation) 358, 454
encapsulated security packet (ESP) 422
EnCase 111
encryption 207, 455
    asymmetrical 306–308
    attacks against 71, 317
    equipment 127–128
    key 148, 455

See also cryptography
English language 203–205
Enigma machine 189–193, 455
entity 19, 100, 455
environmental control 355–357
errors 213
ESIGN (Electronic Signatures in Global and National Commerce Act) 131–132, 455
ESP (encapsulated security packet) 422
estimated annual loss expectancies (EALEs) 82
Ethereal 359, 507
Export Administration Act (EAA) 124, 454
Extensible Authentication Protocol (EAP) 359

F

FATs (file allocation tables) 479
FATs 32 file system 360, 479–481
Feistel ciphers 279–281, 455
file encryption 482
file recovery 489
File Transfer Protocol (FTP) 526
financial institutions 121
Financial Services Modernization Act 100, 456
fire protection 355
firewalls 371–372, 455, 522
flash memory 24
flood protection 355
flooding 64, 455
forecasting 74, 456
fraud 8
Freedom of Information Act 123, 456
Friedman Test 189
Friedman, William 187, 193
function 456

G

GFI LANguard System Integrity Monitor 361
Goner virus 7
Graham-Leach-Bliley Act of 1999 100, 121, 456
graphical user interface (GUI) 149
GUI (graphical user interface) 149

H

hackers 52, 456
hashes 208, 456
hashing algorithms 149
header replacement 371
Health Insurance Portability and Accountability Act (HIPAA) 27, 121, 457
hearsay 110, 456
heating, ventilation, and air-conditioning (HVAC) 356–357
Heisenberg's uncertainty principle 203, 208, 456
Hellman, Martin 301
heuristics 207, 456
hidden addressing 371
hijacking 69, 456
Hill cipher 189, 456
Hill, Lester 189
HIPAA (Health Insurance Portability and Accountability Act) 27, 121, 457
hoax attack 457
hoaxes 70, 457
honeypot 113, 457
host-to-host VPN (virtual private network) 373
host-to-site VPN (virtual private network) 373
HTML (Hypertext Markup Language) 31–33, 413, 457
HTTP (Hypertext Transfer Protocol) 20, 413–417, 457
HTTPD bypass 72, 457
HTTPD overflow 72, 457
HVAC (heating, ventilation, and air-conditioning) 356–357

I

I Love You virus 7
ICMP for Windows 507
IDEA encryption 291
idempodent 457
identity theft 67, 68, 102, 111, 135–137, 457
Identity Theft Act 457

IEC (International Electrotechnical Commission) 164
IETF (Internet Engineering Task Force) 165
illegal IDs 7
image flood 72, 458
IMAP3 (Internet Mail Access Protocol 3) 526
Index of Coincidence 189
infector 398
information 458
  at core of information security model 146–147
information access control 34
information management 33–35
information security 6–9
  application and file protection 358–361
  common myths and misconceptions 42–47
  comparison of 434–439
  effectiveness of 432–433
  intrusion detection 375–379
  network security 364–375
  perpetrators 51–55
  physical security 347–358
    access control 348–354
    environmental control 355–357
    premise security and waste management 357–358
  planning 10–14
  principles 158–160
  risk assessment and vulnerability analysis 74–89
  risks 55–60
  statistics 47–51
  system security 361–364
information security model 144–146
  cryptographic methods layer 147–148
  information at core of 146–147
  information system architecture and design layer 151–152
  OS hardening layer 149–151
  security layer 154–156
  verification and authentication layer 148–149
  Web services protection layer 153–154
information systems 23–27, 151

input 458
integrity 334, 458
integrity analysis 458
integrity factor 149
intellectual property crimes 121–124
International Electrotechnical Commission (IEC) 164
International Standards Organization (ISO) 164
International Traffic in U.S. Arms Regulations (ITAR) 124, 458
Internet 50, 523
  and privacy 100–102
  secure Web protocols 418–432
Internet Engineering Task Force (IETF) 165
Internet fraud 7, 50
Internet Mail Access Protocol 3 (IMAP 3) 526
Internet Protocol (IP) 523–524
Internet Protocol Security (IPSec) 375, 419–422
Internet service providers (ISPs) 46, 458
intranet 523
intrusion attack 66–69, 458
intrusion detection system (IDS) 43, 108, 375–379, 438–439, 457
investor fraud 7
involuntary risks 55, 458
IP (Internet Protocol) 523–524
IP addresses 526
IP tunneling 522
IP version 4 523
IP version 6 523
ISO/IEC 17799 standard 164
isochronous 31, 458
ITAR (International Traffic in U.S. Arms Regulations) 124, 458

J

Jefferson, Thomas 187
JN-25 cipher 193–194, 458

K

Kerberos method 274–276, 458
key 207, 212
key escrow 459

key management 459
key recovery/escrow system 124, 333, 459
key rotation 271, 273, 459
key scheduling 273
keystroke monitors 100, 402, 459
knowledge factor 149, 349–351, 459
known plain text attacks 215

L

L0phtcrack/LC3 81
LAN (local area network) 521
LANguard Network Scanner 81
law enforcement 116–117
Law Enforcement Access Field (LEAF) 125, 459
LDAP (Lightweight Directory Access Protocol) 327, 459
LEAF (Law Enforcement Access Field) 125, 459
LEAP (Lightweight Extensible Authentication Protocol) 359
least privilege 151, 459
Level 2 Tunneling Protocol (L2TP) 374, 459
Lightweight Directory Access Protocol (LDAP) 327, 459
Lightweight Extensible Authentication Protocol (LEAP) 359
local area network (LAN) 521
lockouts 65, 459
logarithm computation attack 317
logging 110–111, 459
logic bomb 70, 396, 402, 459
Lucifer cipher 459

M

MAC (message authentication code) 149, 311–317, 460
MAC address 521
MAC Stumbler 359
mail bombing 65, 460
malformed commands 66, 460
malicious codes 70, 388–389, 460
malicious signatures 151, 460
malware 395–403
  defenses against 403–404

definition of 460
forms of 402–403
mandatory access control 348, 460
man-in-the-middle attack 69, 460
mapping 73, 460
MARS encryption 201, 291, 292
mass market encryption products 127–128
mathematical attacks 71, 460
Mauborgne, Joseph 189
mean 460
medical information 121
memory cards 24
memory sticks 24
mens rea 460
message authentication code (MAC) 149,
        311–317, 460
message digest 208
message substitution 460
metadata 20, 461
metatags 20
misuse models 461
mode 277, 461
monoalphabetic ciphers 183, 209, 461
Monte Carlo simulations 84
Moore's law 211
Morris worm 401
Morris, Robert, Jr. 52, 401
mutation engine 401, 461

N

name spoofing 67, 461
Napster 122
NAT (network address translation) 371, 461,
        523
National Bureau of Standards (NBS) 200, 461
National Information Infrastructure
        Protection Act of 1996 118, 134
National Infrastructure Protection Center
        108, 529
National Institute for Standards and
        Technology (NIST) 164
NBS (National Bureau of Standards) 200, 461
NCP (Network Control Protocol) 365
negligence 104, 461
NETBIOS 150

NetBIOS-NS 526
NETSTAT 526
network address translation 371, 461, 523
network architectures 365–366
Network Control Protocol (NCP) 365
Network Flight Recorder 112
network forensics analysis tools (NFATs) 112,
        461
network interface card (NIC) 521
network layer 29
network mapping attacks 100, 461
Network News Transfer Protocol (NNTP) 526
network security 364–375
    demilitarized zone (DMZ) 368–369
    firewalls 371–372
    network address translation (NAT) 371
    network architectures 365–366
    proxy servers 370–371
    screening routers 366–368
    virtual local area networks (VLANs) 375
    virtual private networks (VPNs) 372–375
    See also information security
Network Stumbler 359
network worm 396, 461
New Technology File System (NTFS) 360,
        479–481
NFATs (network forensics analysis tools) 112,
        461
NIC (network interface card) 521
Nimda virus 7, 402
NIST (National Institute for Standards and
        Technology) 164
NNTP (Network News Transfer Protocol) 526
nonmalicious codes 389–394
nonrepudiation 334, 461
notification agent 376, 462
NTFS (New Technology File System) 360,
        479–481
NTRU cipher 308, 462

O

Office of Homeland Security 357
one-time pad 188, 462
one-way hash 462
online auction fraud 7

operating system hardening 150, 362–363, 436–438, 462
operating systems 149–151, 361
optical disks 24
OSI mode 462
output feedback 279
ownership threat value (OTV) tree analysis 76–80

P

packet redirection 69
passive attacks 61, 72–73, 462
password crackers 402
password cracking 67–68, 462, 485–488
password synchronization 364, 462
PATRIOT Act 134
payload 396, 398, 462
perfectly secure 188
permission-based architecture 463
PGP (Pretty Good Privacy) 201, 427, 463
phreakers 53, 463
ping of death 66, 463
piracy 104, 122, 463
PKCS (public key cryptography standards) 330, 463
plain text 148, 181, 207, 463
plain text attacks 71, 215, 463
Point-to-Point Tunneling Protocol (PPTP) 374, 464
poison cookies 72, 463
policies 155
policy mapping 330, 463
polyalphabetic ciphers 184, 210, 464
polymorphic viruses 399, 464
port scanners 402, 464
port scanning 68–69
ports 525–526
possession factor 149, 351–352, 464
Pouslen, Kevin 53
power management systems 357, 464
PPTP (Point-to-Point Tunneling Protocol) 374, 464
practical irreversibility 307, 464
premise security 357–358
presentation layer 27

primary keys 26
prime numbers 464, 535–537
privacy 97–98
    as a customer or client 99
    and Internet 100–102
    from law enforcement 98–99
    laws 120–121
    policies 102–103
    at work 98–99
Privacy Act of 1974 120, 464
private key 303, 464
PRNG (pseudorandom number generator) 464
procedures 156
process 156, 464
programmable RAM (PRAM) 24
protocols 464
proxy servers 370–371, 464, 522
pseudorandom numbers 86, 464
public 200
public key 303, 465
public key cryptography standards (PKCS) 200, 330, 463
public key infrastructure (PKI) 103, 463
    asymmetrical key cryptography 301–310
    attacks against encryption 317
    CAIN (Confidentiality, Authenticity, Integrity, and Nonrepudiation) 333–334
    digital signatures 310–317, 322–325
    operational issues 331–333
    standards 330–331
    trust and trust relationships 318–322
    verification 149
    X.509 v3 certificates 327–330
Purple cryptographic protocol 193

Q

quantum cryptography 201, 208, 465

R

rabbits 402, 465
Ramen worm 402
random access memory (RAM) 24
random attacks 43

range 465

RATs (remote administrative tools) 396–398, 465

RC6 encryption 201, 291

records 19

relatively prime number 465

release of message content 465

relying party 465

remote administration 432

remote administrative tools (RATs) 396–398, 465

repeaters 521

replay attack 69, 465

Rijndael encryption 201, 291

risk analysis 81–84, 465

risk assessment and vulnerability analysis 74–89

risk management 87–89

risks 55–60, 465

    entities 465

    factors 465

    identification 465

    minimization 466

    mitigation 466

    transference 466

RLOGIN 432

Rocheford, Lt. Cmdr. Joseph 195

Ron's Code encryption 291

root authority 319

rounds 279, 466

routers 521–522, 527

RSA ClearTrust 364

RSA encryption algorithm 200, 309

S

S/MIME (Secure/Multipurpose Internet Mail Extension) certificates 329, 427, 466

sabotage 466

safe labs 473–478

SAINT (security administrator's integrated network tool) 81

SAM (security acceptability metric) 466

SAML (Security Assertion Markup Language) 363, 466

SANs (storage area networks) 24, 466

SATAN (security administration tool for analyzing networks) 81

scanners 466

Scherbius, Arthur 189

screening routers 366–368, 466

script kiddies 43, 466

scytale 182–183

Secure Hypertext Transfer Protocol (S-HTTP) 467

Secure Sockets Layer (SSL) 330, 424–426

Secure/Multipurpose Internet Mail Extension (S/MIME) certificates 329, 427, 466

security acceptability metric (SAM) 85–86, 466

Security and Freedom Through Encryption Act 125

Security Assertion Markup Language (SAML) 363, 466

security context 466

security plan 3–5

    formats and frameworks 164–165

    outline 160–163

    and policy creation 157–158

    principles 158–160

    See also information security

sequence number prediction 69, 467

sequential access method (SAM) 24

serial number 327

Serpent encryption 201, 291, 292

servers 413

session hijacking 69

SET (secure electronic transaction) 427–432, 467

Shannon, Claude 197–198, 211

shared secrets 301

shift cipher 179, 183, 467

shoulder surfing 73, 467

S-HTTP (Secure Hypertext Transfer Protocol) 422–424, 467

signature algorithm identifier 327

signature byte 398

SilentRunner 112

Simple Mail Transfer Protocol (SMTP) 467

single sign-on (SSO) 363, 467

SirCam virus 7
site-to-site VPN (virtual private network) 373
skipjack encryption algorithm 125
small decryption exponent attack 317
SMTP (Simple Mail Transfer Protocol) 65, 467
Smurf attack 65, 467
sniffers 73, 467
social engineering 35
social engineering software 402
social engineers 54, 467
software development 394–395
software keys 272–276
source address 522
specialty industry privacy law 120–121
split secrets 301
springboard attacks 43, 467
SQL (Structured Query Language) 360–361
SSL (Secure Sockets Layer) 330, 424–426
SSL certificates 466
SSO (single sign-on) 363, 467
standard deviation 74
state 468
stateful inspection 371, 468
steganography 201, 208, 468
storage area networks (SANs) 24, 466
storage devices 24
stream cipher 210, 277, 468
Structured Query Language (SQL) 360–361
substitution 468
substitution ciphers 179, 184, 204, 209
switches 522
symmetrical algorithm 208, 276–281, 291–292, 468
symmetrical key cryptography 265–266
    DES (data encryption standard) 287–291
    parts of 267–272
    software keys 272–276
    symmetrical algorithms 276–281, 291–292
    TEA (Tiny Encryption Algorithm) 281–287
    See also asymmetrical key cryptography
    See also cryptography

SYN Flood attack 64, 468
system access control 363–364
system security 361–364

T
tailgating 354
TCP (Transmission Control Protocol) 522, 524–525
TCP/IP (Transmission Control Protocol/Internet Protocol) 365–366
TEA (Tiny Encryption Algorithm) 281–287, 493–494
teardrop attack 64, 468
telephone fraud 7
Telnet 432, 526
TEMPEST 358, 468
Temporal Key Integrity Protocol (TKIP) 359
threat agents 57, 468
time bomb 396, 402, 468
timing attacks 72, 317, 469
TKIP (Temporal Key Integrity Protocol) 359
trade secrets 122
transaction sets 121
Transmission Control Protocol (TCP) 522, 524–525
transport layer 29
transport mode 373, 469
transposition cipher 183, 209, 469
trapdoor 307, 402, 469
travel fraud 7
triggers 43, 398, 469
trigrams 189, 469
triple DES encryption 291
Tripwire 361
Trojans 70, 372, 396–398, 469
trust 318
trust anchor 319, 469
trust relationship 319
trusted authorities 319, 469
trusted insiders 104, 111
trusted third party 13, 149, 319
tunnel mode 373, 469
Turing, Alan 193
Twofish encryption 201, 291

U

uncertainty 74
unconditionally secure 208, 469
uninterruptible power supplies (UPS) 357, 469
unrealized threats 73, 469
URL flood 72, 470
URLs (uniform resource locators) 413, 470
usage policies 102

V

variance 74, 470
VENONA 198
verification 149, 470
Vernam, Gilbert S. 188
Vigenere square 184–187, 470
virtual local area networks (VLANs) 375
virtual private networks (VPNs) 372–375, 470
viruses 7, 470
    anatomy of 398–401
    detection of 495
    See also malware
VLANs (virtual local area networks) 375
voluntary risks 55, 470
VPNs (virtual private networks) 372–375, 470
vulnerabilities 470

W

WAN (wide area network) 521
war driving 358, 470
Wassenaar Arrangement 125
Wave Stumbler 359
weak key 470
Web attacks 72
Web browser 413
Web businesses 411–413
Web pages 413
Web protocols 418–432
Web services 153–154
Websense 81
WEP (Wired Equivalent Privacy) 359, 471
wheel cipher 187
wide area network (WAN) 521
wireless LANs 358
World Wide Web (WWW) 413
worms 7, 396, 401–402, 471

X

X.509 v3 certificates 149, 327–330
XML (Extensible Markup Language) 32

Z

Zimmerman telegram 188
zombies 63, 471